When International Law Works

WHEN INTERNATIONAL LAW WORKS

REALISTIC IDEALISM AFTER 9/11 AND THE GLOBAL RECESSION

Tai-Heng Cheng

For Ben—
Cosmopolitan world
traveller.
Warm wishes.
Tai-Heng Cheng
Aug 22, 2013

OXFORD
UNIVERSITY PRESS

OXFORD
UNIVERSITY PRESS

Oxford University Press, Inc., publishes works that further Oxford University's objective of excellence in research, scholarship, and education.

Oxford New York
Auckland Cape Town Dar es Salaam Hong Kong Karachi Kuala Lumpur Madrid
Melbourne Mexico City Nairobi New Delhi Shanghai Taipei Toronto

With offices in
Argentina Austria Brazil Chile Czech Republic France Greece Guatemala Hungary Italy
Japan Poland Portugal Singapore South Korea Switzerland Thailand Turkey Ukraine
Vietnam

Published by Oxford University Press, Inc.
198 Madison Avenue, New York, New York 10016

Library of Congress Cataloging-in-Publication Data

Cheng, Tai-Heng.
When international law works : realistic idealism after 9/11 and the global recession / Tai-Heng Cheng.
p. cm.
Includes bibliographical references and index.
ISBN 978-0-19-537017-1 (hardback)
1. International law. I. Title.
KZ3410.C47 2011
341—dc23 2011022503

1 2 3 4 5 6 7 8 9

Printed in the United States of America on acid-free paper

Note to Readers
This publication is designed to provide accurate and authoritative information in regard to the subject matter covered. It is based upon sources believed to be accurate and reliable and is intended to be current as of the time it was written. It is sold with the understanding that the publisher is not engaged in rendering legal, accounting, or other professional services. If legal advice or other expert assistance is required, the services of a competent professional person should be sought. Also, to confirm that the information has not been affected or changed by recent developments, traditional legal research techniques should be used, including checking primary sources where appropriate.

(Based on the Declaration of Principles jointly adopted by a Committee of the American Bar Association and a Committee of Publishers and Associations.)

For my teacher W. Michael Reisman, with affection and respect.

Contents

Detailed Contents

Acknowledgments

More so than many other fields of law, international law is situated at the confluence of theoretical research, policy-making, adjudicating, and practice. Mentors and colleagues engaged in these tasks provided gentle encouragement and frank observations throughout my research for this book. I am grateful to them all, and hope that inadvertently-omitted friends will forgive my imperfect recordkeeping over the five years it took to write this book. These friends are in my heart even if their names are not on paper.

Judges Rosalyn Higgins, Stephen M. Schwebel, and Christopher G. Weeramantry provided insights on drafts of the book. I will be forever grateful for their candor and generosity.

For numerous discussions about ideas in the book, and careful reviews of earlier iterations of chapters, I thank Professors Robert Blecker, Daniel Bodansky, Charles H. Brower, Chester Brown, David D. Caron, Simon Chesterman, Maxwell O. Chibundu, Richard Chused, Harlan G. Cohen, Jeffrey L. Dunoff, Stephen J. Ellmann, Ronald H. Filler, Brian T. Fitzpatrick, James Grimmelmann, Jean Gailbraith, Monica Hakimi, Laurence R. Helfer, Chimène I. Keitner, Hari M. Osofsky, Houman B. Shadab, Robert Howse, Janie Chuang, Joseph Landau, Chin Leng Lim, Frank Munger, Mary Ellen O'Connell, Edward Purcell, W. Michael Reisman, Tanina Rostain, David Schoenbrod, David Sloss, Ruti G. Teitel, Fernando Tesón, Marshall Tracht, Romesh Weeramantry, Ingrid Wuerth, Whitmore Gray, Andrew Willard, Rüdiger Wolfrum, and John Yoo. Numerous participants at the New York Law School Faculty Workshops and the Junior International Law Scholars Association Annual Meetings also provided feedback.

From among those who are charged with shaping appropriate conduct of decisionmakers through their policy-making and practice of law, I am especially indebted to Gary Born, Patrick Bumatay, Steven Hill, Devashish Krishan, and Lucy Reed for their comments.

A special note of gratitude is owed to my research assistants over the years: Robert Trisotto, Stuart Barden, Brian Kochisarli, Jeremy Neil, Raymond Girnys, Christopher Harrison, Cynthia Claytor, Colette Siesholtz, Nicholas Turner, Kienan Christianson, Jason Richland, Christoph Doellefeld, and Aaron Julka.

For their professionalism and patience, I thank the staff at Oxford University Press, and especially my editor Kevin Pendergast.

Finally, I acknowledge Abelardo Morell for granting permission to use his photograph on the cover. He has succeeded in using the Renaissance *camera obscura* technique to refresh how we see the world. May this achievement inspire those of us involved in the law to use our venerable methods to revitalize how we perceive the international legal system.

T.H.C.
New York, New York
August 10, 2011

Abbreviations

AIG	American International Group
AMISOM	African Union Mission in Somalia
BIT	Bilateral Investment Treaty
CIA	Central Intelligence Agency
DSU	Dispute Settlement Understanding
FRY	Federal Republic of Yugoslavia
FSB	Financial Stability Board
GATT	General Agreement on Tariffs and Trade
G-7	Group of Seven Finance Ministers and Central Bank Governors
G-20	Group of Twenty Finance Ministers and Central Bank Governors
IAEA	International Atomic Energy Agency
ICC	International Criminal Court
ICJ	International Court of Justice
ICSID	International Centre for Settlement of Investment Disputes
ICTY	The International Criminal Tribunal for the former Yugoslavia
IFRS	International Financial Reporting Standards
ISO	International Organization for Standardization
KLA	Kosovo Liberation Army
NAFTA	North American Free Trade Agreement
NGO	Nongovernmental Organization
NATO	North Atlantic Treaty Organization
OLC	U.S. Department of Justice Office of Legal Counsel
PCIJ	Permanent Court of International Justice
PSYOP	Psychological Operations
SDI	Strategic Defense Initiative
SFRY	Socialist Federal Republic of Yugoslavia
UN	United Nations
UNMIK	United Nations Mission in Kosovo
UNMOVIC	United Nations Monitoring, Verification and Inspection Commission
VCLT	Vienna Convention on the Law of Treaties
WTO	World Trade Organization

1 Confronting Anxieties about International Law

I. WHAT SHOULD DECISIONMAKERS DO?

Sometimes, decisionmakers obey international law; at other times, they do not.[1] This obvious point is nonetheless worth stating because court decisions, laws, and scholarship are often written as if legal rules could fully control outcomes,[2] when in fact no law—whether domestic or international—can make a person do what he does not want to do.[3] Law can only influence decisions and impose consequences

[1] *Cf.*, LOUIS HENKIN, HOW NATIONS BEHAVE: LAW AND FOREIGN POLICY 47 (2d ed. 1979) [hereinafter HENKIN, HOW NATIONS BEHAVE] ("It is probably the case that almost all nations observe almost all principles of international law and almost all of their obligations almost all of the time."); Eric Posner, *Evaluating the Effects of International Law: Next Steps*, 1:3 GLOBAL POLICY 334, 335 (Oct. 2010) ("The empirical work on international law is in its infancy but some of it—particularly the work on human rights treaties—has blasted holes in the Henkin view.").

[2] *See, e.g.*, CMS Gas Transmission Co. v. Argentine Republic, ICSID Case No. ARB/01/8, Award at 139 ¶ 2 (May 12, 2005) ("[Argentina] shall pay [CMS] compensation in the amount of US$133.2 million."); Convention on the Prevention and Punishment of the Crime of Genocide, art. 4, Dec. 9, 1948, 78 U.N.T.S. 1021 ("Persons committing genocide or any of the other acts enumerated in article III shall be punished, whether they are constitutionally responsible rulers, public officials or private individuals."); John B. Bellinger III & Vijay M. Padmanabhan, *Detention Operations in Contemporary Conflicts: Four Challenges for the Geneva Conventions and Other Existing Law*, 105 AM. J. INT'L L. 201, 241 (2011) ("[W]e see the need for new rules where existing rules do not apply or are uncertain in application.").

[3] *See* José E. Alvarez, *The Return of the State*, 20 MINN. J. INT'L L. 223, 244 (2011) ("Whether or not the CMS annulment committee intended the result, the underlying award in this case (as well as

for actions. In domestic activities, each person decides whether to follow laws, and lives with the results of his decisions. In world affairs, each decisionmaker also chooses whether to act according to international law, and faces the consequences of his choices. Remarkably, scholars have not paid much attention to how decisionmakers ought to choose. That is the subject of this book.

This book develops and tests the following framework to guide decisionmakers in problems that implicate international law. Many international laws and other prescriptions promote minimum world order and universally-desired values, such as global banking standards and agreements that enable capital to move across borders to be efficiently deployed to produce goods and services that people want. Decisionmakers ought generally to obey such prescriptions by interpreting and applying them according to accepted procedures and methods. However, some prescriptions threaten basic values or essential interests of communities that decisionmakers serve, such as prescriptions that prohibit a government from taking measures necessary to defend its people against a foreign threat. In those situations, decisionmakers may legitimately choose to disobey international prescriptions or stretch methods of interpreting them, and to bear the consequences of their actions. When they disobey international law, however, decisionmakers ought not to claim a unique exception for themselves, because that encourages others to do the same. This could excessively disrupt world order and diminish basic values. Instead, decisionmakers should explain their reasons for disobedience, so that others can decide if those are good reasons, and shift their expectations of appropriate conduct for the future. This process can help adjust the international legal system to contemporary realities while avoiding unjustified disobedience and disruptions.

Recent academic and political debates about whether international law is really law seem to have lost direct sight of the practical issue of what decisionmakers should do in international problems. Even if there is an answer to whether international law is law, it does not provide all the reasons for obedience or disobedience. This is because many, if not all, of these reasons exist independently of conceptual claims about international law.[4] This book does not examine whether international law is law and what it consequently requires of decisionmakers. Instead, this book explores what decisionmakers should do about international law, whether or not it is law. Hopefully, inverting the prevailing debates will help ease the gridlock between realists who say international law is not law and can be ignored, and idealists who state that international law is law and should be taken seriously.

others rendered against Argentina) have not been paid."). *See also* Jakob Kellenberger, Official Statement of the International Committee for the Red Cross: Sixty Years of the Geneva Conventions: Strengthening Legal Protection for Victims of Armed Conflicts (Sept. 21, 2010), *available at* https://www.icrc.org/web/eng/siteng0.nsf/html/ihl-development-statement-210910 ("What is required in most cases . . . is greater compliance with the existing legal framework, not the adoption of new rules.").

[4] *See, e.g.*, Kofi Anan, A More Secure World: Our Shared Responsibility: Report of the High-Level Panel on Threats, Challenges and Change, UN Doc. A/59/565, ¶ 204 (2004), *available at* https://www/un/org/secureworld, (stating that the use of military force should be "for the right reasons, morally as well as legally").

II. CONTEMPORARY DEBATES

Incredibly, in this century, officials are debating theoretical questions about international law that scholars have long considered.[5] Is international law really law?[6] Is it only politics?[7] Does it control officials, judges, and other decisionmakers?[8] Should it?[9]

Shortly before his appointment as the U.S. Permanent Representative to the United Nations in the George W. Bush administration, John Bolton dismissed as nothing more than myth the view that international law is law:

> International law is not law; it is a series of political and moral arrangements that stand or fall on their own merits, and anything else is simply theology and superstition masquerading as law.[10]

As if in response to Bolton, Harold Koh, shortly before his appointment as U.S. State Department Legal Advisor in the administration of President Barack Obama,

[5] *See* JACK L. GOLDSMITH & ERIC A. POSNER, THE LIMITS OF INTERNATIONAL LAW 201 (2005) ("International law scholars have long grappled with the question of whether international law is law.").

[6] For differing answers to this question, see JOHN AUSTIN, THE PROVINCE OF JURISPRUDENCE DETERMINED 106–08 (David Campbell & Philip Thomas eds., 1998) (1832) (arguing that international law is not law); H. L. A. HART, THE CONCEPT OF LAW, 213–37 (2d. ed. 1994) [hereinafter HART, THE CONCEPT OF LAW] (stating that international law is a primitive legal system); Jeremy Waldron, *Hart and the Principles of Legality*, *in* THE LEGACY OF H. L. A. HART 68 (Matthew H. Kramer et al. eds., 2008) [hereinafter Waldron, *Hart and the Principles of Legality*] (arguing that Hart's characterization of international law as primitive "was wrong in 1960 and it is certainly wrong now").

[7] *Compare* ALEXANDER ORAKHELASHVILI, THE INTERPRETATION OF ACTS AND RULES IN PUBLIC INTERNATIONAL LAW 29 (2008) (stating that international law "must be seen as independent of politics") *with* Burns H. Weston, *The Role of Law in Promoting Peace and Violence: A Matter of Definition, Social Values and Individual Responsibility*, *in* TOWARD WORLD ORDER AND HUMAN DIGNITY 114, 117 (W. Michael Reisman & Burns H. Weston eds., 1976) (stating that international law "is legitimized politics").

[8] *Compare* GOLDSMITH & POSNER, *supra* note 5 ("[S]tates cannot bootstrap cooperation by creating rules and calling them 'law.'") *with* HENKIN, HOW NATIONS BEHAVE, *supra* note 1, at 42.

[9] *Compare* GOLDSMITH & POSNER, *supra* note 5, at 199 ("[W]e cannot condemn a state merely for violating international law.") *with* ROSALYN HIGGINS, PROBLEMS AND PROCESS: INTERNATIONAL LAW AND HOW WE USE IT 1–2 (1994) [hereinafter HIGGINS, PROBLEMS AND PROCESS] ("[I]nternational law [is] a normative system, harnessed to the achievement of common values—values that speak to us all, whether we are rich or poor, black or white, of any religion or none, or come from countries that are industrialized or developing.").

[10] John R. Bolton, *Is There Really "Law" in International Affairs?*, 10 TRANSNAT'L L. & CONTEMP. PROBS. 1, 48 (2000). *See also* JACK GOLDSMITH, THE TERROR PRESIDENCY 41 (2007) (quoting U.S. Attorney General Alberto Gonzales as saying "I don't see how terrorists who violate the laws of war can get the protections of the laws of war."); Henry A. Kissinger, *The Pitfalls of Universal Jurisdiction*, FOREIGN AFFAIRS, July/August 2001, at 86 (arguing against universal jurisdiction over government officials who are alleged to have committed egregious acts). *See also* Harlan Grant Cohen, *Finding International Law: Rethinking the Doctrine of Sources*, 93 IOWA L. REV. 65, 129 (2008) ("To international law skeptics, the gaps between what international law is said to require and what states actually do is proof that international law is a myth, a rhetorical device, or wishful thinking.").

dismissively stated, "The first myth is that somehow 'international law is not really law.'"[11]

Moderate conservatives also expressed their views. The U.S. State Department Legal Advisor in the Bush administration, John Bellinger, III, said that the Bush administration respected international law.[12] President Bush's second-term Secretary of State, Condoleezza Rice, explained that "America's moral authority in international politics also rests on its ability to defend international laws and treaties."[13]

Traumatic world events intensified and broadened these discussions about the nature of international law. The terrorist attacks on the United States on September 11, 2001, created pressure on governments to take extreme international actions that tested the limits of previously held expectations of acceptable behavior in the international legal system.[14] The United States, United Kingdom, and their allies invaded Iraq without specific UN Security Council authorization for that invasion. U.S. Central Intelligence Agency operatives waterboarded terrorists to obtain actionable intelligence to stop another terrorist attack. U.S. officials engaged in other legally questionable tactics, including detentions without judicial review, secret renditions, and wire-tapping without court warrants.

Other actors criticized these actions.[15] Russia, China, and some European countries denounced the invasion of Iraq as ill advised and illegal under international law.

[11] Harold Hongju Koh, *Forward* to MICHAEL P. SCHARF & PAUL R. WILLIAMS, SHAPING FOREIGN POLICY IN TIMES OF CRISIS, at ix, xv (2010) [hereinafter Koh, *Forward*]; *accord* DAVID BEDERMAN, INTERNATIONAL LAW FRAMEWORKS 8–9 (3d ed. 2010) ("Myth #3: International Law is not 'real' law. This statement is the heart of darkness for detractors of this subject. And, I must admit, that it is a pernicious myth and exceedingly difficult to debunk. . . . Repeated enough times, it becomes the proverbial 'big lie.'"). *See also* Harold Hongju Koh, Legal Adviser, U.S. Dep't of State, Remarks at the Annual Meeting of the American Society of International Law (Mar. 25, 2010), *available at* http://www.state.gov/s/l/releases/remarks/139119.htm ("[T]his Administration . . . reaffirmed its commitment to international law.") [hereinafter Koh, Remarks].

[12] John B. Bellinger III, *The Bush (43rd) Administration (2005–2009)*, *in* MICHAEL P. SCHARF & PAUL R. WILLIAMS, SHAPING FOREIGN POLICY IN TIMES OF CRISIS, at 146 (2010) ("In summary, in the Bush Administration's second term, the Office of the Legal Adviser was able to ensure and demonstrate U.S. adherence and respect for international law and institutions in many important cases.") [hereinafter Bellinger, *Bush Administration*]. *See also* John B. Bellinger III, Legal Adviser, U.S. Sec. of State, Luncheon Address at the 6th Annual International Law Conference hosted by the U.S. Naval War College, International Legal Public Diplomacy, 82 INT'L L. STUD. SER. US NAVAL WAR COL. 205 (2007) [hereinafter Bellinger, Address].

[13] Bellinger, *Bush Administration*, *supra* note 12, at 135–36 (quoting U.S. Secretary of State Condaleezza Rice as saying, "This Department, along with the rest of the Bush Administration, will be a strong voice for international legal norms, for living up to our treaty obligations, to recognizing that America's moral authority in international politics also rests on our ability to defend international laws and treaties").

[14] *See* Tony Blair, UK Prime Minister, Speech Spelling Out the Terror Threat Facing the UK and Defending the Iraq War (March 5, 2004), *available at* http://news.bbc.co.uk/2/hi/uk_news/politics/3536131.stm. (expressing frustration with "international law as presently constituted," and asking "[t]his may be the law, but should it be?").

[15] *See* Bellinger & Padmanabhan, *supra* note 2 at 202–03 ("During our respective tenures at the State Department, we responded regularly to concerns raised by foreign governments, nongovernmental and international organizations, and the media that the U.S. policies on [counter-terrorism

Human rights activists were horrified by the waterboarding, calling the interrogations illegal and immoral torture.[16] To be sure, arguments for and against the actions of officials were not only about international law. They were also about domestic law, executive power, normative values, and politics. But there is no denying that international law figured prominently in these debates.

Decisionmakers debated whether international law was law and whether they were required to obey it not because they thought the topic was intellectually important.[17] They argued because the topic was politically relevant.[18] What people think about international law and its obligations affects what government officials, judges, and other decisionmakers do.[19] In liberal democracies, such as the United States and the United Kingdom, governing elites care about what their constituencies think and how they feel. In less liberal or democratic states, such as China, the power and authority of officials and judges are nonetheless ultimately contingent on the minimal support, or at least grudging acquiescence, of their constituencies. When acting in an international dispute, governing elites from states and corporations also bother with whether other elites think they acted lawfully, because that influences how they respond. Whatever critics and supporters of international law say about it, they would all prefer that international law promote their interests than not, and they all try to interpret international laws in their favor.[20]

Reflecting contemporary anxieties about international law, a new wave of scholarship has reexamined questions about the nature of international law.[21] Many scholars

and national security], as implemented by the Bush administration after the 9/11 attacks, violated international law.").

[16] *See infra* ch. 7, pt. II.B. (discussing waterboarding).

[17] Bolton, *supra* note 10, at 1 ("It is hard to imagine a more desperately tedious-sounding topic than whether 'international law' is really law."); R. St. J. MacDonald & Douglas M. Johnston, *International Legal Theory: New Frontiers of the Discipline*, *in* The Structure and Process of International Law 1, 5 (MacDonald & Johnston eds., 1983) ("Very few international lawyers today are seriously interested in the philosophical question whether international law is really law.").

[18] Bolton, *supra* note 10, at 1 (describing the question of whether international law is law as "a political battle of immense significance"); Elizabeth Wilmshurst,: *The Best Defense? Legitimacy & Preventative Force*, 105 Am. J. Int'l L. 390, 394–95 (2011) (book review) ("The perceived legality, or not, of the intervention into Iraq in 2003 was an important factor in the debate on the international community's reactions.").

[19] *Cf.* Harold Hongju Koh, *Bringing International Law Home*, 35 Hous. L. Rev. 623, 628 (1999) [hereinafter Koh, *Bringing International Law Home*] (arguing that when constituents have "internalized the [international law] norm and incorporated it into its own internal value system," officials are more likely to obey international law); *Cf.* Robert Howse & Ruti Teitel, *Beyond Compliance: Rethinking Why International Law Really Matters*, Global Policy (Online), Vol. 1, No. 2; NYU School of Law, Public Law Research Paper No. 10-08, at 13 (Feb. 2010) ("[I]nternational law can affect the way that policymakers view international problems and conflicts . . . and their perception of the constituencies to whom they are accountable in addressing such problems and conflicts."), *available at* http://ssrn.com/abstract=1551923.

[20] *See* Goldsmith & Posner, *supra* note 5, at 184 ("Even as ruthlessly power-hungry a state as Nazi Germany always cloaked its behavior in the garb of international law and political morality.").

[21] *See* Waldron, *Hart and the Principles of Legality*, *supra* note 6, at 69 ("Theoretically [international law] is the issue of the hour."); 2 Rosalyn Higgins, Themes & Theories: Selected Essays,

now agree that there is limited value in discussing whether or not international law is really law.[22] The answer depends on what we pack into the label "international law." It also depends on one's preferred criteria for legality against which to compare international law and what one observes to be international law.[23] The answer seems beyond the reach of purely conceptual analysis.[24]

Inquiries about whether international law is effective and which decisionmakers ought to obey it, however, can yield important insights about the international legal system and provide practical guidance to decisionmakers. Although it can sometimes appear that scholars with differing viewpoints have found limited common ground,[25] their respective perspectives have more in common with each other than appears at first glance.[26] Scholars mostly agree that international law is partially, but not fully, effective. They also generally agree that it is sometimes morally good and sometimes morally bad.

In their widely discussed opus, THE LIMITS OF INTERNATIONAL LAW, Eric Posner and Jack Goldsmith examined treaties and customs and staked a realist claim that "[t]he morality or immorality of international law is exhausted by its content; international legality does not impose any moral obligations,"[27] and "states cannot bootstrap cooperation by creating rules and calling them 'law.'"[28]

SPEECHES AND WRITINGS IN INTERNATIONAL LAW 994 (2009) [hereinafter HIGGINS, THEMES & THEORIES] ("In recent years it has again become respectable to be interested in legal theory."). *See, e.g.*, MARY ELLEN O'CONNELL, THE POWER AND PURPOSE OF INTERNATIONAL LAW 1–16 (2008); ANDREW T. GUZMAN, HOW INTERNATIONAL LAW WORKS: A RATIONAL CHOICE THEORY 18 (2007); GOLDSMITH & POSNER, *supra* note 5; JUTTA BRUNNÉE & STEPHEN J. TOOPE, LEGITIMACY AND LEGALITY IN INTERNATIONAL LAW: AN INTERACTIONAL ACCOUNT 56 (2010).

22 MacDonald & Johnston, *supra* note 17, at 5 ("Most are prepared to treat the question as a rather arid exercise in semantics."); Thomas Franck, *Is International Law Really Law,* Remarks at the American Society of International Law Annual Meeting (March 27, 2009), *in* 103 AM. SOC'Y INT'L L. PROC. 31 (describing the question as a "tired old question").

23 *See* HANS KELSEN, PRINCIPLES OF INTERNATIONAL LAW 3 (1952) ("The answer to this question [of whether international law is law] depends on the definition of the concept of law."). *Compare* AUSTIN, *supra* note 6, at 107 (arguing international law is not law "properly so called" because it does not comprise commands backed by effective sanctions) *with* Peter J. Spiro, *A Negative Proof of International Law,* 34 GA. J. INT'L & COMP. L. 445, 461 (2006) (referring to "regimes that facilitate the creation and entrenchment of behavioral regularities on the ground" and asserting: "There is no institutional logic that precludes conceiving of these regimes as a form of law").

24 *See* GOLDSMITH & POSNER, *supra* note 5, at 201 ("International law scholars have long grappled with the question of whether international law is law. Some express impatience with this question as merely a matter of definition[.]").

25 *See* Bolton, *supra* note 10, at 1 (stating that "much of the intellectual debate" about the legality of international law "consists of two streams of argument that never really engage in actual combat"). *See also* SCHARF & WILLIAMS, *supra* note 12, at xx (2010) (expressing a view that scholars and practitioners have been unable to "precisely articulate the role of international law" because "many authors approach the question as an argument, asserting from the early pages of their work that international law matters, does not matter, should matter, or should not matter").

26 *See infra*, ch. 2, pt. III.C. (discussing in greater detail different contemporary accounts of international law).

27 GOLDSMITH & POSNER, *supra* note 5, at 197.

28 *Id.* at 203.

Other scholars have responded to THE LIMITS OF INTERNATIONAL LAW, attempting to restore faith in and understanding of the international legal system. Among other arguments, they have contended that Goldsmith and Posner adopted an overly narrow legalist account of international law, creating a straw man that seemed ineffective and lacking in inherent legitimacy.[29] Scholars proposed alternate and more sympathetic accounts of international law. Writing in the international law process tradition, Mary Ellen O'Connell published a monograph, THE POWER AND PURPOSE OF INTERNATIONAL LAW, which emphasized enforcement mechanisms in the international legal system and the universal values it promotes. Writing from an international relations perspective, Andrew Guzman published a monograph, HOW INTERNATIONAL LAW WORKS, arguing that complying with international legal prescriptions gives states reputational benefits and avoids reciprocal noncompliance and retaliation by other states. According to Guzman, international law is effective when these benefits outweigh the costs of compliance.[30]

Scholars who respectively favor or criticize international law have more in common than a superficial reading of each of their accounts of international law suggests. One of Goldsmith and Posner's essential points is that because states act rationally, international law "can be binding and robust only when it is rational for states to comply with it."[31] Guzman agrees with this rationalist assumption. Guzman, O'Connell, Goldsmith, and Posner also all agree that the morality of international prescriptions is variable. In a later essay, Guzman acknowledges that "international law is not always effective and it is not always just,"[32] echoing Goldsmith and Posner's argument that the substance of legal prescriptions affects their morality. O'Connell also would agree that the content of prescriptions affects their morality. She argues that it is important for decisionmakers to ensure that "decisions are consistent with the purposes of the international community, especially the higher purposes understood through the application of natural law theory to positive law rules,"[33] thereby implicitly accepting that prescriptions and decisions can be immoral.

There are certainly also important differences among these scholars. O'Connell emphasizes universal values, whereas Guzman, Goldsmith, and Posner focus on self-interest. Guzman argues that when international law functions well it promotes "international order,"[34] whereas Goldsmith and Posner think that the morality of

[29] *See* SCHARF & WILLIAMS, *supra* note 12, at 10–13 (surveying critiques of THE LIMITS OF INTERNATIONAL LAW); Matthew Turk, *The Perils of Global Legalism. By Eric Posner,* 42 INT'L LAW & POL. 344, 348 (2009) (book review).

[30] GUZMAN, *supra* note 21, at 211.

[31] GOLDSMITH & POSNER, *supra* note 5, at 202.

[32] Andrew Guzman, *Rethinking International Law as Law,* 103 AM. SOC'Y INT'L L. PROC. 155, 157 (2009).

[33] O'CONNELL, *supra* note 21, at 370.

[34] Guzman, *supra* note 32, at 157.

prescriptions is limited to their content,[35] implicitly minimizing any independent value in the international legal system as a whole.

Nevertheless, these differences should not obscure the points of agreement among conservative and liberal scholars. Every careful scholar would observe that international law can be effective and just, but is not always so. Every reasonable scholar would also agree that it would be better for international prescriptions to be more moral than less moral. What recent scholarship has not squarely addressed is, given that the international legal system is useful but imperfect, what should decisionmakers do about it, and how can they make it work better to the benefit of their constituencies and other relevant communities?

III. THESIS

Starting from the points of agreement among scholars that international law is partially effective and partially good, this book attempts to move the discussion forward by inquiring, from the respective standpoints of different decisionmakers in international problems, what each of them ought to do to address problems and to make the international legal system as effective and good as it can be in regulating communities and individuals with diverse preferences in a world without centralized authority.

The thesis that was briefly described in the introduction of this chapter is laid out in greater detail here by offering an account of the international legal system that focuses attention on the autonomous role of decisionmakers, and on separate analyses of effectiveness and morality in any international problem. This account is not the only way to think about the international legal system. However, it is useful for present purposes because it provides an analytic framework from which scholars can give realistic guidance to decisionmakers about what they ought to do when confronted with international problems.

A. The Central Case

One way to think about the international legal system is as a process to address international problems. In international problems, government officials, international and domestic judges, corporate officers, and other decisionmakers make decisions about what to do. One consideration in their decisionmaking is whether there are relevant prescriptions, including international laws, guidelines, principles, or even just shared expectations of appropriate conduct.

International law manifests most strongly in situations where decisionmakers have strongly shared expectations about appropriate conduct authorized or required by prescriptions. They also have strongly shared expectations for appropriate methods for identifying, interpreting, and applying laws and other prescriptions to facts.

[35] Goldsmith & Posner, *supra* note 5, at 203.

These methods are not random or arbitrary. Instead, they comport with methods of legalist reasoning and procedures that elites have generally accepted. Borrowing from Aristotelian philosophy, these situations can be termed the "central case" or focal meaning of the idea of the international legal system.

Many central case situations involve international laws because decisionmakers have a strongly shared expectation that the relevant prescriptions are binding as international law and that decisionmakers ought to interpret and apply them according to legalist methods. Examples of such central case situations are decisions of the International Court of Justice (ICJ). The ICJ follows its legalist procedures to reach decisions. It limits its decisions to outcomes justifiable through legalist reasoning. Although it is often possible to identify dicta in ICJ decisions or the out-of-court statements of its judges indicating that they were also concerned about the normative, moral, and political dimensions of international problems,[36] judgments are ultimately expressed as legal decisions and justified by legal prescriptions, not unlike the U.S. Supreme Court's rulings.[37] National and international courts and tribunals refer to ICJ opinions as authoritative or highly persuasive statements of international law.[38]

In other central case situations, there may be informal, but nevertheless widely accepted, prescriptions, methods of reasoning, and procedures. Problems involving such informal shared expectations may not technically involve international laws, but the problems are nevertheless law-like, and the process for identifying, interpreting, and applying these informal shared expectations are often similar to the legalist process. An example of this is the Basel Accords on banking supervision, discussed in Chapter Six, or the informal practices involving the succession of states to preexisting international commercial obligations even in the absence of formal laws governing their transmission.[39] Conceiving of international law to include

[36] *See* Davis R. Robinson, *The Reagan Administration–Davis R. Robinson (1981–1985)*, *in* SCHARF & WILLIAMS, *supra* note 12, at 61 (Davis Robinson, the Legal Adviser of the U.S. State Department, recalled an ICJ judge deciding the *Gulf of Maine* case telling him he "had only one objective, and that was equal disappointment for both the United States and Canada.").

[37] *See* MARK TUSHNET, A COURT DIVIDED: THE REHNQUIST COURT AND THE FUTURE OF CONSTITUTIONAL LAW 360 (2006) ("In short, the deepest truth about how constitutional law develops is that constitutional law is connected to politics, and what happens in the wider political system will determine the [Supreme] Court's legacy."); RICHARD A. POSNER, HOW JUDGES THINK 269 (2008) (" . . . Justices of the U.S. Supreme Court, particularly when they are deciding issues of constitutional law, . . . are political judges[.]").

[38] *See, e.g.*, Medellín v. Texas, 552 U.S. 491, 498 (2008) (accepting ICJ decision as authoritative under international law, but holding that "contrary to the ICJ's determination, the Vienna Convention did not preclude the application of state default rules"); Al-Saadoon v. U.K., App. No. 61498/08, at 2 (Eur. Ct. H.R., Mar. 2, 2010), (following the holding of the ICJ in its *Wall Advisory Opinion* that the International Covenant for Civil and Political Rights applies extraterritorially); R. v. Cook, [1998] 2 S.C.R. 597, ¶ 139 (Can.) (citing the ICJ's *Nottebohm Case* as providing a standard for "determining whether the minimum threshold for nationality has been met in international law").

[39] *See generally* TAI-HENG CHENG, STATE SUCCESSION AND COMMERCIAL OBLIGATIONS (2006); Tai-Heng Cheng, *Why New States Accept Old Obligations*, 2011 U. ILL. L. REV. 1 (2011).

informal prescriptions in this manner helps decisionmakers to consider what is expected of them and whether there ought to be such expectations, more so than focusing only on formal legal rules, which do not fully convey all the expectations of appropriate conduct that decisionmakers expect of each other.

B. Effectiveness

The central case concerns only social facts about shared expectations of appropriate prescriptions and interpretative methods. It says nothing about the effectiveness of these shared expectations in controlling the behavior of decisionmakers or outcomes in international problems.[40]

It is useful to separate the existence of international law from the effectiveness of its prescriptions because many prescriptions are not enforceable against noncompliant decisionmakers. Even prescriptions that have enforcement mechanisms are only enforceable to a degree. Under the Convention on Recognition and Enforcement of Foreign Arbitral Awards (the New York Convention),[41] the awards of international arbitral tribunals are enforced by national courts, subject to limited exceptions for applicable international or national laws and the procedural rules of administering arbitral institutions, as prescribed in the Convention's Article V.[42] Similarly, under the Convention on the Settlement of Investment Disputes between States and Nationals of Other States (the Washington Convention), every signatory state is bound to enforce an arbitration award rendered under the Convention.[43] However, the enforceability of arbitral awards rendered under these two conventions is ultimately contingent on signatory states abiding by provisions of the treaties. Aside from a strongly shared expectation of compliance and pragmatic and moral reasons to comply, there is no centralized authoritative body with coercive force to stop states from breaching their treaty obligations by refusing to enforce awards that do not fall into one of the treaty exceptions for nonenforcement.

The Rome Statute is a multilateral treaty setting up the International Criminal Court (ICC). The statute confers jurisdiction on the ICC over heinous international

[40] *Cf.* Hart, The Concept of Law, *supra* note 6 (postulating that only officials need to have an internal perspective that law and a rule of recognition exists without drawing a strong connection between the existence of law and its effectiveness in controlling conduct or outcomes). *See generally* Hans Kelsen, Pure Theory of Law (Max Knight trans., 1989) (propounding a concept of law based on a *grund norm*, or basic norm, from which all laws emanate, without focusing on the effectiveness of laws).

[41] Convention on the Recognition and Enforcement of Foreign Arbitral Awards, June 10, 1958, 330 U.N.T.S. 3 [hereinafter The New York Convention]. *See also* Federal Arbitration Act, 9 U.S.C. §§ 201–08 (enacting the New York Convention into U.S. law); Arbitration Act of 1996, ch. 23 (Eng.) (enacting New York Convention into UK law).

[42] The New York Convention, art. 5, *supra* note 41; Convention on the Settlement of Investment Disputes Between States and Nationals of Other States, Mar. 18, 1965, 575 U.N.T.S. 159 (entered into force Oct. 14, 1966) [hereinafter The Washington Convention]. *See also* Federal Arbitration Act, *supra* note 41.

[43] The Washington Convention, *supra* note 42.

crimes, such as genocide and crimes against humanity.[44] It obliges signatory states to carry out prison sentences and to enforce fines and forfeiture measures in sentences that the ICC imposes on persons convicted of international crimes.[45] However, should a signatory state decide to violate its treaty obligations under the Rome Statute, the statute contains no legal mechanism for enforcement against the violating state.

Decisions of the ICJ are enforceable against states in contentious disputes, but there are important practical limitations on the effectiveness of court decisions against states that disobey them. Under the Statute of the ICJ, the court's decisions in contentious disputes are enforceable because the UN Security Council can pass a Chapter VII resolution authorizing coercive measures, including military force, to enforce ICJ judgments.[46] Practically speaking, no ICJ decision against a permanent member of the UN Security Council, each which holds a veto on the Council,[47] could ever be enforced, although Security Council member states often comply with the ICJ's decisions.

However, it would be too glib to dismiss the international legal system as thoroughly ineffective in controlling the actions of decisionmakers and outcomes in international problems. In many international disputes, decisionmakers consider international law, which consequently may be one factor in regulating how they act and the outcome of the incident. In 1983, communist revolutionaries in Grenada murdered their head of state and placed his successor under house arrest. The Reagan administration was inclined to invade Grenada. Before a decision was made, officials consulted Davis Robinson, the Legal Advisor of the State Department. Mr. Robinson advised the Reagan administration that the invasion would be legal. As a political matter, Mr. Robinson avoided arguing that there was an inherent right of self-defense or that invasion was lawful as a humanitarian matter, which could have been a strong legal argument. The United States did not rely on this argument in order to avoid legitimizing the Brezhnev Doctrine, which claimed the Soviet Union had the right to militarily support communist movements in third world states.[48] International law is entwined with politics.

Nevertheless, international laws were relevant. President Reagan ordered the invasion of Grenada only after Mr. Robinson advised him that it was lawful. This evidence does not prove that the United States invaded Grenada because its international lawyers advised that the invasion was legal. This evidence does suggest, however, that the requirements of legality imposed some—albeit unquantifiable—constraint

[44] Rome Statute of the International Criminal Court art. 5, U.N. Doc. A/CONF.183/9 (1998) [hereinafter Rome Statute].

[45] *Id.*, arts. 103–11.

[46] *See* Statute of the International Court of Justice art. 41(2), 33 U.N.T.S. 993 (1945) [hereinafter ICJ Statute].

[47] *See* UN Charter art. 27, ¶ 3.

[48] Scharf & Williams, *supra* note 12, at 55–64.

on the use of force by the United States, and that it mattered in subsequently being able to justify the President's actions to Congress.[49]

The international legal system may also succeed in resolving disputes where diplomatic efforts fail. Canada and the United States tried for over 30 years to reach an agreement on the maritime boundary of the Georges Bank, a fertile fishing ground located between the two countries. Eventually, both states decided to submit the dispute to the ICJ. The ICJ's *Gulf of Maine* decision, rendered in 1984,[50] resolved the issue and was respected by both state parties. Similarly, Singapore and Malaysia disagreed about who exercised sovereignty over Pedra Branca, a rocky outcrop located between them. After decades of failed diplomatic negotiations, the respective governments decided to pass the issue to the ICJ. The ICJ rendered its decision in 2008, largely resolving the dispute for the parties and removing this thorn in their bilateral diplomatic relations.[51]

In other international problems involving acute national interests, international law may play only a subsidiary role, if any. When the Reagan administration decided to fund Nicaraguan contras, which the ICJ eventually decided was in violation of customary international law and the UN Charter provision prohibiting the unilateral use of force except in self-defense,[52] the international lawyers at the State Department were not consulted. The CIA directed these activities covertly. Although it is impossible to tell if the CIA considered international law in its secret papers and discussions, Mr. Robinson has stated that as a result of excluding his legal department, which is charged with ensuring U.S. compliance with international law, the Reagan administration was "caught legally off guard" when the covert operation inadvertently became public.[53] This statement is evidence that international law did not play a significant role in shaping U.S. foreign policy in the Nicaragua affair.

Any analysis of the effectiveness of the international legal system therefore requires a highly contextual study of each international problem. No rational government official would comply with international laws restricting when and how military force may be used against a putative enemy if the official was certain that complying with the law would result in his state's annihilation.[54] *Inter arma silent leges.* That same government may, however, decide to comply with an adverse World

[49] *Id.* at 59 (recounting that Senator Patrick Moynihan objected to the invasion, and Mr. Robinson was asked to provide his legal analysis to the Senate).

[50] Delimitation of the Maritime Boundary in the Gulf of Maine Area (Can. v. U.S.), 1984 I.C.J. 246 (Oct. 12).

[51] *See generally* Shunmugam Jayakumar & Tommy Koh, Pedra Branca: The Road to the World Court (2009); Sovereignty Over Pedra Branca/Pulau Batu Puteh, Middle Rocks and South Ledge (Malay./Sing.) Judgment, 2008 I.C.J. 12 (May 23). For a further discussion of this case, *see infra* ch. 4, pt. II.A.

[52] Military and Paramilitary Activities In and Against Nicaragua (Nicar. v. U.S.), Judgment on Merits 1986 I.C.J. 14 (June 27). For a further discussion of this case, *see infra* ch. 4, pt. II.B.

[53] *See* Scharf & Williams, *supra* note 12, at 60.

[54] *See* W. Michael Reisman, *No Man's Land: International Legal Regulation of Coercive Responses to Protracted and Low Level Conflict,* 11 Hous. J. Int'l L. 317, 328 (1988–89) [hereinafter Reisman, *No Man's Land*]; Bellinger, *Bush Administration, supra* note 12, at 146 ("[E]xisting criminal laws and

Trade Organization (WTO) tribunal ruling on an international trade dispute because it derives benefits from favorable WTO tribunal rulings in other disputes, and therefore would not want to undermine the WTO institution with its noncompliance, or present other states with an excuse to reciprocally ignore WTO tribunal decisions.[55]

In order to understand the effectiveness *vel non* of the international legal system, it is necessary to focus on the decisiomaking process in international problems. In broad terms, in every international problem, decisionmakers will tend to identify relevant prescriptions and decide how to interpret and apply a prescription to predicate facts. Its decision will trigger responses from other elites, who go through a similar process of deciding what to do. These decisions collectively produce outcomes in international problems. They also shape expectations about what will happen, and ought to happen, in future problems. However, outcomes in future problems will also ultimately depend on the interpretive decisionmaking process in those problems. It is this process that determines the effectiveness of the international legal system in particular problems and in general.

C. Legitimacy

Building on the foregoing account of the international legal system, this book offers a justificatory framework to help decisionmakers consider relevant prescriptions and what they ought to do. It is justificatory in the sense of shaping the international legal system to more effectively achieve good outcomes in international problems and to provide reasons to promote and obey prescriptions.

Decisionmakers generally ought to abide by prescriptions and shared expectations about how prescriptions should be interpreted and applied, as well as changed, in international problems because, although prescriptions in the international legal system are not necessarily laws, the international legal system is necessary for stability and order. These shared expectations are often expressed as rules about sources of laws and interpreting laws. However, they also include informal expectations that are not actually laws, when the expectations are clear to all decisionmakers. When decisionmakers keep faith with shared expectations and can count on each other to do so, international law coordinates action, promotes some basic shared values, and minimizes the need for destructive actions.[56] Adapting a term from natural law philosophy, such an international order can be called the "common good," which

international humanitarian laws, such as the Geneva Conventions, d[o] not neatly apply to the new threats posed by groups like Al-Qaeda.").

[55] *Compare* Brazil—Measures Affecting Patent Protection, Request for Establishment of a Panel by the United States, WT/DS199/3 (Jan. 9, 2001) *with* Panel Report, United States-Section 129(C)(1) Uruguay Round Agreements Act, WT/DS221/R (July 15, 2002) *and* Jeanne J. Grimmett, Congressional Research Service, WTO Decisions and Their Effect in U.S. Law (2007).

[56] *See also* Koh, *Forward*, *supra* note 11, at xvi (discussing why international law is normatively important); Abram Chayes & Antonia Handler Chayes, The New Sovereignty: Compliance with International Regulatory Agreements 3–4 (1995).

provides conditions for different communities in the world to pursue their respective preferred values and interests.[57]

The relationship between prescriptions and the common good provides a rational, or even moral, reason to promote prescriptions by interpreting them legalistically and by obeying prescriptions. It is this relationship that creates a rebuttable reason for decisionmakers to create, interpret, and apply prescriptions in accordance with the shared expectations of elites.

In order to conclusively decide how to interpret a prescription or even ignore it, a decisionmaker should be cognizant of his institutional functions and the scope and limits of his authority. He should also account for the specific values that are at stake in the international problem and how the interpretation being considered will affect them. Because prescriptions can only make a practical difference if other decisionmakers accept them, the decisionmaker should also consider whether he needs to account for the vital interests of powerful actors, to ensure that the prescription has a minimum degree of effectiveness. Finally, he should pay attention to the pace at which expectations are consolidated. In some instances, leaving prescriptions vague and informal is necessary to accommodate vital interests until circumstances change, or to allow decisionmakers to test tentative prescriptions until they are confident that the outcomes prescribed appropriately serve relevant values and interests.

Where a prescription is archaic or obsolete, a decisionmaker should neither claim that the prescription does not apply only to him or to that situation, nor claim that the prescription has changed without giving reasons. In response, other decisionmakers will tend to also claim exceptions, or they may apply the changed prescription without adequately appraising it. Such arbitrary adjustments to expectations of appropriate conduct undermine the effectiveness of the international legal system and the common good it promotes.

International problems studied later in the book illustrate this negative feedback loop. In the *Nicaragua* case, the International Court of Justice (ICJ) decided to limit the UN Charter prescription permitting self-defense against armed attacks to attacks by or on behalf of other states, even though that limitation does not appear in the prescription's text.[58] The Court did so without sufficient legalist justification.[59] Subsequently, this adjustment was accepted without appraisal by the majority of ICJ judges in the *Wall Opinion*, in which the Court seemed to decide that Israel had no

[57] *See infra* ch. 3, pt. IV (discussing the common good).

[58] Military and Paramilitary Activities In and Against Nicaragua (Nicar. v. U.S.), Judgment on Merits, 1986 I.C.J. 14, 103 ¶ 195 (June 27).

[59] *See* Legal Consequences of the Construction of a Wall in the Occupied Palestinian Territory, Advisory Opinion, 2004 I.C.J. 136, 215 (July 9) (separate opinion of Judge Higgins) ("There is, with respect, nothing in the text of Article 51 that thus stipulates that self-defence is available only when an armed attack is made by a State. That qualification is rather a result of the Court so determining in *Military and Paramilitary Activities in and against Nicaragua* (. . .). It there held that military action by irregulars could constitute an armed attack if these were sent by or on behalf of the State and if the activity 'because of its scale and effects, would have been classified as an armed attack . . . had it been carried out by regular armed forces.'"). *See also infra*, ch. 4, pt. II.B.

right of self-defense against attacks by Palestinians on the basis that Palestine is not a state.[60]

The *Nicaragua* decision also affected international problems not involving the ICJ. When Serbia committed genocide against Muslim Albanians in the late 1990s, the prescription permitting collective self-defense did not permit NATO countries to use force to stop Serbia, because the genocide was an armed attack within a state and not by a state against another state.

In turn, when NATO bombed Serbia in 1999 without UN Security Council authorization, it claimed that the decision was *sui generis*.[61] Although this decision was reasonably justified on humanitarian grounds, NATO states did not clarify their adjustment to the law of force. Instead, they claimed an unregulated exception. Consequently, U.S. Secretary of Defense Donald Rumsfeld and Vice President Richard Cheney persuaded President Bush that he was legally permitted to invade Iraq in 2003 because of the precedent set by the 1999 NATO bombing of Serbia. If NATO countries, the Security Council, or the ICJ had clarified the adjustment to the law of force in 1999, U.S. officials would not have concluded as easily that the bombing of Serbia provided a basis to invade Iraq.[62]

To avoid arbitrary feedback loops, decisionmakers that disobey or change a prescription should explain the reasons for their disobedience and propose changes for other elites to consider. That way, the international legal system could adjust to contemporary needs, continue regulating international problems, and promote the common good. As discussed in Chapter Four, when the United States disobeyed the Vienna Convention on Consular Relations by failing to inform arrested foreign nationals of their right to speak to their consular officers, it did not claim for itself an arbitrary exception to the Vienna Convention.[63] Instead, it explained to the ICJ that it had taken measures to comply, but that the measures were not fully effective in training its local law enforcement officers, due to the practical challenges of educating a broad swath of officers in a large country. Moreover, the federal government could not, under its constitutional structure, force state courts to reexamine the convictions of foreigners whose Vienna Convention rights were violated. Today, no other Vienna Convention state has claimed that the Convention does not apply to it in response to U.S. violations, and the Vienna Convention continues to offer assurances to citizens of all its signatory states who travel overseas.

The foregoing summary of this book's account of the international legal system is necessarily a very rough outline for now. The case studies mentioned briefly above, as well as other case studies, are examined in greater detail in subsequent chapters. They will test and refine the explanatory and justificatory account of the

[60] Legal Consequences of the Construction of a Wall in the Occupied Palestinian Territory, Judgment on Merits, 2004 I.C.J. 136 (July, 9). *See infra*, ch. 4, pts. II.B.1.d & II.B.4.

[61] *Infra*, ch. 8, pt. II.B.

[62] *Infra*, ch. 8, pt. II.C.

[63] *Infra*, ch. 4, pt. II.C.

international legal system, and hopefully clarify and illustrate how this framework of analysis applies to actual problems and how it can help guide elites in future problems. The goal is not to provide algorithms for elites to decide what to do, or to nullify their discretion in making decisions. It is also not principally to provide a predictive model of what officials will do. It is, more modestly, to provide a framework to guide their analysis of problems and their exercise of their judgment and discretion.

Because the account of international law presented here is politically moderate, it will not satisfy readers who hold political views to the far left and right of it. Some of its analysis about controversial international problems will come under intense scrutiny. For example, Chapter Seven offers reasons why legal advisors could authorize government officials to waterboard terrorists in exceptional circumstances and on a case-by-case basis, provided the waterboarding is videotaped for later review. Chapter Eight argues that the invasion of Iraq in 2003 was probably both illegal and illegitimate in retrospect, but nevertheless a reasonable decision in 2003 if U.S. government officials acted in good faith on the best intelligence that was available to them at the time. Some liberals may be shocked that waterboarding could even be countenanced, and others will disagree that the invasion of Iraq could possibly be reasonable. Some conservatives may object to the chilling effect of videotaping the waterboarding of terrorists by interrogators who have to do their duty, and others may reject the idea that U.S. and UK officials who decided to invade Iraq caused their countries to violate international law.

One of the key propositions of this book's thesis is that law is an interpretative process intertwined with morality.[64] Consequently, disagreement is natural and, ironically, is consistent with the thesis. It is hoped that some readers will be persuaded by the analyses in the book, and others will decide that they are reasonable even if they disagree with them. Separate and apart from whatever readers think about the book's conclusions about specific international problems, it is hoped that readers will consider whether the overall thesis about the international legal system explains how it works, and whether it provides a useful framework for elites to think about what they ought to do in international problems.

International law scholars will have detected by now a policy-oriented bent to this book's thesis. National security policies of the United States, which have continued under the Obama administration—such as using unmanned drones to extrajudicially assassinate suspected terrorists in Pakistan[65]—appear to have renewed

[64] Richard Falk, *Legality & Legitimacy: The Quest for Principled Flexibility and Restraint*, 31 Rev. Int'l Stud. 33, 50 (Supp. 2005) (arguing that the "gap between legality and legitimacy is not a matter of substantive standard, but interpretative clarity"). *See also* Wilmshurst, supra note 18, at 393 ("[E]ven the most black-letter of foreign ministry lawyers should recognize the need to call in aid extralegal principles where legal authorities and state practice are divided.").

[65] *See* Mary Ellen O'Connell, *The International Law of Drones*, 14:30 ASIL Insights, (Nov. 12, 2010); Koh, Remarks *supra* note 11 (defending the Obama administration's use of drones).

scholastic debates about different approaches to international law and the political consequences of each approach.[66] It is not the purpose of this book to rehash old debates. Nor is it the purpose of this book to show that one approach is superior to another. Instead, the book seeks to test and validate a framework of analysis under contemporary global conditions, using tools of policy-oriented jurisprudence. Through the course of this book, scholars will see that the analysis also draws on and takes seriously important insights from other international legal theories. Ultimately, it is hoped that the reader will see how the overarching policy-oriented framework of this book situates several other theories in relation to each other and encourages elites to pursue different types of inquiries drawing from different theoretical approaches, according to what is best suited to their particular institutional roles, tasks, and problems.

IV. TERMS

A number of key terms appear throughout this book. Generally, there is no need to use a technical word to express an idea if a plain word would do the job just as well. Nonetheless, in the interest of precision, it is necessary to clarify a few terms. Otherwise, they might carry different special meanings for different scholars. Readers who find definitions tedious may wish to skip this section and return to it later when they encounter ambiguous terms.

"Decisionmakers" refers to human beings who, individually or in collective groups, set policies and make decisions for their constituents and themselves. The most obvious decisionmakers are officials of the executive branch of government. Judges and legislators also set policies and make decisions for their constituents, and these policies and decisions affect international relations and international disputes.

In international law, it is no longer sufficient to focus solely on government officials because many other decisionmakers, such as corporations, nongovernmental organizations (NGOs), and international organizations, interact internationally and affect outcomes in international disputes. Consequently, it is necessary also to consider a wide range of relevant actors in international problems, including senior corporate executives, heads of NGOs, and international civil servants. Nonetheless, because most decisionmaking authority in international problems is most often vested in government officials and judges, this book focuses on these two categories of elites.

[66] *See, e.g.*, Andrew Guzman, Antonia Chayes, Jose Alvarez, Thomas Franck, Sean Murphy, Panel Discussion: *In What Sense is International Law Law?*, 103 Soc'y Int'l L. Proc. 155 (2009). *See also* D. Stephen Mathias, Anthea Roberts, & Carlos M. Vazquez, *An Introduction: International Law as Law*, 103 Am. Soc'y Int'l L. Proc. 1 ("[Contemporary] developments are challenging and transforming traditional visions of international law, sparking new and renewed theoretical and practical debates.").

Occasionally this book refers to "elites" or "governing elites" interchangeably with "decisionmakers." This usage is purely for convenience because "decisionmakers" is a mouthful and to avoid an artificially constricted vocabulary. The word "elite" is not intended to convey an elitist attitude. It simply differentiates, in a realistic fashion, actors who affect outcomes in international disputes, and constituents or other actors who do not directly control outcomes. Notably, constituents may nevertheless exert considerable and even dispositive influence on their governing elites.

"Prescription" means a directive for action. It encompasses laws (if you drive over 50 miles per hour, you will be fined); rules (the principal brief you file in U.S. Federal Appellate court must be 14,000 words or fewer)[67]; principles (treat your counterparty in good faith); and norms (attorneys wear suits in court), which could be social in nature (there is no court rule requiring attorneys to wear dark suits), or legal in nature (a judge might instruct an attorney to wear a suit and may sanction him for disobeying), or even just shared expectations of appropriate conduct (attorneys treat each other with professional courtesies). The word "prescription" is used where it is necessary to convey the idea of a directive that makes a practical difference without debating whether it is legal or nonlegal. Because its component terms, such as laws, norms, and principles, each have different meanings to different scholars, the word prescription is also used when there is no need to get into those definitional debates.

"Effectiveness" refers to making a practical difference, or causing a course of action or outcome to be different, or excluding other potential actions or outcomes.[68] This is observed by what actually happens or could potentially be caused to happen, without any normative appraisal of whether it is good or bad. Policy-oriented jurists and international legal scholars use "effectiveness" and "control" interchangeably.[69]

International law's "legitimacy" is explored throughout this book. Its legitimacy is appraised in terms of whether particular prescriptions are normatively appropriate, that is, whether they promote appropriate values, and whether the process through which law is created, applied, modified, and terminated promotes values, and

[67] Fed. R. App. Proc. 32(B)(i).

[68] *Cf.* John Finnis, Natural Law and Natural Rights 12 (1996) (referring to "practical" as "with a view of decision and action").

[69] Oscar Schachter, Remarks at the American Society of International Law Annual Meeting (Apr. 26, 1985), *in* 79 Am. Soc'y Int'l L. Proc. 266, 268 (1985) (explaining control as "govern[ing] behavior" and "power defined as the capability to influence behavior"); Thomas M. Franck, The Power of Legitimacy Among Nations 41–49 (1990) [hereinafter Franck, Power]. *See also* Rosalyn Higgins, *Integrations of Authority and Control: Trends in Literature of International Law and International Relations, in* Toward World Order and Human Dignity: Essays in Honor of Myers S. McDougal 79–80 (W. M. Reisman & B. Weston eds., 1976) (using the terms "effectiveness" and "control" synonymously).

whether the system as a whole promotes appropriate values.[70] For policy-oriented jurists, this is one component of "authority."[71]

The term "normative" is used in connection with values that are good or bad in a general sense and "that can be participated in or realized in indefinitely many ways on indefinitely many occasions."[72] Normative inquiries, relate, for example, to whether a prescription promotes well-being. Normative goals may be general (well-being is a basic good). Particular interests of a community may be normative because they are generalizable (Official X wants her country to become more militarily powerful to promote the national security necessary to protect the well-being of its citizens; well-being in a general sense is good for every community). Other particular interests may not be obviously normative without further information on why those interests are desired (Official Y wants his country to become more militarily powerful because it desires to be able to do what it wants in international relations). Often, complex normative problems concern conflicts between relevant values and how to balance them in international problems.

"Morality" is discussed at great length in Chapter Three. In a nutshell, it is the reasoned appraisal of action that has consequences for values. Morality is about the relationship between conduct and values. Often, moral appraisals are used interchangeably with normative appraisals. They are concerned with whether the actions of decisionmakers, or whether prescriptions requiring certain actions, promote relevant values and harmonize competing values.

"Politics" carries many different meanings in different contexts.[73] For clarity, this book refers to "politics" or "political" to mean the pursuit of self-interest, power, or preferred values by a community, such as a state, political party, or corporation, and overriding or seeking to override formal and informal regulatory constraints if necessary to achieve the community's goals. When people rhetorically pose the question "Is international law just politics?" they often mean to imply that international law fails to regulate decisionmakers acting in pursuit of self-interest, power, or preferred values. When this chapter referred to "political debates about whether international law is law," it was referring to debates in which each decisionmaker sought to characterize the nature of international law in a certain way that would support

[70] *But cf.* FRANCK, POWER, *supra* note 69, at 24 ("Legitimacy is a property of a rule or rule-making institution which itself exerts a pull toward compliance on those addressed normatively because those addressed believe that the rule or institution has come into being and operates in accordance with generally accepted principles of right process.").

[71] Higgins, *supra* note 69. *See also* Schachter, *supra* note 69, at 267–68 (explaining authority as "a range of decisions that carry with them 'expectations of compliance'" and associating it with "legitimacy").

[72] FINNIS, *supra* note 68, at 61.

[73] *See id.* at 148 ("'Politics' without qualification signifies a field of action and discourse to do with the affairs of complete communities."); TERRY NARDIN, LAW, MORALITY, AND THE RELATIONS OF STATES 35 (1983) (discussing power politics as the pursuit of vital interests over rules governing the relations of states); Arthur A. Stein, *Coordination and Collaboration: Regimes in an Anarchic World*, *in* INTERNATIONAL REGIMES 115, 117 (S. Kranser ed., 2d prtg. 1984) ("International politics is typically characterized by independent self-interested decision making[.]").

that decisionmaker's pursuit of self-interest, power, or preferred values; or constrain other decisionmakers from pursuing their self-interest, power, or preferred values.

"International law," or the "international legal system," refers to a system that seeks to authoritatively regulate human behavior in international problems.[74] In this context, "system" refers to "a regularly interacting or interdependent group of items."[75] International law comprises laws, or formal legal rules, as well as other prescriptions. In an international problem where international law is ineffective, politics may control outcomes. In an international problem where international law is effective, it constrains politics, and decisionmakers are restricted from pursuing self-interest, power, or preferred values in a manner inconsistent with the regulatory framework of the international legal system.

"Theory" is another word that has many different meanings. The theory of international law in this book does not refer to a falsifiable hypothesis about observable phenomena. It does not predict outcomes and the behavior of decisionmakers in international problems through such hypotheses. Instead, the book is an account of the international legal system that offers a way of explaining how the international legal system operates and guides decisionmakers in international problems. It is an interpretative account of international law that seeks to fit and justify the practice it interprets.[76] This book refers to its "account of the international legal system" and its "theory of international law" interchangeably to mean its explanatory and justificatory interpretation of the international legal system.

V. OUTLINE OF INQUIRY

This book develops, tests, and refines its thesis in the following fashion. Chapters Two and Three are more theoretical. They set out, respectively, an analysis of prior theories and a detailed exposition of this book's theory of international law. Chapters Four through Eight apply the book's account to different types of decisionmakers: judges, arbitrators, regulators, legal advisors, and officials, respectively. These chapters focusing on different types of decisionmakers refine the account of international law using case studies. Chapter Nine draws conclusions from the theoretical inquiries and case studies.

Chapter Two surveys extant and apparently conflicting international legal theories to better understand disputes about international law. It concludes that even at the level of theory, disagreements are not purely conceptual. They are, in deep ways, normative and political disagreements. Every theory is based upon assumptions that cannot be taken for granted. These assumptions relate to, for example, the functions of law, what makes up a legal system, and whether a conception of law needs to fit

[74] *Cf.* Finnis, *supra* note 68, at 148 (defining the central case of law as a complete system that "claim[s] authority to regulate all forms of human behavior" without necessarily being effective).

[75] Jennifer Martinez, *Towards an International Judicial System*, 56 Stan. L. Rev. 429, 443 (2003).

[76] *See* Ronald Dworkin, Law's Empire 285 (1986) ("A successful interpretation must not only fit but also justify the practice it interprets.").

with what people think the word "law" means. Theorists have to choose their assumptions before they construct an account of international law, and their choices shape their theories. Further, a study of the personal backgrounds of theorists and social conditions of their respective times indicates that their theoretical assumptions are often conscious or inadvertent choices about appropriate ways to regulate conduct, appropriate allocations of authority among decisionmakers, and what values to prefer over others. Therefore, although legal theories are conceptual, they are also deeply normative as well as being political theories about morality, sovereignty, and how the world should be ordered.

Having argued that theories about international law have political and normative aspects, Chapter Three sets out in detail this book's moderate account of the international legal system that Chapter One introduced. This account is directed toward basic ideals but tempered by realistic expectations about what is achievable and appropriate in a world without a fully effective centralized authority and populated by communities and individuals with diverse preferred values.

Chapter Four applies this account of the international legal system to international judges. It applies the general moral considerations of decisionmakers to judges and examines the extent to which their judicial function tends to justify stronger fidelity to legalism, and the extent to which departures from legalism are warranted. This inquiry is pursued by examining several ICJ decisions: the *Pedra Branca* decision resolving a territorial dispute between Singapore and Malaysia, the *Nicaragua* decision concerning military and paramilitary activities, the *Avena* decision concerning violations of the Vienna Convention on Consular Relations, and the *Wall Opinion* concerning the barrier that Israel erected around the West Bank.

Chapter Five considers how the account of international law applies to arbitrators. In particular, it asks how the framework of analysis addresses the private consensual nature of arbitration and its implications for how arbitrators should decide disputes. Chapter Five refines the account further by examining a WTO award in *United States-Stainless Steel (Mexico)*, the NAFTA award in *Loewen v. United States*, and the ICSID ad hoc Committee decision in *CMS Gas Transmission Co. v. Argentina*.

Chapter Six investigates whether the account of international law provides guidance to regulators. It considers how the focus on shared expectations rather than formal laws enables the theory to accommodate important methods of stabilizing international activities in the absence of international laws. The chapter examines, in particular, the global recession of 2008, and contrasts the regulatory failures in 2008 with the ongoing efforts of the Financial Stability Board convened by the G-20's central bank governors.

Chapter Seven extends the inquiry to legal advisors. It explores the idea that legal advisors serve different functions—namely, advising, authorizing, and advocating. Each function requires different degrees of fidelity to legalism. But in almost every instance, the legal advisor's authority is subservient to elected officials, who retain discretion to obey or disobey prescriptions, and to attract corresponding consequences. These propositions are tested against the inhumane treatment of detainees in Abu Ghraib and the waterboarding of terrorists.

Chapter Eight completes the survey of different types of decisionmakers by studying what guidance the account of international law provides to government officials, with a particular emphasis on the decision to go to war. It shows how the theory of international law accounts for vital national interests, but guides decisionmakers in adjusting obsolete rules on self-defense rather than rejecting them and risking disorder as other decisionmakers similarly abandon this basic strut of world order. These ideas are explored through detailed analyses of the 1990 Gulf War, the 1999 bombing of Serbia by NATO, and the 2003 invasion of Iraq.

Chapter Nine draws conclusions about this book's account of the international legal system in light of the prior case studies.

VI. CONCLUSION

The question "Is international law really law?" is a deeply political question about how the world should be ordered and whether domestic elites should be constrained by an international system. Labeling that system "law" is a political act. It is commonly perceived that laws impose obligations to comply simply because of their legal nature, thereby often minimizing inquiries into whether the content of a specific law, and the legal system as a whole, is good and ought to be followed. Thus, calling the international legal system "law" increases pressure on decisionmakers to comply with its prescriptions because of perceptions that they are obliged to follow those prescriptions as laws. Conversely, denying the legality of the international legal system, and calling it just a political arrangement, increases the freedom of decisionmakers to ignore its claims, or at least to question whether its claims are good and ought to be followed.

When some scholars and pundits express exasperation with the question of whether international law is law, they are not just intellectually bored. They are often frustrated that their political view of world order has not snuffed out all opposing political visions even after centuries of battle.[77] One strategy to silence opponents in a debate is to dismiss the debate out of hand with disbelief that the debate has not ended after all this time, as if it had been settled long ago against the opponent.

It is precisely because the nature of international law raises not just a conceptual issue, but also a political and normative issue,[78] that it must be confronted squarely and not dismissed summarily.[79] But instead of debating whether international law is

[77] *See, e.g.*, José Alvarez, *But is It Law?*, Comments at the American Society of International Law Annual Meeting, *in* 103 Am. Soc'y Int'l L. Proc. 163 (2009) (stating that he was "appalled we are still discussing this 1960s chestnut of a question").

[78] *See* Aaron Fichtelberg, Law at the Vanishing Point: A Philosophical Analysis of International Law, at xiii (2008) ("International law can stand on its own as a field of law and as a field of political analysis.").

[79] Although it is beyond the subject matter of this book, a similar analysis applies to law generally. *See* Liam Murphy, *Better to See Law This Way*, 83 N.Y.U. L. Rev. 1088, 1104 (2008) ("To sum up for a moment, the concept of law is indeterminate, or partially ambiguous. We cannot live with the

law, a productive question to ask is what should decisionmakers do when they face international problems. This book provides a framework of inquiry for decisionmakers to find and appraise answers to that question in each problem they confront.

ambiguity, since we need to be able to make statements about the content of the law in force. So it appears we need to disambiguate. But there are political stakes associated with each possible disambiguation, so we cannot just pick one at random.").

2 The Politics of Theorizing

This chapter makes the point that theories of international law are political. Disagreements among scholars about their respective theories of international law are not just conceptual, as philosphers of analytic jurisprudence often say they are, and they are not just semantic, as practitioners of international law often claim them to be. Instead, disagreements among theorists about different theories of international law are also political. Every theory of international law is inevitably built on non-conceptual choices, including what facts from which to observe the phenomenon of international law, how to describe those facts, and what quintessential system of law against which to compare the description of international law. Embedded in these selections are yet more non-conceptual choices, such as stipluations about the purpose of law, and about whether a theory of law must match what people think the word "law" means. Theorists make their selections at least in part based on their political viewpoints, and the theories of international law that result from their choices have political consequences.

Accordingly, it may be futile for scholars to attempt to use purely conceptual analysis to resolve disagreements about what, if any, parts of international law count as law. Another way to address these disagreements is to try to build a persuasive framework of reasoning to guide elites in deciding what to do about prescriptions in international legal problems, whether or not prescriptions are "law." Subsequent chapters develop that framework.

I. POLITICAL STAKES

Although the discussion about what parts, if any, of international law count as law may seem intellectually tiresome, it is not simply a parlour game. Consider the political stakes involved. People who ask and answer questions about whether international law is law and what counts as international law often have political motivations.[1] They know that what others think about international law affects the potential for international law to guide actions and shape views in international problems.[2] People who believe that a prescription is a part of international law, and that international law is law, will tend to expect decisionmakers to follow that prescription. They will generally anticipate or want to impose consequences on those who disobey that prescription. Conversely, people who believe that a prescription is not part of international law, or that international law is simply not law, will tend not to expect decisionmakers to follow that prescription. They will generally think that there ought not to be consequences for disobeying that prescription.[3]

There are also political stakes in ignoring questions about the nature of international law. Observers might take it that scholars intentionally neglect those questions because they fear that even asking those questions would lead to a conclusion that international law is not law or its rules cannot be concretely determined.[4] Such observers may infer that there is something to the view that international law is not law and need not be taken seriously. Other observers may draw opposite conclusions from the decision to ignore those questions. They may take it that it is so obvious that international law has enough characteristics of law, making it worthwhile to study and promote, that no one thinks it is worth asking questions about its legality anymore. Ignoring questions about the legality of international law in general, and what counts as international law in particular, creates ambiguity about the importance of international law and what to do about it. Simply put, the question of what, if anything, in international law counts as law is important and must be faced squarely.

However, a non-conceptual approach to this inquiry is necessary. For decades, if not centuries, jurists have tried to engage in this inquiry solely through conceptual analysis.

[1] Oona Hathaway & Scott Shapiro, *Outcasting: Enforcement in Domestic and International Law*, 121 YALE L.J. (draft of Nov. 3, 2010 at 4) (forthcoming 2011), *available at* http://www.iilj.org/courses/documents/HC2010Nov10.HathawayShapiro.pdf ("It is no accident that many critics of international law have challenged the jurisprudential status of international law. What better way to discredit international law than by showing that it lacks those properties which make law morally valuable?").

[2] John R. Bolton, *Is There Really "Law" in International Affairs?*, 10 TRANSNAT'L L. & CONTEMP. PROBS. 1, 1 (2000) (describing the question of whether international law is law as "a political battle of immense significance").

[3] Hathaway & Shapiro, *supra* note 1, at 3 ("It might mean that the flouting of international law is justified because the violators would not be breaking *the law*.").

[4] *Id.* ("The anxiety underlying the refusal to engage, perhaps, is that an inquiry into the status of international law is too dangerous to discuss openly. . . Even entertaining the idea that the object of their study is not law threatens to delegitimize it.").

But the answer cannot be reached through conceptual analysis alone. This is beause there are no conceptual answers to certain choices that must be made in constructing any theory of intenational law. These are choices about: (1) what facts in international problems are relevant to describing international law; (2) how to describe the international legal system observed from those facts; and (3) what, if any, system (such as a codified domestic legal system or a customary tribal system) manifests the traits of law, against which international law may be compared, in order to see if international law is sufficiently similar to that other system in enough meaningful ways to count as law.[5] In making those choices, scholars have to also consider the purpose of law and how much of what they describe as law needs to match what people take the word "law" to mean.

For example, as to the first choice, a jurist who decides to study only legal rules will reach different conclusions about the nature of international law than another jurist who focuses on the processes of interaction in international problems.[6] Even if everyone is agreed that the relevant facts are formal rules and not informal practices, the second choice about how to describe facts about formal rules will shape how the international legal system is perceived. A jurist who describes the rules according to their formal sources alone will present a different picture of international law than one who describes rules according to their effectiveness, and both of them will differ in their account of international law from a colleague who chooses to focus on the morality of those rules.[7] As to the third choice, whatever the description of international law, a jurist who compares international law to domestic law will tend to form a different view of international law than another jurist who studies international law as a system onto itself, and both of them will differ from a jurist who compares international law to informal systems of regulation.[8] In deciding which system of

[5] *Compare* John Austin, The Province of Jurisprudence Determined, 77–80, 126 (David Campbell & Philip Thomas eds., 1998) (1832) (comparing international law to domestic law and concluding that is not law because it lacks sanctions such as those that exist in domestic law), *with* Hathaway & Shapiro, *supra* note 1, at 22 (comparing international law to the practices of medieval Iceland and concluding it is law because both systems enforce their norms by ostracizing offenders from the system and depriving them of the benefits of the system).

[6] *Compare* Lassa Oppenheim, International Law: A Treatise (1905) (conceiving of international law as a body of laws) *with* Myres S. McDougal, Remarks at the 79th Annual Meeting of the American Society of International Law, 79 Am. Soc'y Int'l L. Proc. 283, 283 (1985) (describing international law as a process of authoritative decisionmaking).

[7] *Compare* Oppenheim, *supra* note 6 (positing rules without considering their effectiveness or legitimacy) *with* Hans Morgenthau, Politics Among Nations (3d ed. 1960) (emphasizing that states will only act in their interests and questioning the effectiveness of international laws that are contrary to the interests of powerful states) *with* Thomas M. Franck, The Power of Legitimacy Among Nations (1990) [hereinafter Franck, Power] (arguing that states follow international rules when they are legitimate).

[8] *Compare* H. L. A. Hart, The Concept of Law 213–37 (2d. ed. 1994) (comparing international law to the English domestic legal system and concluding that international law is a primitive form of law) [hereinafter Hart, The Concept of Law] *with* Douglas M. Johnston, The Historical Foundations of World Order: The Tower and the Arena 145 (2008) (studying the international system without comparing it to domestic systems of law and concluding that international

law against which to compare international law, the jurist must select criteria for choosing a system. He may consider criteria based on what he thinks is the purpose of law, or he may decide to choose a system that people already regard as exemplifying the meaing of the word "law."

This chapter will show how such choices are unavoidable and that they are not conceptual choices. Therefore, debates about the nature of international law, while important, cannot be resolved by conceptual analysis alone. They must also be addressed politically. By making this point, scholars can move away from seemingly conceptual disputes about international law, to appraising different approaches to international law in political terms, and directly confronting the political stakes involved. Readers can also appraise the policy-oriented approach to international law proposed in this book not according to whether it is "law," but according to whether it is useful and politically attractive.

This chapter develops its thesis in several parts. Part II selects, through the span of history, international events and phenomena that might exemplify facts from which an international legal system could be described. Scholars observing these facts must decide which ones are or are not parts of the international legal system. They must then decide how to describe the international legal system made up of the facts they identified as relevant. Part III studies how scholars have carried out those tasks to devise their respective conceptions of international law. It surveys theories of international law, focusing particularly on theories after World War II, and highlighting differences and similiarties among these theories. Part IV argues that each theory of international law discussed in Part III is built on choices about what facts about the international system are relevant to conceiving intenational law, about how to interpret those facts, and about what are the characteristics of law generally against which to compare their interpretations of facts about the international system. Part V examines the personal backgrounds and geopolitical context of scholars and explores whether each of their contexts helps to explain the respective choices they made in their theories. Part VI builds on the ideas that no theory of international law is purely conceptual and every theory is at least partly political. It suggests that a useful theory of international law in the current geopolitical situation is one that balances realism with idealism.

II. EVIDENCE OF LAW

One way to build a theory of international law is to observe international acts and to interpret these acts as providing evidence of law or the absence of law. This part highlights some international acts that could be relevant in such a theoretical endeavour. There is evidence from antiquity to the present time that certain types of international activities occurred throughout history, and that there were often

law is the "gradual accumulation of elements—ideas, norms, practices, institutions, and especially values") *and* Hathaway & Shapiro, *supra* note 1, at 33–41 (arguing that international law is law because it enforces its behavorial norms through what they call "outcasting").

international arrangements or understandings of one form or another to regulate those activities.[9] These arrangements and understandings addressed, with varied effectiveness, international problems that arose.[10] Although there are different ways to catalogue international activities, and indeed to select relevant activities, many international activities that might plausibly reveal facts concerning international law relate to trade, war, and diplomacy. These activities were regulated by explicit international agreements among decisionmakers, implicit understandings through customary practices, unilateral declarations by governing elites, and tribunals.

International trade may have taken place as long ago as third millennium B.C.[11] However, as one would expect, evidence of how international trade was regulated is more ample only in later centuries. Formal and informal arrangements were concluded between cities or states to protect foreigners, so that merchants could engage in cross-border transactions. The Greek city-states concluded international agreements or *symbola* for the protection of foreigners, which was crucial to facilitate cross border transactions.[12] In 470 B.C., the Amphictyonic League, an international organization comprised of member Greek city-states, ordered inhabitants of Scyros to provide reparations to Thessalian traders whom they had plundered and imprisoned.[13]

During the Tang Dynasty in China (618 A.D. to 907 A.D), the international trade of tea for horses emerged between China and Tibet.[14] Tibetans coveted tea but could not grow it in the elevated altitudes of the Tibetan plateau. China needed Tibetan war horses, which were long-admired for their athletic abilities, in order to boost their military capabilities. To finance its defense budget for calvary, China sold tea to Tibet. These market forces resulted in a thriving international tea-horse trade that lasted for centuries after the Tang Dynasty, via the "tea-horse" routes that ran from China's hinterland to Tibet hundreds of miles away.[15] Whether or not there were formal international agreements between China and Tibet, the fact that these

[9] *Cf.*, David J. Bederman, International Law in Antiquity 279 (2001) (stating that international law in antiquity was designed "to promote predictability and stability, to adequately channel State conduct in ways that were conducive to maintaining power relations, and to nourish the internal legitimacy and sovereignty of polities").

[10] Arthur Nussbaum, A Concise History of the Law of Nations 7–11 (MacMillan 1954) (concluding that there is evidence of the "phenomena" of intenational law in antiquity).

[11] *See* Johnston, *supra* note 8, at 165 ("There is no doubt that Egypt and Mesopotamia were the economic powers of the late third millennium, and had the best opportunity to lay down trade routes with the Orient (Braudel, 2001)"); R. Doak Bishop, James Crawford, & W. Michael Reisman, Foreign Investment Disputes: Cases, Materials, and Commentary 2 (2005) (discussing tin mining in foreign lands by Eyptian pharaohs, and overseas trading posts of Phoenicians); Gary Born, International Arbitration: Cases and Materials 2–4 (2011).

[12] Bederman, *supra* note 9, at 272.

[13] 2 Coleman Phillipson, The International Law and Custom of Ancient Greece and Rome 10 (1911).

[14] Andrew Forbes & David Henley, *China's "Ancient Tea-Horse Road" in Historical Perspective*, CPAmedia, http://www.cpamedia.com/trade-routes/tea-horse-road-historical-perspective/ (last visited Aug. 7, 2011)

[15] *Id.*

cross-broder transactions took place for hundreds of years provides strong circumstantial evidence that Tibet and China had an enduring shared expectation that they would not persecute each others' traders simply because those traders were foreign. Both states, as well as their merchants, must have abided by their intenational tea-horse trade arrangements often enough that whatever political risks existed did not exceed the financial returns from this international trade, and thus this form of trade continued to occur.

In the Middle Ages, the *Magna Carta* of 1215 provided in Clause XXX for the safe passage of foreign merchants in England.[16] In 1495, Henry VII and the Duke of Burgundy, ruler of the Netherlands, concluded the *Intercursus Magnus*, providing for safe travel of their merchants and free trade between the two states.[17] Elaborate customary international trade practices, known as *lex mercatoria*, developed. SELECT CASES CONCERNING THE LAW MERCHANT records various incidents of foreign merchants attempting to secure, and in some instances actually securing, their commercial interests through "law merchants" at county fairs. In 1270, a merchant court required Gerard of Cologne, pursuant to *lex mercatoria*, to produce five oath helpers to corroborate his oath that he owned wine that had been seized as collateral in a dispute.[18]

Although *lex mercatoria* was available to resolve domestic commercial disputes, it also regulated the conduct of international traders. In 1473, in a case involving a foreign merchant requesting to be excepted from English law, the Chancery Court held that the dispute would be decided not under English law but "the law of Nature, which is called by some 'Law Merchant,' which is the law universal throughout the world."[19] In 1622, the merchant Gerard de Malynes described *lex mercatoria* as "customary law, approved by the authority of all kingdoms and commonwealths, and not a law established by the sovereignty of any prince."[20] William Searle Holdsworth described *lex mercatoria* as a "species of *ius gentium*,"[21] or the law of nations, of which Sir John Davies in the seventeenth century wrote: "the laws of all nations do take special knowledge."[22]

Today, the regulation of international commercial activities is achieved through a web of arrangements and prescriptions. The World Trade Organization requires its

[16] NUSSBAUM, *supra* note 10, at 29.

[17] *Id.* at 28–36.

[18] 1 SELECT CASES CONCERNING THE LAW MERCHANT 5 (Charles Gross trans., 1908). *See also* Steven E. Sachs, *From St. Ives to Cyberspace: The Modern Distortion of the Medieval "Law Merchant,"* 21 AM. U. INT'L L. REV. 685, 685 (2006) (discussing the phenomena that "uniformly regulated commerce across Europe" during the Middle Ages known as "Law Merchant").

[19] Anonymous v. Sheriff of London, Y.B. 13 Edw. 2, fol. 9, Pasch, pl. 5 (Ch. 1473).

[20] GERARD MALYNES, LEX MERCATORIA, THE ANCIENT LAW-MERCHANT 3 (Katie F. Hamilton ed., 2d ed. 2001).

[21] WILLIAM SEARLE HOLDSWORTH, A HISTORY OF ENGLISH LAW 529 (7th ed., rev. vol. 1956). *See also* Sachs, *supra* note 18, 685 (questioning whether the law merchant ever achieved the authority independent from national law to the extent that subsequent historians have attributed to *lex mercatoria*).

[22] JOHN DAVIES, THE QUESTION CONCERNING IMPOSITIONS 10 (1656).

member states to comply with trade standards to which they agree when they join the Organization.[23] There are thousands of bilateral investment treaties and free trade agreements between and among states.[24] International tribunals interpret and enforce their prescriptions,[25] which may be explicit, such as mandating the free conversion of currency,[26] or vague, such as the protection of "legitimate expectations."[27] National courts impose domestic trade laws, such as antitrust statutes, on international actors when their commercial actitivies have an impact domestically.[28]

In addition to trade, wars have occurred for as long as territorial communities have existed. Although wars may appear to be completely unregulated because of their rampant violence and destruction, throughout history there have been various international standards regulating when war may be waged and how it was to be waged.[29] These standards achieved varying degrees of compliance.

The ancient Greek city-states had rules governing formalities for declaring war.[30] These city-states also entered into joint defense arrangements, pursuant to which they formed the First and Second Athenian Leagues and the Peloponnesian Confederacy, which were all international security organizations with elaborate decisionmaking processes that were generally followed.[31] Ancient Chinese history was marked by internecine wars. Following wars in the Spring and Autumn Period (722–481 B.C.) and the Warring States Period (403–221 B.C.), China was united by the First Emperor of China, who built the Great Wall of China to defend his nation in life, and the Terracotta Army to guard him in death. After the Qin Dynasty ended, China was once again plunged into wars. Throughout innumerable wars, officials in China appeared to largely follow rules of warfare governing when going to war was justified (what the Romans called *ius ad bellum)* and how war should be conducted

[23] The General Agreement on Tarriffs and Trade, Oct. 30, 1947, 61 Stat. A-11, T.I.A.S. 1700, 55 U.N.T.S. 194. *See also infra* ch. 5, pt. II. A (discussing arbitration in a WTO dispute between the United States and Mexico).

[24] *See* Susan D. Franck, *An Emprical Analysis of Investment Treaty Awards,* 101 Am. Soc'y Int'l L. Proc. 459, 459 (2007).

[25] *See, e.g.,* Metalclad Corp. v. United States, ICSID Case No. ARB(AF)/97/1, Award (Aug. 30, 2000). *See also* Case 323/87, Comm'n v. Italy (taxation of rum), 1989 E.C.R. 2275, 2299 ("The Court has consistently held that the purpose of Article 90 EC [now Article 110], as a whole, is to ensure the free movement of goods between the member states under normal conditions of competition.").

[26] *See, e.g.,* Agreement between the Government of the United States of America and the Government of the Republic of Hondorus Concerning the Encouragement and Reciprocal Protection of Investments art. V(2), July 1, 1995, Senate Treaty Doc. No. 106-27.

[27] *See, e.g.,* North American Free Trade Agreement, art. 1105, U.S.-Can.-Mex., Dec. 17, 1992, 32 I.L.M. 289 (1993).

[28] Sherman Antitrust Act, 15 U.S.C. §§1-7 (1890); United States v. Nippon Paper Industries Co., 109 F.3d 1 (1st Cir. 1997).

[29] Bederman, *supra note* 9, at 278 (concluding, after reviewing evidence from antiquity, that there were rules governing the conduct of warfare). *See also* 1 Philippson, *supra* note 13, at 375–415.

[30] Bederman, *supra* note 9, at 272.

[31] 2 Phillipson, *supra* note 13, at 13–26. *See also generally* Thucydides, History of the Peloponnesian War (R. Warner trans. 1954).

(*ius in bello*).[32] Around 100 B.C., India produced the Hindu Code of Manu. It stipulated rules for warfare, such as prohibiting a warrior from striking a sleeping or fleeing enemy. It is difficult to assess, however, if these rules were enforced or followed on the basis of these prescriptions alone.[33] In the Middle Ages, knights in Europe observed codes of chivalry, which provided for practices such as ransoming prisoners of war.[34]

In 1837, Great Britain attacked the U.S. vessel, the *Caroline*, when it was moored on the American side of the Niagara River, because it was bringing supplies to Canadian insurrectionists against the British.[35] Protesting the attack, U.S. Secretary of State Daniel Webster stated that the use of force was only ever justified when "the necessity of that self-defence is instant, overwhelming, and leaving no choice of means, and no moment for deliberation.'"[36] Additionally, Webster claimed that the use of force had to be proportional to the threat, and the burden of proof was on the aggressor.[37] Eventually, Great Britain apologized for its actions, indicating that it accepted that the use of military force where there had not been a prior attack was impermissible.[38]

The two World Wars severely challenged the legal limits placed on the use of force. Some states thoroughly ignored any purported international restrictions on their use of force. Eventually, these horrors eventually shocked states into reaffirming, through the UN Charter and other international agreements, their commitment to prohibiting the unilateral use of force except in self-defense.[39] Article 2(4) of the UN Charter rejected the view that a sovereign state may use force unilaterally to advance

[32] Johnston, *supra* note 8, at 228.

[33] Nussbaum, *supra* note 10, at 10.

[34] *Id.* at 35.

[35] *See* Kenneth R. Stevens, Border Diplomacy: The *Caroline* and McLeod Affairs in AngloAmerican-Canadian Relations, 1837–1842, at 121 (1989) (arguing that the New York Supreme Court was incorrect in determining that actions of individuals involved in the *Caroline* affair were acts of individuals and not of a sovereign state); David B. Rivkin Jr., et al., *Remember the Caroline!*, Nat'l Rev (July–Dec. 2002), at 17 ("[T]he '*Caroline* incident' spawned the modern international-law doctrine of 'anticipatory self-defense,' a doctrine on which the U.S. now intends to rely heavily to justify military action against terrorist states.").

[36] Letter from Daniel Webster, Secretary of State, United States, to Lord Ashburton, British Plenipotentiary, United Kingdom (Aug. 6, 1842), *in* 2 A Digest of International Law 412 (John Bassett Moore ed., 1906).

[37] Letter from Daniel Webster, Secretary of State, United States, to Henry Fox, Minister, United Kingdom (Apr. 24, 1841), *in* 29 B.S.P. 1129, 1138 (1957) (*quoted in* Lori F. Damrosch et. al., International Law: Cases and Materials 923 (4th ed. 2001)).

[38] *See* R.Y. Jennings, *The Caroline and McLeod Cases*, 32 Am. J. Int'l L. 82, 91 (1938) ("[T]he agreement of the two governments [addressed] the importance of the principle of non-intervention and the narrow limits of the exceptions."); Correspondence Between Great Britain and the United States, Respecting the Destruction of the Steamboat Caroline, 30 B.S.P. 193, 201 (1858) (recording diplomatic letters accepting that force is only authorized in self-defense against attack).

[39] *See* League of Nations Covenant pmbl. (outlining agreements of League of Nations' members, including acceptance of obligation not to resort to war); Charles Hall Davis, *Preamble to Constitution of the League of Nations*, 5 Va. L. Reg. New Ser. 14, 16 (1919) (stressing the importance of the preamble because citizens of all member nations are bound by the agreement).

national interests.[40] Only the Security Council could authorize the use of force pursuant to a resolution under Chapter VII of the UN Charter.[41] Numerous Security Council resolutions have since condemned the unilateral acts of aggression by one state against another.[42] The replacement of a unilateral right to use force by international controls is, however, inoperative if a state consents to another state deploying force, such as to provide assistance in combating insurgents or terrorists,[43] or if a state needs to act in self-defense against an actual or imminent attack.[44] Regardless of the justification for the use of force, the Geneva Conventions of 1949 regulate how military operations are carried out, such as in the treatment of enemy combatants.[45]

Somewhat counterintuitively, powerful states did comply with these rules, albeit imperfectly. At the end of the Cold War, when the United States was at the height of its powers and able to invade almost any country, it chose to seek and obtain a

[40] 60. UN Charter art. 2, para. 4.

[41] UN Charter art. 39; *See also* S.C. Res. 678, ¶ 2, U.N. Doc. S/RES/678 (Nov. 29, 1990) (authorizing force against Iraq for invading Kuwait); S.C. Res. 660, ¶ 2, U.N. Doc. S/RES/660 (Aug. 2, 1990) (determining that Iraq breached international peace by invading Kuwait).

[42] *See, e.g.*, S.C. Res. 686, ¶ 2, U.N. Doc. S/RES/686 (March 2, 1991) (demanding that Iraq return all Kuwaiti property, prisoners of war, and war dead, and that Iraq accept liability for injuries to Kuwait); S.C. Res. 678, ¶ 2, U.N. Doc. S/RES/678 (Nov. 29 1990) (authorizing force against Iraq for invading Kuwait); S.C. Res. 660, ¶ 2, U.N. Doc. S/RES/660 (Aug. 2, 1990) (determining that Iraq breached international peace by invading Kuwait); S.C. Res. 501, ¶ 1, U.N. Doc. S/RES/501 (Feb. 25, 1982) (demanding immediate withdrawal of Israeli forces from Lebanese territory); S.C. Res. 384, ¶ 1, U.N. Doc. S/RES/384 (Dec. 22, 1975) (acknowledging territorial integrity of East Timor).

[43] *See* S.C. Res. 384, ¶2, U.N. Doc. S/RES/384 (Dec. 22, 1975) (condemning Indonesian intervention in East Timor); 1 Oppenheim's International Law 435 (Robert Jennings & Arthur Watts eds., 9th ed. 1996) (discussing "[a]ssistance on request").

[44] UN Charter art. 51. *See also* Mikael Nabati, *International Law at a Crossroads: Self-Defense, Global Terrorism, and Preemption (A Call to Rethink the Self-Defense Normative Framework)*, 13 Transnat'l L. & Contemp. Probs. 771, 790 (2003) (noting that "Article 51 may be read permissively to include a right to anticipatory self-defense"); Rex J. Zedalis, *On the Lawfulness of Forceful Remedies for Violations of Arms Control Agreements: "Star Wars" and Other Glimpses at the Future*, 18 N.Y.U. J. Int'l L. & Pol. 73, 101 (1985) (arguing that "defensive measures in anticipation of an armed attack should be permissible" under UN Charter); High-Level Panel on Threats, Challenges & Change, *A More Secure World: Our Shared Responsibility: Report of the High-Level Panel on Threats, Challenges and Change*, ¶ 188, U.N. Doc A/59/565 (Dec. 2, 2004) [hereinafter *A More Secure World*] (noting that states facing imminent threat can take military action, but questioning use of military action when threat is not imminent); *Cf.* Authorization for Use of Military Force, Pub. L. No. 107-40, S.J. Res. 23, 107th Cong. (2001) (enacted) (authorizing the President to "use . . . force against those nations, organizations, or persons he determines planned, authorized, committed, or aided the terrorist attacks that occurred on September 11, 2001").

[45] Geneva Convention [I] for the Amelioration of the Condition of the Wounded and Sick in Armed Forces in the Field, Aug. 12, 1949, 6 U.S.T. 3114, 75 U.N.T.S. 31; Geneva Convention [II] for the Amelioration of the Condition of the Wounded, Sick and Shipwrecked Members of Armed Forces at Sea, Aug. 12, 1949, 6 U.S.T. 3217, 75 U.N.T.S. 85; Geneva Convention [III] Relative to the Treatment of Prisoners of War, Aug. 12, 1949, 6 U.S.T. 3316, 75 U.N.T.S. 135; Geneva Convention [IV] Relative to the Protection of Civilian Persons in Time of War, Aug. 12, 1949, 6 U.S.T. 3516, 75 U.N.T.S. 287.

Security Council resolution authorizing the use of force to repel Iraq from Kuwait in the Gulf War.[46] It did not act unilaterally.

Today, however, prescriptions regulating when and how states may use military force in or against another state have come under severe pressure because these prescriptions did not anticipate advances in military techonology and the asymmetric methods of violence used by terrorists. Observers have questioned the legality of the invasion of Iraq in 2003, the conduct of military operations in Libya in response to Colonel Muammar el-Qaddafi's violent repression of protestors in 2011,[47] and the use of unmanned drones by the United States to assassinate terrorists in Pakistan.[48]

Wars were historically, and still are, ended by conquest or peace agreements. In the fourth century B.C., the successor of the Macedonian Alexander the Great, Seleucus Nicator, was forced to conclude a peace pact with the Mauryan King Chandragupta, the founder of a new empire in North India.[49] In 1648, European states ended the Thirty Years War with international agreements forming the Peace of Westphalia, which recognized the absolute sovereignty of states and accordingly limited the right of any state to attack another state.[50] The 2003 invasion of Iraq by a U.S.-led international coalition of states ended when Saddam Hussein was removed from power and the UN Security Council recognized the invading forces as an occupying power.[51]

When states were not at war, they engaged in diplomacy, which was achieved through agreements, shared expectations about standards of conduct towards emissaries and foreigners, and dispute resolution by international tribunals.[52] David Bederman reviewed practices in the Near East, Greece, and Rome in antiquity, and

[46] *See infra* ch. 8, pt. II.A.

[47] Lourdes Garcia-Navarro & Stevie Inskeep, *Libya: Coalition Is Overstepping Its U.N. Mandate*, NPR (Mar. 29, 2011) http://www.npr.org/2011/03/29/134943154/Libya-Latest.

[48] Jackie Northam, *Popularity Of Drones Takes Off For Many Countries*, NPR (July 11, 2011) http://www.npr.org/2011/07/11/137710942/popularity-of-drones-takes-off-for-many-countries.

[49] JOHNSTON, *supra* note 8, at 236.

[50] Michael P. Scharf, *Earned Sovereignty: Juridical Underpinnings*, 31 DEN. J. INT'L L. & POL'Y 373, 375 n.20 (2003) (stating that the Treaty of Westphalia is comprised of two treaties). *See also* Treaty of Westphalia, Peace Treaty between the Holy Roman Emperor and the King of France and their Respective Allies, sec. II (1648), *available at* http://avalon.law.yale.edu/17th_century/westphal.asp ("That they shall not act, or permit to be acted, any wrong or injury to any whatsoever; but that all that has pass'd on the one side, and the other, as well before as during the War, in Words, Writings, and Outrageous Actions, in Violences, Hostilitys, Damages and Expences, without any respect to Persons or Things, shall be entirely abolish'd in such a manner that all that might be demanded of, or pretended to, by each other on that behalf, shall be bury'd in eternal Oblivion.").

[51] S.C.Res. 1483, ¶ 9, U.N. Doc. S/RES/1483 (May 22, 2003) ("Supports the formation, by the people of Iraq with the help of the Authority and working with the Special Representative, of an Iraqi interim administration as a transitional administration run by Iraqis, until an internationally recognized, representative government is established by the people of Iraq and assumes the responsibilities of the Authority.").

[52] *See, e.g.*, NUSSBAUM, *supra* note 10, at 28–36 (noting that in 1343, Denmark and Sweden concluded an arbitral compact to arbitrate future disputes before a tribunal compromising twenty-four bishops and knights, with each party appointing twelve).

concluded that there were "norms of international law,"[53] including that "envoys were not to be killed," and "treaties were to be kept in good faith."[54] Sovereigns also granted rights to foreigners. In 537 B.C., the Persian king Cyrus the Great issued the "Cyrus Cylinder", guaranteeing the religious freedoms, traditions, and customs of the nations under his control.[55] Arthur Nussbaum postulated that in the Roman Empire, as a result of Christianity, foreigners received some legal protections.[56] Alexandria in ancient Egypt was a cosmopolitan city in which Egyptians, Greeks, Jews, Romans, Nubians and other people could live together, and the most brilliant students in the Mediterranean attended school at Mouseion.[57] In ancient China, when states were not at war with each other, they subscribed to reciprocal proprieties (*li*) in their diplomatic relations.[58]

The practice of respecting the rights of diplomats and foreigners continued through the centries, even if expectations of protection were violated or threatened. In the late sixteenth century, English officials engaged the jurist Alberico Gentili to advise whether the English government could charge the Spanish ambassador Don Bernardino de Mendoza in English courts for plotting against Queen Elizabeth I. Gentili declared that, based on the law of nations, *ius gentium*, Mendoza was immune from criminal prosecution. The English government then dispatched the conniving Ambassador Mendoza back to Spain without prosecuting him.[59]

[53] Bederman, *supra* note 9, at 279.

[54] *Id.* at 278. *See also* 1 Philippson, *supra* note 13, at 304–35.

[55] *See* James Bennett Pritchard, Ancient Near Eastern Texts: Relating to the Old Testament 315–16 (3d ed. 1969). This remarkable document deserves to be quoted at some length: "Now that I put the crown of kingdom of Iran, Babylon, and the nations of the four directions on the head with the help of (Ahura) Mazda, I announce that I will respect the traditions, customs and religions of the nations of my empire and never let any of my governors and subordinates look down on or insult them while I am alive. From now on, till (Ahura) Mazda grants me the kingdom favor, I will impose my monarchy on no nation. Each is free to accept it, and if any one of them rejects it, I never resolve on war to reign. While I am the king of Iran, Babylon, and the nations of the four directions, I [will] never let anyone oppress any others, and if it occurs, I will take his or her right back and penalize the oppressor. And until I am the monarch, I will never let anyone take possession of movable and landed properties of the others by force or without compensation. While I am alive, I prevent unpaid, forced labor. Today, I announce that everyone is free to choose a religion. People are free to live in all regions and take up a job provided that they never violate other's rights. No one could be penalized for his or her relatives' faults. I prevent slavery and my governors and subordinates are obliged to prohibit exchanging men and women as slaves within their own ruling domains. Such a tradition should be exterminated the world over. I implore to (Ahura) Mazda to make me succeed in fulfilling my obligations to the nations of Iran (Persia), Babylon, and the ones of the four directions." *Id.* at 316.

[56] Nussbaum, *supra* note 10, at 29

[57] Chip Brown, *The Search for Cleopatra*, Nat. Geographic Magazine, July 2011 ("Alexandria soon became the largest, most sophisticated city on the planet. It was a teeming cosmopolitan mix of Egyptians, Greeks, Jews, Romans, Nubians, and other peoples. The best and brightest of the Mediterranean world came to study at the Mouseion, the world's first academy, and at the great Alexandria library.").

[58] Johnston, *supra* note 8, at 228.

[59] *Id.* at 385–87.

In 1619, Russia sent a diplomatic mission to China in an effort to improve relations. Under the Chinese worldview, China was the only kingdom, to which all other territories paid tribute. Because Russia omitted to bring tribute, its mission was summarily sent away. In 1654, Russia attempted to send another ambassador, Fyodor Isakovich Baykov, but he too was not received in the imperial palace because Russia asserted equal status with China. Eventually, however, border disputes between the two states imposed too high a cost and exigencies of interstate relations prevailed. In 1686, China and Russia concluded the Treaty of Nerchinsk, which settled their border dispute, facilitated trade, and established passport controls and extradition. This was followed by a further border treaty, concluded in 1728 at Kiakhta on the Mongolian border.[60]

Even so, Chinese ambivalence to European ideas of sovereign equality persisted. In 1793, Great Britain sent Lord George Macartney as its putative ambassador to China. The 80-year-old Chinese emperor issued an edict, even before Lord Macartney arrived, commanding him to leave.[61] China organized its world affairs around an insular central position, and rejected foreign influences and visitors. It saw no need to participate in the European system of international law built on sovereign equality. However, it is striking that the Chinese emperor did not kill Lord Macartney, but instead sent him away. The emperor's edict also provides colorful evidence of how China treated foreigners. It noted: "Hitherto, whenever men from the various Western Ocean countries have desired to come to the Celestial Empire and to enter the Imperial service, we have allowed them to come to the capital . . . But once having come, they were obliged to adopt the costume of the Celestial Empire, were confined within the Halls, and were never allowed to return home . . ."[62]

Today, a web of international arrangements codify and reinforce expectations among decisionmakers in different countries about how they shoud treat diplomats and foreigners and how they resolve their disagreements peacefully through international dispute resolution mechanisms. The Vienna Convention on Diplomatic Relations provides that diplomats and diplomatic residences are immune from prosecution.[63] The Vienna Convention on Consular Relations provides that foreigners shall be informed of their right to speak to a counsular officer of their home country when they are arrested by the officers of any treaty state.[64] Domestic laws

[60] *Id.* at 474–76.

[61] *Id.* at 478–79 (quoting the edict, which stated, inter alia: "We have perused the text of your state message and the wording expresses your earnestness. From it your sincere humility and obedience can clearly be seen. It is admirable and we fully approve . . . [However,], we have issued these detailed instructions and have commended your tribute Envoys to return safely home. You, O King, should simply act in conformity with our wishes by strengthening your loyalty and swearing perpetual obedience, so as to ensure that your Country may share the blessings of peace. . . .").

[62] *Id.* at 478–79.

[63] Vienna Convention on Diplomatic Relations, Apr. 18, 1961, art. 30, 23 U.S.T. 3227, 500 U.N.T.S. 95.

[64] Vienna Convention on Consular Relations, Apr. 24, 1963, art. 36(1)(b), 21 U.S.T. 77, 596 U.N.T.S. 261 ("[I]f he so requests, the competent authorities of the receiving State shall, without delay, inform the consular post of the sending State if, within its consular district, a national of that

accord sovereign imminuty to foreign governments and heads of state.[65] When a state that is subject to the jurisdiction of the International Court of Justice violates the treaties relating to the treatment of foreigners, the state of the foreigner may bring a lawsuit. Whether or not the lawsuit results in damages, such lawsuits have prompted states to take measures to educate their officers to obey the treaty,[66] and to correct any violations.[67] States with international disputes have tried to resolve their differences through tribunals, succeeding at times and failing on other occasions. The ICJ decision in the *Pedra Branca* dispute largely resolved the dispute between Singapore and Malaysia over sovereignty of the Horsburgh Lighthouse,[68] but the *Ethiopia-Eritrea* commission deciding on the countries' borders did not put an immediate end to violence between the two states.[69]

This cursory glance of international acts throughout history does not purport to even come close to cataloguing all the evidence that is relevant to determining if international law exists. As technology has widened, the range of international activities and formal and informal agreements governing these activities have expanded into the use of the air, sea, and outer space, as well as telecommunications, and the Internet. This brief review of some international practices simply provides an indication that there is a vast universe of facts from which to choose relevant evidence of international law. Theorists have to make choices about which facts are relevant and which are not.[70] They then have to interpret their selected facts.

III. THEORIES FROM FACTS

When describing phenomena, theorists have to decide which facts show the characteristics of that phenomena and how to describe them. This part surveys how scholars have selected and interpreted evidence of international acts along with

State is arrested or committed to prison or to custody pending trial or is detained in any other manner. Any communication addressed to the consular post by the person arrested, in prison, custody or detention shall also be forwarded by the said authorities without delay. The said authorties shall inform the person concerned without delay of his rights under this sub-paragraph.").

[65] *See* Foreign Soverign Immunities Act § 1604, 28 U.S.C. § 1604 (1976).

[66] *See* Case Concerning Avena and Other Mexican Nationals (Mex. v. U.S.), 2004 I.C.J. 12, 17 (March 31).

[67] *See* Medellín v. Texas, 552 U.S. 491, 503 (2008) (quoting former President George W. Bush's memo to the Attorney General implementing Avena by ordering State courts give effect to the decision). *But see* Medellín v. Texas, 544 U.S. at 510–11 (finding President Bush's executive order to be an unconstitutional attempt to assert federal authority over state criminal law systems).

[68] *See infra* ch. 4, pt. II.A.

[69] Western and Eastern Fronts Ethiopia's Claims 1 & 3, Partial Award (Permanent Court of Arbitration 2005) *available at* http://www.pca-cpa.org/upload/files/FINAL%20ET%20FRONT%20CLAIMS(1).pdf.

[70] *Cf.*, Oscar Schachter, *Towards a Theory of International Obligation*, 8 Va. J. Int'l L. 300, 301 (1968) (stating that "we can list at least a baker's dozen of "candidates" which have been put forward as the basis (or one of the bases) of obligation in international law" and listing, *inter alia*, state consent, customary practice, direct intuition, and sanctions).

conclusions they have drawn from this evidence about the nature of international law.

A. Early Modernism

Modern theories about international law emerged in the sixteenth and seventeenth centuries.[71] In this early modern period, jurists tried to conceive of international law as a coherent and rational theory that systematized rules among nations. They thus made a choice to focus only on international acts among states and to ignore international acts by non-state actors. This reflected the assumption made in the Peace of Westphalia that states were sovereign equals and the only relevant legal persons in international affairs.[72]

They also made choices about whether to interpret acts by states as constitutive of international laws, or whether to derive international laws from Christian beliefs. One view focused on the acts of states consenting to international rules and agreements and interpreted these acts of consent as the foundation of international law. In his inaugural lecture as Regius Professor of Civil Law at Oxford University, in 1588, Gentili delivered the core of his important work, DE JURE BELLI LIBRI TRES (On the Law of War), in which he insisted on the separation of law from religion. He favored instead the doctrinal development of law insulated from religious influence.[73] Seventeenth-century English philosopher Thomas Hobbes chose to theorize about international law from his observations of how states behaved. According to Hobbes, international law consisted only of treaties that sovereign states consented to in their self-interest to restrict threats to the state.[74] Hobbes' choice to focus on the agreements among states was not purely conceptual. It was also driven by his view of human nature. According to Nussbaum, Hobbes was skeptical of humanity's virtue; thus, compliance with treaties could only be secured by the self-interest of states, which included stabilizing reciprocal expectations, protecting a state's

[71] JÜRGEN HABERMAS, BETWEEN FACTS AND NORMS: CONTRIBUTIONS TO A DISCOURSE THEORY OF LAW AND DEMOCRACY 107 (1997) ("[I]nternational law commenced its modern career in the 16th and 17th century."); JOHNSTON, *supra* note 8, at 323 (discussing international law from the discovery of the New World in 1492). *But cf.* DAVID BEDERMAN, INTERNATIONAL LAW FRAMEWORKS 2 (3d ed. 2010) (noting that the Treaty of Westphalia in 1648 was "commonly given as the birth of international law" "because of historical serendipity, or (more likely) Western ethnocentrism"); MARTTI KOSKENNIEMI, THE GENTLE CIVILIZER OF NATIONS: THE RISE AND FALL OF INTERNATIONAL LAW 4 (1870–1960) (2001) [hereinafter KOSKENNIEMI, GENTLE CIVILIZER] (arguing that modern international law did not begin at Westphalia, but only emerged in the late nineteenth century); Martti Koskenniemi, *The Politics of International Law*, 1 EUR. J. INT'L L. 4 (1990) (explaining that Koskenniemi's definition of modern international law was Enlightenment libertarianism, which in law meant the rule of law, freedom, and equality).

[72] *See* MICHAEL P. SCHARF & PAUL R. WILLIAMS, SHAPING FOREIGN POLICY IN TIMES OF CRISIS 2 (2010) ("The modern age of international law is said to have been inaugurated with the 1648 treaty of Westphalia.").

[73] JOHNSTON, *supra* note 8, at 385–87.

[74] *See* NUSSBAUM, *supra* note 10, at 112–25 (discussing Hobbes and other positivists).

reputation, and avoiding the consequences of breaching that outweighed the costs of compliance.[75]

Another view minimized observable facts about international activities, and instead drew on theology and derived international law from natural law or religion.[76] Hugo Grotius expounded the view that the law of nations was based on natural law, or law grounded in values and morality, rather than the consent of states. For example, he argued that a war that was just under the law of nature and the law of nations was permitted. In a just war, a nation was permitted to attack the enemy.[77] Natural law scholars have since relied on Grotius' thesis as a foundational work in the natural law tradition of international law.[78] Samuel Pufendorf argued that the law of nations was part of natural law.[79] This was not a conceptual claim divorced from his moral or political outlook. Pufendorf appears to have viewed international law as part of natural law because, unlike Hobbes, he viewed humanity as moral and the state as a moral entity reflecting the collective will of its people. International law was accordingly grounded in a secular form of natural law; neither custom nor treaty had binding force independently of the law of nature.[80]

Scholars also attempted to meditate between the two views by trying to accommodate claims about natural law within observable facts about what states did and agreed to do. Grotius recognized an "internal law of nations" directed by conscience, as well as an "arbitrary law of nations" created by the will of states.[81] Swiss diplomat and international law scholar Emerich de Vattel proposed a pragmatic bridge between positivists and natural law jurists. He grounded international law in natural law by arguing that all men are subject to the law of nature, and states, being the result of the common will of its citizens, remain subject to the laws of nature.[82] Thus,

[75] *Id.*

[76] *See* EMERRICH DE VATTEL, THE LAW OF NATIONS 13–14 (Bela Kapossy & Richard Whatmore eds., Liberty Fund 2009) (noting that Christian Wolff, a contemporary of Vattel, argued that using poisoned weapons in war was justified under natural law); *id.* at Book III, ch. VIII, §156, p. 562–63 (arguing that natural law prohibits the use of poisoned arrows because it is unnecessary to kill a person disabled by an arrow).

[77] JOHNSTON, *supra* note 8, at 397–98; MARY ELLEN O'CONNELL, THE POWER AND PURPOSE OF INTERNATIONAL LAW 21–26 (2008).

[78] *See* O'CONNELL, *supra* note 77, at 27 ("[Grotius] believed in the Christian law of love and the optimistic view of people's capacity embodied in Christianity. He continued the work of the Scholastics but moved farther toward a secular understanding of natural law than they had in order to avoid the swirling religious controversies of his time.").

[79] SAMUEL PUFENDORF, OF THE LAW OF NATURE AND NATIONS, Book II, ch. III, §23 (Basil Kennett trans., 3d ed. 1717).

[80] JOHNSTON, *supra* note 8, at 416.

[81] VATTEL, *supra* note 76, at 8. *See also* H. Lauterpacht, *The Grotian Tradition in International Law*, 23 BRIT. Y.B. INT'L L. 1 (1946) (attempting to reconcile these two strands of thinking in Grotius' work by arguing that the arbitrary law of nations is grounded in the law of nature as expressive of the social nature of man); JOHNSTON, *supra* note 8, at 396–97 (noting that Francisco de Vitoria and Francisco Suarez, Spanish jurists one generation before Grotius, postulated that although the law of nations sprang from natural law, it was also "positive" law in the sense of being posited by society).

[82] VATTEL, *supra* note 76, at 70, §§ 7–9.

he supported Grotius' doctrine of just war.[83] However, he also championed sovereign equality, arguing that it necessarily followed from the equality of men who comprised states. Giving weight to sovereign equality resulted in holding every state beyond the judgment of all other states, which meant that international laws would be the product of state consent and not natural laws that trumped state consent. Natural law seemed only to be pragmatically accommodated in his idea that states are presumed to consent to certain "voluntary" laws.[84]

Grotious, Pudendorf, Hobbes, and Vattel all observed international activities among European states in the sixteenth and seventeenth centuries. Yet they reached different conclusions about what counted as law in the international system. This shows that when conceptualizing international law, scholars make choices about what facts are relevant to determining the nature of international law and about how to interpret those facts. Often, non-conceptual factors motivate those choices, such as the assumptions that human beings are moral or self-interested, which were Pufendorf's and Hobbes' respective views.

B. Late Modernism

In the late modernist period of the nineteenth to mid-twentieth century, international legal theory advanced greatly, and accounts of international law became more nuanced and elaborate. Because there is more scholarship to appraise, and more information about international law scholars, analyzing late modernist theories reveals more non-conceptual choices that scholars make when theorizing about international law. Their respective personal, professional, and geopolitical contexts provide hints about the complex (and perhaps occasionally contradictory) motivations that may have driven those choices.

In the nineteenth century, accounts of international law based purely on natural law became less popular. Positivist accounts of international law continued to develop with the rise of positivism in law generally. Positivist jurisprudence, whether about domestic law or international law, is generally committed to a concept of law as social facts. The content of law and the legality of norms are not usually contingent upon their morality or value.[85] Legality is instead determined by reference to criterial facts. In other words, if certain facts existed, then there was law.

[83] *Id.* at 70, § 7.

[84] *See* Johnston, *supra* note 8, at 418 ("Down the ages Vattel has been a target of criticism by those European jurists who have felt responsible for guarding the European heritage of natural law."); O'Connell, *supra* note 77, at 33 ("Vattel elevated the state and the will of the state to the point that positivism—the doctrine that law is made from positive acts of states—followed naturally from his ideas.").

[85] *See* Hart, The Concept of Law, *supra* note 8, at 240 ("My account is descriptive in that it is morally neutral and has no justificatory aims: it does not seek to justify or commend on moral or other grounds the forms and structures which appear in my general account of law . . ."); Hans Kelsen, General Theory of Law and State xiii (A. Wedberg trans., 1945), *reprinted in* W. Michael Reisman & Aaron M. Schreiber, Jurisprudence 381 (1987) ("[T]he aim of this general theory of law is to enable the jurist concerned with a particular legal order . . . to understand and to

Scholars writing about international law tested if it was law by picking out facts about international activities they thought were relevant, and comparing those facts to their chosen quintessential system of law, which often was domestic law. They would reason that domestic law was law because certain criterial facts for law were present, such as sanctions, and accordingly, international laws would also exist only if those criterial facts existed. Many of the leading postivist scholars reached different conclusions about international law because they picked out different criterial facts from each of their preferred quintessential systems of law.

John Austin developed the "command theory of law."[86] Building on Hobbes, he proposed in 1832 that law was a system of commands issued by the sovereign, backed by sanctions. This concept of law was principally addressed to domestic law. When he applied his criterion for law to international activities, he concluded international law was not really law at all.[87] Starting with the Westphalian notion that all states are equal, there was no sovereign over states to issue commands to states and to enforce those commands by sanction. Accordingly, international law was not "law."

Austin delineated his project as the science of jurisprudence, and set out methodological markers for answering the question: "What is law?"[88] According to Alan Hutchinson, Austin prescribed that the answer was only to be found using analytic jurisprudence, a philosophical mode of inquiry in search of a concept of law that is both universal, transcending any particular or local practices, and general, encompassing and informing all other inquiries into law.[89] Embedded in this research program were value choices about modes of inquiry, presumptions that a concept of law exists, that there can only be one concept of law, and that it does not change. These presumptions foreclose the possibility that there is, or at least need not be, a universal concept of law, and that different communities could have different and equally valid views about what counts as law. Austin's choice to hold up domestic law as the model of law against which the international system should be compared also slanted his inquiry against thinking of informal processes and customs as international law because there was no analog in the domestic legal systems from which he drew his set of relevant facts to interpret into a concept of law.

describe as exactly as possible his own positive law . . ."). Other legal philosophers have since argued that positivism is not entirely free from normativity. *See* Jeremy Waldron, *Normative (or Ethical) Positivism*, *in* HART'S POSTSCRIPT 411, 411–12 (J. Coleman ed., 2001); John Finnis, *H.L.A. Hart: A Twentieth-Century Oxford Political Philosopher: Reflections by a Former Student and Colleague*, 54 AM. J. JURIS. 161, 171 (2009) ("Hart's late-period work also shows the extent to which he was willing to admit, at least by implication, that the asserted autonomy of political from moral philosophy was unsustainable.").

[86] *See generally* AUSTIN, *supra* note 5, at 7–257.

[87] For discussions on Austin's view of international law, *see id.*; NUSSBAUM, *supra* note 10, at 224–25; O'CONNELL, *supra* note 77, at 40–41.

[88] AUSTIN, *supra* note 5, at 77–80, 126.

[89] ALLAN C. HUTCHINSON, THE PROVINCE OF JURISPRUDENCE DEMOCRATIZED 3, 22 (2009).

A generation later in England, Lassa Oppenheim, a committed positivist, challenged Austin's dismissal of international law.[90] Like Austin, Oppenheim was committed to the primacy of state will. Unlike Austin, he did not accept that international law consequently did not exist and was simply positive morality. According to Oppenheim, international law exists when states consent to be bound by a rule of international law "to the same extent and degree as subjects are bound by rules of the municipal law of their state."[91] Unlike positive morality, which was a matter of conscience, Oppenheim postulated that states enforced international law through reprisals and war.[92]

Oppenheim's theory of international law was not free from politics. According to Benedict Kingsbury, Oppenheim thought that international law ought to be promoted in world affairs,[93] and his theory of identifying international laws through state practice promoted that political goal.[94]

Continental Europe also struggled with articulating a concept of international law. German jurist Carl Schmitt viewed the League of Nations as an institutional strategy to promote Anglo-American interests and to suppress Germany. He reflected the Hobbes-Austin view that international law involved "fictions of legality" and accused it of being the product of "the decisions of the powerful."[95] This jurisprudence supported Germany's desire for geopolitical hegemony unconstrained by international law—some legal historians have said that the German Reich installed Schmitt at the University of Berlin because he was sympathetic to Hitler's agenda.[96]

The Austrian Jewish scholar Hans Kelsen did not agree. The preeminent modern monist, Kelsen fixated on conceiving law as a unified and orderly system, even if that was not the case in practice.[97] Under his Pure Theory of Law, every legal rule derived its authority from an antecedent legal rule, until finally, the basic norm of law—the *grundnorm*—was reached. The *grundnorm* thus supplied the central ordering legal authority for the entire legal system.[98] Koskenniemi describes this view as

[90] For discussions of Oppenheim, see Benedict Kingsbury, *Legal Positivism as Normative Politics: International Society, Balance of Power and Lassa Oppenheim's Positive International Law*, 13 EUR. J. INT'L L. 401 (2002); O'CONNELL, *supra* note 77, at 42–45.

[91] Lassa Oppenheim, *The Science of International Law: Its Task and Method,* 2 AM. J. INT'L L. 313, 333 (1908).

[92] O'CONNELL, *supra* note 77, at 43.

[93] *Id. See also* O'CONNELL, *supra* note 77, at 63.

[94] KINGSBURY, *supra* note 90, at 422.

[95] KOSKENNIEMI, GENTLE CIVILIZER, *supra* note 71, at 239.

[96] O'CONNELL, *supra* note 77, at 57–58; Detlev F. Vagts, *International Law in the Third Reich*, 84 AM. J. INT'L L. 661, 671 (1990); KOSKENNIEMI, GENTLE CIVILIZER, *supra* note 71, at 422 (noting Schmitt's "enthusiasm for Hitler's dictatorship").

[97] For a thorough discussion of Kelsen's view of international law, see KOSKENNIEMI, GENTLE CIVILIZER, *supra* note 71, at 238–49.

[98] *Id.* at 241.

"neo-Kantian,"[99] in the sense that international law derived from a fundamental basic obligation.

Even though a positivist, Kelsen's scientific epistemology was markedly different from Austin's and Oppenheim's. Whereas Austin posited there was no international law because it lacked effective sanction, and Oppenheim posited international laws existed through state practices that were enforced through war and reprisals, Kelsen's account of international law did not depend on enforcement or even state practice. Both domestic and international law emanated from the *grundnorm* that organized a unified system of law; however, domestic law was merely a component of the international legal system. This was lofty jurisprudence. Even if in practice, states did not obey international law; it existed at least in concept by logical derivation from the *grundnorm*.

Kelsen eventually conceded that he had made political choices in developing his early theory. In his late scholarship, he accepted that the his theory of law was consistent with either national law being superior to international law or vice versa,[100] and that selecting one over the other was a political decision. According to Kelsen, preferring national law was "an essential element of the political ideology of imperialism," whereas preferring international law "plays a decisive part in the political ideology of pacifism."[101]

For many Anglo-American scholars, Herbert Lionel Adolphus Hart was the greatest positivist of all time.[102] After the Second World War, Hart joined Oxford University to teach and write. Oxford in the late 1940s and 1950s was dominated by philosophers who favored projects concerning the philosophy of ordinary language, and legal scholars who focused on doctrinal work that did not find credence among the philosophers. Hart's biographer, Nicola Lacey, suggests that Hart was a late-starting and insecure academic, and may have pursued analytic jurisprudence to gain intellectual acceptance at Oxford.[103] Whatever his motivation, Hart was hugely successful and earned a chair in jurisprudence in 1952.

Hart's magisterial account of positivism is contained in his signal opus, THE CONCEPT OF LAW. According to Hart, a legal system exists if two social facts exist. First, officials accept secondary rules, the most important of which is the rule of recognition that prescribes the validity of primary rules. Second, there is a general acceptance by the community, to whom rules are addressed, of primary rules identified as valid by secondary rules and the rule of recognition.[104] The rule of

[99] *Id.*

[100] HANS KELSEN, PURE THEORY OF LAW 333–44 (Max Knight trans., 1989) [hereinafter KELSEN, PURE THEORY] (arguing that a monist construction was inevitable whether national or international legal orders had primacy over the other).

[101] *Id.* at 346–47.

[102] For a biography of Hart, see generally NICOLA LACEY, A LIFE OF H. L. A. HART: THE NIGHTMARE AND THE NOBLE DREAM (2004).

[103] *Id.* at 3, 35, 112.

[104] HART, THE CONCEPT OF LAW, *supra* note 85, at 100–23. *See also* Stephen R. Perry, *Hart's Methodological Positivism, in* HART'S POSTSCRIPT, *supra* note 85, at 319.

recognition is a social rule or custom constituted by a regular pattern of conduct and by a "distinctive normative attitude" accepting the rule of recognition. This normative attitude is the rule of recognition's "internal aspect."[105]

In his infamous Chapter Ten, Hart dismisses international law as a primitive system of law because it lacks a unified rule of recognition and secondary rules. International law was merely a hodgepodge of primary rules.[106] Hart chose the English domestic legal system as the set of facts from which to interpret and describe a theory of law. His criterial facts for the existence of law were facts present in the English system. Accordingly, his conclusion that international law was at most a primitive legal system because it lacked those criterial facts also flowed from his initial choice to select facts from England's legal system. However, his choice to hold up the English legal system as the exemplar of law was not a conceptual choice.

If Hart established law as a serious philosophical discipline within the intellectual milieu at Oxford University by moving beyond the cataloguing work of law professors at the time, his contemporary, Hersch Lauterpacht, successfully promoted international law by systematizing its rules and decisions at Cambridge University.[107] Lauterpacht was closely associated with positivism because he conceived of international law as a complete system of rules.[108] Lacunae in laws were filled by analogy to ensure correspondence with facts and consistency with laws.

As a positivist, Lauterpacht observed international acts and interpreted them as evidence of international laws *vel non* by examining whether those acts complied with criterial facts for the existence of international laws, such as state consent. For example, when the Universal Declaration of Human Rights was adopted, Lauterpacht insisted that it was not a legal document; it was merely a UN General Assembly resolution lacking the state consent necessary for it to have any legal effect.[109]

Because Lauterpacht was a leading posivitist, it is useful for present purposes to examine his scholarship to see if he had made any non-conceptual choices in his theory of international law. As it turns out, for Lauterpacht's ultimate criterial fact of state consent for international law was not contingent on states consenting to it.[110] He does not explain why this choice of consent as the ultimate criterial fact was conceptually necessary.[111]

[105] Hart, The Concept of Law, *supra* note 85, at 56.

[106] *Id.* ch. X, p. 213–37. *But see* Jeremy Waldron, *Hart and the Principles of Legality*, *in* The Legacy of H. L. A. Hart 68 (Matthew H. Kramer et al. eds., 2008) [hereinafter Waldron, *Hart and the Principles of Legality*] (arguing that the observation that international law lacks secondary rules is inaccurate).

[107] For biographical information about Lauterpacht, see Robert Jennings, *Hersch Lauterpacht: A Personal Recollection*, 8 Eur. J. Int'l L. 301 (1997); First Interview with Professor Sir Elihu Lauterpacht, Squire Law Library, Cambridge University, questions 1, 2 (Jan. 29, 2008).

[108] *See generally* Oppenheim's International Law (Lauterpacht ed., Cambridge Univ. Press 1970).

[109] *Id.* at 395.

[110] Hersch Lauterpacht, Private Law Sources and Analogies of International Law 54–59 (1927).

[111] Martti Koskenniemi, From Apology to Utopia 364 (2005) (questioning the consistency of Lauterpacht's position that even though state consent was the ultimate test of whether an

Indeed, in some of his scholarship, Lauterpacht accepts that international law could exist without state consent or be modified by non-consensual principles.[112] Like Grotius, Lauterpacht urged that "ethics and reason" affected the content of international laws.[113] He argued that in order to protect against anarchy, reason and principle should temper purely consensual lawmaking. In his view, this "explains the pertinacity, in the international sphere, of the idea of natural law as a legal source."[114]

Lauterpacht's personal experiences might explain his non-conceptual choice to modify the criterial fact of state consent with ethics. His whole family, with the exception of one niece, was murdered during the Holocaust. Israeli President Chaim Herzog, who married the aunt of Lauterpacht's wife, stated:

> The loss of [Lauterpacht's] own family in Poland during the Holocaust undoubtedly influenced the development of his own ideas regarding individual responsibility for war crimes and crimes against humanity.[115]

For someone who experienced so personally the horrors of the Holocaust, the political dangers of allowing states to make whatever international laws they wanted based solely on their consent could not have been clearer.

The foregoing survey of theories about international law in the late modern period highlights some of the choices that scholars made in constructing their theories. Austin and Hart, who constructed positivist theories about law, questioned whether international law was law because they selected criterial facts for the existence of law from their observations of domestic law, and international law did not appear to them to have those facts. It was open to them, however, to have chosen intead to use the international legal system as their quintessential system and to find its own criterial facts. As Kelsen conceded in his late work, the choice of prioritizing domestic law over international law, or vice versa, was a political choice.

Scholars who contended that international law was law under their positivist approaches also made political or non-conceptual choices in their theorizing. Oppenheim believed that international law ought to be promoted and that identifying laws through state consent advanced this goal. In comparision, Lauterpacht believed that state consent ought to be moderated by ethics and reason in order to avoid creating international laws that resulted in anarchy.

international law existed, states did not have to consent to state consent being the criterial fact of international law).

112 O'Connell, *supra* note 77, 52–55. *See also* Koskenniemi, From Apology to Utopia, *supra* note 111, at 406–11.

113 *See* Lauterpacht, *supra* note 81, at 22.

114 *Id.* at 23.

115 Chaim Herzog, *Sir Hersch Lauterpacht: An Appraisal*, 8 Eur. J. Int'l L. 299, 299–300 (1997).

C. Postmodernism

Theories about international law after 1945 are even more diverse than from previous eras. The proliferation of theories makes it impossible to devote sufficient attention here to each theory. This section is however neither intended as a catalogue of international legal theories nor as a guidebook to any one of them.[116]

The purposes of this section are simply to continue the exploration of the choices that scholars make in selecting facts of international acts and interpreting them to theorize about international law, and whether these choices are conceptual, personal, or political. For these limited purposes, it may be sufficient to offer thumbnail accounts of contempory theories along with brief biographical information of scholars who promote them. This inquiry reveals the different choices that scholars made in their respective theories, which resulted in divergent accounts of international law, each with different political and normative consequences. The personal backgrounds and geopolitical contexts in which each scholar engaged in research help to explain their respective choices.

The period of international legal theory after 1945 has some times been labeled "postmodern," which is a convenient term to express uncertainty about theory. Scholars have identified two forms of uncertainty. The first is uncertainty about basic values. According to O'Connell, postmodernists "contemplate no metanarrative, no conception of human good to be universally espoused and ultimately achieved."[117] Postwar thinkers rejected Enlightenment libertarian and rational ideals because the Reich had co-opted them to implement and justify the Holocaust.[118] The second form of uncertainty is about whether international law actually controls outcomes. According to critical legal studies scholars, or "crits," the techniques for creating and applying international laws are inherently malleable and are tools for the powerful to perpetuate their domination.[119]

In this author's view, there is a third form of uncertainty, which is uncertainty about whether a concept of international law even exists and if such a concept could ever be found even if it existed. Before 1945, scholars of international law believed that there there could be a single theory of international law, even if they disagreed about what that theory was. Today, the diversity of theories about international law makes it reasonable to question whether there could ever be a conclusive theory of international law. This book's thesis is post-modern in this sense: It takes the view that all theories of international law ultimately make political choices and therefore

[116] For a detailed discussion of contempory theories of international law, see generally THE METHODS OF INTERNATIONAL LAW (Steven R. Ranter & Anne-Marie Slaughter eds., 2004).

[117] O'CONNELL, *supra* note 77, at 92 (quoting Barbara Stark, *Women and Globalization: The Failure and Postmodern Possibilities of International Law*, 33 VAND. J. TRANSNAT'L L. 503, 546 (2000)).

[118] *See* JACK L. GOLDSMITH & ERIC A. POSNER, THE LIMITS OF INTERNATIONAL LAW 167–84 (2005) (discussing Hitler's use of international law).

[119] Andreas L. Paulus, *International Law After Postmodernism: Towards Renewal or Decline of International Law?*, 14 LEIDEN J. INT'L L. 727, 732 (2001).

no theory is purely conceptual. The following survey of the postmodern theories of international law illustrates this.

Critical legal scholars, as exemplified by David Kennedy and Martti Koskenniemi, question prior theories of international law that conceived of it as a system of legal rules. They believe legal rules are indeterminate because they obtain practical meaning only through application, which is open to endless semantic interpretation and contingent on choices exogenous to law.[120] Kennedy argues that:

> international law is not a bundle of rules governing relations among states. International law is a profession, a discipline, in which people . . . pursue projects, projects of affiliation or disaffiliation, of commitment and aversion, of power and submission—pursue them in a shared vocabulary, through the apparatus of shared professional practices and institutions. As they do so, they lay behind them evidence of both their shared and individual styles.[121]

According to Kennedy, law is a rhetorical system that becomes "an international regime" because "[e]ach doctrine seems to free ride somewhat on this overall systemic image—an image which is sustained by continual reference elsewhere for authority or decisiveness." [122]

Koskenniemi has recently taken a slightly different view about the indeterminacy of legal rules. In 2009, he argued that within specific international regimes, such as trade or human rights, outcomes are somewhat predictable because the vocabulary and styles of reasoning in each regime create structural biases in favor of the normative values of that regime. Indeterminacy results from the lack of control over how officials select regimes in which to press their interests. Although he attempted some doctrinal harmonization in the International Law Commission's report on fragmentation, which he authored as Special Rapporteur,[123] in subsequent academic writing he has continued to despair about indeterminacy resulting from political choices to frame an international incident under one regime or another in a fragmented international legal system.[124]

[120] DAVID KENNEDY, INTERNATIONAL LEGAL STRUCTURES 294 (1987) ("In fact, the pattern of repetitions, associations and references which characterise public international law seems suited to a practice of interminable discourse."); KOSKENNIEMI, FROM APOLOGY TO UTOPIA, *supra* note 111; Martti Koskenniemi, *Letter to the Editors of the Symposium*, 93 AM. J. INT'L L. 351, 355 (Steven R. Ratner & Anne-Marie Slaughter eds., 1999) ("[I]nternational law consisted in a small number of argumentative rules through which it was possible to justify anything . . .").

[121] David Kennedy, *Tom Franck and the Manhattan School*, 35 N.Y.U. J. INT'L L. & POL. 397, 398–99 (2003). *See also* KOSKENNIEMI, FROM APOLOGY TO UTOPIA, *supra* note 111, at 548 ("[L]aw is what lawyers do and think and that the problem of the law cannot be disassociated from the identity of the lawyer.").

[122] KENNEDY, *supra* note 120, at 293.

[123] International Law Commission, Fragmentation of International Law: Difficulties Arising from the Diversification and Expansion of International Law, U.N. Doc. A/CN.4/L.682 (Apr. 13, 2006) (*finalized by* Martti Koskenniemi).

[124] Martti Koskenniemi, *The Politics of International Law—20 Years Later*, 20 EUR. J. INT'L L. 7, 10 (2009).

Kennedy and Koskenniemi, on the one hand, and the theorists that came before them, on the other hand, all observed that states made rules among themselves, either by their consent as the positivists emphasized, or by reason and ethics, as natural law philosophers stressed. However, Kennedy and Koskenniemi assessed the relevance of these facts about the international actions of states differently from prior scholars. Crits did not interpret those rules as constituting international law on their own. Instead, Kennedy chose to select as relevant facts the actions and interactions of legal professionals and elites in institutions in discussing, interpreting, and applying international prescriptions to give them meaning, and Koskienniemi chose to focus on the decisions of elites to situate an international problem within one legal regime or another. Kennedy and Koskienniemi chose different facts as evidence of international law than the facts preferred by positivists or natural law scholars. However, there is no way to determine conceptually which sets of facts are more relevant in theorizing about international law.[125]

Like crits, realists challenge theories of international law that view it as a body of binding legal rules, but they do so for different reasons. Realists do not focus on the intedeteminacy of rules. Instead, they emphasize that states act only in self-interest and argue rules that do not serve that self-interest do not, cannot, or should not bind states. Sitting on the shoulders of Hobbes and Austin, Hans Morgenthau focused on "the concept of interest defined in terms of power."[126] Based on this principle, he argued in 1948 in his book Politics Among Nations that "the only bond of union that endures among nations is the absence of all clashing interests."[127] He understood international law to comprise only positive laws to which states had consented, but regarded its lack of sanction and imprecision as a "debilitating vice."[128] He also rejected the theory of common values, explaining that "[p]olitical

[125] Other branches of "crits" do not necessarily offer a unique conception of international law. Instead, they question the normative underpinnings of international laws as insufficiently promoting the interests of certain groups, such as women, gays, or the Third World. Because these approaches do not address the choices that must be made in conceptualizing international law, they are not discussed in this chapter. For general discussions about femimist theory and Third World Approaches to International Law, see generally, Hilary Charlesworth, *Feminist Methods in International Law*, *in* The Methods of International Law, *supra* note 116, at 159; Antony Anghie & B. S. Chimni, *Third World Approaches to International Law and Individual Responsibility in Internal Conflict*, *in id.* at 185; B. S. Chimni, International Law and World Order: A Critique of Contemporary Approaches (1993) (critiquing the international law theories proposed by Morgenthau, McDougal-Lasswell, Richard Falk, and Grigory Tunkin); R. P. Anand, Studies in International Law and History: An Asian Perspective (2004); International Law and the Third World (R. Falk et al. eds., 2008); Anthony Carty, *Critical International Law: Recent Trends in the Theory of International Law*, 2 Eur. J. Int'l L. 66, 68 (1991); Anthony Carty, The Decay of International Law?: A Reappraisal of the Limits of Legal Imagination in International Affairs (1988).

[126] Morgenthau, *supra* note 7, at 5.

[127] *Id.* at 8 (internal quotations omitted).

[128] *Id.* at 279–81.

realism refuses to identify the moral aspirations of a particular nation with the moral laws that govern the universe."[129]

Morgenthau's work was ultimately unable to ignore common values entirely. The third edition of POLITICS AMONG NATIONS was published in 1960, at the height of the Cold War. He concluded with a plea for "international peace" and a proposal to engage in formal diplomatic processes with the Soviet Union as the best chance of avoiding war.[130] It is easy to justify peace as a goal of international relations because it was in the interests of the United States. However, the coincidence of Morgenthau's position with the fundamental value ascribed to peace under the natural law tradition is also difficult to ignore.[131]

Realism reached a new pinnacle with the publication in 2005 of Eric Posner and Jack Goldsmith's book THE LIMITS OF INTERNATIONAL LAW.[132] Although they began by stating that the claim that international law is not really law is misleading, scholars have accused them of "dismissing international law as something less than real law."[133] Like Morgenthau, Posner and Goldsmith view interstate relations as a function of state interest and power, thus "states cannot bootstrap cooperation by creating rules and calling them 'law.'"[134] The value of any international rule, in their view, is determined by its content alone. Consequently, "[t]he mortality or immorality of international law is exhausted by its content; international legality does not impose any moral obligations."[135]

Like positivists, realists observe that states make legal rules among themselves through treaties or customary practices. However, they have chosen to interpret the

[129] *Id.* at 11.

[130] *Id.* at 570.

[131] *See generally* INTERNATIONAL REGIMES (Stephen D. Krasner ed., 1983); Richard H. Steinberg & Jonathan M. Zasloff, *Power and International Law*, 100 AM. J. INT'L L. 64, 74 (2006) (stating that Kranser viewed international law as "merely an epiphenomenon of underlying power").

[132] For reviews and discussions of THE LIMITS OF INTERNATIONAL LAW, *see generally* 34 GA. J. INT'L & COMP. L. (2005–06) (symposium discussing and responding to THE LIMITS OF INTERNATIONAL LAW); O'CONNELL, *supra* note 77, at 105–31; Andrew T. Guzman, *The Promise of International Law*, 92 VA. L. REV. 522 (2006); Edward T. Swaine, *Restoring (and Risking) Interest in International Law*, 100 AM. J. INT'L L. 259 (2006); David Gray, *Rule-Skepticism, "Strategery," and the Limits of International Law*, 46 VA. J. INT'L L. 563 (2005-06); Paul Schiff Berman, *Seeing Beyond the Limits of International Law*, 84 TEX. L. REV. 1265 (2005-06); John Ikenberry, *The Limits of International Law*, FOREIGN AFFAIRS, Mar./Apr., 2005, at 150 (book review); SCHARF & WILLIAMS, *supra* note 72, at 10–13 (surveying critiques of THE LIMITS OF INTERNATIONAL LAW).

[133] SCHARF & WILLIAMS, *supra* note 72, at 11 (restating Peter Spiro's view that Goldsmith and Posner "dismiss[] international law as something less than real law . . .").

[134] GOLDSMITH & POSNER, *supra* note 118, at 203.

[135] *Id.* at 197. *But see* Kenneth Anderson, *Remarks by an Idealist on the Realism of the Limits of International Law*, 34 GA. J. INT'L & COMP. L. 253, 272 (2006) ("[W]e might have an instance within international law in which a body of international law exerts independent moral weight, tugging toward compliance, not because of state interest, nor even because of state interest taking account of certain values, but instead because the individual actors within the system, . . . accept the legitimacy of the international rules, law and morality."); Oona A. Hathaway & Ariel N. Lavinbuk, *Rationalism and Revisionism in International Law*, 119 HARV. L. REV. 1404, 1442 (2006) (book review) ("[U]tility seeking and law-abiding behavior is often identical.").

significance of these facts differently. Positivists end their inquiry with the creation of legal obligations when criterial facts exist. In contrast, realists ask a further question of whether and when states ought to obey international legal obligations. Their answer is that states ought to obey legal obligations when it is in their interests to do so, and states ought not to follow customary practices that do not promote the values of their citizens.

Policy-oriented jurisprudence developed in response to realism. Myres S. McDougal and Harold Lasswell pioneered this approach to international law in the 1940s.[136] As the policy-oriented approach developed, observers conferred upon it the appellation "The New Haven School," in recognition of its geographical and intellectual locus and its worldwide epistemic community of New Haven associates.[137] The New Haven School conceived of law not as a system of rules, but approached it as a process of decision achieved through a constant stream of communications among international decisionmakers issuing demands backed by authority and control.[138] Normative concerns are explicitly considered and included in the criteria for legal validity. The New Haven School's solution to the indeterminacy of law was to embrace it and make policy recommendations to stabilize international relations to promote minimum order and human dignity.[139] Policy-oriented jurisprudence was a way forward from the realism of Morgenthau. For Morgenthau, law was purely a function of effectiveness or control, without necessary normative content. It was thus indistinct from pure power. New Haven scholars distinguished law from politics by insisting that legality did not come from its effectiveness alone. It also had to be authoritative and legitimate.[140]

[136] *See generally* Harold D. Lasswell & Myres S. McDougal, *Legal Education and Public Policy: Professional Training in the Public Interest,* 52 Yale LJ. 203 (1943). For McDougal's biography, see Johnston, *supra* note 8, at 116; Richard A. Falk et al., *Myres Smith McDougal (1906–1998), in* 2 Rosalyn Higgins, Themes and Theories: Selected Essays, Speeches and Writing in International Law (2009) [hereinafter Higgins, Themes and Theories] 975–76 (2009).

[137] They include Burns Weston and Douglas Johnston, as well as Florentino Feliciano, the first chairman of the Appellate Body of the World Trade Organization and the president of the Supreme Court of the Phillipines; and Rosalyn Higgins, former president of the International Court of Justice.

[138] *See* Siegfried Wiessner & Andrew R. Willard, *Policy-Oriented Jurisprudence & Human Rights Abuses in Internal Conflict: Toward a World Public Order of Human Dignity*, 93 Am. J. Int'l L. 316, 319 (1999) ("First, law is conceived of as an ongoing process of authoritative and controlling decision.").

[139] For an expansive bibliography of New Haven jurisprudence, see David Kennedy, *The Mystery of Global Governance*, 34 Ohio N.U. L. Rev. 827, n.1 (2008). The author would add to the list Rosalyn Higgins, Themes and Theories: Selected Essays, Speeches and Writing in International Law, vols. 1 & 2 (2009) [hereinafter Higgins, Themes and Theories]; Johnston, *supra* note 8.

[140] Koskenniemi thus mischaracterizes the New Haven school when he asserts that its view was "if it works let it be law, and let it be law as long as and to the extent that it does work." Gentle Civilizer, *supra* note 71, at 485.

From its inception, the New Haven School has provoked strong responses.[141] This may have been due in part to McDougal's iconoclastic persona.[142] But leaving that aside, there were real theoretical disagreements within the Academy that were not amenable to conceptual resolution. Whereas positivists choose to focus on law as a system of rules derived from facts,[143] the New Haven jurists choose to focus on the normative content of legal rules when interpreting them and deciding whether to follow them.[144]

Other scholars revealed that their concerns were not conceptual, but political. They were disturbed by what they perceived to be the political consequences of applying the New Haven approach to legal problems. Oscar Schachter criticized policy-oriented jurisprudence for appearing to permit decisionmakers to substitute their subjective judgments for sound policy appraisals in determining the legality *vel non* of actions and decisions.[145] It did not take long for Schachter to reveal that his methodological complaints were also proxies for normative disagreements about whether it was desirable to specify universal values for a world community in all its diversity,[146] and, relatedly, about the propriety of apparently

[141] *See* David J. Bederman, *Appraising a Century of Scholarship in the American Journal of International Law*, 100 Am. J. Int'l L. 20, 41 (2006) ("So powerful was this new approach—and generally unprecedented and subversive—that it naturally started to draw sharp critiques.").

[142] *See* W. Michael Reisman, *Theory About Law: Jurisprudence for a Free Society*, 108 Yale L.J. 935, 939 (1999) ("McDougal's image . . . in the collective mind of the academy and the profession [was that of an] enfant terrible and destroyer of the law . . .").

[143] *See* Bruno Simma & Andreas L. Paulus, *The Responsibility of Individuals for Human Rights Abuses in Internal Conflicts: A Positivist View*, 93 Am. J. Int'l L. 302, 304 (1999) ("Law is regarded as a unified system of rules[.]"); Ulrich Fastenrath, *Relative Normativity in International Law*, 4 Eur. J. Int'l L. 305, 307 (1993) ("Legal positivism identifies law with legal propositions (Rechtssätze), i.e., the wording of positive rules. . . .").

[144] *See* Harold Hongju Koh, *Is there a "New" New Haven School of International Law?*, 32 Yale J. Int'l L. 559, 561 (2007) ("The New Haven School expressly intended to criticize both legal formalism and legal positivism in international law."); Rosalyn Higgins, *Introductory Statement: Diverging Anglo-American Attitudes to International Law*, 2 Ga. J. Int'l & Comp. L. 1 (1972) (recording Rosalyn Higgins' observations about skepticism of British scholars toward mixing policy with legal rules); Julien Cantegreil, *Legal Formalism Meets Policy-Oriented Jurisprudence: A More European Approach to Frame the War on Terror*, 60 Me. L. Rev. 98, 99 (2008) (noting that the policy-oriented approach is "diametrically opposed to the Kelsenian spirit").

[145] Oscar Schachter, Remarks at the American Society of International Law Annual Meeting (Apr. 26, 1985), *in* 79 Am. Soc'y Int'l L. Proc. 266, 272 (1985) ("The dangers of this approach become still more apparent when the higher goals are determined by the particular policies of a national state."). Notably, Schachter had been one of the "creators of the policy-oriented frame of jurisprudence" when he was a guest lecturer at Yale Law School from 1955 to 1971. Myres S. McDougal, *Remarks at the 79th Annual Meeting of the American Society of International Law*, 79 Am. Soc'y Int'l L. Proc. 283 (1985).

[146] *Id.* at 270 ("Mac nearly always finds that his own preferences are the key to what is in the common interest and in accord with the shared expectations of 'all peoples.' . . . [b]ut how does one discover the values that some 4 billion people actually hold?"); Koskenniemi, Gentle Civilizer, *supra* note 71, at 476 ("[T]heir repetitive lists of variables of policy analysis failed to protect their postulated goal values from a critique of being either an old-fashioned naturalism in disguise or a smoke screen for a defense of American foreign policy.").

using the New Haven approach to justify U.S. interests under the banner of world values.[147]

W. Michael Reisman, Myres S. McDougal Professor of International Law at Yale Law School, has continued to clarify and develop the New Haven approach.[148] Rebutting Schachter's argument that referring to policy and effectiveness outside of legal rules rendered law even more indeterminate, Reisman distinguished myth systems of rules from operational codes of actual practices. Where myth and code coincided with each other and with relevant values, the New Haven School recommended fidelity to rules.[149] In *LCIA Case No. 81010*, Reisman opined that a prior award had no persuasive authority because it failed to apply a strictly textualist approach to treaty interpretation, as required under Articles 31 and 32 of the Vienna Convention on the Law of Treaties.[150] Positivism's legalist methods of reasoning were appropriate in that dispute to stabilize treaty texts against the changing and imagined subjective views of a state.[151]

Where myth and code deviated, however, it was necessary for a lawyer to consider both and to offer guidance on the normative implications of any decision so that good decisions could be made.[152] When U.S. President George W. Bush announced his eponymous doctrine of preemptive force, he claimed to establish an operational code on the use of force that deviated from the myth system of Article 2(4) and 51

[147] Schachter, *supra* note 145, at 272–73. *See also* Hari M. Osofsky, *A Law and Geography Perspective on the New Haven School*, 32 YALE J. INT'L L. 421, 424 (2007) ("The School has been accused of . . . serving as apologists for U.S. foreign policy."); O'CONNELL, *supra* note 77, at 70 ("The harsher criticism of the New Haven School was aimed at McDougal's evident promotion of United States policy."); Reisman, *supra* note 141, at 939 (noting that critics have accused policy-oriented jurisprudence of promoting American values).

[148] *See* Rosalyn Higgins, *Closing Remarks at the Conference To Honor the Work of Professor Michael Reisman*, 34 YALE J. INT'L L. 605, 613 (2009) ("[Reisman] remains the keeper of the flame, the one among us with probably the most profound understanding of what had instinctively attracted us [to New Haven jurisprudence] as our ideas were being shaped."); Harold Hongju Koh, *Michael Reisman, Dean of the New Haven School of International Law*, 34 YALE J. INT'L L. 501, 501 (2009) (stating that Reisman "has been the acknowledged Dean" of the New Haven School). *See also* Siegfried Wiessner, *Law as a Means to a Public Order of Human Dignity: The Jurisprudence of Michael Reisman*, 34 YALE J. INT'L L. 525, 532 (2009) (describing Reisman as "the realistic idealist, [] a beacon of hope, a bridge between cultures, a light in troubled waters"); James E. Baker, *Use of Force: Jupiter as Everyman: Michael Reisman and the Scholar as Teacher*, 34 YALE J. INT'L L. 533 (2009).

[149] W. Michael Reisman, Panel Remarks, *McDougal's Jurisprudence: Utility, Influence, Controversy*, 79 AM. SOC'Y INT'L L. PROC. 266, 273 (1985) ("If international law were working as it is supposed to be working, McDougal and his associates would have been among the first to use it in that fashion.").

[150] W. Michael Reisman, United States of America v. Canada, Opinion with Respect to Selected International Legal Problems in LCIA Case No. 7941 (May 1, 2009), *available at* http://ita.law.uvic.ca/documents/ReismanExpertOpinion.pdf. *Accord* Pac Rim Cayman LLC v. El Salvador, expert opinion of W. Michael Reisman, ICSID Case No. ARB/09/12 (Mar. 22, 2010) (urging strict textual interpretation as prescribed by Articles 31 and 32 of the Vienna Convention on the Law of Treaties) (copy on file with author).

[151] Reisman, *supra* note 150, at 12.

[152] Reisman, *supra* note 149, at 275.

of the UN Charter constraining the use of force except in self-defense. In response, Reisman and Andrea Armstrong, a New Haven associate, warned that the Bush doctrine could pose a threat to world order because it encouraged other states to claim similar preemptive rights.[153] In addition to underscoring the necessity of policy calculus in shaping international law when operational codes, myth systems, and values are not synchronous, this appraisal contradicts the claim that New Haven jurisprudence blindly promotes U.S. foreign policies.[154]

Rosalyn Higgins, the first female president of the Interantional Court of Justice and an eminient scholar, also clarified the New Haven approach. After studying law at Cambridge University in the late 1950s, she served as an intern at the Legal Department of the UN, which at that time was barely over a decade old, and became acquainted with Oscar Schachter, the head of the legal department.[155] Higgins visited Harvard and Yale Law Schools and found herself so taken by Yale generally and McDougal in particular that she determined to pursue her doctoral work there,[156] which she completed in three years, in 1961. She emerged a policy-oriented jurist, convinced that "law is not an abstract application of rules: it is a process directed towards the implementation of policy goals for the common good."[157]

Higgins clarified how policy appraisals were part of law, and not part of politics. Because formal rules were often indeterminate, and a judge would have to make choices about how to interpret the law, she urged that those choices should be informed by the "humanitarian, moral, and social purposes of the law" and "therefore, policy-considerations . . . are an integral element of that decision-making process which we call international law."[158] Policy was "pre-articulated, not just ex post facto, and intellectually systematized," and "that distinguishes policy choices from politics."[159] With precision, Higgins explicitly rejected Koskenniemi's charge that

[153] *See generally* W. Michael Reisman & Andrea Armstrong, *The Past and Future of the Claim of Preemptive Self-Defense*, 100 Am. J. Int'l L. 525 (2006).

[154] Other New Haven scholars have also take positions contrary to U.S. foreign policies or interests. *See* Rosalyn Higgins, *The Benign First Mate*, *in* Law in the Service of Human Dignity: Essays in Honour of Florentino Feliciano 11 (S. Charnovitz et al. eds., 2005) ("Feliciano's life in the law is a silent rebuttal to those who contend that a policy-oriented approach to law is but a façade for politics. . . ."); Tai-Heng Cheng, *Power, Authority and International Investment Law*, 20 Am. U. Int'l L. Rev. 465, 508–12 (2005) (criticizing the *Loewen* award for refusing to find jurisdiction over NAFTA dispute arising from lack of due process in Mississippi courts); Julien Cantegreil, *The Final Award* in *Mondev International v. United States of America*, *in* The Reasons Requirement in International Investment Arbitration 33, 50–57 (W. M. Reisman & G. A. Alvarez eds., 2008) (criticizing the *Mondev* award for finding in favor of the United States based on inadequate reasoning).

[155] 2 Higgins, Themes and Theories, *supra* note 139, at 992 (stating at Schachter was her "closest friend in the world of international law").

[156] E-mail from Rosalyn Higgins, former President of the ICJ, to Tai-Heng Cheng, Professor of Law, New York Law School (Feb. 15, 2011, 10:35 EST) (on file with author).

[157] 1 Higgins, Themes and Theories, *supra* note 139, at 3.

[158] *Id.* at 22.

[159] *Id.* at 18.

the New Haven School was an apology for state interests.[160] New Haven scholars observed, as crits did, that legal rules did not have fully determinate content until elites interpreted them, but New Haven scholars proposed a detailed approach to address that indeterminacy. They chose to focus, as realists did, on what decisionmakers ought to do in response to legal rules, but New Haven scholars proposed a unique approach to deciding what to do by taking into account basic values and not just self-interest. These features of the New Haven approach are not the only way to conceive international law. They are choices about how to perceive and shape it.

Another theory of international law emerged in response to realists and the New Haven School: international legal process. Its progenitors include many leading first-generation scholars of the postmodern era: Louis Henkin and Oscar Schachter at Columbia Law School, Thomas Franck at New York University Law School, and Abram Chayes at Harvard Law School. Like the New Haven School, international legal process recognizes the indeterminacy of rules that realists emphasize and the role of process in controlling outcomes. Unlike the New Haven School, their solution is not to focus on process rather than rules, but to use process to improve compliance with rules.

In his pathbreaking book published in 1968, How Nations Behave, Henkin observed that even though international laws often did not have sanctions, states nonetheless complied with them most of the time.[161] The reason for this was that it was in the self-interest of states to do so, including the protection of a state's reputation that was necessary to credibly conduct foreign affairs, international order, reciprocity, and to avoid a communal response.[162] Henkin acknowledged that states would observe international law so long as it was in their utilitarian interests to do so, but would not if the costs of compliance in a particular incident outweighed the benefits.[163] Two decades later, Henkin concluded:

> All law, of course, is political: nations make law (rather than leave a matter unregulated) from a political judgment that it will be in their respective or common interests. How existing law would be interpreted, whether it should be violated, what kind or degree of violation should be perpetrated, are also political decisions subject to the constraints of law and the costs of violation in international society.[164]

Observing the same facts in international problems as the realists, crits, and New Haven Scholars, Henkin interpreted them in a similar way: laws were made, interpreted and applied by elites who each exercised discretion after taking into account the costs and benefits of their decisions.

Building on Henkin's insights, Schachter recommended that decisionmakers engage in international processes that buttress the legitimacy of international rules.

160 Koskenniemi, Gentle Civilizer, *supra* note 71, at 476.

161 Louis Henkin, How Nations Behave: Law and Foreign Policy 45–46 (2d ed. 1979).

162 *Id.* at 46–50.

163 *Id.* at 48–49.

164 Louis Henkin, *Comment*, *in* Abram Chayes, The Cuban Missile Crisis 149–50 (1974).

The goals were to minimize ambiguity in the meaning of rules and to entrench state interests in compliance. Schachter thought that building on Henkin's ideas would enable him to harness process to take politics out of international legal rules.[165]

Abram Chayes also contributed to the development of the international legal process school. He and his wife Antonia Chayes observed that states tended to comply with treaty rules because of efficiency, national interest, and regime norms.[166] These interests, and thus compliance, could be improved by international processes that involved transparency, verification, active management, and review.[167] Through this "iterative process of discourse among parties, the treaty organization, and the wider public," an acceptable level of compliance could be obtained without sanctions.[168] Including sanctions in treaty regimes was a poor strategic choice because they would discourage states from entering into treaties.[169]

Thomas Franck built on the international legal process tradition. In his major work POWER AND LEGITIMACY AMONG NATIONS, Franck took as his jumping-off point Reisman's New Haven perspective that law is "the fruit of communications between elites and politically relevant groups which shapes wide expectations about appropriate behavior."[170] Avoiding debates about whether or not international law was really "law," Franck theorized that international law is "not law in the sense in which it is used in the national context."[171] He added that although "it is perfectly possible to call the international system of rules 'law' . . . this is neither necessary nor particularly helpful."[172] Unlike Hart, who chose to investigate whether international law was "law" by comparing it to domestic legal systems, Franck chose not to compare it to domestic law but instead to focus on how to make international law legitimate as an independent system of international regulation.

According to Franck, four factors determined the legitimacy of international law: (1) determinacy (echoing Schachter's call for clarity in what rules meant and how they applied),[173] (2) symbolic validation (echoing Reisman's analysis of the "authority signal" of prescriptions),[174] (3) coherence (application of a rule in a rational and consistent manner),[175] and (4) adherence (creating rules in accord with established

[165] *See* Schachter, *supra* note 70, at 308, 322 (proposing processes to establish legal obligations and concluding that "the specific features of that structure must be identified and validated in terms of shared expectations and attitudes, rather than in trans-empirical terms").

[166] ABRAM CHAYES & ANTONIA HANDLER CHAYES, THE NEW SOVEREIGNTY: COMPLIANCE WITH INTERNATIONAL REGULATORY AGREEMENTS 3–9 (1995).

[167] *Id.*

[168] *Id.* at 25.

[169] *Id.* at 2–3.

[170] FRANCK, POWER, *supra* note 7, at 39 (quoting W. Michael Reisman, *International Lawmaking: A Process of Communication*, 75 AM. SOC'Y INT'L L. PROC. 101 (1981)).

[171] *Id.* at 33.

[172] *Id.* at 206.

[173] *Id.* at 84.

[174] *Id.* at 91.

[175] *Id.* at 136.

procedures that states support and believe in, i.e., Hart's rule of recognition).[176] Where international laws were legitimate, they were likely to attract compliance. In a later work, he thickened his concept of compliance by adding to procedural legitimacy the requirement that substantive rules achieve fairness in the form of distributive justice.[177]

Second-generation scholars Mary Ellen O'Connell, Harold Koh, and Anne-Marie Slaughter took international legal process in different directions. O'Connell argued that international law was authoritative because the international community accepted law, and sanctions and legally regulated reprisals contributed to the power of international law.[178] O'Connell's strong response to the realism of Posner and Goldsmith is that even under an Austinian conception of law, international law is law. It "is a legal system worthy of the name" because sanctions exist "in the form of armed measures, countermeasures and judicial measures."[179] By appending sanctions to the compliance theories of her first-generation mentors, O'Connell refreshed the positivism of Austin and Oppenheim.[180]

Koh focused on ways to improve compliance with international law through domestic processes that internalized international norms among domestic elites and their constituencies.[181] Acknowledging Franck as one of his "intellectual polestars,"[182] as well as the influence of Chayes,[183] Koh deepened international legal process scholarship with his brand of "transnational legal process." He observed that states did not simply comply with international law in the sense of consciously accepting a rule. In some instances, they actually obeyed an international law, in the sense of "internaliz[ing] the norm and incorporat[ing] it into its own internal value system."[184] A transnational legal process secured obedience when government

[176] *Id.* at 183–84, 194.

[177] *See generally* THOMAS M. FRANCK, FAIRNESS IN INTERNATIONAL LAW AND INSTITUTIONS (1995).

[178] *See* O'CONNELL, *supra* note 77, at 16 ("This book's general conclusion is that sanctions play a significant—if not essential—role in why international law has power to bind both nations and individuals. The real basis of international law's authority is not sanction per se, but the international community's acceptance of law regardless of sanctions.").

[179] *Id.* at 369.

[180] *Id.* at 16 (presenting a theory that combines "a belief in higher things" with "positivist and legal process theory").

[181] *See* Harold Hongju Koh, *Why Do Nations Obey International Law?*, 106 YALE L.J. 2599 (1997) (explaining transnational legal process). Philip Jessup coined the term "transnational law" in 1956. PHILIP C. JESSUP, TRANSNATIONAL LAW (1956). Henry J. Steiner and Detlev F. Vagts developed the idea. HENRY J. STEINER & DETLEV F. VAGTS, TRANSNATIONAL LEGAL PROBLEMS (1968). But it was under Koh that the term gained widespread usage.

[182] Harold Hongju Koh, *The 1988 Fraenkel Lecture: Bringing International Law Home*, 35 HOUS. L. REV. 623, 624 (1998).

[183] Interview by Harry Kreisler with Harold Hongju Koh, Legal Adviser, in Berkeley, Ca. (Oct. 3, 2003), *available at* http://globetrotter.berkeley.edu/people3/Koh/koh-con1.html (stating that Abram Chayes was a mentor to Koh when Koh attended Harvard Law School).

[184] Koh, *supra* note 182, at 628.

officials and other domestic actors entrench the international law into the domestic order by legislation, court decisions, and other political strategies.[185]

In her major work A NEW WORLD ORDER, Slaughter described an emerging world order dominated not by interstate relations, but by global networks of bureaucrats—regulators, judges, and legislators—who exchange information, influence each other's ideas and values, and shape international decisions.[186] Slaughter applied ideas from liberalist international relations theory to international law. In particular, she disaggregated states into their substate actors. This move was consistent with the focus of policy-oriented jurisprudence on identifying actual decisionmakers and not simply treating states as monolithic entities, and also Koh's emphasis on the interactions among domestic and international factors in implementing international norms.

A subdiscipline of international law and international relations soon developed around the four major schools of international relations theory: realist, institutionalist, liberal, and constructivist.[187] Andrew Guzman, writing from the institutionalist international relations perspective, published a rebuttal of Goldsmith and Posner's rejection of international law's effectiveness.[188] Like first-generation international legal process scholars, and the Austin-Morgenthau-Posner line of realists, Guzman assumed that states are rational actors that will make rational choices to maximize their self-interest. Guzman argued that that even without any assumption of an inherent pull toward compliance, the benefits of reputation, reciprocal noncompliance, and retaliation would make international law effective if they outweighed the costs of compliance with treaties and customary law. In this fashion, Guzman showed that some of the benefits of complying with treaties that Chayes had identified also applied to customary law.

All this time, positivism continued to burn brightly in Europe. Like their positivist cousins in legal philosophy, positivists in international law see their conceptual function as "not to facilitate the decisionmaker's dilemma between law and politics

[185] *See generally id. See also* Koh, *supra* note 181, at 2645–59; *accord* ROGER FISHER, IMPROVING COMPLIANCE WITH INTERNATIONAL LAW 141 (1981) ("[O]ne of the best ways of causing respect for international law is to make it indistinguishable from domestic law.").

[186] *See generally* ANNE-MARIE SLAUGHTER, A NEW WORLD ORDER (2004).

[187] *See* Kenneth W. Abbott, *International Relations Theory, International Law, and the Regime Governing Atrocities in Internal Conflicts*, 93 AM. J. INT'L L. 361, 364–68 (1999); Kenneth W. Abbott, *Modern International Relations Theory: A Prospectus for International Lawyers*, 14 YALE J. INT'L L. 335 (1989) (describing various sub-branches of international relations theory in international law). *See also* ROBERT KEOHANE, INTERNATIONAL INSTITUTIONS AND STATE POWER, 10–11 (1989) (explaining institutionalism as focusing on "international institutions, constructed by states, in facilitating mutually beneficial policy coordination among governments"); MICHAEL BYRES, CUSTOM, POWER AND THE POWER OF RULES 15 (1999) (explaining his project as "one way in which disciplines of international relations and international law might together explore and conceptualize the functional character of power within international society generally").

[188] ANDREW T. GUZMAN, HOW INTERNATIONAL LAW WORKS: A RATIONAL CHOICE THEORY 18 (2007) (describing his theory as institutionalist).

(and, occasionally, law and morals), but to clarify the legal side of things."[189] Bruno Simma, the German judge on the International Court of Justice since 2003; and Andreas L. Paulus, the chair of general international law at the University of Göttingen, reasserted a theory of international law as a body of rules determined by the criterial social fact of state consent:

> Law is regarded as a unified system of rules that, according to most variants, emanate from state will. This system of rules is an "objective" reality and needs to be distinguished from law "as it should be."[190]

Postmodern positivists are, however, divided on how sharply to draw the line between law as it is and law as it should be, and, relatedly, whether law can be created by criteria (whether factual or normative) other than state consent. Hard positivists insist on a strict separation of what law *is* from what law *ought* to be.[191] In the language of legal philosophy, this is what Brian Leiter has termed the Separation Thesis (what law is and what law ought to be are separate questions), and the Social Thesis (what counts as law is fundamentally a question of social fact).[192] Joseph Weiler and Paulus have coined the label "Pantheon *vue*," to describe Prosper Weil's hard positivism that is committed both to law as a social fact and to the criterial social fact being exclusively state consent.[193] For Weil, who is professor emeritus of the University of Paris II: Panthéon-Assas law school, international law is derived from state action alone in accord with the canonical secondary rules on the sources of international law contained in Article 38 of the ICJ statute,[194] and "the distinction between *lex lata* (formal law) and *lex feranda* (law as it ought to be) must be maintained with vigor."[195] Although he acknowledges that the tendency to recognize *jus cogens* as peremptory human rights norm "is certainly inspired by unimpeachable moral concerns," "it also carries, in both its criterion and its content, some germs of alarming portent for the future of the international normative system."[196]

189 Simma & Paulus, *supra* note 143, at 307.

190 *Id.* at 304.

191 *Id.* (stating that classical positivism "[d]emands rigorous tests for legal validity. Extralegal arguments, e.g., arguments that have no textual, systemic or historical basis, are deemed irrelevant to legal analysis; there is only hard law, no soft law.").

192 Brian Leiter, *Legal Realism, Hard Positivism, and the Limits of Conceptual Analysis*, *in* Hart's Postscript, *supra* note 85, at 356–57.

193 *Accord* Brigitte Stern, *Custom at the Heart of International Law*, 11 Duke J. Comp. & Int'l L. 89, 93–94 (2001) (refusing to "refer to an extra-legal element justifying the passage from fact into law in the customary phenomenon as an approach which is foreign to a veritable legal science" and concluding "law is nothing but a particular factual modality, a legal order that can define itself as a factual order considered as law, without anything needing to be added to this definition").

194 Statute of the International Court of Justice, art. 38, June, 26, 1945, 33 U.N.T.S. 993, 994 [hereinafter ICJ Statute]; Prosper Weil, *Towards Relative Normativity in International Law?*, 77 Am. J. Int'l L. 413, 420 (1983) ("Absent voluntarism, international law would no longer be performing its functions.").

195 Weil, *supra* note 194, at 421.

196 *Id.* at 424.

Other postmodern positivists are softer. They acknowledge that "soft law" may be a sort of law even though their criteria for validity is more open-textured both in terms of looking for facts other than state consent and admitting value criteria.[197] Simma and Paulus appear to accept the introduction of policy as long as it is prescribed as a relevant consideration by a law. They state that in circumstances where there does not appear to be only one correct legal answer, the positivist may derive a legal answer by injecting his "ethical standpoint," for instance, through the application of "general principles of law," or in so far as "global values . . . find sufficient expression in legal form."[198] German scholar Ulrich Fastenrath perhaps moves a step further away from hard positivism. He accepts that "soft law" is a new form of lawmaking that is open to "subjective auto-determination," because it enables international law to accommodate "conflicting interests and divergent goals, stemming from different cultures." By acknowledging that "soft law" can make a practical difference to decisionmaking but designating it as formally "extra-legal," it saves "legal positivism . . . from extinction in a pluralist world."[199]

International law theories after World War II have proliferated. Taken as a whole, the varying accounts of international law are now entirely postmodern in their diversity of viewpoints about the nature of international law and in their rejection of conceptual certainty. Although the universe of facts about international problems is the same for every scholar studying international law, scholars have built their respective theories of international law based on different selections and interpretations of relevant facts. Crits, such as Kennedy and Koskenniemi, have focused on the practice of legal technicians and concluded that international law results from their interactions and not from the formal actions of states in making legal rules. Realists, like Morgenthau and Posner, studied how states behave in their self-interest, and concluded that international relations are largely a function of power, not law. New Haven jurists have chosen to address the indeterminacy of rules and the self-interests of elites by approaching international law as a process of decisionmaking and providing guidance to decisionmakers about how to promote basic values. International legal process scholars see law as a combination of rules, process, and sanctions, with the precise combination depending on which international legal process scholar you ask. Positivists focus on formal sources of law and accordingly approach international law as a system of rules, although even among positivists there is no agreement as to whether rules must be pure social fact or whether values can be incorporated. This variation of theories should not cause despair that scholars are talking past each other. Scholars can have a meaningful discussion about

[197] Simma & Paulus, *supra* note 143, at 306; Ian Brownlie, Principles of Public International Law 4 (7th ed. 2008) (acknowledging that although unratified treaties and reports of the ILC are not formal sources of law, yet "they may stand for a threshold of consensus and confront states in a significant way").

[198] Simma & Paulus, *supra* note 143, at 316.

[199] Fastenrath, *supra* note 143, at 339.

international law by making explicit the choices that underlie each of their theories.

IV. CHOICES IN THEORIES

The theories surveyed above made foundational choices that shaped each respective theory. In addition to focusing on different facts in international problems, each theory interpreted those facts differently based on choices about the function of inquiry, the ideal type to observe, and the value of semantics. Whenever scholars make different choices, they will disagree about the conceptualization of objects under inquiry.

A thought experiment illustrates these points. Suppose that the conception of a table is the subject of philosophical inquiry. Philosopher A is interested in putting forth the best interpretation of a table to enable carpenters to build dining tables, whereas Philosopher B is interested in describing criteria for a table as it exists in its various forms. A's conception of a table may well specify that tables must be large enough to seat at least two persons and strong enough to bear the weight of china and silverware. B's conception of a table may specify that a table simply needs to be a piece of furniture in which a flat surface is elevated about four feet from the ground by one or more vertical legs. It is not possible for A and B to meaningfully disagree on their concepts of a table because their function of inquiries are different. They may certainly debate their preferred purposes of philosophizing, but this is not a conceptual debate.

Philosopher C enters into a debate with B. B's ideal type of a table is extrapolated from the salient characteristics common among tables in his home. C, however, comes from a different culture in which people sit cross-legged on the floor and designate as a table what we might ordinarily call a tray. C's conception of a table will be radically different than B's conception because their ideal types, or the representative data they conceptualize, are different. Again, to assert then that B and C disagree about the conception of a table is not meaningful because they are simply speaking about different things.

C leaves in a huff, and in comes D. D is a scientist with aesthetic pretensions. He has invented a stable platform that is suspended in the air by magnetic fields created by a machine installed beneath the floorboards. B, who is committed to the semantic usage of the word "table" insists that the conception of a table cannot be extrapolated from the floating platform because no one in the community would use the word "table" in that way. D, however, does not share the same commitment to semantic usage of words. In his view, what matters more is whether the platform serves the same function as a table. Because it is a stable flat surface parallel to the ground on which a person could eat, read, and write, the conception of a table must include his platform.

The point here about disagreements over commitments to semantics is different from Ronald Dworkin's semantic sting argument. Dworkin argued that philosophers must agree on roughly the same criteria for a conception denoted by a word before they can have a meaningful disagreement about that conception. So, according to

Dworkin, if you do not count his copy of Moby Dick as a book because in your view novels are not books, "any disagreement is bound to be senseless" because you and Dworkin are using the word "book" in completely different ways.[200] Joseph Raz disagreed with Dworkin. In Raz's view, in the ordinary course of human interaction, you would not insist that Moby Dick is not a book, and you would apologize for your mistake.[201] According to Raz, "[c]riterial explanations of concepts are consistent with the fact that people who use the rules setting out these criteria may make mistakes about which criteria are set by the rules."[202]

Although Raz is correct that people can make mistakes about semantic criteria without invalidating criterial explanations, he seems to miss Dworkin's point. If a person is committed to different semantic criteria, then it is impossible to engage in a meaningful disagreement with him about the conception denoted by the word being used. Take, for example, the word "consideration." A person committed to the semantics of its ordinary usage may say the conception of consideration entails deliberately thinking about an idea. A lawyer, who does not share those semantics, but is committed to the specialized semantics of his profession, asserts that the concept of consideration is a bargained-for exchange of something of legal value. The lay person and the lawyer may disagree about their concepts of consideration, but they are speaking past each other.

In any event, the author's point about the semantics does not stand or fall on whether Dworkin or Raz is correct, because the author's point is slightly different. The author's point is that for there to be meaningful conceptual disagreement, the disagreeing parties must share roughly the commitment to the semantics (as opposed to the semantic criteria for a concept, which was the topic of Raz and Dworkin's debate). Without this commitment, a philosopher may determine a conception by the functions ascribed to it by the community, rather than by its ordinary semantic meaning of the word representing the conception. This conception could be quite different from the conception shackled to the semantic usage of the word representing the conception. So, Philosopher D is not committed to semantics about how an object appears, but instead focuses on how an object functions, so he designates his platform as a table. B, who is committed to semantics, does not believe the word table and its associated conception include platforms. Yet D and B cannot have a meaningful conceptual disagreement. They could certainly have a meaningful disagreement about their respective views on the importance of semantics, but this would be anterior to conceptual debate.

This discussion of choices anterior to conceptualizing applies to the accounts of international law. Using New Haven jurisprudence and positivists as comparative examples, it appears that New Haven jurists and positivists cannot engage each

[200] *See* Ronald Dworkin, Law's Empire 45 (1986).

[201] *Id.;* Joseph Raz, *Two Views on the Nature of the Theory of Law, in* Hart's Postscript, *supra* note 85, at 17 (making the point with reference to a disagreement about tables and drawing-boards).

[202] *Id.* at 18.

other about the fundamental differences in their accounts of international law because they disagree about all three choices anterior to theorizing.[203]

Regarding the function of jurisprudence, the New Haven account of law seeks to guide decisionmakers about what to do to authoritatively secure maximum human dignity. Not surprisingly, the New Haven School takes as its starting point law as the process of decisionmaking. Some positivists believe the key functions of jurisprudence are describing law as distinct from policy, ethics, or morality, and providing the best explanatory or descriptive account of law.[204] They conclude that the best way to do this is to take as their starting point law as a body of rules.[205]

International law positivists—even very hard ones—have thicker normative goals than merely description. Weil views the purpose of international law as "governing international relations,"[206] and specifically "to regulate the relations between . . . co-existing independent communities or with a view to the achievement of common aims."[207] Depending on the content of "common aims," they can be as thick as the commitments of policy-oriented jurisprudence and liberal international relations theories to achieving a world order of common human dignity, somewhat thinner, like the commitments of international relations rational choice/institutionalist theory to common interest, or even as bare as commitments of realists to nothing more than overlapping self-interest. Choices about the purposes of theorizing do not therefore necessarily drive accounts of international law on their own.

Choices about the ideal type of law moves the analysis forward. Because the New Haven School is committed to offering practical guidance to decisionmakers, it selects as its ideal type the entire global decisionmaking process in which power and authority are diffused rather than concentrated in lawmakers; in which claims and norms may be, to varying degrees, authoritatively controlling, and in which formal legal rules may not tell the whole story about the actions and deliberations of decisionmakers.[208] In contrast, international law positivists designate as their ideal type the body of international legal rules concerning international relations that are legally validated by reference to limited sources specified through an international rule of recognition because they believe this ideal type best achieves their normative

[203] *See* Jules Coleman, *Incorporationism, Conventionality, and the Practical Difference Thesis*, *in* Hart's Postscript *supra* note 85, at 106 ("A theory of law is a contestable conception of law, reflecting, as it must, an account of law's function or purpose. Disputes between or among conflicting legal theories are ultimately normative disputes, resolvable by substantive moral and political argument.").

[204] In the extreme, methodological positivism "maintain[s] that legal theory is a purely descriptive, non-normative enterprise that sets out, in the manner of ordinary science, to tell us what one particular corner of the world we inhabit is like." Stephen R. Perry, *The Varieties of Legal Positivism*, 9 Can. J. L. & Juris. 361, 361 (1996).

[205] *See* Liam Murphy, *The Political Question of the Concept of Law*, *in* Hart's Postscript, *supra* note 85, at 373 (noting that Hart "takes for granted that law should be conceived in a positivist manner, and then proceeds to describe the complex structure of law, so understood").

[206] Weil, *supra* note 194, at 413.

[207] *Id.* at 419.

[208] *See* Reisman, *supra* note 149, at 274.

purposes of theorizing.[209] Weil believes that his goals of regulating state conduct to achieve common aims are best served by conceiving of law as a "self-contained, self-sufficient world" of state consent.[210] In contrast, soft positivist Fastenrath believes that because the world is pluralistic, divergent goals stemming from different cultures need accommodating with international law, necessitating the idea of "soft law" alongside purely statist hard norms.[211] With different respective ideal types, accounts of international law can hardly engage each other in a meaningful way.

As regards the value of semantics, it follows from the New Haven School's commitment to offering functional guidance that it draws into its scope of inquiry factors that affect international conduct, even if those factors would not in ordinary usage be termed as law. Reisman has explained:

> Arrangements and processes which may not have been assigned the sobriquet, "international law," by the people who fashioned them; yet from the perspective of a disengaged observer, it will be apparent that these processes and arrangements functioned as the struts of world or regional order in specific contexts.[212]

This rejection of descriptive semantics in favor of functional criteria is an anathema to positivists, who choose to describe only those phenomena that ordinarily would fall within the normal usage of the word "law."[213]

These disagreements about the purpose of jurisprudence, the ideal type of international law, and the relevance of semantics cannot be properly addressed at the conceptual level. The resultant differences between the New Haven School and positivists respective accounts of law are accordingly not really conceptual disagreements. They are, more fundamentally, disagreements about underlying choices that drive their respective theories.[214] A similar analysis applies to all the other accounts of international law: realism, crits, international legal process, and international relations theory.

[209] *See* Alexander Orakhelashvili, The Interpretation of Acts and Rules in Public International Law 53 (2008) ("Positivism and consensualism are necessary in international law owing to the need for coherency and predictability in the legal system, the legitimacy of which rests on the expression of the will of States which know of no sovereign government over and above them."). *See also* Charles De Visscher, Theory and Reality in Public International Law 67 (P.E. Corbett trans., 1968) (describing "contemporary tendency to limit arbitrarily, on pretext of science or unity of method, the subject matter of law, narrowing or distorting legal reality").

[210] Weil, *supra* note 194, at 413 (stating that the functions of international law lie in "governing international relations").

[211] Fastenrath, *supra* note 143, at 339.

[212] W. Michael Reisman, *Preface to* Douglas M. Johnston, The Historical Foundations of World Order vii (2008). *See also generally* W. Michael Reisman, Law in Brief Encounters (1999).

[213] Nicos Stavropoulos, *Hart's Semantics*, *in* Hart's Postscript, *supra* note 85, at 70 ("It seems natural to suppose that conceptual analysis aims at articulating the existing, *common* understanding of the terms whose extension constitutes the field of inquiry.").

[214] *See* Leiter, *supra* note 192, at 367 (noting the view that "[c]onceptual analysis, by itself, gives us no reason to prefer one concept to the other; only a further, normative argument can do that. . . .").

This does not mean, however, that there cannot be any meaningful discussion or examination of competing accounts of international law. It simply means that it is necessary to discuss the choices regarding semantics, the function of inquiry, and ideal types.

V. REASONS FOR CHOICES

Because choices that must be made to develop an account of international law are anterior to conceptualizing, a scholar's reasons and motivations for his choices are relevant. Reasons and motivations are complex, and it is often futile to try to prove that there was one reason in particular for a choice. However, understanding the choices necessary for theorizing in the context of the personal, professional, and geopolitical contexts of the theorist can deepen one's understanding of those choices and the international legal theory that results from them.

Theorizing international law often implicates political and normative values, which inform the choices discussed in Part IV that must be made to develop an account of international law. Normative commitments are choices about which values are important. Political commitments, in the sense that the word "politics" is used in this book, are choices about how national or international communities should be organized and how authority should be allocated among them.[215]

Many accounts of international law emerged from the social and intellectual experiences of the jurist developing the theory and the broader political context in which he or she lived. Gentili's efforts to separate law from religion, or at least to derive it from reasoning from values, were consonant with his politics seeking independence from the Catholic Church. He was a Protestant, and for some years practiced law as a judge in Northern Italy in the mid-sixteenth century. By 1579, he had to flee from the Inquisition, and lectured at Oxford University from 1580.[216] In this context, it is unsurprising that Gentili favored the development of international law free from religion. By comparison, Vattel's pragmatic accommodation of natural law and state consent was a political and normative choice that validated and supported the diplomatic practices in which he was steeped.[217]

In the postmodern era, Kelsen insisted on a Pure Theory of Law that, at least in its early iterations, appeared to elevate international law over national law within a unified theory of law. It can be better understood in light of the horrific national laws imposed by Hitler's Reich and Kelsen's left-leaning politics.[218] Koskenniemi also observed that Kelsen and his followers were mostly liberals opposed to the rise of the

[215] *Cf.*, Murphy, *supra* note 205, at 409 (noting that underlying Dworkin's and Hart's accounts of law "is a fundamental disagreement about the politically most desirable way to conceive of law's domain").

[216] JOHNSTON, *supra* note 8, at 385.

[217] *Id.* at 418 (Vattel was a diplomat).

[218] *See generally* HANS KELSEN, THE COMMUNIST THEORY OF LAW (1999) [hereinafter KELSEN, COMMUNIST THEORY]. *See also* KOSKENNIEMI, GENTLE CIVILIZER, *supra* note 71, at 244–45 (discussing Kelsen's left-leaning politics).

German extreme right and forced to leave Germany because of their race or left-leaning politics. Kelsen himself was fired from his Professorship at the University of Cologne in 1933, and after a sojourn in Geneva, traveled to Harvard at Roscoe Pound's invitation, eventually ending up at the University of California at Berkeley.[219] If a scholar wished to remove the power to make law from state governments that opposed his politics, the Pure Theory of Law that elevated international law over national law would certainly support that agenda.

Eventually, Kelsen revised his view. In his last edition of the PURE THEORY OF LAW in 1989,[220] he explicitly conceded that his Pure Theory was equally consistent with international law being superior to domestic law, or vice versa.[221] By that time, the Nuremburg trials had ended, Germany was split in two, and there was no threat of a repeat of the Jewish Holocaust. That might explain his intellectual ambivalence, in the end, about whether his Pure Theory of Law held up international law as the superior to domestic law.

Morgenthau's choice to view law's effectiveness as a function of national self-interest, which led him to develop a realist account of international law, was forged from World War II, and could have reflected his belief that the United States needed maximum discretion in foreign policy to prevail in the Cold War, the urgent issue of the day. Johnston also suggests that it was the failure of the League of Nations that hardened Morgenthau's skepticism about consensual international law.[222]

McDougal's normative choices to view law as functional rather than formalist, value-driven rather than based solely on consent, led him to develop policy-oriented jurisprudence. McDougal's normative choices that resulted in his jurisprudence can be better understood in the context of the Cold War and deep anxiety about competing world accounts of the United States and the Soviet Union.[223] The Yale of McDougal's era was a bastion of American Legal Realism, and the United States of his time would soon be consumed in the Cold War. Given the frustration that realists faced with the indeterminacy of rules, it was reasonable to search for determinacy in law from sources outside of rules. The turn to policy and values was a natural decision. In light of the contending world orders during the Cold War—that of Soviet totalitarianism and American democracy—it was understandable that McDougal made a normative and perhaps even a political choice for the latter.[224]

[219] KOSKENNIEMI, GENTLE CIVILIZER, *supra* note 71, at 249.

[220] KELSEN, PURE THEORY, *supra* note 100.

[221] *Id.* at 333–44 (arguing for a monist or unified theory of law, regardless of whether the national legal order was superior to the international legal order, or vice versa).

[222] JOHNSTON, *supra* note 8, at 706. *See also* KOSKENNIEMI, GENTLE CIVILIZER, *supra* note 71, at 446 (discussing Morgenthau's unpublished work, *The Significance of Being Alone*, in which Morgenthau describes three elements that shaped him: his authoritarian father, anti-semitism in school, and an "almost neurotic desire to get the highest marks at every subject…").

[223] *See* KOSKENNIEMI, GENTLE CIVILIZER, *supra* note 71, at 482 (describing McDougal's jurisprudence as an "anti-communist crusade").

[224] Falk et al., *supra* note 136, at 979 (stating that McDougal "made the conflict between democracy and totalitarianism—'contending systems of world public order'—a foundation of his work").

Henkin, Schachter, and Franck's choice to turn back to rules and buttress them with process were not solely intellectual decisions. They were political claims to restrain what they perceived to be overreaching U.S. interests propelled by the New Haven School. They also made a normative choice favoring libertarian and cosmopolitan ideals that embraced diversity of values worldwide and therefore rejected a policy orientation that they believed could too easily be abused to impose values on distant lands and different cultures. Higgins, a life-long friend of Schachter's, notes that "Oscar emphasized his distaste for any enforced uniformity. . . . Diverse cultures are to be encouraged."[225] Schachter was also formerly the head of the UN's legal unit. With his personal values and professional experiences, it is easy to see why Schachter initially participated in developing the New Haven account of law as process, but turned back to rules when he believed that McDougal deployed policy-oriented jurisprudence in support of a uniform, and, in Schachter's opinion, American worldview.

Weil's seminal English language essay on hard positivism in international law was published in 1983[226] at the height of the Cold War. U.S. President Reagan began the Strategic Defense Initiative (SDI), or "Star Wars," in order to protect the United States from nuclear attack. *Perestroika* and *glasnost* had not yet arisen. Weil made a normative choice to adhere to law as social fact. The reason for his adherence was political. In his view, it was the only way to achieve coordination "between equal, but disparate, entities."[227]

With the end of the Cold War, liberal democratic ideals of the United States triumphed over communist totalitarianism. Eastern bloc countries everywhere gained independence and embraced democracy. This political context is reflected in the confidence of soft positivist Fastenrath's assertion in 1993 that there was "an emerging global society," and accordingly, *jus cogens* (peremptory norms) ought to be recognized as a cognate concept through which "worldwide perceptions of justice may be expressed."[228] Even though realistically "such perceptions have to date been crude and inconsistent," he expressed optimism that "this merely points to the fact that we are but at the beginning of a process which has hitherto led us from the law of coexistence to the law of cooperation; the path to a true constitution of the global society remains open and untrodden before us."[229]

Slaughter began writing her book A New World Order in 1993. Germany had reunited three years earlier.[230] The Soviet Union had dissolved away.[231] President William J. Clinton, a Democrat, was elected to his first term in the White House. Her liberal optimism projected a political account of a world community discovering

[225] 2 Higgins, Themes and Theories, *supra* note 139, at 995.

[226] *See* Weil, *supra* note 194.

[227] *Id.* at 421. *See also id.* at 420 ("[I]deological neutrality is also necessary to guarantee the coexistence of heterogeneous entities in a pluralistic society.").

[228] Fastenrath, *supra* note 143, at 340.

[229] *Id.*

[230] *See* Treaty on the Establishment of German Unity 1990, 30 I.L.M. 463 (1991).

[231] Tai-Heng Cheng, State Succession and Commercial Obligations 344 (2006).

and embedding shared liberal ideals through networks of officials interacting with each other across borders.[232] By the time the book was published in 2004, genocide had occurred in the Balkans,[233] and NATO troops were still deployed there. The United States had been attacked in New York and Washington D.C. by Islamist terrorists. The Bush administration was mired in two armed conflicts in Afghanistan and Iraq. However, when the book was conceived, the world was washed in the glow of liberal optimism.

Koh articulated his powerful account of transnational legal process in 1995. Its optimism for the ability of domestic processes to internalize norms was in accord with the renewed vigor of the human rights movement in a post-Cold War world.[234] His account was also a politically urgent project because the United States had emerged as a hegemon that could and would ignore international law if it wished to, unless its internal norms matched the values that international law promoted. Koh's emphasis on domestic legal processes to inculcate in governing elites a habit of obedience to international norms may also be a result of his professional experiences in the State Department and the White House.[235]

The end of the Cold War and hope of a new world order also created the right conditions for a scholastic détente. In 1998, Jonathan Charney and W. Michael Reisman, the editors in chief of the *American Journal of International Law*, decided to bring together thought leaders of various accounts of international law in a symposium to engage and understand each other's perspectives better. This resulted in an impressive volume of nine essays in the journal a year later.[236] The editors of

[232] David Kennedy, *The Last Treatise: Project and Person (Reflections onMartti Koskenniemi's From Apology to Utopia)*, 7 German L. J. 982, 990 (2006) ("After the end of the Cold War, the promises of a broadly liberal cosmopolitan order again felt shiny and new.").

[233] *Harold Hongju Koh Biography*, U.S. Dep't of State, http://www.state.gov/r/pa/ei/biog/143262.htm (last visited Aug. 7, 2011).

[234] *See also*, Brandt Goldstein, Storming the Court 30–32 (2005) (describing how Koh was influenced by his father's experiences of campaigning for democracy in Korea and subsequently fleeing to the United States after a military coup); Interview by Harry Kreisler with Harold Hongju Koh, *supra* note 183 (Q: "Looking back, how did your parents shaped your thinking about the world? A: "Totally. My father came at the time when Korea was controlled by the Syngman Rhee dictatorship. When it was overthrown, he went back to campaign for the first democratic government of Korea. When that government was elected, he was appointed ambassador to the United Nations, and then minister to the United States. Then his government, the new democratic government, was overthrown by military coup, and my father refused to serve the dictatorship and spent the rest of his life in America. That's how I grew up here.")

[235] Harold Hongju Koh, Legal Adviser, U.S. Dep't of State, Remarks at the American Society of International Law Annual Meeting: *The Obama Administration and International Law* (Mar. 25, 2010), *available at* http://www.state.gov/s/l/releases/remarks/139119.htm (revealing the influence of his professional experiences on his scholarly views in the following terms: "I had never really thought about the question: 'can you attach a panda?' Or the question, can Mu'ammar al-Qadhafi erect a tent in Englewood, New Jersey, notwithstanding a contrary local ordinance? To be honest, I had never really thought about those questions. But rest assured, in the future, many Yale law students will.").

[236] *Symposium on Method in International Law: Appraising the Methods of International Law: A Prospectus for Readers*, 93 Am. J. Int'l L. 291–570 (1999). *See also generally* The Methods of

that volume, Anne-Marie Slaughter and Steven Ratner, concluded that the symposium

> demonstrated not only the relative merits of [the respective] methods, but also the value of having a wide range of methods to bear on issues that stir the conscience and move us to professional and personal action.[237]

It became apparent that disagreements about accounts of international law were not just conceptual disagreements, but also disagreements about methods that were not necessarily mutually exclusive.[238]

The truce proved propitious. Cosmopolitan international legal scholars had to go on the defensive with leading conservatives in the administration of U.S. President George W. Bush skeptical about international law, so it was just as well that those scholars closed ranks. Regrettably, geopolitical events ended the truce.

Following a growing public awareness that Islamist terrorism posed grave threats to national security, conservative-governing elites in the United States who had always favored American hegemony over liberal ideals gained the political support they needed to push their agenda. Posner and Goldsmith's conservative politics were in accord with their realist manifesto THE LIMITS OF INTERNATIONAL LAW. Eric Posner was born in 1965, the son of Richard Posner, whom Republican President Ronald Reagan appointed to the Court of Appeals for the Seventh Circuit. Jack Goldsmith was born in 1962 in Memphis, Tennessee. At Yale Law School, Goldsmith developed "an allergic reaction to Yale's political correctness and left-wing jurisprudence."[239] After Goldsmith had clerked for a conservative federal judge, Harvie Wilkinson, Justice Anthony Kennedy of the U.S. Supreme Court selected Goldsmith to clerk for him. He was a professor at the University of Virginia Law School when U.S. President George W. Bush appointed him to head the Office of Legal Counsel in the Department of Justice. By his own description, he became "the chief advisor to the President and the Attorney General about the legality of presidential actions."[240] He saw firsthand the difficulties that the U.S. administration faced daily in keeping the United States safe from attack, and faced personal pressures to interpret away perceived limits on presidential powers imposed by international and constitutional law. Viewed in this context, THE LIMITS OF INTERNATIONAL LAW was not a purely conceptual monograph free from political values.

INTERNATIONAL LAW, *supra* note 116 (republishing essays and adding a further essay on Third World Approaches to International Law).

[237] THE METHODS OF INTERNATIONAL LAW, *supra* note 116, at 263–64.

[238] Steinberg & Zasloff, *supra* note 131, at 86 ("Increasingly, the great metatheories either operate in the background, or lend themselves to a conscious engagement across isms, with a focus on midlevel analysis of international legal and political developments using hybrid theories."). *See also generally* INTERNATIONAL RULES: APPROACHES FROM INTERNATIONAL LAW AND INTERNATIONAL RELATIONS (R. Beck et al eds., 1996) (comparing different accounts of international law).

[239] JACK L. GOLDSMITH, THE TERROR PRESIDENCY 20 (2007).

[240] *Id.* at 9.

Like Morgenthau, Posner and Goldsmith's legal theory reflected their preference for U.S. interests and the concern about international law potentially constraining U.S. foreign policy.[241]

O'Connell's thesis in her monograph THE POWER AND PURPOSE OF INTERNATIONAL LAW that international law is law because it has sanctions that support compliance is not apolitical either. She devotes 30 pages, or 10 percent of her text, to a rebuttal of Posner and Goldsmith.[242] Her account of international law is not only intellectual. It is a political account motivated by a belief in "higher things" that seeks to order the world according to natural law values discovered through rational inquiry and expressed through international law *qua* law.[243] This is a political account of international law as an effective and appropriate way to order international society, and she goes to great lengths to support this account. Guzman's book HOW INTERNATIONAL LAW WORKS is similarly at least in part a political and intellectual response to THE LIMITS OF INTERNATIONAL LAW. It is an attempt to wrestle rational-choice theory and utilitarian method away from U.S. sovereigntists and deploy them in support of liberal and cosmopolitan ideals.

Across the Atlantic, theories of international law reflected European perceptions of U.S. power run amuck and international relations gone awry. Western European states were the dominant powers in the nineteenth and first half of the twentieth century. After World War II and decolonization, their geopolitical influence faded. Concurrently, the United States rose in status and power. Its economy outpaced Europe, its military was unmatched except perhaps by the Soviet Union, and its diplomatic influence accordingly expanded. With the dissolution of the Soviet Union at the end of the Cold War, the United States was the sole remaining hegemon, and Western Europe was a shadow of its glorious past. It is in this geopolitical context that, in 2002, Koskenniemi derided American accounts of international law as "Empire's Law,"[244] and the functional jurisprudence developed in the United States as "pax Americana."[245]

European feelings were hurt when U.S. Secretary of Defense Donald Rumsfeld dismissed Western Europe as "old Europe," in January 2003.[246] The unpopular

[241] Some realist neoconservatives were more explicit. *See* Bolton, *supra* note 2, at 10 ("We should be unashamed, unapologetic, uncompromising American constitutional hegemonists. International law is not superior to, and does not trump, the Constitution. The rest of the world may not like that approach, but abandoning it is the first step to abandoning the United States of America.").

[242] O'CONNELL, *supra* note 77, at 105–31.

[243] *Id.* at 370.

[244] KOSKENNIEMI, GENTLE CIVILIZER, *supra* note 71, at 480. The inversion of the title of American legal philosopher Ronald Dworkin's signal opus, LAW'S EMPIRE, is also obvious, and it is difficult not to infer an implied and mischievous criticism of that work. In LAW'S EMPIRE, Dworkin rejected European positivism in favor of a justificatory theory of law that sought to interpret legal prescriptions in their best light. *See generally* DWORKIN, *supra* note 200. *See also* Ronald Dworkin, *Response*, *in* EXPLORING LAW'S EMPIRE 305–06 (2006) (rejecting Simon Gardner's claim that LAW'S EMPIRE reveals Dworkin to be a legal positivist).

[245] KOSKENNIEMI, GENTLE CIVILIZER, *supra* note 71, at 482.

[246] *Outrage at "Old Europe" Remarks*, BBC NEWS WORLD EDITION (Jan. 23, 2003), http://news.bbc.co.uk/2/hi/europe/2687403.stm.

U.S.-led invasion of Iraq later that year, against the wishes of France and constituents all across France, Germany, and the United Kingdom, was the last straw that broke the scholastic accord that Charney, Reisman, Slaughter, and Ratner had achieved in 1998. European international law scholars unsheathed their positivistic knives.

In a book published in 2008, positivist Alexander Orakhelashvili criticized, apparently on conceptual grounds, New Haven jurisprudence and the international relations approach to international law. He argued that these accounts of international law simply "cannot be accommodated within the discipline of international law," because "international law is not what 'lawyers, political scientists and policymakers use to describe the world they study and *seek to manipulate*,' but what States agree about."[247] Orakhelashvili made a normative choice to designate the ideal type of international law as having an "independent existence and profile" from politics.[248] He was driven to positivism because he believed that such a conceptualization of international law was "inevitable" based on his choice to sharply distinguish delineate law from politics.[249] For him, positivism was the best method of "ensuring the determinacy of the relevant provision by enabling its application to facts,"[250] as opposed to "an approach that justifies indeterminacy being used for political interests."[251]

Orakhelashvili revealed the politics behind his normative commitments 550 pages later. He favored textual interpretations of international legal prescriptions over policy-driven interpretations because, at least in part, he objected to the U.S. administration's "reference to the 'war on terror,'" in order to "assert some approaches regarding change and modification of the relevant international legal regulation, without adducing evidence that such change is feasible or material."[252] His emphasis on determinacy in law appears to be driven by a desire to curb U.S. attempts to change law, which he regarded as infeasible.

Vaughan Lowe, Chichele Professor of Public International Law at Oxford University and one of the keepers of the positivist flame,[253] was more direct. He appraised the invasion on explicitly political and normative grounds:

> It is simply unacceptable that a step as serious and important as a massive military attack upon a State should be launched on the basis of a legal argument dependent

[247] Orakhelashvili, *supra* note 209, at 29–30 (2008) (criticizing both New Haven jurisprudence and the international relations theory of Anne-Marie Slaughter) (emphasis in original).

[248] *Id.* at 583.

[249] *Id.*

[250] *Id.* at 584.

[251] *Id.* at 583.

[252] *Id.* at 583.

[253] Vaughan Lowe, *Preface* to Matthew Craven, The Decolonization of International Law (2007) (stating that the "theoretical foundations" of international law are "in the consent of States").

> upon dubious inferences drawn from the silences in [Security Council] Resolution 1441. . . .[254]

European criticisms of U.S. accounts of international law were at their core political and normative judgments about the U.S. foreign policy of launching a "massive military attack" on Iraq.

Orakhelashvili's criticism of the New Haven approach missed its mark. Rather than directly arguing, like Lowe, that the invasion of Iraq as a normatively bad decision and objecting to the United States apparently riding roughshod over the Security Council, Orakhelashvili rehashed 1970s and 1980s criticisms of the policy-orientated approach as being a fig leaf for U.S. foreign policies,[255] and resurrected arguments favoring positivism as a method of controlling powerful states. The fact of the matter was that scholars applying policy-oriented jurisprudence criticized the U.S. invasion. Following the U.S. invasion of Iraq in 2003, Reisman used the Manley O. Hudson lecture to deliver the following critique of regime change:

> [L]et the strongest and best-intentioned government contemplating or being pressed to undertake regime change remember that not everything noble is lawful; not everything noble and lawful is feasible; and not everything noble, lawful, and feasible is wise.[256]

In contrast, the UK government defended its support for, and participation in, the invasion on purely formalist grounds. On March 17, 2003, UK Attorney General Lord Peter Goldsmith advised his parliament:

> Resolution 1441 would in terms have provided that a further decision of the Security Council to sanction force was required if that had been intended. Thus, all that Resolution 1441 requires is reporting to and discussion by the Security Council of Iraq's failures, but not an express further decision to authorize force.[257]

If the invasion of Iraq was objectionable, and its legalist justifications were unpersuasive, criticism should have been directed at the use or misuse of formalism, rather than policy-oriented jurisprudence.

The fact that criticism was instead directed at policy-oriented jurisprudence indicates that the apparent disagreements today about policy-oriented theories of international law are not conceptual. Rather, they appear to reflect preferences for some normative and political values over others, and possibly also for alternate distributions

254 Vaughan Lowe, *The Iraq Crisis: What Now?*, 52 INT'L & COMP. L.Q. 859, 866 (2003).

255 Schachter, *supra* note 145, at 267.

256 W. Michael Reisman, *The Manley O. Hudson Lecture: Why Regime Change Is (Almost Always) A Bad Idea*, 98 AM. J. INT'L L. 516, 525 (2004).

257 Lord Goldsmith, Legal Basis for Use of Force Against Iraq (Mar. 17, 2003) (responding to parliamentary questions), *available at* http://www.number10.gov.uk/Page3287. U.S. legal advisors deployed similarly positivist arguments supporting the invasion. *See infra* ch. 8, pt. II.C.

of power among states. These preferences do not map cleanly onto conceptual debates about theories of international law.

VI. CONCLUSION

This chapter has shown that in order to develop international legal theories, scholars often observe international activities and select and interpret facts that they regard as relevant evidence of international law. They also compare international law to other systems of regulation that they identify as quintessentially legal. All of these intellectual decisions involve choices that are not conceptual in nature. They are political or normative choices. Thus, scholars and decisionmakers conceive of international law according to their political and normative values, their personal and professional experiences, and in light of the geopolitical contexts in which they make decisions.[258]

Consequently, whatever else international legal theories might be, they are also normative and political accounts of what values ought to be promoted and what decisionmakers should be free to pursue, encouraged to do, and stopped from doing. Decisionmakers and some scholars tend to view international law in ways that promote their political preferences.

The fact that international law is political and normative does not automatically nullify its legitimacy. It simply makes it necessary to explicate what values are embedded in each account of international law, so that decisionmakers and their constituents may appraise these values and examine whether a decisionmaker adopting a particular view of international law appropriately promotes relevant values.

Some realists in strong states favor liberating state elites to do whatever they want in the pursuit of national interests and conceive of international law as political arrangements without any incentive to compliance except self-interest.[259]

Some idealists and pragmatists from weaker states favor equalizing the power of strong states by bolstering the legitimacy and effectiveness of international law.[260]

[258] *Cf.* KOSKENNIEMI, FROM APOLOGY TO UTOPIA, *supra* note 111, at 615–16 ("To commit oneself to international law is to allow its grammar to enter as one's second nature but still maintain the position of choice—at a minimum a choice to work with colleagues with certain preferences in institutions with a certain bias. Those may be the right preferences, of course, but they are not produced or even strongly supported by legal argument—that is, any more strongly than opposite preferences. Legal work will require choice."); HANS KELSEN, PRINCIPLES OF INTERNATIONAL LAW 447 (3rd prtg. 1959) ("It may be that our choice [of how to conceive international law], though not determined by the science of law, is guided by ethical or political preferences.").

[259] *See* KELSEN, *supra* note 258, at 447 ("A person whose political attitude is that of nationalism and imperialism may be inclined to accept as a hypothesis the basic norm of his own national legal order; in other terms, he may proceed on the primacy of national law.").

[260] *See* Koskenniemi, *supra* note 71, at 5 ("The fight for an international Rule of Law is a fight against politics, understood as a matter of furthering subjective desires and leading into an international anarchy."); SHUNMUGAM JAYAKUMAR, DIPLOMACY: A SINGAPORE EXPERIENCE 76 (2011) ("Strategically, small states can ill-afford to have the international arena degenerate into the law of

Positivism in international law supports this political ideal by emphasizing legal rules based on state consent, in the hope of achieving determinacy.[261] International legal process and international relations theories tend also to find favor among liberal idealists because they focus on strategies to secure obedience to prescriptions and fidelity to cosmopolitan ideals. Cosmopolitans would tend to favor these accounts of international laws, but sovereigntists may not.[262]

For international law to be effective and legitimate in an international dispute, decisionmakers must mediate between realism and idealism when confronted with international problems. They should idealistically promote world order and basic human values while embracing diverse cultural values and choices. Decisionmakers should also realistically recognize the limits of international law in a world still dominated by power and interests. Such realistic idealism is needed now, as it was in the past. The optimism following the end of the Cold War has waned. There are many urgent problems. Some that stand out are internecine wars and Islamist terrorism, on the one hand, and disruptions to global financial markets and the world economy, on the other hand. All these problems require a greater international cooperation and shared values to address them. Their persistence suggests cooperation and shared values will not be easily obtained. The project of international law, now 5000 years old from the first evidence of international relationships, needs to adjust to contemporary realities. It must be directed toward ideals, but its methods will have to be tempered by a sense of realism that a world community will not soon come into being. This is the geopolitical context in which this book develops its justificatory theory of international law.

the jungle. . . . [Singapore's] survival . . . is dependent on advancing the rule of law and establishing codes of conduct and civilised norms of behaviour among nations, large and small.").

261 Conversely, positivists criticize "an approach [to international law] that justifies indeterminacy being used for political interests." ORAKHELASHVILI, *supra* note 209, at 583.

262 *See* KELSEN, *supra* note 258, at 447 ("A person whose sympathy is for internationalism and pacifism may be inclined to accept as a hypothesis the basic norm of international law and thus proceed from the primacy of international law.").

3 Legalism and Morality

I. FRAMING THE INQUIRY

Chapter Two explored how theories of international law explicitly or implicitly make political choices about how the world should be ordered and whether decisionmakers should be constrained by an international regulatory system.[1] Rather than attempt to construct a purely conceptual theory of international law, this chapter develops a justificatory theory of international law, which was outlined in Chapter One.[2]

This book's theory is designed to be politically moderate and normatively balanced. Whether or not a reader agrees that it is indeed moderate and balanced may depend on his or her political and normative values. However, it is hoped that most readers will see that this account gives decisionmakers an analytic framework to be evenhanded, even if the reader does not always agree with the substantive conclusions that this author draws in his case studies.

The account of the international legal system is directed toward the ideal of promoting human dignity by balancing minimum world order with optimum world order. Writing from the policy-oriented perspective, Steven Ratner defines minimum order as "minimal coercion . . . with a set of authoritative procedures for the

[1] *Cf.* Liam Murphy, *The Political Question of the Concept of Law*, *in* HART'S POSTSCRIPT 371, 409 (Coleman ed., 2001) (noting that accounts of law are about "the politically most desirable way to conceive of law's domain").

[2] *Supra* ch. 1, pts. I & III.

deployment of force in situations when it is necessary," so that "human beings can best advance their individual and collective goals[.]"[3] Optimum world order refers to the global conditions necessary for maximizing the worldwide production and distribution of basic values important to everyone, such as wealth and well-being.[4]

The idealism in this book's account of the international legal system is not naïve. It is bounded by the necessity of achieving some modicum of effectiveness; otherwise, the international legal system cannot secure the values it seeks to promote. In the international legal system, there is no centralized world authority to force compliance with international laws. Therefore, decisionmakers should be concerned about the effectiveness of any prescriptive claim they make on other decisionmakers. In some international problems, pragmatic accommodations of ideals and interests are necessary to secure minimum effectiveness, especially where shared expectations of appropriate conduct are a product of a collective decisionmaking process among elites.[5]

Further, the idealistic aspiration of balancing minimum world order with optimum world order to promote human dignity is bounded by an appreciation of moral ambiguities in many real-world problems. Prescriptions of baselines of appropriate conduct for minimum world order appear more self-evidently justified than prescriptions aimed at optimum world order. The framework for minimum world order includes prescriptions outlawing heinous conduct that irreparably harms the most basic value of life, such as the prohibitions of torture, genocide, and baseless aggression against other countries; and corresponding prescriptions authorizing appropriate measures to restrain heinous conduct. Protecting minimum world order also includes prescriptions that prohibit conduct that destroys the foundations of peaceful international relations, such as state sovereignty. These prescriptions include prohibiting military attacks except where necessary to defend communities against unlawful aggression. Finally, minimum world order requires decisionmakers to agree on the struts for international cooperation and competition, such as prescriptions for making agreements and coordinating market activities.

Prescriptions aiming at optimal world order are more contested. Although everyone believes in human dignity and basic freedoms, these values are capacious in the abstract.[6] In many international problems, the basic value of freedom of decisionmaking and communities' abilities to make decisions for themselves and to

[3] *See* Steven Ratner, *Between Minimum and Maximum World Public Order, An Ethical Path for the Future, in* Looking to the Future: Essays in Honor of W. Michael Reisman 195, 196 (Arsanjani et al. eds., 2011).

[4] *Id.* at 197.

[5] *Cf.* W. Michael Reisman, *On the Causes of Uncertainty and Volatility in International Law, in* The Shifting Allocation of Authority in International Law: Considering Sovereignty, Supremacy and Subsidiarity 33, 48 (Broudy & Shany eds., 2008) ("Normative arrangements require power to support and implement them.").

[6] *See* Ratner, *supra* note 3, at 203 ("[E]ach [philosophical approach to justice] can create sharply contrasting visions of the balance between minimum order and optimum public order.").

compete—the freedom to win as well as to lose—hangs in the balance with other values. Different individuals and communities around the world, who each view the world from their respective standpoints, often reasonably disagree on the content of all these values and their prioritizations.[7] They also disagree on how best to secure them in actual international problems and the ideal balance between minimum world order and optimum world order. Therefore, a moderate justificatory account of the international legal system may not always limit the freedom of decisionmakers to choose among differing interpretations of prescriptions—and to make other decisions—where there are several reasonable normative outcomes, and the optimal outcome is contested.

Finally, different decisionmakers in international problems have specific institutional responsibilities. Therefore, even where there is a reasonable set of optimal outcomes, it is necessary to consider who ought to authoritatively prescribe those outcomes. In many international problems, significant decisionmaking authority is allocated to government and other officials, and the role of legal advisors and judges is not to make executive decisions but to restrain executive discretion within legalist limits. This idea is taken up in detail in subsequent chapters.

This chapter will proceed in the following fashion. Part II states and discusses the choices that underlie the account of the international legal system in this book. Part III proposes that in the central case of the international legal system, decisionmakers make, interpret, and apply prescriptions according to procedures commonly accepted by other relevant decisionmakers. Oftentimes, formal procedures are the most widely accepted modes of making and applying formal laws. But that is not always the case. In some instances, elites expect each other to follow informal procedures and informal prescriptions in a legalistic, if not legal, fashion. The central case of international law is thus one grounded in social facts about strong shared expectations of appropriate conduct expressed as prescriptions—whether in the form of laws or not—and accompanied by common legalist methods of interpreting, applying, and adjusting prescriptions that decisionmakers generally accept.

Part IV explores the idea that there is a moral obligation to promote this legalist central case, because it maintains the minimum global order that supports the common good necessary for every person worldwide to reasonably pursue his preferred values. This moral obligation, however, should not exhaust a decisionmaker's moral calculus when deciding what to do in an international problem.

Where legalism permits various outcomes, decisionmakers ought to exercise their judgment in selecting an interpretation of prescriptions within the bounds of legalism that achieves the outcome that best balances the interests of their constituencies with basic goods for other communities.

[7] *Cf. id.* at 201–03 ("[C]ommunitarians do not give short shrift to human dignity, instead they see that dignity as defined by the community itself. For them, justice is about allowing a significant degree of toleration of diversity in order to allow communities to flourish and individuals to realize their goals in them.") (citing Michael Walzer and John Rawls).

Where the legalism would lead to an outcome that unacceptably damages basic goods, decisionmakers should change the legal prescription. They should explain the reasons for changing the prescription so that other decisionmakers can assess and respond to the proposal. What decisionmakers ought not to do is to claim an unregulated exception for their conduct, because that encourages other decisionmakers to do so the same, destabilizing minimum world order.

Where decisionmakers have not fully worked out the normative implications of an outcome that would result from a highly legalist process, or where there is no practical possibility of achieving that outcome because it would undermine the vital interests of powerful decisionmakers, they may reasonably opt for informal prescriptions with vague content or with only very modest expectations of compliance. This alternative approach enables decisionmakers to test and adjust tentative prescriptions before finally settling, when the time is right, for a stronger prescription that effectively consolidates shared expectations of appropriate conduct to promote a normatively desirable outcome.

Finally, because prescriptions that lack a minimum degree of effectiveness cannot achieve the moral goals to which they are directed, decisionmakers must consider whether their proposed interpretation of a prescription will gain the support of other decisionmakers. In some instances, the vital interests of powerful actors must be accommodated in order for a prescription to become effective. It is necessary to consider, therefore, how far to go with pragmatic accommodations before prescriptions become entirely arbitrary and lose their law-like character entirely.

II. CHOICES

Choices underlying this account of international law should be stated at the outset so that the reader can assess them and decide whether he agrees with them and the account of international law that they support.

First, a key purpose of the theory of international law developed in this book is to justify the regulation of decisionmakers through a theory that gives them guidance on how they ought to make decisions to promote values with a minimum degree of effectiveness. In other words, the theory seeks to present an account of international law that has the potential to be normatively desirable when the decisionmakers follow the guidance provided in that account.

For readers interested in legal philosophy, the justificatory project here is similar to, but not identical with, Ronald Dworkin's project to develop a justificatory account of law. Dworkin's justificatory account of law in LAW'S EMPIRE focused on domestic law, where the legal system monopolizes force to coerce individuals to follow laws.[8] In a sense, his account sought to justify a strong form of coercion. By comparison, in international law, coercion by force to follow laws is often but

[8] RONALD DWORKIN, LAW'S EMPIRE 110 (1986).

not universally absent. Instead, decisionmakers are often—but not always—most effectively compelled to follow prescriptions because of costs other than the force imposed on them for noncompliance and/or the benefits from complying. Although this is one form of coercion, it is different than the sort of coercion that police officers, jailors, and court marshals use in domestic legal systems to force compliance with domestic laws. The justificatory project of this book is thus more accurately characterized as an attempt to justify the international regulation of decisionmakers rather than an attempt to justify coercing them.

The justificatory goal of this book's theory is achieved by guiding decisionmakers to make decisions within the international legal system that promote normatively desirable goals. It does not seek to force them to do so. Although forcing compliance with laws is one way to secure outcomes, that is not generally possible in an international system without centralized authority. The justificatory account of international law, therefore, does not seek to issue coercive instructions about what laws are or ought to be, as surely it cannot. Instead, this account of international law acknowledges the reality that decisionmakers are more likely to consider and follow appropriate prescriptions through reasoning and by harmonizing, where possible, their interests with the values at stake in an international problem. This approach may not effectively secure compliance with prescriptions in some international problems, and it may not lead to normatively ideal prescriptions in others. But it may provide the best justification possible given the limitations of the international legal system.

Second, to provide decisionmakers with guidance, a theory of international law must first explain how the international legal system operates. This goal of deepening the understanding of the international legal system is important in and of itself. It is also a necessary exercise that makes it possible to give guidance to decisionmakers on what they should do within the international legal system to justify its actual, or potential for, authoritative control of decisionmakers. Because the theory seeks to explain how the international legal system operates, it focuses on what actually happens in international problems and not just on what legal rules say.

Importantly, although the explanatory aspects of this book's theory may provide some tools to anticipate the actions of decisionmakers, it does not seek to present a comprehensive schema to predict how decisionmakers will behave in every problem. There are too many variables to control in the abstract. The mammoth task of comprehensive mapping would require collaborative efforts among generations of scholars. The theory in this book, therefore, simply tests and refines a framework of analysis that scholars and decisionmakers can apply in actual international problems to anticipate what other decisionmakers could do. Under this theory, it is appropriate for decisionmakers to use their judgment in light of the context of each problem because their constituents expect them to do so. The exercise of discretion naturally introduces uncertainty in the outcomes of international problems.

Third, an account of the international legal system need not confine itself to traits that are equally manifest in every international legal problem. A descriptive account can instead posit what John Finnis termed the "central case," or ideal type, of international law from incidents which may depart from it.[9] The central case is a description of international law's focal meaning, to use Aristotle's term, or ideal type, to use Max Weber's term. Joseph Raz also accepted that "general traits which mark a system as a legal one are several and each of them admits, in principle, of various degrees."[10] Applying the idea of the central case to the international legal system, specific international problems may thus be more like international law or less like it, but collectively international incidents constituting the central case illustrate the focal meaning of the international legal system. In this manner, international law can be distinct from politics even if not every incident deserving of legal analysis is equally distinct from politics, so long as the international legal system as a whole has a unique focal meaning.

The choice to describe international law through a central case is not universally shared by philosophers. Hans Kelsen insisted that explanatory terms must extend equally to all legal incidents. Alexander Orakhelashvili shares this Kelsenian view. In Orakhelashvili's opinion, "the threshold of international law is defined as 'a point where non-law ends and law begins.'"[11] He rejects the view that there is "no clear cut threshold between what is legal and what is not in the international legal society."[12]

Orakhelashvili is free to make his methodological choice. However, it is not a choice that advances a project to explain and justify the complex phenomena of international law. If one were to insist on sharp threshold traits that distinguish a footstool from a coffee table, there would simply be no way to describe an ottoman, which could be both. The futility of formalistic categorization is amplified when addressing not simply a static physical object, but the concept of that object that includes countless variations of that object. Even if a specific ottoman could be said to be a footstool and not a coffee table, insisting that the concept of an ottoman always be one or the other in every type of ottoman is simply impossible and consequently precludes a meaningful description of the nature of ottomans. This analysis applies with even greater force to social phenomena like international law. Insisting on a sharp line between international law and international politics undermines any ability to richly describe the nature of international law.

Leading hard positivist Raz proposes that the better approach when "faced with borderline cases . . . is to admit their problematic credentials [and] to enumerate their similarities and dissimilarities to the typical cases[.]"[13] In a similar vein, H. L. A. Hart explains that, although there may be plain cases or exemplars of a general term that clearly fit the term, there are unclear cases that have "only some of the

[9] *See generally* John Finnis, Natural Law and Natural Rights 9–11, 277 (1996) (discussing the central case heuristic in general legal philosophy).

[10] Joseph Raz, Practical Reason and Norms 150 (1999).

[11] Alexander Orakhelashvili, The Interpretation of Acts and Rules in Public International Law 51 (2008).

[12] *Id.*

[13] Raz, *supra* note 10, at 150.

features of the plain cases. . . ."[14] It is not possible to say whether an unclear case fits the term or not. Instead, the better analysis studies what characteristics the unclear case shares with the exemplars.[15] Nicos Stavropoulos shares this view of unclear cases, stating that "a judgment of resemblance constitutes a *choice* between open alternatives [ ]: it is neither true nor false that the term correctly applies to such cases."[16] Applying this analysis to the inquiry about international law, some international incidents will clearly resemble the central case of international law and a fine, but sharp, line may demarcate law from politics; other international incidents may exhibit characteristics of international law and politics, and it may not be possible to designate whether that incident is either law or non-law.

Fourth, because this account of the international legal system seeks to justify the regulatory claims that international law makes over decisionmakers, the ideal type or central case of international law comprises international problems in which there are prescriptions that claim to authoritatively regulate decisionmakers.

Some critics may insist that international law must be measured against a central case of law in general, derived from common understandings of what law means in domestic contexts. This view finds parallels in the approaches of legal philosophers studying law in general. Hart, for example, built his concept of law on the domestic English legal system.[17] However, the present inquiry is explicitly not about whether international law is law. Therefore, it is unnecessary and unhelpful to refer to any other system of law as another central case of law that is antagonistic to international law.

Other critics may contend that the central case ought not to be identified according to what shared expectations decisionmakers consider in making decisions in international problems, but according to what people think falls within the ordinary semantic meaning of the term "international law." Such a central case may include only formal international laws and exclude informal prescriptions and other shared expectations of appropriate conduct.

However, for the purposes of an account of how international problems are, or have the potential to be, addressed in a regularized fashion, focusing on social phenomena relevant to shaping the conduct of decisionmakers is more useful. In contrast, studying only formal laws excludes from the field of inquiry swaths of important decisionmaking processes in international problems, especially where there are no formal laws or where the shared expectations deviate from the text of formal laws.

Prescriptions within the central case of international law include, but are not limited to, the decisions of the ICJ, especially in contentious disputes; and UN Security

[14] H. L. A. Hart, The Concept of Law 126 (2d ed. 1994) [hereinafter Hart, The Concept of Law].

[15] *Id.* at 126–27.

[16] Nicos Stavropoulos, *Hart's Semantics*, *in* Hart's Postscript, *supra* note 1, at 59, 92 (emphasis in original).

[17] Hart, *supra* note 14, at 26 (looking at laws "in a modern system such as English law"); *id.* at 79 (pointing to "certain familiar features of municipal law in a modern state. . . .").

Council resolutions, especially its Chapter VII resolutions. The ICJ may not itself enforce its sanctions or orders, and its contentious jurisdiction is contingent on the consent of state parties. Nevertheless, it represents part of the central case of international law, because it is regarded by many decisionmakers as a "court of law" with general subject matter jurisdiction and "is considered by international lawyers to be the central judicial body of the international community."[18] Its general pronouncements of law are often regarded as authoritative statements of shared expectations, especially by other ICJ judges in subsequent cases and, to a lesser extent, government officials and domestic and international judges sitting on other tribunals. The UN Security Council is a political organ but when it exercises its Chapter VII powers, its resolutions are regarded by decisionmakers as authoritative. Chapter VII resolutions may authorize economic sanctions or military force. All member states are obliged to comply with the resolutions, and the Security Council can sanction noncompliance.[19] Decisionmakers, especially government officials, tend to have a strong expectation of compliance with Chapter VII resolutions.

There are many other social settings or arenas that decisionmakers regard as part of the system of international law, albeit generally to a lesser extent than the central case. These include the UN General Assembly, which issues nonbinding resolutions; bilateral negotiations between states; informal prescriptions issued by international organizations; the decisions of arbitral tribunals and national courts; and internal deliberations in governments. For illustrative purposes, however, this chapter focuses on, albeit not exclusively, the UN Security Council and the ICJ.

III. LEGALISM

In the central case of international law,[20] decisionmakers make, interpret, and apply prescriptions legalistically in international problems to shape actions and influence outcomes. That is, they claim to apply prescriptions neutrally through accepted procedures and methods of reasoning to the problem at hand. The use of the word "legalism" is not intended to disparage international law. Rather, it is intended to express social facts about a specialized mode of interaction in the process of

[18] Mohamed Sameh M. Amr, The Role of the International Court of Justice as the Principal Judicial Organ of the United Nations 42–43 (2003). *See also* James Crawford, *The International Court of Justice, Judicial Administration and the Rule of Law*, *in* Bowett et al., The International Court of Justice: Process, Practice and Procedure 112, 113 (1997) ("The Court is the principal judicial organ of the organized international community as a whole, and not less than that.").

[19] UN Charter art. 24. *See also* Juergen Dedring, The United Nations Security Council in the 1990s 54 (2008) ("[T]he total UN membership value the given tools [of the Security Council] as legally based . . ."); Chinmaya R. Gharekhan, The Horseshoe Table: An Inside View of the UN Security Council 3 (2006) ("The Security Council is unique in the sense that it combines in itself both legislative and executive functions."); Kenneth Manusama, The United Nations Security Council in the Post-Cold War Era: Applying the Principle of Legality 12 (2006) (describing the UN Security Council as an "executive organ bound by law").

[20] *See supra* ch. 1, pt. III.A.

decisionmaking in international problems, without engaging in unnecessary conceptual debates about whether or not this mode of interaction is actually "law." As later parts of this chapter will show, it is possible for decisionmakers, who are trying to make up their minds about what to do in an international problem, to analyze the effectiveness and morality of the international legal system without answering questions about whether international law is law.[21] That is why this theory of international law focuses on the legalism and not legality of the central case of international law.

In a functioning domestic legal system, authority to make decisions is largely centralized in the government. Simplistically stated, the legislative branch makes laws, the executive branch interprets and applies legislation and passes regulations, and the judiciary interprets laws and prior cases. In legal disputes that parties cannot resolve among themselves, they may bring their claims to a court. Judges then interpret the law and issue an authoritative decision, enforceable by marshals and other officials. Scholars and decisionmakers seeking to understand outcomes in domestic legal disputes would therefore make significant headway by focusing on the process of creation, interpretation, and application of law by judges. If further inquiry is desired, analysis of decisionmaking by officials and legislators will bear fruit. Although there are other actors who may influence decisionmaking in domestic legal disputes, including the media, corporations, lobbyists, scholars, and professional associations, the principal decisionmakers are usually officials of the three branches of government who largely make decisions in defined arenas such as courts and Congress. Therefore, it is possible to understand and guide decisionmakers in domestic law by focusing on the interpretive processes of a relatively narrow group of decisionmakers in clearly defined arenas.

By comparison, in the international system, centralized authority to make and enforce decisions is largely absent. There is no legislature charged with comprehensively making formal laws binding and enforceable on everyone in the world. Although the UN Security Council passes binding Chapter VII resolutions enforceable by force, Chapter VII authority concerns only peace and security. Although the UN General Assembly passes resolutions on a broad range of topics, which may be persuasive or help to consolidate expectations of appropriate conduct, these resolutions are not formally law in and of themselves and are not, *ipso jure*, binding. The International Criminal Court is a creation of treaty, and its judicial authority extends only over signatory states.[22] Although it issues criminal convictions of individuals from those states, there is no international military or police force to enforce those convictions should a signatory state breach its treaty obligations to abide by the

[21] *Infra* pts. IV, V.C.

[22] *See* Rome Statute of the International Criminal Court art 4(2), Jul. 17, 1998, U.N. Doc A/Conf. 183/9 [hereinafter Rome Statute]. *See also* Commentary on the Rome Statute of the International Criminal Court: Observers Notes, Article by Article 124-27 (2d ed. O. Triffterer ed., 2008) [hereinafter commentary on the rome statute].

convictions or choose to exit the treaty.[23] It also has no jurisdiction over noncriminal matters. The ICJ has general jurisdiction over international disputes, but its formal authority is contingent on the consent of states to its jurisdiction in advance. Its decisions are enforceable only if the UN Security Council decides to issue a Chapter VII resolution. Passing a resolution requires a majority of votes in favor by members of the Security Council and no veto by a permanent member of it.

In the absence of comprehensive centralized authority in the international legal system, in many international problems, authority to make and apply prescriptions is diffused over a wide range of decisionmakers, including government officials, judges, corporations, and international bureaucrats. It is rare that a single decision maker, acting alone, succeeds in authoritatively making or enforcing an international law. Frequently, each decisionmaker can only make a claim as to what the relevant prescription is and what it instructs, regardless of whether the prescription takes the form of a law or informal practice. Although some decisionmakers are more influential than others, ultimately, the content of the prescription most often depends on a sufficiently influential group of decisionmakers negotiating through words or acts, and finally accepting a shared interpretation of the prescription. That equilibrium lasts only until the next international problem, when the process of interpretation begins anew. The prior shared expectation of appropriate conduct can have a strong influence on, or even authoritatively control, subsequent interpretations of prescriptions.

The central case of the international legal system comprises incidents in which the decisionmakers share strong expectations about relevant prescriptions and procedures for making, interpreting, modifying, and terminating them. Decisionmakers accept that certain procedures are necessary to make prescriptions authoritative, and they accept that a prescription so made is authoritative. They also accept that if prescriptions are to be interpreted and applied to facts, then the outcome prescribed in a particular international problem is legal. These social facts are observed in four aspects of communication and decision among decisionmakers in international problems.

First, decisionmakers in an international problem claim that a certain prescription is law or expresses shared expectations of appropriate conduct. An example of a prescription that is also formally law is Article 51 of the UN Charter, which expresses a strong shared expectation among decisionmakers that a state may use force in self-defense against an armed attack. An example of a prescription that expresses shared expectations of appropriate conduct beyond what the text of a prescription says is Article 38 of the ICJ statute, which in terms states the choice of law for the ICJ, but which decisionmakers have widely come to accept represents formal sources of international law beyond judicial decisionmaking by the ICJ. An example of a prescription that has no basis in formal law, and indeed is clearly not law, but nevertheless expresses a strong expectation of appropriate conduct, are the capital

[23] Rome Statute, art. 127. *See also* Commentary on the Rome Statute, *supra* note 22, at 1777.

requirements for banks worldwide stated in the Basel Accords on banking supervision among the Group of Twenty Finance Ministers and Central Bank Governors. In other incidents beyond the central case, an elite may accept that a prescription is not law strictly speaking, but nonetheless claim there is a shared expectation that elites will comply with it because it was made through commonly accepted informal procedures. These soft norms of international financial standards among bank regulators[24] are examples of prescriptions that are not law but are nevertheless law-like. Decisionmakers who invoke an international law in support of a proposed action claim that the relevant prescription justifies or requires that action because of the shared expectation of appropriate conduct, which is often, but not always, expressed as law. They do not justify the proposed action solely on the basis that it is expedient or moral.

Second, decisionmakers explicitly or implicitly reason that their prescription demands compliance because it results from procedures for making prescriptions that decisionmakers have accepted as an appropriate process for reaching a prescription that demands compliance, and because compliance represents the shared view of decisionmakers. These include the voting system of the UN Security Council to pass resolutions, procedural rules of the ICJ to render judicial opinions, and the procedures under the Vienna Convention on the Law of Treaties (the VCLT) to make binding international agreements.[25] It also includes processes for making prescriptions that are not formally international law but nevertheless strengthen and express shared expectations of appropriate conduct, such as informal financial regulations issued by the Bank of International Settlements.

Third, elites interpret and apply that prescription according to modes of legalist reasoning.[26] Legalist reasoning is a specialized method of communication familiar to lawyers and judges, as well as to some other decisionmakers.[27] U.S. Federal Appellate Judge Richard Posner defined legalism as "a neutral application of rules not made up for the occasion to facts fairly found."[28] It is reasonable to wonder whether it is possible for a judge or other decisionmaker to ever be totally neutral. The answer to that debate, however, is not crucial to explain the central case of international law. This book defines legalist reasoning slightly differently from Judge Posner. It defines legalist reasoning as a *claim* to apply prescriptions, through a process of reasoning and logic, neutrally to facts in an international problem.

[24] *See infra* ch. 6, pt II.B (discussing Basel III prescriptions).

[25] *See* Vienna Convention on the Law of Treaties art. 7, May 14, 23, 1969, 1155 U.N.T.S. 331 [hereinafter VCLT].

[26] *See* David Kennedy, *The Last Treatise: Project and Person*, 7 German L. J. 982, 984 (2006) ("International law is a professional practice of arguing."); Martti Koskenniemi, From Apology to Utopia 615–16 (2005) ("International law is what international lawyers make of it. To commit oneself to international law is to allow its grammar to enter as one's second nature but still to maintain the position of choice . . .").

[27] For an exemplar of legalist reasoning, *see generally* Richard K. Gardiner, Treaty Interpretation (2008).

[28] Richard A. Posner, How Judges Think 370 (2008).

Methods of legalist reasoning include inductive and deductive reasoning to identify and interpret prescriptions; to extend, limit, or modify them; to select relevant facts from a universe of data; and to apply prescriptions to facts in a rational fashion to each proposed outcome. Legalist reasoning differentiates international law from raw power politics, which seeks outcomes that promote immediate self-interest, without necessarily applying prescriptions uniformly to similarly situated communities in similar problems.[29]

Fourth, other governing elites and constituents accept these claims as authoritative prescriptions because they manifest fidelity to legalist reasoning and accepted procedures for authoritative prescription. This does not mean, however, that they will obey the prescription. In international law, as in domestic law, one can recognize a law or prescription, as the case may be, without obeying it.[30]

Although decisionmakers may pursue vital national interests and other self-interested goals through the international legal system, the social facts about legalist reasoning and procedures for making legal prescriptions make it distinctive from politics plain and simple. When governing elites make political demands on other decisionmakers or constituents, they do not necessarily make claims to be legalistically authoritative and do not necessarily use legalist reasoning. They may of course do so as a cloak for their political agendas, but they do not have to. In contrast, decisionmakers acting within the central case of international law must make legalist claims. In other words, politics and law overlap, but politics is not coextensive with the central case of international law.

When assessing legalist claims, decisionmakers will often consider what the claims mean in terms of self-interest and values. However, they will also consider the claims on legalist grounds. A claim that departs from legalism is less likely to be accepted as a prescription, even though a decisionmaker may nevertheless accept it as a desirable political goal if it serves that decisionmaker's interests.[31]

The extent to which international law is distinct from politics, however, varies from incident to incident. In incidents that make up the central case of international law, that is, exemplars of the ideal type of international law, the social facts described

[29] *Cf.* Richard Falk, *The Role of Law in World Society*, *in* Toward World Order and Human Dignity: Essays in Honor of Myres S. McDougal 132, 148 (Weston & Reisman eds., 1976) ("[T]he more highly articulated the social order, the more likely it is that the legal system will achieve a measure of autonomy from immediate political pressures.").

[30] *Cf.* Burns H. Weston, *The Role of Law in Promoting Peace and Violence: A Matter of Definition, Social Values, and Individual Responsibility*, *in* Toward World Order and Human Dignity, *supra* note 29, at 117 ("To turn a phrase, [international] law is legitimized politics—a Hydra-headed process of social decision, involving persons at all levels and from all walks of public and private life who, with authority derived both explicitly and implicitly from community consensus or expectation, and supported by formal and informal sanction, effect those codes or standards of everyday conduct by which we plan and go about our lives.").

[31] *Cf.* Thomas M. Franck, The Power of Legitimacy Among Nations 134 (1990) [hereinafter Franck, Power] ("When validating cues are generally perceived to be misapplied . . . then the symbolic validation would not occur; instead, the symbol and its bestower would both suffer the erosion of their authority to confer legitimacy.").

above are most clearly in evidence. As incidents deviate from the central case, the four features of the central case fade. The claim that a prescription accords with procedures for making law becomes progressively weaker, and fewer and fewer elites accept any claim that the prescription is law-like. Claims are accordingly less and less legal until finally, international law shades away to international politics.

Although it is impossible to draw a bright line dividing the end of international law and the start of politics, it is also unnecessary to do so to understand international law's separate existence. The social phenomena of international law exists because there is a distinctive central case of international law, and there are enough incidents close enough to the central case that governing elites claim to be both empowered and constrained by legal and law-like international prescriptions. Some of these social facts are illustrated below by examining the UN Security Council and the ICJ.

A. The UN Security Council

The UN Security Council claims to be legally authoritative on the basis that there is a strong shared expectation among decisionmakers that its Chapter VII resolutions passed in accordance with its procedures create binding legal obligations on states. It does not simply command other states to comply with a Council resolution because five powerful states and at least four others sitting on the Council voted in favor of a prescription in a Security Council resolution. It also does not simply claim that its resolutions must be followed because the course of action is moral or expedient. Although resolutions may indeed be moral, and it may be expedient for weaker states to generally do what powerful states want them to do, every time the Security Council issues a mandatory resolution, it claims, especially, that member states must comply because they are legally obliged to do so under international law.

This claim is predicated not solely on politics or power but on the UN Charter, which is widely regarded as codifying shared expectations of appropriate conduct in international relations. The Charter is a constitutive treaty with almost 200 signatory states as of September 1, 2010.[32] It provides that the Council is one of six principal UN organs, which are a General Assembly, a Security Council, an Economic and Social Council, a Trusteeship Council, an International Court of Justice, and a Secretariat.[33] The Charter allocates primary binding executive authority to the Security Council. The General Assembly may consider any matters within the scope of the UN Charter, which practically speaking is any international topic, but it can only make recommendations to member states[34] and is prohibited from making recommendations when the Security Council is seized of a matter.[35] The Economic

[32] *See Member States of the United Nations*, The United Nations, http://www.un.org/en/members/index.shtml (last visited Aug, 7 2011).

[33] *See* UN Charter art. 7.

[34] *See id.* art. 10–11.

[35] *See id.* art. 12.

and Social Council may only make recommendations on economic and social matters.[36] The Trusteeship Council is vested with authority to oversee the trusteeship of territories that have not achieved statehood. Its contemporary relevance has greatly diminished with the completion of decolonization. Although international law remains concerned with international territorial administration to manage post-Cold War successions and self-determination movements other than decolonizations, most transitional administrations are created pursuant to Chapter VII resolutions adopted by the Security Council, and they report to it.[37] Pursuant to Article 92 of the UN Charter, the ICJ is the "principal judicial organ of the United Nations."[38] It is not vested with executive authority. While it has general advisory authority when certain organs of the UN ask for its opinion on a legal question,[39] its binding judicial authority is only triggered by the consent of disputing states.[40] The sixth organ in the UN Charter is the Secretariat, which is headed by the Secretary General, the UN's chief administrative officer.[41] The Secretary General wields influence through his administrative functions and can persuade member states to his point of view. He does not however have binding authority over states, the Security Council, or the ICJ.

The Security Council is vested with discretionary legal authority to make decisions binding on member states.[42] Article 25 provides that they "agree to accept and carry out the decisions of the Security Council in accordance with the present Charter."[43]

[36] *See id.* art. 62.

[37] *See, e.g.*, S.C. Res. 1272, ¶ 1, U.N. Doc. S/RES/1272 (Oct. 25, 1999); S.C. Res. 1244, U.N. Doc. S/RES/1244 (June 10, 1999). *See also generally* Ralph Wilde, International Territorial Administration: How Trusteeship and the Civilizing Mission Never Went Away (2008); Bernhard Knoll, The Legal Status of Territories Subject to Administration by International Organisations (2008).

[38] UN Charter art. 92.

[39] *See id.* art. 96. *See, e.g.*, Admission of a State to the United Nations (Charter, art. 4), Advisory Opinion, 1948 I.C.J. 57 (May 28); International Status of South-West Africa, Advisory Opinion, 1950 I.C.J. 128 (July 11); Reservations to the Convention on the Prevention and Punishment of the Crime of Genocide, Advisory Opinion, 1951 I.C.J. 15 (May 28); Legal Consequences for States of the Continued Presence of South Africa in Namibia (South-West Africa) Notwithstanding Security Council Resolution 276 (1970), Advisory Opinion, 1971 I.C.J. 16 (June 21); Western Sahara, Advisory Opinion, 1975 I.C.J. 12 (Oct. 16); Legality of the Use by a State of Nuclear Weapons in Armed Conflict, Advisory Opinion, 1996 I.C.J. 66 (July 8); Legal Consequences of the Construction of a Wall in the Occupied Palestinian Territory, Advisory Opinion, 2004 I.C.J. 136 (July 9).

[40] *See* UN Charter art. 94.

[41] *See. id.* art. 97.

[42] *See* The United Nations Security Council and War: The Evolution of Thought and Practice since 1945, at 4–10 (Vaughan Lowe et al. eds., 2008) (describing legal authority of the Security Council under relevant provisions of the UN Charter); David L. Bosco, Five to Rule Them All: The UN Security Council and the Making of the Modern World 3 (2009) ("When the Council is united, its members can wage war, impose blockades, unseat governments, and levy sanctions, all in the name of the international community. There are almost no limits to the body's authority.").

[43] UN Charter art. 25.

Through the Charter, member states confer upon the Security Council "primary responsibility for the maintenance of international peace and security."[44] By the terms of the UN Charter, the Security Council has legal authority for matters relating to peace and security.

This authority is exercised pursuant to, and is contingent upon, the Security Council complying with the Charter's provisions. The Council has many powers, including recommending to the General Assembly to appoint the Council's choice for UN Secretary General,[45] calling up states to settle disputes,[46] and investigating any situation that might lead to international friction.[47] The starkest of its legal powers are its discretion to authorize force under Chapter VII of the UN Charter to restore peace and security. There are legalistic requirements for the exercise of this authority. First, under Article 39, it must satisfy itself that there is "any threat to peace, breach of the peace, or act of aggression."[48] If any of these threshold conditions exist, the Council may call upon states to comply with provisional measures under Article 40.[49] Pursuant to Article 41, the Council may also command member states to take measures not involving the use of armed force, including economic sanctions and severing diplomatic relations.[50] If it deems such non-armed measures to be inadequate, it may order or authorize, under Article 42, military force against or in a state in order to restore international peace and security.[51]

UN Secretary General Kofi Annan underscored the social belief in the legal authority of the Council's power to authorize military force in his statement:

> When States decide to use force, not in self-defense but to deal with broader threats to international peace and security, there is no substitute for the unique legitimacy provided by the United Nations Security Council. States and peoples around the world attach fundamental importance to such legitimacy, and to the international rule of law.[52]

[44] *See id.* art. 24.

[45] *See id.* art. 97.

[46] *See id.* art. 33.

[47] *See id.* art. 34. *See also* Edward C. Luck, UN Security Council: Practice and Promise 18–19 (2006) (listing 25 subsidiary bodies of the Security Council addressing a wide range of responsibilities).

[48] UN Charter art. 39. *See also* Erika de Wet, The Chapter VII Powers of the United Nations Security Council 133–77 (2004) (interpreting the threshold requirements for the exercise of Chapter VII powers).

[49] *See* UN Charter art. 40.

[50] *See id.* art. 41.

[51] *See id.* art. 42. *See also generally* de Wet, *supra* note 48, at 178–368 (surveying the Security Council's powers under Chapter VII); Jeremy M. Farrall, United Nations Sanctions and the Rule of Law (2007) (appraising the Security Council's legal authority to impose sanctions regimes).

[52] Press Release, Secretary-General Says United Nations Has Duty to Exhaust All Possibilities of Peaceful Settlement Before Resorting to Use of Force, U.N. Doc. SG/SM/8600 (Feb. 12, 2003) (*cited in* Ralph Zacklin, The United Nations Secretariat and the Use of Force in a Unipolar World 143 (2010)).

The issue of international law's legitimacy or morality is taken up in Part IV of this chapter. For now, it is sufficient to note the association with the Council's Chapter VII powers with an international rule of *law*. This substantive legal framework of the rule of law comprises in the main an absolute prohibition on the use of force under Article 2(4) by states, except in self-defense until the Security Council is seized of the threat of peace, act of aggression, or breach of international peace and security.[53]

In addition to legalistic triggers and bases for the Council's authority to prescribe forcible measures to restore international peace and security, there are also regularized and legalistic procedures that must be followed to render its resolutions lawful. Key procedural requirements for the exercise of its authority are codified in the Charter. According to Article 27(2), procedural matters are passed by affirmative votes of at least 9 of its 15 members.[54] Under Article 27(3), substantive resolutions, including Chapter VII resolutions, are adopted only if its draft wins 9 votes, and none of the permanent members—China, France, Russia, the United Kingdom, and the United States[55]—vetoes the draft resolution.[56]

Other procedural matters are not explicitly codified in the Charter but are nonetheless necessary for the Council to issue legal resolutions. It must meet, and it must discuss what resolutions it wants to adopt. These procedures are regularized in a legalistic fashion. The obligatory nature of the procedures is grounded in Article 30, which provides that the Security Council "shall adopt its own rules of procedure. . . ."[57] The Council thus adopted its Provisional Rules of Procedure at its first meeting in 1946. They have been amended just over half a dozen times since, and are in effect the Council's rules of procedure in spite of their provisional title.[58] These rules provide, inter alia, that the president of the Council has sole authority to convene meetings,[59] but that he shall do so at the request of any member of the Council.[60] He has authority to approve the provisional agenda of each meeting, which the UN Secretary General prepares,[61] and the Security Council then adopts the provisional agenda as the agenda as its first order of business at its meetings.[62] Pursuant to Rule 48, the meetings of the Council are generally held in public, and verbatim records of meetings are prepared for Council members.[63] The Provisional Rules cover the minutiae of procedure for the Security Council. They provide evidence that the Council is not just an unruly forum for power politics. On the contrary, it is a highly regularized

[53] *See* UN Charter art. 2, ¶ 4; UN Charter art. 51. *See also* Christine Gray, *The Charter Limitations on the Use of Force: Theory and Practice*, *in* The United Nations Security Council and War, *supra* note 42, at 86–87.

[54] *See* UN Charter art. 27, ¶ 2.

[55] *See id.* ¶ 3. *See also id.* art. 23, ¶ 1.

[56] *See id.* art. 27, ¶ 3.

[57] *See id.* art. 30.

[58] *See* Provisional Rules of Procedure of the Security Council, U.N. Doc. S/96/Rev.7 (1983).

[59] *See id.* R. 1.

[60] *See id.* R. 2.

[61] *See id.* R. 7.

[62] *See id.* R. 9.

[63] *See id.* R. 48–49.

forum for communication and decisionmaking, which is achieved by legalistic written rules.

Notably, the Security Council's informal meetings are also regularized through informal habitual practices that, although not formally law, fall within the central case of prescriptions accompanied by strong shared expectations of appropriate conduct.[64] In addition to the formal meetings of the Security Council, its permanent members often convene informal meetings. These meetings are not contemplated in the Charter or Provisional Rules and therefore are unregulated by them. Nevertheless, they are important venues because the permanent members and other members invited to attend use informal meetings to try to reach consensus prior to the formal meetings, which the members tend to use to give speeches rather than to engage in actual substantive decisionmaking.[65] Chinmaya Gharekhan, the Secretary General's personal representative to the Security Council from 1993 to 1996, and India's representative from 1991 to 1992, described informal meetings in the following terms:

> The implication of this silence on informal consultations in any official document is that they are not governed by any rules. This is not to suggest that informal meetings are unruly. Over time, practices have developed which, as a body, like the unwritten British constitution, have served the meetings quite well.[66]

For example, Gharekhan reports that there is an informal prescription that forbids nonmembers of the Council from participating in the informal consultations. Although nonmembers have tried to attend those informal meetings, decisionmakers never deviated from that prescription. Instead, nonmembers try to participate in Security Council decisionmaking by persuading the president or Security Council members of their views outside the informal consultation meetings.[67]

Even this method of departing from established informal procedural practices in informal meetings is regularized and based on strong shared expectations about appropriate conduct. Gharekhan documented that when permanent members wished to deviate from established practices, they would invoke the legalist claim that the "Security Council is the master of its procedures."[68] The motivations for departing from established procedure are often political. However, the method of

[64] *See* Shunmugam Jayakumar, Diplomacy: Singapore Experience 66 (2011) ("Unlike other UN bodies, the UNSC operates in a very closed and secretive manner and has its own set of informal practices and procedures. . . . We needed to understand the trade-offs that took place behind the scenes, which cannot be observed from the set-piece open meetings of the UNSC.").

[65] *See* Luck, *supra* note 47, at 17 ("In practice, the Council meets either in formal meetings that are public and largely devoted to speechmaking or in private meetings and informal consultations where most of its deliberative work is accomplished out of the public eye.").

[66] Gharekhan, *supra* note 19, at 15. *See also* Dedring, *supra* note 19, at 1–4 (describing the detailed consultation process that the president uses to decide whether to place an item on the Council's agenda and stating that the "practice of these 'informals' continues until our time").

[67] *See* Gharekhan, *supra* note 19, at 31.

[68] *Id.* at 15.

advancing those political goals is not simply to assert raw power according to the exigencies of a situation. Instead, a legalist reason is provided by referring to an established norm that the Council controls its own procedures.

The Security Council also uses a legalistic style of communication to formulate legal prescriptions in the form of resolutions to terminate, to extend, or to modify them, and to apply them to international disputes. Undoubtedly the content of a Council communication is also political, and political styles of communication are often used as well.[69] However, whatever else the Security Council is, it is also a legal institution in which legalist language and reasoning is ever present.[70] Consider a typical Chapter VII resolution, Security Council Resolution 1863 (2009), which extends prior authorizations of military intervention in Somalia. It states in relevant part:

> The *Security Council*,
>
> *Recalling* its previous resolutions concerning the situation in Somalia
>
> [. . .]
>
> *Further reaffirming* that the Djibouti Peace Agreement represents the basis for a resolution of the conflict in Somalia, and *stressing* the importance of broad-based and representative institutions reached through a political process ultimately inclusive of all,
>
> *Welcoming* the guiding principles agreed by the parties to the Djibouti Peace Agreement on 25 November 2008, in particular the establishment of a Unity Government and an inclusive Parliament,
>
> *Recognizing* the need for all parties to contribute to an enhanced political process, *calling on* the Somali parties to the Djibouti Peace Agreement to fulfil [sic] their obligations set out therein, and *taking note* of the request from the parties for United Nations authorization and deployment of an international stabilization force,
>
> [. . .]
>
> *Reiterating* its serious concern at the worsening humanitarian situation in Somalia, and *calling on* all Member States to contribute to current and future consolidated humanitarian appeals,
>
> *Recognizing* that serious crimes have been committed against civilians in the ongoing conflict in Somalia and *reaffirming* the importance of the fight against impunity,
>
> [. . .]
>
> *Determining* that the situation in Somalia constitutes a threat to international peace and security in the region,
>
> *Acting* under Chapter VII of the Charter of the United Nations,
>
> [. . .]

[69] *Cf.* Dedring, *supra* note 19, at 33 ("As a forum for the complete airing of arguments, conflicts, and allegations, the Council continues to be indispensable.").

[70] *See also* Manusama, *supra* note 19, at 46 (noting that the Council uses "the language of international law to address a particular situation" and thereby "automatically interprets the relevant body of international law").

2. *Decides* to renew for up to six months from the date of this resolution the authorization of Member States of the African Union to maintain a mission in Somalia, which shall be authorized to take all necessary measures to carry out the mandate set out in paragraph 9 of resolution 1772 (2007); and *underlines*, in particular, that AMISOM is authorized to take all necessary measures to provide security for key infrastructure and to contribute, as may be requested and within its capabilities and existing mandate, to the creation of the necessary security conditions for the provision of humanitarian assistance;

3. *Calls upon* the Somali parties and other stakeholders to uphold the principles of the Djibouti Peace Agreement, to cease hostilities, to ensure without delay unhindered humanitarian access and assistance to the Somali people, to terminate all acts of armed confrontation, to reach agreement on permanent ceasefire mechanisms, and to use the Joint Security Committee to resolve disputes over military issues; and *requests* the Secretary-General to report on ways to improve the implementation of the Djibouti Peace Agreement, including the option of an international peace conference to include local, regional and international actors. . . . [71]

The resolution is a political decision. It emphasizes the "political process" to achieve peace, recognizes the need for an "enhanced political process," and reaffirms the "political independence" of Somalia.

By its terms, it is also a normative and ethical statement. It expresses "serious concern at the worsening humanitarian situation in Somalia," calls on states to "contribute to . . . humanitarian appeals," and reaffirms "the importance of the fight against impunity."

But above all, the resolution is a decision within the central case of international law. It refers to its legal authority and communicates using a specialized legalistic mode of reasoning. It is replete with legalistic language. Consistent with other Council resolutions, Resolution 1863 begins with the invocation of prior resolutions concerning its subject matter, thereby situating the resolution within a larger corpus of law. Resolution 1863 also affirms the Djibouti Peace Agreement between warring internecine parties in Somalia, recognizing that it is the basis for resolving the civil war. It implicitly refers to the substantive threshold in Article 39 for the Council to exercise its Chapter VII authority by stating that the Council has determined that the situation in Somalia "constitutes a threat to international peace and security in the region."[72]

Crucially, in comparison to the preamble that refers to legal, political, and normative considerations, the operative paragraphs authorizing military force are explicitly taken only under the legal authority of Chapter VII of the UN Charter. As with all other Chapter VII resolutions, Resolution 1863 incants with capitalized formality

[71] S.C. Res. 1863, U.N. Doc. S/RES/1863 (Jan. 16, 2009).

[72] *Id.*

that the Council is "*Acting* under Chapter VII of the Charter of the United Nations."[73] Pursuant to that legal authority, paragraph 1 requests military reinforcements, paragraph 2 prescribes six months as the period of legal authority for the international military mission to "take all necessary measures," and paragraph 3 issues a legal command to uphold the Djibouti Peace Agreement and to cease hostilities.

This foregoing analysis of a Chapter VII resolution shows how the Security Council's resolutions typify the four social facts in the central case of international law. First, Resolution 1863 made prescriptive claim to control warring parties based on legalist authority and not just political or moral considerations. Second, the basis of this legalist claim was that it had followed legalist procedures that other decisionmakers accept as a precondition for the Security Council's legal authority. Third, the Security Council interpreted the source of its authority, the UN Charter, in the legalist fashion, in order to further consolidate expectations among decisionmakers that Resolution 1863 was legally authoritative. Fourth, the Security Council referred to and accepted its prior prescription in Resolution 1772 as legally authoritative because that resolution was also legalistically adopted (even though that was not explicitly stated in the text of Resolution 1863).

Although Resolution 1863 provides an illustrative vignette of the central case of international law, a complete analysis of the process of decisionmaking around Resolution 1863 requires observing how other decisionmakers have interpreted and responded to its prescriptive claims. It is beyond the scope of this book to do so. However, in Chapter Six, a similar decision process involving and responding to Chapter VII resolutions is analyzed in detail in the context of the 1990 Gulf War, the 1999 NATO bombing of Serbia, and the 2003 invasion of Iraq.

B. International Court of Justice

The decisionmaking process of the ICJ is another illustration of the central case. The ICJ claims to issue legally authoritative decisions in accordance with its legalist process and based on legal reasoning. In its decisions, it accepts other prescriptions as lawful if they comply with shared expectations of appropriate conduct, most often, but not exclusively, expressed as laws. Parties in contentious disputes accept the ICJ's decisions as legally authoritative where the decision was based on accepted legalist reasoning or procedures; whether the parties comply is another matter entirely. It thus exhibits the central case characteristics. The unique legal nature of the ICJ is evident in its constitutional and procedural texts, its decisions, and the responses of governing elites to ICJ decisions.[74]

As stated earlier, the UN Charter recognizes the ICJ as its principal judicial organ.[75] Its ultimate claim to legal authority is thus derived from the Charter. However, the

[73] *Id.*

[74] *See generally* Robert Jennings, *The Role of the International Court of Justice*, 68 Brit. Y.B. Int'l L. 1 (1998) & sources cited at n.1 therein.

[75] *See* UN Charter, art. 92.

Statute of the ICJ also makes a claim to authority, by prescribing in detail the basis of its legal jurisdiction. Article 34 provides that only states may be parties in cases before the court.[76] Article 35 provides that the ICJ shall be open to any state party to the ICJ Statute.[77] Article 36 states the ICJ's authority in disputes. Its personal jurisdiction lies in the consent of state parties who subject themselves to the court's adjudication.[78] Its subject matter jurisdiction extends to treaty interpretation, any question of international law, the breach of an international obligation, or the nature of reparation for breach.[79] Article 65 provides that the court may give advisory opinions on any legal question at the request of bodies authorized to ask for a legal opinion.[80] Advisory opinions are therefore not obligatory in and of themselves, although they may indirectly claim to be authoritative by claiming to have identified authoritative legal prescriptions in their opinions.[81]

The ICJ Statute also claims to control the reasoning through which disputes are adjudicated. Article 38 requires the court to decide disputes in accordance with sources of prescriptions that Article 38 identifies principally as treaties, customs, and general principles of law.[82] The court may refer to judicial decisions and the teachings of the most highly qualified publicists as a subsidiary means of identifying prescriptions, which it characterizes as "rules of law."[83] Finally, Article 38 permits the court to decide *ex aequo et bono*, or according to the right and good, if the parties permit it to do so.[84]

In addition to the ICJ Statute, the ICJ has also issued Rules of Court and Practice Directions, which regulate the minutiae of court procedure, including the ceremonial declarations that judges have to incant on their election,[85] guidance that written pleadings should be concise,[86] and the methods by which written documents are to be provided to the court.[87]

Collectively, the texts of the ICJ communicate when and how it claims to be legally authoritative, the procedure that must be followed to make its adjudicatory or advisory legal prescriptions, and the methods of legalist reasoning used to reach its decisions. In general, parties before the ICJ and observers who are not parties tend to accept the ICJ's decision as expressing shared expectations of appropriate conduct

[76] Statute of the International Court of Justice art. June 34, 26, 1945, 33 U.N.T.S. 993 [hereinafter ICJ Statute].

[77] *See id.* art. 35.

[78] *See id.* art. 36(1).

[79] *See id.* art. 36(2).

[80] *See id.* art. 65.

[81] For a discussion of the procedures in an ICJ case, see BOWETT ET AL., *supra* note 18, at 1–20.

[82] *See* ICJ Statute, *supra* note 76, art. 38(1)(a)–(c).

[83] *See id.* art. 38(1)(d).

[84] *See id.* art. 38(2).

[85] *See* Rules of the International Court of Justice, 1978 I.C.J. Acts & Docs. 4, art. 40 (as amended Apr. 14, 2005).

[86] *See* I.C.J. Practice Directions, Practice Direction III (Order of Oct. 2001) (as amended Jan. 20, 2009).

[87] *See id.* at Practice Direction IX (Order of Oct. 2001) (as amended Jan. 20, 2009).

when the ICJ exhibits greatest fidelity to legalist reasoning and procedures and appropriately balances competing considerations. This is the central case of international law in the adjudicatory processes of the ICJ. As the Court departs from legalist reasoning and procedures, acceptance of its decisions tends to diminish, moving it decisions further from the central case.

The decisionmaking processes in international problems involving the ICJ are examined in detail in Chapter Seven, which studies the peaceful resolution of disputes in three ICJ cases.

C. Conclusions About Legalism

In summary, in the central case, such as in decisions by the ICJ and the UN Security Council, decisionmakers claim that their judgments and resolutions, respectively, are legally authoritative not simply because they are backed by power, are moral, or are expedient. Judges and permanent representatives of UN Security Council member states make decisions and prescribe legal outcomes through highly regularized procedures and practices designed to symbolically validate those decisions as legal or, at a minimum, consonant with the shared expectations of other elites and appropriate decisionmaking processes. Any departure from those procedures can render the outcomes less legal unless the departures are justified by reference to other procedural rules and practices permitting deviation. When decisionmakers invoke resolutions of the Security Council and decisions of the ICJ to empower or constrain actions, they communicate using a legalistic mode of reasoning, with a view of limiting the discretion of other actors in ignoring the claims of elites that those prescriptions create rights or obligations to act in a certain way. In general, governing elites and their constituencies accept that resolutions of the Security Council and the decisions of the ICJ in contentious disputes are legally authoritative, even if they choose to disobey them.

This is not to say that every claim to be legally authoritative counts as an international law or even a law-like prescription. The claim must be credibly justified, either explicitly or implicitly, by fidelity to accepted procedures for making prescriptions and accepted legalist reasoning for interpreting and applying them to facts. It is the shared belief in legalism, whether formally expressed as laws or informally as law-like prescriptions, that provides a basis for assessing how legal a claim is and, at the extremes, that a claim is not legal and entirely political.

This belief in legalism exists as a social fact. It is in a sense a functional myth. Bronislaw Malinowski has explained the meaning of functional myths at length, and not all the traits he ascribed to functional myths map perfectly to the myth of law. However, some traits are relevant. According to Malinowski, myth is "a pragmatic charter of primitive faith and moral wisdom."[88] It fulfills "an indispensable function: it expresses, enhances and codifies belief; it safeguards and enforces morality;

[88] Martin S. Day, The Many Meanings of Myth 251–52 (1984) (quoting Malinowski).

it vouches for the efficiency of ritual and contains practical rules for the guidance of man."[89] Conceived as myth, international law is based on a primitive faith that the legal procedures and legalistic reasoning create laws. These prescriptions may express moral values or coordinate action to facilitate international interactions,[90] which is the topic of the next part of this chapter. One of the key points of this book is that decisionmakers ought not to promote and obey international law simply because they believe in the myth, but because the myth serves a useful function and thereby justifies international law. This move from the mythological to the rational permits decisionmakers to appraise when, why, and the extent to which they should promote international law. This appraisal concerns international law's morality, which is addressed below.

IV. THE MORALITY OF INTERNATIONAL LAW

The explanation of the international legal system as social facts about shared expectations of appropriate conduct so far provides no explicit justification for an obligation to obey and promote it. However, the justification is embedded in its legalism, which creates a moral obligation to obey and promote international laws and law-like prescriptions.

As discussed above, in the central case, there are clearly articulated procedures for making laws and other prescriptions and widely accepted modes of legalist reasoning for interpreting them. The system of making and applying prescriptions, if obeyed, coordinates the conduct of decisionmakers and enhances global order, which is necessary for the common good, that is, conditions for constituents worldwide to reasonably optimize their preferred values. For practically reasonable decisionmakers and constituents, there is therefore a general moral obligation to obey and promote international law.

Importantly, however, this general moral obligation can be outweighed by specific countervailing moral considerations: in particular, international disputes. If legal obligations are nothing more or less than a special type of moral obligation to obey laws and other prescriptions, then legal obligations exist because it is moral to obey international law, albeit legal obligations should in some cases be ignored if other moral considerations outweigh the legal obligation.

The foregoing argument applies ideas about value, common good, and morality addressed in general legal jurisprudence to international law. It is therefore useful to

[89] *Id.*

[90] *See* Stephane Beaulac, The Power of Language in the Making of International Law 31 (2004) ("[M]yths are also powerful social productions, often themselves expressed through language, which provide a shared explanatory structure for the substantial areas of socially constructed reality."); *id.* at 41 (noting that "Philip Alott opined that law is nothing more, or less, than the continuing structure-system of human socializing"); *cf.* W. Michael Reisman, Systems of Control in International Adjudication and Arbitration: Breakdown and Repair 135 (1992) ("Modern law is increasingly a complex and nuanced social instrument designed to achieve a wide range of quite detailed social and economic objectives.").

explain each step of the argument, generally discussing the nature and relationships among value, morality, and justice and applying that discussion to international law.

A. Basic Values

Natural law theory postulates that there are basic general goods or values common to human beings.[91] "Good" is not used in its personal sense (I think this dish is good) but in a general sense (food is good). A personal sense of good may be an example of its general sense; however, where a personal sense of good contradicts the general sense, it does not necessarily invalidate it. (Hitler did not personally think the human dignity of Jews was good/valuable; yet the human dignity of Jews and all humans are nevertheless basic goods/values.)[92]

The claim that something is generally good does not mean it is in all situations good (food is good, too much food is bad) or that it trumps other goods in specific contexts (food is valuable; potable water on a desert island is more valuable). The values that this book is principally, although not exclusively, concerned about are order, i.e., avoiding destruction and harm from violence and promoting conditions necessary for international cooperation and competition; and dignity, i.e., maximizing the well-being of each human being consonant with the well-being of all other human beings.

Basic goods are self-evident to rational and reasonable human beings.[93] Jurists with different scholarly perspectives share this basic commitment. Myres McDougal and Harold Lasswell postulated that all human beings are concerned with human dignity.[94] Rosalyn Higgins agrees that there are "common values—values that speak to us all, whether we are rich or poor, black or white, of any religion or none, or come from countries that are industrialized or developing."[95] More recently, Mary Ellen O'Connell postulates that there are, across "diverse cultures . . . moral norms that we should commonly live by."[96]

Agreement about what constitutes basic goods or values is more difficult to obtain than agreement that there are basic values. In general jurisprudence, Finnis proposes that basic goods are life; knowledge; play; aesthetic experience; sociability; practical reasonableness; and "religion," or a belief in a divinity.[97] He explains that all of these seven basic goods are valuable in and of themselves, regardless of their

[91] Finnis, *supra* note 9, at 61 (1980).

[92] *Id.* at 61–62 (providing explanations of "good" and "value" that this book generally adopts).

[93] *Id.* at 69.

[94] Myres S. McDougal & Harold D. Lasswell, *Identification and Appraisal of Diverse Systems of Public Order, in* International Law Essays: A Supplement to International Law in Contemporary Perspective 15, 15 (McDougal & Reisman eds., 1981) [hereinafter McDougal & Lasswell, *Identification and Appraisal*].

[95] Rosalyn Higgins, Problems and Process: International Law and How We Use It 1–2 (1994) [hereinafter Higgins, Problems]; *id.* at 97 ("I believe, profoundly, in the universality of the human spirit.").

[96] Mary Ellen O'Connell, The Power & Purpose of International Law 370 (2008).

[97] Finnis, *supra* note 9, at 86–90.

instrumental value. In the international law context, McDougal and Lasswell postulated eight shared values: power, wealth, respect, well-being, skill, enlightenment, rectitude, and affection.[98] Some of McDougal and Lasswell's values map roughly with Finnis' values: life with well-being, friendship with affection (congeniality, freedom of choice of partner, and group affiliation), knowledge with enlightenment (transmission of information), and religion with rectitude (freedom of worship and religious propaganda).

Higgins, too, has a list:

> Individuals everywhere want the same essential things: to have sufficient food and shelter; to be able to speak freely; to practice their own religion or to abstain from religion belief; to feel that their person is not threatened by the state; to know that they will not be tortured; or detained without charge; and that, if charged, they will have a fair trial.[99]

More recently, O'Connell has proposed her list of common values. She subscribes to the basic good of religion or social value of rectitude when she states: "People everywhere . . . believe in higher things."[100] She specifies additional shared goals. These goals are: "peace, respect for human rights, prosperity, and the protection of the natural environment."[101]

Even Alexander Orakhelashvili, a positivist, accepts that values "possess certain normative relevance in the international legal system" and that they are "goals to be achieved."[102] He specifies as basic values: "peace and security," "sustainable development," "democracy and democratic society," "considerations of humanity," "security and survival of states."[103]

It is unnecessary to reconcile these different basic shared values, or to determine if there are other values that should be included or excluded, in order to make the argument that international law ought to matter in a general sense. Finnis concedes that there is no need to accept his list as exhaustive or definitive, and that other jurists may have different lists, or designate similar basic values with different words or nomenclature.[104] Here, if it were possible to prove that the values promoted in international law include an exhaustive list of basic values, this would make a stronger moral case to obey international law. However, even if that were not possible, so long as there are some values that all readers agree are basic values, this is a sufficient basis to reason that a system that promotes those values ought to be followed in the absence of stronger moral reasons not to do so.

98 Harold D. Lasswell & Myres S. McDougal, Jurisprudence for a Free Society 375–86 (1992) [hereinafter Lasswell & McDougal, Jurisprudence]; McDougal & Lasswell, *Identification and Appraisal, supra* note 94, at 25–26.

99 Higgins, Problems, *supra* note 95.

100 O'Connell, *supra* note 96, at 370.

101 *Id.*

102 Orakhelashvili, Interpretation, *supra* note 11, at 180.

103 *Id.* at 181–94.

104 Finnis, *supra* note 9, at 92.

It appears self-evident and consistent with many of the values that other scholars have specified that life (or well-being), freedom, sociability (or friendship), and wealth are basic values that all human beings value, even though they may value other goods as well, and they may prioritize their values differently. However, even if the reader disagrees that there are basic goods, or that the values specified below are fundamentally important, and has her own basic goods, the account of international law developed here may still be justificatory, so long as the common good, as explained below,[105] is necessary to secure those basic goods.

Life refers not only to living but to every aspect of well-being necessary for personal self-determination. This includes health, the minimization of pain and physical hurt, and the enjoyment of living. Basic conditions for life are a roof over our heads, food on our tables, and clothes on our back. Health care and education are also important. It seems difficult to dispute that everyone would want life, so conceived.[106]

Freedom is another basic good. It entails the liberty to pursue other values, to prioritize some values over others, to make choices and decisions, and to adopt or reject spiritual beliefs (religion or rectitude). Debates about freedom, of course, are not about whether freedom in the abstract is good. They are often discussions about what sorts of freedoms matter more than others, how best to promote the preferred freedoms, and how much freedom an individual or community should have without unduly limiting the freedoms of others.

Sociability is related to life and freedom. Humans are social creatures, and without community or personal bonds to other human beings, the enjoyment of life is curtailed. Nobody wants other people around them all the time, and some persons might not want anyone around them at any time, but every human being wants to be able to form social bonds of friendship, marriage, and family should he desire such bonds. It is in these senses that sociality is a basic good.[107]

Finally, it seems difficult to dispute that people everywhere would prefer to be wealthy than not. We would all want more resources, whether in the form of capital, income, or other assets: to acquire other possessions we desire or need, to pass onto our children, or to trade with others.

B. Moral Obligations

Basic values or goods do not, in themselves, entail any assertion about morality. According to Finnis:

> The principles that express the general ends of human life do not acquire what would nowadays be called a 'moral' force until they are brought to bear upon definite

[105] *Infra* pt. IV.B.

[106] Finnis, *supra* note 9, at 86–87; McDougal & Lasswell, Id*entification and Appraisal, supra* note 94, at 25–26, 37.

[107] *See* Finnis, *supra* note 9, at 88; McDougal & Lasswell, Id*entification and Appraisal, supra* note 94, at 38.

ranges of project, disposition or action, or upon particular projects, dispositions or actions.[108]

In other words, morality is a reasoned appraisal of action that has consequences for basic values.[109] For example, consider the following: Life is a basic good, but it is not in itself moral or immoral. Because life is good, killing is generally immoral and ought not to be done, unless there is an overriding moral reason to do so, such as in the case of inadvertently killing an attacker in proportionate self-defense.

This definition of morality does not permit capricious views of appropriate and inappropriate conduct to masquerade as morality. Admittedly, the precise contours of morality are not sharply delineated, and its application to facts can lead to differing moral judgments. However, the method of moral debate is rational and involves practical reasoning from basic values common to all humans, and not just some narrow community.[110] A purely subjective impulse of personal "conscience," so to speak, is not moral reasoning;[111] and what Tom Tyler has termed "personal morality" is not morality at all if it is subjective or irrational, at least under the conception of morality adopted in this book.[112]

The appraisal of action or a decision to act by connecting facts to basic values through reasoning permits moral judgments about the application of international legal prescriptions for disputes.[113] The UN Charter prohibits the use of military force against another state[114] unless in self-defense.[115] Because life is good, unilaterally launching a military attack on another state is generally immoral because people will die. It may, however, be moral if there are overriding moral reasons to do so, such

108 FINNIS, *supra* note 9, at 101.

109 *Cf.* JOSEPH RAZ, *supra* note 10, at 15–16 ("Reasons are referred to in explaining, in evaluating, and in guiding people's behaviour."). *But cf.* TERRY NARDIN, LAW, MORALITY, AND THE RELATIONS OF STATES 224–25 (1983) (clarifying that "the words 'morality' and 'morals' are used differently in different contexts," and explaining morality as "an authoritative practice, and moral conduct is conduct that conforms to its standards").

110 *See* PRACTICAL REASONING: READINGS IN PHILOSOPHY 5 (Joseph Raz ed., 1978) (stating that practical reasoning "is the transition (not necessarily conscious) from belief in the premises to acceptance of the putative conclusion of a practical inference").

111 This view of morality is different than that advanced by Hersch Lauterpacht, who stated that "morality operates within the realm of conscience," as opposed to law, which in his Austinian account is "command made effective, if necessary, by external compulsion." 1 HERSCH LAUTERPACHT, INTERNATIONAL LAW 46 (1970).

112 TOM TYLER, WHY PEOPLE OBEY THE LAW 3–4 (1990). *See also* DWORKIN, *supra* note 8, at 97 (identifying "the 'popular morality' of a community" as "the set of opinions about justice and other political and personal virtues that are held as matters of personal conviction by most of the members of that community, or perhaps of some moral elite within it"); Harry Wellington, *Common Law Rules and Constitutional Double Standards: Some Notes on Adjudication*, 83 YALE L.J. 221, 244 (1973) (defining "conventional morality" from HART, *supra* note 14, at 162–63 as "standard of conduct . . . which are widely shared in a particular society").

113 *Cf.* RAZ, *supra* note 10, at 18 (stating that reasons "determine what ought to be done").

114 UN Charter art. 2, ¶ 4.

115 UN Charter art. 51.

as in proportionate self-defense against an attacking state, in order to protect one's own constituents.

This analysis, however, only addresses the morality of the use of force in a particular dispute. It goes no further than John Bolton's position that international law is "a series of political and moral arrangements that stand or fall on their own merits,"[116] or Eric Posner and Jack Goldsmith's assertion that the "morality or immorality of international law is exhausted by its content; international legality does not impose any moral obligations."[117]

A thought experiment illustrates this point. Imagine that there was no law regulating recourse to force, but the supreme religious leader of Iran made a political decision not to unilaterally attack Israel. That decision, although political and not legal, would be just as moral because it was a practically reasonable act to respect the value of life. In the real world, however, there is a law prohibiting force except in self-defense. Suppose that the supreme leader decided to obey the law and not attack Israel. The substantive morality or legitimacy of his action as derived by reasoning practically from the value of life remains unchanged. Thus, the moral argument made so far does not address whether international law is moral because it is law, independently of the content of prescriptions and their application to disputes.

In order to determine whether a prescription has a general morality independently of its content, it is necessary to turn to the idea of the common good. Finnis points out that there are different meanings to common good. Every basic value is a common good because they are good for all human beings, and each human being can potentially attain every basic value. But the sense in which the common good is used for present purposes is different. The common good is:

> a set of conditions which enables the members of a community to attain for themselves reasonable objectives, or to realize reasonably for themselves the value(s), for the sake of which they have to collaborate with each other (positively and/or negatively) in a community.[118]

Finnis clarifies that this conception of the common good does not require each member of the community to have the same personal values or objectives. It only requires that there must be a set of conditions—the common good—that permits each member to attain his objectives.[119]

[116] John Bolton, *Is there Really "Law" in International Affairs*, 10 Transnat'l L. & Contemp. Probs. 1, 48 (2000).

[117] Jack L. Goldsmith & Eric A. Posner, The Limits of International Law 197 (2005). *See also* Lauterpacht, *supra* note 111, at 46 ("In the first instance, like any other law, international law is to a large extent the expression of dictates of morality.").

[118] Finnis, *supra* note 9, at 155.

[119] *Id.* at 156. *See also* Lon Fuller, The Morality of Law 183 (Revised ed. 1969) (arguing that "we should aspire to enlarge that community at every opportunity and to include within it ultimately, if we can, all men of good will").

In the international context, the common good allows every constituent worldwide to reasonably pursue basic values that all human beings want.[120] Conditions of common good include peace;[121] arrangements that permit economic and other forms of cooperation, as well as competition; and respect for certain essential human rights.[122] In order to promote and pursue values, decisionmakers have to collaborate in many ways, such as agreeing not to attack each other, taking turns to use shipping and air lanes, protecting foreigners who visit a state, permitting bank transfers of money across borders, cooperating to apprehend criminals and terrorists, and so on.[123] So conceived, the common good is another way of expressing minimum world order.

If it is moral to comply with prescriptions independent of their content, it is because the international legal system is an appropriate method of promoting the common good.[124] As Christopher Weeramantry, the former vice president of the International Court of Justice, has explained, international law "provides the foundations of . . . world order."[125] Whatever one thinks about world order, such as it is, at a minimum, international law is a system that exists for solving international coordination problems for the common good. As the survey in Chapter Two

[120] *See* President Barack Obama, Speech to the United Nations General Assembly (Sept. 24, 2009) ("[I]t is my deeply held belief that in the year 2009—more than at any point in human history—the interests of nations and peoples are shared.").

[121] *See* C.G. Weeramantry, Universalising International Law 329 (2004) ("Peace is the paramount objective of international law.").

[122] *Cf.* Thomas M. Franck, Fairness in International Law and Institutions 7 (1995) [hereinafter Franck, Fairness] ("[P]eople expect more than food. They expect peace, good order, security, and to be free of the stress of perpetual revolution, even if that revolution has benevolent redistributive intent."); President Obama, *supra* note 120 ("Today, let me put forward four pillars that I believe are fundamental to the future that we want for our children: non-proliferation and disarmament; the promotion of peace and security; the preservation of our planet; and a global economy that advances opportunity for all people.").

[123] Parenthetically, justice, then, is simply a theory about how to allocate resources and correct conduct, in order to promote optimal conditions for the common good. *See* Finnis, *supra* note 9, at 164–93. It is unnecessary here, however, to develop a theory of justice in order to explain the general morality of complying with international laws.

[124] *See, e.g.*, Jan Paulsson, John E.C. Brierley Memorial Lecture at McGill University, Montreal: *International Arbitration is Not Arbitration* (May 28, 2008) (quoting from the U.S. President's transmission to the Senate regarding accession to the New York Convention on the Recognition and Enforcement of Foreign Arbitral Awards. The transmission noted that the Convention "contributes in many ways to the promotion of international trade and investment. For example, it provides greater flexibility for the arranging of business transactions abroad; . . . and it strengthens the concept of safeguarding private rights in foreign transactions"); Weeremantry, *supra* note 121, at 43 ("[T]he process of international adjudication is a valuable safety valve which has on many an occasion helped avert conflict and maintain international peace."). *Cf.* Abram Chayes, *A Common Lawyer Looks at International Law,* 78 Harv. L. Rev. 1396, 1413 (1965) ("The appeal to rationality and order depends on a perception of common values and common interests."). Although the effectiveness of the appeal to rationality and order depends on perceptions of a common good, the moral argument made here does not depend on those perceptions, because the morality of international law is not contingent on its effectiveness.

[125] Weeramantry, *supra* note 121, at 38.

showed, since antiquity, the international legal system provided a means of dispute resolution among states, including diplomacy and peace agreements among states, that reduced the recourse to war, which often all but destroys the common good because war threatens basic values.[126] International law also provides a means of establishing diplomatic relations that enable trade and other cross-border economic exchanges to occur peacefully.[127] These features of the international legal system that support the common good exist regardless of whether a prescription in an international dispute emphasizes values pursued by one set of constituents over another.[128]

Studies of why states comply with international law also reveal how the international legal system promotes coordination for the common good. Abram and Antonia Chayes identify three reasons why there is a propensity to comply with international law. First, it is efficient to follow prior legal decisions about appropriate conduct because making new decisions incurs costs of decisionmaking and deliberation. Second, treaties are bargained-for exchanges in which treaty parties have allocated and exchanged resources according to their preferred values, and so there is a tendency to abide by those exchanges. Third, people "whether as a result of socialization or otherwise—accept that they are obliged to obey the law."[129]

The third observation, to the extent to which it refers to the unquestioning belief in obligations as a result of socialization, does not provide a reason to obey international laws. The first two observations, however, explain how the international legal system promotes the common good and provide practical reasons why that system is a desirable or appropriate method of solving coordination problems that must be overcome to promote the common good.[130] International relations are highly complex processes, and constituencies worldwide are highly interdependent for trade, finance, mutual defense, and social and cultural interactions. Therefore, coordination can only be achieved through a high level of deference to international laws and law-like prescriptions, and there is accordingly a fairly weighty moral obligation to comply with them and to promote the international legal system.[131]

[126] *Supra* ch. 2, pt. II.

[127] *Id.*

[128] *See* Shabtai Rosenne, Practice and Methods of International Law 2 (1984) (explaining that international law is a "law of coordination" in which "it is created and applied by its own subjects, primarily independent states (directly or indirectly), for their own common purposes") *Cf.* Daniel Bodansky, *The Legitimacy of International Governance: a Coming Challenge for International Environmental Law*, 93 Am. J. Int'l L. 596 (1999) (discussing the extents to which consent or democracy provide bases for international law's legitimacy).

[129] Abram Chayes & Antonia Handler Chayes, The New Sovereignty: Compliance with International Regulatory Agreements 8 (1995).

[130] *See also* Finnis, *supra* note 9, at 243 (arguing that customary international law creates legal obligations only if there is a practical judgment that the process of creating customary laws "is a desirable or appropriate method of solving interaction or co-ordination problems in the international community").

[131] *See generally id.* at 319 (explaining that because law can only succeed in regulating complex social interactions "inasmuch as individuals drastically restrict the occasion on which they trade off their legal obligations against their individual convenience or conceptions of social good," there is a "relatively weighty" moral obligation to obey law); Fuller, *supra* note 119, at 30 (explaining

Louis Henkin also identified reasons why states observe international law. He explained:

> Nations have a common interest in keeping the society running and keeping international relations orderly. They observe laws they do not care about to maintain others which they value, and to keep "the system" intact; they observe law when it "hurts" so that others will observe laws to their benefit.[132]

The practical reasons identified by Henkin and Chayes relating to the common good make it generally moral to comply with international laws and prescriptions.

International law positivists also identify ways that international law coordinates international relations for the common good. Alexander Orakhelashvili explains that international law creates "reliability in international dealings" and "promote[s] international cooperation."[133]

The inquiry can be pushed further by asking how it is that legalism creates reliability and orderliness in international relations. Thomas Franck's research into legitimacy in international law provides a more granular explanation of how legalism maintains the stability and manages the change that Henkin, Chayes, and Orakhelashvili identify as necessary for the common good.[134] In Franck's view, stability is maintained through "textual determinacy," that is, laws have "a readily accessible meaning,"[135] which thereby "are more likely to have a real impact on conduct."[136] Textual determinacy is achieved through legalist reasoning because legalism restricts the range of meanings in text, ensuring predictability in how the prescription will be interpreted and applied in international disputes. This contributes to perceptions by governing elites and constituents that international law is fair

morality of law as the morality of duty "to maintain the integrity of its domain and to protect that domain from the erosions threatened by a view that attempts to solve too many simultaneous equations at once"). *See also* Thomas Burgenthal, *Proliferation of International Courts and Tribunals: Is It Good or Bad?*, 14 LEIDEN J. INT'L L. 267, 270 (2001) ("Globalization and privatization can function effectively only within the legal infrastructure consistent of an amalgam of different national and international laws and institutions . . . ."); Senate Testimony of John B. Bellinger, III, Legal Advisor, Dep't of State, Apr. 15, 2008 at 3, 110th Cong. Rec. 2007–2008 (stating that ratifying treaties encourages other states to also ratify, "with the result that overall implementation of and compliance with these norms will improve over time, which ultimately helps to protect our forces").

132 LOUIS HENKIN, HOW NATIONS BEHAVE: LAW AND FOREIGN POLICY 48 (1968).

133 ORAKHELASHVILI, *supra* note 11, at 491. *See also* Theodor Meron, *Judicial Independence and Impartiality in International Criminal Tribunals*, 99 AM. J. INT'L L. 359, 359 (2005) (stating that "predictability allows the political and economic actors to plan their behavior accordingly, contributing greatly to the political stability and economic prosperity of a society").

134 FRANCK, FAIRNESS, *supra* note 122, at 11 ("The laws in a community thus evince not only the generally held belief that each must do what he or she is legally required to do, but also that each will discharge towards all others those obligations arising from the shared moral sense.").

135 *Id.* at 30–34; FRANCK, POWER, *supra* note 31, at 50–66. *See also* ORAKHELASHVILI, *supra* note 11, at 584 (stating that the ultimate purpose of strict textual interpretations is to "ensure the effectiveness of legal regulation").

136 FRANCK, FAIRNESS, *supra* note 122, at 31.

because they can understand the prescription and anticipate the outcome it mandates,[137] and such determinacy enables them to plan their activities.[138]

Legalism also promotes the common good by rendering laws and other prescriptions coherent. If governing elites, including legal advisors and judges, apply legalist procedures and reasoning equally to all prescriptions in all disputes, the interpretation and application of prescriptions will be more consistent and international relations will be more stable,[139] thereby permitting elites to engage in international activities in the pursuit of their respective preferred values. Even where a prescription is interpreted to require different outcomes in different situations, factual differences between the situations must be explained according to legalist principles as supplying rational reasons to differentiate between the disputes. Additionally, prescriptions must be interpreted as a whole, so that each is given meaning and they are all harmonized.[140] Legalism so conceived reduces subjectivity, fears that political interests have caused arbitrary distinctions between disputes or constituents, and confusion about apparent contradictions among legal prescriptions.[141]

Franck's final reason for international law's legitimacy is what he calls "adherence."[142] Whereas coherence refers to the consistent application of prescriptions horizontally among disputes, adherence ensures that prescriptions are created, modified, and terminated in accord with established procedures or secondary rules, in H. L. A. Hart's terminology. Adherence thus manages change in international law in an orderly fashion, thereby maintaining stability and minimizing arbitrary alterations to laws.[143] Fidelity to legalist procedures thus improves international law's ability to coordinate governing elites in an orderly fashion for the common good.

Accordingly, these qualities of determinacy, coherence, and adherence not only enable the international legal system to promote the common good, they also do so in a manner that is more fair by ensuring that rules are applied consistently and that

[137] *Id.* at 33.

[138] *See* Stephen M. Schwebel, *Reflections on the Role of the International Court of Justice, Jurisprudential Lecture at the University of Washington*, 61 Wash. L. Rev. 1061, 1068 (1985) ("[P]eaceful settlement on the basis of law builds expectations of consistency and stability in international life.").

[139] *See* Marrakesh Agreement Establishing the World Trade Organization annex 2, art. 3(2), Apr. 15, 1994, 33 I.L.M. 1144, 1238 (1994) [hereinafter DSU art. 21.3] (noting that dispute resolution in accord with WTO laws provide "security and predictability to the multilateral trading system").

[140] Luiz Olavo Baptista, *Interpretiton and Application of WTO Rules: Florentiono Feliciano and the First Seven, in* Law in the Service of Human Dignity: Essays in Honour of Florentino Feliciano 127, 134 (Charnovitz et al. eds., 2005) (citing Appellate Body Report, *Korea- Definitive Safeguard Measure on Imports of Certain Dairy Products*, ¶ 81, WT/DS98/AB/R (Jan. 12, 2000)) (stating that international law requires interpreting "all applicable provisions of a treaty in a way that gives meaning to all of them, harmoniously").

[141] Franck, Fairness, *supra* note 122, at 38–41; Franck, Power, *supra* note 31, at 150–82. *See also* Dworkin, *supra* note 8, at 190–92 (arguing that law which has integrity, Dworkin's synonym for coherence, "has a better case for legitimacy than one that does not").

[142] Franck, Power, *supra* note 31, at 183–94. Franck also argued that symbolic validation increases legitimacy. *Id.* at 91–134. However, although symbolic validation may increase perceptions of legitimacy, this is a psychological attitude rather than a rational moral judgment.

[143] Franck, Fairness, *supra* note 122, at 41–46.

change to rules is carried out in an orderly manner.[144] For these reasons, the international legal system is at present a useful system to promote the common good of worldwide constituents.[145] This connection with the common good creates a general moral obligation on governing elites to comply with and promote international law through legalism and legalist procedures.[146]

C. Realist Critiques

Realists may oppose the argument that there is a moral obligation to obey and promote international law because it provides a system to promote the common good in order to permit communities to pursue basic goods for themselves. Jack Goldsmith and Eric Posner offer a counterargument that when states act consistently with international law, they have made a "prudential decision" to do so out of self-interest. They have not complied with international law because of their moral obligation to do so.[147]

Admittedly, it is possible in theory to semantically insist on a distinction between prudence and morality. Rationalists could argue that just because there are rational reasons to promote the "common good" through international law in order to overcome coordination problems that would otherwise plague everyone, this rational reason does not therefore become a moral one. However, even if this argument were accepted, it does not undermine the argument here that there are good reasons to obey international law because it is the best system to solve coordination problems.

But, in any event, the realist argument should be rejected. The semantic distinction between prudence and morality is analytically unhelpful and perhaps conceptually unsound. There is no reason why prudent actions cannot also be moral. In any event, at a minimum, in order to differentiate between a reason to act because it promotes personal preferences (self-interest) and a reason to act because it promotes the common good (collective interests), it is useful to designate the latter as a special type of rational reason by calling it a moral reason. It also stands to reason that because the common good is necessary to promote basic values for everyone,

[144] *Cf.* Lauterpacht, *supra* note 111, at 47 ("For the occasional rigidity of the law, although it may result in hardship in individual cases, is, like law itself, part of the moral order of society.").

[145] 1 James Brown Scott, Law, the State, and the International Community 8 (2002) (citing Cicero as stating "Ubi societas, ibi ius" (where there is society there must be law)); Philip C. Jessup, A Modern Law of Nations 3 (1959) ("Law is indeed a human necessity. . . . Law must govern world relationships if they are to be peaceful[.]"); Jan Paulsson, *Moral Hazard in International Dispute Resolution*, Inaugural Lecture at University of Miami School of Law (Apr. 29, 2010), *available at* http://www.artbitrationicca.org/media/0/12773749999020/paulsson_moral_hazard.pdf. (noting that "common objectives can be more effectively pursued" when "our institutions are legitimate").

[146] *See* Fuller, *supra* note 122, at 96 (describing the inner morality of law as a "procedural version of natural law"). *See also* Charles Brower, *The Ethics of Arbitration: Perspectives from a Practicing International Arbitrator*, Keynote Address at the Riesenfeld Symposium, *in* 5 Berkeley J. Int'l L. Publicist 1, 1 (2010) (noting that "ethics and transparency better ensure legitimacy—general public acceptance that any rule-based system is authoritative and binding").

[147] Goldsmith & Posner, *supra* note 117, at 192–93.

including states' constituents, there is a basis to make the normative or moral claim that governing elites *ought* to promote the common good, and not simply that they can be expected as rational actors to do so.

Consider the three reasons that Andrew Guzman, who agrees with the rational choice assumptions that Posner and Goldsmith make,[148] identifies for why states comply with international law. First, compliance bolsters a state's reputation for compliance and enables it to bargain more effectively in future disputes.[149] It also "makes [the state's] promises more credible and, therefore, makes future cooperation both easier and less costly."[150] Second, noncompliance risks reciprocal noncompliance by other states, such as withdrawals from treaties.[151] Third, noncompliance encourages retaliation in the form of economic, diplomatic, and military sanctions.[152] Guzman essentially argues that these three reasons make international law effective, without necessarily making it moral.[153]

Although Guzman rightly explains that the importance of reputation, reciprocity, and retaliation promotes the self-interests of states, and thus they rationally provide reasons for compliance, the three "R's" also provide moral reasons for complying with international law because they individually and collectively promote coordination in the common good. Compliance that bolsters reputation not only decreases the costs for the complying elite in negotiating future agreements, it decreases costs for its bilateral and multilateral elites in those agreements as well, because they can trust the elite with a good reputation and can enter into agreements with it more easily. This reduces transaction costs overall, leaving more net resources for everyone to further promote basic values. Thus, it is in the common good for a governing elite to have a strong reputation for compliance. Regarding reciprocity, a complying governing elite increases the likelihood that other elites will reciprocally comply, thus making coordination more effective, which is in the common good. As Guzman points out, retaliation is not a cost-free enterprise.[154] It imposes costs on both the elite sanctioned and the elite imposing the sanction. Given that global resources are

[148] Andrew T. Guzman, *The Promise of International Law*, 92 VA. L. REV. 533, 534 (2006) (reviewing GOLDSMITH & POSNER, *supra* note 117) ("I agree with the basic assumptions made in [*The Limits of International Law*] [.]").

[149] HENKIN, *supra* note 132, at 48 ("Every nation's foreign policy depends substantially on its 'credit,'—on maintaining the expectation that it will live up to international mores and obligations.").

[150] ANDREW T. GUZMAN, HOW INTERNATIONAL LAW WORKS: A RATIONAL CHOICE THEORY 33 (2007). *See also* HENKIN, *supra* note 132, at 48 ("Nations generally desire a reputation for principled behavior, for propriety and respectability.").

[151] GUZMAN, *supra* note 150, at 33. *See also* JOHN YOO, WAR BY OTHER MEANS 68 (2006) ("Reciprocity is an important principle at work in law and policy.").

[152] GUZMAN, *supra* note 150, at 33–34. *See also* O'CONNELL, *supra* note 96, at 229–94 (describing unilateral and collective countermeasures as a contemporary form of regulated retaliation).

[153] Guzman, *supra* note 150, at 35 ("[T]he assumption of rational states is entirely consistent with a world in which international law constrains state conduct in important ways, including ways that Goldsmith and Posner explicitly reject.").

[154] GUZMAN, *supra* note 150, at 32–33.

scarce, it is preferable to all constituents not to use resources to rectify deviating conduct through sanctions. Therefore, compliance that makes sanctions unnecessary is in the common good. Accordingly, reputation, reciprocity, and retaliation do not only explain compliance. Practical reasoning reveals that they also supply moral reasons to comply with international law.

Further, even if governing elites are motivated by self-interest when they comply with international law, that does not negate the moral obligation to do so. The source of the moral obligation is practical reasoning from basic values and the common good. It is contingent neither on whether elites comply with or ignore international law, nor on whether elites comply with international law because they recognize their moral obligation to do so or purely out of self-interest.

Leaving aside the flawed argument that elites act in self-interest, and therefore there is no moral obligation to comply with international law, critics of international law make a better normative argument that international law has no moral content as law because it is not a desirable or appropriate method of solving international coordination problems. For example, Goldsmith and Posner distinguish between the moral obligation to "promote the good of all individuals in the world" and "the moral obligation to comply with international law." They reject the latter by hypothesizing:

> In our world, we cannot say that if a particular state complies with international law—regardless of the normative value of the law, regardless of what other states do, and maybe regardless of the interests of its own citizens—or even treated compliance as a presumptive duty, the world would be a "better place."[155]

This argument merely knocks down a straw man. The argument in support of a moral obligation to obey and promote international law does not claim that the international legal system maximizes international coordination or the common good. Such a claim would be false because the international legal system is deficient in many ways. However, this claim need not be made in order to support the morality of complying with international laws and prescriptions.

The argument is simply that there is a general moral obligation to comply with international laws and prescriptions because the international legal system addresses coordination problems by providing an accepted and understood method of making and anticipating decisions in each international dispute, and that system permits governing elites to reach bargained-for exchanges through treaties, which all promote the common good.[156] Because of this, and because there is no other worldwide

[155] Goldsmith & Posner, *supra* note 117, at 197.

[156] *See* Condoleezza Rice, U.S. Sec'y of State, Remarks at the 99th Annual Meeting of the American Society of International Law (Apr. 1, 2005), *reported in* 21:3 Am. Soc'y Int'l L. Newsletter 7 (May/July 2005) ("When we observe our treaties and other international commitments, other country—other countries are more willing to cooperate with us and we have a better chance of persuading them to live up to their own commitments. And so, when we respect our international

system of coordination beyond the international legal system—as broadly defined in this book—it is moral to comply with and promote prescriptions and the international legal process for their creation, interpretation, and application. Nothing in this argument claims that international law always makes the world a better place, which is too tall an order.

In other words, Goldsmith and Posner's views should prevail against a claim that there is always an overriding moral obligation to obey international law because it is untrue that international law always makes the world a better place. However, their argument does not prevail against the claim that is made in this book: that international law carries with it some moral obligation to comply with it, even if the weight of that obligation is not always established in the abstract. Their argument also fails to establish that there is never a moral obligation to obey international law. Neither does their argument show that the general morality of complying with international law to promote the common good should not conclusively guide the actions of elites in disputes where the content of a relevant prescription is morally neutral. In sum, whether or not the general moral obligation to obey international law ought to guide action in an international dispute depends on the particulars of that dispute, and a decisionmaker should balance his general moral obligation to promote international law with the specific morality of applying or ignoring a relevant prescription in that dispute.

D. Liberal Critique

Liberals may also criticize the account of international law's inherent morality as too thin. Some academics wish to expand human rights to claims that are not universally accepted, such as emphasizing some civil and political rights, gay rights, and certain forms of democracy, as well as prohibiting the death penalty and cruel and inhuman treatment. The argument that the moral obligation to obey international law stems from its unique ability to solve coordination problems and create conditions necessary for communities to cooperate and compete does not go far enough to promote their agenda. The liberal argument is that morality is not simply the obligation to promote the common good. It is instead the obligation to conform to standards of accepted conduct.[157] Therefore, for example, if it is unacceptable to deny gays their equal rights to marriage, international law ought to protect gay rights, and the moral obligation to do so is not contingent upon the common good.

The author is sympathetic to many human rights that remain contested globally, including most of those described in the paragraph above. He is also in principle

law obligations and support an international system based on the role of law, we do the work of making the world a better place, [and making the United States] a more secure place[.]").

[157] *See* Ratner, *supra* note 3 at 30–31 (noting that "cosmopolitans" "focus on the limits of diversity," and "[c]osmopolitan scholars are committed to justice based on equal moral concern for individuals everywhere, regardless of whether the individual is in one's community or in another community").

committed to the ideal of optimum world order. However, liberal arguments tend to inadequately address difficulties in determining standards of accepted conduct, especially where two or more human rights are in conflict with each other in a given situation. According to Terry Nardin, morality based on accepted conduct relates to the "standards of conduct by which the acts and character of the members of a particular community are judged."[158] In international relations, the diversity of viewpoints about contested human rights norms often precludes, as a factual matter, shared expectations about global standards of conduct relating to those rights.[159] Therefore, while it is possible to assert values and their prioritization when they conflict with each other, it is often difficult to prove those assertions and to argue accordingly that that there are moral obligations to promote and obey international prescriptions favoring those prioritizations.

There are only a small handful of values and standards of conduct shared globally, such as the universal condemnation of genocide and torture as wholly incompatible to the basic good of life, as well as the shared commitment to the common good to enable communities and individuals to reasonably pursue their preferred values. Beyond those most basic values and standards of conduct, the international legal system's legalist reasoning and accepted procedures are a method for decisionmakers to negotiate on behalf of their constituents international standards of conduct that may reflect a diversity of viewpoints rather than cultural or ideological homogeneity.[160]

Even if liberals do not accept the supposedly thin conception of morality of international law presented here, they may accept the overall account of international law because it requires decisionmakers to balance against the general morality of international law the impact of any legalist interpretation of prescriptions on basic goods preferred by constituents and other communities. This moral calculus requires elites to give some weight to human rights, although the weight that decisionmakers give to contested rights may be less than proponents of those rights would want.

E. Legal Obligations

Having explained why it is generally moral to comply with international law (in the sense that there are moral reasons to do so), it is now possible to explain why international legal prescriptions impose legal obligations to comply. A legal obligation is commonly said to exist when a legal prescription exists. However, the fact that a legal prescription has been created in accord with legalist procedures and reasoning does

[158] Nardin, *supra* note 109, at 225.

[159] *See id.* at 305 ("Shared beliefs, values, and purposes can provide the basis of association only where they exist."). *See also* Chayes, *supra* note 124, at ("The appeal to rationality and order depends on a perception of common values and common interests.").

[160] *See* Nardin, *supra* note 109, at 323 ("International law, and especially customary international law, embodies the minimum principles of mutual accommodation required for the coexistence not only of separate states but of different *kinds* of states.") (emphasis in original).

not, without more, explain why there is a moral obligation to obey the prescription. If legal obligations are special moral obligations relating to law,[161] then further explanation is required.

An answer can be derived from the practical judgment that international law is an appropriate or desirable system to achieve international coordination necessary for the common good, and this answer provides a reason why legal obligations exist as moral obligations. It does not, however, explain how to identify when there is a legal obligation. This practical judgment can apply specifically to laws and other prescriptions. In that form, it is a judgment that legalist procedures and reasoning are appropriate or desirable ways to derive prescriptions and thereby promote coordination for the common good. It flows from that judgment that there is a moral obligation or, more specifically, a legal obligation to obey prescriptions created by such legalism.

This practical reasoning applies to treaties. The VCLT creates rules to recognize when agreements are binding treaties. It contains basic rules that states may freely enter into binding bargains,[162] and make their intentions concrete through the plain and ordinary meanings of words in light of the objects and purposes of the treaty.[163] It is necessary to have rules to enable treaties to be made and interpreted, and these rules are as good as any. Therefore, the law of treaties is moral, and there is a legal obligation to obey the legalist rules on making and applying treaties because these rules enable coordination for the common good.[164]

Finnis makes a similar argument about customary law. Customary international laws are widely accepted as legal prescriptions supported by widespread state practice and *opinio juris*, or a belief that there is a legal rule mandating that practice.[165] By combining the practical judgment that "it is desirable that in this domain there be some determinate, common, stable pattern of conduct and corresponding

[161] Finnis, *supra* note 9, at 318 (stating "moral theorem . . . that one of the forms of moral obligation is legal obligation").

[162] VCLT, *supra* note 25, arts. 26 & 51.

[163] *Id.* art 31(1).

[164] Franck, Fairness, *supra* note 122, at 42 ("[S]tates regard themselves as bound by their treaty commitments, whether or not they are parties to the Vienna Convention, because they recognize that their obligation to act in accordance with those commitments derives not from their specific consent to the secondary rule of recognition, but rather from their membership of a community of which the sanctity of treaty obligations is the normative cornerstone.").

[165] ICJ Statute, *supra* note 76, art. 38(1) ("The Court, whose function is to decide in accordance with international law such disputes as are submitted to it, shall apply:

a. international conventions, whether general or particular, establishing rules expressly recognized by the contesting states;

b. international custom, as evidence of a general practice accepted as law;

c. the general principles of law recognized by civilized nations;

d. subject to the provisions of Article 59, judicial decisions and the teachings of the most highly qualified publicists of the various nations, as subsidiary means for the determination of rules of law.

2. This provision shall not prejudice the power of the Court to decide a case *ex aequo et bono*, if the parties agree thereto.").

authoritative rule" with the practical judgment that "the emergence and recognition of customary rules [according to the two legalist criteria] is [*sic*] a desirable or appropriate method of solving international and co-ordination problems," a practically reasonable basis for complying with customary law is provided. This argument instantiates the moral and legal obligation that attaches to customary laws identified through accepted legalist procedures and reasoning.[166]

Jus cogens are also accommodated within the rubric of practical reasoning specified here. Formally speaking, *jus cogens* are preemptory norms that override contradictory treaty provisions and customary laws.[167] They are universal in character and binding on all governing elites, regardless of whether the elites consented to them.[168] There is only a limited set of *jus cogens* that prohibit the most heinous conduct, such as genocide, torture, and slavery.[169] Alexander Orakhelashvili and Larry May both argue that the source of *jus cogens* is morality.[170]

That is well and good, but how do the moral obligations to abide by *jus cogens* transform into legal obligations? An answer could be that *jus cogens* impose overriding moral obligations to obey them because they are directed at behavior that causes direct and irreparable harm to either basic values or the common good. It is necessary to have some way of identifying *jus cogens*, so that it is not left to the personal caprices or convictions of governing elites. Legalism, in legal practice and as provided for in the customary rules on sources of law codified in Article 38 of the ICJ statute, supplies a way to identify *jus cogens* that involves canvassing judicial decisions and the writings of highly regarded publicists.[171] A practical judgment can be made that this is an acceptable—or, in the absence of an alternative—the best way to identify *jus cogens*. As with Finnis' reasoning regarding customary law, the combination of practical judgments that *jus cogens* are necessary to protect values and the common good, and that legalist rules for identifying *jus cogens* are a desirable way of invoking and applying *jus cogens*, create a legal obligation to obey *jus cogens*.

This analysis of legal and moral obligations also explains the nature of soft norms and their justifications. Soft norms, such as the Basel Accords on banking supervision, discussed in Chapter Eight, are prescriptions that are not formally laws. They do not conform with established legalist procedures and reasoning for creating

[166] *Cf.* Nardin, *supra* note 109, at 234 (arguing that customary international law is "the common morality of international society because it contains the authoritative practices and rules according to which that society is defined and the conduct of its members directed and judged").

[167] VCLT, *supra* note 25, art. 53.

[168] The Barcelona Traction, Light, and Power Co., Limited (Belg. V. Spain), Second Phase, 1970 I.C.J. 3 (Feb. 5).

[169] *Id.*

[170] Larry May, *Jus Cogens and Procedural Rights in International Law*, Presentation at the Foundation of International Law Conference 13–37 (Apr. 24, 2010); Alexander Orakhelashvili, Peremptory Norms in International Law 577 (2006) [hereinafter Orakhelashvili, Peremptory Norms] (explaining *jus cogens* "as a concept embodying the community interest and reinforced by its link with public morality exists in modern international law as a matter of necessity").

[171] ICJ Statute, *supra* note 76, art. 38(1)(b).

formal laws. They nonetheless adjust the conduct of governing elites. This phenomenon has puzzled jurists.

The distinction between moral and legal obligations explains this puzzle. Soft norms do not entail fully formed legal obligations because they do not conform to procedures for making laws, and governing elites have made a practical judgment that it is not yet reasonable to legalize soft norms. This practical judgment may involve determinations that the effect of a tentative prescription on basic values or the common good is insufficiently certain. For example, the costs of internal disruptions to comply with soft norms may not yet have been fully calculated. Therefore, a collective decision among elites is made not to legalize a soft norm until the appraisal of the norm is more complete.

However, a simultaneous practical judgment is made that the soft norm may promote basic values or common good, and elites accordingly articulate that soft norm in accord with commonly accepted procedures for prescribing soft norms. As a result of following those prescriptive procedures, there is a moral obligation to abide by the soft norm. This also permits elites to test the extent to which the soft norm actually optimizes the values at stake.[172] Accordingly, decisionmakers, acting with practical reasoning, ought to abide by the moral obligation attached to the soft norm, even if there is not yet a corresponding legal obligation.

There are at least two other types of situations where decisionmakers may justifiably prefer informal prescriptions with weak shared expectations to formal laws. First, in situations requiring swift adjustments to shared expectations of appropriate conduct in response to rapid changes of facts on the ground, such as the regulation of financial markets in times of crisis, informal prescriptions may be made and agreed to more quickly than formal laws. Here, the shared expectations of appropriate conduct accompanying informal prescriptions can be just as strong, if not stronger, than those accompanying some other formal laws.

Second, in some international problems, the vital interests of powerful decisionmakers are at stake, and it would be impossible, as a practical matter, to obtain a formal prescription. For example, no Security Council resolution can be passed if a permanent member assesses that the draft resolution undermines a key interest of the member or one of its allies. In such circumstances, decisionmakers may achieve a lesser, different form of cooperation through informal prescriptions that circumvent the powerful decisionmaker or which may be sufficiently weak to win the tentative support of the powerful decisionmaker. At a later point in time, if circumstances or the powerful decisionmaker's perception of his interests change, decisionmakers may collectively transform the informal prescription to a formal law, or they may simply consolidate expectations around the informal prescription without formalizing it as a law.

[172] *Cf.* Reisman, *supra* note 90, at 31 (explaining that soft agreements "are important phases in the lawmaking process, permitting states to establish target goals, to begin to adapt national behavior to them and to accommodate internal disruptions that may ensue, giving all parties respite before they decide whether to proceed toward a more binding form of agreement").

V. GUIDANCE TO OFFICIALS

In an international problem, a decisionmaker should balance competing considerations when deciding what to do. Specifically, he ought to balance the general morality of international law with specific moral considerations particular to the problem at hand and the values at stake, within the limits of his institutional authority and functions. A decisionmaker would do well to remember at all times that his decisions will only secure the values it aims at if other decisionmakers support and agree with his decision. Therefore, he ought to consider what accommodations of other decisionmakers' preferred values are necessary to achieve at least a minimum degree of effectiveness and at what point pragmatism would unacceptably undermine the morality of a decision.

A. Morality

As discussed at length above, the central case of international law is inherently valuable because it is necessary for the common good. Therefore, decisionmakers have a moral obligation to interpret and apply prescriptions legalistically, in order to maintain the minimum world order that enables communities and individuals to cooperate and compete for their respective preferred values. This is a general moral obligation because it exists in every international problem and is not contingent on the content of any relevant prescription.

However, the general moral obligation is not the only consideration when decisionmakers face an international problem. In each international problem, there is also a specific moral obligation to promote optimum world order, that is, the regulation of conduct to promote the optimum attainment and distribution of values worldwide in the resolution of that problem. This book's account of international law does not dictate in the abstract what optimum attainment and distribution of values are. Indeed, the author is skeptical that there is one correct view about distributive justice and the prioritization of values in most international problems. Nevertheless, these ambiguities do not absolve decisionmakers from aiming at optimum world order. Instead, the ambiguities make it all the more important that decisionmakers explicitly consider the reasons for preferring one set of values over another, along with considerations of the common good, when deciding which interpretation of a prescription to adopt.[173]

B. Institutional Functions

The discretion of decisionmakers to interpret prescriptions is not only limited by considerations of morality. They should also be mindful of the institutional

[173] Franck conceived of general and specific morality as legitimacy and justice, respective. *See* Franck, Power, *supra* note 31, at 206 ("Legitimacy is the standard by which the community measures rules' capacity to obligate."); *id.* at 208 (stating that justice is not "include[ed] among the factors making for legitimacy").

functions they discharge and the limits of their authority. A judge tasked with settling disputes according to law has a duty to be especially faithful to legalism, and has less discretion in creating and adjusting prescriptions than government officials concluding treaties. The judge ought to take legalism more seriously than some other decisionmakers because courts are special custodians of legalism. An arbitrator should also decide disputes legalistically because parties that consented to the jurisdiction of the international tribunal have delegated authority to the arbitrator to decide by applying laws. A legal advisor charged with authorizing the executive decisions of officials may stray further from legalism in order to support his client's goals but has to nevertheless advise the official of lines that cannot be crossed without making the official's acts illegal. A regulator may lack the formal authority to make international laws with regulators of other states, but she may have significant discretion in concluding agreements that create informal prescriptions expressing strong shared expectations of compliance with agreed-upon standards of international conduct.

C. Effectiveness

A decisionmaker must also take into account the likely effectiveness of any legalist claim he may make. A justificatory account of international law must establish some link between law's morality and its effectiveness; otherwise, there is no general moral justification for decisionmakers to participate in a system that always fails as a practical matter to promote the common good.[174] The effectiveness *vel non* of an international legal prescription depends first and foremost on a decisionmaker identifying the prescription, interpreting it, applying it to an international dispute, and claiming that the prescription requires a certain outcome. Without application by a governing elite, a legal prescription has no existence as a social fact. It only exists as an abstract idea until someone says what it means and instructs other people on what the prescription requires them to do.

The effectiveness of any claim based on a prescription is then contingent on whether or not other governing elites accept the invocation of a prescription. In addition to the personal preferences of decisionmakers (which cannot be accounted for in the abstract), acceptance by other elites of a legalist claim depends on its fidelity to legalism, the power of governing elites, and their respective interests and perceptions of the values at stake.

Fidelity to legalism can increase the likelihood of effectiveness for at least three reasons. The first reason derives from international law as an elaborate social

[174] *Accord* W. Michael Reisman, *Law from the Policy Perspective*, *in* International Law Essays: A Supplement to International Law in Contemporary Practice 1, 7 (Myres S. McDougal & W. Michael Reisman eds., 1981) ("[L]awful acts, to be such, will require a minimum degree of effectiveness."); Harlan Cohen, *Finding International Law: Rethinking the Doctrine of Sources*, 93 Iowa L. Rev. 67, 95 (2008) ("Law need not be universally followed in order to qualify as law. . . . but if 'law' is commonly disregarded and seems to have little impact on action, the meaningfulness of 'law' must be doubted. Perhaps the 'law' isn't law at all.").

myth.[175] Like the ancients who followed myths without questioning if there was a rational basis to do so, constituents may believe the myth of international law and tend to expect their elites to follow anything that is faithful to legalism and thereby identified as international law.[176] As with legalism, physical manifestations of legal authority such as the UN flag or diplomatic formalities serve as mythic symbols to validate the legal prescriptions they represent, and exert what Thomas Franck called a "pull towards compliance."[177] He explained that symbolism positively affects the legitimacy of legal prescriptions that are symbolically validated.[178]

However, it appears to this author that legalism and symbolism, to the extent they trigger irrational psychological reactions in governing elites to comply with international law, are merely social myths. They do not, without more, supply reasons to comply with international law. This explanation of why legalism and its associated symbols exert pressure on governing elites to comply with international law is interesting from a sociological standpoint. However, it does not provide a reason to follow international law, let alone a moral reason to do so.

This mythological explanation presumes that governing elites are unthinking actors who are unable to see through myths and do not demand rational reasons for actions. Although such a presumption may be accurate about some elites some of the time, it seems a stretch to think that the presumption holds with enough elites enough of the time to sustain international law as a social myth without additional functional reasons to do so.[179] Further inquiry is necessary.

A more cogent reason for thinking that fidelity to substantive and procedural legalism is a factor in effectiveness is that decisionmakers, as rational actors, believe that it is in their long-term self-interest to comply with international law because that bolsters their reputation for trustworthiness. They calculate that it is necessary to protect their credibility because it is an important component of "soft power,"

[175] *See generally* Lasswell & McDougal, Jurisprudence, *supra* note 101 (describing law generally as a myth system, i.e., "stable patterns of personal as well as group perspectives [in which] systems of identification (identity), demand and expectation are involved"). *Cf.* Bolton, *supra* note 116, at 48 (stating that international law is "theology and superstition"); for other discussions of international law as a myth, see *supra* pt. III.C.; *infra*, pt. VI.

[176] If myth systems are sustained by lore, that is, "popular legends, anecdotes, poems and other folk elements embellishing the basic themes of the myth," then legalism could be viewed as a key mode of communicating and developing lore (such as judicial decisions or justifications that elites give their constituents for action according to legal doctrine). *See* Lasswell & McDougal, Jurisprudence, *supra* note 98, at 353–55. *See also* Tyler, *supra* note 112, at 176–78 (1990) (discussing how people are socialized to believe that law is fair and correspondingly they "obey the law because they believe that it is proper to do so").

[177] Franck, Fairness, *supra* note 122, at 34.

[178] *Id.* at 34–36; Franck, Power, *supra* note 31 at 91–134.

[179] *See, e.g.*, Hillary Clinton Senate Confirmation Hearing as Nominee for Secretary of State (2009), *video available* at http://foreign.senate.gov/hearings/hearing/?id=7b16fc93-0c92-41f5-5e17-a09abc461b1c ("[F]oreign policy must be based on a marriage of principles and pragmatism, not rigid ideology, on facts and evidence, not emotion or prejudice."). *See also* Tyler, *supra* note 112, at 178 (noting that people "react to their experiences by evaluating their justice or injustice, and in evaluating the justice of their experiences they consider factors unrelated to outcome[.] . . .").

which enables them to more effectively pursue their interests in future bargains with other elites.[180] Accordingly, in an international dispute, when an interpretation of a legal prescription is faithful to legalism, a decisionmaker may decide to adopt and follow that interpretation to bolster its reputation for taking international law seriously and keeping its legal promises. This explanation provides a reason to comply with international law. It also provides a justification to do so, because, as subsequent chapters will argue, it is moral for governing elites to pursue the interests of constituents, who delegated power and authority to elites to promote those interests in an international system that, by design, permits communities to compete and exchange values according to their respective wants.

A third reason why elites may follow prescriptions is that decisionmakers, if they are rational, will tend to promote prescriptions that support the common good because the common good provides minimum conditions necessary for elites to attain values for their constituencies. To the extent that legalist reasoning and prescriptive procedures promote the common good by ensuring stability, consistency, and adherence in international relations, the moral obligation to obey and promote international law also provides a rational reason to do so, thereby connecting international law's morality to its effectiveness.[181]

Although these are all good reasons for decisionmakers to accept claims that are faithful to legalism, these reasons are not necessarily dispositive of what they will do, or ought to do. Every decisionmaker will have to decide whether legalism is outweighed by other moral considerations, including his duty to his constituents who appointed or elected him to promote their interests and preferred values. In some instances, these other moral considerations outweigh the general morality of legalism, and the claim has little chance of acceptance and effectiveness. Where vital interests of elites or their constituents are at stake, pragmatic accommodations may become necessary to balance idealistic goals with the reality of obtaining acceptance from those elites. A practical and ethical challenge for decisionmakers is to determine the right balance, without reducing the international legal system to a series of arbitrary political arrangements and destroying the common good that requires stability and shared expectations that prescriptions will be applied consistently to all decisionmakers.

D. The Indeterminacy Paradox

Although it is necessary for every governing elite in every international dispute to make a particularized decision about how to interpret or modify prescriptions, it is

[180] *See* Paul Schiff Berman, *Seeing Beyond the Limits of International Law*, 84 Texas L. Rev. 1265, 1291–92 (2005-06) (discussing correlation between compliance with international law and soft power); Clinton, *supra* note 179 ("We must use what has been called smart power.").

[181] *Cf.* Tyler, *supra* note 112, at 178 (presenting findings of a domestic study showing that "people [] evaluate laws and the decisions of legal authorities in normative terms, obeying the law if it is legitimate and moral and accepting decisions if they are fairly arrived at").

impossible to fully determine, in advance, the optimal moral decision before making that decision. This book calls this conundrum the indeterminacy paradox. The indeterminacy paradox prevents a complete answer to whether an international legal prescription is legitimate in a specific international dispute until the moment for decision about what to do about the prescription is in the past.

The international legal system is inherently unstable. Its abstract prescriptions, such as rules governing when military force is authorized against another sovereign state, consular relations, or territorial boundaries do not carry fully determinate meaning in the abstract. A prescription only has fully concrete meaning after governing elites have interpreted it, applied it, and reached consensus about what it means in any given international dispute.[182] Until that happens, there cannot be a complete appraisal of whether a decisionmaker should comply with a relevant prescription because the content of that prescription is not completely fixed.

Consequently, it is never possible to completely determine the morality of a prescription before it has been applied. It is only possible to retroactively determine whether international law should have mattered in a decision that has been made.

Because the morality of a prescription is usually one factor that affects its effectiveness, its moral indeterminacy before it has been applied makes it impossible to determine its effectiveness in advance. Once a legal prescription has been applied in an international dispute, its effectiveness can be observed as a historical fact. However, by that time, the inquiry has lost much of its prospective practical use to a decisionmaker who needs to decide whether or not to comply with an international prescription, since that issue is also rendered moot.

The solution to the indeterminacy paradox is not conceptual but practical. A decisionmaker in an international dispute should not be paralyzed by philosophical problem that he cannot know his moral obligation to obey a prescription until he has obeyed, interpreted, or disobeyed it and given the prescription concrete meaning, and he cannot know how effective his actions are until other decisionmakers have responded. The decisionmaker is himself an applier of legal prescriptions and not just a passive observer. He is, in a sense, also a creator of law because the elite gives prescriptions concrete meaning by applying them to disputes. In deciding how to apply prescriptions, he simultaneously affects international law's morality and effectiveness. Therefore, he should simply consider various interpretations of the prescriptions and, in good faith and with his best judgment, pick the interpretation and course of action that he anticipates would be most effective in balancing the general and specific moral obligations at issue.

[182] *Cf.* Dworkin, *supra* note 8, at 410 ("Law is an interpretive concept. Judges should decide what the law is by interpreting the practice of other judges deciding what the law is."); Arthur Corbin, *The Judicial Process Revisited: Introduction*, 71 Yale L.J. 195, 199 (1971) ("A rule of law has no content divorced from its application: . . . every application to new facts adds to (or subtracts from) its content."); Aharon Barak, Judicial Discretion 139 (1989) ("Even the most simple and clear rules appears to us in its simplicity, only after we have passed it consciously or unconsciously, through the melting pot of our interpretive conception . . . Every text requires interpretation . . . To understand means to interpret.").

This interpretive process in international law is akin to the judicial decisionmaking of Ronald Dworkin's Herculean judge.[183] The intricacies of Dworkin's philosophy and the jurisprudential debates it has engendered[184] are beyond the scope of this book. In a nutshell, however, Dworkin proposed that judges ought to interpret and apply legal prescriptions by giving them their best normative content reflecting the values of their community, within the limits of legalism, thereby providing the best justification for law while maintaining its integrity.[185] Arguably this analysis applies to other governing elites in domestic law, ranging from the solicitor general interpreting law for other government agencies,[186] to a police officer interpreting the Vienna Convention on Consular Relations when he arrests a foreigner.[187] All decisionmakers operating under law interpret and apply laws to discharge their functions.[188] However, it is not the purpose of this book to discuss the breadth of application of Dworkin's jurisprudence in the domestic context.

Whatever the implications of Dworkin's jurisprudence domestically, in international law, his Herculean judge is transformed into the Herculean decisionmaker. It is not just judges and arbitrators in international courts and tribunals that interpret and apply legal prescriptions. The vast bulk of interpretative work is conducted outside of judicial settings in international disputes, where legal advisors guide government officials on what they may or may not do under international law and whether or not to abide by legal prescriptions. Officials, in turn, explicitly or implicitly make claims about prescriptions when they act.[189] In every international dispute, all governing elites involved ought to engage in the interpretative deliberation of Dworkin's Herculean judge, to simultaneously contribute to international law's morality and effectiveness.

The similarities between Dworkin's Herculean judge and the Herculean decisionmaker in international law should not be overstated, however. Dworkin's Herculean judges operate in fairly stable institutional settings with relatively clear legalist rules of interpretation and established judicial norms about respect for legalism. Herculean governing elites in international disputes may perceive interpretive rules to have varying degrees of malleability. Respect for legalism also varies considerably in international disputes and depends on a governing elite's role, the nature of the

[183] DWORKIN, *supra* note 8, at 254–58.

[184] *See generally* EXPLORING LAW'S EMPIRE: THE JURISPRUDENCE OF RONALD DWORKIN (Scott Hershovitz ed., 2006).

[185] *See* DWORKIN, *supra* note 8, at 177–224.

[186] *See* John O. McGinnis, Review Essay, *Principle versus Politics: The Solicitor General's Office in Constitutional and Bureaucratic Theory*, 44 STAN. L. REV. 799, 801 (1992) (declaring the solicitor general as the "Tenth Justice" of the U.S. Supreme Court).

[187] *See infra* ch. 4, pt. II.C (discussing violations of the Vienna Convention on Consular Relations by local law enforcement officials).

[188] *See* Kevin M. Stack, *The Concept of Law in the Age of Administration* (Oct. 14, 2009) (on file with author).

[189] *See* DWORKIN, *supra* note 8, at 413 (explaining that law "is a protestant attitude that makes each citizen responsible for imagining what his society's public commitments to principle are, and what these commitments require in new circumstances").

relevant prescriptions, his view of international law, and the institutional setting in which he operates.

A judge in an international tribunal has an institutional responsibility to accept the legalist procedures and modes of reasoning entrenched in the legal culture of his tribunal. However, in an international tribunal where judges come from different legal cultures and traditions, individual judges may have differing views about fidelity to legalism. Experienced practitioners seeking success on behalf of their client will try to persuade every judge on the tribunal hearing a dispute by appealing to each judge's respective legalist procedures and modes of reasoning.

In a nonadjudicative setting, the flexibility available to a Herculean governing elite increases. A legal advisor counseling government officials about what actions to take in a legal dispute is unburdened by the institutional constraints of an international tribunal, especially if the dispute is unlikely to lead to international arbitration before the ICJ or a private tribunal. Some advisors may interpret a legal prescription more liberally to serve the interests of his government and to promote relevant values, thereby concluding that a normatively ideal outcome can be accommodated within or even mandated by law. Other advisors who subscribe to a higher degree of legalism may interpret legal prescriptions more narrowly and conclude more often that the law falls short of a normative ideal, and leave it to their political masters to determine whether to ignore the law, rendering it ineffective.

In order to understand and apply Dworkin's interpretive technique to justify international law in international problems, it is necessary, therefore, to examine in detail each of the different roles of decisionmakers and their responsibilities. International law today involves many different types of decisionmakers: domestic judges, international judges, arbitrators, legal advisors, outside counsel, and in-house counsel in corporations, NGOs, and international organizations. This book applies its theory to some of the main types of decisionmakers in later chapters.

VI. CONCLUSION

Although politics is inseparable from international law, the international legal system is most distinct from pure politics when decisionmakers make, apply, and adjust prescriptions according to accepted legalist procedures and reasoning. As these shared expectations diminish, so too does the distinction between international law and politics.

Decisionmakers ought to promote the legalist central case because it is generally moral to do so. Legalism confers stability to international relations and manages change according to shared expectations of appropriate conduct.

However, this general morality—the morality of minimum world order—is not necessarily dispositive of actions or outcomes. When deciding what to do in an international problem, decisionmakers should balance other specific moral considerations—the morality of optimum world order—including the impact of their decision on the interests of their constituencies. Given normative ambiguities of what constitutes optimum world order, it may be possible to propose and debate what the right balance of values ought to be in actual international problems, but it seems futile to attempt to assess that balance in the abstract. Correspondingly, a justificatory account of the international legal system can help decisionmakers to justify international regulation by considering general and specific morality in international problems, and it can provide reasons for whether a particular decision is better or worse than another in an actual problem. But it seems both impossible and inappropriate to instruct decisionmakers as to what the right balance among values must be in the abstract.

The justificatory theory of international law also provides decisionmakers with guidance about what else to consider when deciding how to make, interpret, and modify prescriptions. These considerations are their institutional function and the limits of their authority, as well as the need to accommodate vital interests if necessary to ensure that the preferred interpretation of a prescription is at least minimally effective. This book's account does not seek to, and indeed cannot, instruct decisionmakers on what balance to strike among these considerations in every situation. However, this account can provide guidance by illustrating how these considerations guided, or ought to have guided, different decisionmakers in past and ongoing international problems. These problems are confronted in the chapters that follow.

The account presented of the international legal system builds upon insights from several schools of international law. The recognition that international law exists through social facts is emphasized in positivism. Notably, however, positivists look for different criterial social facts, such as state consent, than those identified here, that is, shared expectations of appropriate conduct among decisionmakers. Skepticism about whether prescriptions are fully determinate before elites interpret and apply them is shared with the critical legal school led by David Kennedy and Marti Koskenniemi. The idea that legalist procedures and reasoning legitimize prescriptions and outcomes is one of the oeuvres of the international legal process school, especially in the late works of Thomas Franck.[190] The inquiry into whether prescriptions are effective or inherently moral is a leitmotif of the realist school and recurs in the recent works of Eric Posner and Jack Goldsmith.[191] The commitment to legalism as a way to promote effectiveness of prescriptions in securing stability is shared with those positivists who believe that formal rules are desirable.[192] However, the theory presented here does not accept that stability is the only consideration when decisionmakers face international problems.

Overall, the attempt to understand and anticipate decisions as a function of prescriptions, power, interest, and morality is a focus of inquiry of the New Haven School, which is concerned with divergences between the myth system that make claims to control what actors do and an operational code that actually guides their action, and with shaping the operation code to authoritatively control decisionmakers in order

[190] *See generally* Franck, Fairness, *supra* note 112; Franck, Power, *supra* note 31.

[191] *See generally* Goldsmith & Posner, *supra* note 117.

[192] *See* Orakhelashvili, *supra* note 11, at 584 (arguing that prescriptions must be "interpreted in accordance with pre-determined legal rules . . . to ensure the effectiveness of legal regulation").

to maximize human dignity.[193] Leading contemporary positivists also seem to agree that international law's effectiveness cannot be determined by looking at only its prescriptions. Vaughan Lowe acknowledges that "actual practice of states and international bodies is seen as at least as important as prescription or theory."[194]

It is hoped that by drawing on multiple rich scholarly traditions in international law, this chapter has clarified the essential characteristics of the international legal system, and the relationship between legalism and morality. The stage is now set to test this book's account in the chapters that follow.

[193] *See* W. Michael Reisman & Andrew R. Willard, International Incidents: The Law that Counts in World Politics 12 (1988).

[194] The United Nations Security Council and War, *supra* note 42, at 18. *See also id.* at 2 ("[T]he actual practice of the Security Council is richer, more complex, and more paradoxical than can be captured by any single prescriptive document or theory.").

4 Judges

I. THEORY

This chapter applies the general theory of international law, developed earlier, to judges. Judges have a special moral duty to be faithful to legalism because they are appointed to resolve disputes according to law. However, legalism does not eliminate their discretion. In some international disputes, they ought to resolve interpretative ambiguities by considering the specific moral implications of applying relevant prescriptions to resolve disputes. These propositions are tested against several decisions of the ICJ in this chapter. Although international courts have proliferated, the ICJ remains the only court of general jurisdiction. It is the main judicial institution of the UN and is still thought of as the preeminent World Court. For these reasons, as well as considerations of space in this book, the examination of whether and how the justificatory theory of international law applies to judges focuses on decisionmaking in the ICJ.

A. Judicial Functions

When deciding cases, judges ought to direct their efforts at discharging their judicial functions. The principal function of an international judge, just as a domestic judge, is resolution of disputes in cases that come before him.[1] This function applies with

[1] *See* Florentino P. Feliciano, *The Application of Law: Some Recurring Aspects of the Process of Judicial Review and Decision Making*, 37 Am. J. Juris. 17, 34 (1992) ("The first function [of a judge] is an

full force in contentious disputes because that is explicitly what the parties before the judge have asked him to do. In courts that lack enforcement powers, such as—for most practical purposes—the ICJ, judges concerned with resolving disputes according to law should interpret and apply prescriptions to disputes in a legalist fashion with an eye toward the effectiveness of their decisions.[2]

When the ICJ is called to render an advisory opinion, there is no explicit dispute resolution function. Indeed, the Statute of the ICJ states that an advisory opinion is not binding on the parties. However, requests for advisory opinions are not made in a geopolitical vacuum. Most often, a request is made to head off an incipient dispute or to address a dispute that one party is unwilling to submit to contentious adjudication. It is reasonable to question whether the ICJ should accept advisory requests of the latter type.[3] If it does accept an advisory request, ICJ judges should be conscious that their opinions will indirectly affect how other decisionmakers, such as government officials and international bureaucrats, behave in a dispute. Generally speaking, no decisionmaker wishes to be seen to violate international law or an opinion of the ICJ, if he can avoid it. Consequently, through its advisory opinions, the ICJ may indirectly prevent or resolve disputes, or inadvertently precipitate or exacerbate them.

Another function of an international judge is to clarify and develop international legal prescriptions.[4] This is the main purpose of advisory opinions. It is also a function of judgments in contentious disputes. A judgment is binding only on the parties in the disputes addressed in the judgment.[5] However, legalism dictates that in ICJ decisionmaking, judicial decisions are additionally subsidiary sources.[6] In reality, decisionmakers, including arbitrators, judges, practitioners, and government officials often look to prior judicial decisions and their reasoning to help them understand and apply the law to guide their actions in future disputes.[7] Consequently,

intensely practical one: the resolution of the case pending before him, within definite time limits.").

[2] *See also* Tom Ginsburg, *Bounded Discretion in International Judicial Lawmaking*, 45 VA. J. INT'L L. 631, 651 (2004–05) (noting that when the WTO appellate body authorizes sanctions, "it is playing a coordinating role by setting a focal level of retaliation").

[3] *See, e.g.*, Accordance with International Law of the Unilateral Declaration of Independence in Respect of Kosovo, Advisory Opinion, 2010 I.C.J. 141 (July 22).

[4] *See* Feliciano, *supra* note 1, at 34; Stephen M. Schwebel, *Reflections on the Role of the International Court of Justice*, Jurisprudential Lecture at the University of Washington, 61 WASH. L. REV. 1061, 1068 (1986) ("[The] application of the law by an impartial international court not only solves particular disputes but also contributes to the development of the law."); Ginsburg, *supra* note 2, at 651 ("The secondary role of the WTO trade dispute settlement system is to clarify and articulate rules.").

[5] *See* Statute of the International Court of Justice art. 59 June, 26, 1945, 33 U.N.T.S. 993 [hereinafter ICJ Statute]; Convention on the Settlement of Investment Disputes Between States and Nationals of Other States, Mar. 18, 1965, 575 U.N.T.S. 159 [hereinafter Washington Convention]; 1 GARY B. BORN, INTERNATIONAL COMMERCIAL ARBITRATION 563–849, 1003–57 (2009).

[6] ICJ Statute, *supra* note 5 art. 38(1)(d).

[7] Jan Paulsson, *International Arbitration and the Generation of Legal Norms: Treaty Arbitration and International Law* 2–3 (May 21, 2006) (Unpublished draft, presented at the ICCA Annual Congress)

ICJ decisions informally shape expectations of appropriate behavior and generally regulate the international conduct of decisionmakers.[8]

B. General Morality

When adjudicating and elaborating on legal prescriptions, judges have a general moral duty to apply international legal prescriptions using legalist reasoning and procedures.[9] There are strong moral reasons to exercise their decisionmaking powers and judgment within limits permitted by legalist reasoning and procedure. These constraints apply to judges more than they apply to some other decisionmakers. Because life and its basic freedoms are values shared by every human being, no judge should exercise his judicial authority to limit the freedom of decisionmakers and constituents, including the parties in a case and other observers, without justification.

The justification for exercising judicial powers also limits how they may be exercised. States consent to international adjudication by signing the Optional Protocol of the ICJ or, alternatively, by forming a special agreement to refer a dispute to the ICJ. In both situations, they consent in a limited way to permitting the ICJ to resolve the dispute by applying and interpreting international laws using legalism.[10] The parties have a strongly shared expectation that judges will do so without substituting personal choices for the legalist reasoning they are expected to apply.[11] It would be

(on file with author); Ian Brownlie, Principles of Public International Law 19–20 (7th ed. 2008) ("[T]he literature of the law contains frequent reference to decisions of arbitral tribunals. The quality of arbitral tribunals have varied considerably, but there have been a number of awards which contain notable contributions to the development of the law by eminent jurists sitting as arbitrators, umpires, or commissioners."); Ginsburg, *supra* note 2, at 638 (providing statistics on the ICJ's references to its prior cases in support of its decisions and concluding: "Whatever the formal role of precedent in the international system, a glance at the decisions of international tribunals shows a tendency to reference and abide by earlier decisions."). *See, e.g.*, Armed Activities on the Territory of the Congo (Democratic Republic of the Congo v. Uganda), Judgment, 2005 I.C.J. 168, ¶ 160 (Dec. 19) (applying control test from *Nicaragua* case to determine whether a state is responsible for nonstate actors); W. Michael Reisman, Systems of Control in International Adjudication and Arbitration: Breakdown and repair 32–34 (1992) [hereinafter Reisman, Systems of Control] (explaining that the *Nicaragua* case applied the *Corfu Channel* case to decide what to do about the absence of the United States from the *Nicaragua* proceedings).

[8] *See* Ginsburg, *supra* note 2, at 673 ("International judges exercise lawmaking power.").

[9] *See* Reisman, Systems of Control, *supra* note 7, at 31 (1992) ("The morality of case law, like that of all law, rests on respect for expectations that have been established and authorized by appropriate community processes.").

[10] In theory, parties could ask the court to decide the issue according to equity and justice, but in practice that almost always never is the case. *See* ICJ Statute, *supra* note 5, art. 38(2).

[11] *See* Feliciano, *supra* note 1, at 48 ("The judicial process should make possible and reinforce the *stability* of expectations in the community by enhancing the predictability of outcomes of recourse to system of application of law."); Robert Jennings, *The Role of the International Court of Justice*, 68 Brit. Y.B. Int'l L. 1, 40 (1998) ("The justice a court of law should seek is not a subjective notion of what appears to be just in the instant case between the particular parties, but that most effective and

therefore immoral for a judge to entirely ignore legalist procedures and reasoning in deciding disputes.

Aside from restraining judges from overreaching the delegation of dispute resolution authority from parties, legalism supplies another main justification for judicial authority. The common good enables decisionmakers and constituents to reasonably pursue their interests because it stabilizes international arrangements. Legalism supports the common good by providing a method of regularizing the claims that decisionmakers make on each other and the expectations that they have of each other. Judges ought to promote the common good,[12] and legalism provides them with a way to do so.[13]

Further, ignoring legalist strictures may also cause parties who are dismayed that judges exceeded the limited powers delegated to them to withdraw their support for and participation in international adjudicatory institutions. For example, when the ICJ arguably exceeded its powers in finding jurisdiction over the United States in a case brought by Nicaragua,[14] the United States responded by no longer participating in the proceedings and ignoring the court's decisions in that dispute. A decision ought not to undermine the effectiveness of international law by exceeding the bounds of legalism without overriding reasons for that departure.

C. Specific Morality

Although there is a strong moral reason to apply legalism when judging, legalism alone should not control outcomes in adjudication.[15] Exogenous calculi are necessary because legalism alone often does not provide one answer.[16] Where legalism does not resolve interpretative ambiguity, judges ought to supplement legalism with moral reasoning. A judge ought to employ practical moral reasoning to identify and balance the basic values and interests at stake within legalist limits.

general justice which is achieved by ordering matters generally in accordance with the rule of law.").

[12] *See* 2 Rosalyn Higgins, Themes & Theories: Selected Essays, Speeches and Writings in International Law 1261–63 (2009) [hereinafter Higgins, Themes & Theories] (noting that courts often attempt to harmonize their interpretations of prescriptions with other courts); *id.* at 1268 ("We must try to preserve unity among us [judges] unless context really prevents this.").

[13] *Cf.* Laurence R. Helfer & Anne-Marie Slaughter, *Why States Create International Tribunals: A Response to Professors Posner and Yoo*, 93 Cal. L. Rev. 899, 932 (2005) (noting that international tribunals "act as trustees" for governments and "enhance the credibility of the promises that governments make to one another").

[14] *See* Reisman, *supra* note 7, at 22–25, 33–34. *See also generally* Military and Paramilitary Activities in and against Nicaragua (Nicar. v. U.S.), Judgment on Merits, 1986 I.C.J. 14 (June 27) [hereinafter Nicaragua Case].

[15] *Cf.* Richard Posner, How Judges Think 228 (2008) ("Judges . . . . want to understand the real stakes in a case. They want the lawyers to help them dig below the semantic surface.").

[16] *See* Schwebel, *supra* note 4, at 1068 (stating that the view that the "content of international law is uncertain, that is to say, the law to be applied by the Court is uncertain . . . . may have some basis in fact"). *See also generally* Karl Llewellyn, *How Appellate Courts Decide Cases*, 17 Penn B. Ass'n Q. 54 (Oct. 1945).

In any event, many legal prescriptions explicitly require decisionmakers to balance the values at stake, and it is only consistent with legalism for a judge to use moral reasoning when those prescriptions apply. Article 31 of the Vienna Convention on the Law of Treaties (the VCLT) instructs interpreters of treaties to read the ordinary words of a treaty in light of its objects and purposes, which invariably are directed at allocating values among different constituents.

Even if legalism alone could determine outcomes because a prescription admits no ambiguity, and a dispute fits squarely into the situation envisaged by the prescription, a judge should nevertheless, as a moral matter, consider the values that are at stake in a dispute, as well as the impact of his decision on the allocation of values in future disputes where his prescriptions may be invoked by other courts, government officials, and legal advisors. Although the effect of legalism on the common good provides a weighty reason to follow legalism strictly, it does not always provide the conclusive reason to do so. In exceptional circumstances, such as where a law is unjust, or archaic, or did not anticipate the factual situation to which it is subsequently applied, there may be other supervening considerations that require legalism to be stretched. In order to be alert to such exceptional disputes, a judge ought to anticipate and appraise the impact of his legalist ruling on the allocation of values before finally deciding to issue that ruling.

This view is shared by judges and scholars of different jurisprudential persuasions, from different cultures, and with different political values. Christopher Weeremantry, a former vice president of the ICJ, has explained that "the medium of the law" involves "sensitivity of lawyers to their social responsibilities," which requires "divert[ing] attention from the letter of the law to the spirit and principles lying behind the letter of the law."[17] Rosalyn Higgins, a former president of the ICJ, has stated: "The function of international law is to find that fine balance between legal expectations generated by the experiences of the past and the solving of problems as they present themselves today,"[18] and "the attainment of values (or the assessment of motives) must be part of the analysis[.]"[19]

Even judges who appear at first glance to reject moral appraisals when judging may in fact adopt them by folding such moral appraisals into legalism. Stephen Schwebel, a former U.S. ICJ judge, in his dissent to the decision on the merits of the *Nicaragua* case, stated that "the proper function of a judge of this Court is limited to an appraisal of what the law permits or requires, and does not extend to passing judgment on the merits of policies which are pursued within those confines."[20] He did not, however, explain whether moral or value considerations factor into his appraisals of what the law permits or requires, only that it is not the role of judges to

[17] Christopher Weeramantry, Acceptance Speech at The Right Livelihood Awards (Dec. 7, 2007), *available at* http://www.rightlivelihood.org/weeramantry_speech.html (last visited Aug. 7, 2011).

[18] 2 Higgins, Themes & Theories, *supra* note 12, at 1125.

[19] *Id.* at 1295. *See also generally* Shabtai Rosenne, *The Influence of Judaism on the Development of International Law*, 5 Neth. Int'l L. Rev. 119 (1958) (expressing dismay at dicta of the ICJ that appeared to divorce law from morality).

[20] Nicaragua Case, *supra* note 14, at 268 (dissenting opinion of Judge Schwebel).

constrict governing elites who act within the four corners of the law. Hersch Lauterpacht, the great positivist who believed that the "decisive consideration [to deciding a case based on a rule] is that it is the rule or principle in force,"[21] nevertheless accommodated his "neo-Grotian" attitudes in legalism.[22] He stated in his separate opinion in the *South-West Africa—Voting Procedure* case that "the highest international interest . . . . can never be legally irrelevant."[23]

Engaging in moral appraisals to try to determine the morally optimal judicial decision does not usually contradict legalist reasoning. Moral reasoning provides guidance to choose among equally plausible legalist interpretations and applications of the laws to facts.[24] Shabtai Rosenne explained Hersch Lauterpacht's judicial approach: "Lauterpacht was extremely careful to emphasize that the burden of his remarks was confined to legal issues, howsoever broadly conceived, and 'did not transcend the limits of judicial propriety' by entering the political field."[25]

However, this does not mean that where a substantive outcome required by legalism is immoral, the judge should do nothing. In an extreme case, where a court has run amuck, or the law has been perverted beyond recognition by other elites, such as during the Reich, a judge may resign rather than participate in a morally abhorrent adjudication. In less extreme circumstances, the judge may determine an issue according to legalist reasoning, even if it does not promote the optimal moral outcome. Subsequently, outside the courtroom, the judge may write articles and give speeches to other elites empowered to change the law, such as government officials, encouraging them to reexamine the issue.[26] He may call on scholars to undertake research that is required to project alternatives and to appraise them against applicable values.

[21] Hersch Lauterpacht, International Law: Collected Papers 235 (1975).

[22] Shabtai Rosenne, *Sir Hersch Lauterpacht's Concept of the Task of an International Judge*, 55 Am. J. Int'l L. 825, 829 (1961) [hereinafter Rosenne, *Lauterpacht's Concept*].

[23] Voting Procedure on Questions Relating to Reports and Petitions Concerning the Territory of South-West Africa, Advisory Opinion, 1955 I.C.J. 67, 122 (June 7) (separate opinion of Judge Lauterpacht).

[24] 2 Higgins, Themes & Theories, *supra* note 12, at 1295 ("International law has never been about the automatic and mechanical application of a single 'rule' governing a situation. We now have an ever thickening and deepening corpus of law. The decision-maker has several norms among which to choose, in any given situation, the appropriate governing law."); *id.* (noting that in choosing among potentially applicable legal norms, "several desirable values—human dignity, security of person, the environment, intergenerational considerations—can be jostling for our attention.").

[25] Rosenne, *Lauterpacht's Concept*, *supra* note 22, at 854. *See also* Ronald Dworkin, Law's Empire 401 (1986) ("If Hercules had decided to ignore legislative supremacy and strict precedent whenever ignoring these doctrines would allow him to improve the law's integrity, judged as a matter of substance alone, then he would have violated integrity overall. For any successful general interpretation of our legal practice must recognize these institutional constraints.").

[26] *See* Feliciano, *supra* note 1, at 51 (noting that the judge "may and should bring the inconsistency he has discovered to the notice of the legislature, the Bar, and the law schools").

A judge may also append a separate opinion or a dissent,[27] to explain why, even though legalism justified the majority's decision, the law ought to be changed.[28] An early example of this practice is the issue of "automatic reservations" to the ICJ's jurisdiction. In the United States' original consent to the ICJ's jurisdiction, it made an automatic reservation that, practically speaking, undermined its consent. Although it purported to consent to the ICJ's jurisdiction, it withheld consent for domestic matters and reserved the right to determine if a matter was domestic. Therefore, the United States claimed the right to decide, in any dispute, that the matter was domestic, and the ICJ had no jurisdiction.

Lauterpacht strongly opposed the automatic reservation in his separate opinion in the *Certain Norwegian Loans* case from 1957 and the dissenting opinion in the *Interhandel* case from 1959. Although he based his opinions on legalist reasoning, he also explained his moral reasoning. In *Norwegian Loans*, he stated:

> A purported obligation, however apparently comprehensive, which leaves it to the will of the State to determine the very existence of the obligation, cannot be the basis of an instrument claimed to found the jurisdiction of the Court. That view seems to be drastic and startling only if it is assumed that principles of law which generally apply in respect of the validity of texts purporting to create a legal obligation do not apply in the case of Governments. Any such assumption is inconsistent with the function of a Court of Justice.[29]

From this passage, it is clear Lauterpacht conceived of the ICJ not just as the World Court but a court of justice. He objected to automatic reservations because it hampered the functioning of adjudication that, in his view, was directed at promoting justice.

In the *Interhandel* case, Lauterpacht sharpened his moral objection to automatic reservations. He stated that it was "juridically repugnant" to accept the idea of automatic reservations. It would render "odious and offensive a finding by the Court" that the subject matter of the dispute was not domestic even though the United States claimed it was, because the court would have to find that "the reservation had been invoked unreasonably and in bad faith." If there was any doubt about his reasoned outrage, he clarified:

[27] Nicaragua Case, *supra* note 14, at 267 (dissenting opinion of Judge Schwebel) ("A dissent in a court of last resort is an appeal to the brooding spirit of the law, to the intelligence of a future day, when a later decision may possibly correct the error into which the dissenting judge believes the court to have been betrayed.").

[28] *See* Weeramantry, *supra* note 17 ("I have also written a series of Separate and Dissenting Opinions in the International Court of Justice, seeking to make international law a more universal discipline.").

[29] Certain Norwegian Loans (Fr. v. Nor.), 1957 I.C.J. 9, 65 (July 6) (separate opinion of Judge Lauterpacht).

> Any such construction of the function of the Court which is calculated to put the Court in the invidious position of having to make pronouncements of that kind in the matter of its own jurisdiction is, for that additional reason, open to objection.[30]

According to Rosenne, the practical effect of Lauterpacht's opinions was indicated by the trends that states thereafter withdrew their automatic reservations, and states that subsequently consented to jurisdiction did not insert automatic reservations.[31]

For a more recent example of the practice of using dissenting opinions to express moral dimensions of a problem that are absent in majority opinions bound by legalism, consider the ICJ's advisory opinion that Israel's construction of a wall around the Occupied Palestinian Territory was illegal.[32] On December 8, 2003, the UN General Assembly at a Tenth Emergency Special Session requested an advisory opinion from the ICJ on the legal consequences of Israel's construction of the wall.[33] The ICJ rendered its advisory opinion on July 9, 2004. Fourteen out of fifteen judges found that Israel had violated international law.[34] Judge Buergenthal from the United States was the exception because he decided that the ICJ should not have rendered an advisory opinion at all, even though he agreed with much of the majority's substantive decision.[35]

The majority's opinion is rich in analysis and controversial at parts. For present purposes, it is sufficient to focus on its determination that Israel violated international law by constructing the wall.[36] It found, inter alia, that Israel had violated international humanitarian law,[37] that its actions were inconsistent with human rights law,[38] and that the illegality of constructing the wall was not excused by self-defense[39] or necessity.[40]

Judge Higgins voted with the majority but wrote a separate opinion disagreeing with some of the court's findings. Higgins' opinion is a useful illustration of the uses and limits of moral reasoning in adjudication. Her separate opinion took pains to explain the need for "balance," to recount the obligations of both Israel and Palestine, and to acknowledge the obligations that Israel had violated along with those that

[30] Interhandel Case (Switz. v. U.S.), 1959 I.C.J. 6, 112 (Mar. 21) (dissenting opinion of Judge Lauterpacht).

[31] *See* Rosenne, *Lauterpacht's Concept*, *supra* note 22, at 853.

[32] Legal Consequences of the Construction of a Wall in the Occupied Palestinian Territory, Advisory Opinion, 2004 I.C.J. 136 (July 9) [hereinafter Wall in the Occupied Palestinian Territory].

[33] G.A. Res. A/ES-10/14, U. N. Doc. A/RES/ES/10/14 (Dec. 8, 2003).

[34] Wall in the Occupied Palestinian Territory, *supra* note 32, at 201–03, ¶ 163.

[35] *See generally id.* (declaration of Judge Buergenthal).

[36] Wall in the Occupied Palestinian Territory, *supra* note 32, at 201.

[37] *Id.* at 183–84, ¶ 120 (finding Israel violated Article 49 of the Fourth Geneva Convention); *id.* at 189, ¶ 132 (finding Israel violated Articles 46 and 52 of the Hague Regulations and Article. 53 of the Fourth Geneva Convention).

[38] *Id.* at 188–89, ¶¶ 129–31 (finding rights guaranteed under the International Covenant on Civil and Political Rights, International Covenant on Economic, Social, and Cultural Rights, United Nations Convention on the Rights of the Child to be impeded).

[39] *Id.* at 194, ¶ 139.

[40] *Id.* at 195, ¶ 142.

it had not.[41] According to Higgins, this "[c]ontext is usually important in legal determinations," and here, the ICJ ought to have more fully considered the broader context of the Israel-Palestine conflict.[42]

Although Higgins does not explain why this context and balance was important, a reason to consider context and balance is because they are necessary to maintain coherence in the law. Explicitly considering fairness helps a judge decide if the relevant facts in a particular situation are sufficiently similar to other situations where a legal prescription was applied, and to ensure that the prescription was intended to apply in order to rectify the type of conduct at issue. If the relevant conduct of the parties is not completely considered, there is a risk that a prescription may be misapplied where it was not designed to correct the particular conduct in the dispute. Such a misapplication would render international law incoherent and not promote the common good.

Higgins' opinion demonstrates the uses and limits of context because it showed how context led her to agree with some of the majority's views and disagree with others. She found that context prevented her from agreeing with the majority's finding that Israel's construction of the wall violated Palestinian self-determination rights. In contrast, context was largely irrelevant in humanitarian violations; and accordingly, she endorsed the majority's finding that Israel violated humanitarian law.

Regarding human rights violations, Higgins disagreed with the majority's finding that the wall impeded the Palestinian's right to self-determination. She explained:

> But it seems to me quite detached from reality for the Court to find that it is the wall that presents a "serious impediment" to the exercise of this right. The real impediment is the apparent inability and/or unwillingness of both Israel and Palestine to move in parallel to secure the necessary conditions—that is, at one and the same time, for Israel to withdraw from Arab occupied territory and for Palestine to provide the conditions to allow Israel to feel secure in so doing. The simple point is underscored by the fact that if the wall had never been built, the Palestinians would still not yet have exercised their right to self-determination.
>
> It seems to me both unrealistic and unbalanced for the Court to find that the wall (rather than "the larger problem", which is beyond the question put to the Court for an opinion) is a serious obstacle to self-determination.
>
> [. . .]
>
> And to bring to an end that circumstance, it is necessary that both sides, simultaneously, accept their responsibilities under international law.[43]

[41] *See generally id.* at 207 (separate opinion of Judge Higgins) [hereinafter Higgins, Wall in the Occupied Palestinian Territory].

[42] *See id.* at 210, ¶ 14. *But see* Wall in the Occupied Palestinian Territory, *supra* note 32, at 195, ¶ 141 ("The fact remains that Israel has to face numerous indiscriminate and deadly acts of violence against its civilian population. It has the right, and indeed the duty, to respond in order to protect the life of its citizens. The measures taken are bound nonetheless to remain in conformity with applicable international law.").

[43] *See* Higgins, Wall in the Occupied Palestinian Territory, *supra* note 41, at 214, ¶¶ 30–31.

Regarding humanitarian law, although she criticized the majority for failing to consider context, she ultimately voted with the majority. She concluded that Israel's actions violated humanitarian law, which, in her view, imposes "absolute" obligations and "diminishes [the] relevance of context."[44] She emphasized that "the protection of civilians remains an intransgressible obligation of humanitarian law, not only for the occupier but equally for those seeking to liberate themselves from occupation."[45] This strict legalist position was appropriate, in this author's view, because it outlawed actions that strike at the very heart of the basic good of life.

Through her different analyses of humanitarian law and self-determination, Higgins' separate opinion addresses the rhetorical question she posed two years later in her keynote lecture at the 100th anniversary of the American Society of International Law: "Is there a point at which reliance on 'context' can change the illegal into the normative?"[46] The answer is decidedly that there is such a point, but a judge ought to consider the values at stake along with legalist reasoning to determine that point in any given dispute before her.

D. Effectiveness

Judges should also be concerned about the effectiveness of their decisions because a decision that is ignored is useless. The concern about effectives is especially acute given the lack of enforcement powers of the ICJ, except through a Chapter VII resolution of the UN Security Council, and given the history of disobedience in some ICJ cases.[47]

Eric Posner and John Yoo have argued that judges should promote the national interests of the parties in order to bolster the effectiveness of their decisions. They argue that judges should not be independent, because it is only with prescribed "outcomes that are satisfactory to both parties" that courts may achieve "widespread compliance."[48] According to Posner and Yoo, judges therefore ought not to "allow moral ideals . . . to influence their judgments."[49]

A careful review of Posner and Yoo's article suggests another reason why they believe that judges should balance the interests of the parties rather than exercise moral judgment. As conservative scholars, they are critical of international courts that "are continuing to undermine democratic institutions and to enact the agenda

[44] *Id.* at 210, ¶ 14. *See also id.* at 212, ¶ 19 ("[T]he protection of civilians remains an intransgressible obligation of humanitarian law, not only for the occupier but equally for those seeking to liberate themselves from occupation.").

[45] *Id.* at 212, ¶ 19.

[46] 2 Higgins, Themes & Theories, *supra* note 12, at 1295. *See also id.* ("Let me put a related question: when does 'creativity' in the face of adverse circumstances cross the line into the unpermitted?").

[47] *See* Reisman, Systems of Control *supra* note 7, at 20 (1992) (noting that Albania withdrew from the *Corfu Channel* case and refused to accept the ICJ's decision on the merits).

[48] *Id.* at 72.

[49] *Id.* at 27. *But see* Ginsburg, *supra* note 2 (criticizing Posner and Yoo's thesis).

of the liberal Left or New Class," and they criticize that agenda for containing "a toxic measure of anti-Americanism."[50]

Leaving aside concerns about whether their political viewpoint skewed their empirical assertion that biased courts are more likely to be effective, scholars have nevertheless not agreed with their hypothesis. Anne-Marie Slaughter and Larry Helfer have argued, in response to Posner and Yoo, the "most effective tribunals in the international legal system are independent tribunals."[51] Based on the case studies discussed later in this chapter,[52] it appears that Slaughter and Helfer's assessment of the relationship between legalism and effectiveness is more correct.

In any event, whether or not biased courts are more likely to be effective than independent courts ought not to be the operative consideration for judges in their decisionmaking. Placing effectiveness before morality is like placing the cart before the horse. In order to justify their authority, judges ought to strive first and foremost to balance the common good with the specific values at stake in each dispute. Being biased does not usually achieve that balance.

Generally speaking, judges ought to be faithful to legalism in an independent fashion to promote the coherence, adherence, and stability necessary for the common good.[53] As Posner and Yoo recognize, international judging is designed to promote the common interest. They acknowledge that "international adjudication can play a useful role by enabling states to overcome a limited set of cooperation problems in international affairs." They also recognize that courts improve adherence by "providing . . . rules of conduct."[54] Judges are unlikely to effectively promote those values if states do not trust them to resolve disputes according to states' expectation that the disputes will be resolved according to law and not politics.[55]

This is not to say that judges should never consider the interests of constituents affected by their decisions. As discussed above, the basic goods that every human

[50] Eric A. Posner & John C. Yoo, *Judicial Independence in International Tribunals*, 93 Cal. L. Rev. 1, 5 n.8 (2005) (quoting Robert H. Bork, Coercing Virtue: The Worldwide Rule of Judges 10 (2003)). *See also id.* at 4 n.7 (citing John R. Bolton, Under Secretary for Arms Control and International Security, American Justice and the International Criminal Court, Remarks at the American Enterprise Institute (Nov. 3, 2003) (favoring "national independence" over regulation by the international criminal court)).

[51] Helfer & Slaughter, *supra* note 13, at 955 (arguing that the "most effective tribunals in the international legal system are independent tribunals.").

[52] *Infra*, pt. II.

[53] *See* Alexander Orakhelashvili, The Interpretation of Acts and Rules in Public International Law 583 (2008) (spending almost 600 pages "demonstrat[ing] the deficiency and shortcomings of an approach that justified indeterminacy being used for political interests").

[54] Posner & Yoo, *supra* note 50, at 72.

[55] *See* Helfer & Slaughter, *supra* note 13, at 936 ("Indeed, international tribunals can *only* make state commitments more credible if they are independent. If a tribunal were dependent . . . defections would increase and the long- term benefits of interstate cooperation would quickly unravel."). *See also infra*, pt. II(C) (discussing how judicial fidelity to legalism was one factor why U.S. President Bush accepted the judgement against the United States in the *Avena* case, and contrasting *Avena* against the *Nicaragua* case where the ICJ's deviation from legalism made it easlier for President Reagan to ignore the ICJ decision).

being values, and the common good that creates conditions to attain those basic goods, should always factor in the judges' deliberations. To this extent, the interests of constituents of states that appear before courts are accommodated.

Additionally, a judge may also consider a party's interests, separate from the common good, where the legal prescription permits the judge to do so. What a judge should not do, however, is to accommodate a party's interests when no reasonable legalist interpretation of applicable prescriptions permit that outcome.

II. PRAXIS

It is relatively easy to state in a general sense how this book's justificatory theory of international law applies to judges. It is more difficult to specify how judges ought to balance competing considerations of general morality, specific morality, and effectiveness in discharging their judicial functions. Although the right balance in any case is open to debate, the justificatory theory provides a framework to both appraise judicial decisions and guide judges. The case studies below show how, when deciding cases, judges ought to consider the values at stake and the likely effectiveness of their decisions, but they should especially emphasize legalism because that is the basis for their authority, and legalism is likely to make their decisions more effective.

The first case is the *Case Concerning Sovereignty over Pedra Branca/Pulau Batu Puteh, Middle Rocks and South Ledge (Malaysia/Singapore)* (the "*Pedra Branca* case"). It involves a dispute between Singapore and Malaysia over several rocky outcrops in their territorial waters. In this case between two relatively smaller states with some global influence, the ICJ effectively resolved the principal dispute using legalist reasoning, even though the states involved were not completely satisfied with the outcome prescribed. This case is an illustration that where the parties share a strong expectation that the court will make a decision according to law, and both parties are interested in resolving their dispute whatever the outcome of the case, the moral duty to interpret and apply prescriptions legalistically is at its strongest.

The second case, *Military and Paramilitary Activities in and Against Nicaragua* (the "*Nicaragua* case") illustrates how deviating from legalism undermines the legitimacy of the international legal system and its effectiveness. In the *Nicaragua* case, Nicaragua brought a claim before the ICJ against the United States because the Reagan administration provided training and arms to contras in Nicaragua and mined the harbors around that country. The ICJ found it had jurisdiction even though serious questions existed about whether Nicaragua had complied with formal requirements of consenting to the ICJ's jurisdiction, and whether the United States was reciprocally bound. After the decision on jurisdiction, the United States withdrew from the case entirely. Thereafter, the ICJ issued a decision on the merits, finding that the United States had violated international law by indirectly using force against Nicaragua and that its actions were not justified by self-defense based on the court's narrow interpretation of the right to self-defense. There were also serious procedural concerns about this decision. The United States ignored it.

It is possible that the United States would have ignored the ICJ's decision even if the court had been faithful to legalism, because the decision was contrary to the United States' vital interests and its Cold War efforts against the Soviet Union, which supported the Nicaraguan government. However, it seems credible to infer that the ICJ's infidelity to legalism made it less costly for the United States to ignore the decision, and that the *Nicaragua* case undermined the common good by departing from legalism.

Additionally, the dangers of departing from legalism and failing to balance the values at stake are illustrated by subsequent decisions adopting the court's unreasoned restriction of the right to self-defense to only armed attacks by another state. This restriction anachronistically conceived of war as between two states, when increasingly violence is perpetrated through proxy by nonstate forces. Rather than perpetuate an earlier error, judges ought to correct prior deviations through their dicta or decisions in subsequent cases, as Judge Higgins tried to do in a portion of her opinion in the *Wall Opinion* that this chapter will discuss later.

The third case concerns another dispute before the ICJ, which is commonly referred to in international legal circles as "*Avena*," but comprises a series of related decisions. This chapter focuses on the *Case Concerning Avena and Other Mexican Nationals* (the "*Avena* case") and the *Request for Interpretation of the Judgment of March 31, 2004 in the Case Concerning Avena and Other Mexican Nationals (Mexico v. United States of America)* (the "*Avena Interpretation*"). These two decisions illustrate the importance of fidelity to legalism and how decisions that are legalist are more likely to be effective.

In *Avena*, Mexico brought a lawsuit against the United States because U.S state courts had sentenced Mexican nationals to death for criminal convictions, even though their rights under the Vienna Convention for Consular Relations had been violated. In a well-reasoned decision that strictly followed legalist prescriptions and procedures, the ICJ found that the United States had violated the Vienna Convention and ordered the United States to rectify its violations. The Bush administration accepted the ICJ decision and the responsibility of the United States under the Vienna Convention. President Bush instructed state governments to comply with the ICJ's decision. The U.S. Supreme Court, however, held that President Bush's actions were unconstitutional, and Texas executed one of the *Avena* convicts. Nevertheless, the Bush State Department continued its efforts to implement the ICJ decision and had some success persuading U.S. states to comply with it. The *Avena* case thus adds another layer of complexity to the analysis of how judges ought to make decisions. Unlike the *Nicaragua* case, the same powerful respondent state attempted to obey the ICJ decisions in *Avena*, albeit the United States only partially complied due to domestic legal constraints. The reasons for U.S. attempts to comply include U.S. interest in reciprocal compliance of other states with the Vienna Convention, the ICJ's fidelity to legalism, as well as the previous acceptance of the United States of the ICJ's decisions in the *Avena* line of cases.

Even though the three ICJ cases presented here far from exhaust the complexity and variety of adjudication in international law, they do, collectively, indicate that the justificatory theory of international law presented here applies to judges.

A. The Pedra Branca Case

The dispute between Singapore and Malaysia over the rocky outcrop called Pedra Branca must be explained by reference to their geographical locations and a brief political history of the two countries. Singapore is a small island state in South East Asia, on the tip of the Malaysian peninsula. Malaysia is its larger neighbor, whose territory encompasses the entire peninsula. Indonesia is located south of Singapore. A map showing the geographical relationship among these three states is produced as Figure 1.[56]

Both Singapore and Malaysia were formerly British colonies. After World War II, the Federation of Malaya, which included Singapore, gained independence. Its population comprised mainly ethnic Malays, whereas Singapore was mainly ethnically Chinese. In short order, the governing elites of Malaya decided it was not tenable for Singapore to remain part of Malaya and rejected Singapore from the federation. Singapore ultimately achieved independence and separated from Malaysia in 1965.[57]

On December 21, 1979, Malaysia published a map titled "Territorial Waters and Continental Shelf Boundaries of Malaysia," which claimed sovereignty over Pedra Branca.[58] Pedra Branca, as Singapore called it, was called Pulau Batu Puteh by Malaysia. Solely for brevity, it is referred to as Pedra Branca in this book since that is the name that appears first in the name of the ICJ case.

Pedra Branca is a rocky outcrop in the South China Sea that is merely 137 meters long and 60 meters wide.[59] It lacked resources and was not usable. However, as indicated in Figure 1, it is located right in the center of the maritime channel between Malaysia and Indonesia and so is the entry point to Singapore by sea.[60] As a trading nation with a busy seaport, it was vital for Singapore to control these rocks to help protect free sea travel through the channel to Singapore.

Singapore registered a formal protest with Malaysia by a diplomatic note dated February 14, 1980.[61] Singapore claimed that Pedra Branca was its sovereign territory. Singapore's Prime Minister Lee Kuan Yew attempted to resolve the dispute bilaterally with Malaysia throughout the 1980s but without success.[62]

Lee proposed to his Malaysian counterpart Mahathir Mohammed in 1989 that if they could not resolve the dispute by exchanging their respective evidence for sovereignty over Pedra Branca, the two states should submit the dispute to the ICJ. Lee has subsequently explained that he suggested ICJ adjudication because he

[56] *See* Sovereignty over Pedra Branca/Pulau Batu Puteh, Middle Rocks and South Ledge (Malay./Sing.), Judgment, 2008 I.C.J. 12, 24 (May 23) [hereinafter Judgment, Pedra Branca Case].

[57] *See generally* Lee Kuan Yew, The Singapore Story 13–24 (1998).

[58] *See* Judgment, Pedra Branca Case, *supra* note 56, at ¶ 30.

[59] *See id.* at ¶ 16.

[60] *See id.* at ¶ 19.

[61] *See id.* at ¶¶ 30–31.

[62] Lee Kuan Yew, *Forward*, *in* Shunmugam Jayakumar & Tommy Koh, Pedra Branca: The Road to the World Court xi–xiii (2009).

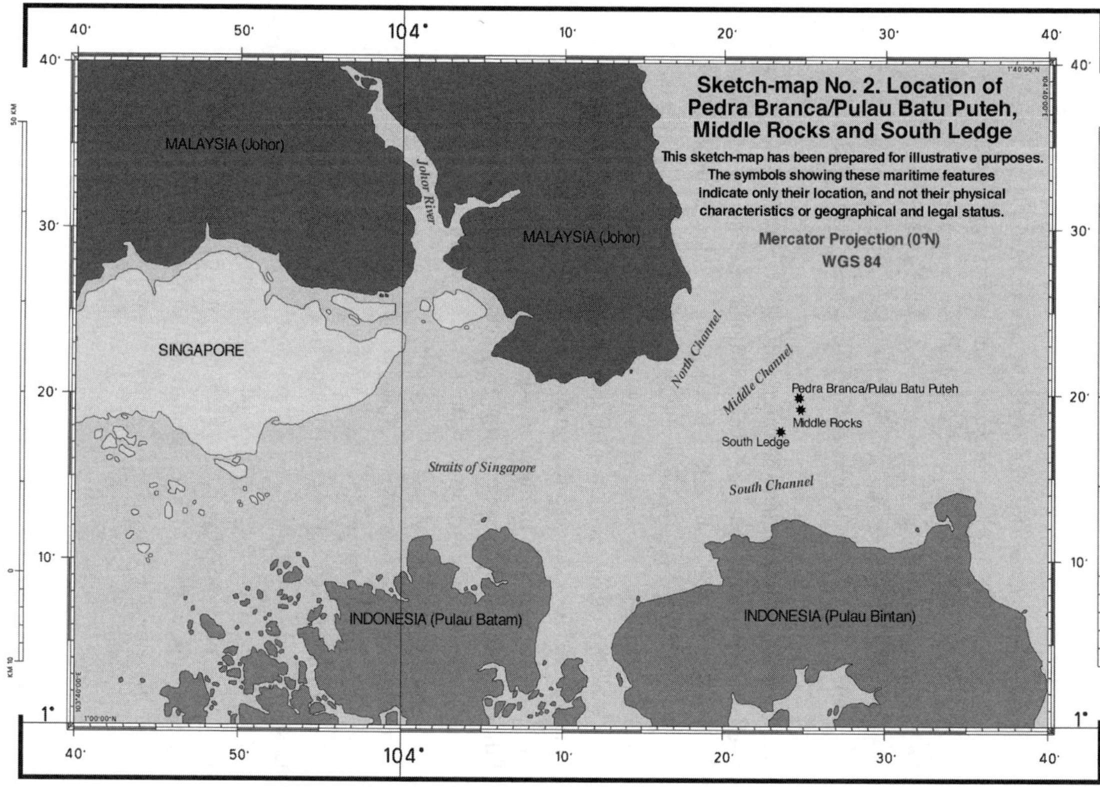

FIG 1: Sketch map: Location of Pedra Branca, Singapore, and Malaysia. This map is reproduced from the Judgment, Pedra Branca Case.

"understood that it was difficult for any leader to give up sovereignty claims unilaterally."[63] An ICJ decision that claimed to authoritatively settle the dispute as a matter of law would give the elites of the losing state political cover with its electorate. Lee also proposed ICJ adjudication because, in his view, "[i]f a dispute cannot be resolved by negotiations, it is better to refer it to a third party dispute settlement mechanism, than to allow it to fester and sour bilateral relations."[64]

In 1993, the two states engaged in intense negotiations. In the course of their diplomatic exchanges, they added Middle Rocks and South Ledge to their dispute. These two rocky outcrops near Pedra Branca were even smaller, and South Ledge was only visible at low tide. Negotiations did not settle the dispute.[65]

On July 24, 2003, Singapore and Malaysia submitted the dispute to the ICJ via a Notification of a Special Agreement.[66] The Agreement provided that the two states submitted the dispute to the ICJ pursuant to Article 36(1) of the ICJ Statute,[67] that the parties agreed to accept the judgment of the court as final and binding upon them,[68] and that the applicable law was the law recognized in Article 38 of the ICJ Statute.[69]

1. Legalism

The decision of the court in the *Pedra Branca* case was highly legalist. It found that Malaysia was originally sovereign over Pedra Branca and Middle Rocks.[70] Under international law, however, sovereignty can pass to another state by the sovereign state's agreement.[71] That agreement can be evinced by words, conduct, or silence.[72] The ICJ justified these prescriptions with legalist references to the *Temple of Preah Vihear Case* and the *Island of Palmas Case*.[73] Although Article 38 of the ICJ statute provides that judicial decisions are only subsidiary sources of law, the operational practice of the ICJ is to seek consistency with its prior decisions.

[63] *Id.* at xii.

[64] *Id.* at xiii.

[65] Jayakumar & Koh, *supra* note 62, at 20–43 (discussing the long period of negotiations between Singapore and Malaysia).

[66] *See* Sovereignty over Pedra Branca/Pulau Batu Puteh, Middle Rocks and South Ledge (Malay./Sing.), Special Agreement, 2003 I.C.J. 2 (July 24) [hereinafter Special Agreement, Pedra Branca Case].

[67] *See id.* at 6. *See also* ICJ Statute, *supra* note 5, art. 36 (1).

[68] *See* Special Agreement, Pedra Branca Case, *supra* note 66, at 8. *See also* ICJ Statute, *supra* note 5, art. 36.

[69] *See* Special Agreement, Pedra Branca Case, *supra* note 66, at 8. *See also* ICJ Statute, *supra* note 5, art. 38.

[70] *See* Judgment, Pedra Branca Case, *supra* note 56, at 31–32.

[71] *Id.* at 42.

[72] *Id.*

[73] *See id.* at ¶ 120–21 (citing Temple of Preah Vihear (Cambodia v. Thai.), Preliminary Objections, 1961 I.C.J. 17, 31 (May 26)); Island of Palmas Case (Neth./U.S.), Award of the Tribunal, 2 R.I.A.A. 828, 839 (1928).

Applying its legal prescriptions to the facts, it found sufficient evidence of Singapore's use of Pedra Branca and Malaysia's acquiescence to this use that sovereignty had passed to Singapore by 1980.[74] In 1953, during the colonial era, the colonial secretary of Singapore wrote to the British advisor to the Sultan of Johor, asking to "clarify the status of Pedra Branca" and whether "it has been ceded by the Government of the State of Johore," the predecessor entity that later became part of Malaysia.[75] The Sultan of Johor did not claim ownership of Pedra Branca.[76]

In particular, in 1978, Malaysia requested permission from Singapore, which Singapore granted, to enter Singapore's territorial waters to inspect tide gauges, and among the points identified was the lighthouse on Pedra Branca. This inspection was pursuant to a prior agreement that the states conduct joint maritime studies.[77] The conduct of Singapore, giving permission to Malaysia, impressed upon the court that title had passed to Singapore.[78] The court considered this exchange "of central importance" to its conclusion that title over Pedra Branca had passed to Singapore.[79]

As regards Middle Rocks, the ICJ found that because the evidence of Singapore and Malaysia's conduct related to Pedra Branca and not Middle Rocks, there was no evidence of any agreement to pass sovereignty of Middle Rocks to Singapore. Sovereignty therefore remained with Malaysia.[80]

As regards South Ledge, the court invoked Article 13 of the United Nations Convention on the Law of the Sea, defining low tide elevations.[81] It found that South Ledge met the definition of a low tide elevation in Article 13.[82] The ICJ relied on *Qatar v. Bahrain*'s statement that low tide elevations belong to the state in whose territorial waters the elevation is found. South Ledge fell into the overlapping territorial waters of Malaysia and Singapore, because of the ICJ's decision finding that Singapore and Malaysia were respectively sovereign over Pedra Branca and Middle Rocks, which are both right beside South Ledge. The ICJ was unable to determine which state was sovereign over the South Ledge without delimiting the territorial waters of Singapore and Malaysia. The ICJ concluded, by 15 out of 16 votes in favor, including both party appointed ad hoc judges, that territorial delimitation was beyond the scope of jurisdiction granted by the Special Agreement, and thus did not decide the issue.[83] Apparently avoiding a decision was a compromise acceptable to even the ad hoc judges.

[74] *See* Judgment, Pedra Branca Case, *supra* note 56, at ¶ 276.

[75] *See id.* at ¶ 192 (quoting the 1953 letter).

[76] *See id.* at ¶ 196 (quoting the letter from Acting State Secretary of Johor of Sept. 21, 1953).

[77] *See id.* at ¶ 238.

[78] *See id.* at ¶ 239.

[79] *See id.* at ¶ 203.

[80] *See* Judgment, Pedra Branca Case, *supra* note 56, at ¶ 300.

[81] *See id.* at ¶ 292.

[82] *See id.* at ¶ 299.

[83] *See id.* at ¶¶ 296–99.

The issues were undoubtedly of key national interests to Singapore and Malaysia, and the legalism that justified the outcome was arid. This is not a criticism of the decision. The more legalist an international decision, the greater is its differentiation from purely political decisions. Singapore and Malaysia took a strategic decision to settle the dispute under international law to avoid the political fallout of a negotiated settlement, or the diplomatic costs of continuing disagreement. As a court with jurisdiction contingent on state consent, the ICJ appropriately did what the parties wanted it to do. It appeared to take the dispute out of politics by engaging in legalist reasoning. Legalist reasoning is necessary to claim that the disputes are decided according to law and not politics or policy, even if other considerations operate in the background of judicial decisionmaking.[84]

2. Morality

Even though legalism was important in the *Pedra Branca* case, it did not exhaust the decisionmaking of judges. Legalism did not resolve all ambiguities in the interpretation of prescriptions, and therefore other moral considerations should also guide judicial decisions.

Judge Parra-Aranguren wrote a separate opinion stating that Pedra Branca belonged to Malaysia. He did not agree that the 1953 letter from the Sultan of Johor ceded title over Pedra Branca to Great Britain, which was the colonial ruler of Singapore at the time. Rather than explain any substantive concern over the communication, Judge Parra-Aranguren invoked a different legalist principle that because Singapore had not argued that the 1953 letter ceded title, the ICJ should not have relied on it as "the main basis to conclude on Singapore's sovereign title to Pedra Branca/Pulau Batu Puteh."[85] Further, unlike the majority, he did not interpret Johor's silence and inaction as evidence that it had given up title over Pedra Branca. Instead, "Johor authorities and their successors were under no international obligations to undertake any action at all, because Johor had historical title."[86] Consistent with the theories of critical legal studies scholars, Judge Parra-Aranguren conceded that he was able to reach a different decision because, in his view, "[j]uridical reasons can always be found to support any conclusion."[87]

[84] *Cf.* Rosalyn Higgins, Problems and Process: International Law and How We Use It 4 (1995) [hereinafter Higgins, Problems and Process] (quoting Judges Fitzmaurice and Spender in the *South-West Africa* cases in 1962. "'We are not unmindful of, nor are we insensible to, the various considerations of a non-judicial character, social, humanitarian, and other . . . but these are matters for the political rather than for the legal arena. They cannot be allowed to deflect us from our duty of reaching a conclusion strictly on the basis of what we believe to be the correct legal view.'").

[85] Judgment, Pedra Branca Case, *supra* note 56, at ¶ 14 (separate opinion of Judge Parra-Aranguren).

[86] *Id.* at ¶ 26.

[87] *Id.* at ¶ 1. *But cf.* Neil MacCormick, Rhetoric and the Rule of Law 15 (2009) ("[S]o far as law is that which underlies legal claims or accusations and legal defenses, law is something arguable, sometimes, but not always, conclusively, always at least persuasively.").

If juridical reasons do not wholly determine outcomes in adjudication, judges should elaborate in their decisions what their exogenous considerations were, rather than leave observers to guess. Judges Simma and Abraham explicitly considered the values at stake in this dispute. Like Judge Parra-Aranguren, they found the evidence insufficient to demonstrate that Malaysia or its predecessors had consented to giving up sovereignty of Pedra Branca. They emphasized the central importance in international law and relations of State sovereignty over territory and of the stability and certainty of that sovereignty. Because of that, any passing of sovereignty over territory on the basis of conduct of the Parties . . . . must be manifested clearly and without any doubt by that conduct and the relevant facts.[88]

Chapter Two discussed Judge Simma's positivist academic writing, which stated that law is derived from rules and not values unless the rules allow reference to values.[89] It is striking that, as a judge, he explicitly made value choices alongside legalist reasoning.[90]

Although judges should engage in value judgments alongside legalist reasoning where legalist interpretations leave the meaning of prescriptions unclear, value judgments may be similarly indeterminate. Judge Ranjeva appended a declaration agreeing that title had passed to Singapore based on the conduct of Singapore and Malaysia, but sharply criticized the ICJ's interpretation of the Sultan of Johor's concession of Pedra Branca to Great Britain. Judge Ranjeva pointed out that given the power disparity between the Sultan and his colonial overlord, it was "surreal to speak of the international transfer of title by acquiescence" because had the Sultan claimed continuing sovereignty over Pedra Branca he would have had to "organize a war for the liberation of Pedra Branca/Pulau Batu Peteh!"[91] In this dispute, the

> reduction of the reality of facts to suit the interpretation of concepts and techniques of international law does not tally with the legal and political order which prevailed when sovereignty was transferred.[92]

Similarly, Judge Bennouna objected to the majority's emphasis on the 1953 colonial interaction because "legal categories of the colonial period cannot be recycled to

[88] Judgment, Pedra Branca Case, *supra* note 56, at ¶ 20 (Joint Dissenting Opinion of Judges Simma and Abraham (quoting majority opinion at ¶ 122)).

[89] *Supra* ch. 2, pt III.C.

[90] This view that value choices are entrenched in judicial decisions is shared even by conservative judges in the domestic context. *See* Posner, *supra* note 15, at 220 ("Rarely is it effective advocacy to try to convince the judges that the case law compels them to rule in one's favor. . . . In a case that is not controlled by precedent, the task of the advocate is to convince the judges that the position for which he is contending is the more reasonable one in light of all relevant circumstances, which include but are not exhausted in the case law, the statutory text and the other conventional materials of legal decision making.").

[91] Judgment, Pedra Branca Case, *supra* note 56, at ¶ 5 (separate declaration of Judge Ranjeva).

[92] *Id.* at ¶ 4.

make them presentable today as though it were just a matter of words."[93] Even apparently neutral applications of prescriptions and interpretations of facts may involve normative judgments.

3. Effectiveness

The *Pedra Branca* decision was largely effective in settling the dispute between Singapore and Malaysia. The countries have established a Joint Technical Committee to delimit the maritime boundary around Pedra Branca and determine ownership of South Ledge. Although the *Pedra Branca* case did not resolve all ancillary issues, it addressed the principal issues and established a legal framework under which the parties can negotiate and cooperate with each other in a peaceful manner, thereby securing both the interests of the parties and the common good of world order.[94]

The effectiveness of the legalist decision supports the general proposition in this chapter that judges ought to be legalist in their decisionmaking. One key consideration is that the parties consented to and sought ICJ dispute resolution under law.[95] Thus, when the court decided the dispute legalistically, the parties were more likely to accept the decision. Even though the opinions in the *Pedra Branca* cases considered normative issues concerning colonialism and explicitly took into account the common good in the form of stability of international relations and order, the Court's opinions were also explicitly legalist. This legalist reasoning enabled Singapore and Malaysia to resolve their territorial dispute in a way that avoided disruptions to bilateral relations and minimized domestic political costs.[96] Singapore's Prime Minister Lee Hsien Loong explained:

> We fully accept the judgment of the ICJ. I am glad that Malaysia has also consistently said that it will accept the ICJ judgment. This is a good way for us to resolve disagreements

[93] *Id.* at ¶ 15 (separate declaration of Judge Bennouna).

[94] *See* Joint Press Statement on the 5th Malaysia-Singapore Joint Technical Committee (MSJTC) Meeting on the Implementation of the ICJ Judgment on Pedra Branca, Middle Rocks and South Ledge, 29–November 30, 2010 (Dec. 2, 2010), *available at* http://app.mf.gov.sg/2006/press/ view_press.asp?post_id=6585 ("Both sides reiterated their commitment to honour and abide by the ICJ's judgment and fully implement its decision by continuing the discussions following from the Fourth MSJTC Meeting held in Kuala Lumpur, Malaysia on 26–July 27, 2010.").

[95] Colter Paulson, *Compliance with Final Judgments of the International Court of Justice Since 1987*, 98 AM J. INT'L L. 434, 460 (2004) (updating and revalidating Charney and Gross' observation "that willingness to appear before the Court relates directly to compliance").

[96] *See* Malcolm N. Shaw, *The International Court of Justice: A Practical Perspective,* 46 INT'L & COMP. L.Q. 831, 832 (1997) ("The advantage of third party judicial settlement is that the ultimate responsibility for the decision lies elsewhere than with the states concerned. [The ICJ] thus constitutes an important mechanism to enable a state to come to terms with a losing position in a manner that often entails less political cost than a negotiating strategy producing the same result. International political forces are more often inclined to accept losing if the decision has been imposed from elsewhere than if the state concerned had simply conceded from the start.").

> or problems while maintaining good relations with each other. . . . I am glad that this problem is now cleared. I will be writing to [Malaysia Prime Minister] Abdullah to express my thanks to him that both our countries have been able to work together to resolve this problem, and we can now go on to develop our cooperation in many areas, such as the Iskandar Malaysia project.[97]

The direct link between legalism and effectiveness was underscored by Lee's explicit references to the ICJ adjudication as "a good way of resolving disputes" and the importance of "maintaining good relations."[98] Contrary to Posner and Yoo's hypothesis that independent courts are less likely to be effective, Singapore's deputy prime minister stated that "Singapore must remain committed to upholding the rule of law in relations between States."[99] This indicates that it was impartial legalism that was a factor in the effectiveness of the *Pedra Branca* decision. Accordingly, this case study underscores the importance of legalism in judicial decisionmaking, not only because it is moral to support the common good through legalism, but because it helps to make judicial decisions effective.

B. The Nicaragua Case

The *Nicaragua* case is a good test case for this book because the ICJ departed from legalism, and its decisions were ineffective in resolving the dispute between the United States and Nicaragua, a dispute in which both countries vital interests' were implicated. The case highlights the importance of legalism in judicial decisionmaking because legalism helps secure the effectiveness of judicial prescriptions, and, conversely, departures from legalism undermine effectiveness and justifications for international law.

The *Nicaragua* case also was the first time the ICJ issued rulings on an ongoing military conflict and only the second time it issued a ruling on any military conflict.[100] The decisions in jurisdiction and merits are hundreds of pages long, and have spurred probably thousands of pages of commentary.[101] The great interest in the *Nicaragua* case was due in part because it was brought against one of two superpowers

[97] Jayakumar & Koh, *supra* note 62, at 138–39.

[98] *Accord* Lee, *Forward*, *in* Jayakumar & Koh, *supra* note 62, at xii–xiii ("Naturally we were disappointed because we believed, as did our foreign counsel, that any Court would decide that sovereignty over all three features Pedra Branca, Middle Rocks and South Ledge went together. Nonetheless, the Government accepted the Court's judgment without any qualification. Whichever way the judgment went, it is better for bilateral relations that a conclusive judgment has been made. This allows us to put this issue aside and move on to other areas of cooperation.").

[99] Jayakumar & Koh, *supra* note 62, at xiii ("Singapore must remain committed to upholding the rule of law in relations between States.").

[100] The first decision was the *Corfu Channel* case. *See* Corfu Channel (U.K. v. Alb.), 1949 I.C.J. 244, 248 (Dec. 15) [hereinafter Corfu Channel].

[101] *See, e.g.*, Herbert W. Briggs, *Nicaragua v. United States: Jurisdiction and Admissibility*, 79 Am J. Int'l L. 373 (1985); Thomas M. Franck, *Icy Day at the ICJ*, 79 Am. J. Int'l L. 379 (1985); Herbert W. Briggs et al., *Appraisals of the ICJ's Decision: Nicaragua v. United States (Merits)*, 81 Am. J. Int'l

at the time (the United States), in part because it concerned covert intelligence and military operations in the Cold War, and in part because the United States walked away from the World Court and ignored its decisions.

Although the Nicaraguan decisions are now over two decades old, and everything that could be said about the decisions at the time they were made has probably been said, the *Nicaragua* case nevertheless helps refine this book's account of international law. The passage of time has proven or disproven scholarly speculations about what, if any, impact the *Nicaragua* case would have on international law and international relations. With this new data, it is possible to appraise whether the account of international law proposed provides guidance to international judges deciding cases on how to best justify international law.

Nicaragua is a country in Central America bordered by Honduras to the north and Costa Rica to the south. It was formerly a Spanish colony. In 1821, it achieved independence from Spain and eventually came under the rule of the Somoza family, which was pro-United States and anti-communist. In 1979, the Somoza government collapsed. The leftist Sandinista government, led by Daniel Ortega, seized power and aligned itself with the Soviet Union.

Change was also afoot in the United States, albeit not quite revolutionary in nature. President Ronald Reagan was elected the 40th president of the United States and took office in 1981. The Cold War intensified. President Reagan took a hard-line stance against the Soviet Union, which he called the "evil empire."[102] In the 1985 State of the Union Address, Reagan declared:

> We must not break faith with those who are risking their lives—on every continent, from Afghanistan to Nicaragua—to defy Soviet aggression and secure rights which have been ours from birth . . . Support for freedom fighters is self-defense.[103]

This policy, which Charles Krauthammer called the Reagan Doctrine,[104] involved overtly and covertly supporting rebels in socialist or communist foreign sovereign countries. It was this policy that landed the United States before the ICJ in the *Nicaragua* case, and it was this policy's implementation in Nicaragua that President Reagan unabashedly promoted in his State of the Union Address during the pendency of the ICJ's decision.

After the Sandinista government came to power, the CIA gathered intelligence that Nicaragua was supporting leftist militias in Honduras and El Salvador to undermine those governments, just as the Sandinistas had achieved in Nicaragua.

L. 77–183, John Norton Moore, *The Secret War in Central America and the Future of World Order*, 80 AM. J. INT'L L. 43 (1986).

[102] Ronald Reagan, Address at the National Association of Evangelicals (Mar. 8, 1983) (using the term for the first time).

[103] Ronald Reagan, Address Before a Joint Session of the Congress on the State of the Union (Feb. 6, 1985).

[104] Charles Krauthammer, *The Reagan Doctrine*, TIME, Apr. 1, 1985.

These actions were carried out with the backing of Cuba, which provided arms and other support.

President Reagan responded. In 1981, the U.S. government ended all economic aid to the Nicaraguan government. The CIA began supporting anti-Sandinista rebels in Nicaragua by providing them with paramilitary training and arms. The United States also mined the harbors of Nicaragua.[105] With the aid of the United States, contras raided Nicaraguan ports and set fire to oil storage facilities.[106]

Although the goals of the Reagan administration may have been noble, or at least consistent with U.S. foreign policy goals, the implementation of the Reagan Doctrine in Nicaragua was not savory. The CIA training manual provided to the contras instructed them that "judges, police officials, tax collectors, etc.—may be removed for PSYOP [psychological operations] effect. . . ."[107] The contras took their training seriously. They also took it too far.[108] However, whether or not the ends justified the means, the U.S.-sponsored attacks achieved their intended purposes of undermining the authority of the Sandinista government and the Nicaraguan economy, and played a role in stopping the spread of communism in Central America.

On April 9, 1984, while the United States was still supporting contras and carrying out its covert operations in Nicaragua, Nicaragua filed a lawsuit against the United States before the ICJ, the *Nicaragua* case, claiming that the United States violated international laws, including prohibition on armed attacks, by arming contras and directly participating in attacks against Nicaragua.

1. Legalism

Unlike the *Pedra Branca* cases, the decisions and orders of the ICJ in the *Nicaragua* case departed from legalism, contrary to this book's thesis that judges ought to be faithful to legalism. It is useful to investigate therefore what consequences flowed from the ICJ's deviations from legalism.

The ICJ issued two decisions in the *Nicaragua* case. The first decision found that the court had jurisdiction over the United States in the dispute. The second decision found that the United States had violated international law by assisting Nicaraguan contras and through U.S. covert operations in Nicaragua. The Court also issued several orders. Two of them are important. The first one granted provisional measures to Nicaragua. The second rejected El Salvador's request to intervene at the jurisdictional stage. These decisions and orders appeared to rely on legalist

[105] Nicaragua Case, *supra* note 14, at ¶ 78.

[106] Frederick Henry Gareau, State Terrorism and the United States: From Counterinsurgency to the war on Terrorism 166 (2004); Nicaragua Case, *supra* note 14 at ¶ 86.

[107] James Bouvard, Terrorism and Tyranny 21 (2003).

[108] *See* Gregory Grandin, Empire's Workshop 90 (2007) ("U.S.-backed Contras decapitated, castrated, and otherwise mutilated civilians and foreign aid workers. Some earned a reputation for using spoons to gorge their victims' eyes out. In one raid, Contras cut the breasts of a civilian defender to pieces and ripped the flesh off the bones of another.").

reasoning, but on closer inspection, the reasoning was flawed. Instead, the various opinions and decisions of the majority, to varying degrees, rely on policy and moral reasoning exogenous to legalism.

a. Provisional Measures When Nicaragua filed the lawsuit against the United States, it also requested provisional measures ordering the United States "to immediately cease and desist from providing, directly or indirectly, any support" to the contras, and from itself carrying out military or paramilitary activities or threatening the use of force against Nicaragua.[109] Later that month, on April 25 and 27, the ICJ conducted public hearings. Abram Chayes and Ian Brownlie were among those who represented Nicaragua. U.S. State Department legal advisor Davis Robinson and others represented the United States.

On May 10, 1984, the ICJ judges unanimously ordered the United States to stop blockading Nicaraguan ports and laying mines in the harbors, and ordered both the United States and Nicaragua not to take any actions that would aggravate the dispute or prejudice the rights of either party. The ICJ also ordered by 14 votes to 1, with U.S. Judge Stephen Schwebel dissenting, that the sovereignty and political independence of Nicaragua should be fully respected and not jeopardized by prohibited military and paramilitary activities.

Responding to the United States' argument that Nicaragua was not properly a party to the ICJ statute and therefore that the court did not have jurisdiction in the case, the ICJ reasoned that it was not required to make a final decision that it had jurisdiction before it had the authority to order provisional measures. It only needed to satisfy itself that Nicaragua had made a prima facie case showing that the ICJ had jurisdiction, and the court found that this lower standard had been met.[110]

Further, it reasoned that Article 41 of the ICJ Statute gave it authority to order provisional measures if it considered it necessary to do so to preserve the parties' respective rights.[111] The ICJ decided that provisional measures were necessary to protect the life and liberty of Nicaraguans and accordingly granted Nicaragua's request.

The foregoing reasoning appears faithful to legalism. Further analysis of the order, however, reveals gaps in legalist reasoning. One of the arguments that the United States made was that the legal dispute was

> but one facet of a complex of interrelated political, social, economic, and security matters that confront the Central American region. Those matters are the subject of a regional diplomatic effort, know as the "Contadora Process," which has been endorsed by the Organization of American States and in which the Government of Nicaragua participates . . . . The concern of

[109] Military and Paramilitary Activities in and against Nicaragua (Nicar. v. U.S.), Order on Provisional Measures, 1984 I.C.J. 169, ¶ 2 (May 10) [hereinafter Provisional Measures, Nicaragua Case].

[110] *Id.* at ¶¶ 24–26.

[111] *Id.* at ¶ 39.

> the United States is that bilateral judicial proceedings initiated by Nicaragua would impede this ongoing multilateral diplomatic process . . . .
>
> In the present situation in Central America, the indication of such measures could irreparably prejudice the interests of a number of states . . . .[112]

The United States sought to explain to the ICJ that the dispute was at core a Cold War dispute that required more than just judicial resolution, and that the stability of other Central American states was also at stake because Nicaragua was financing leftist rebels in those states.[113]

Nicaragua responded that its legal claims against the United States could not be resolved through the Contadora Process and that judicial resolution would neither disrupt the process nor prejudice the rights of other states.[114]

Both sides made serious arguments concerning both the proper allocation of international authority between political and judicial bodies to supervise and stop ongoing armed attacks, and the impact of court decisions on nonparties to the lawsuit.

The ICJ ought to have addressed these arguments and stated its reasons for deciding in favor of Nicaragua. Article 56 of the ICJ Statute provides that the "judgment shall state the reasons on which it is based." Arguably, the order was not a judgment, but that would be too literal a reading of Article 56. The Vienna Convention on the Law of Treaties requires treaty provisions to be interpreted according to the plain meaning of words in light of the treaty's object and purpose.[115] The ICJ Statute is a treaty, and its purpose is to establish the ICJ as "the principal judicial organ of the United Nations."[116] A key feature of judicial decision is explaining legal reasons for the decision. Accordingly, Article 56 should apply to the Provisional Order, and the ICJ ought to have explained its view of the arguments raised about the proper scope of judicial authority in an ongoing military, political, and ideological dispute.

The ICJ failed to do so. It simply stated the arguments of the United States and Nicaragua about the Contadora Process, without explaining why it favored Nicaragua, or why it decided the arguments were not relevant to provisional measures. Although it is understandable that the court did not fully resolve this difficult issue in its order, rendered roughly two weeks after oral argument, because there could have been insufficient time to fully consider the issue and obtain consensus or majority support of the judges, it is nevertheless regrettable that the ICJ did not address it at all. This aspect of the order was a departure from legalism.

The individual opinions reveal that the decisions in the central case of international law are not exclusively legalist. Judges Jennings and Mosler appended a brief separate opinion stating that both parties ought to refrain from the use or threat of

[112] *Id.* at ¶ 33 (quoting letter by U.S. Ambassador in The Hague, dated April 13, 1984).

[113] *See also id.* at ¶¶ 35–36.

[114] *Id.* at ¶ 38.

[115] Vienna Convention on the Law of Treaties art. 31 May 23, 1969, 1155 U.N.T.S. 331 [hereinafter VCLT].

[116] ICJ Statute, *supra* note 5, art. 1.

force, which was a more balanced view than the Provisional Order that ordered only the United States to cease using force. Those two judges also acknowledged that the situation in Central America was "complex and delicate," and emphasized the obligation of both parties to pursue "good faith negotiations within the context of the regional arrangements approved by the Security Council of the United Nations and endorsed by the Organization of American States."[117]

Judge Schwebel's dissenting opinion disagreed only with the portion of the order granting the provisional measure that spoke only to the sovereignty of Nicaragua but not the corresponding right of the United States to be free from military and paramilitary activities. In his view, the ICJ ought to have imposed that provisional measure against military and paramilitary activities in Nicaragua as well as in El Salvador, Honduras and Costa Rica.[118] Invoking legalist prescriptions in the ICJ statute and legalist precedents of ICJ decisions, he argued that the ICJ had the authority to fashion provisional measures to apply to both parties even though only one party requested such measures, and that it ought to have done so here because the prohibition on force against territorial integrity and political independence are rights *erga omnes* that every state holds universally and that do not depend on privity to a judicial dispute.[119]

Judge Schwebel's dissent was not just legalist, however. He explicitly criticized the majority "as a matter of law, as a matter of equity, and as a matter of the place of the Court as the principal judicial organ of the United Nations."[120] The conjunction "and" suggests that Judge Schwebel regarded "equity" as distinct from "law" or legalism, and a view of the ICJ as the World Court was not a legalist view. One interpretation of his statement is that judicial decisionmaking must be concerned with specific moral considerations relating to equity beyond legalism.[121]

b. El Salvador's Intervention On August 15, 1984, El Salvador filed a declaration of intervention, seeking to intervene in the lawsuit for the "sole and limited purpose of arguing that this Court [did] not have jurisdiction" over the case, and to "make it a matter of record that contrary to what Nicaragua . . . asserted in its allegations in this case, El Salvador considers itself under the pressure of an effective armed attack on the part of Nicaragua."[122] El Salvador explained that it requested "assistance

[117] Provisional Measures, Nicaragua Case, *supra* note 109, 189 (Separate Opinion of Judges Mosler and Jennings).

[118] *Id. at* 194 (dissenting opinion of Judge Schwebel) [hereinafter Schwebel Dissent on Provisional Measures, Nicaragua Case].

[119] *Id.* at 195–96.

[120] *Id.* at 194.

[121] *Cf. id.* at 195 (referring approvingly to "a balanced Order" in another case and "even-handed authority").

[122] Military and Paramilitary Activities in and against Nicaragua (Nicar. v. U.S.), Declaration of Intervention of the Republic of El Salvador art. I (Aug. 15, 1984) [hereinafter Declaration of Intervention, Nicaragua Case].

of [its] defence from the United States," pursuant to the rights to individual and collective self-defense under Article 51 of the UN Charter.[123]

A majority of the ICJ rejected the declaration. The court explained that the substance of the declaration related to the merits of Nicaragua's claims and whether the United States avoided responsibility under the doctrine of collective self-defense. Accordingly, the declaration served no purposes for the jurisdictional phase of the proceedings.[124] The court noted, appropriately, that El Salvador reserved the right to intervene in the merits phase.[125] This aspect of the decision is difficult to fault on legalist grounds.

More controversially, a majority of 9 out of 15 judges denied El Salvador an opportunity to be heard before making its decision.[126] This decision departed from strict fidelity to legalist procedures. In a separate opinion, Judges Ruda, Mosler, Ago, Jennings, and de Lacharrière explained that "it would have been more in accordance with judicial propriety if the Court had granted a hearing to the State seeking to intervene, and had not decided only on the basis of the written communications."[127] Judge Schwebel's also dissented because in his view El Salvador should have had the opportunity to be heard as a basic principle of due process.[128]

c. Decision on Jurisdiction In the jurisdiction phase of the Nicaragua case, the U.S. legal team was bolstered with Myres McDougal, Louis Sohn, and John Norton Moore, among other scholars. Nicaragua added Alain Pellet to its counsel of Abram Chayes and Ian Brownlie. With the exception of U.S. Judge Schwebel, all the other judges found that they had jurisdiction over the case.[129] On November 26, 1984, by 11 votes to 5, a majority of the judges found that the ICJ had jurisdiction under Articles 36(2) and (5) of the ICJ Statute.[130] By 14 judges to 2, a majority of the judges found that the ICJ had jurisdiction over aspects of the dispute that related to the 1956 Treaty of Friendship, Commerce and Navigation between the United States and Nicaragua.[131]

[123] *Id.* art. XII.

[124] Military and Paramilitary Activities in and against Nicaragua (Nicar. v. U.S.), Order on Intervention of the Republic of El Salvador ¶ 5 (Oct. 4, 1985) [hereinafter Order on Intervention, Nicaragua Case].

[125] *Id.* at ¶ 3.

[126] *Id.* at ¶ 4.

[127] *Id.* at ¶ 4 (separate opinion of Judges Ruda, Mosler, Ago, Jennings, and de Lacharrière).

[128] Declaration of Intervention, Nicaragua Case, *supra* note 122, at 223 (dissenting opinion of Judge Schwebel), *id.* at 231 [hereinafter Schwebel, Dissent on Jurisdiction, Nicaragua Case] ("If the Court is to deserve and maintain the confidence of States, it must act with scrupulous regard to the letter and spirit of its Rules.").

[129] Military and Paramilitary Activities in and against Nicaragua (Nicar. v. U.S.), Judgment on Jurisdiction of the Court and Admissibility of the Application, 1984 I.C.J. 392 (Nov. 26) [hereinafter Judgment on Jurisdiction, Nicaragua Case].

[130] *Id.* at ¶ 113 (a).

[131] *Id.* at ¶ 113 (b).

For illustrative purposes, and because the decision on jurisdiction under the ICJ Statute has wider implications than jurisdiction under the bilateral U.S.-Nicaragua treaty, this section will focus on a key Article 36 issue in the decision about whether Nicaragua had properly consented to the the jurisdiction of the League of Nation's Permanent Court of International Justice (PCIJ), the ICJ's predecessor court, which would provide a basis for ICJ jurisdiction as the PCIJ's successor.[132]

Article 36(2) provides that states may consent to the compulsory jurisdiction of the ICJ in disputes involving other states that have reciprocally granted that consent.[133] Article 36(5) provides that declarations accepting the jurisdiction of the PCIJ are acceptances of the ICJ's jurisdiction if the PCIJ declarations remain in force.[134]

The United States argued that even though they had previously consented to the ICJ's compulsory jurisdiction, the court lacked jurisdiction over the dispute because Article 36(2) jurisdiction was contingent upon Nicaragua also having reciprocally consented to the ICJ's compulsory jurisdiction. Nicaragua had never made an Article 36(2) declaration. It had made a declaration accepting the PCIJ's jurisdiction, but it failed to comply with the formalities of the PCIJ by not depositing with the UN Secretary General a Protocol of Signature to the Statute of The Court, even though the Minister of Foreign Affairs of Nicaragua stated in 1939 that Nicaragua had done so. The last PCIJ report covering the period of 1939 to 1945 recorded that Nicaragua was not bound by the PCIJ because it had not ratified the Protocol.[135]

Curiously, however, although the PCIJ did not treat Nicaragua as having submitted to its compulsory jurisdiction, the Registrar of the ICJ did. From the first yearbook of the ICJ in 1946–47, Nicaragua was listed as a state that had consented to the ICJ's jurisdiction by virtue of its PCIJ declaration "deemed to be still in force."[136] This characterization continued in subsequent yearbooks. A majority of the ICJ concluded that Nicaragua's failure to protest the yearbook records since the very first yearbook indicated that Nicaragua had accepted the ICJ's jurisdiction.

Whether a declaration without binding force during the time of the PCIJ satisfied the consent to jurisdiction under Article 36(5) of the ICJ Statute was a novel issue.[137] The ICJ reasoned that Article 36(5) should be construed widely, and because Nicaragua had for decades not protested the yearbook's claim that it had consented to the ICJ's jurisdiction,[138] it held that Nicaragua's conduct confirmed that its PCIJ declaration was in force sufficient to grant the ICJ compulsory jurisdiction.[139]

[132] For a discussion of other arguments on jurisdiction, *see* Reisman, Systems of Control, *supra* note 7, at 23–24; John F. Murphy, The United States and the Rule of Law in International Affairs 255–60 (2004); D.W. Greig, *Nicaragua and the United States: Confrontation Over the Jurisdiction of the International Court*, 62 Brit. Y.B. Int'l L. 119 (1991).

[133] ICJ Statute, *supra* note 5, art. 36(2).

[134] *Id.* art. 36(5).

[135] Judgment on Jurisdiction, *supra* note 129, at ¶ 19.

[136] Schwebel Dissent on Provisional Measures, Nicaragua Case, *supra* note 118, at 201.

[137] Judgment on Jurisdiction, *supra* note 129, at ¶ 29.

[138] *Id.* at ¶¶ 37–39.

[139] *Id.* at ¶ 42 ("It should therefore be observed that the conduct of Nicaragua in relation to the publications in question also supports a finding of jurisdiction under Article 36, paragraph 2, of the

The legalism of this reasoning is opaque. The court did not support its assertion of jurisdiction based on Nicaragua's conduct with a single customary law, treaty, scholarly writing, or judicial decision—the sources of legal prescriptions under the ICJ's choice of law clause in Article 38 of the ICJ Statute. Although this was not the only argument of the majority, and it was admittedly a novel issue, the complete absence of any invocation of legal prescription to interpret or apply by extension to the present case was conspicuous. Judge Jennings, who dissented on this point, made a more cogent argument: because the Nicaragua declaration was never in force in the PCIJ, it could not be "still in force" as required under Article 36(5).[140] The absence of legal prescriptions in the majority's decision and Judge Jennings' logical argument support a conclusion that the ICJ departed from the central case of legalism in its decision on jurisdiction.

The United States also made an alternative argument that the ICJ lacked jurisdiction over the United States because on April 6, 1984, three days before Nicaragua filed suit, the U.S. Secretary of State modified its consent to compulsory jurisdiction to exclude disputes with Central American States. The ICJ rejected this argument because the U.S. Optional Clause of 1946, through which it had previously granted jurisdiction, required the United States to give six months' notice of any change. Because the United States accepted the compulsory jurisdiction for, under the express words of the Optional Clause, "five years and thereafter until the expiration of six months after notice,"[141] the majority reasoned that therefore Secretary Schultz's letter was ineffective to divest the ICJ of jurisdiction over the lawsuit brought by Nicaragua against the United States.[142]

Judge Jennings also disagreed on this point. In his view, the United States could change its declaration before the lawsuit was filed in spite of the six-month notice period in its Optional Protocol. He did not principally base his argument on the U.S. claim of a reciprocal right of immediate termination of consent because Nicaragua could do the same. Instead, he simply eliminated the six-month notice period.

He reasoned:

> Law develops by precedent, and it is that which gives it consistency and predictability. But legal precedents like any other must be seen in the light of history and of changing times. In the period of the Permanent Court and even in 1946 when the United States Declaration was made, an important proportion of States had subscribed to the Optional-Clause system. Today that is no longer the case. The Optional-Clause States are distinctly in the minority and very many of the most important and powerful States

Statute independently of the interpretation and effect of paragraph 5 of that Article"). *Accord* Nicaragua Case, *supra* note 14 (separate opinion of Judge Lachs, at 155) [hereinafter Lachs, Separate Opinion on Merits, Nicaragua Case].

[140] Judgment on Jurisdiction, Nicaragua Case, *supra* note 129, at 536 (separate opinion of Judge Jennings) [hereinafter Jennings, Separate Opinion on Jurisdiction, Nicaragua Case].

[141] *Id.* at 398 (quoting U.S. Optional Clause).

[142] Nicaragua Case, *supra* note 14, at ¶ 271.

> have not accepted compulsory jurisdiction and show little indication of any ambition to do so. Any assessment of the position in contemporary practice must take into account the position of this majority of States which do not subscribe to the Optional-Clause system.[143]

Judge Jennings also noted the unfairness of holding the United States to the six-month notice period when Nicaragua could withdraw from the ICJ's jurisdiction at will because its declaration did not contain a notice period:

> In this climate it would in my view be as impracticable as it would be inequitable to hold that a State whose declaration, like that of the United States, is expressed as subject to six months' notice, is bound by that statement of intention in respect of all corners, including those very many States which have declined to risk even a potential liability to jurisdiction.[144]

He concluded:

> In face of the unmistakable trend of recent developments, I feel bound to conclude that States now—though the position was probably different during the earlier, more promising period of the Optional Clause jurisdiction—have the right, before seisin of the Court, to withdraw or alter their declarations of acceptance, with immediate effect, and, moreover, even in anticipation of a particular case or class of cases. If this is so, then it follows that the Shultz letter was effective to deprive the Court of jurisdiction under Article 36, paragraph 2, of the Court's Statute.[145]

This reasoning is remarkable because Jennings in important ways appeared to be a committed positivist.[146] In his scholarly writing, he argued: "The justice a court of law should seek is not a subjective notion of what appears to be just in the instant case between the particular parties, but that most effective and general justice which is achieved by ordering matters generally in accordance with the rule of law."[147] He stressed: "Even where the court develops the law . . . the decision must be seen to emanate reasonably and logically from existing and previously ascertainable law."[148]

Arguably, his innovation of nullifying the express six-month notice period of the U.S. Optional Protocol was a reasonable and logical derivation from previously ascertainable law. However, it is equally plausible, if not more tempting, to observe that his brand of positivism is one that accounted for—*pace* policy-oriented jurisprudence—trend analysis, with a focus on powerful states, that authoritatively

143 Jennings, Separate Opinion on Jurisdiction, Nicaragua Case, *supra* note 140, at 547.

144 *Id.* at 548.

145 *Id.* at 553.

146 *Accord* Lachs, Separate Opinion on Merits, Nicaragua Case, *supra* note 139, at 168 ("The Court's primary task is to ascertain the law, and to leave no doubt as to its meaning.").

147 Jennings, *supra* note 11.

148 *Id.* at 43.

shapes the expectations of appropriate conduct for elites and their constituencies, and an appraisal of the inequities of current prescriptions on Optional Protocols, all of which led him to conclude, as a matter of law, that the express six-month notice period in the U.S. Optional Clause was now a nullity. There is much to commend in the candor of Judge Jennings' reasoning.

d. Merits After the ICJ issued its decision on jurisdiction, the United States withdrew from the case. This response is discussed at length below in the section on effectiveness and legitimacy. The ICJ nevertheless continued to have hearings and to receive submissions without the United States participating.

On June 27, 1986, the ICJ rendered its judgment finding that the United States committed numerous violations of international law by mining Nicaraguan harbors, arming and training contras, and directly attacking Nicaragua.[149] This section will focus on the arguments of the judges relating to U.S. violations of the prohibition against the use of force through its assistance to contras indirectly constituting "armed attacks" and the unavailability of self-defense as a legal justification in this case because, inter alia, Nicaragua's assistance of El Salvador rebels did not constitute armed attacks on El Salvador.

A majority of 12 judges of the tribunal decided that U.S. assistance to contras constituted armed attacks in violation of the prohibition on the use of force. Judges Schwebel, Jennings, and Oda voted against this decision. The majority reasoned that the customary law against force was expressed in Article 2(4), which states:

> All Members shall refrain in their international relations from the threat or use of force against the territorial integrity or political independence of any state, or in any other manner inconsistent with the Purposes of the United Nations.[150]

The ICJ reasoned further that armed attacks constituted illegal uses of force and could only be justified by individual or collective self-defense against another armed attack.[151] This is well established in customary law, and as expressed in Article 51 of the UN Charter, which states in relevant part:

> Nothing in the present Charter shall impair the inherent right of individual or collective self-defence if an armed attack occurs against a Member of the United Nations, until the Security Council has taken measures necessary to maintain international peace and security. . . . [152]

So far, none of this is controversial. What is controversial is the court's definition of "armed attack" and its application to the facts. The court inserted an additional

[149] Nicaragua Case, *supra* note 14.

[150] UN Charter art. 2, ¶ 4.

[151] *See* Nicaragua Case, *supra* note 14, at 110–11.

[152] UN Charter art. 51.

requirement for self-defense under Article 51 and for its corresponding customary law that the armed attack must be by or on behalf of another state.[153] The majority in the *Nicaragua* merits judgment properly acknowledged that the exercise of self-defense "is subject to the State concerned having been the victim of an armed attack."[154] It then circumscribed the right by limiting an armed attack to an attack by or on behalf of a state.[155] It stated:

> [A]n armed attack must be understood as including not merely action by regular armed forces across an international border, but also "the sending by or on behalf of State of armed bands, groups, irregulars or mercenaries, which carry out acts of armed force against another State of such gravity as to amount to" (*inter alia*) an actual armed attack conducted by regular forces, "or its substantial involvement therein."[156]

The court added, however, that although armed attacks included acts by "armed bands where such acts occur on a significant scale," it did not extend to "the provision of weapons or logistical or other support."[157]

This key aspect of the majority's decision surprisingly lacks legalist support. It did not refer to the methods of interpretation of treaties in the Vienna Convention on the Law of Treaties that control the interpretation of Article 51. The only purported legalist prescription that the court gave for its assertion was Article 3(g) of the Definition of Aggression annexed to UN General Assembly Resolution 3314 (XXIX).[158] The court's justification is questionable on formal legalist grounds. UN General Assembly resolutions are not legally binding. They are not one of the sources of law applicable to ICJ decisions, as stated in Article 38 of the ICJ Statute. Resolution 3314 is not in and of itself evidence of customary law because it was adopted without a vote by the General Assembly.[159]

Even if Resolution 3314 were a legal prescription reflecting strongly shared expectations of conduct, it refers in terms to aggression and not an armed attack.

[153] *See* Judge Higgins, Wall in the Occupied Palestinian Territory, *supra* note 41, at 215 ("There is, with respect, nothing in the text of Article 51 that thus stipulates that self-defence is available only when an armed attack is made by a State. That qualification is rather a result of the Court so determining in *Military and Paramilitary Activities in and against Nicaragua* (. . .). It there held that military action by irregulars could constitute an armed attack if these were sent by or on behalf of the State and if the activity "because of its scale and effects, would have been classified as an armed attack . . .had it been carried out by regular armed forces.").

[154] *See* Nicaragua Case, *supra* note 14, at 103, ¶ 195 ("In particular, it may be considered to be agreed that an armed attack must be understood as including not merely action by regular armed forces across an international border, but also the sending by or on behalf of a State of armed bands, groups, irregulars or mercenaries, which carry out acts of armed force against another State of such gravity as to amount to (inter alia) an actual armed attack conducted by regular forces, or its substantial involvement therein.") (quotation marks and citations omitted).

[155] *See id.*

[156] *Id.* (quoting G.A. Res. 3314 (XXIX), art. 3, para. g, U.N. Doc. A/3314 (Dec. 14, 1974)).

[157] Nicaragua Case, *supra* note 14, at 104.

[158] *See id.* at 103. *See also* G.A. Res. 3314 (XXIX), art. 3, para. g, U.N. Doc. A/3314 (Dec. 14, 1974).

[159] *See* Dietrich Rauschning et al., Key Resolutions of the United Nations General Assembly 1946–1996, at 13 (1997).

Article 3(g) defines "aggression," not "armed attack," as "[t]he sending by or on behalf of a State of armed bands, groups, irregulars or mercenaries, which carry out acts of armed force against another State of such gravity as to amount to the acts listed above, or its substantial involvement therein."[160] Under the ordinary meaning of these words, aggression is wider in scope than an armed attack. The court does not explain why it conflates the meaning of the two terms, much less provide a legal justification.

Having failed to explain why it defined an armed attack as an act of aggression and thus appearing to decide arbitrarily, it then proceeded to exclude from the scope of an "armed attack" the supply of weapons or other support. It did so without providing any reason or invoking and interpreting any legal prescription for its view. It is troubling that the court decided a holding of a case without any law at all in support of its view.[161] This comes close to violating the court's own choice of law provision, Article 38(2) of the ICJ Statute, which explicitly permits the court to decide a case *ex aequo et bono* only if the parties agree,[162] which they did not in this case.

As to the facts, the court's findings also appear less than faithful to legalist standards of proof. Based on its distinction between effectively controlling militias so that they act on behalf of a state, versus merely supplying them with arms and providing other support, the court concluded that the United States had engaged in armed attacks against Nicaragua in the scale of its assistance of contras. However, Nicaragua had not engaged in armed attacks against El Salvador that could otherwise have justified collective self-defense by the United States against Nicaragua. The court explained that the provision of arms did not as a legal matter constitute an armed attack, and, in fact, Nicaragua was not responsible for the flow of arms from its territory to El Salvadorian rebels.[163]

Judge Schwebel questioned in his dissent the findings of fact based on testimony from witnesses for Nicaragua that it did not provide assistance to rebels in El Salvador of such a scale as to amount to an armed attack.[164] Although the Nicaraguan foreign minister testified that Nicaragua never supplied arms or assistance to rebels in El Salvador,[165] this testimony was implausible given that there was aircraft that took off from Papalonal Airport in Nicaragua to deliver weapons to rebels in El Salvador.[166] After the fall of the Sandinista regime, the new Nicaragua government admitted that the prior regime had indeed supplied arms to El Salvadorian rebels.[167]

Judge Schwebel also pointed out that had the court permitted El Salvador to intervene when it requested to do so, the ICJ would have received direct evidence from

[160] G.A. Res. 3314 (XXIX), art. 3 para. g, U.N. Doc. A/3314 (Dec. 14, 1974).

[161] *See* Higgins, Problems and Process, *supra* note 84, at 250 ("The Court found this to represent customary international law (without elaborating how it reached that view)[.]").

[162] ICJ Statute, *supra* note 5, art. 38 (2).

[163] *See* Nicaragua Case, *supra* note 14, at 119.

[164] *See id.* at 276–77 (dissenting opinion of Judge Schwebel) [hereinafter Schwebel, Dissent on Merits, Nicaragua Case].

[165] *See id.*

[166] *See id.* at 330–31.

[167] *See id.* at 164.

El Salvador about the extent to which Nicaragua assisted El Salvadorian rebels, as was made amply clear in El Salvador's declaration that the ICJ had rejected at the jurisdictional stage of proceedings.[168]

Likewise, Michael Reisman questioned whether the majority properly satisfied itself that the facts supported their distinction between respective acts of the contras and the United States.[169] The majority invoked Article 53 of the ICJ Statute, which permitted the court to proceed even when a party does not appear, but which required the court to satisfy itself that the "claim is well founded in fact and law."[170] Quoting the *Corfu Channel* case, the court adopted the following interpretation of Article 53:

> While Article 53 thus obliges the Court to consider the submissions of the Party which appears, it does not compel the Court to examine their accuracy in all their details; for this might in certain unopposed cases prove impossible in practice.[171]

As Michael Reisman pointed out, the court selectively quoted the *Corfu Channel* case, which immediately after the quoted passage stated: "It is sufficient for the Court to convince itself by such methods as it considers suitable that the submissions are well-founded."[172] In his view, the omission of the operative language of the *Corfu Channel* case on this point "leaves the impression that . . . the court is entitled to reach judgment in Article 53 cases without satisfying itself that the factual claims made by the applicant state are well-founded. It is not."[173] If Reisman's analysis is accepted, the ICJ's infidelity to its prior case law is a serious failure of procedural legitimacy in a legalist sense, a failure that undermined the prescriptive force of the decision on the merits in the *Nicaragua* case.

Without legalist guidance on the law and the facts, an observer of the *Nicaragua* case is left to scour the judges' opinions for clues on what motivated their decisions. ICJ President Nagendra, in his separate opinion fully supporting the operative holdings of the Court explained that the essential points were important legally, as well as "for promoting peaceful community existence of sovereign States."[174] To promote "sound public order," nonintervention was "sanctified [as an] absolute rule of law."[175] Based on the foregoing, it appears that the majority decision was not strictly legalist, and there are indications in dicta that they were also motivated by exogenous appraisals of appropriate conduct.

[168] *See* Schwebel, Dissent on Jurisdiction, Nicaragua Case, *supra* note 128, at 606–08.

[169] *See* Reisman, Systems of Control, *supra* note 7, at 32.

[170] ICJ Statue, *supra* note 5, art. 53, ¶ 2.

[171] Corfu Channel, *supra* note 100, at 248.

[172] Reisman, Systems of Control, *supra* note 7, at 34 (quoting *Corfu Channel*, *supra* note 100).

[173] *Id.*

[174] Nicaragua Case, *supra* note 14, at 151 (separate opinion of President Nagendra Singh).

[175] *Id.* at 156.

2. Effectiveness

The *Nicaragua* case was ineffective in resolving the dispute between the United States and Nicaragua.[176] It appears that the Reagan administration ignored the Order for Provisional Measures. The majority of the ICJ found at the merits stage that the United States continued to conduct overflights after the order was issued, in November 1984. The court also determined that the United States funded contras until September 30, 1984. Thus, the United States breached its obligations to cease activities that would affect the rights of Nicaragua and to respect the political sovereignty of Nicaragua.

The decision of jurisdiction produced a dramatic result. The United States simply withdrew from the case entirely. As quoted earlier, Ronald Reagan publicly reiterated U.S. support for Nicaraguan contras in his 1985 State of the Union address. The nonappearance of the United States in the ICJ merits phase also directly contradicted the decision on jurisdiction and made fact-finding by the ICJ significantly more challenging.

The decision on the merits was likewise ignored. Following the order for the United States to pay reparations, Nicaragua submitted a claim for $17 billion. The United States resisted pressure from European countries to pay.[177] It also vetoed a Security Council resolution against it for not complying with the ICJ decision.[178] The U.S. Congress approved a further $100 million in aid to the contras in 1986 after the decision.[179] The dispute was only resolved when the Sandinista government fell from power, and the new regime abandoned its claim for reparations in exchange for trade and foreign aid from the United States.[180]

3. Morality

The decisions of the ICJ were ineffective in part because of its departures from legalist reasoning and procedures, in part because the legal decision prescribed bad outcomes, and in part because of the great power and interest of the United States to ignore the ICJ's decisions in this dispute.

As discussed above, the court's decisions were insufficiently supported on legalist grounds. This undermined the credibility of the decisions and weakened the moral obligation to obey the rulings, which is strongest when rulings are based on

[176] Aaron Fichtelberg, Law at the Vanishing Point: A Philosophical Analysis of International Law 165 (2008) ("In many ways the *Nicaragua* case is an abject failure of law, to use Henkin's terminology."). *But cf.*, Paul Reichler, *Holding America to Its Own Best Standards, Abe Chayes and Nicaragua in the World Court*, 42 Harv. Int'l L. J. 15, 34, 42, 44 (2001) (arguing that the ICJ's decision on interim measures contributed to decisions of the U.S. Congress not to finance aid to contras, but conceding that the Regan administration nonetheless supplied contras in secret, and that by the time of the decision on the merits, Congress had once again authorized aid to contras).

[177] *Id.* at 164.

[178] *See* S.C. Draft Res. 18250, U.N. Doc. S/18250 (July 31, 1986).

[179] *See* Fichtelberg, *supra* note 176, at 167.

[180] *See id.* at 164.

established legal prescriptions. This is perhaps what Reisman has referred to as the "morality of case law."[181] The court declined to hear El Salvador before rejecting its declaration of intervention. It then seized jurisdiction based on questionable legalist reasoning, interpretations of fact, and departures from the Statute of the ICJ.[182] Finally, at the merits stage, on key issues of whether the United States carried out armed attacks through contras and whether Nicaragua did the same in El Salvador, the court invented an artificial distinction completely unsupported by law to reach findings of fact based on inadequate evidence.

In addition to the weakness of reasoning and procedures identified above, there were also procedural pathologies. Nicaragua's counsel subsequently admitted that a judge of the ICJ was in contact with Nicaragua before the case was submitted.[183] This fact suggests serious deficiencies of fairness in process. Davis Robinson, the legal advisor to the U.S. State Department during the *Nicaragua* case, emphasized this when discussing the *Nicaragua* case almost 15 years later,[184] indicating that governing elites are concerned with formalist procedures as a way to ensure procedural fairness, when deciding whether or not to accept the prescriptive claims of another elite, such as the ICJ.

Worse, while the decision of the ICJ was pending and three weeks before the United States announced its decision to withdraw from the ICJ case, the president of the ICJ gave an interview with the Associated Press. He is reported to have threatened:

> It is not acceptable in a civilized system of international law that any nation withdraws without notice from a solemn undertaking like that . . . A State that defies the Court will not get away with it.[185]

[181] Reisman, Systems of Control, *supra* note 7, at 31. *See also* Jennings, *supra* note 11, at 40 ("'[J]ustice is very seldom achieved by directly aiming at it: rather it is a by-product of the application of legal rules and principles, a consequence of the general order, certainty and stability introduced into human and international relationships through the regular and systematic application of known legal rules and principles, even if these rules and principles are not always perfect and do not always achieve ideal results in every case.'") (quoting Sir Gerald Fitzmaurice).

[182] *See generally* Judgment on Jurisdiction, Nicaragua Case, *supra* note 129. *See also* Reisman, Systems of Control, *supra* note 7, at 22–25 (criticizing jurisdictional reasoning of the ICJ in the *Nicaragua* case for deviating from legalist reasoning and the Statute of the ICJ).

[183] *See* Michael P. Scharf & Paul R. Williams, Shaping Foreign Policy in Times of Crisis 62–64 (2010); Reichler, *supra* note 176 at 34 (recollecting, as a member of Nicaragua's legal team, that prior to filing the lawsuit, "a meeting was arranged with one of the judges of the Court, from a nonaligned nation, to inquire whether, in his opinion, the Court would render an impartial judgement in a case brought by Nicaragua against the United State, or whether the judges would feel obliged, for whatever reason, to favor the United States. The answer was inequivocal: the composition of the Court was such that it could be counted upon to decde the case on its merits.").

[184] *Id.* at 62 ("The lawyer in charge of the Nicaragua case has since admitted in a remarkable article that a Judge of the Court was in communication with Nicaragua before its application was submitted.").

[185] Schwebel, Dissent on Jurisdiction, Nicaragua Case, *supra* note 128, at 314–15.

He added that the U.S. invasion of Grenada was not "according to the rule of law," and "[s]maller nations wonder what happened to the rule of law when the United States can behave like this."[186]

As Judge Schwebel pointed out, a jurist no less eminent than Shabtai Rosenne noted:

> Public comment on a pending case by any judge, let alone the President, is absolutely unprecedented and contrary to all standards of judicial propriety . . . That interview, which was given before the United States announced its intention not to participate in further proceedings . . . and indeed may have precipitated it, was reported in the Press.[187]

The ICJ president's departure from legalist procedures through his out-of-court statements stoked U.S. suspicions of judicial bias in the ICJ and provided administration officials with a further reason to ignore the court's rulings.

In addition to defects in legalism, the decision of the ICJ on the merits regarding armed attacks, if followed, would have resulted in a substantively poor outcome. It would have prevented the United States from protecting El Salvador and other small states from insurgents financed and assisted by other states. Sovereign states would be undermined, rather than protected. As discussed in the section on feedback loops, below, this aspect of the *Nicaragua* case has not promoted world order against terrorism and destructive violence by insurgents and militias in post-Cold War conflicts. It was thus understandable that the United States appraised the ICJ decision poorly and elected to ignore it.

That said, infidelity to legalism and the substantive problems posed by the decision for the common good and basic values do not fully explain the ineffectiveness of the ICJ in the *Nicaragua* case. National interests, the power of the United States, the Republican Party's hard line during the Cold War and its robust view of executive power also aligned to undermine the ICJ's effectiveness. Robinson subsequently revealed that "[s]ome political forces in Washington argued that the United States should not have shown up in the Hague at all," and U.S. attorneys were not allowed to make certain persuasive arguments.[188] U.S. actions after the Order for Provisional Measures were issued provide strong indications that U.S. power and interests played a key role in the court's ineffectiveness in this case. Unlike the decisions on jurisdiction and merits, the Order for Provisional Measures was largely faithful to legalism, even if not beyond reproach. There was no known procedural impropriety at that time. Nevertheless, the United States ignored the order by violating Nicaraguan airspace through low overflights of U.S. aircraft from November 7 to 11, 1984, after the Order for Provisional Measures but before the decision on jurisdiction. Therefore, the decision to carry out these overflights was more likely taken

[186] *Id.*

[187] *Id.* (quoting Shabtai Rosenne, *The Changing Role of the International Court*, 20 Israel L. Rev. 196, n.33 (1985)).

[188] Scharf & Williams, *supra* note 183, at 61.

because the U.S. administration determined they was necessary to protect U.S. interests and world order, rather than because the order of provisional measures was defective on legalist grounds. These facts indicate that although legalism and substantive legitimacy play some role in securing the effectiveness of international legal decisions, national interests and power cannot be ignored.

4. Feedback Loops

Even though the *Nicaragua* decision was ineffective in settling the dispute concerning Nicaragua, it did adjust international legal prescriptions on the use of force because the decision created an authoritative feedback loop in the ICJ's future cases. This feedback loop has proven that some of the criticisms of the decision were justified.

When the *Nicaragua* decision on the merits was rendered, several dissenting judges warned that its holdings would not promote peaceful international relations. Judge Schwebel suggested that the court's distinction between the unlawful sending of contras on behalf of a state and the purportedly lawful supply of arms and other support to contras appeared to "justify foreign intervention in furtherance of 'the process of decolonization.'"[189] In his view, this distinction was "inconsonant with . . . the realities of international relations"[190] and ignored "the realities of modern warfare."[191]

Judge Jennings, in a passage that contradicts any characterization of his jurisprudence as purely positivistic, explained the policy concern well:

> This looks to me neither realistic nor just in the world where power struggles are in every continent carried on by destabilization, interference in civil strife, comfort, aid and encouragement to rebels, and the like. The original scheme of the United Nations Charter, whereby force would be deployed by the United Nations itself, in accordance with the provisions of Chapter VII of the Charter, has never come into effect. Therefore an essential element in the Charter design is totally missing. In this situation it seems dangerous to define unnecessarily strictly the conditions for lawful self-defence, so as to leave a large area where both a forcible response to force is forbidden, and yet the United Nations employment of force, which was intended to fill that gap, is absent.[192]

Judge Jennings' observation that the UN Security Council failed to exercise its Chapter VII powers was salient at the time because during the Cold War, either the United States or the Soviet Union would veto any Chapter VII resolution, thoroughly paralyzing the Security Council. Even after the Cold War, however, when the Security Council has exercised its Chapter VII powers, it has not always done so in

[189] Schwebel, Dissent on Jurisdiction, Nicaragua Case, *supra* note 128, at 266.

[190] *Id.* at 271.

[191] *Id.* at 346.

[192] Jennings, Separate Opinion on Merits, Nicaragua Case, *supra* note 140, at 543–44.

disputes with limited geopolitical interest, or it has intervened too late. Therefore, Judge Jennings' exhortation that states must be able to act to protect themselves when the Security Council fails to act remains relevant.

Scholars commenting after the case was decided were divided.[193] History appears to have sided with the critics. Rosalyn Higgins warned that the distinction between sending militias so as to be tantamount to an armed attack, versus supporting them without constituting an armed attack, is operationally unworkable. She asked rhetorically:

> When a state has to decide whether it can repel incessant low-level irregular military activity, does it really have to decide whether that activity is the equivalent of an armed attack by a foreign army—and, anyway, is not *any* use of force by a foreign army entitled to be met by sufficient force to require it to withdraw? Or is that now in doubt also?[194]

Abraham Sofaer and Michael Reisman shared this view, pointing out that the holding of the *Nicaragua* decision on the merits created an incentive for state-sponsored terrorism because the victim state cannot use force in self-defense against it.[195]

These criticisms were directly borne out when Israel fenced the West Bank in response to numerous suicide attacks upon civilians by Palestinians. The majority of the ICJ in the *Wall Opinion* concluded that Israel's actions were not in self-defense because the attacks by the Palestinians were not armed attacks by a state.[196] Implicitly validating the *Nicaragua* decision, the ICJ in the *Wall Opinion* reasoned that Article 51 of the UN Charter permitting self-defense did not authorize force against any armed attack, but only armed attacks by another state. The *Wall Opinion* thus illustrates how the *Nicaragua* decision's departure from legalism created an unjustified feedback loop on the law of self-defense that arguably adjusted the original prescriptions on self-defense.

This feedback loop that was created by a prior decision of the court on questionable legalist grounds raises several important issues. It shows that the legalist procedures for interpreting and identifying legal prescriptions do not necessarily fully explain how governing elites—in this instance, judges—actually interpret or change the law. Article 38 of the ICJ Statute states that judicial decisions are only subsidiary sources of law that do not supersede treaties and customary law.[197] If Article 38 were followed strictly, the court in the *Wall Opinion* should not have accepted the

[193] *See, e.g.*, Briggs, *supra* note 101, at 373; Moore, *supra* note 101, at 151 (1987); Briggs et al., *supra* note 101, at 78 (1987).

[194] Higgins, Problems and Process, *supra* note 84, at 251.

[195] *See* Abraham D. Sofaer, *Terrorism and the Law*, Foreign Affairs, Summer 1986, at 901, 919. *See also* W. Michael Reisman, *Old Wine in New Bottles: The Reagan and Brezhnev Doctrines in Contemporary International Law and Practice*, 13 Yale J. Int'l L. 171, 195–96 (1988).

[196] Wall in the Occupied Palestinian Territory, *supra* note 32.

[197] *See* ICJ Statute, *supra* note 5, art. 38(1).

Nicaragua decision's insertion into Article 51, without legalist authority, that an armed attack must come from a state. In the alternative, at the very least, the *Wall Opinion* should have explained how that aspect of the *Nicaragua* decision, as a source of law subsidiary to treaties and custom, was consistent with either the methods of interpreting treaties prescribed by the Vienna Convention on the Law of Treaties, or with the customary law of self-defense. The fact that the court in the *Wall Opinion* decision did not provide such an explanation indicates that the *Nicaragua* decision had effectively become the controlling authority in ICJ decisions at least on par with treaties and custom. This contradicts the formalist choice of law prescriptions in Article 38 of the ICJ's own statute and validates an informal shared expectation among ICJ judges and other elites that prior cases often serve a function akin to precedent.

This feedback loop substantiates Robert Jennings' explanation of how legal rules change in international law—at least in the context of ICJ decisions. He explained:

> [T]here is no gainsaying the practical authority and power of that precedent of the International Court. It would be wrong, of course, to try to treat all judgments, even of the International Court, as being of equal authority. It depends upon a number of factors; and one is that one must look to see how they wear in later practice.[198]

Although legalism may play a role in interpreting, changing, and applying law, it appears that judges are not simply passive receivers of the law but through their practice, create new laws and confirm those prescriptions by referring to them in subsequent cases.

The *Nicaragua* decision also created feedback loops in unforeseen ways beyond the dislocating of international law from the realities of combating terrorism militias. It hamstrung the ability of the international legal system to rectify internecine abuses. The court in the *Nicaragua* merits judgment found that the United States was responsible for the armed attacks of the contras because it exercised "effective control" over the contras.[199] Anything short of effective control over militias did not create state responsibility, such as the supply of arms from Nicaragua to El Salvadorian rebels. In the *Case Concerning the Application of the Convention on the Prevention and Punishment of Genocide* (Bosnia & Herzegovina v. Serbia & Montenegro) (the *Genocide* case), the ICJ had to decide whether Serbia was responsible for genocide committed by militias. It applied the *Nicaragua* standard and found insufficient evidence that President Slobodan Milosevic effectively controlled the militias to impute direct responsibility on Serbia for carrying out genocide of Muslims in Bosnia.[200]

[198] Robert Jennings, *The Judiciary, International and National, and the Development of International Law*, *in* 102 Int'l L. Reports ix, xvii–xviii (E. Lauterpacht et al. eds.,1996).

[199] *See* Nicaragua Case, *supra* note 14, at 64, 118–19.

[200] The Application of the Convention on the Prevention and Punishment of the Crime of Genocide (Bosn. & Herz. v. Serb. & Mont.), 2007 I.C.J. 1, 138–45 (Feb. 26).

The strength of feedback loops can depend, however, on the elite making a decision. In the *Tadic* case, an appeals chamber of the International Criminal Tribunal for the Former Yugoslavia rejected the *Nicaragua* standard of effective control in determining whether an individual Serbian official was criminally liable for genocides committed by militias. The ICTY appeals chamber invented a different test of "overall control" and on the basis of this lower evidentiary threshold, found the official responsible.[201] In contrast, the ICJ in the *Genocide* case found the *Tadic* case to not apply because the *Tadic* case addressed individual liability for international crimes and not state responsibility. The ICJ chose instead to follow the *Nicaragua* case, which it described as "settled jurisprudence of the Court."[202] As an operational matter, it appears that feedback loops will tend to be stronger within institutions but weaker between them.[203] This is similar to how U.S. district courts regard appellate decisions within their circuit as settled and binding jurisprudence, and appellate decisions in other circuits as only persuasive or unpersuasive.[204]

When faced with an unjustified departure from legalism in a prior case, a judge should correct that deviation rather than reinforce it. Judge Higgins provides a good example of judicial decisionmaking that balances legalism and moral considerations to correct deviations and to give the practice of judicial decisionmaking a good interpretation. In the *Wall Opinion*, Judge Higgins disagreed with the majority's interpretation of Article 51 of the UN Charter. The majority held that Article 51 applied only to armed attacks from other states, as had been its interpretation of Article 51 since the *Nicaragua* case in 1986. Because Palestine was a territory occupied by Israel, it was not a state, and Israel could not find shelter under Article 51.[205] Judge Higgins stressed the relevance of context in moral deliberation but also acknowledged its limits in legalist reasoning that she was morally obliged as a judge to apply. She stated:

> While accepting, as I must, that this [limitation that Article 51 applies only to armed attacks by another state] is to be regarded as a statement of the law as it now stands, I maintain all the reservations as to this proposition that I have expressed elsewhere.
>
> I also find unpersuasive the Court's contention that, as the uses of force emanate from occupied territory, it is not an armed attack "by one State against another." I fail to understand the Court's view that an occupying Power loses the right to defend its own civilian citizens at home if the attacks emanate from the occupied territory—a territory which it has found not to have been annexed and is certainly "other than" Israel. Further, Palestine cannot be sufficiently an international entity to be invited to these proceedings, and to benefit from humanitarian law, but not sufficiently

201 *See id.* at 143–45 (discussing the Judgment of the ICTY Appeals Chamber in the *Tadic* case.).

202 *See id.* at 145.

203 *See* Jennings, *supra* note 198, at xv ("[T]he Court pretty rigidly eschews the citing of decisions other than those of the two World Courts [the ICJ and PCIJ].").

204 *Cf. id.* at xiv (noting that among international tribunals, "[t]here is not even the semblance of any kind of hierarchy or system.").

205 *See* Wall in the Occupied Palestinian Territory, *supra* note 32, at 194, ¶ 139.

> an international entity for the prohibition of armed attacked on others to be applicable. This is formalism of an uneven handed sort.[206]

She ultimately voted with the majority because she concluded that constructing the wall was a nonforcible measure, and such measures did not fall within self-defense under Article 51 "as that provision is normally understood,"[207] and in any event it would need to be justified as "necessary and proportionate"[208]: two legalist (and, in this author's view, morally appropriate) criteria for self-defense. Yet embedded in her *dictum* is an invitation for the court, at some future point, to change its interpretation of Article 51, both based on the moral considerations she espoused, as well as the legalist argument that nothing in the words of Article 51 limited it to armed attacks by states, which was a limitation adopted by the ICJ in the *Nicaragua* case.[209]

C. The Avena Case

The United States has a history of violating the Vienna Convention on Consular Relations. The treaty requires, under Article 36, that U.S. officials inform a foreigner when he is arrested of his right to request contact with his consulate. It also requires officials to inform the consulate if the arrestee so chooses to request it.[210] A purpose of this reciprocal duty is to ensure that U.S. citizens traveling overseas and foreigners in the United States receive the protections of their states when they are arrested and subjected to unfamiliar criminal justice systems. State law enforcement officials in the United States, however, have not always complied with Article 36. One can speculate that may be because of lack of knowledge of the Vienna Convention, inadequate training, or even disrespect for international law. Some of these foreigners were subsequently convicted and sentenced to death.

In three ICJ cases, foreign states filed suit against the United States for violating Article 36. The first case involved Angel Francisco Breard, a Paraguay citizen, who, in 1993, was convicted in Virginia of murder and attempted rape and sentenced to death. Paraguay was never told about Mr. Breard until 1996. The State Department acknowledged the failure of the United States to observe its Article 36 obligations. Paraguay then filed a lawsuit before the ICJ on April 3, 1998. The court issued provisional measures ordering the United States not to execute Mr. Breard until it decided the case.[211] U.S. Secretary of State Madeline Albright urged the governor of

[206] *See* Higgins, Problems and Process, *supra* note 84, at 250–51 (1995). *See also* Higgins, Wall in the Occupied Palestinian Territory, *supra* note 41, at 215, ¶¶ 33–34.

[207] *Id.* at 216, ¶ 35.

[208] *Id.*

[209] *Id.* at 215, ¶ 33.

[210] Vienna Convention on Consular Relations, Apr. 24, 1963, 21 U.S.T. 77, 596 U.N.T.S. 261, art. 36(1)(b). *See also* LaGrand (Ger. v. U.S.), Judgment, 2001 I.C.J. 466 ¶ 77 (June 27).

[211] *See* Vienna Convention on Consular Relations (Para. v. U.S.), Provisional Measures, 1998 I.C.J. 248 (Apr. 9).

Virginia to stay the execution, expressing concern for U.S. citizens who live and travel abroad and that the execution of Mr. Breard would limit the ability of the United States to protect its citizens abroad. The U.S. Supreme Court denied Mr. Breard's petition for habeas corpus relief.[212] The governor declined to stay the execution, explaining that the "safety of those residing in the Commonwealth of Virginia" was his primary responsibility. Mr. Breard was killed on April 14, 1998. Paraguay discontinued the ICJ lawsuit on November 10 that year.[213]

In 1984, Karl and Walter LaGrand were sentenced to death in Arizona for a failed bank robbery during which they murdered the bank manager. They were both U.S. permanent residents and German citizens, but were not told of their right to request contact with the German consulate under Article 36. Germany learned of their arrest in June 1992, but for seven years, it did nothing. On January 15, 1999, the Arizona Supreme Court set the execution dates of Karl LaGrand for February 24, 1999 and of Walter LaGrand for March 3, 1999. Germany then sought a diplomatic solution but to no avail. After Karl LaGrand was executed, and one day before Walter LaGrand was to be killed, Germany filed a lawsuit before the ICJ at 7:30 P.M. Hague time, and also before the U.S. Supreme Court. The ICJ issued a provisional measure ordering the United States to delay the execution until the ICJ could decide the case. Germany then petitioned the U.S. Supreme Court to enforce the order, two hours before the scheduled execution, which the court denied.[214] Walter LaGrand was executed. Germany did not, however, terminate the ICJ case, and the ICJ in due course rendered a judgment finding the United States in violation of the Vienna Convention. The court continued, however, to find that the efforts by the U.S. State Department to educate federal, state, and local law enforcement officers of the Vienna Convention and measures to comply with it, was sufficient to satisfy Germany's request for nonrepetition of the violation.[215]

These efforts of the State Department did not end violations of the Vienna Convention. In 2003, Mexico brought a lawsuit, the *Avena* case, against the United States before the ICJ, alleging violations of Article 36.[216] Article 36(1)(b) provides that a signatory state "shall inform the [foreigner arrested] without delay of his rights under this subparagraph," which includes informing the foreigner's consular post of his arrest and passing any communications from the suspect to the consular post. In 51 cases, state police officers arrested Mexican nationals and did not inform

212 *See* Breard v. Greene et al., 523 U.S. 371 (1998).

213 *See* Murphy, *supra* note 132, at 270–74. *See also* W. Michael Reisman et al., International Law in Contemporary Perspective 120 (2d ed. 2004) (reprinting letter by Madeline Albright and statement by the governor of Virginia).

214 *See* Fed. Rep. Germany v. United States, 526 U.S. 111 (1999).

215 LaGrand *supra* note 210 at 511, 516. *See also* Murphy, *supra* note 132, at 274–75.

216 *See* Case Concerning Avena and other Mexican Nationals (Mex. v. U.S.), Application (Jan. 9, 2003) [hereinafter Application, Avena Case]. *See also* Avena and other Mexican Nationals (Mex. v. U.S.), 2004 I.C.J. 12 (Mar. 31) [hereinafter Avena Case].

the suspects of their rights under Article 36. In one case, a Mexican national was informed of his Article 36 rights 40 hours after arrest.[217]

1. Legalism

The *Avena* case raises many important issues, and scholars have appraised various aspects of the case.[218] For present purposes, it is sufficient to focus on the United States' conduct in relation to the Vienna Convention and the lawsuit, and the ICJ's interpretation of Article 36.

The United States objected to the jurisdiction of the ICJ.[219] This is unremarkable. A silver bullet for defendants in litigation is to persuade the court not to hear a plaintiffs' claim. The ICJ found that it had jurisdiction because the case concerned the interpretation of the Vienna Convention, a subject matter properly within its competence under the terms of Article 36 of the ICJ Statute. Further, the United States had signed the Vienna Convention's Optional Protocol granting the ICJ personal jurisdiction over the United States for disputes concerning the Vienna Convention.[220] Unlike the *Nicaragua* case, in which the United States rejected the ICJ's jurisdictional finding, here, the United States accepted the court's determination of jurisdiction.

As regards whether the United States had violated Article 36(1)(b), the ICJ had to interpret the meaning of "without delay" in the obligation to inform an arrested foreign suspect of his consular rights. The court's reasoning was strictly legalist. It identified its prescription for interpretation: Articles 31 and 32 of the VCLT.[221]

[217] *See* Avena Case, *supra* note 216.

[218] *See, e.g.*, Dinah L. Shelton, *Case Concerning Avena and Other Mexican Nationals (Mexico v. United States)*, 98 Am. J. Int'l L. 559 (2004); Mark J. Kadish, *Article 36 of the Vienna Convention on Consular Relations: The International Court of Justice in Mexico v. United States (Avena) Speaks Emphatically to the Supreme Court of the United States about the Fundamental Nature of the Right to Consul*, 36 Geo. J. Int'l L. 1 (2004); Reynaldo Anaya Valencia et al., *Avena and the World Court's Death Penalty Jurisdiction in Texas: Addressing the Odd Notion of Texas' Independence from the World*, 23 Yale L. & Pol'y Rev. 455 (2005).

[219] *See* Avena Case, *supra* note 216.

[220] *Id.* at 30–33, ¶¶ 27–35.

[221] *Id.* at 48, ¶ 83. Given the canonical status of Articles 31 and 32, it is useful to quote them verbatim:

Article 31

General rule of interpretation

1. A treaty shall be interpreted in good faith in accordance with the ordinary meaning to be given to the terms of the treaty in their context and in the light of its object and purpose.

2. The context for the purpose of the interpretation of a treaty shall comprise, in addition to the text, including its preamble and annexes:

(a) any agreement relating to the treaty which was made between all the parties in connection with the conclusion of the treaty;

(b) any instrument which was made by one or more parties in connection with the conclusion of the treaty and accepted by the other parties as an instrument related to the treaty.

Applying the cannons of interpretation in Article 31, the ICJ defined "without delay" as "normally understood," and in the context of "its object and purpose."[222] The court concluded that it did not mean "immediately upon arrest and before interrogation."[223] But the court did not rely on Article 31 to venture a meaning. Instead, it looked at the *travaux préparatoires* to confirm that Article 32 of the VCLT did not mean immediately upon arrest.[224] This was a departure from the structure of Articles 31 and 32, which mandate that *travaux* should only be consulted to confirm the meaning derived from Article 31 or if Article 31 leaves a term unclear or leads to an absurd interpretation. The ICJ did not determine that any of these threshold criteria for invoking Article 32 had been met.

Having turned in error to Article 32 to confirm its Article 31 noninterpretation of "without undue delay" as not meaning "immediately," the ICJ made up its own interpretation of "without undue delay" without relying on any of the canons in Article 31 or 32. The Court simply stated, *mirabile dictu*, that the phrase created "a duty upon the arresting authorities to give that information to an arrested person as soon as it is realized that the person is a foreign national, or once there are grounds to think that the person is probably a foreign national."[225] Based on this interpretation, the Court concluded that the United States had violated Article 36(1)(b) and ordered that the United States "provide, by means of its own choosing, review and reconsideration of the convictions and sentences of the Mexican nationals[.]"[226] The court's departure from the VCLT does not bring it too far from the central case because its reasoning was still legalist, even if it was insufficiently faithful to canons of interpretation.

3. There shall be taken into account, together with the context:
   (a) any subsequent agreement between the parties regarding the interpretation of the treaty or the application of its provisions;
   (b) any subsequent practice in the application of the treaty which establishes the agreement of the parties regarding its interpretation;
   (c) any relevant rules of international law applicable in the relations between the parties.
4. A special meaning shall be given to a term if it is established that the parties so intended.

Article 32
Supplementary means of interpretation
Recourse may be had to supplementary means of interpretation, including the preparatory work of the treaty and the circumstances of its conclusion, in order to confirm the meaning resulting from the application of article 31, or to determine the meaning when the interpretation according to article 31:
   (a) leaves the meaning ambiguous or obscure; or
   (b) leads to a result which is manifestly absurd or unreasonable.

VCLT, *supra* note 115, arts. 31–32.

222 *See* Avena Case, *supra* note 216, at 48, ¶85.

223 *Id.*

224 *See id.* at 48–49, ¶ 86.

225 *Id.* at 49, ¶ 88.

226 *Id.* at 72, ¶ 153(9).

2. Effectiveness

The ICJ was partially effective in securing the compliance of the United States with the *Avena* Decision. Contrary to critics who accuse the United States of disregarding international law, the U.S. administration accepted the ICJ decision and its finding that the United States had breached international law.[227] On February 28, 2005, President Bush issued a memorandum instructing state courts to give effect to the *Avena* judgment by reconsidering sentences of foreign nationals whose Article 36 rights were violated.[228] When the constitutionality of President Bush's order was challenged in the U.S. Supreme Court case of *Medellín*,[229] the United States argued that it had

> an international law obligation to comply with the ICJ's decision in *Avena*. That decision requires the United States courts to provide review and reconsideration of the convictions and sentences of the 51 Mexican nationals addressed in that decision.[230]

This executive order is all the more remarkable because President Bush was a Republican former governor of Texas, a supporter of the death penalty, and because Mr. Medellín had been convicted of murdering and raping two teenage girls.[231] President Bush chose to comply with the *Avena* case against his personal convictions and political interests.

The U.S. administration also engaged state officials and succeeded in securing the commitment of Texas Governor Rick Perry that if an *Avena* defendant had not previously received judicial determination of prejudice from a Vienna Convention violation and sought a habeas review, Texas would ask the reviewing court to address the claim of prejudice on its merits.[232] The Bush administration also received a similar commitment from Nevada.[233]

[227] *See* Further Written Observations of the United States of America, Request for Interpretation of the Judgment of 31 March 2004 in the Case Concerning Avena and Other Mexican Nationals (Mex. v. U.S.) 2008 I.C.J. ¶ 7–8 (Oct. 6) [hereinafter U.S. Further Written Observations, Avena Interpretation Case].

[228] Order of July 16, 2008, Request for Interpretation of the Judgment of 31 March 2004 in the case concerning Avena and other Mexican Nationals (Mex. v. U.S), 2008 I.C.J. 311, 312 & n.3 [hereinafter Provisional Measures, Avena Interpretation Case] (quoting the memorandum as stating: "I have determined, pursuant to the authority vested in me as President by the Constitution and laws of the United States, that the United States will discharge its international obligations under the decision of the International Court of Justice in [*Avena*], by having State courts give effect to the decision in accordance with general principles of comity in cases filed by the 51 Mexican nationals addressed in that decision.") (citing Memorandum from George W. Bush, Compliance with the Decision of the International Court of Justice in *Avena*, to Alberto Gonzales, Attorney General (Feb. 28, 2005)).

[229] *See* Medellín v. Texas, 552 U.S. 491 (2008).

[230] U.S. Further Written Observation, Avena Interpretation Case, *supra* note 227, at 4, n.8.

[231] Scharf & Williams, *supra* note 183, at 140.

[232] *See* U.S. Further Written Observation, Avena Interpretation Case, *supra* note 227, at 11.

[233] *Id.* at 24 (describing federal efforts to obtain compliance from states with the *Avena* decision).

Ultimately, the U.S. Supreme Court recognized that the United States had obligations under international law, but as a matter of U.S. constitutional law, the President's memorandum had overstepped his executive authority and was invalid.[234] Following that decision, Texas scheduled the execution of Ernesto Medellín, one of the *Avena* defendants.

In an attempt to stop the execution, Mexico filed a request for interpretation of the *Avena* judgment, pursuant to Article 60 of the ICJ Statute. Article 60 states: "The judgment is final and without appeal. In the event of dispute as to the meaning or scope of the judgment, the Court shall construe it upon the request of any party."[235] Although facially styling its submission as a request for interpretation, Mexico apparently intended to obtain provisional measures to stay the execution. The ICJ granted that request.[236] It needed to file an Article 60 request because the United States withdrew from the Optional Protocol after the *Avena* case decision in 2004, as was its legal right to do, thereby precluding ICJ jurisdiction over the United States in any new case, but not invalidating the ICJ's residual authority to interpret the *Avena* case that was decided when the United States had consented to the ICJ's jurisdiction.

Texas ignored the ICJ order to stay the execution and killed Mr. Medellín.[237] Consequently, the ICJ found in the *Avena Interpretation* that the United States had breached its obligations to stay Medellín's execution as ordered in the court's provisional measures decision.[238] However, it concluded that there was no dispute in the interpretation of the *Avena* case.[239] Mexico and the United States agreed that the latter had an obligation to ensure compliance with the Vienna Convention and to make reparation by providing review of the cases of the *Avena* defendants, by means of its own choosing.[240] Consequently, the Court denied Mexico's request for interpretation, and simply reaffirmed "the continuing binding character of the obligations" of the United States in the *Avena* case.[241]

In sum, the *Avena* case was effective but only partially so. The United States did not reject the authority of the ICJ in the *Avena* case and the *Avena Interpretation* decision. It also did not reject the ICJ's decisions finding it had breached the Vienna Convention. Instead, the United States tried various measures to comply with the decision and make reparations, even though not all measures were successful.

[234] *See Medellín*, 552 U.S. at 525–26.

[235] ICJ Statute, *supra* note 5, art. 60.

[236] *See* Request for the Indication of Provisional Measures, Request for Interpretation of the Judgment of 31, March 2004 in the Avena Case *supra* note 216, at 5, ¶ 15 (June 5, 2008) [hereinafter Request, Avena Interpretation Case].

[237] *See* Request for Interpretation of the Judgment of 31 March 2004 in the case concerning Avena and other Mexican Nationals (Mex. v. U.S.), 2009 I.C.J. 1, 16, ¶ 52 (Jan. 19) [hereinafter Avena Interpretation Case].

[238] *See id.* at 18, ¶ 61(2).

[239] *See id.* at 18, ¶ 61(1).

[240] *See id.* at 18, ¶ 61(3); Provisional Measures, Avena Interpretation Case, *supra* note 180, at 64, ¶ 153(9).

[241] Avena Interpretation Case, *supra* note 237, at 18, ¶ 61(3).

3. Morality

One partial explanation of why the *Avena* decisions were somewhat effective is that U.S. national interests required taking the Vienna Convention seriously. The United States desired that its nationals receive the same reciprocal protections contained in the Vienna Convention when traveling overseas, as explained in Secretary of State Albright's exhortations to the governor of Virginia not to kill Mr. Breard.

However, it is too simplistic to explain the compliance measures undertaken by the United States solely in terms of its national interest that U.S. citizens abroad be accorded rights under the Vienna Convention. This explanation is not fully persuasive because, as the most powerful nation, the United States could asymmetrically insist that foreign states accord its citizens Vienna Convention rights while itself flouting those rights. The compliance of the United States with the *Avena* case must be explained by something more than national interest.

Another possible explanation is that it was moral to comply with the *Avena* case because it was faithful to legalism and promoted the common good. The court properly exercised its jurisdiction under the Vienna Convention's Optional Protocol in the *Avena* case. The ICJ used accepted methods of legalist reasoning to interpret Article 36 and apply it to the United States' treatment of arrested foreign suspects. In the *Avena Interpretation* decision, the court properly rejected Mexico's Article 60 request. Under the terms of Article 60, there needed to be a dispute over what the *Avena* decision meant. Because there was no dispute between Mexico and the United States, there was nothing to interpret. By acting within the bounds of appropriate conduct that the United States expected from the ICJ, the court made its decision procedurally legitimate. This legitimacy, which aligned with U.S. national interests, secured U.S. acceptance of the ICJ's decisions in the *Avena* case. A reasonable hypothesis is thus that the *Avena* case and the *Avena Interpretation* were effective because they were highly legitimate as a result of their fidelity to legalism.

Another consideration that could have promoted the court's effectiveness was that the *Avena* decisions properly balanced the values at stake, and therefore it was moral to obey the decisions. Like *Pedra Branca* and the *Nicaragua* cases, seemingly determinate legalist reasoning conceals normative considerations. The dissenting opinion of Judge Sepulveda-Amor in the *Avena Interpretation* managed to tease out points of disagreement between the United States and Mexico. He noted that "[i]t is also instructive to read the views expressed by the United States Supreme Court in the *Sanchez-Llamas* case, views which diverge substantially from Mexico's contentions and from what this Court decided in the *LaGrand* and the *Avena* cases[.]"[242] The answer to whether or not there were interpretive disagreements depends on how searching the inquiry is. Absent prescriptions controlling the interpretation of Article 60, the choice as to how detailed an inquiry to conduct is a policy choice. Judge Sepulveda-Amor found differences in the United States' and Mexico's positions in the hope that this would enable him to "make an invaluable contribution to

[242] *Id.* at 5, ¶ 17 (dissenting opinion of Judge Sepulveda-Amor).

the settlement of a dispute which runs the risk of self-perpetuation."[243] He tried to achieve this by prescribing further particulars for the United States to comply with the *Avena* case.

By implication, the overwhelming majority of the ICJ decided that interpreting the *Avena* case would be counterproductive. The United States had shown in its pleadings that it had undertaken efforts to comply and had succeeded in making changes to its treatment of foreign suspects to comply with the Vienna Convention. Interpreting the *Avena* case would not have led the United States to do more. It was also fairly obvious that Mexico sought further enforcement action through the Article 60 backdoor. Indulging this tactic would have disregarded the consensual nature of the ICJ's jurisdictional authority at a time when the United States had, in exercise of its sovereign rights, withheld consent to ICJ jurisdiction, just as many other states have withheld consent.[244]

Scholars can speculate whether the ICJ was circumspect in exercising its authority because a more aggressive approach would have risked provoking the United States to further reject international adjudication and thereby weaken the international legal system. Scholars can also debate whether, if this in fact was an important consideration for the ICJ, the ICJ's decision was normatively appropriate. Under this book's account of international law, the *Avena* decisions fall within the range of outcomes that the ICJ could have prescribed without exceeding the bounds of legalism, general morality, specific morality, and the judicial function.

The general morality of obeying a decision because it is faithful to legalism, and the specific morality of obeying the decision because it properly balances the values at stake do not, however, without more, explain the outcome in the *Avena* case. This book's account of international law requires the interests and power of governing elites to be considered. The sheer power of the United States, its domestic allocation of criminal powers to states in the federal system, and the constitutional authority of its Supreme Court limited the *Avena* cases' effectiveness.

The *Avena* case has yet to achieve full effectiveness because not all U.S. states have complied with the *Avena* case. Under the U.S. constitutional structure, even if the United States has incurred international responsibility, there are limits to what a federal government can do to regulate state criminal law and procedure in order to avoid continuing Article 36 violations. This analysis validates the shared perspective of policy-oriented jurisprudence and transnational legal process that when considering the interests and power of governing elites in an international incident, it may be necessary to disaggregate a state to identify the powers and interests of different governing elites within a nation state if they each have the power to influence outcomes in an international incident.

[243] *Id.* at 18, ¶ 68.

[244] *See also* Reisman, Systems of Control, *supra* note 7 (counseling against extending ICJ jurisdiction beyond the consent of states because that would ultimately undermine the ICJ's legitimacy and effectiveness).

4. Feedback Loops

The *Avena* decision reveals several feedback loops. The most obvious feedback loop is the ICJ's reliance on its prior interpretations of Article 36 of the Vienna Convention of Consular Relations in the *LaGrand* case. The court relied on its prior decision in *LaGrand* to similarly hold in *Avena* that the purpose of Article 36 was to "facilitate the implementation of the system of consular protection,"[245] to determine the appropriate remedies for violations by the United States of the Vienna Convention,[246] and that the procedural rule under U.S. law that the criminal defendant's failure to plead a violation of Article 36 as a defense at trial waived the right to raise it on appeal violated the United States' obligations under the Vienna Convention as regards several Mexican nationals in *Avena*.[247]

This operational practice contrasts against the absence of any formal procedural rule of precedent in the ICJ. Article 38 of the ICJ Statute explicitly states that prior judicial decisions are only a subsidiary source of law, and Article 59 provides that decisions are binding only on the parties in the disputes.[248] However, in light of the court's practice—as illustrated in the feedback loops in the *Nicaragua* case, the *Wall Opinion*, and the *Genocide Case*—it is unsurprising that the court decided the *Avena* case consistently with *LaGrand*.[249]

There were other less obvious, albeit important, feedback loops in *Avena*, relating to the conduct of the United States. The United States accepted its obligations under Article 36 of the Vienna Convention, in both proceedings on the merits and the request for interpretation. It may have done so for the reasons of legitimacy analyzed in the part above.[250] But there may be a further complementary reason having to do with feedback loops. By accepting its Article 36 obligations in the *Breard* and *LaGrand* disputes, the U.S. government created an internal feedback loop to do so again in *Avena*,[251] a process that Harold Koh has described as internalizing international norms.[252]

There are several reasons why prior decisions by government officials create feedback loops in international judicial disputes. As an external foreign policy matter, having previously accepted its Article 36 obligations, the United States could not now reject them without undermining its credibility.

[245] *See* Avena Case, *supra* note 216, at 39–40, ¶ 50 (quoting *LaGrand*).

[246] *See id.* at 56, ¶ 111–12.

[247] *See id.* ¶¶ 120, 128, 143, 150.

[248] *See* ICJ Statute, *supra* note 5, art. 38, ¶1 & art. 59.

[249] *Cf.* Jennings, *supra* note 198, at xvii ("But there is no gainsaying the practical authority and power of that precedent of the International Court. It would be wrong, of course, to try to treat all judgments, even of the International Court, as being of equal authority. It depends upon a number of factors; and one is that one must look to see how they wear in later practice.").

[250] *Supra,* pt. II.C.3.

[251] *See* Avena Case, *supra* note 216, ¶ 51 ("The United States as the receiving State does not deny its duty to perform these obligations.").

[252] *See* Harold Hongju Koh, *Why Do Nations Obey International Law*, 106 Yale L.J. 2599 (1997). *See also* ch. 2, pt V (discussing Koh's transnational legal process).

As an internal matter, consistent foreign policy positions are important for coherence and consistency within the government policies. Government officials tend to highly value consistency and coherence. Past institutional decisions tend to influence future decisions to avoid the costs of reevaluating every decision, to bolster the credibility of the institution's system of decisionmaking, and even out of respect for prior officials that determined the institutional position. Thomas Franck's argument that international law seeks stability applies equally to foreign policy positions of governments.

This is not to say that decisions will never change. They clearly do, such as when Jack Goldsmith retracted prior Department of Justice memoranda relating to interrogation techniques, which is discussed in Chapter Seven.[253] However, absent a change in circumstances or strong arguments that prior internal decisions were wrongly decided, a state's position in a prior judicial dispute can be a strong predictor of its position in a future, similar dispute.

Just as domestic feedback loops can reinforce international law, domestic decisions by governing elites rejecting international law can also create feedback loops to ignore international law in future disputes. After the U.S. Supreme Court decided in response to Mr. Breard's petition for habeas corpus that U.S. law did not require the governor of Virginia to obey the ICJ's provision order,[254] and the governor rejected Secretary of State Albright's request to do so, it is unsurprising that the U.S. Supreme Court similarly rejected Germany's petition to enjoin Walter LaGrand's execution following the ICJ's provisional order that the United States not execute Mr. LaGrand while the *LaGrand* case was pending.[255] It was also unsurprising that the governor of Arizona similarly refused to stay Mr. LaGrand's execution, as the governor of Virginia had declined to do so years before. By the time of the *Avena Interpretation* proceedings, the pattern of state conduct indicated that Texas would likely ignore the ICJ's provisional order to stay the execution of Mr. Medellín, which was exactly what happened.

The *Avena* case also demonstrates feedback loops concerning consent to the jurisdiction of the ICJ. An unintended consequence of the ICJ's decisions in the *Avena* case was that the United States withdrew consent to the jurisdiction of the ICJ for disputes alleging violations of the Vienna Convention. When President Bush issued the executive order to states, he also withdrew from the Optional Protocol of the Vienna Convention.[256] Because of the federalist nature of the U.S. constitution, and the practical difficulty of implementing the Vienna Convention in all police stations

[253] *Infra*, ch. 7, pt.II.B.

[254] *See* Breard v. Greene, 523 U.S. 371, 378 (1998) ("If the Governor wishes to wait for the decision of the ICJ that is his prerogative. But nothing in our existing case law allows us to make that choice for him.").

[255] *See* Fed. Rep. Germany v. United States, 526 U.S. 111, 112 (1999) (*citing* Breard, 523 U.S. 371).

[256] *See* Scharf & Williams, *supra* note 183, at 140; John R. Crook, *Contemporary Practice of the United States Relating to International Law: U.S. Strategy for Responding to ICJ's Avena Decision*, 99 Am. J. Int'l L. 489, 489–90 (2005).

around the United States, the U.S. Attorney General and Secretary of State advised President Bush that it would be unwise to expose the United States to new Vienna Convention international lawsuits.[257] In international law, as in contract law, no party will bargain against its own interests.[258] It is impossible to prove that this decision to withdraw from the Optional Protocol of the Vienna Convention when it became apparent that the United States was unable to perfectly comply with Article 36 was influenced by President Reagan's decision to withdraw from the Optional Protocol of the ICJ Statute when the ICJ decided it had jurisdiction against the United States in the *Nicaragua* case. However, given the careful nature and high quality of U.S. government lawyers, it would be surprising if they did not consider U.S. actions in the *Nicaragua* case as an informal institutional precedent for withdrawing from the Vienna Convention's Optional Protocol.

Ironically, however, the U.S. withdrawal from the Optional Protocol was not clearly immoral—in the sense of damaging the common good—because the United States followed the formalist strictures of the Vienna Convention's prescriptions on withdrawing consent to jurisdiction. Whatever one's appraisal about whether this was a good outcome resulting from the ICJ's adverse finding against the United States, the moral imperative to promote determinacy in law through legalism was vindicated (even though in the long run the common good could be harmed by the weakened shared expectation that the ICJ is an appropriate venue for dispute resolution).[259]

III. CONCLUSION

Because the account of the international legal system in this book is justificatory, it seeks to provide guidance to decisionmakers on how to make decisions in international problems to justify the regulatory claim of international law. Accordingly, if the account is to apply to the judges it must guide them in their decisions. The analysis of *Pedra Branca*, *Nicaragua,* and *Avena* validates the hypothesis at the start of this chapter that judges ought to give special emphasis to legalism, but ought not to ignore the values at stake and the effectiveness *vel non* of their decisions.

When the authority of the tribunal is contingent on the consent of the parties, judges would do well to remain within the strict limits of that consent and avoid deciding issues beyond the dispute that the parties submitted to adjudication, as the ICJ did in *Pedra Branca.* This not only increases the likelihood that the parties will accept the decision and make it effective, it is also morally appropriate to do so because sovereign states have allocated power and authority to judges only for those limited purposes.

[257] *See* Scharf & Williams, *supra* note 183, at 140–41.

[258] *See* Browning v. Johnson, 422 P.2d 314, 318 (Wash. 1967) ("[T]he law must presume that no man bargains against his own interest.").

[259] *See* Orakhelashvili, *supra* note 53, at 583 (2008) (stating policy preference for determinacy as basis for positivist vision of international law).

This analysis applies to even powerful states. In *Avena*, the ICJ's scrupulous fidelity of the limits of its authority in deciding the dispute but not interpreting its decision where there was no real dispute as to its meaning helped secure the partial compliance of the United States with its decisions. In contrast, in *Nicaragua*, the ICJ's overly aggressive reading of its jurisdiction, though Nicaragua had never complied with formalities necessary to confer jurisdiction, made it easier for the United States to justify rejecting the authority of the ICJ entirely midway through the lawsuit.

Importantly, interpreting consent to jurisdiction narrowly is not simply a matter of prudence or pragmatism. It is morally appropriate for judges to do so. Their authority is not derived from any comprehensive legal order superior to states, but from states themselves, as expressed in the ICJ Statute. Overreaching the legal authority of judges to decide disputes also overreaches their moral authority. It undermines the international constitutional structure that by design respects the autonomy of territorial communities organized as states. At stake is the freedom of every constituent to pursue its preferred values through the decisions of its governing elites to interact and compete with foreign communities.

If judges properly conclude that they have jurisdiction over a dispute, this book's account of international law, as tested in the three cases in this chapter, provides guidance on how decisions on the merits ought to be made, or at least gives judges something to think about. Judges should be conscious of the range of decisions permissible by legalism through the appreciation of relevant facts and evidence as well as the identification, interpretation, and application of legal prescriptions to those facts. Fidelity of legalism is crucial to maintain the moral authority of international law that comes from promoting the common good through a stable and coherent set of rules. The infidelity to legalism in *Nicaragua*, in contrast with the fidelity to legalism in *Pedra Branca* and *Avena*, shows the relevance of legalism to not just effectiveness but also to the general morality of international law.

Because prior decisions can create feedback loops when they are unquestioningly accepted in later cases, as was the situation in the *Wall Opinion*'s acceptance of the *Nicaragua* case's limitation of self-defense against armed attacks to only attacks by other states, judges should strive to examine and appraise the bases of prior decisions in deciding whether to validate or reject them. Admittedly, examining prior cases is not a cost-free endeavor. Judges with heavy caseloads and an insufficient number of clerks may find it impractical to appraise prior cases afresh before applying them to ongoing judicial disputes. Scholars lighten this judicial burden through their analysis of decisions, which may help judges decide what weight to give to those decisions.

Within the range of decisions possible under legalist grounds, judges ought to be aware of the moral implications of each possible decision. This requires them first to anticipate the consequences of their decisions. Such an appraisal should consider the immediate impact of their decisions on the parties, bearing in mind their power and interests that will determine their reactions. In addition, this appraisal should also consider the feedback loops that might be created from the decision itself, as well as the reactions of the parties. The manifold feedback loops in *Nicaragua* and *Avena* underscore the long-term consequences of judicial decisions, and it is better to anticipate them in advance. Having anticipated the consequences of decisions, judges can then aim to reach a decision that is not just faithful to legalism but also substantively legitimate.

Once a decision has been made that comports with legalism, promotes substantive legitimacy, and anticipates effectiveness, judges should explain their decisions and must identify and apply legal rules to facts in their judgments, so that governing elites understand that judges have acted according to law and within their legal authority. It is also helpful to explain whether the judgment leads to good outcomes, to persuade litigants that they ought to comply with the decisions of judges because there is a moral imperative to obey and promote law, and also because the outcome is desirable. Such normative appraisals are replete in the opinions in *Pedra Branca*, *Nicaragua,* and *Avena*, as discussed earlier.

In exceptional cases, a judge may decide that there is no way to reach a normatively appropriate outcome under applicable legal prescriptions without exceeding the legalist bounds of interpretation. Here, the judge ought to reject the prescription, in a dissent if necessary, and to explain why it ought to be changed, as Judge Higgins did in the *Wall Opinion* and as Judge Schwebel did in the *Nicaragua* judgment on the merits. Such judicially responsible opinions may trigger feedback loops that alter legal prescriptions if elites are persuaded by the opinions.

It is hoped that the analysis of three contrasting ICJ cases has validated, or at least illustrated, how the account of the international legal system developed in this book applies to judging by explaining how decisions are made and with what effect, and by providing guidance on how decisions ought to be made.

In situations where it is unclear what the best decision is, and there are a number of reasonable decisions, even if they are not all equally reasonable, the moral obligation of the judge might be simply to choose one of those decisions in good faith. It is not the purpose of this chapter to set out some mathematical formula to balance competing practical reasons that favor one decision or another in a dispute.[260] Its goal is simply to set out the ideals that judges ought to promote, to mark decisions that should be clearly off limits, and to provide guidance on how to identify a range of reasonable decisions. Governing elites and constituents delegate authority to judges to choose among reasonable decisions because they trust that judges will do so based on "experience and study and reflection,"[261] as Judge Cardozo put it, and with "courage and sensitivity and commitment to the values of free human beings

[260] *See* Jan Paulsson, Symposium, *Making the Most of International Investment Agreements: Indirect Expropriation: Is the Right to Regulate at Risk?* at 1 (Dec. 12, 2005), *available at* http://www.oecd.org/dataoecd/5/52/36055332.pdf ("In a phrase, perfect predictability is an illusion.").

[261] Benjamin N. Cardozo, The Nature of the Judicial Process 113 (1921).

in a society that is both productive and caring[,]"[262] as Justice Feliciano stated. In this book's account of international law, judges should try to be Herculean,[263] but everyone understands that Hercules was partly human after all and therefore can only exercise his best, but often imperfect, judgment.

[262] Feliciano, *supra* note 1, at 56.

[263] *See supra*, ch. 3, pt. V.D (discussing Dworkin's Herculean judge and Herculean decisionmakers in international law).

5 Arbitrators

I. THEORY

This chapter applies the justificatory theory of the international law to decisionmaking by arbitrators in international disputes. It explores the extent to which the theory provides a framework of analysis for guiding arbitrators in their decisions and for helping observers and elites understand and explain the decisions that arbitrators make.

In order to justify international legal regulation, which limits the freedom of actors to do whatever they want, when deciding what to do and what claims to make in international problems, decisionmakers ought to balance several considerations. As set out in Chapter Three, these are: (1) their institutional responsibilities and the limits of authority allocated to them, (2) the general morality of promoting the common good through prescriptions and legalism, (3) the specific morality of promoting the values directly at stake in an international problem, and (4) the effectiveness of their decision in controlling the actions of other decisionmakers.

These factors should also generally apply to guide arbitrators in deciding disputes before them. However, to provide more useful guidance to arbitrators, a more granular analysis is necessary to develop and apply the theory to the specific context of arbitration involving nation states. Specifically, this chapter considers the weight of each factor, how they relate or conflict with each other, and possible ways to balance a conflict when it occurs.

A. Arbitral Functions

The responsibilities of an arbitrator and the limits of his authority are prescribed and proscribed by the arbitral functions in disputes. These functions are in turn closely tied to the interests of the constituencies in arbitrations, which are the parties in the dispute who pay for the arbitration, as well as, arguably, other actors who look to arbitral awards for guidance on appropriate conduct and the meaning of prescriptions.

A primary function of international arbitrators is to resolve disputes before them.[1] International arbitration is a privately sponsored system of dispute resolution designated through arbitration agreements and paid for by the parties in the dispute. The responsibilities and, correspondingly, the limits of arbitrators' decision function, ought to be determined in large part by the parties who appoint them and pay for their services. Such a view of arbitration is grounded in the basic value of freedom of choice of decisionmakers in a dispute in seeking and structuring dispute resolution by agreement. This view also supports the common good by promoting minimum order through private dispute settlement, which is ultimately contingent on decisionmakers having confidence that arbitrators will do what they are paid and agreed to do, and no more.

There is a view that another function of an arbitrator is to interpret prescriptions not just to settle disputes between the parties in the arbitration, but also to consolidate expectations among decisionmakers not involved in that dispute about appropriate standards of conduct expressed through prescriptions and arbitral awards interpreting and applying them. Although awards are formally binding only on parties in those disputes,[2] there is some shared expectation among decisionmakers, including arbitrators, judges, practitioners, and government officials, that awards help them understand and apply prescriptions to generally guide their actions in future disputes.[3]

This shared expectation for arbitrators to develop the law generally is minimal when awards are confidential between the parties, which are therefore unavailable to influence third parties in later disputes. In any event, the parties who pay for the

[1] *Cf.* Florentino P. Feliciano, *The Application of Law: Some Recurring Aspects of the Process of Judicial Review and Decision Making*, 37 Am. J. Juris. 17, 34 (1992) ("The first function [of a judge] is an intensely practical one: the resolution of the case pending before him, within definite time limits."). *See also* Tom Ginsburg, *Bounded Discretion in International Judicial Lawmaking*, 45 VA. J. Int'l L. 631, 651 (2004–05) (noting that when the WTO Appellate Body authorizes sanctions, "it is playing a coordinating role by setting a focal level of retaliation").

[2] *See* 1 Gary B. Born, International Commercial Arbitration 563–849, 1003–57 (2009).

[3] *See* Jan Paulsson, *International Arbitration and the Generation of Legal Norms: Treaty Arbitration and International Law* 2–3 (May 21, 2006) (presented at the ICCA Annual Congress), *available at* http://www.transnational-dispute-management.com/article.asp?key=883; Ian Brownlie, Principles of Public International Law 19–20 (7th ed. 2008) ("The literature of the law contains frequent reference to decisions of arbitral tribunals. The quality of arbitral tribunals has varied considerably, but there have been a number of awards which contain notable contributions to the development of the law by eminent jurists sitting as arbitrators, umpires or commissioners.").

services of arbitrators often have no interest in developing the law. Even though clarifying the law promotes the common good for the parties and everyone else, parties are justifiably uninterested in bearing a disproportionate burden—in terms of arbitration expenses—in order to reap these positive externalities for society at large.

Conversely, the shared expectation that arbitrators ought to clarify the meaning of prescriptions increases where arbitral awards are public. This is the case with many investor-state arbitrations under the North American Free Trade Agreement and other investment treaties. This is also the case with WTO arbitration. If the reality is that decisionmakers and practitioners look to those public awards for guidance in future disputes, it would be irresponsible for arbitrators to completely ignore the broader impact of their awards on the common good when they make decisions.

In many disputes, these two functions of arbitrators are complementary. If arbitrators decide disputes on narrow grounds, they will spend less time deliberating about and charging for decisions on extraneous issues. The holdings of their awards will both discharge their dispute resolution responsibilities and influence—but not necessarily control—interpretations of prescriptions in future disputes.

There are, however, instances when the two functions are in conflict. When arbitrators stray into obiter dicta, their statements are not strictly necessary to resolve the dispute. Although the dicta may be wise interpretations of prescriptions generally, the parties did not pay for that dicta and did not necessarily want them. The conflict between the two functions is especially strong when extraneous dicta diminish the likelihood that the award will resolve the dispute. For example, where dicta implicitly or explicitly criticize a holding but leave it intact, the dicta may encourage the losing party to not pay or to look for other forums that may block enforcement.

Ultimately, the proper balance between the functions when they conflict may depend on an arbitrator's appraisal of his responsibilities. An arbitrator who appraises his job as focused on dispute resolution will criticize dicta that undermine the persuasiveness of the holding, even if they preserve its formal authority. An arbitrator who believes his job is to also to develop the law even for those who did not pay for his services, or who believes that he was paid to fully explain his reasoning (including dissenting reasons) will tend to appraise more favorably dicta that serve these functions.

B. General Morality

Arbitrators have a strong moral duty to take prescriptions as they are and interpret them strictly according to legalism. This duty is often stronger than the duty of government officials and legal advisors to generally promote the common good through legalism. Because freedom is a basic good, no arbitrator should claim to constrain the parties in dispute through their procedural orders and awards, unless there is a justification to do so. Unlike government officials and legal advisors to whom constituents have allocated general authority to make decisions in a broad range of problems, the authority of arbitrators is entirely contingent on the consent of the parties in a dispute and is limited to that dispute. Except in very rare instances when the parties explicitly request a tribunal to decide a dispute according to a sense of justice and not according to law, the parties expect those arbitrators to decide the disputes by interpreting and applying prescriptions in a legalist fashion.[4]

Arbitrators also have a special duty to promote the common good. Decision-makers look to their awards, especially those that are public, as authoritative or persuasive interpretations of prescriptions for future disputes. Therefore, arbitral awards have a special place in maintaining the minimum world order established through prescriptions and legalism, which promotes stability and coherence, in order for the legal system to serve its function of promoting the common good to enable governing elites to reasonably pursue their constituents' interests.

C. Specific Morality

The moral reason for arbitrators to promote the common good through fidelity to prescriptions and legalism does not exhaust the moral calculus that arbitrators ought to conduct when deciding disputes. In a specific international dispute, the moral obligation to promote the common good through legalism may not carry the day.

In a specific dispute, the range of reasonable interpretations of applicable legal prescriptions may not permit a course of action necessary to optimally, or even minimally, secure basic goods at stake.[5] International prescriptions do not necessarily promote the most normatively desirable outcomes. This is because prescriptions are also the product of imperfect legalist procedures, partisan interests, and power.

Further, where there is only a weak shared expectation of appropriate conduct expressed as a prescription, the general morality of interpreting that prescription according to legalism is correspondingly weak because there are fewer settled expectations that would be disrupted by a novel interpretation of the prescription. For example, the obligation to accord foreign investments "fair and equitable treatment" was in the past ambiguous, and early arbitral awards justifiably reached different conclusions about its meaning.[6]

Even positivist Alexander Orakhelashvili acknowledges that international law involves margins of appreciation,[7] equity,[8] proportionality, and legitimate expectations, as well as basic values. Legalist interpretative methods, by his reckoning, "cannot

[4] *See, e.g.*, Convention on the Settlement of Investment Disputes Between States and Nationals of Other States, Mar. 18, 1965, 575 U.N.T.S. 159, art. 42(3) (entered into force Oct. 14, 1966) [hereinafter Washington Convention].

[5] *See* John Finnis, Natural Law and Natural Rights 318 (1996) ("[T]he moral obligation to obey *each* law is variable in force. It will vary according to the subject-matter of the law and the circumstances of a possible violation[.]").

[6] *See* Tai-Heng Cheng, *Precedent and Control in Investment Treaty Arbitration*, 30 Fordham Int'l L.J. 1014, 1031–37 (2007) (discussing differing interpretations of the fair and equitable treatment standard in arbitral awards).

[7] *See* Alexander Orakhelashvili, The Interpretation of Acts and Rules in Public International Law 197–207 (2008).

[8] *See id.* at 222–54.

provide a straightforward definition of the relevant terms," and can only provide guidance that the adjudicator ought to act in "good faith" and to ensure the "effectiveness" of international law.[9] Because legalism permits various interpretations of legal prescriptions[10] and only provides vague guidance on how to resolve ambiguity, arbitrators cannot avoid applying exogenous considerations in their interpretation of prescriptions.

Therefore, it is often the case that an arbitrator cannot discharge his duties of good faith and cannot ensure international law will be effective without engaging in moral reasoning. Practical moral reasoning, which identifies the basic values and interests at stake and balances competing moral considerations, is one way to resolve the ambiguities in legalism. It is preferable to randomly selecting an outcome for no reason at all, or uncritically adopting an outcome that an arbitrator personally likes more than the other outcomes.

In any event, many legal prescriptions explicitly require governing elites to balance the values at stake, and legalism requires the arbitrator to engage in moral reasoning to interpret those prescriptions. Article 31 of the Vienna Convention on the Law of Treaties (the VCLT) instructs interpreters of treaties to read the ordinary words of a treaty in light of its objects and purposes, which invariably are directed at allocating values among different constituents.[11] For example, most, if not all, investment treaties explain in their preambles that the purpose of the treaty is to promote investment.[12]

D. Effectiveness

An international legal system that does not achieve some degree of effectiveness does not promote the common good or any basic value. An arbitrator concerned with promoting basic values must therefore be concerned with the effectiveness of his decisions as well as the values promoted in his award. On the one hand, a decision that reaches an optimal balance of values but which the parties reject will be ineffective, and is hardly worth the arbitrator's fees. On the other hand, a decision that is pragmatically drafted to secure compliance without regard for the damage that pragmatic accommodations inflict on relevant values or the common good secured through legalism is perhaps no better than an idealistic award that is not followed.

Concerns about effectiveness in arbitral decisions are significantly alleviated in private commercial international arbitrations because of strongly shared expecta-

[9] *See id.* at 584.

[10] *See id.*

[11] Vienna Convention on the Law of Treaties, May 23, 1969, 1155 U.N.T.S. 331, art. 31(1) (entered into force January 27, 1980) [hereinafter VCLT].

[12] *See, e.g.*, Agreement on Encouragement and Reciprocal Protection of Investments, Czech/Slovk.-Neth., Aug. 1, 1975 ("Desiring to extend and intensify the economic relations between them particularly with respect to investments by the investors of one Contracting Party in the territory of the other Contracting Party.").

tions that awards will be enforced if they are made in accordance with laws and legalism within the formal authority of arbitrators granted to them by arbitral agreements. In an international commercial arbitration, an award rendered in accord with the Convention on the Recognition and Enforcement of Foreign Arbitral Awards (the New York Convention) will tend to be enforced by any court of a New York Convention signatory state.[13] Although domestic courts have some margin of appreciation in determining whether the requirements of the New York Convention have been met in an award, and signatory states are free to both violate the New York Convention or withdraw from it,[14] decades of arbitral practice in conjunction with domestic court enforcement has consolidated expectations among decision-makers that New York Convention awards will be enforced.[15] Consequently, awards that strive to promote relevant values will tend to be effective in resolving disputes so long as they are made within the legalist framework of the New York Convention and applicable domestic laws of the state in which domestic enforcement may be sought.

Questions of effectiveness in investment treaty arbitrations are more vexing. Although the Convention on the Settlement of Investment Disputes between States and Nationals of Other States (the ICSID or Washington Convention) provides that International Centre for Settlement of Investment Disputes (ICSID) awards are enforceable,[16] in practice, some host states that have lost arbitrations have taken a long time to pay their awards. Investors have had to sell their rights under investment treaty awards for cents on the dollar to third parties, leaving it to them to subsequently recover what they can from the host states.[17] Additionally, the possibility of states exiting from investment treaty regimes, including NAFTA and ICSID, is ever present.[18] Add to these difficulties ambiguity in investment treaty standards of protection for investments, and arbitrators face a complex decisionmaking process.

An award that fails to adequately balance the values at stake and preserve the essential interests of the states involved risks becoming ineffective, undermining the whole point of the arbitration to resolve the dispute, and risking damage to the common good that depends on shared expectations that the investment treaty regime will be effective in stabilizing international investment relationships.

[13] Convention on Recognition and Enforcement of Foreign Arbitral Awards, June 10, 1958, 330 U.N.T.S. 38, art. v (entered into force June 7, 1959) [hereinafter New York Convention].

[14] *Id.* art. XIII.

[15] *See also* Federal Arbitration Act, 9 U.S.C. §§ 201 ("The Convention on the Recognition and Enforcement of Foreign Arbitral Awards of June 10, 1958, shall be enforced in United States courts in accordance with this chapter.") (enacting the NY Convention into domestic law).

[16] Washington Convention, *supra* note 4, arts. 53–54.

[17] *See* Susan D. Franck, *An Empirical Analysis of Investment Treaty Awards*, 101 Am. Soc'y Int'l L. Proc. 459 (2007) (surveying recovery on investment treaty awards).

[18] North American Free Trade Agreement, art. 2205, U.S.-Can.-Mex., Dec. 17, 1992, 32 I.L.M. 289 (1993), [hereinafter NAFTA]; Washington Convention, *supra* note 4, art. 71.

An award that departs too far from legalist reasoning and procedures or which adopts an interpretation of substantive prescriptions that strays too far from shared expectations of what the prescription means also risks becoming ineffective if the parties reject the award as invalid, a court refuses to enforce it, or an ad hoc committee convened by the administering institution to review the award annuls it.[19]

II. PRAXIS

Applying the account of the international legal system offered in this book, arbitrators are called to exercise their judgment about the appropriate balance among the competing considerations discussed above.

In some disputes, the considerations do not conflict with each other to any significant degree. In these easy cases, arbitrators should strive to render awards that optimize the values at stake without deviating too far from legalism that promotes the common good and which the parties expect the arbitrators to apply, triggering their shared expectation that the award is authoritative. The *United States-Stainless Steel (Mexico)* arbitration award by Florentino Feliciano is an illustrative case, as explained below.

Other cases are more difficult because some of the considerations that an arbitrator ought to promote in his decisionmaking conflict with each other. In such cases, the arbitrators are called upon to exercise their best judgment, and they have significant discretion in determining the best balance among completing considerations. Observers may disagree about whether their decisions provide international law with its best justification. Because these disagreements often implicate choices that are not obviously right or wrong, such as the views about the functions of arbitration, the account of international law here does not provide a way to determine the best justification for international law in arbitral awards, if indeed there is even a "best" justification. Instead, this account simply provides a framework of analysis for arbitrators to reach a reasonable justification for international law that identifies and seeks to balance competing considerations.

A. United States-Stainless Steel (Mexico), Implementing Award

The award that Feliciano rendered in the *United States-Final Anti-dumping Measures on Stainless Steel from Mexico* WTO dispute ("the *Implementing Award*"), dated October 31, 2008,[20] is an easy case. It is also a good test case because it is one of the few international decisions by Feliciano alone, and this is a practical application of his stated jurisprudential approach. Because his approach to adjudication also calls for a balance of competing policy concerns, along with legalist imperatives, his

[19] Washington Convention, *supra* note 4, art. 52(1)(e).

[20] Final Anti-Dumping Measures on Stainless Steel from Mexico, Arbitration Report, WT/DS344/15 (Oct. 31, 2008).

award in this dispute also serves as a proxy for testing the account of international law presented in this book.

In Feliciano's view, a judge should consider broader community values when making decisions. He stated in his 1990 Sherrill lecture:

> The most important task of the judge is to become very clear as to what community values or interests are engaged, and in what degree, in the case before him, given the facts provisionally designated as operative and the legal norms tentatively deemed applicable. . . . [T] he task of clarifying and specifying community interests requires the judge to consider both competing interests and to choose and give effect to the requirements of the interest deemed more insistent and important in the total circumstances of the case.[21]

However, he also has explicitly counselled:

> Where the community values involved are less urgent or less dramatic and immediate in their requirements—the reliability and efficiency of the legal system, for instance—he should comply with his oath of office and apply the legal norm because it was authoritatively prescribed.[22]

In other words, in disputes where it is possible to find an interpretation of prescriptions within legalist limits that acceptably harmonizes the values at stake, the arbitrator ought not to stray from legalism in order to promote the common good that requires stability in the international legal system.

The *United States-Stainless Steel (Mexico)* award he rendered illustrates this point. In the *Implementing Award*, the Appellate Body of the World Trade Organization had found that the United States violated the General Agreement on Tariffs and Trade of 1994 (GATT) and its associated anti-dumping agreement, through its anti-dumping determinations by the U.S. Department of Commerce concerning Mexican steel exports.[23] The Appellate Body ordered the United States to change its anti-dumping measures so that they complied with GATT and the anti-dumping agreement.[24]

Under Article 21.3(c) of the Dispute Settlement Understanding, the sole issue for Feliciano to decide was how much time the United States was permitted to comply with the decision of the WTO appellate panel. The legal prescription he was bound to apply provided limited guidance. Article 21.3 states in relevant part:

> 3. At a DSB [the Dispute Settlement Board] meeting held within 30 days after the date of adoption of the panel or Appellate Body report, the Member concerned shall inform the DSB of its

[21] Feliciano, *supra* note 1, at 42, 52.

[22] *Id.*, at 51. *Cf.* 2 Rosalyn Higgins, Themes & Theories: Selected Essays, Speeches and Writings in International Law 1295 (2009).

[23] Final Anti-Dumping Measures on Stainless Steel from Mexico, Appellate Body Report, WT/DS344/AB/R, ¶ 3 (Apr. 30, 2008).

[24] *Id.*

intentions in respect of implementation of the recommendations and rulings of the DSB. If it is impracticable to comply immediately with the recommendations and rulings, the Member concerned shall have a reasonable period of time in which to do so. The reasonable period of time shall be:

[. . .]

(c) a period of time determined through binding arbitration within 90 days after the date of adoption of the recommendations and rulings. In such arbitration, a guideline for the arbitrator should be that the reasonable period of time to implement panel or Appellate Body recommendations should not exceed 15 months from the date of adoption of a panel or Appellate Body report. However, that time may be shorter or longer, depending upon the particular circumstances.[25]

Article 21.3(c) thus provides that Feliciano was to set the period of time for implementation, and the only guidance it gave was that the time should be "reasonable," "depending on the particular circumstances."[26] It did not state what facts are relevant considerations of the circumstances and how those facts were to be interpreted to decide what was reasonable.

As one would expect, the United States and Mexico both advocated their respective interests. The United States argued that Feliciano was only to determine what a reasonable time was and was not mandated to determine how the United States was to implement the Appellate Body's decision.[27] The United States could choose whether to do so through legislative amendment or administrative regulations.[28] The United States contended that Feliciano was required to consider the complexity of U.S. legislative and administrative processes and the delays that would be caused by the 2008 presidential elections.[29] In light of these considerations, the United States requested 15 months to implement the decision of the Appellate Body.[30]

Mexico conceded that Feliciano should account for the legal system of the United States, but argued that he should determine a reasonable time as the "shortest possible time within the legal system,"[31] using "all the flexibility and discretion available within the legal system."[32] It also argued that Feliciano should take into account the fact that there had been similar anti-dumping cases brought against the United

[25] Marrakesh Agreement Establishing the World Trade Organization annex 2, art. 21.3, Apr. 15, 1994, 33 I.L.M. 1144, 1238 (1994), *available at* http://www.wto.org/english/docs_e/legal_e/04-wto.pdf [hereinafter DSU art. 21.3].

[26] *Id.*

[27] United States—Final Anti-dumping Measures on Stainless Steel From Mexico, Award of the Arbitrator, WT/DS344/15, ¶¶ 1–3 (Oct. 31, 2008) [hereinafter United States—Stainless Steel Award].

[28] *Id.* at ¶ 11.

[29] *Id.* at ¶¶ 12–20.

[30] *Id.* at ¶ 21.

[31] *Id. at* ¶ 23.

[32] *See id.*

States by other states, and the United States had been under an obligation since at least May 9, 2006, to comply with anti-dumping rulings in *U.S-Zeroing (EC)*.[33]

Feliciano decided that the United States had a little over 11 months to comply with the Appellate Body decision and ordered the United States to implement the decision by April 30, 2009.[34] He accepted that he was not authorized to decide how the United States was to implement the decision but only the time in which it was to do so. However, he reasoned that in order to decide the time period, he needed to consider how the United States proposed to do so, consistent with the approach taken by the arbitrators in *Japan-DRAMs (Korea)*.[35] Although the United States had discretion to choose the method of implementation, its discretion was not "unfettered," based on the decision in the *Brazil-Retreaded Tyres* and other awards.[36] The United States was required to use the method requiring the shortest time possible.[37] Applying these principles, Feliciano decided that the United States could not claim it would need more time to make legislative changes because it could use administrative measures that would take less time,[38] and that it could begin making those changes immediately, without waiting for the new Congress and President to take office, even if the changes would need to be completed under the new administration.[39] Finally, Feliciano explained that it was inappropriate to take into account prior anti-dumping cases against the United States because they were insufficiently similar to the present dispute.[40] In light of these considerations, Feliciano decided that the United States would have until April 30, 2009, to implement the Appellate Body decision.[41]

This award is a straightforward example of how arbitrators should interpret and apply prescriptions. A function in this arbitration was to contribute to the resolution of the dispute between the United States and Mexico. Another function was to develop the shared expectations of WTO signatory states about appropriate reasoning to determine deadlines for implementing WTO decisions. Although WTO arbitration is contingent on the consent of signatory states, and states finance the operations of the WTO, there is some expectation among decisionmakers that WTO decisions should not just address the dispute at hand, and that they should also contribute to the consolidation of trade norms that promote the common good

[33] *See id.* at ¶ 24; United States—Laws, Regulations and Methodology for Calculating Dumping Margins ("Zeroing"), Appellate Body Report, WT/DS294/R (May 9, 2006).

[34] *See id.* at ¶ 65.

[35] *See id.* at ¶ 41; Japan—Countervailing Duties on Dynamic Random Access Memories From Korea, Award of the Arbitrator, WT/DS336/16, ¶ 26 (May 5, 2008) [hereinafter Japan–DRAMs].

[36] United States—Stainless Steel Award, *supra* note 26, ¶ 42 (citing Brazil—Measures Affecting Imports of Retreaded Tyres, Award of the Arbitrator, WT/DS332/16, ¶ 48 (Aug. 29, 2008)); EC—Measures Concerning Meat and Meat Products (Hormones), Award of the Arbitrator, WT/DS26/15 & WT/DS48/13, ¶ 38 (May 29, 1998); Japan—DRAMs, *supra* note 34, ¶ 27)).

[37] United States—Stainless Steel Award, *supra* note 26, at ¶ 43.

[38] *See id.* at ¶ 53.

[39] *See id.* at ¶ 62.

[40] *See id.* at ¶ 64.

[41] *See id.* at ¶ 65.

through stabilizing international trade relations. Feliciano discharged both these functions by balancing the values at stake, promoting the common good through legalism, and accommodating the interests of the parties to ensure a minimum degree of effectiveness.

The common good was satisfied through legalism because Feliciano reached his decision relying on Article 23 of the DSU and prior awards interpreting what that provision meant.

In addition to the stability necessary for the common good, Feliciano's award also promoted relevant values. Detailed economic analysis of the trade goals of GATT are beyond the scope of this book. However, assuming that the substantive outcomes required under GATT generally promote the common good by creating conditions for trade that allow constituents worldwide to pursue their preferred values, then this award increasing the practical effectiveness of GATT was substantively moral, even if it did not secure the immediate compliance of the United States with the underlying WTO decision. It was also moral because it promoted the common good by ensuring that the award was consistent with prior awards, even though Feliciano was not formally bound by precedent, and by adhering to the procedures of the DSU. In this fashion, it promoted stability in the international legal system that is necessary for the common good.

Sovereigntists who argue that judges must account for the interests of states involved should also be content. Feliciano accommodated U.S. interests by making allowances for complex and slow U.S. legislative and administrative processes. He also protected Mexico's interests by requiring the United States to use the method that was the swiftest, rather than to leave the choice entirely up to the United States.

Although his award did not result in the United States necessarily complying with the time limits he set, it did achieve a minimum degree of effectiveness. At the time this book was drafted in December 31, 2010, the dispute was ongoing, and Mexico had commenced compliance proceedings.[42] Superficially, this suggests that the award was ineffective. However, although the award was not fully effective, Mexico and the United States remained within the WTO system of dispute resolution and are utilizing its legal mechanisms to resolve their trade dispute in an orderly manner, which is ultimately one of the key goals of the WTO. The better view is that the award discharged its function within a broader and customarily lengthy dispute resolution process in the WTO.[43]

In addition to being an easy case, it is a useful case for the present study of the international legal system. In disputes such as the *U.S.-Stainless Steel (Mexico)*

[42] United States—Final Anti-Dumping Measures on Stainless Steel from Mexico, World Trade Org., *available at* http://www.wto.org/english/tratop_e/dispu_e/cases_e/ds344_e.htm.

[43] *Cf.* Tai-Heng Cheng, *Power, Norms and International Intellectual Property Law*, 28 Mich. J. Int'l L. 109 (2009) (surveying the long time periods for compliance with WTO decisions in IP disputes).

case, arbitrators can reach decisions that reasonably harmonize the completing considerations that justify the regulatory demands of international law. The ability of such a decision to promote effectiveness depends in part on satisfying elites that a minimum quantum of their respective preferred values are protected. Effectiveness here also depends on whether the arbitral decision defends legalism and its attendant virtues of stability, coherence, and adherence, all of which, in turn, depend on confining a decision within the bounds of legalist reasoning and procedures. Finally, an effective decision is one that is not so substantively unjust that the judge should not enforce it. It appears that the bulk of international disputes can be resolved in a manner that accommodates these considerations, and it is incumbent upon arbitrators to do so.

B. Loewen Group, Inc. v. United States of America

Not all cases are easy. There are also hard cases where legalism, moral concerns, interests, and functions of arbitration are sufficiently divergent or ambiguous to make decisionmaking difficult for arbitrators. *Loewen Group, Inc. v. United States of America* is one such case.[44]

The Canadian Loewen Group was embroiled in a dispute with Mississippi companies owned by the O'Keefes over contracts worth around $1 million and the exchange of two O'Keefe funeral homes worth $2.5 million, for a Loewen insurance company valued at $4 million.[45] At the end of the trial, the jury awarded to the U.S. plaintiff $500 million in damages, including $75 million in emotional distress and $400 million in punitive damages.[46] The Mississippi court that adjudicated the dispute allowed racial and class biases to infect the trial.[47] Unable to appeal this decision without going into bankruptcy because the bond for appeal under Mississippi law was $625 million, Loewen settled the case for $175 million.[48] The Loewen Group, comprising the Loewen Group, Inc. and Loewen Group International, Inc., as well as Raymond Loewen, then brought a proceeding against the United States under NAFTA for beaching its obligations to provide Loewen's investment in the United States with the "minimum standard of treatment," including "fair and equitable treatment and full protection and security."[49]

The award was surprising. The tribunal comprised Sir Anthony Mason, the former Chief Justice of the Australia High Court; Judge Abner J. Mikva, a former federal judge on the U.S. Court of Appeals for the D.C. Circuit; and Lord Michael Mustill,

[44] Loewen Group, Inc. v. U.S., ICSID Case No. ARB(AF)/98/3, 42 I.L.M. 811 (June 26, 2003) [hereinafter Loewen Award]. *See also* Tai-Heng Cheng, *Power, Authority and International Investment Law,* 20 AM. U. INT'L L. REV. 465, 508–12 (2005) (discussing the Loewen award).

[45] Loewen Award, *supra* note 44, at ¶ 3.

[46] *See id.* at ¶ 4.

[47] *See id.* at ¶ 138.

[48] *See id.* at ¶¶ 6–7.

[49] NAFTA, art. 1105, ¶ 1.

a retired English law lord. They found that Loewen had been completely denied a fair trial. They stated:

> By any standard of measurement, the trial involving O'Keefe and Loewen was a disgrace. By any standard of review, the tactics of O'Keefe's lawyers, particularly Mr. Gary, were impermissible. By any standard of evaluation, the trial judge failed to afford Loewen the process that was due.[50]

However, the tribunal stated that the United States was not responsible for what appeared to be breaches of NAFTA. It reasoned that Loewen failed to exhaust local remedies, which in its view was a precondition to pursuing a NAFTA claim. Although the tribunal acknowledged Loewen's claim that it was unable to post the $625 million bond,[51] the tribunal reasoned that Loewen nonetheless failed to exhaust local remedies because Loewen could have gone into Chapter 11 bankruptcy and appealed against the state court decision.[52] Alternatively, the tribunal decided Loewen could have petitioned to the U.S. Supreme Court with an application for a stay of execution of the judgment against the bond requirement.[53]

The tribunal additionally found that it did not have jurisdiction over the Loewen Group. After the initial hearing on the merits in Mississippi, the Loewen Group, Inc. had filed for Chapter 11 bankruptcy.[54] It had been reorganized as a U.S. corporation, and its NAFTA claims were assigned to a Canadian corporation, Nafcanco, created to pursue this claim. The tribunal concluded that since Loewen Group, Inc. was no longer a Canadian corporation, and NAFTA claims could only be brought against the United States by Canadian or Mexican corporations, the tribunal lacked jurisdiction to hear the claims of the Loewen Group, Inc.[55]

With remarkable non-legalist candor, the tribunal ended its award with a lengthy dictum explaining its hyper-technical decision that consciously avoided correcting the injustice in the case:

> We think it right to add one final word. . . . There was unfairness here towards the foreign investor. Why not use the weapons at hand to put it right? What clearer case than the present could there be for the ideals of NAFTA to be given some teeth?
>
> This human reaction has been present in our minds throughout but we must be on guard against allowing it to control our decision. Far from fulfilling the purposes of NAFTA, an

[50] Loewen Award, *supra* note 44, ¶119. *See also id.* ¶ 138 ("We take the view that the judge, for reasons which do not clearly appear, failed to discharge his paramount duty to ensure that Loewen received a fair trial.").

[51] *See id.* at ¶ 6.

[52] *See id.* at ¶ 209.

[53] *See id.* at ¶ 217.

[54] *See id.* at ¶ 234.

[55] *See id.* at ¶ 240(2). The tribunal also found it had no jurisdiction over Raymond Loewen because he failed to prove that he owned any stock in the Loewen Group when at the time when NAFTA proceedings were brought. *See id.* at ¶ 239.

> intervention on our part would compromise them by obscuring the crucial separation between the international obligations of the State under NAFTA, of which the fair treatment of foreign investors in the judicial sphere is but one aspect, and the much broader domestic responsibilities of every nation towards litigants of whatever origin who appear before its national courts. . . . Too great a readiness to step from outside into the domestic arena, attributing the shape of an international wrong to what is really a local error (however serious), will damage both the integrity of the domestic judicial system and the viability of NAFTA itself. The natural instinct, when someone observes a miscarriage of justice, is to step in and try to put it right, but the interests of the international investing community demand that we must observe the principles which we have been appointed to apply, and stay our hands.[56]

Some scholars and arbitrators have soundly criticized the tribunal's reasoning. The tribunal's finding that Loewen could have petitioned to the Supreme Court to reconsider the Mississippi court's application of the bond requirement on due process grounds, which was unlikely to succeed, rather than settle for a third of the verdict, prompted Swiss arbitrator Jacques Werner to exclaim: "In what world does the Arbitral Tribunal live?"[57] The notion that an international law claim can only be pursued by going into bankruptcy similarly bears no relation to commercial realities or business practices, and many scholars think the tribunal simply got the law wrong.[58]

Allegations have now arisen about the United States' actions behind the scenes, and about the tribunal's deliberations, which raise graver concerns.[59] According to one academic, the U.S.-appointed arbitrator, Judge Mikva, apparently revealed at an academic conference in 2004 that after he agreed to serve on the Loewen tribunal,

[56] *Id.* at ¶¶ 241–42.

[57] *See* Michael D. Goldhaber., *NAFTA Suit* is *Alive, Kicking*, NAT'L L.J., Mar. 1, 2004, at 1. *See also* Jan Paulsson, *Moral Hazard in International Dispute Resolution*, Inaugural Lecture as Holder of the Michael R. Klein Distinguished Scholar Chair, at 8 (Apr. 29, 2010) (quoting Jacques Werner), *available at* http://www.arbitration-icca.org/media/0/12773749999020/paulsson_moral_hazard.pdf.

[58] On the holding that there was no jurisdiction because Loewen was reorganized as a U.S. corporation, *see* Paulsson, *supra* note 57, at 6 ("Let me just stress that it was highly abstruse point of public international law, which the three arbitrators, most specialists agree, got quite wrong."). On the holding that there was no jurisdiction because Loewen had not exhausted local remedies, *see* Cheng, *supra* note 44 at 510 & n. 193 (2005) (discussing awards holding that exhaustion of local remedies was not a requirement). *See also* Helnan Int'l Hotels A/S/ v. Arab Republic of Egypt, Decision of the Ad Hoc Committee, ICSID Arb/05/19, at 26, ¶ 73(1) (June 14, 2010) (annulling portion of award that applied exhaustion of local remedies requirement).

[59] The claim that Judge Mikva said at a conference that he had ex parte conversations was first made by David Schneiderman. *See* David Schneiderman, *Judicial Politics and International Investment Arbitration: Seeking an Explanation for Conflicting Outcomes*, 30 NW. J. INT'L L. & BUS. 383, 404–05 (2010). Other scholars have since referred to Schneiderman's claim in their own scholarship. *See* Jason Webb Yackee, *Book Review*, 103 AM. J. INT'L L. 629, n.12 (2009) (reviewing THE REASONS REQUIREMENT IN INTERNATIONAL INVESTMENT ARBITRATION: CRITICAL CASE STUDIES (Guillermo Aguilar Alvarez & W. Michael Reisman eds., 2008)); Susan D. Franck, *Development of Outcomes of Investment Treaty Arbitration*, 50 HARV. INT'L L. J. 435, 486, n.7 (2009). However, the transcripts and audio tapes of Judge Mikva's remarks at the conference are no longer publicly available, and the accuracy of Schneiderman's claims is difficult to assess.

Department of Justice officials met with him privately. They told him, "You know, judge, if we lose this case we could lose NAFTA." Judge Mikva replied, "Well, if you want to put pressure on me, then this does it."[60] Judge Mikva told his audience that he was "on the dissenting side of a difficult problem," and that Lord Mustill and Sir Mason wanted to find in favor of Loewen.[61] These U.S. actions, if true, were especially galling because the United States had previously moved to disqualify Yves Fortier, QC, as a member of the tribunal because of a proposed merger of Mr. Fortier's firm with a firm that had previously acted for Loewen in connection with their bankruptcy reorganization under Chapter 11 of the United States Bankruptcy Code. Mr. Fortier resigned, and Lord Mustill replaced him.[62] For the Department of Justice officials, it was not the independence of the arbitrators that they sought. Rather, it was their bias toward the United States that mattered.

Although there is no information about how Judge Mikva persuaded his co-arbitrators to change their minds, Jan Paulsson, a preeminent arbitrator, has speculated that Judge Mikva secured a unanimous award by bartering with the rest of the tribunal that he would go along with their conclusions of judicial impropriety in exchange for a technical finding of no jurisdiction.[63]

By any judicial standards in developed legal systems, ex parte communications that apply pressure on a judge are inappropriate.[64] The appraisal of most legal scholars and lawyers is that the judge should have recused himself and, having failed to do so, his refusal raises serious questions about the integrity of the arbitral process and the resulting award. Thus, if the United States had contacted Judge Mikva ex parte, Judge Mikva should have recused himself or at least disclosed the conversation to the parties soon after it occurred and well before issuing an award, not years after the award was handed down. The award was consequently illegitimate under this book's account of international law because it unjustifiably departed from legalist procedures and expectations of appropriate party and arbitrator conduct. It damaged the common good when the departures were revealed only after the arbitration was decided, because it undermined confidence in NAFTA dispute settlement.[65] The award also raises questions about whether the tribunal had appropriately balanced the specific values and interests at stake. In short, the *Loewen* award is an easy case of an unjustified award if Judge Mikva had spoken with Department of Justice officials ex parte, in contrast to the *United States-Stainless Steel (Mexico)* award of Judge Feliciano, which was an easy case of a properly decided award.

[60] Schneiderman, *supra* note 59 at 405.

[61] *See id.*

[62] *See* Loewen Award, *supra* note 44, at ¶ 21.

[63] *See* Paulsson, *supra* note 57, at 9.

[64] For other examples of states applying improper pressure on arbitrators, see *id.* at 2–5.

[65] *See* Paulsson, *supra* note 57, at 2 ("Ultimately, if there is no faith in the legitimacy of adjudication—which we all surely accept as better than violence or corruption—suppliers of goods, services, and know how will prefer to disengage.").

If, however, the ex parte conversation with Judge Mikva never occurred, the *Loewen* award presents a harder case under this book's account of international law, contrary to criticisms that have been made against the award, including some criticisms that this author made in an earlier work.[66]

The outcome of the case was unfair to Loewen and perhaps failed to properly balance the values at stake. Had the tribunal found against the United States, such a finding could have been, by the tribunal's own reckoning, more just.[67] Such a finding would also have been faithful to legalism. The tribunal could have decided that it had jurisdiction over the Loewen Group because it was Canadian when it commenced its claim, or that Nafcanco was a proper successor to the claims because it was Canadian. It could also have held that Loewen did not need to exhaust local remedies, as other awards have held.[68]

It is not clear, however, that the tribunal damaged the common good by excessively departing from legalist reasoning. The award was perhaps at the outer margins of legal reasoning but probably did not cross the line into illegality and depart too far from shared expectations that arbitrators should make decisions using legalist reasoning. Lord Mustill and Sir Mason, who served on their respective countries' highest courts, would not have signed off on an award that was completely indefensible on legalist grounds.

In an important way, the award protected the common good by reducing the risk that the United States would withdraw from NAFTA, which is a basic strut of regional economic order. Unlike domestic law, which is mandatorily applied, NAFTA allows any party to withdraw from it. Even absent an intervention from the Department of Justice with Judge Mikva, the tribunal would have known that some domestic elites in the United States opposed NAFTA, and a decision against the United States would risk agitating those elites to undermine NAFTA or withdraw from it. While it is far less than ideal to have to accommodate powerful interests to ensure that the international legal system maintains a modicum of effectiveness to achieve any regulation at all (and contrary to some conceptions of the rule of law), that pragmatic accommodation may be the least suboptimal alternative in some situations. Whatever one's views of the extent to which law can accommodate power and interests before it ceases to be law, reasonable minds can disagree about the extent to which arbitrators should be concerned with effectiveness of their rulings when deciding what outcomes to prescribe in their awards.

NAFTA benefits Mexico, the United States, and Canada. If the tribunal in good faith believed that a finding that U.S. courts acted improperly, unless there was no

[66] Cheng, *supra* note 43 at 509–11.

[67] *See id.* (stating that there was a "miscarriage of justice" and they instinctively wanted "to try to put it right").

[68] GAMI Investments, Inc. v. United Mexican States, Final Award ¶ 38 (B) (UNCITRAL, Nov. 15, 2004), *available at* http://www.state.gov/documents/organization/38789.pdf (stating that a foreign investor "is entitled to seek international relief from a NAFTA tribunal on account of wrongful expropriation" even though investor had not sought any relief before the host state's courts).

other legalist alternative, would "damage . . . the viability of NAFTA itself,"[69] then it is at least debatable that their decision was appropriately made to protect the common good within the technical limits of legalism.

On final analysis, if it is true that the Department of Justice tried to influence Judge Mikva ex parte, his failure to recuse himself or at least disclose the conversation rendered the award illegitimate under this book's account of international law. However, if the Department of Justice had not contacted Judge Mikva ex parte, he and his co-arbitrators could have independently decided that it was necessary to accommodate the U.S. interests by insulating its domestic legal system from NAFTA, in order to achieve minimum effectiveness and to protect the stability of the regional economic order. Judge Mikva could also have persuaded his co-arbitrators that this was an overriding consideration, and it was in any event consistent with legalist reasoning, so such a finding would not damage the integrity of international law. For these reasons, the *Loewen* award was a hard case, but a good illustration of how this book's justificatory theory would provide guidance to arbitrators.

C. CMS Gas Transmission Co. v. Argentine Republic, Decision on Annulment

Another hard case, and a good test of this book's theory of international law, is the annulment decision of the ad hoc committee in *CMS Gas Transmission Co. v. Argentine Republic.*[70] After the arbitration tribunal found that Argentina had violated the U.S.-Argentina bilateral investment treaty (BIT),[71] an ad hoc committee annulled a portion of the award and left another portion intact, after harshly criticizing it. For the reasons discussed below, the ad hoc decision to both find the standard for annulment had not been met but nevertheless criticize the award is a hard case because it turns on contested views about the appropriate function of arbitrators.

During Argentina's financial crisis, it took emergency financial measures to protect its economy that resulted in losses to foreign investors.[72] CMS Gas Transmission Company was one such foreign investor. CMS filed an ICSID arbitration against Argentina under the Argentina-U.S. BIT. In the tribunal's award of May 12, 2005, the tribunal found that Argentina had breached the fair and equitable treatment standard and umbrella clauses of the BIT, and that Argentina did not have a valid necessity defense. The tribunal awarded CMS $133.2 million.[73]

Argentina requested that an ad hoc committee annul the award under Article 52 of the ICSID Convention. Article 52 provides that a party "may request annulment

[69] Loewen Award, *supra* note 44, at ¶ 242.

[70] CMS Gas Transmission Co. v. Argentine Republic, ICSID Case No. ARB/01/8, Annulment Proceeding (Sept. 1, 2006) [hereinafter CMS Annulment Decision].

[71] CMS Gas Transmission Co. v. Argentine Republic, ICSID Case No. ARB/01/8, Award (May 12, 2005 [hereinafter CMS Award].

[72] *Id.* at § 4 ¶¶ 59–67.

[73] *Id.* at ¶ 468.

of the award by an application in writing addressed to the Secretary-General (of ICSID) on one or more of the following grounds . . . that the award has failed to state reasons on which it is based."[74]

The ad hoc committee explained that the possibility of annulment for failure to state reasons did not open the door for appellate review and to reverse the award on the merits. The "failure to state reasons" basis for annulment was a high threshold requiring that the tribunal had failed to provide reasons to enable the parties to understand the award. If reasons were provided and the award could be understood, the award could not be annulled even if the reasons were wrong.[75]

Applying this high threshold for annulment to the award, the ad hoc committee annulled the portion of the award finding that the umbrella clause of the BIT had been violated[76] but rejected all other requests for annulment.[77] This effectively left the award intact because the breach of the fair and equitable treatment standard was sufficient to justify the damages awarded.[78]

The portion of the CMS decision that presents a hard case is its denial of the request to annul the portion of the award that rejected Argentina's necessity defense alongside its harsh criticism of that holding. Article XI of the Argentina-U.S. BIT provided a defense of necessity that absolved Argentina of responsibility for breaches of the BIT if Argentina took only measures that were deemed necessary under the BIT.[79] The tribunal found that Argentina did not meet the criteria for necessity under Article XI because it did not satisfy the conditions for necessity under the general customary law of necessity, as expressed in Article 25 of the ILC's Articles on State Responsibility.[80]

The ad hoc committee found that the tribunal had made "manifest errors of law."[81] The tribunal had essentially conflated Article 25 of the ILC Articles with Art XI of the BIT. The ad hoc committee thus stated that the tribunal "should have been more explicit in specifying, for instance, that the very same reasons that disqualified Argentina from relying on the general law of necessity meant that measures it took could not be considered 'necessary' for the purposes of Article XI either[.]"[82] The committee held, however, that it was possible to follow the tribunal's implicit reasoning, and therefore there was no failure to state reasons, and the tribunal's manifest errors of law were insufficient to annul its rejection of Argentina's necessity defense.

[74] Washington Convention, *supra* note 4, art. 52(1)(e).

[75] CMS Annulment Decision, *supra* note 70, at ¶ 97.

[76] *Id.* at ¶ 100.

[77] *Id.*

[78] *Id.* at ¶ 161.

[79] Bilateral Investment Treaty Concerning the Reciprocal Encouragement and Protection of Investment, U.S.-Arg., art. XI, Nov. 14, 1991, 31 I.L.M. 124 (1992).

[80] Draft Articles on the Responsibility of States for Internationally Wrongful Acts, Report of the ILC on the Work of its Fifty-third Session, art. 25, U.N. GAOR, 56th Sess, Supp No 10, U.N. Doc. A/56/10, at 49 (2001).

[81] CMS Annulment Decision, *supra* note 70, at ¶ 45.

[82] *Id.* at ¶ 95.

At first glance, the *CMS* annulment decision may seem appropriate. It appears sufficiently faithful to legalism and the moral obligation to promote the common good through legalism. Its high standard for annulment is consistent with many, although not all, other annulment decisions. Because the standard for annulment is not uniform,[83] and the *CMS* committee associated itself with the high threshold for annulment adopted by other committees, it did not deviate from shared expectations about the standard for annulment.[84] There also does not appear to be grave imbalances in allocating the values at stake and in protecting the vital interests of CMS, the United States, or Argentina.

However, the *CMS* annulment decision presents a hard case because the committee's obiter criticisms of the tribunal's findings on necessity greatly reduced the effectiveness of the tribunal's decision—and indeed the entire arbitration process—in resolving the dispute between CMS and Argentina. Had Argentina succeeded in raising the necessity defense, it would not have had any responsibility for damages. Thus, criticizing the tribunal's findings on necessity greatly increased the opposition of Argentinean constituencies to paying an award that an eminent committee of arbitrators had found made manifest errors of law on a crucial holding. Even though the award was left formally intact, the statements of the ad hoc committee unsettled shared expectations that Argentina should have paid the award, which could otherwise have coalesced more easily. Critics who made this argument would say that the ad hoc committee's decision failed to adequately promote effectiveness, which under this book's general theory of law, is one of the key considerations in proper decisionmaking.

This aspect of the ad hoc committee's decision presents a hard case because whether or not its failure to adequately account for effectiveness reduced the justificatory power of the decision depends on one's view of the function of arbitrators in general and ad hoc committees in particular. From one view, the arbitral function is dispute resolution. From this standpoint, the ad hoc committee's decision was indeed lacking because it undermined the effectiveness of an award that it chose to leave essentially intact as a formal matter. From another view, the arbitral function, especially that of an ad hoc committee, is to clarify the law that the parties paid the committee to deliberate and, crucially, to fully provide the reasons for its decision. From this standpoint, effectiveness is a secondary consideration, if at all. Although the author sees merit in the view that emphasizes effectiveness, it cannot

[83] *See* Tai-Heng Cheng & Robert Trisotto, *Reasons and Reasoning in Investment Treaty Arbitration*, 32 Suffolk Transnat'l L. Rev. 409, 414–23 (2009) (discussing uncertainties in the reasons requirement).

[84] *See* Guillermo Aguilar Alvarez & W. Michael Reisman, *How Well are Investment Awards Reasoned?*, *in* The Reasons Requirement in International Investment Arbitration: Critical Case Studies 1, 20 (G.A. Alvarez & W. M. Reisman eds., 2008) ("The Committee explicitly associated itself with the annulment decisions in *MTD v. Chile*, *MINE*, *Vivendi*, and *Wena Hotels*."). *But* see Klöckner Industrie-Anlagen GmBH v. Rep. Cameroon, 1 ICSID Rev. FILJ 89 (1986) (setting high reasons requirement making annulment easily obtained).

be said that that view is necessarily correct and the other necessarily wrong. Accordingly, the *CMS* ad hoc decision presents a hard case.

III. CONCLUSION

The foregoing analysis has shown that the general justificatory account of the international legal system applies to arbitrators. The chapter has also demonstrated how that account provides guidelines to help arbitrators make decisions and to identify easy and hard cases. That approach neither eliminates the arbitrator's discretion in making difficult moral and normative decisions in hard cases, nor is it intended to.[85] However, it provides a framework of analysis to puzzle through competing considerations in international arbitration involving states.

[85] *See* Jan Paulsson, Symposium, *Making the Most of International Investment Agreements: Indirect Expropriation: Is the Right to Regulate at Risk?* 1 (Dec. 12, 2005), *available at* http://www.oecd.org/dataoecd/5/52/36055332.pdf ("In a phrase, perfect predictability is an illusion.").

6 Regulators

I. THEORY

This chapter studies whether and how the justificatory theory of international law extends to regulators. After discussing how the theory applies to regulators generally, this chapter examines the actions and decisions of international bank regulators in the 2008 global financial crisis.

In this book, "regulators" refers to the category of officials that Anne-Marie Slaughter has described as "appointed top officials or career civil servants who possess a special expertise in a particular subject."[1] In international problems, regulators are officials charged with authoritatively controlling the actions of specialized industries, such as banking, in a coordinated fashion. Although they engage in a range of actions, as this book is principally concerned with the regulation of international problems through authoritative prescriptions,[2] the focus of inquiry is on how regulators ought to make, apply, and modify prescriptions. Regulators do not represent states in making international laws. Instead, they use informal prescriptions, which may or may not involve enforcement mechanisms. Benedict Kingsbury has referred to this type of regulation as global administrative law.[3]

[1] Anne-Marie Slaughter, A New World Order 38 (2004).

[2] *See id.* at 63 (explaining that, in addition to harmonizing state action, regulators exchange information and assist each other in enforcing national laws).

[3] Benedict Kingsbury, Nico Krisch, & Richard B. Stewart, *The Emergence of Global Administrative Law*, Law & Contemp. Probs., Summer/Autumn 2005, at 15, 17 ("[G]lobal administrative action

An example of such a regulatory body is the International Organization for Standardization (ISO).[4] The ISO comprises regulators from standard setting bodies of over 150 states who nonetheless do not represent the state in the ISO. Instead, these regulators establish technical standards through committees of experts. Corporations and other domestic entities can then voluntary agree to meet the ISO standards. This process regulates international standards without formal international laws.

The justificatory theory of international law provides guidance to regulators in their decisionmaking. Because the theory conceives of the international legal system broadly to include informal prescriptions and other shared expectations of appropriate conduct, the fact that regulators do not directly make international laws is not an obstacle to applying the theory to them. The four considerations of the justificatory theory that provide guidance to officials—function, general morality, specific morality, and effectiveness—also apply to regulators, albeit differently than they apply to judges and arbitrators.

The primary functions of regulators is to set and make effective international standards that coordinate the actions of private and government actors in domestic settings. This function shapes the general moral obligation of regulators to promote the common good in their particular spheres of expertise. Although all decisionmakers have an obligation to promote the common good by interpreting, applying, and modifying prescriptions, regulators have a special duty to additionally create prescriptions and to alter them when global conditions require different standards. When engaging in informal lawmaking, they have only a weak duty to remain faithful to prior prescriptions because the point of their lawmaking exercise is to promote the common good by setting international standards rather than slavishly keeping them the same. Put differently, actors share an expectation that regulators ought to be prescriptive. Thus, when regulators make new prescriptions, they generally promote the common good, not damage it.

The role of regulators in making international standards also informs their specific moral obligation to make prescriptions that optimize the values at stake. Because of their special expertise in the technical fields that they are charged with regulating, and their positions of authority to do so, they have a strong moral obligation to engage in a careful appraisal of relevant values and of how best to harmonize and promote them.

is rulemaking, adjudications, and other decisions that are neither treaty-making nor simple dispute settlements between parties."). *See also* Nico Krisch & Benedict Kingsbury, *Introduction: Global Governance and Global Administrative Law in the International Legal Order*, 17 Eur. J. Int'l L. 1, 3 (2006) (describing global administrative law as "the setting and application of rules by bodies that are not legislative or primarily adjudicative in character").

[4] *See generally* Aseem Prakash & Matthew Potoski, *The International Organization for Standardization as a Global Governor: A Club Theory Perspective, in* Who Governs the Globe? 72 (Avant ed., 2010) (describing the international organization for standardization and its role in international regulation).

The goal of regulation is to authoritatively guide the actors to whom regulation is directed. Therefore, regulators should pay special attention to the effectiveness of their regulation. Given the voluntary nature of the type of regulation within the scope of this chapter, prescriptions are unlikely to be effective unless they adequately harmonize and accommodate the vital interests of relevant decisionmakers and their constituents. Most often, these interests are expressed as national policies. International regulatory prescriptions are most likely to be effective when they do not require national policies to change. Prescriptions that require adjustments to national policies are less likely to be effective unless government officials believe that these changes directly benefit their constituencies and would have been made absent the prescription, or that the prescriptions are necessary tradeoffs to obtain other benefits.

For some regulators of critical industries, such as finance, a secondary function is to manage international crises when they emerge, to stabilize global order, and to restore normal patterns of activities. In a crisis, the time available for them to make decisions is short. Although the moral obligation to promote the common good is arguably stronger because coordination can be critical to solving a global crisis, the potential for effective coordination also diminishes in the heat of crisis management. Where regulators fail to coordinate their actions, and instead create ad hoc arrangements or act unilaterally, they become less like legal actors and more like political ones. This is not a criticism of what they have to do in exigent circumstances; it is simply an observation of the inverse relationship between the coherence of law and the arbitrariness of politics, as those terms are used in this book.

II. PRAXIS

The application of the justificatory theory of international law to regulators that is set out above is tested here by studying the efforts of central bank governors and other financial regulators to restore stability to world financial markets during and after the global recession. In the last quarter of 2008, financial regulators were in crisis management mode as credit froze, financial institutions collapsed, and global markets plummeted. This account of international law provides a framework to appraise their actions and shows that while the need for coordination was critical, effective coordination was also difficult as each state perceived its vital economic interests to be in danger and was unsure of how best to secure those interests.

After global markets stabilized from March 2009 onwards, however, regulators were better able to discharge their regulatory functions in the international legal system through the Financial Stability Board (FSB). The FSB is an international organization that is not legally authoritative.[5] Its guidelines are not international laws in any traditional sense. Nevertheless, the FSB's prescriptions are accompanied

[5] Kern Alexander, *Global Financial Standard Setting, the G10 Committees, and International Economic Law*, 34 BROOK. J. INT'L L. 861, 879 (2008–09) ("These international bodies [including the Financial Stability Board] lack the requisite attributes of an international organization, namely, they

by strongly shared expectations that they prescribe appropriate conduct for banks and bank regulators, and ought to be followed.

The FSB comprises international financial institutions, international regulatory bodies, and 24 national regulators, but not states themselves.[6] The Group of Seven Finance Ministers and Central Bank Governors (G-7) had created a Financial Stability Forum in 1999.[7] A decade later, on April 2, 2009, in response to the financial crisis, the Group of Twenty Finance Ministers and Central Bank Governors (G-20) expanded the forum and gave it a broader mandate, and renamed it the FSB.[8] According to the FSB Charter, its purpose is to "develop and promote the implementation of effective regulatory, supervisory, and other financial sector policies" in key financial markets worldwide, in order to promote "global financial stability."[9] It does this through various methods, including coordination and sharing information among its members.[10] It also sets guidelines[11] but does not make laws in the sense of treaties, custom, or domestic law.

The FSB prescriptions, which are a principal subject of investigation here, are a form of soft law.[12] In the international legal system, soft laws are not legal rules such as those identified in Article 38 of the ICJ Statute but are informal prescriptions that

are not subject to international law, and do not have international personality, the capacity to conclude treaties, or international legal immunities.").

[6] Financial Stability Board Charter art. 4 [hereinafter FSB Charter]. Member Jurisdictions include Argentina, Australia, Brazil, Canada, China, France, Germany, Hong Kong, India, Indonesia, Italy, Japan, Korea, Mexico, Netherlands, Russia, Saudi Arabia, Singapore, South Africa, Spain, Switzerland, Turkey, United Kingdom, and United States. In addition to governmental and non-governmental organizations within the jurisdictions above, many other international financial institutions and regulatory organizations are members, including European Central Bank, European Commission, Bank for International Settlements, International Monetary Fund, Organisation for Economic Co-operation and Development, World Bank, Basel Committee on Banking Supervision, Committee on Payment and Settlement Systems, Committee on the Global Financial System, International Accounting Standards Board, International Association of Insurance Supervisors, International Organization of Securities Commissions and several Standing Committees and ad hoc working groups. Financial Stability Board Charter, annex A, *available at* http://www.financialstabilityboard.org/publications/r_090925d.pdf.

[7] *Id.* pmbl. ¶ (1). *See also* Alan Greenspan, The Age of Turbulence 336 (2008) (stating that the G-20 was "an organization of finance ministers and central bank governors that had been put together after several tumultuous years in global finance" and that it was "seen as a way to help make sure that emerging-market countries were fully involved in discussions of global economic developments").

[8] FSB Charter, *supra* note 6, pmbl. ¶¶ (2) & (3). *See also* Robert B. Ahdieh, *After the Fall: Financial Crisis and the International Order*, 24 Emory Int'l L. Rev. 1, 7–8 (2010) (describing the creation of the FSB).

[9] FSB Charter, *supra* note 6, art. 1.

[10] *Id.* arts. 2(1)(b) & 2(2).

[11] *Id.* art. 2(1)(f).

[12] Alexander, *supra* note 5, at 869 ("[T]hese Committees have resolved not to adopt legally binding international standards in a public international law sense, but rather to influence domestic regulatory law, practices and standards by adopting what has become known as 'international soft law.'").

nonetheless authoritatively shape expectations of appropriate conduct by governing elites and can control outcomes in international problems.[13]

Scholars have explained soft norms in several international problems.[14] After the global recession of 2008, scholars have begun applying and refining their ideas about informal prescriptions by studying post-crisis global financial regulation.[15] This portion of the book adds to this corpus of scholarship. It is an early effort to assess in real time the efforts of the FSB using the justificatory theory of international law, although it is surely not the last effort as reappraisals will become necessary in the future as new facts develop. Examining ongoing processes in the international legal

[13] *See supra*, ch. 3, pt. III (explaining soft law using the justificatory theory of international law). *See also* Janet Koven Levit, *A Bottom-Up Approach to International Lawmaking: The Tale of Three Trade Finance Instruments*, 30 Yale J. Int'l L. 125, 172 (2005) (describing soft norms as "not binding international law, for it does not fit into the technical international law categories"); Christine Chinkin, *Normative Development in the International Legal System, in* Commitment and Compliance: The Role of Non-Binding Norms in the International Legal System, 21 (Shelton ed., 2000); Edith Brown Weiss, *Introduction, in* International Compliance with Nonbinding Accords 1 (Weiss ed., 1997); *A Hard Look at Soft Law*, 82 Am. Soc'y Int'l L. Proc. 371 (1988); Joseph Gold, *Strengthening the Soft International Law of Exchange Agreements*, 77 Am. J. Int'l L. 443, 452 (1983); W. Michael Reisman, Systems of Control In International Adjudication & Arbitration 31 (1992) (Soft norms "are important phases in the lawmaking process, permitting states to establish target goals, to begin to adapt national behavior to them and to accommodate internal disruptions that may ensue, giving all parties respite before they decide whether to proceed toward a more binding form of agreement.").

[14] *See, e.g.*, Levit, *supra* note 13 (studying soft norms in private international commercial relations, such as Bern Union regulation); Janet Koven Levit, *Bottom-Up Lawmaking though a Pluralist Lens: The ICC Banking Commission and the Transnational Regulations of Letters of Credit*, 57 Emory L.J. 1147 (2008) (studying Uniform Customs and Practice for Documentary Credits as soft norms that effectively regulate international banking); Tai-Heng Cheng, State Succession and Commercial Obligations (2006) (observing and proposing informal but authoritative norms for the transmission *vel non* of commercial obligations when state succession occurs); Tai-Heng Cheng, *Renegotiating the Odious Debt Doctrine*, 70 Law & Contemp. Probs. 7 (2007) (extending thesis to the doctrine of odious debt in government and state succession); Tai-Heng Cheng, *Why New States Accept Old Obligations*, 2011 U. ILL. L. REV. 1 (2011) (testing thesis of soft norms against the succession of Kosovo). *But cf.* Chris Brummer, *Post-American Securities Regulation*, 98 Cal. L. Rev. 327, 327–32 (2010) (expressing skepticism over the effectiveness of soft norms in international securities regulation).

[15] *See generally* Anupum Chander & Randall Costa, *Clearing Credit Default Swaps: A Case Study in Global Legal Convergence*, 10 Chi. J. Int'l L. 639 (2009-10) (studying informal international regulation of credit default swaps as a result of the financial crisis); Ahdieh, *supra* note 8, at 8–9 (noting efforts to harmonize accounting standards worldwide, including in the United States, following the financial crisis); David Zaring, *International Institutional Performance in Crisis,* 10 Chi J. Int'l L. 475 (2009-10) (appraising different informal international arrangements in managing the financial crisis); Eric J. Pan, *Challenge of International Cooperation and Institutional Design in Financial Supervision: Beyond Transgovernmental Networks*, 11 Chi J. Int'l L. 243, 248–50 (2010-11) (surveying soft norms and international institutions coordinating global markets). *See also* Kenneth W. Dam, *The Subprime Crisis and Financial Regulation: International and Comparative Perspectives*, 10 Chi J. Int'l L. 581 (2009-10); Detlev F. Vagts, *The Financial Meltdown and its International Implications*, 103 Am. J. Int'l L. 684, 685–90 (2009) (noting international financial standards that the United States adopted after the crisis).

system in arenas of decisionmaking is discomforting to observers who prefer the security of hindsight from the academic tower. This analysis is necessarily subject to some imprecision because the data examination analysis is neither complete nor stable. Nevertheless, this current global problem was selected as a case study to illustrate how the account of international law here can provide guidance to elites while they are involved in international problems, and not just explain historical events and suggest how officials ought to have acted in the past, as previous chapters have already done.

A. The Global Financial Crisis

It is necessary to recount briefly key events and causes of the global financial crisis.[16] According to George Soros, the financial crisis began in August and September 2007. He recounts the following events: On August 6, American Home Mortgage, one of the largest U.S. independent home loan providers, filed for bankruptcy after laying off the majority of its staff. The Company said it was a victim of the slump in the U.S. housing market that had "caught out many subprime borrowers and lenders."[17]

On August 9, short-term credit markets froze up after a large French bank, BNP Paribas, suspended three of its investment funds worth €2 billion, citing problems in the U.S. subprime mortgage sector. BNP said it could not value the assets in the funds because the market had disappeared. The European Central Bank pumped €95 billion into the eurozone banking system to ease the subprime credit crunch. The U.S. Federal Reserve and the Bank of Japan took similar steps.

The next day, the European Central Bank provided an extra €61 billion to funds and banks. The U.S. Federal Reserve said it would be needed to combat the credit crunch.

On August 13, the European Central Bank pumped €47.7 billion into the money markets, its third cash injection in as many working days. Central banks in the United States and Japan also topped up earlier injections. Goldman Sachs said it would pump $3 billion into a hedge fund hit by the credit crunch to shore up its value.

On August 16, Countrywide Financial, the Largest U.S. mortgage originator, drew down its entire $11.5 billion credit line. Australian mortgage lender Rams also admitted to liquidity problems. A day later, the U.S. Federal Reserve cut the

[16] For first person accounts of the financial crisis by key officials, *see generally* Henry M. Paulson, Jr., On the Brink (2009); George W. Bush, Decision Points 452–72 (2010). For a detailed journalistic report of the financial crisis, see generally Andrew Ross Sorkin, Too Big to Fail (2010). *See also* Randall D. Guynn, *The Global Financial Crisis and Proposed Regulatory Reform*, 2010 BYU L. Rev. 421, 422–34 (2010).

[17] *See Chronology of the Financial Crisis: USA–Europe–Switzerland*, Institut für Bankrech, http://www.ibr.unibe.ch/unibe/rechtswissenschaft/ibr/content/e9490/e9491/files9571/total.ChronologyoftheFinancialCrisis.pdf.

discount rate, which is the interest rate it charges to banks when it lends money to banks, by half a percentage point to help banks deal with credit problems. This did not help. Subsequently, the central banks of the developed world ended up injecting funds on the largest scale for longer periods and accepting a wider range of securities as collateral than ever before in history.

On September 13, it was disclosed that Northern Rock, the largest British mortgage bank prior to the subprime mortgage crash, was bordering on insolvency due to a run on the bank in which customers withdrew their funds rapidly when they feared that the bank was on the brink of bankruptcy.[18]

A complete analysis of the causes of the financial crisis will have to be left to economists.[19] For the purposes of the legal project here, it is sufficient to sketch out, in a manner that may seem simplistic to financial experts, some relevant reasons for the crisis. Following the bursting of the Internet bubble in 2000, the U.S. Federal Reserve cut interest rates. In response to the terrorist attack of September 11, 2001, interest rates were reduced further to encourage credit and economic activity in the United States. The sustained low interest rate environment led to a housing bubble, where U.S. home owners and investors overleveraged their personal balance sheets to purchase property, driving up property prices. Banks made riskier and riskier loans, in part because they did not hold those loans on their balance sheets, but packaged them together with other loans and sold off slices of those loans to other investors. The securitization of loans prevented investors and banks from fully knowing the amount of aggregate risk that they were incurring through these loans to overleveraged borrowers.

Eventually, the housing market began to turn down in the fourth quarter of 2006. Investments that were secure in a rising housing market required greater capital to sustain. Investors suffered losses from the subprime mortgages they extended to borrowers or purchased from lenders. In February 2007, HSBC Holdings, the UK-based bank and the third largest bank in the world, announced that it was setting aside $10.6 billion to cover U.S. subprime debts on its books.[20] In June 2007, two large mortgage hedge funds at Bear Stearns could not meet their mortgage obligations.[21] The bank bailed out one fund with a $3.2 billion credit line; but the other failed, wiping out $1.5 billion in investor equity.[22] One month later, Germany

[18] George Soros, The New Paradigm for Financial Markets, xiii–xxiv (2008).

[19] *See id.* at xiv–xxiii, 123–29; Paulson, *supra* note 16, at 64–73; Ben S. Bernanke, Chairman of the Bd. of Governors of the Fed. Reserve Sys., Statement before the United States Senate Committee on Banking, Housing, and Urban Affairs (Sept. 23, 2008); Henry M. Paulson, Jr., Sec'y of the Treasury, Testimony Before the Senate Banking Committee on Turmoil in US Credit Markets: Recent Actions Regarding Government Sponsored Entities, Investment Banks and other Financial Institutions (Sept. 23, 2008).

[20] Soros, *supra* note 18, at xx.

[21] *Id.*

[22] *Id.*

organized a €3.5 billion bank-led rescue of IKB Deutsche Industriebank, which could not meet its debt obligations.[23]

Markets tightened. Investors who lost confidence in financial institutions sold their shares. Around the world, banks and other financial institutions found themselves overexposed to subprime debts that they could no longer pass on to others and with insufficient capital to meet those debt obligations.

In February 2008, the UK government nationalized Northern Rock.[24] In March, 2008, Bear Stearns was also on the brink of collapse. It had overleveraged. For every dollar it held in capital, it owed 30 dollars, and had invested most of that debt in subprime mortgages. When the housing market declined and Bear became overexposed, investors moved their accounts from the firm, beginning a run on that bank. The U.S. government put together a bailout under which JPMorgan purchased Bear Stearns, but only after the Federal Reserve Bank of New York lent $30 billion against Bear Stearns' mortgage holdings, essentially guaranteeing those bad loans.

Six months later, the U.S. government put the national mortgage lenders, Fannie Mae and Freddie Mac, under conservatorship. It did not, however, act to save Lehman Brothers, the next bank unable to meet its subprime obligations. In September 2008, Lehman Brothers hurtled to the brink of collapse. Lehman funded itself through the short-term repurchase agreements or "repo" agreement,[25] and had to borrow tens or hundreds of billions of dollars daily from repo markets. Creditors were losing confidence in the value of Lehman's mortgage-related assets, and the moment they refused to roll over Lehman's daily funding through short-term repos, Lehman would be unable to fund itself and continue to operate.[26] Shareholders lost confidence and sold off their shares, driving down Lehman's stock price.

There were several potential purchasers for Lehman Brothers, but a deal never panned out. Barclays, the UK bank, considered purchasing the troubled bank. However, the UK Financial Services Authority had issued a regulation requiring Barclays to obtain shareholder approval for the purchase before the FSA would approve the purchase. The shareholder vote would take 30 to 60 days, far too long

[23] *See* Günther Bräunig et al, *Financial Statements and Management Report 2007/2008*, IKB Deutsche Industriebank AG, 16-17 (Jul. 4, 2008), *available at* http://www.ikb.de/content/en/ir/financial_reports/annual_report_2007_2008/AG_englisch_080814_sicher.pdf.

[24] *See Alistair Darling's Northern Rock Statement Text*, The Telegraph, (Feb. 17, 2008), *available at* http://www.telegraph.co.uk/news/uknews/1578940/Alistair-Darlings-Northern-Rock-statement-text.html.

[25] *See* Bevill, Bresler, & Schulman v. Spencer Sav. & Loan, 878 F.2d 742, 743 (3d Cir. 1989) ("A standard repurchase agreement, commonly called a 'repo,' consists of a two-part transaction. The first part is the transfer of specified securities by one party, the dealer, to another party, the purchaser, in exchange for cash. The second part consists of a contemporaneous agreement by the dealer to repurchase the securities at the original price, plus an agreed upon additional amount on a specified future date.").

[26] *See* Anton R. Valukas, Report of Anton R. Valukas Volume 1, 6–8 (Mar. 2010), *available at* http://online.wsj.com/public/resources/documents/LehmanVol1.pdf.

to save Lehman. UK Chancellor of the Exchequer, Alistair Darling, would not waive the requirement for a Barclays shareholder vote before approving the sale, effectively ending the deal. UK banks were facing their own liquidity crisis, and the banking system was even more important to their national economy.[27] UK bank assets were four times the size of the UK GDP, whereas U.S. bank assets were roughly the same as the U.S. GDP.[28] On Monday, September 15, Lehman Brothers Holdings, Inc. filed for bankruptcy.

The next day, the U.S. government announced it would bail out the global insurer American Insurance Group (AIG) with an $85 billion bridge loan.[29] With innumerable business units internationally and insurance policies worldwide, AIG's collapse could have unhinged the world economy. President Bush, who was opposed to bailouts, concluded that the U.S. government had no choice but to prop up AIG with taxpayer dollars.[30]

Global markets nevertheless went into a tailspin. As indicated in Figure 2, the Chicago Board Options Exchange Volatility Index (the VIX Index), a measure of fear in the market, shot up dramatically, and global stock indexes plummeted.[31]

Credit markets seized up, and lending all but stopped, bringing economic activity close to a halt.

B. Responses and Decisions of Regulators

The international response to the widening global financial crisis had mixed success. At the height of the crisis in 2008, although the need for coordination was great, it was more difficult to achieve, because regulators perceived their vital national interests to be precarious. After the immediate crisis subsided in April 2009, regulators were better able to discharge their prescriptive function.

1. Crisis Management

Regulators responsible for domestic financial regulation in different countries were in close contact, but their efforts did not initially stabilize markets.[32] In August 2008, the U.S. Federal Reserve loaned $52 billion to banks, and the European

[27] Paulson, *supra* note 16, at 188 (quoting UK Chancellor of the Exchequer Alistair Darling stating to Paulson: "I understand one of your possible buyers is a British Bank. . . . I want you to know that we have some concern, because our banks are already under a lot of stress. We don't want them to become overextended and further weakened.").

[28] *Id.* at 210–11.

[29] *Id.* at 240.

[30] Bush, *supra* note 16, at 457–58.

[31] This chart was generated with Bloomberg Professional service.

[32] Paulson, *supra* note 16, at 18 (describing telephone conversation with the head of China's central bank, Zhou Xiaochuan).

FIG 2: Vix Index and Dow Jones Industrial Index: 1/1/08—12/31/09. This chart was generated with Bloomberg Professional service.

Central Bank loaned €61 billion. That did not stop the Dow Jones Index from falling 400 points in a single day in August, the second-biggest one-day drop in five years.[33]

Amidst the crisis, states also secretly pursued actions to undermine each other. In August 2008, Paulson learned from Chinese officials that high-level Russian officials suggested to the Chinese that Russia and China collectively sell their stock holdings of Fannie Mac and Freddie Mae, which would have driven their prices down and forced the United States to take emergency action to prop up the two government-sponsored entities. The Chinese rejected this proposal.[34] In any event, the U.S. government did place the two entities into conservatorship and injected more capital into them.

Other actions may not have been malevolent, but simply were taken to protect national interests. Nevertheless, they could have increased the risk of global collapse, which would have undermined every national economy. In September 2008, after Lehman collapsed and the U.S. government bailed out AIG, Chinese officials began pulling out their funds from money markets and reducing their secured lending. After U.S. officials spoke to China's Central Bank Governor, Zhou Xiaochuan, he agreed to instruct lower-ranking officials in China not to reduce lending or to pull out their funds from money markets.[35] Through its sovereign wealth fund, China Investment Corporation, China also held a 9.9 percent stake in Morgan Stanley, the U.S. bank with the largest risk of failure after Lehman Brothers. Although Paulson tried to persuade the Chinese Vice Premier, Wang Qishan, to increase its stake in Morgan, Wang was unmoved.

In early October 2008, French President Nicolas Sarkozy convened a summit of European leaders to coordinate European efforts to stabilize markets. Europeans officials, however, could not agree on how far they should support their significant financial institutions. German Chancellor Angela Merkel arranged a €48 billion bailout of the German institution Hypo Real Estate, and, apparently without warning her European counterparts, stated publicly that Germany would guarantee personal savings accounts in the amount of roughly €704 billion[36] Although Chancellor Merkel quickly clarified a few days later that her statement was not an announcement of government action, the damage had been done. To prevent savings and funds from fleeing, the United Kingdom announced a £500 billion program to shore up its banks.[37]

[33] *Id.* at 63–64.

[34] *Id.* at 161.

[35] *Id.* at 242.

[36] *Id.* at 333; *Germany Seeks to Reassure Savers*, BBC News (Oct. 5, 2008), http://news.bbc.co.uk/2/hi/7653317.stm; *Germany Clinches Bank Rescue Deal*, BBC News (Oct. 06, 2008), http://news.bbc.co.uk/2/hi/7653868.stm.

[37] *See Timeline: Banking Crisis*, CNN (Oct. 22, 2008), http://edition.cnn.com/2008/BUSINESS/09/30/us.bailout.timeline/index.html.

After these missteps, international cooperation improved. On October 8, 2008, in an unprecedented act of coordination, the six central banks, including the U.S. Federal Reserve, the Bank of England, and the European Central Bank all reduced their interest rates. This was intended to maximize the impact of rate cuts, and it had some, albeit limited, effect. European stocks rallied but U.S. stocks opened lower.[38] While these rate cuts were not made pursuant to any international prescription from the international legal system, the cuts were made with a shared expectation among regulators that central banks would coordinate their rate cuts. In this sense, the rate cuts were as much political decisions as international legal ones under this book's theory of international law.

In order to avoid collapsing after Lehman's bankruptcy, Morgan Stanley needed additional capital to meet its debt obligations. Mitsubishi UFJ, a Japanese bank, was a potential investor in Morgan Stanley. However, with markets crashing, Mitsubishi now worried that if it invested, the U.S. government would nonetheless have to bail out Morgan Stanley, a step that could wipe out stock holders and Mitsubishi's investment. At the G-7 meeting on October 10, 2008, Paulson met bilaterally with the Japanese Finance Minister, Shoichi Nakagawa, to reassure him. The U.S. Treasury also indicated that any subsequent bailout of Morgan Stanley would be structured to not punish existing investors. On October 13, Mitsubishi purchased 21 percent of Morgan Stanley for $9 billion.[39]

The G-7 meeting on October 10, 2008 also produced results. The finance ministers and governors of central banks of seven key economies agreed on a five-point plan to protect significant financial institutions, unfreeze credit and money markets, restart lending by banks, insure deposits, and restart the secondary market for mortgages.[40] A few days later, 15 eurozone states agreed to inject billions of euros into their respective banks through equity purchases and to guarantee new bank debt through 2009. European markets responded by jumping around 10 percent, and the interbank interest rate fell by 7 basis points to 4.75 percent.[41]

UK Prime Minister Gordon Brown favored a broader meeting of the G-20 countries,[42] which was a group established to involve key emerging market countries in global economic developments.[43] President Bush agreed. On November 15, 2008,

[38] Paulson, *supra* note 16, at 339.

[39] *Id.* at 347, 354, 360.

[40] Press Release, G-7 Finance Ministers and Central Bank Governors Plan of Action (Oct. 10, 2008), *available at* http://www.treasury.gov/press-center/press-releases/Pages/hp1195.aspx.

[41] Paulson, *supra* note 16, at 360–61; Jean-Claude Trichet, President of the ECB; Lucas Papademos, Vice President of the ECB; Statement at Frankfurt am Main: Introductory Statement with Q&A (Oct. 2, 2008); Jean-Claude Trichet, President of the ECB, Statement at the European American Press Club Paris: The ECB's Response to the Crisis (Feb. 20, 2009).

[42] Paulson, *supra* note 16, at 336.

[43] Greenspan, *supra* note 7, at 334.

the G-20 convened and reached agreement on common principles to regulate global financial markets.[44]

Eventually, markets bottomed out in January 2009, and the VIX index calmed down. Credit unfroze, and stock markets recovered dramatically in 2009 and 2010, albeit with dramatic declines along the way before resuming recovery. At the end of 2010 when this book was written, the world economy still faced significant tailwinds, but the acute risks of systemic failure in 2008 had diminished.

2. Regulatory Reform

As markets calmed down in 2009, the G-20 regulators turned their attention to international regulatory reform to minimize the risks of another global financial meltdown. After the G-20 created the Financial Stability Board at their London summit in April 2009, the FSB began coordinating regulatory reform efforts with national regulators and international financial organizations.[45] Its report to G-20 leaders dated September 25, 2009, listed a wide array of global financial reform initiatives. These included: (1) correcting distortions in the financial markets; (2) promoting adherence to international standards; (3) higher capital requirements in quantity and quality at financial institutions; (4) reducing moral hazard in systemically important institutions that are "too big to fail" and therefore expect to be bailed out and take excessive risks; (5) strengthening accounting with a single set of global accounting standards; and (6) improving compensation practices in corporations to align compensation of executives with long-term profitability of the corporation and to reduce incentives for them to take excessive risks.[46]

There is evidence from 2009 and 2010 that the FSB was moving towards meeting these goals through a consultative process among FSB members (officials from 24 key economies and 10 international financial organizations) to develop and implement financial prescriptions at the national level and to monitor compliance at the international level. One early achievement was the orderly withdrawal of central banks from deposit guarantees that they extended during the crisis. An IMF report prepared for the FSB at the FSB's request noted that during the crisis 46 countries adopted enhanced deposit protections, and 18 countries in that group offered full

[44] *Cf.* Chander & Costa, *supra* note 15, at 683 (tracing a similar evolution of international relations concerning credit default swaps from "competition, to experience, to logic, and ultimately to coordination").

[45] Financial Stability Board, Progress since the Washington Summit in the Implementation of the G20 Recommendations for Strengthening Financial Stability, 1 (2010) [hereinafter Report of the Financial Stability Board to G20 Leaders] *available at* http://www.financialstability-board.org/publications/r_101111b.pdf (describing FSB as "a central locus of coordination" for national authorities and international bodies to design and implement financial reforms).

[46] Financial Stability Board, Improving Financial Regulation: Report of the Financial Stability Board to G20 Leaders, 4–12 (2009).

guarantees for deposits.[47] Because these emergency measures distorted global capital flows, they needed to be wound down.[48] However, withdrawals also needed to be coordinated to avoid surprises and spillover effects on other countries, and to generally promote stability in financial markets.

To that end, in June 2009, FSB members agreed to exchange notes on planned exits from exceptional financial support measures adopted during the crisis.[49] The IMF report recorded that as of September 2009, out of 25 countries that adopted temporary enhanced guarantees, all but 7 had announced expiration dates on the emergency measures. Malaysia, Singapore, and Hong Kong created a tripartite working group to coordinate the termination of their respective measures. The EU coordinated its deposit guarantees through EU Directive 2009/14/EC. Other countries, including the United States and Russia, expressed their willingness to collaborate regionally to withdraw emergency measures.[50] Although it is impossible to prove whether the withdrawals resulted from FSB action or whether national regulators would have withdrawn even if the FSB did not exist, it is reasonable to infer that, at a minimum, the FSB improved coordination of withdrawals by exchanging information among FSB member regulators.

In 2010, the FSB also made progress in improving compliance with international financial standards. In March, it announced prescriptions to promote adherence to substantive standards. The FSB established a framework, which committed member regulators to "lead by example," implement international financial standards, disclose their degree of compliance, and subject themselves to periodic peer reviews.[51] Mexico voluntarily submitted to peer review in September 2010, and reviews of Spain and Italy were taking place at the end of 2010. By December 31, 2010, reviews of Canada, Australia, and Switzerland were planned for 2011.[52]

Although it remains to be seen whether states found to fall short of international financial prescriptions through peer reviews or other disclosures will thereby rectify their deviations from these prescriptions, the ability of the FSB to secure peer reviews, which intrude on domestic matters and which states do not have to submit to, is in itself a measure of effectiveness in securing compliance.

[47] José Viñals & Martin J. Gruenberg, Report to the Financial Stability Board: Note by the Staffs of the International Association of Deposit Insurers and the International Monetary Fund on Unwinding Temporary Deposit Insurance Arrangements, 1–3 (2009) [hereinafter Unwinding Temporary Deposit Insurance Arrangements].

[48] Christopher Towe & Martin J. Gruenberg, Exit from Extraordinary Financial Sector Support Measures: Note for G20 Ministers and Governors Meeting, 6 (2009) ("Members recognized, however, that emergency measures have distortionary effects on the allocation of capital across borders as well as within them.").

[49] *Id.* at 1.

[50] *See* Unwinding Temporary Deposit Insurance Arrangements *supra* note 47, at 4–5. *See also* Appendix to the report (providing details of each country's withdrawal plan).

[51] Financial Stability Board, Promoting Global Adherence to International Cooperation and Information Exchange Standards, 4–14, 7 (2010).

[52] *See* Report of the Financial Stability Board to G20 Leaders, *supra* note 45, at 19.

The Basel Committee on Banking Supervision, which is comprised of central bank regulators, is another non-state international body that is involved in global financial regulation. Working in coordination with the FSB, the Committee has promulgated new international prescriptions for capital requirements in what is known as Basel III, or the third iteration of the Basel Accords. The governing body of the G-20, the Group of Governors and Heads of Supervision, approved the new Basel III regulatory framework at its July 26, 2010, meeting.[53] Less than two months later, at their September 12, 2010, meeting, the Group approved prescriptions for new minimum requirements and capital buffers.[54] In December, the Basel Committee issued detailed rules about these liquidity requirements.[55] Basel III more than doubled the minimum capital requirements of common equity of banks from 2 percent to 4.5 percent. It also increased Tier 1 capital requirements from 4 percent to 6 percent and also requires banks to hold a further buffer of 2.5 percent of common equity for future periods of stress. It focused on capital reserves of common equity, because common equity is the highest quality capital. Basel III also no longer permits banks to meet capital requirements with capital of questionable quality, such as goodwill.[56]

In regard to reducing moral hazard at significant financial institutions, the FSB planned to issue prescriptions in 2011.[57] It also requested that the Basel Committee complete by mid-2011 a study of additional loss capacity that significant financial institutions ought to have.[58] Therefore, it is premature at the time of this writing to assess the FSB's effectiveness in reducing moral hazard.

As for its project of achieving a single global set of accounting standards, FSB has made significant progress in securing compliance with the International Financial Reporting Standards (IFRS). Nearly all member FSB jurisdictions, that is, the G-20 countries, have adopted the IFRS or have programs underway to harmonize their accounting standards with IFRS. The U.S. Securities and Exchange Commission announced that it was considering incorporating IFRS into the financial reporting

[53] Press Release, Bank for International Settlements, Group of Governors and Heads of Supervision reach broad agreement on Basel Committee capital and liquidity reform package, (July 26, 2010), *available at* http://www.bis.org/press/p100726.htm; *id.* at annex, *available at* http://www.bis.org/press/p100726/annex.pdf.

[54] Press Release, Basel Committee on Banking Supervision, Group of Governors and Heads of Supervision announces higher global minimum capital standards (Sept. 12, 2010), annex 1 & 2, [hereinafter BASEL III] *available at* http://www.bis.org/press/p100912.pdf. *See* Report of the Financial Stability Board to G20 Leaders, *supra* note 45, at 3.

[55] Basel Committee on Banking Supervision, Basel III: International Framework for Liquidity Risk Measurement, Standards and Monitoring, 18 (2010), *available at* http://www.bis.org/publ/bcbs188.pdf.

[56] BASEL III, *supra* note 54. *See also* Report of the Financial Stability Board to G20 Leaders, *supra* note 45, at 3.

[57] Report of the Financial Stability Board to G20 Leaders, *supra* note 45, at 8.

[58] Financial Stability Board, Reducing the Moral Hazard Posed by Systemically Important Financial Institutions: FSB Recommendations and Time Lines, 6 (2010), *available at* http://www.financialstabilityboard.org/publications/r_101111a.pdf.

system for U.S. issuers of security. There is a long way to go before the U.S. accounting standards converge with the IFRS, if ever, and corporate or accounting constituents in the United States may persuade SEC officials that it is not in the U.S. public interest to do so. Nonetheless, the fact that the SEC is even considering such a "substantial incursion" of international standards into U.S. accounting practices is remarkable.[59]

Regarding the international standards for executive compensation, the FSB appears also to have achieved a measure of effectiveness. In April 2009, the FSB's predecessor organization, the Financial Stability Forum, published principles to align compensation with risks. These principles included adjusting compensation to account for all types of risk; making payouts sensitive to the time horizon of risks; and allocating compensation in a mix of cash, equity, and other forms of compensation to further align overall compensation with risks.[60] The FSB elaborated on the principles contained in a report dated September 25, 2009. Concrete prescriptions included requiring an annual report from corporations disclosing compensation policy, the remuneration committee, and criteria for compensation. The FSB also called on regulators to ensure the effective implementation of FSB compensation principles, especially as regards significant financial institutions whose failure would be a systemic risk to capital markets.[61]

To encourage and monitor compliance with its compensation prescriptions, the FSB conducted a peer review of members in March 2010. The peer review team comprised members from Australia, Canada, the Netherlands, Singapore, South Africa, Switzerland, the Basel Committee, and the OCED.[62] The report of the review concluded that "[m]ost FSB members have incorporated in their regulatory and supervisory frameworks the requirement that compensation be aligned with prudent risk taking, though differences remain in approach, emphasis, and degree of detail."[63] Some jurisdictions, such as the United Kingdom, are considering legislative changes that would give their regulators the enforcement and sanction powers under domestic law to ensure the corporations comply with international

[59] Vagts, *supra* note 15, at 687 ("This would represent a substantial international incursion into the way that the American accounting profession conducts its business. It has been termed 'the most revolutionary development in securities regulation since the New Deal.'") (quoting Lawrence A. Cunningham).

[60] Financial Stability Forum, Report of the Financial Stability Forum on Addressing Procyclicality on the Financial System, 13 (2009), *available at* http://www.financialstabilityboard.org/publications/r_0904a.pdf. *See generally* Financial Stability Forum, Principles for Sound Compensation Practices (2009), *available at* http://www.financialstabilityboard.org/publications/r_0904b.pdf.

[61] Report of the Financial Stability Board to G20 Leaders, *supra* note 45, at 5–6.

[62] Financial Stability Forum, Thematic Review on Compensation: Peer Review Report, 1 (2010), *available at* http://www.financialstabilityboard.org/publications/r_100330a.pdf [hereinafter Thematic Review on Compensation].

[63] *Id.*, at 9. *See also* Paulson, *supra* note 16, at 450 ("And on politically sensitive matters such as compensation, the FSB has already shown an ability to develop nuanced and constructive proposals.").

compensation standards.[64] The U.S. Securities and Exchange Commission amended its disclosure rules to require listed companies to discuss compensation practices as they relate to risk, if the policies are reasonably likely to have a material adverse effect on the company.[65] This evidence does not prove that national regulators adjusted their compensation oversight practices because of the FSB, but it does suggest some relationship between the FSB's efforts and changes in domestic regulation.

C. Guidance to Regulators

The justificatory theory of international law provides guidance to financial regulators. It provides a way to understand FSB guidelines as law-like prescriptions even though they are not laws. The FSB is not formally a legally authoritative international body; its members are not states, and therefore no state has consented to its charter or prescriptions. In any event, its charter provides that the FSB issues only guidelines.[66] However, FSB prescriptions are law-like because they express appropriate conduct for financial regulators to implement domestically. One reason for this shared expectation is that FSB prescriptions are common standards for states rather than ad hoc and arbitrary measures that apply unequally to different states. They are general in scope, addressed to all members, and created in accordance with the FSB's charter and institutional processes. They meet Thomas Franck's criteria for legitimacy, that is, determinacy, adherence, and coherence.[67]

Because FSB guidelines are prescriptions in the international legal system, the justificatory theory provides guidance to financial regulators about how to make the prescriptions and what to do about them once they are made. The general moral obligation to promote the common good creates a duty to promote minimum order, including global financial order. This general moral obligation to systemically promote global order is aligned with the specific obligations to make detailed prescriptions to ensure the global financial markets function smoothly. Here, the general and specific moral obligations of FSB regulators are almost coextensive.

[64] Thematic Review on Compensation, *supra* note 62, at 4, 13; Regulatory Enforcement and Sanctions Act (c. 13, 2008). *See also* Robert Thompson, *The SEC After the Financial Meltdown: Social Control Over Finance?*, 71 U. Pitt. L. Rev. 567, 580 (2010) ("The Federal Reserve announced broad compensation guidelines for banks under its control that reflects discussions among the G-20 countries and the Financial Stability Board.") (citing Press Release, Bd. of Governors of the Fed. Reserve, Board Policy on Incentive Compensation (Oct. 22, 2009), *available at* http://www.federalreserve.gov/newsevents/press/bcreg/20091022a.htm.).

[65] Thematic Review on Compensation, *supra* note 62, at 13; Proxy Disclosure Enhancements, Exchange Act Release Nos. 33–9089; 34–61175; Investment Company Act Release No. IC-29092 (Dec. 16, 2009).

[66] FSB Charter, *supra* note 6, art. 2.

[67] *See supra* ch. 2, pt. III.C.

In order to discharge those obligations, regulators need to ensure that their prescriptions secure some modicum of effectiveness. Because their prescriptions are not backed by enforcement mechanisms, regulators must accommodate the interests of states within their prescriptions while still pursuing their regulatory goals. Balance is more easily achieved here because the financial crisis has made states acutely aware of their strong interest in global financial stability and reforms necessary for stability.[68]

Historical and contemporary practice suggests that the convergence of the general morality of promoting the common good, the specific morality of complying with FSB prescriptions to secure the values they aim at, and national interests in doing so will help secure the effectiveness of prescriptions, which in turn will promote the common good and values at stake. Historically, national regulators largely complied with Basel II and implemented it within the time frames provided for them to comply with the lower capital requirements in Basel II.[69] At the time of the writing of this book, regulators appear to have begun making changes to national standards in conformity with FSB prescriptions. This data bolsters the hypothesis that Basel III is likely to be at least somewhat effective because national interests are aligned with the common good.

Projecting into the future, it is too soon to tell if all FSB prescriptions will be fully effective. Basel III standards are to be phased in over several years, with 2019 as the target date for full implementation.[70] In the intervening time period, the demands of constituents can distort the implementation of some of the more politically sensitive FSB prescriptions, such as the regulation of compensation, especially if the political climate in states changes in the decade to come.

To enhance the effectiveness of their prescriptions, and thereby further promote the common good and the specific morality of their prescriptions, regulators ought to continue legalistically following procedural prescriptions for passing financial regulation standards. These prescriptions are contained in the FSB Charter. Regulators ought to follow these legalist procedures that are part of a web of rules that undergird the common good by managing the process for making prescriptions,

[68] *See, e.g.*, U.S. Dep't of the Treasury, Financial Regulatory Reform: A New Foundation 81 (2009) (stating the Obama administration's focus, among other regulatory reforms, on strengthening the financial stability board and improving oversight of global financial markets).

[69] Report of the Financial Stability Board to G20 Leaders, *supra* note 45, at 5 ("Most countries have already fully adopted Basel II, and the remaining countries are still in the process. The effects of the financial crisis became manifest in 2007 and built-up prior to the implementation of Basel II."). According to Alan Greenspan, "BASEL II [is] the international consensus on banking regulation first published in 2004 [that] mirrored the risk valuation models of the private markets." Greenspan, *supra* note 7, at 524.

[70] BASEL III, *supra* note 54. *See also* Hervé Hannoun, Presentation: The Basel III Capital Framework: A Decisive Breakthrough, at 2 (Nov. 22, 2010), *available at* http://www.bis.org/speeches/sp101125a.htm (summarizing timeline for implementation of Basel III).

and because compliance with them improves the effectiveness of financial regulations, further enhancing the common good.[71]

Prescriptions are also more likely to be effective if regulators make prescriptions that minimize the need to alter domestic standards, where it is possible to do so, while promoting the common good and relevant values. Writing in 2008, Alan Greenspan speculated that any new Basel capital requirements would simply mirror the private sector's already revised practices.[72] Greenspan was partly correct. After the G-20 approved Basel III, financial analysts concluded that the largest U.S. banks are already in compliance with Basel III, but Basel III would increase the cost of borrowing from small community banks.[73] A legal analysis conducted by the U.S. law firm Morrison and Foerster in 2010 also concluded that various countries would have to make regulatory adjustments.[74] These analyses provide a basis to anticipate that the United States will be more likely to comply with Basel III unless small banks mobilize against the new capital standards.

Although this chapter focused on regulators, the justificatory theory also provides guidance to other decisionmakers to whom regulatory prescriptions are directed. FSB prescriptions are made by the central bankers of over 20 major economies, through a process of international decision. As a result of this multilateral process, they agreed by consensus to new common financial standards and have begun to implement these prescriptions in private corporations and national regulators. The prescriptions thus carry with them a strongly shared expectation of appropriate conduct and are critical to the stability of global financial markets, which is intrinsic to the common good. Other decisionmakers—bank executives and national regulatory agencies—thus have a strong general moral obligation to abide by FSB prescriptions.

As to the specific morality of abiding by FSB regulations, it is presently unclear whether the post-crisis FSB standards will actually achieve their aims of global stability and whether, if these aims are met, they will come at the cost of unintended consequences such as the undermining of economic development, distorting wealth distribution among constituents worldwide, or damaging the interests of non-G-20 countries that are excluded from the FSB process.[75]

[71] Some observers question the legitimacy of FSB processes because they excludes many states from its decisionmaking processes. However, they do not provide persuasive reasons why the benefits of including states beyond the G-20, which make up nearly 90 percent of the world economy, would outweigh costs of a more cumbersome process of prescription that would inevitably result from involving more governing elites.

[72] Greenspan, *supra* note 7, at 524.

[73] Michael Corkery, *Basel III: And the Biggest Winners Are . . .*, Wall. St. J. (Sept. 13, 2010), http://blogs.wsj.com/deals/2010/09/13/basel-iii-and-the-biggest-winners-are/; Greg Keller & Frank Jordans, *Basel III Rules: Banks Given Until 2019 to Fully Comply with Global Regulations,* Huffington Post (Sept. 13, 2010), http://www.huffingtonpost.com/2010/09/13/basel-iii-rules-market-we_n_714263.html.

[74] Morrison Foerster, Basel Framework 17 (March 2010).

[75] *Compare* Unwinding Temporary Deposit Insurance Arrangements, *supra* note 47, at 4–5 (stating that Basel III will not have negative macroeconomic effects) *and* Mario Giovanoli, *The*

Until there is more clarity about outcomes, government officials ought to be guided by presumptive moral obligations to comply with FSB guidelines. The FSB prescriptions are directed toward global financial stability, and there is presently no other alternative international system to coordinate global capital requirements and other financial standards. Accordingly, it is both in the common good and the interest of states to promote the FSB prescriptions. Government officials ought to promote the FSB prescriptions by interpreting them narrowly and obeying them, in order to promote global order. This is particularly necessary when prescriptions are clear instructions for action, as opposed to vague principles that are subject to interpretation in their application to facts on the ground.

The guidance to corporate officers provided by the general account of the international legal system is more complex. There is an argument that corporate officers have a legal and moral fiduciary duty to their shareholders to maximize profits. If a financial institution is so large that its failure would pose systemic risks and therefore government regulators would likely take action to prevent its failure, a corporate officer may take a rational business decision to incur large risks, in violation of the spirit, or even the letter of FSB prescriptions, before domestic regulators have implemented the prescriptions into domestic laws and regulations. On the other hand, the common interests in global financial stability may provide an overriding moral reason not to take those risks, even if they could enhance profits for shareholders. Given this moral ambiguity about FSB prescriptions that are not laws, government officials ought to enact FSB prescriptions into domestic laws and regulations with all due speed. When that happens, it would be illegal for corporate officers to deviate from the prescriptions, and it would be immoral to do so, because it is neither in the common good nor in shareholder interests for corporate officers to violate laws in their conduct of business.

III. CONCLUSION

The foregoing analysis has shown how the justificatory theory of international law applies to regulators even though they do not formally make laws. The case study about financial regulators in the 2008–2009 global financial crisis illustrates how the

Reform of International Financial Architecture After the Global Crisis, 42 N.Y.U. J. INT'L L. & POL. 81, 110–11 (2009) ("One of the most frequently heard critiques of the FSF in its former composition was of its restrictive membership, which some believed deprived this body of sufficient legitimacy to impose its recommended IFSs on a worldwide scale. . . . This criticism now appears to be moot, as the FSF/FSB has attained a significantly broader membership since March 2009, a fact that will no doubt enhance its legitimacy.") *with* Alexander, *supra* note 5, at 881 (stating, without citation or other direct evidence "as a matter of economic policy, if those designing the standards maintain the fiction that they are voluntary when in fact they are not, the content of the standards is likely to be suboptimal for economic growth and financial development, as is demonstrated with the recent financial crisis"). *See also* Eric C. Chaffee, *Finishing the Race to the Bottom: An Argument for the Harmonization and Centralization of International Securities Law*, 40 SETON HALL L. REV. 1581, 1603–18 (2010) (surveying arguments for and against greater international harmonization of securities regulation).

framework of analysis helps them make regulatory decisions. It also shows the limits of the international legal system in effectively regulating and coordinating actions in times of acute crisis, such as in the last quarter of 2008.

Based on this case study, it is reasonable to suggest that the justificatory theory applies to regulators generally, and not just financial regulators. The particulars of how it applies to other regulators, however, will have to be determined in research beyond the scope of this book. For example, this chapter has not examined regulators who are not government officials, such as business executives on the International Chamber of Commerce, which sets international standards for the Uniform Customs and Practice for Documentary Credits. Although these "private" regulators serve an important function in international law, a detailed study of how the justificatory theory applies to private regulators is left for another day.

7 Legal Advisors

I. THEORY

This chapter applies the justificatory theory of international law to legal advisors. Legal advisors are important to consider in developing and testing the theory because they have to interpret and apply legal prescriptions to facts in international problems.[1] Most of their decisions are not scrutinized by tribunals after the fact.[2] Any rectification must come from the responses of other decisionmakers in the dispute, and those responses will determine the effectiveness and legitimacy of the international legal system.

Examining the role of legal advisors is also important because they have different institutional responsibilities than judges, arbitrators, and regulators. Their moral calculi in interpreting and applying legal prescriptions must therefore account for different considerations and possibly lead to different conclusions than what other

[1] *See* C.G. Weeramantry, Universalising International Law 78 (2004) (noting that the opinions of legal advisors "do count"); Jack L. Goldsmith, The Terror Presidency 155 (2007) (noting that when the U.S. Department of Defense accepted his withdrawal, as head of the Department of Justice Office of Legal Counsel, of memoranda permitting enhanced interrogation techniques, the Defense Department immediately ordered officers not to rely on the withdrawn authorizations).

[2] *Cf.* John O. McGinnis, Review Essay, *Principle versus Politics: The Solicitor General's Office in Constitutional and Bureaucratic Theory*, 44 Stan. L. Rev. 799, 801 (1992) (describing the Solicitor General as the "Tenth Justice" because of his duty to interpret the law for the rest of the executive branch).

decisionmakers reach. Thus, it is relevant to ask whether the view of the international legal system presented in this book, which tries to explain and justify international law, provides a sufficient account of and guidance for legal advisors in executive decisionmaking.

A. The Legal Advisor's Functions

For purposes of this book, legal advisors include more than government officials who have formal appointments as legal counsel. It refers to any government official who provides guidance to other governing elites in his government by drawing at least in part on international prescriptions. Legal counsel falls into this definition. In the United States, this includes the Legal Advisor to the State Department, lawyers in the Department of Justice Office of Legal Counsel (OLC), White House Counsel, and Department of Defense attorneys. But legal advisors also include officials who are not legal counsel, when they provide guidance by drawing at least in part on international legal prescriptions. Accordingly, a military official who assesses military operations from a legal standpoint, or by relying on international legal prescriptions, falls within the analysis of this book when he does so.

Given the great variety of officials that fall under this definition of legal advisor, it is unsurprising that there is not just one legal advisor's function. Instead, legal advisors discharge several different but overlapping functions.[3] These are, generally speaking: advising, authorizing, and advocating.[4]

Legal advisors are frequently asked to advise government officials about what action is permitted or required under international law in an international dispute.[5] Officials may also ask advisors what they ought to do, taking international law

[3] *See The Role of the Legal Adviser of the Department of State*, 85 Am. J. Int'l L. 358, 358–62 (1991) (describing legal adviser's duties); Stephen Schwebel, Remarks on the Role of the Legal Adviser of the U.S. State Department, 2 Eur. J. Int'l L. 131 (1991) (surveying responsibilities of legal advisors); UK Office of Legal Advisor to the Ministry of Foreign Affairs, Report to Committee of Legal Advisors on Public International Law, Council of Europe at 3 (citing sources discussing the role of UK legal advisors to the Ministry of Foreign Affairs).

[4] *Cf.*, UK Office of Legal Advisor *supra* note 3, at 1 (March 2006) ("The principal function of FCO Legal Advisers is to provide legal advice to Ministers and officials within the FCO. . . . The Legal Advisers [also] act as agent for the Government before international tribunals.").

[5] *See* Weeramantry, *supra* note 1, at 78 (stating that legal advisors "have a responsibility to advise on the law as it really is"); Sir Frank Berman, *Foreign Legal Advisers' Roundtable*, *in* Michael P. Scharf & Paul R. Williams, Shaping Foreign Policy in Times of Crisis 169, 171 (2010) [hereinafter Scharf & Williams] (stating that the Attorney General's role is to "provide ministerial-level advice on all areas of the law, including international law"); John B. Bellinger, Speech to the Int'l Law Assoc: Reflections on Four Years as Legal Advisor (Oct. 17, 2008) (stating that in his role as legal advisor to the State Department during the Bush administration, among several responsibilities "[t]he *first*—it almost goes without saying—was to provide the best possible legal advice to the Secretary, to the Department of State, and to the U.S. government. A key part of carrying out that duty for me as legal adviser was to ensure that international law is considered and respected in decision-making by every component of the Department of State and by every department of the U.S. government.") (copy on file with author).

into account. Although both types of questions seek advice, they seek different advice. The first question solicits information about the range of possible interpretations of legal prescriptions in the factual matrix at issue, leaving it to the official to decide which interpretation to select and apply. The second question solicits not only information about the range of possible interpretations, but also guidance on the best interpretation for the official to adopt.

In other international problems, a government official may have preliminarily decided to take a certain action or selected a small number of alternative courses of action as appropriate policies to adopt. He may call on a legal advisor not for instruction on how the law can be interpreted generally, but for a legal authorization to proceed with the official's preferred action.

This function of the legal advisor is often overlooked but cannot be overstated. The majority of executive decisions are not litigated in court, and there are few court decisions to guide the interpretation of prescriptions. Therefore, even officials who reserve policymaking functions to themselves and do not share it with their lawyers, but who wish nevertheless to act lawfully, will often seek legal permission from their legal advisors. If permission is not forthcoming, officials may abandon the policy that their legal advisors determined to be illegal.[6] This desire for authorization can be especially acute in highly legalist systems of government where line officers fear prosecution in domestic courts or administrative proceedings for actions they take in the field of operations.[7] Seeking and obtaining clear authorization from legal advisors can in some situations immunize them from findings of wrongdoing, and in other situations at least give them comfort when they act.[8]

In all of these circumstances, legal advisors offer legal advice, but they are not just advising. They are also making a decision about whether the proposed action is legal and authorized, or illegal and prohibited.[9] Although they lack the formal authority of judges, in these situations they play a role functionally similar to judges rendering advisory opinions or stating the law in an actual dispute with an eye to guiding

[6] *See* Conrad Harper, *Foreign Legal Advisers' Roundtable*, *in* Scharf & Williams, *supra* note 5, at 176 (2010) (stating that after he advised the Clinton administration in his capacity as Legal Advisor to the State Department that a U.S. intelligence practice violated the Chicago Convention, the administration discontinued that practice).

[7] *See* Goldsmith, *supra* note 1, at 92–95 (describing officials' fear in acting when legal advice does not clearly authorize action).

[8] *Compare id.* at 79–80 (describing the U.S. Federal Bureau of Investigation's reliance on the opinions of the government's legal advisor's opinions over the President's to allay fears of criminal prosecution for their actions), *with id.* at 23 (describing how memoranda of legal advisors on authorizing aggressive counterterrorism methods "gave counterterrorism officials the comfort of knowing that they could not easily be prosecuted later for the approved actions").

[9] *See id.* at 38 (describing the legal advisor's "duty to define the legal limits of executive action in a neutral manner *and* the President's desire to receive the legal advice that helps him do what he wants.") (quoting Jimmy Carter's Attorney General, Griffin Bell). *See also* Schwebel, *supra* note 3, at 134 (stating that a legal advisor must interject his opinions in the decision process especially where the action considered is illegal).

action in similar situations in the future.[10] It is an open question, however, whether an advisor discharging his authorizing function ought to be as impartial as a judge, and the extent to which he ought to seek to promote his official's goals. This question is addressed in detail below when discussing whether legal advisors ought to authorize waterboarding.[11]

Once an official has acted, he may call upon his legal advisors to advocate the legality of his previous actions. In a small minority of disputes, other domestic or international governing elites may challenge the legality of official action under international law before domestic or international courts and tribunals, and may seek criminal or civil redress. In many more disputes, other domestic and international elites may challenge the action in venues other than courts, such as in the media or the chambers of international organizations. The purposes of these challenges are to restrain the official and to persuade other elites to oppose the challenged actions. These actions are often criticized on a variety of grounds, one of which is its purported illegality. Although these exchanges do not occur in court, they are nonetheless legalist confrontations that call for legalist arguments, along with political or policy responses, to be deployed in a procedurally strategic fashion.[12]

In these situations, the legal advisor represents his government, whether in court or some other less ritualized arena, and is no longer called to advise on the range of legal outcomes or to offer his views on the best interpretation of the law.[13] Instead, he is called to advocate that his government's actions were the best interpretation of the law or, at a minimum, a lawful interpretation of international law.[14]

B. General Morality

Legal advisors have a general moral obligation to determine the range of actions permitted under legalist reasoning and procedures. Protecting the common good, which includes the national interests of their constituents but extends far beyond as well, requires that when legal advisors are called upon to render legal advice, they give advice that takes into account laws and other shared expectations of

[10] *Cf.* Trevor Morrison, *Stare Decisis in the Office of Legal Counsel*, 110 Colum. L. Rev. 1448 (2010) (discussing the function of U.S. Office of Legal Counsel memoranda serving as precedent).

[11] *Infra* pt. II.B.

[12] *See generally* Davis R. Robinson et al., *Some Perspectives on Adjudicating Before the World Court: The Gulf of Maine Case*, 79 Am. J. Int'l L. 578 (1985) (describing efforts of U.S. legal advisors to gain procedural advantages in the *Gulf of Maine* case against Canada).

[13] *See The Role of the Legal Adviser of the Department of State*, *supra* note 3, at 363 (noting the view that "the Legal Adviser, like other attorneys with respect to their clients, can properly serve as the Secretary's advocate and make the best case possible in support of the Administration's position—at least so long as the arguments presented are in good faith and legally responsible").

[14] *See, e.g.*, Davis R. Robinson, *The Reagan Administration—Davis R. Robinson (1981–1986) in* Scharf & Williams, *supra* note 5, at 59 (describing the incident where he defended the legality of the invasion of Grenada before a U.S. senator). *See also generally* Antonio Cassese, *The Role of Legal Advisers in Ensuring that Foreign Policy Conforms to International Legal Standards*, 14 Mich. J. Int'l L. 139 (1992) (discussing various roles that legal advisors play).

appropriate conduct upon which the international order depends. Legalist reasoning distinguishes actions that are legal from those that are not. Although the line between the two may often be less than sharp, it is often possible to identify those actions that fall clearly on one side of the line or the other. It is only by taking legalism seriously and drawing a reasonable line that the coherence, adherence, and stability of international law, which are the *sine qua non* of its support of the common good, are maintained.

The general moral obligation to be faithful to legalism is stronger when a legal advisor is advising or authorizing and is weaker when he is advocating. When advising or authorizing, his opinion can effectively permit or constrain the actions of government officials relying on his advice. Because his advice on disputes implicating foreign policy or national security are often secret and not subject to scrutiny by the public or by courts as neutral adjudicators, there is an enhanced responsibility to protect the stability, coherence, and adherence of international law through fidelity to legalism. Simply put, there is often no one to correct him when he is wrong.

In contrast, when advocating a government's position in the diplomatic arena or courts, the moral duty to apply legalist reasoning is weaker. The consequences of getting it wrong on legalist grounds are diminished because there are other decisionmakers, such as courts or foreign and domestic governing elites, who will appraise his reasoning and may reject it if it is unpersuasive on legalist grounds. This is not to say that the legal advisor may not choose to be legalist for instrumental reasons. He may well do so because he appraises that the judges or other elites he wishes to persuade subscribe to legalism. That strategic choice would, however, be an instrumental goal to achieve his constituent's national objectives rather than a moral consideration about promoting the common good through international law.

C. Specific Morality

A legal advisor also has a specific moral obligation to interpret prescriptions to maximize relevant values, whether he is advising, authorizing, or advocating. He ought to consider the outcomes of his decision in terms of its impact on basic goods and whether the decision under consideration maximizes the attainment of basic goods and the conditions of common good under which every human being may pursue basic values, in addition to the conditions provided by international law.

For example, a legal advisor may ask whether the national policy he is asked to authorize or help formulate would maximize economic development or geopolitical stability, as considerations independent of whether the policy promotes the stability of international law for the common good. This vision of law is not just a liberal ideal; it is a view shared by conservative lawyers as well.[15]

[15] *See* John Yoo, War by Other Means xii (2006) ("But the law is not the end of a matter; indeed, it is often the beginning. Sometimes people look to the law as if it were a religion or a fully articulated ethical code that will make these decisions for us, relieving us of the difficult job of making a choice. The law sets the rules of the playing field, but it does not set policy within that field.").

These moral considerations exogenous to legalism should not ordinarily lead the legal advisor to ignore legalism. In most cases, these moral considerations should factor in the legal advisor's selection of policy options among the range of alternatives that are permissible under the ambiguity inherent in legal prescriptions. How these moral considerations are presented will depend on the advice that officials have sought from him. If invited to play a role in policymaking, the advisor might present his analysis in terms of the legalist options available, followed by the moral reasoning (or, if a different term would be more persuasive to his audience, policy reasoning) that favors a particular option. If asked to authorize an unwise policy permissible under legalist reasoning, the advisor may explain why it is legal but unwise.

It is only in an extreme case that no legalist interpretation is sufficiently moral. The advisor will have to judge for himself when such a rare tipping point is reached: for example, where nuclear weapons are deployed not in self-defense or, if in self-defense, against a nonnuclear threat.[16] But when the advisor has decided that the balance is tipped, he should as a moral matter resign rather than authorize the policy, because the morality of promoting legalism for the common good is unambiguously outweighed by the immorality of the action that would be permitted under legalism.

D. Interests and Effectiveness

Too often, legal advisors have cast national interests at odds with the morality of the common good or the morality of promoting relevant values.[17] However, the two are not so often at odds. Constituencies have an interest in the common good because it is necessary for them to cooperate and compete internationally in pursuit of their preferred values.

The specific moral requirement to optimize relevant values also includes values preferred by the constituencies that the advisor serves: in other words, the national interest. Governing elites and their legal advisors have an ethical duty to represent the interests of their constituencies because that is often the main reason the constituencies have allocated decisionmaking authority to their elites. It would be immoral to ignore national interests because that undermines the basic goods sought by the national community.

Promoting national interests is moral even if the scope of a community is expanded to a notion of world community and not just a sovereign state. The general morality of international law is a morality of obligation, that is, the obligation to take or not

[16] *Cf.* Legality of the Threat or Use of Nuclear Weapons, Advisory Opinion, 1996 I.C.J. 226, 266 (July 8) (concluding that it was not possible to state generally that nuclear weapons were illegal).

[17] *See* Goldsmith, *supra* note 1, at 58 (discussing "lawfare," or the use of law by terrorists to gain military advantage over states); *id.* at 79 (noting officials "felt the same imperatives of responsibility that led Roosevelt and many other presidents to blow through 'legalistic' restrictions on presidential authority during times of crisis").

take actions that are necessary to preserve conditions that make it possible to pursue basic goods.[18] It is not a morality of aspiration, that is, the optimal attainment of goods that maximizes everyone's basic goods.[19] It might be nice if international law had a morality of aspiration, as defined by Lon Fuller. However, this is simply unrealistic because of the diversity of cultural viewpoints among territorial communities about what goods and mix of goods they desire. There are also disagreements about how those goods should be allocated among communities and in what mix. Some states may prefer social and economic rights over political and civil ones, while other states may have the inverse preference. Additionally, there is ambiguity about what process should be used to allocate values without undermining efficiencies gained from free competition. It is also normatively unappealing to impose a detailed morality of aspiration among diverse communities because that would undermine the basic good of life itself by constricting the liberty value of freely choosing for oneself and striving to attain those choices.

Because international law creates a morality of obligation, but not much of a morality of aspiration, it leaves wide discretion to decisionmakers to decide for themselves what to do to promote their preferred values. By design, the international legal system permits communities with constituencies, whether states and their citizens or corporations and their shareholders, to compete with each other, to barter interests, and to succeed as well as fail. It is permissible for legal advisors to act in the national interest within the broad parameters of a general moral obligation to preserve the common good through legalism and to consider specific moral obligations to balance the values at stake in any international problem. Indeed, it is morally appropriate for them to do so.

The legal advisor should also be concerned that his advice has a modicum of effectiveness. Without effectiveness, no matter how morally optimal his advice would have otherwise been, the advice does not make any practical difference in international problems and therefore does not achieve the moral ends to which it is directed. In order to be effective, a legal advisor will often have to give advice that promotes national interests and the goals of the officials he advises. To some extent, it is appropriate for advisors to pragmatically adjust or sequence their advice in order to ensure that the advice is at least minimally effective. The legal advisor therefore is fully justified in promoting national interests within the balance of general and specific morality, and in many situations, there is no true conflict among them.

In a minority of disputes, there could be a true or perceived conflict. It is often because a government official demands authorization that he has determined is in the national interest but which comes close to exceeding the limits of legalism. The legal advisor is often less equipped to determine what is in the national interest than his official, because his official usually has access to a broader scope of relevant information than the advisor. The advisor ought, in general, to defer to the official's

[18] *See* Lon L. Fuller, The Morality of Law 5–6 (rev. ed. 1969) (discussing morality of obligation and morality of aspiration).

[19] *See id.*

determination of national interest because constituencies have allocated authority to the official, usually through elections or acquiescence, to determine and pursue their common interests. They have not correspondingly appointed the advisor, and the role expected by constituents of the legal advisor is narrower. Therefore, the advisor is not equipped to disagree about the national interests.

The advisor is, however, appropriately concerned that the limits of legalism are not exceeded. When he appraises that a policy he is asked to authorize is clearly illegal, he should usually refuse to authorize it.[20] If, however, the illegal policy is necessary to protect key national interests, he can counsel the official to violate international law and incur the costs of doing so. Law, after all, is not a suicide pact.[21] For example, Jack Goldsmith, the head of the Office of Legal Counsel for U.S. Department of Justice under the George W. Bush administration, advised his Attorney General, as well as the counsel for the Vice President, that although Goldsmith could not find any legal authorization for a counterterrorism initiative that the President thought was essential, "the President can also ignore the law and act extralegally."[22] He would, however, have to let his constituents decide if "the emergency was severe enough to warrant extralegal action."[23]

In other situations, a legal advisor may appraise that a proposed action is not only illegal, but that it is also unwarranted on grounds of morality or interest. In such a case, the legal advisor should resign. Elizabeth Wilmshurst, the Deputy Legal Advisor of the United Kingdom, did just that when the United Kingdom participated in the invasion of Iraq. She issued a legal opinion that the invasion was illegal, and thereafter promptly resigned.[24] Across the Atlantic, Goldsmith as head lawyer for the U.S. Office of Legal Counsel, withdrew several overbroad legal opinions authorizing interrogation tactics, and resigned when the Vice President's legal counsel criticized him for doing so.[25]

A conflict among national interests and specific and general morality is less likely to be reached when the legal advisor is advocating a national policy before other foreign elites or a court. The advisor is not called upon to decide on its legality. That task falls on judges and other elites appraising the actions after the fact. Because advocating is not authorizing, it is appropriate—indeed, there is an ethical duty to constituents—to present the best argument in the interests of the advisor's constituencies to assist the judge or other authoritative elites in considering all viewpoints

[20] *See* Gerald Fitzmaurice, *Legal Advisers and Foreign Affairs*, 59 Am. J. Int'l L. 72, 73 (1965) ("[I]t is [the legal advisor's] first duty to tell his government what courses it cannot take without running foul of the law, and to refuse as a lawyer to endorse any such course[.]").

[21] *See* W. Michael Reisman, *NATO's Kosovo Intervention: Kosovo Antinomies*, 93 Am. J. Int'l L. 860, 860 (1999) ("The Constitution is not a suicide pact.") (quoting Justice Holmes).

[22] Goldsmith, *supra* note 1, at 80 (citing Thomas Jefferson and John Locke).

[23] *Id.* at 81. *See also* George W. Bush, Decision Points 164 (2010) (stating that he chose to engage in a domestic surveillance program and to order enhanced interrogation techniques knowing that they would be "controversial," because he decided it was more important to promote national security).

[24] *See* Scharf & Williams, *supra* note 5, at 180.

[25] *See* Goldsmith, *supra* note 1, at 161.

and in making an informed decision about the legality of the actions under examination.

This does not mean that the goal of presenting the best case is unbounded. The ethical rules of advocacy that are designed to ensure that adjudication is fair and unbiased must still be followed. The allegations that Nicaragua's counsel contacted an ICJ judge ex parte in the *Nicaragua* case,[26] and allegations that Department of Justice officials contacted an arbitrator ex parte in the *Loewen* arbitration,[27] if true, are both equally immoral because these actions cut to the core of the international system and its effectiveness in securing conditions of the common good.

II. PRAXIS

Legal advisors in different countries,[28] as well as various international law scholars studying legal advisors,[29] agree that the responsibility of the legal advisor is to find some balance among competing considerations.

This observation also holds true for legal advisors of different political persuasions in the United States. Conrad Harper, who was Legal Advisor to the State Department under President William J. Clinton, has stated that "a Legal Advisor must come to the best legal conclusion whether or not it is sympathetic to the objective of what the policy maker wants," and acknowledges that a legal advisor may "speak as a policy advisor" so long as he is clear that he is speaking in that capacity.[30] He also acknowledged the demands of ethics, stating: "When there is a very important matter and the government refuses to follow advice that you consider to be essential, you are supposed to resign."[31]

Jack Goldsmith, who was the head of the Department of Justice's Office of Legal Counsel under the Bush administration, explained:

[26] *Supra* ch. 4, pt. II.B.

[27] *Supra* ch. 5, pt. II.B.

[28] *See* P.S. Rao, *Foreign Legal Advisers' Roundtable, in* Scharf & Williams, *supra* note 5, at 172 (stating that legal advisors in India stand "supreme and independent when an issue concerns international law advice"); Frank Berman, *Foreign Legal Advisers' Roundtable, in* Scharf & Williams, *supra* note 5, at 174 (stating that a legal advisor in the United Kingdom must be sensitive to the needs and interests of government officials, but "still owes an allegiance to the law and to his own professional conscience"); Xue Hanqin, *Foreign Legal Advisers' Roundtable, in* Scharf & Williams, *supra* note 5 at 174–75 (stating that legal advisors in China "work as diplomats" and should "see the broader context of the law" but "must still give sound legal analysis and opinion as a lawyer" and "should not simply give the client the legal conclusions he wants to hear").

[29] *See* Weeramantry, *supra* note 1, at 78 ("I would submit that the true international lawyer does not take his or her eyes off the ideals underlying the discipline, and aims at being something more than a mere black-letter craftsman."); Douglas M. Johnston, The Historical Foundations of World Order 69 (2008) (stating that legal advisors "are often called upon to find a balance . . . between the policy suggested by the national interest that the legal advisor is bound to serve and the policy of progressive development of international law in the common interest of world society").

[30] *See* Conrad Harper, *Foreign Legal Advisers' Roundtable, in* Scharf & Williams, *supra* note 5, at 175.

[31] *Id.* at 180.

> Legal advice to the President from the Department of Justice is neither like advice from a private attorney nor like a politically neutral ruling from a court. It is something inevitably and uncomfortably, in between.[32]

John Yoo, one of the authors of the so-called "torture memos" under the Bush administration, has tried to explain why the legal memoranda were not only legal, they set policies that were "the right thing to do."[33]

Although it is easy to simply state that a balance must be struck among general and specific morality and effectiveness, bearing in mind the particular function that an advisor plays in a particular international problem, this does not, without more, provide much practical guidance to legal advisors. The issue is always what balance ought to be struck, or, at a minimum, how ought that balance be found? The studies below of an easy case—Abu Ghraib Prison—and a hard case—waterboarding—explore this question.

A. Abu Ghraib Prison

The easy test of the justificatory theory of international law is the degrading treatment of captives in Abu Ghraib Prison by U.S. military officers. It is an easy test because the answer is clearly that no legal advisor should authorize those abuses or counsel the U.S. President that those abuses are acceptable. This case is made even easier because it appears that, in fact, no advisor did so.

After the United States invaded Iraq in March 2003, and during its occupation, the United States established 17 detention facilities in Iraq. The largest facility was Abu Ghraib, which housed 7,000 detainees.[34] From October through December 2003, during the night shift at Abu Ghraib, military officers committed acts "of brutality and purposeless sadism."[35] An independent review panel of the U.S. Department of Defense condemned them in its report, the Schlesinger Report.[36] Another military investigation, called the Fay-Jones Report, detailed these acts. They included sexually assaulting female detainees, stripping other detainees and forcing them to simulate sex or masturbate and photographing them, and photographing yet others covered in feces.[37] These cruel acts were not inflicted on detainees for any military purpose, such as intelligence gathering.[38]

[32] Goldsmith, *supra* note 1, at 35.

[33] John Yoo, *supra* note 15 at x (2006).

[34] *See* Schlesinger Report, Final Report of the Independent Panel to Review Department of Defense Detention Operations (Aug. 2004), *in* The Torture Papers: The Road to Abu Ghraib 909, 913 (Greenberg & Dratel eds., 2005) [hereinafter Torture Papers].

[35] *Id.* at 909.

[36] *Id.*

[37] The Fay-Jones Report, Investigation of Intelligence Activities at Abu Ghraib (Aug. 2004), *in* Torture Papers, *supra* note 34, at 1073–95.

[38] *See* Yoo, *supra* note 15, at 194–95.

These abuses are horrific. Their senseless cruelty, ironically, make the Abu Ghraib abuses an easy case under the justificatory theory of international law. It is one thing if a government lawyer is asked to defend the perpetrators of those abuses. In that advocate's role, his duty is to protect the due process rights and interests of the accused. But it is entirely a different matter if a legal advisor is asked to authorize or give advice about Abu Ghraib. When exercising the authorizing or advising functions, legal advisors can look to this book's justificatory theory for guidance in condemning the Abu Ghraib abuses, because general morality, specific morality, and effectiveness all point toward disallowing those abusive actions.

The general moral obligation to respect legalism, which is a basic strut of the common good, requires legal advisors to condemn the Abu Ghraib abuses because no legalist interpretation of applicable prescriptions permits those abuses. The abuses were violations of international laws. Specifically, they violated Common Article III of the Geneva Conventions,[39] which provides that all detainees "shall in all circumstances be treated humanely."[40] Article III also prohibits "violence to life and person, in particular murder of all kinds, mutilation, cruel treatment, and torture," as well as "outrages upon personal dignity, in particular humiliating or degrading treatment."[41] The abuses at Abu Ghraib contravene many of these prohibitions and are without excuse. There was no operational purpose to them, even if one took the view that there could be operational exceptions to Common Article III. That is not to say that they only violated Common Article III, but, whatever one's views of customary international law, at a minimum, they were clear violations of a fundamental legal prescription enacted or codified in Common Article III.

The specific moral obligation to balance the values at stake also required legal advisors to prohibit the abuses at Abu Ghraib, because those abuses fundamentally damaged the basic good of life for detainees and utterly reduced their human dignity. Even if one took the view that cruel and degrading treatment can be justified in a moral calculus if it is necessary to protect other basic goods in some situations, this was not such a situation. There was no extenuating reason for the abuses.

Legal advisors should also consider national interests and preferred values in their balancing of the values at stake, and national interests and values were damaged by the abuses.[42] On February 7, 2002, President Bush issued a memorandum ordering

[39] *See* Exec. Order No. 13,491 § 3, 74 Fed. Reg. 4893 (Jan. 22, 2009) (subsequently ordering that Common Article III apply to all detainees); Hamdan v. Rumsfeld, 548 U.S. 557 (2006) (holding that Common Article III applied to Al-Qaeda detainees in their conflict with the United States).

[40] Geneva Convention [III] Relative to the Treatment of Prisoners of War, Aug. 12, 1949, 6 U.S.T. 3316, 75 U.N.T.S. 135 [hereinafter Geneva Convention].

[41] *See id.* art. 3. *See also* American Bar Association Report to the House of Delegates, *in* Torture Papers, *supra* note 34, at 1140–44 (discussing how Abu Ghraib abuses violated the Geneva Conventions).

[42] *See* Bush, *supra* note 23, at 88–89 (condemning abuses at Abu Ghraib as contrary to U.S. values and interests in the following terms: "In defiance of their orders and military law, American soldiers had severely mistreated detainees at an Iraqi prison called Abu Ghraib. I felt sick, really sick. This was not what our military or our country stood for. While the perpetrators were court-martialed, America's reputation took a severe hit.").

that Al-Qaeda and Taliban detainees be treated humanely and consistent with the principles of the Geneva Conventions in a manner consistent with military necessity.[43] There was no military necessity here. President Bush affirmed that the humane treatment of detainees was a national value, as it is in many nations.[44] U.S. Secretary of State Colin Powell assessed that U.S. national interests were served by treating detainees humanely because this would "preserve[] U.S. credibility and moral authority," putting it in a "'better position to demand and receive international support,' and that it 'supports the U.S. objective of ensuring its forces are accorded protection under the Convention,' and 'reduces incentives for international criminal investigations directed against U.S. officials and troops.'"[45] The Abu Ghraib abuses undermined these national interests and values.

The issue of a legal advisor's effectiveness is not implicated in this case because elected officials condemned the abuses, and it would be unreasonable to think that officials would ignore advice from the advisor that the abuses were unlawful and immoral.

The confluence of general and specific morality and effectiveness makes the Abu Ghraib abuses an easy example of how the justificatory account of international law provides guidance to legal advisors.

B. Waterboarding

A difficult case, contrary to what some zealous human rights advocates or strident sovereigntists may respectively claim, concerns whether legal advisors should have authorized waterboarding of high-level Al-Qaeda operatives to obtain actionable intelligence that senior U.S. officials believed likely prevented terrorist attacks. There is a vast and polarized literature debating U.S. methods against terrorism, with one side characterizing these efforts as part of a "war on terror,"[46] and the other calling U.S. officials the "torture team."[47] It is neither within the scope of this book to even begin to address this debate on Islamist terrorism, nor is it necessary to subscribe to the choice of emotive framing phrases or name calling that each side has tactically selected.

For present purposes of testing how the justificatory theory of international law applies to legal advisors, it is sufficient to focus on a series of memoranda the Office of Legal Counsel produced from August 1, 2002, to May 10, 2005, regarding standards of conduct for interrogation (the "interrogation memoranda"), authorizing, among other enhanced interrogation techniques, waterboarding.

[43] *See* Memorandum for the Vice President et al., Humane Treatment of al Qaeda and Taliban Detainees (Feb. 7, 2002), *in* Torture papers, *supra* note 34, at 134–35.

[44] *Id.*

[45] *See* Memorandum from Colin L. Powell to Counsel to the President, Draft Decision Memorandum for the President on the Applicability of the Geneva Convention to the Conflict in Afghanistan, *in* Torture Papers, *supra* note 34, at 122–25.

[46] *See generally* Yoo, *supra* note 15.

[47] Philippe Sands, Torture Team (2008). *See also* Torture Papers, *supra* note 34.

It is useful to summarize this book's analysis before developing it in the sections that follow. Initially, the analysis is confined to the following factual assumptions reasonably drawn from government documents and recollections of officials: Waterboarding is carried out in a controlled and regulated manner that is apparently designed, based on medical knowledge provided by the CIA's *Office of Medical Services*, to prevent serious physical or prolonged mental suffering.[48] Further, it is used only in restricted circumstances when all other interrogation methods have failed to obtain crucial intelligence to stop a terrorist attack that the U.S. officials reasonably believe the detainee knows about.[49]

Under these parameters, waterboarding arguably is not illegal torture or morally impermissible. Because a legal advisor lacks the intelligence information, national security expertise, and direct responsibilities for national security that elected officials have, the legal advisor is not better placed than elected officials to decide if waterboarding would maximize national security and moral goals in a specific situation within those parameters. Therefore, when asked by officials to authorize waterboarding, a legal advisor should legally authorize it on a case-by-case basis to ensure that these acts of interrogation fall within the parameters described above, and leave it to the President's executive discretion to decide whether it should be conducted in a case that the advisor has authorized.

In alternate scenarios where the methods of waterboarding were changed and made more extreme to constitute torture, or if medical science discovered that waterboarding as currently practiced did cause long-term physical or mental harm so that it constituted torture, a legal advisor ought not to legally authorize torture. However, he should also advise the President that in a specific situation, if the President reasonably believes, in spite of the illegality and immorality of torture, that a national security threat in that particular situation is so grave—such as a terrorist biological attack that would kill thousands of constituents and cause untold physical suffering—that it outweighs considerations against waterboarding, the

[48] *See* Memorandum from Steven G. Bradbury, Principal Deputy Assistant Attorney General, to John A. Rizzo, Senior Deputy General Counsel, Central Intelligence Agency, at pt. I.B.13 (May 10, 2005) (describing procedures for waterboarding described by the CIA Office of Medical Services as "medically acceptable") (redacted copy on file with author). *Cf.*, Fax to Office of Legal Counsel, Latest OMS Guidelines, Jan. 15, 2005 at 19 ("A series (within a 'session') of several relatively rapid waterboard applications is medically acceptable in all healthy subjects, so long as there is no indication of some emerging vulnerability.") (partially redacted copy on file with author); *id.* at 18 ("The SERE training program has applied the waterboard technique (single exposure) to trainees for years, and reportedly there have been thousands of applications without significant or lasting medical complications. This procedure nonetheless carries some potential risks, particularly when repeated a large number of times or when applied to an individual less fit than a typical SERE trainee.").

[49] *See* Memorandum from Steven G. Bradbury, *supra* note 48 at pt. I.B.13 (stating that waterboarding is only used if other interrogation techniques have failed, that the CIA has credible intelligence that a terrorist attack is imminent, and there are substantial indicators that the detainee has actionable intelligence that can prevent, disrupt or delay that attack) (redacted copy on file with author).

President may decide that there is an overriding moral obligation to carry out torture in the reasonable expectation that it will help officials neutralize the threat. The President would be acting illegally but morally in that situation—just as NATO acted illegally but morally in the bombing of Serbia in 1999, as discussed in the next chapter. If the President makes that choice, he should be prepared to face the political and possible legal consequences of his illegal action, but it is ultimately his choice to make.

Finally, this section considers a further scenario where government officials have run amok and carry out waterboarding in situations unwarranted on national interest grounds, such as simply to inflict recrimination on terrorists, or are doing so without a reasonable basis to believe that the detainee has useful intelligence, or in violation of the strict controls that are operationally required when using it as an enhanced interrogation technique. The legal advisor should neither legally authorize nor condone such acts. He should also advise the President against acting illegally by ordering waterboarding in such situations, because there could be no moral justification for so doing.

To minimize the risk of such abhorrent situations occurring, the legal advisor could insist on granting authorizations on a case-by-case basis. This should be operationally feasible, because it appears from the history of CIA waterboarding that it was only necessary to use this technique on three detainees out of thousands. The legal advisor should also insist that the interrogation be videotaped and reviewed later by an official, perhaps even a judge with appropriate security clearance, to ensure that that the interrogation was carried out within the strict limits of what was authorized.

If government officials do not respect those internal checks or insist on broader authorization, the legal advisor could instead resign rather than acquiesce. If the executive conduct is beyond the pale, the legal advisor should also consider resigning in as much public fashion as permitted by law, in order to draw attention to illegal and immoral acts of government officials, so that constituents and courts can decide if officials should be held accountable for their acts.

Importantly, nothing in the foregoing generally condones or condemns torture or even cruel and inhuman treatment, on legal, moral, or national interest grounds. This chapter also does not address whether waterboarding is a violation of international or domestic laws prohibiting cruel, inhuman, and degrading treatment. These are topics of grave importance and great sensitivity, and require lengthy discussions of their own to do them justice. The analysis here focuses solely on the question of whether waterboarding is illegal torture under international law to provide a detailed illustration how this book's theory of international law provides guidance to legal advisors on a narrow question. Legal advisors could also apply the theory to questions about whether waterboarding constitutes cruel, inhuman, and degrading treatment, or about whether other forms of interrogation constitute torture, but those applications are not carried out here. This section is confined narrowly to a discussion of whether waterboarding, as carried out by the CIA during the Bush administration, constitutes illegal torture.

The analysis summarized above is developed in more detail below.

1. Factual Assumptions

Given the atmospherics surrounding the subject of waterboarding, it is necessary to state the presumed facts upon which the analysis will be built. The purpose of this section is neither to indict nor absolve the authors of the interrogation memoranda, the officials who ordered them, or the ground officers who conducted waterboarding. Such an effort cannot be done without access to complete evidence and expert opinions to assess and make findings of fact determined by a preponderance of evidence. It is beyond the scope of this book to do so. It is also unnecessary to do so for the present purposes of illustrating how the justificatory view of international law might apply in an international problem. So, the analysis that follows will be based on certain facts that are presumed. After that, this section will examine whether the conclusion changes if any of those facts are altered.

First, the facts about waterboarding itself. Waterboarding simulates the feeling of drowning in the detainee being questioned.[50] The procedure for waterboarding, according to a memorandum produced for the CIA, is as follows:

> In this technique, the detainee is lying on a gurney that is inclined at an angle of 10 to 15 degrees to the horizontal, with the detainee on his back and his head toward the lower end of the gurney: A cloth is placed over the detainee's face, and cold water is poured on the cloth from a height of approximately 6 to 18 inches. The wet cloth creates a barrier through which it is difficult—or in some cases not possible—to breathe. A single "application" of water may not last for more than 40 seconds, with the duration of an "application" measured from the moment when water—of whatever quantity—is first poured onto the cloth until the cloth is removed. . . .
>
> During the use of the waterboard, a physician and psychologist are present at all times. The detainee is monitored to ensure that he does not develop respiratory distress. If the detainee is not breathing freely after the cloth is removed from his face, he is immediately moved to a vertical position in order to clear the water from his mouth, nose, and nasophraynx. . . .
>
> [T]he waterboard may be approved for use with a given detainee only during, at most, one single 30-day period, and that during that period, the waterboard technique may be used on no more than five days. We further understand that in any 24-hour period, interrogators may use no more than two "sessions" of the waterboard on a subject with a "session" defined to mean the time that the detainee is strapped to the waterboard—and that no session may last more than two hours. Moreover, during any session, the number of individual applications of water lasting 10 seconds or longer may not exceed six. As noted above, the maximum length of any application of water is 40 seconds (you have informed us that this maximum has rarely been reached). Finally, the total cumulative time of applications of whatever length in a 24-hour period may not exceed 12 minutes.[51]

The same memorandum describes the effect of waterboarding on the detainee:

[50] *See* Bush, *supra* note 23, at 169 (stating that waterboarding is "simulated drowning").

[51] Memorandum from Steven G. Bradbury, *supra* note 48.

> We understand the effect of the waterboard is to induce a sensation of drowning. This sensation is based on a deeply rooted physiological response. Thus, the detainee experiences this sensation even if he is aware that he is not actually drowning. We are informed that based on extensive experience, the process is not physically painful, but that it usually does cause fear and panic.[52]

Crucially, "in the many years of use on thousands of participants in SERE training, the waterboard technique (although used in a substantially more limited way) has not resulted in any cases of serious physical pain or prolonged mental harm."[53]

Readers may disagree with the description of waterboarding or its effects. However, for the purposes of analyzing what the legal advisors asked to authorize waterboarding should have done, it is appropriate to consider the facts as they were provided by military officials, which were the basis on which the legal opinion requested was rendered.

As to when waterboarding is used, it is only used if:

> (1) the CIA has credible intelligence that a terrorist attack is imminent; (2) there are 'substantial and credible indicators the subject has actionable intelligence that can prevent, disrupt or delay this attack'; and (3) other interrogation methods have failed or are unlikely to yield actionable intelligence in time to prevent the attack.[54]

President Bush has revealed in his memoirs that of the thousands of suspected terrorists captured after 9/11, only three were waterboarded. He discusses two of these detainees. The first was Abu Zubaydah, a senior recruiter and operator who ran a camp in Afghanistan where some of the 9/11 hijackers were trained and whom the CIA believed had been planning another attack against the United States. The second detainee was Khalid Sheikh Mohammed, the mastermind of 9/11.[55]

According to President Bush, all other interrogation techniques on Zubaydah failed to obtain useful information from him. After he was waterboarded, he provided information about Al-Qaeda's structure and operations, and this information contributed to the capture of Khalid. Waterboarding Khalid after all other interrogation techniques failed caused him to reveal information about Al-Qaeda's biological weapons program, and plans to attack the United States with anthrax. The information he provided also led to the capture of key Al-Qaeda operatives planning another attack on the United States using hijacked planes, but this time on the West Coast. President Bush concluded:

> The intelligence he provided, which proved vital to saving American lives, almost certainly would not have come to light without the CIA's enhanced interrogation program.
>
> Of the thousands of terrorists we captured in the years after 9/11, about a hundred were placed into the CIA program. . . . Three were waterboarded. The information the detainees in the

[52] *Id.*

[53] *Id.*

[54] *Id.*

[55] Bush, *supra* note 23, at 170–71.

> CIA program revealed constituted more than half of what the CIA knew about al Qaeda. Their interrogations helped break up plots to attack American military and diplomatic facilities abroad, Heathrow Airport and Canary Wharf in London, and multiple targets in the United States. Experts in the intelligence community told me that without the CIA program, there would have been another attack on the United States.
>
> [. . .] The CIA interrogation program saved lives.[56]

Readers may also disagree that waterboarding provided actionable intelligence, believing extreme interrogation does not result in credible information.[57] This ignores the fact that intelligence is always triangulated and corroborated, so U.S. officials will check the information offered before acting on it.

In any event, the President has stated that the intelligence obtained from waterboarding helped prevent specific terrorist attacks. Absent evidence that he lied, or was lied to, in this regard, there ought to be a presumption that statements by the President are truthful and carry weight.

2. International Legal Prescriptions

There are several soft international agreements prohibiting torture, including the Universal Declaration of Human Rights[58] and the International Covenant on Civil and Political Rights.[59] Some courts have also stated that the prohibition of torture is also a customary international law and *jus cogens*.[60]

The United States has signed the Torture Convention but with modifications. The United States is obliged to abide by only those provisions it consented to, which are the Convention as modified and enacted into a domestic statute known as the Torture Convention Implementation Act or Torture Act, which prohibits torture.[61]

[56] *Id.* at 171.

[57] *See* Sands, *supra* note 47, at 118–19.

[58] *See* Universal Declaration of Human Rights, G.A. Res. 217A, art. 5, U.N. GAOR, 3d Sess., 1st plen. mtg., U.N. Doc. A/810 (Dec. 12, 1948).

[59] *See* International Covenant on Civil and Political Rights, G.A. Res. 2200A (XXI), art. 7, U.N. Doc. A/6316 (Dec. 16, 1966).

[60] *See* Prosecutor v. Furundija, Int'l Crim. Trib. Former Yugoslavia, Case No. IT-95–17/1-T, ¶ 144–47, 153–54 (Dec. 10, 1998) (prohibition of torture is *jus cogens*); Al-Adsani v. United Kingdom, Eur. Ct. Hum. Rt., Application No. 35763/97, ¶ 30 (Nov. 21, 2001).

[61] 18 U.S.C. § 2340A ("Whoever outside the United States commits or attempts to commit torture shall be fined . . . or imprisoned not more than 20 years, or both, and if death results . . . shall be punished by death or imprisoned for any term of years or for life."); United States v. Belfast, 611 F.3d 783, 801 (11th Cir. 2010) ("Congress passed the Torture Act to implement the United States' obligations under the Convention Against Torture.").

The Torture Convention defines torture in the following way:

> [T]orture means any act by which severe pain or suffering, whether physical or mental, is intentionally inflicted on a person for such purposes as obtaining from him or a third person information or a confession, punishing him for an act he or a third person has committed or is suspected of having committed, or intimidating or coercing him or a third person, or for any reason based on discrimination of any kind, when such pain or suffering is inflicted by or at the instigation of or with the consent or acquiescence of a public official or other person acting in an official capacity. It does not include pain or suffering arising only from, inherent in or incidental to lawful sanctions.[62]

The Torture Act defines torture more narrowly by providing that mental pain and suffering must be prolonged to be severe. Section 2340 of the United States Code Title 18 states:

(1) "torture" means an act committed by a person acting under the color of law specifically intended to inflict severe physical or mental pain or suffering (other than pain or suffering incidental to lawful sanctions) upon another person within his custody or physical control;
(2) "severe mental pain or suffering" means the prolonged mental harm caused by or resulting from—
   (A) the intentional infliction or threatened infliction of severe physical pain or suffering;
   (B) the administration or application, or threatened administration or application, of mind-altering substances or other procedures calculated to disrupt profoundly the senses or the personality;
   (C) the threat of imminent death; or
   (D) the threat that another person will imminently be subjected to death, severe physical pain or suffering, or the administration or application of mind-altering substances or other procedures calculated to disrupt profoundly the senses or personality[.].[63]

3. The Interrogation Memoranda

The first interrogation memorandum (the "2002 Blanket Interrogation Memorandum") provided, in August 2002, broad authorization for extreme interrogation

[62] Convention Against Torture and Other Cruel, Inhuman or Degrading Treatment or Punishment art. 1, 1465 U.N.T.S. 85 (Dec. 10, 1984).

[63] *See* 18 U.S.C. § 2340(1), (2) (2010). *See also* Belfast, 611 F.3d at 801–02 (discussing legislative history of the Torture Act and noting that President George H.W. Bush, acting for the United States, expressed his understanding that "'in order to constitute torture, an act must be specifically intended to inflict severe physical or mental pain or suffering'") (quoting S. Exec. Rep. 101–30 at 9, 35 (1990).

techniques.[64] It addressed both domestic U.S. law and international law. Regarding international law, it interpreted the Torture Convention as the U.S. ratified it with reservations and enacted it into U.S. law. The 2002 Interrogation Memorandum interpreted Section 2340 to prohibit only "extreme acts" in the following manner:

> [W]e conclude that torture as defined in and proscribed by Sections 2340–2340A, covers only extreme acts. Severe pain is generally of the kind difficult for the victim to endure. Where the pain is physical, it must be of an intensity akin to that which accompanies serious physical injury such as death or organ failure. Severe mental pain requires suffering not just at the moment of infliction but it also requires lasting psychological harm, such as seen in mental disorders like post-traumatic stress disorder. Additionally, such severe mental pain can arise only from the predicate acts listed in Section 2340. Because the acts inflicting torture are extreme, there is significant range of acts that though they might constitute cruel, inhuman, or degrading treatment or punishment fail to rise to the level of torture.
>
> Further, we conclude that under the circumstances of the current war against al Qaeda and its allies, application of Section 2340A to interrogations undertaken pursuant to the President's Commander-in-Chief powers may be unconstitutional. Finally, even if an interrogation method might violate Section 2340A, necessity or self-defense could provide justifications that would eliminate any criminal liability.[65]

The effect of this interpretation was to generally authorize the extreme interrogation techniques used by the U.S. military, including waterboarding.

A second memorandum (the "2002 Specific Interrogation Memorandum") was issued on the same day, August 2, 2002, specifically authorizing 10 enhanced interrogation techniques, including waterboarding, to be used against a key Al-Qaeda operative.[66] It reasoned that although waterboarding "constitutes the threat of imminent death" it did not cause "prolonged mental harm," such as "mental harm lasting months or years," and therefore did not cause "severe mental pain or suffering" and accordingly did not meet the requisite elements of torture.[67] Further, it explained that an interrogator who had a good faith belief that waterboarding would not cause severe mental pain or suffering would not have the requisite specific intent necessary for torture under the U.S. enactment of the Torture Convention.[68] The memorandum concluded that its authorization of waterboarding was based on

[64] *See* Memorandum from Jay S. Bybee, Assistant Attorney General, U.S. Department of Justice, to Alberto R. Gonzales, Counsel to the President, U.S. Department of Justice, (Aug. 1, 2002), *in* Torture Papers, *supra* note 34 at 172 [hereinafter Interrogation Memorandum I]. *See also* Memorandum for John Rizzo, Acting General Counsel of the Central Intelligence Agency, (Aug. 1, 2002) (Memorandum entitled "Interrogation of al Qaeda Operative") (on file with author) [hereinafter 2002 Al-Qaeda Interrogation Memorandum].

[65] Interrogation Memorandum I, *supra* note 64, at 213–14.

[66] *See* 2002 Al-Qaeda Interrogation Memorandum, *supra* note 64.

[67] *Id.* pt. III.

[68] *See id.*

the advisors' "best reading of the law," in the absence of "cases construing this statute" and "prosecutions brought under it."[69]

Almost immediately, U.S. military legal advisors expressed concerns about these memoranda. U.S. Navy General Counsel Alberto Mora warned that the techniques "could rise to the level of torture, and probably will cause significant harm to our national, legal, political, military and diplomatic interests."[70] Under pressure, U.S. Secretary of Defense Donald Rumsfeld rescinded authority for the enhanced interrogation techniques on January 15, 2003.[71]

However, he also simultaneously established a working group to review these techniques and asked for another legal opinion from Office of Legal Counsel in light of the concerns expressed by military lawyers.[72] State Department legal advisors were excluded from the working group. On March 24, the working group issued a memorandum that John Yoo had been actively involved in drafting, repeating many of the broad conclusions that he had drawn in the August 1, 2002, interrogation memorandum (the "2003 Blanket Interrogation Memorandum"). The new memo also concluded that customary international law prohibitions were not binding on the U.S. President, and he was free to override them at his discretion.[73] Based on this broad authorization, Secretary Rumsfeld authorized 24 specific interrogation techniques.[74]

The 2003 memorandum and Secretary Rumsfeld's authorization of 24 techniques represented the high-water mark for broad authorization of enhanced interrogation. The Legal Advisor for the State Department, William Howard Taft IV, subsequently stated that it was "highly regrettable" that the State Department had been excluded from the working group, and had his office been involved, "several conclusions not consistent with our treaty obligations under the Convention against Torture and our obligations under customary international law would not have been reached."[75]

Jack Goldsmith, who had become the head of OLC in October 2003, concluded two months later in December that the 2002 Interrogation Blanket Memorandum and the 2003 Blanket Interrogation Memorandum were overbroad and prone to abuse. In his view, authorization of interrogation techniques should be narrowly

[69] *Id.*

[70] *See* Scharf & Williams, *supra* note 5, at 190.

[71] Memorandum from Donald Rumsfeld, U.S. Secretary of Defense, to Commander USSOUTHCOM (Jan. 15, 2003), *in* Torture Papers, *supra* note 34, at 239.

[72] Memorandum from William J. Haynes II, General Counsel, U.S. Department of Defense, to General Counsel of the Department of the Air Force (Jan. 17, 2003), *in* Torture Papers, *supra* note 34, at 240.

[73] *See* Working Group Report on Detainee Interrogation in the Global War on Terrorism: Assessment of Legal, Historical, Policy, and Operational Considerations (Mar. 6, 2003), *in* Torture Papers, *supra* note 34, at 241, 243.

[74] *See* Memorandum from Donald Rumsfeld, U.S. Secretary of Defense, to James T. Hill, Commander, U.S. Southern Command (Apr. 16, 2003), *in* Torture Papers, *supra* note 34, at 360.

[75] *See* Scharf & Williams, *supra* note 5, at 192–93 (citation omitted).

tailored with safeguards to ensure that actual techniques used were lawful. He withdrew these two memoranda but kept in place the 2002 Al-Qaeda Interrogation Memorandum permitting 10 specific interrogation techniques, including waterboarding.[76]

On December 30, 2004, OLC, now led by Daniel Levin because Goldsmith had resigned soon after withdrawing the 2002 and 2003 Interrogation Memoranda, issued a new memorandum on interrogation (the "2004 Blanket Interrogation Memorandum"). It provided that torture "is abhorrent to both American law and values and international norms."[77] It superseded the withdrawn 2002 Interrogation Memorandum in its entirety, specifically disagreeing that torture required severe pain amounting to "excruciating and agonizing pain."[78]

However, it is remarkable in its lack of guidance. It stated that prolonged mental harm is of "some lasting duration" without specifying that duration. In addressing "severe pain," it stated that there was no "precise, objective scientific criteria for measuring pain"[79] and proceeded to provide examples of severe pain but did not inductively draw out any guiding principle, other than the unhelpful observation that pain was to be determined by "its persistence as well as intensity," and could not be only "mild or transitory."[80] As to specific intent, it stated that the term "is ambiguous," and "it would not be appropriate to rely on parsing the specific intent element of the statute to approve as lawful conduct that might otherwise amount to torture," thereby effectively minimizing this element that Congress enacted into the statute.[81]

Given the lack of clarity in the 2004 Interrogation Memorandum, it is unsurprising the OLC was once again asked, in 2005, to specifically authorize enhanced interrogation techniques. It did so in two memoranda issued on May 10, 2005: one authorizing 13 enhanced techniques, including waterboarding, when used individually (the "2005 Specific Interrogation Memorandum") and one authorizing the 13 techniques used in certain combinations (the "2005 Combined Interrogation Memorandum").

Describing waterboarding as the closest call, Steven Bradbury of OLC nonetheless concluded that waterboarding was legal. Although it caused panic associated with the feeling of drowning, the technique was "not physically painful," did not cause "prolonged mental harm," and, as applied by U.S. military officers, was not "specifically intended to cause severe physical harm or mental pain or suffering."[82] The 2005 Combination Memorandum authorized the combinations specified in the memorandum but did not express a view on other combinations that it had not

[76] *See* Goldsmith, *supra* note 1, at 151–53.

[77] Memorandum from Daniel Levin, Acting Assistant Attorney General, to James B. Comey, Deputy Attorney General 1 (Dec. 30, 2004) (on file with author).

[78] *Id.* at 2.

[79] *Id.* at 8.

[80] *See id.* at 12.

[81] *Id.* at 17.

[82] Memorandum from Steven G. Bradbury, *supra* note 48, at pt. III.13.

addressed. It concluded by stating: "Our task has been made more difficult by the imprecision of the statute and the relative absence of judicial guidance, but we have applied our best reading to the specific facts you have provided."[83]

In December 2008, a U.S. Senate Armed Services Committee Report stated that the OLC opinions

> distorted the meaning and intent of anti-torture laws, rationalized the abuse of detainees in U.S. custody and influenced Department of Defense determinations as to what interrogation techniques were legal for use during interrogations conducted by U.S. military personnel.[84]

Finally, two days after taking office, on January 22, 2009, President Obama issued an executive order rescinding all the OLC interrogation authorizations from September 11, 2001, to January 20, 2009.[85]

It may be tempting to conclude under this sequence of events that this is an easy case of legal advisors behaving immorally, illegally, and against national interests. Such an evaluation would be too simplistic. For the reasons started below, under the view of international law presented here, OLC ought not to have rendered its general interpretations of the Torture Convention as enacted into U.S. law in its 2002, 2003, and 2004 Blanket Interrogation Memoranda. Its specific authorizations of waterboarding, however, present a difficult case.

4. General Morality

The legal advisors who wrote the 2002 and 2005 Specific Interrogation Memoranda, as well as the 2003 Combined Interrogation Memorandum did not clearly violate their general moral obligation to interpret prescriptions legalistically because their memoranda provided arguably reasonable legalist interpretations of an ambiguous text and applications of that text to facts. Confining the present analysis to waterboarding, which, in any event, the memoranda state are the harshest form of interrogation considered in them, it can hardly be said that legalism prohibits, with no room for textual doubt, waterboarding.

The Torture Convention as enacted into U.S. law requires "prolonged mental harm." The mental distress from the feeling of suffocating that waterboarding produces is acute, but it lasts only for the seconds that waterboarding is applied. On that basis, arguably the mental harm is not prolonged. The same law requires, in the

[83] *Id.* concl.

[84] Senate Armed Services Committee, 110th Congress, Inquiry into the Treatment of Detainees in U.S. Custody xxvii (Nov. 20, 2008), *available at* http://armed-services.senate.gov/Publications/Detainee%20Report%20Final_April%2022%202009.pdf.

[85] Exec. Order No. 13,491, 74 Fed. Reg. 4893 (Jan. 22, 2009). *See also* Dick Jackson, *Interrogation and Treatment of Detainees in the Global War on Terror*, *in* The War on Terror and the Laws of War: A Military Perspective 125, 137–58 (Lewis ed., 2009) (describing the authorizations for enhanced interrogations and their application by military officers).

alternative, severe "physical . . . pain or suffering." Waterboarding is "not physically painful."[86] Therefore, it arguably does not meet the physical harm test. The law also requires that the official "specifically intended" to inflict severe physical or mental pain or suffering. Arguably, an official who has no reason to know that waterboarding causes severe physical or mental pain or suffering (statutorily defined as "prolonged mental pain or suffering"), and conducts waterboarding solely to obtain information, does not have that *mens rea*. Thus, it would be difficult to contend that waterboarding is prohibited by legalism.

Critics will be quick to point out that such legalism is formalism gone awry. A teleological interpretation of text would counsel for a broader reading of the prohibition on torture, and anything that comes close to the line is too close. There is an argument that the legal prescription must be interpreted in light of the other conventions and customary international law prohibiting torture and that doing so would indicate that a literalist interpretation of texts is too narrow. However, such a contextual approach should not override the express reservation that the United States made in accepting a treaty obligation prohibiting torture that is more narrowly defined than the general text of the Torture Convention.

Another criticism of the legal reasoning in the memoranda is that they failed to consider *jus cogens* and customary international law prohibiting torture, which some international tribunals have stated defines torture as it appears in the Torture Convention,[87] and not narrowly as the United States defined it the Torture Act. The *jus cogens* prescription accordingly prohibited acts causing severe mental suffering, even if it was not prolonged. Therefore, waterboarding, which caused severe mental suffering, albeit brief, constituted torture in violation of customary law and *jus cogens*. The criticism that John Yoo improperly ignored customary law seems particularly justified because elsewhere he has acknowledged that customary law is a form of law binding on the United States.[88]

On close examination, however, it is not clear that waterboarding violated the customary international law prohibiting torture. While few would dispute that the customary law and even *jus cogens* prohibit torture, the outer limits of torture under customary law and *jus cogens* are unclear. International courts have stated that the *jus cogens* prohibition of torture is coextensive with the definition of torture under the Convention Against Torture.[89] Court decisions are, however, only a subsidiary

[86] Memorandum from Steven G. Bradbury, *supra* note 48, at pt. I.B.13.

[87] *See* Prosecutor v. Furundija, Int'l Crim. Trib. Former Yugoslavia, Case No. IT-95–17/1-T, ¶ 160 (Dec. 10, 1998).

[88] John Yoo, *Using Force*, 71 U. Chi. L. Rev. 729, 761–62 (2004) (recognizing that "customary international law . . . may identify limits of the use of force in the international legal system"); John Yoo, *International Law and the War in Iraq*, 97 Am. J. Int'l L. 563 (2003) ("The customary international law right to use force in anticipatory self-defense is a well-established aspect of the 'inherent right' of self-defense.").

[89] *See* Prosecutor v. Furundija, Int'l Crim. Trib. Former Yugoslavia, Case No. IT-95–17/1-T, ¶ 160 (Dec. 10, 1998) (citing Prosecutor v. Jean Paul Akayesu, Case No. ICTR-94-T, ¶ 593 (Sept. 2, 1998). *See also* Jutta Brunnée & Stephen J. Toope, Legitimacy and Legality in International Law 228–30 (2010) (surveying cases recognizing international prohibition on torture).

source of law and not a substitute for examining whether there is state practice and *opinio juris* supporting the definition of torture proposed.

The bases provided for asserting that the customary prohibition was coextensive with the Convention Against Torture are summarized by the International Criminal Tribunal for Former Yugoslavia in *Prosecutor v. Furundija*. That court argued that that the UN General Assembly accepted by consensus a resolution in 1975 that torture was prohibited, and that the European Court of Human Rights, the Human Rights Committee, and the Inter-American Convention all have adopted substantially similar definitions.[90] Of these pieces of evidence, only the UN General Assembly resolution reflected a consensus of *opinio juris*. The *opinio juris* expressed, however, was not that its definition of torture was law, but that, in terms, it was only a "guideline for all States and other entities exercising effective power."[91] Further, torture is reported to take place in Syria, Egypt, Russia, China, Pakistan, Iran, Uzbekistan, North Korea, Myanmar, Zimbabwe, Equitorial Guniea, Cameroon, Gambia, Mexico, Venezuela, and Paraguay.[92] This state practice hardly supports the contention that states agree on the definition of torture.

Further, the claim that the definition of torture in the Torture Convention is a *jus cogens* that overrides the United States' reservation is contradicted by state practice. States negotiating the Convention permitted reservations, and around 40 states made reservations.[93] This indicates that states did not believe that there was a *jus cogens* prohibiting them from derogating from the text of the Convention Against Torture. Further, although some states objected to the United States' reservations, none did so on the grounds that the U.S. reservations were inconsistent with *jus cogens*, indicating the absence of *opinio juris* that the definition of torture in the Torture Convention was *jus cogens*.[94] Accordingly, the criticism that the memoranda failed to consider customary law fails to prove that the omission was more than harmless error.

5. Specific Morality

When faced with ambiguity in the scope of the prohibition of torture that legalism alone cannot resolve, OLC lawyers ought to have applied moral reasoning to select the interpretation that best optimized the values at stake. There was a failure of moral reasoning with regard to the 2002, 2003, and 2004 Blanket Interrogation Memoranda. They were overbroad because officials could have interpreted them to apply to techniques that lacked adequate checks to prevent abuse. This, indeed, was a conclusion

[90] Prosecutor v. Furundija, Int'l Crim. Trib. Former Yugoslavia, Case No. IT-95–17/1-T, ¶ 160 (Dec. 10, 1998).

[91] UN Gen. Assembly Res. 3452 (XXX) (Dec. 9, 1975).

[92] *See* Brunnée & Toope, *supra* note 89, at 260–61.

[93] *See* UN Convention Against Torture, Declarations, *available at* http://treaties.un.org/Pages/ViewDetails.aspx?src=TREATY&mtdsg_no=IV-9&chapter=4&lang=en.

[94] *See* UN Convention Against Torture, Objections to Declarations, *available at* http://treaties.un.org/Pages/ViewDetails.aspx?src=TREATY&mtdsg_no=IV-9&chapter=4&lang=en.

that Goldsmith drew and which led him to withdraw the 2002 and 2003 Interrogation Memoranda.[95] The need to prevent abuse was particularly acute because of the widespread interrogations that U.S. line officers were carrying out in Afghanistan, Iraq, Guantanamo Bay, and elsewhere in their national security efforts. The need to prevent abuse was also critical because if torture was intentionally or inadvertently inflicted on detainees through techniques that were not specifically authorized, it would fundamentally undermine their basic good of life and, indeed, the human dignity of the torturers as well.

The criticism of these memoranda as overbroad is heightened because national interest did not require issuing them, even assuming that national interest required enhanced interrogation to obtain actionable intelligence to prevent another terrorist attack. The memos were unnecessarily broad because OLC or the Department of Defense also issued specific authorizations for the techniques of interrogation carefully prescribed under CIA and military doctrine with checks and balances. The only residual effect of the overbroad memoranda was therefore to inadvertently authorize techniques that fell outside the scope of procedures vetted and institutionalized as safe and appropriate by the CIA and the Department of Defense.

John Yoo defended the 2002 memoranda by explaining that he intended to draw "bright lines" providing field officers with guidance and clarity about what they were authorized to do.[96] Certainly a blanket authorization is a bright line. However, clarity is not the only goal and should not be pursued at any cost, especially where it is possible to provide clarity without being overbroad, as discussed below.

The specific authorizations of waterboarding in the 2002 and 2005 Specific Interrogation Memoranda and the 2005 Combined Interrogation Memorandum are more difficult cases. From a legalist standpoint, every memorandum specifically authorizing waterboarding carefully considered the impact of the technique on the detainee and applied a reasonable interpretation of the text of the U.S. law prohibiting torture. It was not the only interpretation, to be sure, and the text is open to a narrower interpretation prohibiting waterboarding. However, the fact that there are two interpretations, one prohibiting and the other permitting waterboarding, makes it impossible to say that the memoranda specifically considering and authorizing waterboarding were wrong on strictly legalist grounds.

Moral reasoning about the specific values that hung in the balance also does not provide a clear answer on the best interpretation of the law to resolve the ambiguity of legalism here.[97] There is an absolutist moral view, ably explained by Jeremy Waldron and Philippe Sands, that torture is absolutely prohibited no matter what good outcomes it produces,[98] and anything that comes close to it should not even be

[95] *See* Goldsmith *supra* note 1, at 151.

[96] *See* Yoo, *supra* note 15, at 171.

[97] *See generally* Yuval Ginbar, Why Not Torture Terrorists 10–156 (2010) (surveying various viewpoints about the morality or immorality of torture).

[98] *See* Jeremy Waldron, Torture, Terror, and Trade-Offs 25 (2010) ("Talk of balance—particularly talk of changes in the balance as circumstances and consequences change—may not be appropriate in the realm of civil liberties."); *id.* at 16 (quoting President Obama as stating: "I believe

countenanced.[99] Applying this view, since OLC concluded that waterboarding was a close call, it should have erred on the side of prohibiting it.

Another view, however, is consequentialist. Alan Dershowitz, Adrian Vermeule, and Eric Posner all subscribe to different versions of consequentialism.[100] Generally speaking, under that view, the moral harm from torture or something close to torture can and must be balanced against the good that can only be achieved through enhanced interrogation to obtain intelligence that can stop another terrorist attack.[101] Under this view, because terrorism undermines the common good for every community in the world, both in terms of the lives of constituencies from different nations in any terrorist attack in a metropolitan area, and in terms of the disruptions to international actions and the psychic fear that likely results in constituencies everywhere, there can be a calculus that justifies enhanced interrogation in carefully circumscribed situations narrowly tailored to obtain actionable intelligence.

The absolutist view and the consequential view are diametrically opposed. They simply cannot engage with each other. Therefore, unless one view is proven correct and the other wrong, moral reasoning does not conclusively guide the legal advisor who has to make a decision about whether to authorize waterboarding.[102]

Moral critics who accept consequentialism may nevertheless object to waterboarding. They argue that, even accepting consequentialism as the right approach, the moral costs of waterboarding are simply too high and always outweigh the benefits. They say enhanced interrogation does not produce useful intelligence.[103] That is a factual claim that is not ordinarily for a legal advisor to decide. If advised by military experts that enhanced interrogation produces results, he should accept that view unless there is evidence that the experts are acting in bad faith or have clearly formed a view without foundation.

that waterboarding was torture. And I think—whatever the legal rationales were used, it was a mistake"); SANDS, *supra* note 47, at 144 ("[V]iolations of the Torture Convention, cannot be justified on the grounds that they produced useful material."). *See also* WILLIAM SCHULZ, TAINTED LEGACY 170 (2003) ("The irony is that torture stains the torturer almost as much as it wounds his victim.").

[99] MARK OSIEL, THE END OF RECIPROCITY: TERROR, TORTURE AND THE LAW OF WAR 164 (2009) (explaining Waldron's argument that interrogators should not attempt to "push the envelope" by using techniques that approach torture, even if those techniques do not reach the legal threshold for torture because "law's gravitational force rightly extends beyond its formal letter").

[100] *See generally* ALAN DERSHOWITZ, SHOUTING FIRE: CIVIL LIBERTIES IN A TURBULENT AGE (2002); ALAN DERSHOWITZ, WHY TERRORISM WORKS: UNDERSTANDING THE THREAT, RESPONDING TO THE CHALLENGE (2002); ERIC A. POSNER & ADRIAN VERMEULE, TERROR IN THE BALANCE 187 (2007).

[101] *See* Sanford H. Kadish, *Torture, the State and the Individual*, 23 ISR. L. REV. 345, 346 (1989). *See also* SANDS, *supra* note 47, at 224 n.1 ("Ex post following another terrorist attack that might have been prevented through the exercise of coercive interrogation—the price of my scruple might simply seem too high. This is a risk I am prepared to take, but frankly, a majority of fellow citizens is unlikely to concur.").

[102] POSNER & VERMEULE, *supra* note 101, at 187 (noting that the "absolutist deontological view . . . may ignore [the consequentialist] argument").

[103] SCHULZ, *supra* note 98, at 163.

Critics argue that even if waterboarding produces useful intelligence, the risks of abuses are too great, and they believe the abuses at Abu Ghraib were in part the result of lax restrictions on interrogation.[104] This claim ignores that fact that the officers at Abu Ghraib violated military restrictions and broke the law. The fear of a slippery slope also need not be addressed by banning waterboarding and by forsaking the benefits that inure when it is absolutely necessary. The proper course of action to prevent abuses is stronger oversight and training of officers. The U.S. military made these and other operational recommendations after Abu Ghraib.[105] Since that time, there has not been another repeat of Abu Ghraib, even though waterboarding was permitted throughout the years of the Bush administration. This analysis suggests that even consequential moral reasoning does not conclusively guide legal advisors when deciding whether to authorize waterboarding.

Resorting to considerations of national interest also does not offer clear guidance. One view, expressed by Colin Powell, argues that enhanced interrogation techniques undermine U.S. credibility and its soft power to garner international support for its national security efforts, and endanger U.S. troops abroad who are exposed to reciprocal harsh treatment.[106] On another view, stated by President Bush, he only authorized waterboarding three high-level Al-Qaeda detainees out of the thousands of suspected terrorists who were interrogated, because he believed those three detainees had actionable intelligence, and all other interrogation techniques had failed.[107] According to President Bush, waterboarding those three detainees succeeded in extracting information that likely prevented other terrorist attacks in the United States and elsewhere by Al-Qaeda,[108] who do not respect international law and the common good.[109] The correct balance of national interests between the two views is ultimately a judgment call.

6. Guidance to Advisors

As discussed above, legalism is vague on what constitutes torture, considerations of morality—if one accepts that torture can be balanced against other moral concerns—do not provide a universal answer, and national interests can be appraised differently in many situations. Whether or not to authorize waterboarding in a specific instance therefore requires judgment.

[104] *See id.* at 200–03 (discussing and responding to slippery slope arguments).

[105] Schlesinger Report, Final Report of the Independent Panel to Review Department of Defense Detention Operations (Aug. 2004), *in* Torture Papers, *supra* note 34, at 909, 951–54.

[106] *See* Memorandum from Colin L. Powell, to Counsel to the President, Draft Decision Memorandum for the President on the Applicability of the Geneva Convention to the Conflict in Afghanistan, *in* Torture Papers, *supra* note 34, at 122–25.

[107] *See* Bush, *supra* note 23, at 171.

[108] *Id.*

[109] *See* Yoo, *supra* note 15, at 23 (noting Al-Qaeda's failure to observe international law and values); Goldsmith, *supra* note 1, at 71–76 (describing security threats to the United States).

The issue then is whether the legal advisor or his government official is best suited to make that judgment. The author submits that in so far as a government has a track record of generally not abusing its authority, decisions in hard cases that involve national security ought to be made by officials and not their legal advisors. Key officials have access to information that the advisor does not, and the officials have relevant policy or military expertise that the advisor does not. Ultimately, elected officials also have direct responsibilities for the security of their constituencies that the advisor does not. All these reasons favor granting legal authorization and permitting the official to determine, as a matter of policy, whether waterboarding should be carried out. The advisor can and should prescribe restrictions and require monitoring of the executive to prevent abuse and to authorize waterboarding only when it is strictly necessary. This is especially important because many interrogations take place secretly. However, once those checks are assured, there are strong practical reasons to authorize waterboarding or other similar techniques that may come close to torture but do not clearly constitute torture.

Applying this analysis to the 2002 and 2005 Specific Interrogation Memoranda and the 2005 Combined Interrogation Memorandum, one can conclude that these memoranda, while better than the 2002, 2003, and 2004 Blanket Interrogation Memoranda because they are less overbroad, are nevertheless not beyond reproach. There is a narrower approach that could still have achieved the operational purposes of waterboarding and preserved executive discretion to make good faith assessments of moral need and national interest in deciding whether to order waterboarding, while further minimizing the risks of abuse.

OLC could have proposed that in every instance of waterboarding, or at least with every detainee that officials are considering waterboarding, intelligence supervisors were required to obtain specific authorization from the legal advisors. This narrower approach would ensure that legal advisors make individual determinations in every instance as to whether waterboarding falls into the proper scope of executive discretion that is bounded by limits of legalism, moral reasoning, and national interests. This narrower approach would also enable legal advisors to remain actively involved in the operationalization of their authorizations to waterboard so that they can monitor the implementation of their orders to ensure compliance and to adjust their authorizations if necessary.

The checks against abuse could have been further enhanced if the advisors insisted that interrogations were videotaped and appropriately classified, and subject to review by legal advisors or even judges when the information contained in them was less sensitive. This provides a layer of oversight to correct and deter illegal conduct, without compromising national security or intelligence through information leaks or delays from legalist review in operational situations that require secrecy and immediate action.

Critics may argue that videotaping interrogations would have a chilling effect on officials conducting them. However, it would not be such a bad thing to deter officials who would otherwise act unlawfully. As for officials who seek to remain within the confines of their legal authorization, adequate training in interrogation and education about the purpose of videotaping should ameliorate their concerns.

Individual authorizations would not have imposed an unbearable administrative burden because only very few detainees are waterboarded. President Bush has stated that he authorized the waterboarding of only three out of thousands of detainees. Officials might nevertheless be concerned that legal advisors would not be able to make rapid decisions in the heat of operations when authorization to waterboard a detainee is necessary. However, it does not appear that the decision to waterboard any of the three Al-Qaeda detainees was made hastily, so that concern seems academic. In any event, in a ticking-time-bomb situation, if the legal advisor has prepared in advance a memorandum on the criteria that must be met before he will authorize waterboarding in any specific case, it should not take very long for officials to appraise him of relevant facts and for the advisor to ascertain whether the criteria he has established in advance are satisfied in that situation. Finally, in a truly unforeseen emergency, the President can always choose to act without explicit legal authorization and explain his actions to other domestic elites after the emergency has passed for them.

7. Qualifications

The foregoing discussion addresses how a legal advisor could decide whether or not to authorize waterboarding if he took into account only the prescriptions against torture. This exercise was intended to illustrate how the theory of international law would apply specific prescriptions to limited facts. It chose to apply prescriptions regulating torture to waterboarding as a difficult test case. This exercise was not intended to exonerate or condemn the interrogation memoranda produced by the Office of Legal Counsel, in large part because a complete appraisal of those memoranda would require many more pages to consider all applicable domestic and international laws, as well as other shared expectations of appropriate conduct, including prescriptions on cruel, inhuman, and degrading treatment. Although such a complete analysis can be carried out using this book's theory of international, just as the discussion of waterboarding in light of prescriptions against torture was conducted here, a comprehensive appraisal of those memoranda is not the focus of this book and must be left to another day.

The analysis in the section above was also based on factual assumptions made relying on statements from U.S. officials and declassified government documents. This reliance is reasonable, in the absence of proof they lacked credibility. Further, the impulse to make self-serving statements is diminished in documents that were classified when they were written, because there is less risk of the analysis becoming public and subject to external scrutiny.

For the sake of further illustrating how the justificatory view of international law might apply to different situations, some of the factual assumptions are changed in the analysis that follows. Suppose waterboarding did cause prolonged mental suffering, and the CIA through its interrogation experiences knew that. Waterboarding would under these circumstances be illegal under any textual interpretation of the Torture Convention as enacted into U.S. law. This is a harder case in which to justify authorizing waterboarding. In these scenarios, waterboarding is both illegal and highly immoral because it constitutes torture.

In such an instance, the legal advisor ought to advise the President that waterboarding is illegal. There is an especially strong reason to do so because the Military Commissions Act of 2006 provides a defense from suit for any official who interrogates terrorists that he did not know the interrogation technique was unlawful, especially where he relied on the advice of counsel in good faith.[110]

However, in the absence of an operational emergency, the executive branch may also seek legislative amendments explicitly authorizing waterboarding, thereby placing the technique on legal footing under domestic law, although this may not render waterboarding either moral or legal under international law.[111]

The President may also decide to act illegally by authorizing waterboarding, and face the consequences for so doing, if he appraises that there is an overriding moral reason or national interest to carry out waterboarding.[112] The President may decide, for example, that a high-level Al-Qaeda operative has crucial information to stop an imminent terrorist attack, and waterboarding is the only way to obtain information that can then be swiftly corroborated and the attack can be stopped.[113] In this case, the government official authorizing torture against the legal advice of his lawyers should satisfy himself that immediate national security needs, and the moral demands of saving his constituencies from the death and suffering that inevitability accompany a successful terrorist attack, outweigh the immorality of torture and the damage to international standing and relations when other states realize that torture was carried out.

Suppose, further, that a legal advisor has received credible information that government officials wish to carry out waterboarding in situations unwarranted on national interest grounds, such as simply to inflict recrimination on terrorists, or are doing so without a reasonable basis to believe that the detainee has useful intelligence, or in violation of the strict controls that are operationally required when using waterboarding as an enhanced interrogation technique. The legal advisor should not authorize such acts. He should also advise the President against acting illegally because there could be no moral justification for so doing. Should the President insist on proceeding, the legal advisor should also consider resigning in protest. In extreme cases of abuse, the advisor should consider resigning in as public a fashion as permitted by law, if doing so would not compromise national security, not unlike a co-conspirator's "noisy withdrawal" from a conspiracy to make clear he has no further part in the scheme. The purpose of publicity is to draw attention to

[110] 42 U.S.C. § 2000dd-1(a).

[111] *Cf.* Bush, *supra* note 23, at 177 (arguing that at his urging Congress passed legislation making the U.S. terrorism surveillance program legal).

[112] *See supra* pt. I (suggesting that an advisor may counsel his official to act illegally if there are overriding reasons to ignore the law).

[113] *Cf.* Bush, *supra* note 23, at 164 (acknowledging that the Terrorist Surveillance Program in the United States was legally controversial but nevertheless authorizing it because President Bush "believed it was necessary" to combat terrorism).

illegal and immoral acts of government officials so that constituents and courts can decide if officials should be held accountable for their actions.

This strategy is justified both by moral considerations as well as by the need to effectively restrain decisionmakers. If, acting within the bureaucracy, the advisor claims that the techniques used are prohibited and immoral torture but is ignored (and therefore ineffective), a noisy withdrawal increases the likelihood that he will be effective. If successful, he will mobilize constituents to accept his claims and to exert influence over officials to stop torturing terrorists.

III. CONCLUSION

The foregoing discussion has illustrated how the justificatory theory of international law provides legal advisors with guidance about how to make decisions that justify the regulatory claim that international law makes. By contrasting the easy case of Abu Ghraib with the difficult case of waterboarding, it is hoped that this chapter has shown how the account of international law offered parses different decisions that legal advisors are asked to make.

Like other decisionmakers, legal advisors should balance the general morality of legalism with the specific morality of what they are asked to authorize, as well as the necessity of achieving some degree of effectiveness in their decisions. To properly balance these competing considerations, they should account for whether ultimate decisionmaking authority in an international problem properly resides in advisors charged with interpreting international law, or with other officials responsible to their constituents or who have the expertise in policymaking or other fields necessary to make a fully informed decision with input from their legal advisors. In situations where legal advisors have a less operational role, they should confine their advice to demarcating the limits of action, taking into account legalism, as guided by moral reasoning and national interest where legalism is ambiguous. It is then for officials to make operational decisions to act within that advice, or even to choose to act illegally and explain their actions to constituents or judges, and face the consequences of their actions.

This approach may not sit well with readers who are cynical about the integrity or judgment of officials. Such cynicism can have a strong emotional pull in a popular culture that cherishes aphorisms such as "absolute power corrupts absolutely," and in a legal culture that takes checks and balances from separation of powers very seriously. Skepticism about human nature is understandable.

However, checks and balances are not without costs. They delay or even make impracticable executive action to take measures that may be operationally urgent and necessary. The costs of inaction or impeded action can result in terrorist attacks and other disasters.

Therefore, the author would urge readers to consider whether there is proof, or at least evidence, that government officials acted in bad faith or with poor judgment. If such evidence is strong, the justificatory account of international law would require greater checks against abuse than proposed here in the context of waterboarding. However, if the evidence is weak or nonexistent, then perhaps the approach to waterboarding suggested here is appropriate. Officials were elected for their judgment and to represent and lead constituents. The legal system must let them do their job, within legal limits. If they do a poor job, constituents can elect other candidates at the next election, or even press for criminal sanctions if there is a basis to believe that the officials acted illegally.

Deciding when to authorize harsh interrogation techniques, or when to go to war knowing that people will die as a result of that decision—the topic of the next chapter—is one of the most difficult decisions any official or advisor has to make.[114] Some readers may feel that the approach here may lead to outcomes that instinctively strike them as not the decisions they would make. Indeed, the author would not necessarily find it easy to authorize waterboarding if given the authority to do so. Yet, we all would do well to remember that these decisions are difficult because the stakes of acting and not acting are both high.

Jeremy Waldron has published in graphic detail a first person account of harsh detention conditions to draw attention to one set of considerations in making difficult choices about executive power. For balance and to illustrate why it is truly a difficult decision, this chapter concludes by quoting both Waldron's selected first person account of detention, and a first person account of September 11, 2001, that motivated controversial decisions by the Bush administration, including waterboarding.

An unnamed FBI agent recounted what he saw in detention facilities:

> I entered interview rooms to find a detainee chained hand and foot in a fetal position to the floor, with no chair, food or water. Most times they had urinated or defecated on themselves, and had been left there for 18–24 hours or more. . . . On another occasion. . . . the detainee was almost unconscious on the floor, with a pile of hair next to him. He had apparently literally been pulling his own hair out throughout the night.[115]

Theressa Tobin, a New York Police Department officer, remembers these details about September 11:

> There was a huge explosion and massive fireballs. . . . Try to imagine these huge windows breaking into shards and falling to the ground. We would be walking along, and then crash—glass and debris were falling everywhere. . . . Some people jumped alone and others in groups and at one point someone said twenty people held hands and jumped. . . . I saw a man who looked as if he were scaling down the outside of the building. He made it down at least one floor and then, whether he lost his grip or it got too hot, I don't know, but he came flying down.[116]

[114] *See* Bush, *supra* note 23, at 184 ("I felt the gravity of the decision [to invade Afghanistan]. I knew the war would bring death and sorrow. Every life lost would devastate a family forever . . . My anxiety about the sacrifice was mitigated by the urgency of the cause.").

[115] Waldron, *supra* note 98, at 8.

[116] Theresa Tobin, *A Terrorist Attack: Response and Reflection*, *in* Perspectives on 9/11, at 3, 5 (El-Ayouty ed., 2004).

The justificatory theory of international law presented here ultimately attempts to provide a methodical way for legal advisors and officials to chart a reasonable course that minimizes the likelihood of both situations described above.

Even if readers disagree with the proposed balance among specific and general moral considerations and effectiveness, the justificatory theory of international law nevertheless is useful. For decisionmakers and scholars focused on the morality or immorality of torture, the justificatory theory highlights that whatever their views about the morality of torture in exigent circumstances,[117] they ought consider, additionally, the morality of promoting prohibitions against torture simply because they are prescriptions and part of the minimum global order.[118] For decisionmakers and scholars who argue that Bush administration officials should not have authorized waterboarding because this violated international laws, the justificatory theory bolsters their point of view by showing that the reason for not violating those international laws is not just that they are laws, but that these laws promote the common good which everyone has a general moral obligation to support.[119] However, the theory also shows that arguments against waterboarding based on international laws against torture have their limits because legalism does not definitively establish that it falls into the definition of torture under those laws. Therefore, decisionmakers ought to engage in moral reasoning to choose their definition of torture and to decide whether waterboarding falls into that definition. Accordingly, even if readers disagree with this chapter's position on waterboarding, this book's framework for analysis helps legal advisors consider the issue more fully when they have to decide whether or not to authorize interrogators to use this technique.

[117] Both critics and supporters of enhanced interrogation techniques have debated the morality of torture, but they have not considered the general morality of prescriptions prohibiting torture that is independent of the content of the prescriptions. *See* Posner & Vermeule, *supra* note 101 at 186–93 (considering morality of torture, but not addressing whether international prescriptions against torture have any value independent of their content); *id.* at 207 (considering legal regulation but neither addressing international prescriptions nor the inherent value of regulation); Ginbar, *supra* note 97, at 10–154 (discussing morality of torture but not the inherent morality of prescriptions about torture that is not contingent on their content).

[118] Waldron's thesis comes close to this argument, but ultimately does not make it. *See* Waldron, *supra* note 98 at 257 ("Undermining an archetype will usually have an effect on the general morale of the law in a given area. It may become much harder for us to hang on to a proper sense of why the surrounding law is important and to convey that sense to the public."). A close reading of his work reveals his is concerned ultimately with the public's sense of the *normative values in law*. *Id.* at 260 (concluding that his analysis of the relevance of law provides a "clear and more substantive sense of what we aspire to in our jurisprudence: a body of law and a Rule of Law that renounce savagery . . ."). In contrast, the focus on the general morality of law helps decisionmakers consider, additionally, the *normative value of law*, independent of its content, because it coordinates actions and stabilizes expectations, whatever those expectations may be.

[119] *Cf.*, Ginbar, *supra* note 97, at 270–301 (discussing content of legalist prescriptions but not addressing their value independent of their content).

8 Officials

I. THEORY

Having applied the justificatory theory of international law to judges, arbitrators, regulators, and legal advisors, this chapter conducts a final test of the theory by examining how the theory offers guidance to government officials. This chapter uses "officials" to refer to key officials of the executive branch, such as the president, prime minister, and top cabinet ministers, when they act in international problems on behalf of their state. Thus, even though legal advisors and regulators are officials of the executive branch, they do not usually fall within the scope of this chapter.

Like other decisionmakers, officials ought to strive to balance the general moral duty to promote the common good through legalism, the specific moral duty to balance the values at stake in an international problem, and the need for a minimum level of effectiveness on the claims they make in the international decisionmaking process to address that problem. Perhaps uniquely to officials, however, considerations of specific morality and effectiveness ought to weigh more heavily in their deliberations.

Officials have a particularly weighty obligation to promote the preferred values of their constituents when considering the specific morality of any course of action. This is because, more than any other decisionmaker, elected leaders and other key government officials owe a direct responsibility for the well-being of their constituents, whom they represent internationally and from whom they derive their authority to lead.

Officials also have to be particularly concerned about the effectiveness of their claims, because they are often the final decisionmaker for a government in an international problem. Having decided what claim best promotes the specific values at stake, they would fail to discharge their duty to their constituents if their claims are totally ineffective and do not secure the desired outcomes.

As a result of the emphasis that officials ought to place on specific morality and effectiveness, it is often all too easy to slip into ad hoc decisionmaking that undervalues the common good. This would be a mistake. World order is necessary for peaceful international relations and international economic activities that benefit constituents. Therefore, officials ought not take actions that unjustifiably depart from legalism and damage the common good. Where they decide that there are good reasons to deviate from prescriptions, officials ought not claim exceptions for themselves only. Such a strategy encourages other decisionmakers to do the same, or else it risks other decisionmakers misapplying the adjustment to the prescription. Instead, officials ought to clarify their new interpretation of the existing prescription or propose an entirely new one, specifying the reasons for the change and its limits. Other decisionmakers can then respond with their own claims until there is a shared consensus about appropriate conduct. This process allows prescriptions to adjust to changing conditions without undermining legalism entirely and leaving unregulated lacunae in the international legal system.

II. PRAXIS

The justificatory theory is here applied to officials in three wars. This chapter contrasts the 1990 war against Iraq by multilateral partners, the 1999 bombing of the Federal Republic of Yugoslavia (FRY, or Serbia) by NATO, and the 2003 invasion of Iraq by the United States and its coalition partners.

The 1990 Gulf War and 2003 invasion of Iraq, which bookend the major wars from the end of the Cold War to the present time, and the 1999 NATO campaign against Serbia are all signal incidents in the international law of war. As UN Secretary General Kofi Annan noted:

> [T]he 1990 Gulf War was the beginning of a period of the exercise of power which called into question the use of force principles in the Charter in a variety of circumstances: the reversal of aggression in Kuwait; the imposition of peace in the Balkans; the imperative of humanitarian intervention in Kosovo; and regime change in Iraq.[1]

The authorization of military force in 1990 was the first time the Security Council did so since the end of the Cold War, and the second time in its history that it did so, the first being the authorization of force in the Korean War.[2] The NATO

[1] Kofi Annan, *Forward in* Ralph Zacklin, The United Nations Secretariat and the Use of Force in a Unipolar World. Power v. Principle xiii (2010).

[2] *Id.*

invasion was only the second time that NATO had been activated to wage a military campaign. The 2003 invasion is the last major war that the United States, or any country, has waged at the time of this writing.

There have been other important military operations, including the invasion of Afghanistan, several other bombings of Iraq between 1990 and 2003, air campaigns in Libya in 2011, and international military deployments in Rwanda and Somalia. However, the three wars covered in this chapter provide especially good comparisons to test this book's account of the international legal system.

The officials from the international coalition that liberated Kuwait in the 1990 invasion properly balanced general morality, specific morality, and effectiveness. They obtained Security Council authorization, and their invasion was legal and legitimate.

NATO-country officials departed from legalism when deciding to bomb Serbia in 1999 without Security Council authorization because this violated the prohibition on the use of force except in self-defense. However, their deviation from their general moral duty to promote the common good through legalism was justified by the specific moral duty to protect Muslim Albanians from the mass killings that Serb forces were carrying out. Had NATO officials clarified then that they were adjusting the law of force to permit humanitarian intervention, they would have helped to minimize damage to the common good because their clarifications would have constrained future interpretations of their actions. However, they did not do so. Their omission unjustifiably damaged the legalist struts of world order, creating an unregulated feedback loop in which U.S. officials later relied on the 1999 bombing of Serbia as precedent for the 2003 invasion of Iraq even though the two situations were dissimilar.

U.S. and UK officials deviated from strict fidelity to legalism when they stretched a Security Council Resolution from the 1990 Gulf War to claim that they were authorized in invading Iraq in 2003. In retrospect, it has become clear that Saddam Hussein did not have weapons of mass destruction. This appears to indicate that the 2003 invasion of Iraq was also not justified by the specific moral consideration that required officials to protect their constituents against attacks using weapons of mass destruction. However, if observers believe that officials believed in good faith that Iraq had not disarmed, in light of the attacks on the United States on September 11, 2001, one might appraise the decision to invade Iraq as nonetheless reasonable. Looking to the future, in order to discharge the continuing general moral obligation to promote the common good through legalism, officials should clarify adjustments to the law of force that enable decisionmakers to protect their security interests while restraining unwarranted aggression and minimizing the risk of poor judgments of military risk that lead to unnecessary wars.

A. The 1990 Gulf War

On August 2, 1990, Iraq illegally invaded Kuwait. With the end of the Iran-Iraq war, Iraq's tensions with Kuwait had previously intensified. Iraq had a territorial dispute with Kuwait over two islands off Kuwait's border. Iraq declined Kuwait's suggestion to refer the dispute to the ICJ. The United States had not officially taken a position on this border dispute. Iraq's finances were in shambles. These problems were deepened because one of its main sources of revenue was the sale of its oil, but oil prices fell from $20 to $14 a barrel from January to June 1990. On July 18, Iraq's Deputy Prime Minister and Foreign Minister, Tariq Aziz, issued a memorandum to the Arab League accusing Kuwait of stealing oil from the Rumaila fields contiguous to Iraq and Kuwait, and conspiring to lower oil prices. Aziz argued that these actions in combination constituted an act of aggression. Barely two weeks later, Iraqi tanks rolled into Kuwait.[3]

In response to Iraq's illegal invasion of Kuwait, government officials around the world acted in concert, galvanizing a multilateral military force that repelled Iraq and restored Kuwait's sovereignty. These actions were political, moral, and legal in nature. The responses of the United States, the United Kingdom, their allies, and the Security Council thus illustrate the role of legalism alongside morality and politics in international disputes.

It was evening in New York when the invasion occurred. The U.S. ambassador to the UN, Thomas Pickering, was having dinner with his British counterpart, Crispin Tickell. Restaurant staff were contacted urgently, and Pickering took a call in the restaurant's kitchen, informing him of the invasion. He left immediately for the U.S. mission, where his team of advisors drafted Security Council resolutions in consultation with Washington. Pickering tracked Mohammed Abulhassan, the Kuwait ambassador, to the Russian Tea Room, where he was dining with Arab friends. By the time Pickering escorted Abulhassan to the U.S. mission opposite the UN Headquarters along the East River of Manhattan, the first resolution was drafted.[4]

The full Council assembled that evening in the consultation room. After eight hours of negotiations, and communications between each ambassador and his capital, the emergency meeting concluded with a resolution demanding that Iraq withdraw immediately from Kuwait.[5] Resolution 660 stated that the Council was "alarmed by the invasion of Kuwait on 2 August 1990 by the military forces of Iraq," "determine[ed] that there exists a breach of international peace and security," and, "[a]cting under Articles 39 and 40 of the Charter of the United Nations," demanded Iraq's immediate and unconditional withdrawal.[6]

[3] *See* David M. Malone, The International Struggle Over Iraq: Politics in the UN Security Council, 1980–2005, at 56–57 (2006); Chinmaya R. Gharekhan, The Horseshoe Table: An Inside View of the UN Security Council 44–45 (2006). *See also* Kaiyan Homi Kaikobad, *Self Defence, Enforcement Action and the Gulf Wars*, 63 Brit. Y.B. Int'l L. 300, 302–03 (1992) (discussing the history of the conflict between Iraq and Kuwait going back to Kuwait's independence in 1961).

[4] *See* Gharekhan, *supra* note 3, at 44; David L. Bosco, Five to Rule Them All: The UN Security Council and the Making of the Modern World 155 (2009); Alexander Thompson, Channels of Power: The UN Security Council and U.S. Statecraft in Iraq 48–51 (2010).

[5] Bosco, *supra* note 4, at 155–56.

[6] S.C. Res. 660, U.N. Doc. S/RES/660 (Aug. 2, 1990).

Resolution 660 was a political act with a desired geopolitical outcome, that is, the withdrawal of Iraqi forces. The process of obtaining the resolution was also political. Britain and France backed the United States. China was less supportive but did not obstruct the resolution. The nonpermanent members voted in favor, except for Yemen, which did not participate in the vote and whose president was friendly with Saddam Hussein.[7]

But the resolution also claimed to be a legal act. It also referred not to political will, military might, or values as the basis of its prescription that Iraq withdraw. The explicit basis for its prescription was legalist: Articles 39 and 40 of the UN Charter. Its implicit reasoning was legalist, that the invasion had met the threshold requirement for Chapter VII legal authority, a breach of international peace and security. The Security Council had also followed its internal legalist procedure of voting in order to act and provided a legalistic justification for its prescription.

The next morning, Pickering flew to Washington for instructions from President George H.W. Bush and his national security team. Washington decided to continue pursuing the UN route. Bush then flew to Colorado for a planned conference with UK Prime Minister Margaret Thatcher. In her memoirs, Thatcher recalled that she tried to dissuade Bush from relying on the Council. Instead, once the Council had issued its resolution condemning the invasion and recognizing the principle of collective security, the United States and Britain should proceed with whatever actions they deemed fit without further Council authorization. She explained:

> I did not like unnecessary resort to the UN, because it suggested that sovereign states lacked the moral authority to act on their own behalf. If it became accepted that force could only be used—even in self-defence—when the United Nations approved, neither Britain's interests nor those of international justice and order would be served. The UN was a useful—for some matters vital—forum. But it was hardly the nucleus of a new world order. And there was still no substitute for the leadership of the United States.[8]

Thatcher did not appear to regard the issue of military force as principally a legal one. It was a question of "moral authority,"[9] international justice and order, and national interest. Legal authority was not even mentioned.

However, international law as a system depends on claims by decisionmakers that prescriptions are authoritative because they comport with legalist and other shared expectations of appropriate conduct, and that those prescriptions are neither sustained nor destroyed by the views of one actor alone, even if it is an important one. At Washington's instruction, Pickering continued from August through November to obtain a series of increasingly stronger resolutions from the Security Council.[10]

[7] *See* Bosco, *supra* note 4, at 156.

[8] Margaret Thatcher, The Downing Street Years 821 (1993).

[9] *Id.* at 821.

[10] *See* S.C. Res. 661, U.N. Doc. S/RES/661 (Aug. 6, 1990); S.C. Res. 662, U.N. Doc. S/RES/662 (Aug. 9, 1990); S.C. Res. 664, U.N. Doc. S/RES/664 (Aug. 18, 1990); S.C. Res. 665, U.N. Doc. S/RES/665

After Iraq ignored Resolution 660 and did not withdraw from Kuwait, on August 6, 1990, the Security Council issued Resolution 661, with Cuba and Yemen abstaining. The language of Resolution 661 was just as legalistic as 660. It "affirm[ed] the inherent right of individual and collective self-defense," not as a moral right, but as a legal right "in accordance with Article 51 of the Charter." The Security Council here referred to its prior prescription, by explicitly "[r]eaffirming its resolution of 660 (1990) of 2 August 1990." Resolution 661 ordered member states to impose comprehensive sanctions, and the reason it provided for this order was explicitly legalist: the Security Council stated it was "[a]cting under Chapter VII of the Charter."[11]

On August 25, 1990, Resolution 665 was passed, with Yemen and Cuba voting against it, calling upon member states to use military force to enforce an embargo in the Gulf. The reasoning justifying the prescription in Resolution 665 was again legalistic. It did not explicitly invoke Chapter VII nor, indeed, any provision of the UN Charter. However, Resolution 665 did explicitly refer to the prior decision of Resolution 661 to impose sanctions, and thereby derived its implementing authority from Resolution 661 and that prior invocation of Chapter VII.[12]

Resolution 662, adopted previously on August 9, was more unusual from the standpoint of legalist reasoning. In that resolution, the Council "decide[d] that annexation of Kuwait by Iraq under any form and whatever pretext has no legal validity, and is considered null and void."[13] This claim is remarkable because it does not explicitly refer to any legal source of the Council's authority to make determinations of legal validity. Under the UN Charter, legal disputes are the province of the ICJ. Article 92 provides that it is the principal judicial organ of the UN Charter.[14] Article 96 provides that the Security Council may request an advisory opinion on "any legal question."[15] Article 36 of the ICJ Statute provides that it has jurisdiction when states consent to "any question of international law."[16] In contrast, nothing in Chapter VII of the UN Charter authorizes the Security Council to make any legal determination. Instead, it is charged with maintaining peace and security and is authorized to take measures to do so. Arguably, making a legal determination could

(Aug. 25, 1990); S.C. Res. 666, U.N. Doc. S/RES/666 (Sept. 13, 1990); S.C. Res. 667, U.N. Doc. S/RES/667 (Sept. 16, 1990); S.C. Res. 669, U.N. Doc. S/RES/669 (Sept. 24, 1990); S.C. Res. 674, U.N. Doc. S/RES/674 (Oct. 29, 1990); S.C. Res. 677, U.N. Doc. S/RES/677 (Nov. 28, 1990); S.C. Res. 678, U.N. Doc. S/RES/678 (Nov. 29, 1990).

[11] S.C. Res. 661, *supra* note 10. *See also* Jeremy Matam Farrall, United Nations Sanctions and the Rule of Law 261–82 (2007) (describing the sanctions regime imposed by Resolution 661).

[12] S.C. Res. 665, *supra* note 10, pmbl.

[13] S.C. Res. 662, *supra* note 10.

[14] UN Charter art. 92 ("The International Court of Justice shall be the principal judicial organ of the United Nations. It shall function in accordance with the annexed Statute which is based upon the Statute of the Permanent Court of International Justice and forms an integral part of the present Charter.").

[15] *Id.* art. 96; Statute of the International Court of Justice art. 65, June 26, 1945, 33 U.N.T.S. 993 [hereinafter ICJ Statute] (stating the court may give an advisory opinion on "any legal question").

[16] ICJ Statute, *supra* note 15, art. 36(2)(b).

be one such measure, but that is not an obvious interpretation of Chapter VII in light of Articles 92 and 96 of the UN Charter.

In any event, the vote in favor of Resolution 662 was unanimous.[17] There were no objections raised in the UN General Assembly. As far as this author can tell, no scholar writing in English has criticized Resolution 662 as *ultra vires*. These facts suggest that the legal authority of the Security Council is not always based solely on legalistic claims it makes from the Charter, but also on the acquiescence of decisionmakers to its claims to authority in particular incidents. In some cases, as with Resolution 662, legal authority rests on the shared faith of other decisionmakers in the Security Council's authority. This shared expectation is manifested and reinforced by acceptance of the resolution that arguably exceeded the legalist authority conferred on the Security Council by the UN Charter. The international response to Resolution 662 validates this book's hypothesis that legalism exists not just in legalistic reasoning and procedures, but also in informal shared expectations.

To be legalistic is not the same as achieving effectiveness. Iraq ignored sanctions and the Security Council. It continued to occupy Kuwait. Thus, it quickly became clear to the United States that Iraq would only give up its campaign if forced to do so by a military operation against it. As the super-hegemon at the time, the United States had the operational capability to invade Iraq. It had the ability to ignore the legal prohibitions on the use of force contained in Articles 2(4) and 42 of the UN Charter. But it did not do so. Instead, the Bush administration set about obtaining Security Council authorization for its invasion, Operation Desert Storm, with Pickering working tirelessly and Secretary of State James Baker reaching out to his counterparts of Security Council member states.[18]

On November 29, the Security Council passed Resolution 678 with China abstaining and Cuba and Yemen opposed. Resolution 678 authorized member states to use military force against Iraq if it did not withdraw by January 15, 1991, and fully comply with prior resolutions.[19] This is a legal document within the central case of international law.[20] It claimed to provide legal authorization to use force. The basis of the claim was explicitly stated as "Chapter VII of the Charter." Resolution 678 also recalled the Council's "duties and responsibilities under the Charter of the United Nations for the maintenance and preservation of international peace and security." The Security Council here reaffirmed its prior resolutions against Iraq, and it issued the new resolution to "secure full compliance with its decisions."[21]

[17] *See* Malone, *supra* note 3, at 63 (noting that the annexation of Kuwait "had clearly exceeded the tolerance even of Cuba and Yemen. . . .").

[18] *See id.* at 67; Gharekhan, *supra* note 3, at 46–62 (describing in detail diplomatic maneuvers leading up to the resolution); Bosco, *supra* note 4, at 157–63.

[19] *See* S.C. Res. 678, *supra* note 10, ¶ 2.

[20] *Cf.* Malone, *supra* note 3, at 69 ("SCR 678, [was] almost certainly the most important text agreed by the Security Council in the immediate post-Cold War period. . . .").

[21] S.C. Res 678, *supra* note 10, pmbl.

Resolution 678 was also adopted pursuant to the procedures of the Security Council in the UN Charter. It exhibited all the key traits of legalism: it claimed to be authoritative, and decisionmakers accepted that claim; it used legalistic reasoning to make that claim; and it followed established legalistic procedures to reach its prescriptive decision.

The legalistic nature of the Security Council's decisionmaking was further confirmed by the manner in which its prescriptive claims were communicated to world audiences. The UK House of Commons expressed "full support for British forces in the Gulf . . . as authorized by United Nations Security Council Resolution 678."[22] As early as August 1990, Bush stated to Thatcher and NATO Secretary General Manfred Wörner that the will of the world would be to "enforce these sanctions."[23] After Resolution 678, Bush stated to the press that Iraq would only be permitted to rejoin the world community after "its full compliance with all twelve Security Council Resolutions."[24] These communications are replete with prescriptive words, such as "authorized," "enforce," and "compliance."

Although the account of this central case of international law not contingent on its effectiveness, Resolution 678, together with its associated resolutions, were effective in several important ways. Resolution 678 provided an explicit legal basis for the air campaign at 3 a.m. local time on January 15, 1991. Two days after ground forces were launched on February 24, Baghdad Radio announced that Iraqi troops were withdrawing from Kuwait in accordance with Resolution 660. The United States was able to continue its invasion by using the legalist reasoning that Iraq had not complied with all 12 of the other resolutions that the Security Council had passed.[25]

President George H.W. Bush also revealed in his memoirs that the United States did not advance to Baghdad to overthrow Saddam Hussein because in his view the Security Council Resolutions did not authorize that objective.[26] Norman Schwarzkopf, commander of the military operation, also stated that, aside from a political concern that the military coalition would have fallen apart if the United States pressed onto Iraq, "point number one" was that the resolutions "[d]id not say one word about going into Iraq. . . ."[27] On March 2, a formal ceasefire was negotiated under Resolution 686, which required Iraq to "[a]ccept . . . liability under international law" for war damages and cease hostilities.[28]

Thus, the Security Council resolutions in response to Iraq's invasion of Kuwait represented the central case of international law because they were prescriptions made in accord with shared expectations about appropriate legalistic procedures

[22] 184 Parl. Deb., H.C. (6th ser.) (1991) 24.

[23] THOMPSON, *supra* note 4, at 74. *See also* Rochelle L. Stanfield, *Looking Beyond the Guns of August*, 22 NAT'L J. 1959, 1959–60 (1990).

[24] THE IRAQ WAR READER: HISTORY, DOCUMENTS, OPINIONS 176 (Sifry & Cerf eds., 1991).

[25] MALONE, *supra* note 3, at 72–73.

[26] *Id.* at 74. *See* GEORGE BUSH & BRENT SCOWCROFT, A WORLD TRANSFORMED 464 (1998).

[27] *Frontline: The Gulf War: Part B* (PBS television broadcast Feb. 4 1997) *transcript available at* www.pbs.org/wgbh/pages/frontline/gulf/script_b.html (cited in THOMPSON, *supra* note 4, at 65).

[28] *See* S.C. Res. 686, ¶ 2(b), U.N. Doc S/RES/686 (Mar. 2, 1991).

and reasoning. In addition, they were effective: they provided the basis for, as well as the limits of, military operations.

The legalist nature of the resolutions does not negate their political dimensions. Indeed, a deeper understanding of the law and politics of Resolution 678 requires examining both in conjunction. President Bush's memoir reveals that he believed that the United States had sufficient legal grounds to act under Article 51 of the UN Charter,[29] a view shared by James Baker.[30] This fact is a further affirmation of international law, evinced by a belief of decisionmakers that it makes a unique justificatory claim for action.

Even though Bush believed the international prescriptions permitted him to go to war without a further resolution, he nonetheless sought and obtained Resolution 678. This suggests that the reasons for seeking an explicit resolution for the use of force were not therefore purely legal but also political. Richard Cheney, the U.S. Secretary of Defense; Brent Scowcroft, the U.S. National Security Advisor; and Thatcher preferred not seeking an explicit resolution mandating a military invasion, because they feared seeking another resolution risked amendments and preferred to go to war on the terms of the United States.[31] These were real risks assessed by seasoned policymakers.

Yet President Bush, a former U.S. ambassador to the UN, understood the legitimizing effect of a UN Security Council Resolution. He sought Resolution 678 because coalition partner governments faced significant domestic opposition for what was perceived to be U.S. military action.[32] By November 1990, except for Thatcher's government, Canada, the Soviet Union, and every European and Arab coalition member insisted on explicit Council authorization as a *sine qua non* for invasion.[33] The resolution provided coalition governments with the cover of supporting an international decision rather than a U.S. invasion.[34] President Francois Mitterrand of France stated to Baker that although he believed that Article 51 alone provided enough legal justification for the invasion:

> Article 51 does not mind public opinion. Fifty-five million French people are not international lawyers. We need that resolution . . . to ensure that consequences will entail.[35]

[29] *See* Bush & Scowcroft, *supra* note 26, at 345; *id.* at 355–36.

[30] *See* James A. Baker, The Politics of Diplomacy: Revolution, War, and Peace, 1989–1992, at 278 (1995).

[31] *Id.* at 279. *See* Bush and Scowcroft, *supra* note 26, at 384 (discussing Thatcher's view).

[32] *See* Bush and Scowcroft, *supra* note 26, at 489 (stating that President Bush believed the UN "could provide a cloak of acceptability to our efforts and mobilize public opinion behind the principles we wished to project"). *See also* James Cockayne & David M. Malone, *The Security Council and the 1991 and 2003 Wars in Iraq*, *in* The United Nations Security Council and War: The Evolution of Thought and Practice Since 1945 398 (Vaughan Lowe et al. eds., 2008) (suggesting an additional political reason was to generate domestic congressional support for the invasion by obtaining a Security Council resolution mandating force).

[33] Thompson, *supra* note 4, at 67.

[34] *Id.* at 67–73.

[35] Baker, *supra* note 30, at 315.

German Chancellor Helmut Kohl stated to the *New York Times* in September 1990: "As a member of the United Nations, we cannot stand aside when the United Nations calls on us to take responsibility."[36] President Bush issued a statement along similar lines after Resolution 679 was passed:

> The United Nations Security Council has endorsed 12 resolutions to condemn Iraq's unprovoked invasion and occupation of Kuwait, implement tough economic sanctions to stop all trade in and out of Iraq, and to authorize the use of force to compel Saddam to comply. . . . The fact is that it is not the United States against Iraq; it is Iraq against the world. And there's never been a clearer demonstration of a world united against appeasement and aggression.[37]

Even though Resolution 678 was a central case prescription, it was not just a legal prescription. It was also a political tactic and a public relations communiqué that framed the invasion not as a decision of the United States but as a collective mission of a world community to promote a shared policy against aggression and to restore peace.[38] The Security Council makes a unique claim to legal authority, but that authority will be used in accord with values, politics, and interests, and in response to the political actions of international actors.

1. Specific Morality

The 1990 Gulf War presents an easy case for the justificatory theory of international law because specific morality, effectiveness, and general morality were aligned toward using military force to remove Iraq from Kuwait.

Officials had a specific moral obligation to rectify Iraq's unlawful invasion of Kuwait. One consideration was their duty to their respective constituents to protect the values and interests their constituents cared about. The United States and other oil-consuming, developed nations had a strong interest in a stable Middle East so that oil could flow freely. Kuwait was rich in oil, and a sovereign Kuwaiti government served global interests in access to oil more than a hostile Iraq controlling Kuwait's oil fields. Further, protecting sovereignty and territorial boundaries are key struts of global order. Decisionmakers were united in protecting the emerging

[36] Serge Schmemann, *Confrontation in the Gulf: Kohl Says He'll Seek to End Curb on Army's Role*, N.Y. Times, Sept. 10, 1990 (quoting German Chancellor Helmut Kohl).

[37] Thompson, *supra* note 4, at 74–75.

[38] *Accord id.*, at 75 ("The passage of various UN resolutions allowed U.S. leaders to portray it to the publics as a justified response to violations of international rules."). *See also* S.C. Provisional Records, S/PV.2693, at 92 (Nov. 29, 1990) (recording Soviet foreign minister Shevardnadze statement about the relevance of law and values: "[I]t is so important to parry this blow and to prevent it from inflicting irreparable damage to the institutions of freedom and democracy and plunging humankind into chaos. . . . The fact that today we respond to these challenges in a different way that we did yesterday is extremely important. We give preference to law, to acts based on the UN Charter, at the Security Council, and to collective efforts.").

post-Cold War order from the damaging actions of Iraq.[39] Additionally, it was moral to protect Kuwaitis from the aggression of Saddam Hussein and his violations of the liberties and property rights of Kuwaitis. Had it been immoral to repel Saddam's forces, military action by a broad coalition may not have occurred so decisively.

2. General Morality and Effectiveness

Officials also discharged their general moral obligation to protect the common good through legalism by obtaining authorization to use force in the form of Resolution 678. This consolidated shared expectations worldwide that the invasion of Kuwait was illegal and that force ought to be deployed to rectify Iraq's actions.

This legalist strategy thus increased the effectiveness of the decision to use force against Iraq. Resolution 678 rallied states in support of the military option, provided the legal framework for repelling Iraq, and stopped powerful states from exceeding the limited authorization to use force. Resolution 678 is thus a riposte to the constitutional hegemonists who fear international law is a form of "lawfare" that enemies use to constrain discretion in foreign policy. In some international problems, such as Resolution 678, international law enables, rather than limits, a state's ability to pursue its foreign policy.

Officials appropriately complied with Resolution 678 because it was adopted under the legalist procedures of the Security Council. Because the procedures of the Security Council require no vetoes by any permanent member and at least nine votes in total in order to pass a resolution, one that is adopted also has an imprimatur of fairness because it survived the scrutiny of the great powers and nonpermanent members, who each review draft resolutions from their own standpoints. In the case of Resolution 678, legitimacy was grounded in the manifest shared expectations of decisionmakers because all members of the Council voted in favor of it aside from China, which abstained; and two nonpermanent members who opposed.

Fidelity to legal procedures in adopting Resolution 678 and to legalist reasoning in interpreting and applying it to the invasion of Kuwait was an important factor in making it effective. There was a belief among constituencies in the Arab world that a UN Resolution made invasion legal and indeed obligatory, thereby allowing Saudi Arabia and other states to join the U.S. military effort. Absent Resolution 678, the coalition would not have been obtained.

The U.S. Congress was also swayed by Resolution 678. President George H.W. Bush believed that this resolution helped him persuade Congress to authorize war. The legitimating effect of international law prescriptions, derived from following

[39] *See* Bosco, *supra* note 4, at 167–68 (quoting speech by UK Prime Minister stating that "we must show that the Security Council is working with a common purpose," and noting that other powerful states responded with favorable "dramatic gestures").

Security Council procedures and legalist reasoning, helped the United States form a multinational force that effectively repelled Saddam from Kuwait.[40]

Resolution 678's effectiveness as a legal prescription is further indicated in that the United States did not invade Iraq after the Iraqi army left Kuwait, even though it was in U.S. interests to topple Saddam Hussein. The United States had the military power to continue into Baghdad. It also probably had sufficient diplomatic capital to do so. Yet Bush stopped his forces at the border of Kuwait and Iraq.

Legalist reasoning arguably could have interpreted Resolution 678 to authorize removing Saddam Hussein. Paragraph 2, its operative paragraph, states that the Security Council:

> Authorizes Member States co-operating with the Government of Kuwait, unless Iraq on or before 15 January 1991 fully implements, as set forth in paragraph 1 above, the above-mentioned resolutions, to use all necessary means to uphold and implement resolution 660 (1990) and all subsequent relevant resolutions and to restore international peace and security in the area[.][41]

By its terms, Resolution 678 authorized the use of military force to implement Resolution 660. Resolution 660 demanded that Iraq withdraw from Kuwait. The conjunctive "and" in paragraph 2 of Resolution 678 could indicate that there was further authorization to use force to "restore international peace and security in the area." Although there is ambiguity as to whether "area" is confined only to Kuwait, in order for the conjunctive "and" to make sense, restoring peace must mean something more than forcing Iraq out of Kuwait to comply with Resolution 660. It could, quite reasonably, as a matter of textual interpretation, have meant that Resolution 678 permitted coalition forces to invade Iraq to remove Hussein from power if that was necessary to restore international peace and security in the Gulf region.[42]

However, officials took a different view of Resolution 678. President Bush explained that he made this decision because he believed that there was a shared expectation in the international community that Resolution 678 did not permit coalition forces to go further. He feared that exceeding shared expectations about Resolution 678 could cause the coalition to fall apart.[43] This view was shared by the UK Secretary of Defense, who explained:

[40] Bush & Scowcroft, *supra* note 26 at 303 ("Decisive UN action would be important in rallying international opposition to the invasion and reversing it."). *See* Thompson, *supra* note 4, at 79 ("Some argue that the UNSC stands as the *only* international institution that can legitimize the use of force.") (emphasis in original) (citing multiple scholars).

[41] SC Res 678, *supra* note 10, ¶ 2.

[42] *See* Christine Gray, *After the Ceasefire: Iraq, the Security Council and the Use of Force*, 65 Brit. Y.B. Int'l L. 135, 136–37 (1994) (arguing that the Security Council could have "destroy[ed] Saddam Hussein's regime under the cover of the authorization to use 'all necessary measures . . . to restore peace and security'").

[43] *See* The United Nations Security Council and War, *supra* note 32, at 388.

> [W]e we were part of a coalition acting under the authority of the United Nations, for the purposes authorised by the Security Council and none other. Had we tried to go beyond the scope of those authorised purposes, the coalition would have fallen apart.[44]

Shared expectations about what prescriptions mean must be determined in fact-specific inquiries and may control the content of prescriptions even where text appears to be clear. Because President Bush believed that Resolution 678 did not authorize coalition forces to go beyond the border of Iraq, he acted appropriately and consistently with the general moral obligation to respect legalism, by terminating the military campaign once Iraq was expelled from Kuwait.

3. Feedback Loops

Decisions whether or not to accept the invocation of a prescription create feedback loops. If decisionmakers accept the invocation and comply with it, international law is effective in the sense that it controls outcomes. It may also increase the power of the governing elite to take action that the prescription mandates. Beyond that, constituents and decisionmakers who accept the prescription may find their values adjusting toward the values embedded in the prescription. When this happens, the interpretation and application of the prescription shapes not just outcomes in a specific international dispute to which it is applied, it also shapes expectations of appropriate conduct in future international problems. This is what the policy-oriented approach refers to as "authoritative"[45] and what transnational legal process scholars refer to as securing "obedience."[46]

If decisionmakers reject another elite's interpretation of a prescription, a different feedback loop is created. An elite who is viewed as misapplying the prescription may find that his power is diminished, because the failure to garner support for his interpretation damages his credibility and crystallizes opposition to his proposed actions that he sought to justify legalistically. The U.S. invasion of Iraq in 2003, discussed later in this chapter, is an example of this negative feedback loop.[47]

The U.S. invasion of Iraq in 1990 was an international incident that created a positive feedback loop.[48] Resolution 678 was a constitutive decision because it

[44] 216 Parl. Deb., H.C. (6th ser.) (1993) 917.

[45] *See* Rosalyn Higgins, Problems and Process: International Law and How We Use It 4 (1994) ("By authority is meant expectations of appropriateness in regard to the phases of effective decision processes.") (quoting Myres S. McDougal, Harold D. Lasswell & W. Michael Reisman, *The World Constitutive Process of Authoritative Decision*, 19 J. Legal Educ. 253, 256 (1967)).

[46] Harold Hongju Koh, *Transnational Legal Process*, 75 Nebraska L. Rev. 181, 204 (1996) ("As transnational actors interact, they create patterns of behavior and generate norms of external conduct which they in turn internalize. . . . It is thought this repeated process of interaction and internalization that international law acquires its 'stickiness[.]'").

[47] *Infra*, pt. II.C.

[48] International disputes that create feedback loops form a special category of disputes that scholars call "incidents." Incidents are not merely "an overt conflict between two or more actors in the international system." W. Michael Reisman & Andrew R. Willard, International Incidents: The

shaped the expectations of constituencies worldwide that it was appropriate and necessary to restrain Saddam Hussein so long as he remained in power. It thereby gave the United States and its allies support to seek and obtain Resolution 687 from the Security Council to contain Saddam. Resolution 687 established what Cheney called "the most intrusive systems of arms control in history."[49] There is no doubt that this comprehensive regulatory regime over Iraq could have been established and maintained only with Security Council authorization and supervision, and Resolution 678 was pivotal in the sequence of decisions against Iraq. It shaped perceptions of constituents about what outcome would be good and bolstered the power of the United States and the Security Council to take strong measures. In this fashion, the procedural legitimacy of adopting and applying a legal prescription such as Resolution 678—and its uniquely legalist nature—played a role in the effectiveness of international law in repelling Saddam and in a feedback loop that enhanced international law's effectiveness in subsequent decisions that were taken to contain Iraq.

B. 1999 NATO Bombing of the Federal Republic of Yugoslavia

In 1999, NATO bombed the Federal Republic of Yugoslavia (FRY) to stop Slobodan Milosevic's murderous rampage through Kosovo, which was then part of the FRY. The bombing deviated from the legalist central case of international law. NATO intentionally avoided seeking Security Council authorization, fearing that Russia or China would veto any Chapter VII resolution permitting NATO to act. The military campaign was not in self-defense, because no NATO country was under attack or even threatened. Therefore, the bombing violated the legal prohibition on using military force except in self-defense or with the Security Council's Chapter VII authorization. However, NATO's invasion is widely regarded as morally legitimate. All other measures short of force had not stopped FRY President Milosevic from killing Muslim Albanians in Kosovo. The bombing succeeded in ending his slaughter. Although there are questions about whether the bombing resulted in further displacements of Kosovars, had NATO not acted on humanitarian grounds, many more innocent Kosovars would have been killed or displaced from their homes. The 1999 bombing of Serbia thus presents an interesting test case for this book's account of international law, to determine if it can explain the invasion that contravened legal prescriptions, and if it can guide decisionmakers to give the law authorizing war its best justification.

Law that Counts in World Politics 15 (1988). The resolution of the conflict provides "some indication of what elites in a variety of effective processes consider to be acceptable behavior." *Id.* It is the shaping of authority—expectations of appropriate conduct—that distinguishes an incident from a mere dispute, and which makes an incident an epistemic unit of international law broadly configured.

[49] *Eyes on Iraq; In Cheney's Words: The Administration Case for Removing Saddam Hussein*, N.Y. Times (Aug. 27, 2002), http://query.nytimes.com/gst/fullpage.html?res=9505E3D9113CF934A1575BC0A9649C8B63.

To understand why NATO bombed the FRY in 1999, it is necessary to briefly review the geopolitical history of the Balkans.[50] The Balkans is a multiethnic and multireligious region. It has been ruled at different times by the "Byzantines, Croats, Serbs, Hungarians and Turks."[51] In the mid-fourteenth century, the Ottoman Empire was expanding, and in 1369, Sultan Murad I advanced his army deeper into Serbia. The Serbian Prince Lazar, together with other noblemen and their troops, met the Ottoman force at Kosovo. The Serbs were heavily outnumbered, and the Ottoman army prevailed, but both sides suffered heavy causalities, including the Prince and Sultan. The Battle of Kosovo became a symbol of Serbian independence, for it temporarily halted the Ottoman's advance.[52] To some Serbs, Kosovo is considered the birthplace of their identity,[53] the cradle of the great Serbian medieval empire, and a symbol of Serbian civilization and culture.[54]

In World War II, the Axis forces occupied Yugoslavia.[55] In 1943, the Socialist Federal Republic of Yugoslavia (the SFRY), firmly under the Soviet sphere of influence, was proclaimed. It comprised six republics: Bosnia-Herzegovina, Croatia, Slovenia, Montenegro, Macedonia, and Serbia, which included the autonomous region of Kosovo.[56] Except for Bosnia, each of the republics roughly represents a distinct ethnic group. Today each of the republics of the former Yugoslavia uses its own language, but they are all Slavic languages similar to Serbo-Croatian.[57]

By the end of the 1980s, communism was waning. When Slobodan Milosevic came to power in 1987, Serbian nationalism was on the rise and the fall of the Berlin Wall and Soviet communism was imminent. He became a hero in Serbia when in 1987 he went to Kosovo to calm the fears of local Serbs amid a strike by Kosovar Albanian miners that was paralyzing the province. By 1989, Milosevic was firmly in

[50] *See generally* Jure Vidmar, *International Legal Responses to Kosovo's Declaration of Independence*, 42 Vand. J. Transnat'l L. 779 (2009); Milena Sterio, *The Kosovar Declaration of Independence: "Botching the Balkans" or Respecting International Law*, 37 Ga. J. Int'l & Comp. L. 267 (2009); *Kosovo: Historical Chronology*, UN Security Council, http://www.securitycouncilreport.org/site/c.glKWLeMTIsG/b.2693009/ (rev. Nov. 1, 2010); Independent International Commission on Kosovo, The Kosovo Report: Conflict, International Response, Lessons Learned pt. I.1–.2 (2000) [hereinafter Kosovo Report] (describing history of the Kosovo crisis); Paul R. Williams, *Earned Sovereignty: the Road to Resolving the Conflict Over Kosovo's Final Status,* 31 Denv. J Int'l L & Pol'y 387, 394–405 (describing history of Kosovo from 1918 until UN Security Council Resolution 1244 establishing UN administration in Kosovo); Vidmar, *supra* note 50, at 781–806 (listing events over the past 30 years that have lead to Kosovo's declaration of independence).

[51] *See* Tai-Heng Cheng, State Succession and Commercial Obligations 268 (2006).

[52] *See* Hajredin Kuci, *The Legal and Political Grounds for, and the Influence of the Actual Situation on, the Demand of the Albanians of Kosovo for Independence*, 80 Chi.-Kent L. Rev. 331, 336 (2005); Vidmar, *supra* note 50, at 784; Sean D. Murphy, *Contemporary Practice of the United States Relating to International Law*, 93 Am. J. Int'l L. 161, 167–68 (1999).

[53] *See* Sterio, *supra* note 50, at 270.

[54] Henry H. Perritt, Jr., *Final Status for Kosovo*, 80 Chi.-Kent L. Rev. 3, 6 (2005).

[55] *See* Vidmar, *supra* note 50, at 785.

[56] *See* The Economist, Economist Intelligence Unit, Country Profile: Bosnia and Herzegovina 1998 (1998).

[57] *See generally* Robert D. Greenberg, Language and Identity in the Balkans: The Serbo-Croatian Disintegration (2004).

control of the Serbian republic and embarked on a campaign to consolidate his power throughout Yugoslavia. On the 600th anniversary of the Battle of Kosovo, Milosevic presided over a massive rally attended by more than a million Serbs at Kosovo Polje, the location of the historic battle.[58] One of his first acts following this historic event was to rescind the autonomy enjoyed by Kosovo and institute draconian martial law in the province. Kosovar Albanians were fired from their jobs, their schools were closed, they were denied access to state-run health care, and they lost administrative control of the province.[59]

As Milosevic pushed for more power over Yugoslavia, the other republics began to break away. In 1990, Slovenia, Croatia, and Macedonia issued declarations of independence. Efforts by Slovenia and Croatia to secede led Serbia to invade them. Eventually, however, Slovenia and Croatia achieved succession. Bosnia-Herzegovina followed suit. More civil wars followed until the Dayton Peace Agreement in 1995. The SFRY had broken up into the FRY, Slovenia, Croatia, and Bosnia-Herzegovina.[60]

Kosovo, too, began to agitate against Milosevic's oppression.[61] In 1998, fighting broke out between Serbian forces and Kosovar Albanian forces, resulting in mass murders of Kosovars by Milosevic's regime.[62] After student demonstrations in Kosovo at the beginning of 1998, on February 27, Serb forces attacked the Drenica village of Likosane with armored units and helicopter gunships. A street protest was organized in Pristina in response on March 2, which Serb forces broke up, injuring 289 people.[63]

These events invigorated the Kosovo Liberation Army, a political and paramilitary group in Kosovo that opposed Serbian rule. The KLA carried out abusive activities, causing Serbian residents to flee their villages and homes.

KLA activities, in turn, escalated Serbian reprisals. Amnesty International described frequent extrajudicial executions and disappearances of Kosovars.[64] Throughout July and August 1998, Serb incursions increased. They bombed and burned villages in Prizen and Djakovica. Further clashes between the KLA and Serb

[58] Robert F. Carolan, *An Examination of the Role of Hybrid International Tribunals in Prosecuting War Crimes and Developing Independent Domestic Court Systems: The Kosovo Experiment*, 17 TRANSNAT'L L. & CONTEMP. PROBS. 9, 13 (2008).

[59] *See* Sterio, *supra* note 50, at 271; Christopher J. Borgen, *The Language of Law and the Practice of Politics: Great Powers and the Rhetoric of Self-Determination in the Cases of Kosovo and South Ossetia*, 10 CHI. J. INT'L L. 1, 3 (2009); Michael T. Kaufman, *Crisis in the Balkans: The History; Two Distinct Peoples With Two Divergent Memories Battle Over One Land*, N.Y. TIMES, April 4, 1999.

[60] Application of the Convention on the Prevention and the Punishment of the Crime of Genocide (Bosn. & Herz. v. Serb. & Montenegro), 2007 I.C.J. 1, 83–84, ¶¶ 231–34 (Feb. 26).

[61] *See* Colin Warbrick & Dominic McGoldrick, *Kosovo: The Declaration of Independence*, 57 INT'L & COMP. L.Q. 675, 675–77 (2008) (describing history of violence in Kosovo from 1991 to 1999).

[62] *Id.*; Prosecutor v. Tadic, Judgement, Case No. IT-94–1-A (July 15, 1999) (making findings of fact about the genocide that occurred).

[63] Kosovo Report, *supra* note 50, pt. I.2.

[64] AMNESTY INTERNATIONAL, EUR 70/046/1998, FEDERAL REPUBLIC OF YUGOSLAVIA: A HUMAN RIGHTS CRISIS IN KOSOVO PROVINCE: DOCUMENT SERIES A, LJUBENIC AND POKLEK: EXTRAJUDICIAL EXECUTIONS, EXCESSIVE USE OF FORCE AND "DISAPPEARANCES" 20 (June 1998).

forces occurred in the Kosovo provinces of Rahovec and Mitrovica. The Independent International Commission on Kosovo estimated that as of the beginning of August, 200,000 to 300,000 Kosovar Albanians had been displaced from their homes as a result of sustained Serb attacks.[65]

On October 13, 1998, NATO voted to authorize air strikes if Milosevic did not withdraw from Kosovo within 96 hours. Under this threat of military action, Milosevic agreed to withdrawal terms with Richard Holbroke, the U.S. Special Envoy. On October 24, 1998, the Security Council endorsed the agreement under its Chapter VII powers.[66]

Although Milosevic initially observed his commitments, the KLA did not cease its military activities and moved into positions as Serbian forces withdrew. Violence broke out again. From October to December 1998, Serbian forces detained 1,500 to 2,000 Kosovar Albanians, and their military forces once again entered Kosovo. On January 15, 1999, Serb forces assaulted Racak village and executed 45 ethnic Albanians.[67] According to the UN High Commission for Human Rights, from January to March 1999, another 150,000 to 200,000 Kosovars were driven from their homes in Kosovo.[68]

By early 1999, as violence escalated in Kosovo with the massacre at Racak, the United States developed a plan to use the threat of air strikes to apply pressure on Milosevic to agree to a political settlement on Kosovo. If the Serbs did not negotiate in good faith, NATO would begin air strikes. Hubert Vedrine, the French Foreign Minister and UK Foreign Secretary Robin Cook wanted to be sure a NATO peacekeeping force would fill the void in Kosovo left by the withdrawal of Serbian troops once settlement was reached, to avoid the KLA seizing power.[69]

Concurrently, the United States, France, and the United Kingdom tried to negotiate a peace agreement between the FRY and the KLA. However, the FRY resumed its military movements in Kosovo in March 1999. Albright sent U.S. Special Envoy Richard Holbroke to Belgrade in a final attempt to negotiate peace. That failed as well.[70]

In March 1999, UN Secretary General Kofi Annan demanded that Serb armed forces cease their offensive in Kosovo. On March 23, NATO Secretary General Javier Solana wrote to Annan warning of a humanitarian catastrophe.[71]

On March 24, at 8 p.m. local time, NATO aircraft started a bombing campaign against the FRY. The invasion continued until June 10, 1999. NATO aircraft from

[65] Kosovo Report, *supra* note 50, pt. I.2.

[66] S.C. Res. 1203, U.N. Doc. S/RES/1203 (Oct. 24, 1998).

[67] *See* Williams, *supra* note 50, at 391 (noting that U.S. ambassador William Walker described the massacre at Racak as a crime against humanity); Dino Kritsiotis, *The Kosovo Crisis and NATO's Application of Armed Force against the Federal Republic of Yugoslavia*, 49 Int'l & Comp. L.Q. 330, 337 (2008) (describing Racak massacre).

[68] Kosovo Report, *supra* note 50, pt. 2. *See also* Prosecutor v. Tadic, Judgment, Case No. IT-94–1-A (July 15, 1999).

[69] Madeleine Albright, Madam Secretary: A Memoir 501 n.2 (2003).

[70] *Id.* at 517–18.

[71] Kosovo Report, *supra* note 50, pt. 2.

13 countries flew almost 40,000 sorties, including almost 10,500 strike sorties, deploying over 26,500 munitions.[72]

In Rambouillet, France, in early June 1999, EU envoy Martti Ahtisarri and Russian envoy Victor Chernomydin reached an agreement with Milosevic providing for an end to the NATO invasion and for the FRY to withdraw its forces from Kosovo, granting Kosovo substantial autonomy under UN administration.[73] On June 3, 1999, the Serb parliament approved the peace plan, and on June 10, NATO ended its military campaign after verifying Serbia's troop withdrawals from Kosovo.[74] That day, the Security Council adopted Resolution 1244, establishing the UN Mission in Kosovo (UNMIK), a UN provisional authority, to administer Kosovo.[75]

Resolution 1244 struck a careful balance between self-determination and sovereignty. It reaffirmed both: "the sovereignty and territorial integrity of the Federal Republic of Yugoslavia and the other States of the region," as well as "substantial autonomy and meaningful self-administration for Kosovo."[76] It also set in motion a process for Kosovo's self-governance. It established an international civil presence, which would be responsible for "[p]romoting the establishment, pending a final settlement, of substantial autonomy and self-government in Kosovo."[77]

1. General Morality

The 1999 bombing of Serbia presents a more difficult case for the justificatory theory of international law because officials deviated from their general obligation to promote the common good through legalism. The decision to bomb the FRY was moral and political. It was not legal. Legalist reasoning and procedures hardly played any role in guiding the decision before it was made, and law was never applied to authoritatively appraise the invasion after it ended.

The Security Council, which was the only international body that could legally authorize military force to maintain peace and security, was completely cut out of the decisionmaking process to unilaterally attack the FRY. In late spring of 1998, the United States approached NATO to consider military options against the FRY, "including preventative deployments in Albania and Macedonia . . ., air strikes . . ., and a peace plan implementation force" if a political settlement on Kosovo was achieved.[78] At that time, there was some hope that international law would play a role in regulating any eventual military action against the FRY. UK lawyers had advised their Foreign Secretary, Robin Cook, that any NATO action required Security Council

[72] *Id. supra* note 50, pt. 3; W.J. Fenrick, *Targeting and Proportionality during the NATO Bombing Campaign against Yugoslavia,* 12 Eur. J. Int'l L. 489, 489–90 (2001) (providing details of NATO's military actions).

[73] *See* Darrel Menthe, *Legalization and the Mediation of International Disputes: The Balkan Experience*, 23 Conn. J. Int'l L. 83, 112–13 (2008) (describing peace agreement negotiations).

[74] Kosovo Report, *supra* note 50, pt. 3.

[75] *See* S.C. Res. 1244, U.N. Doc. S/RES/1244, ¶ 10 (June 10, 1999).

[76] *Id.* pmbl.

[77] *Id.* at ¶11(a).

[78] Albright, *supra* note 69, at 488–89.

approval. Cook accordingly circulated a draft Council resolution.[79] These facts indicate that international law initially had a degree of effectiveness in restraining and regularizing political and military decisionmaking about the Kosovo problem.

In her autobiography, U.S. Secretary of State Madeline Albright recounted that in response to Cook's actions, she told him "he should get himself new lawyers." She opposed seeking Security Council authorization. If a resolution was adopted, "it would have set a precedent that NATO required Security Council authorization before it could act. This would give Russia, not to mention China, a veto over NATO." If the resolution failed, it would have made it "that much harder for NATO to move." A third possibility was that the resolution would pass but only after significant compromises with Russia.[80]

In any event, none of the NATO states, including three permanent members of the Security Council, the United States, France and the United Kingdom, sought or obtained Security Council authorization for its air campaign. Thus, when NATO decided to bomb the FRY, it did so unilaterally without Chapter VII authorization.[81] International law played no role in controlling whether and when NATO would attack the FRY.

Scholars on both sides of the Atlantic are divided on whether NATO's bombing without Chapter VII approval was legal.[82] However, overall, the majority view is that it was not.[83]

[79] *Id.* at 489.

[80] *Id.*

[81] Tarcisio Grazzini, *NATO Coercive Military Activities in the Yugoslav Crisis (1992–1999)*, 12 Eur. J. Int'l L. 391, 431 (2001) ("NATO deliberately ignored the Security Council and unilaterally assumed entire control over the operations.").

[82] *Compare* Louis Henkin, *Kosovo and the Law of Humanitarian Intervention*, 93 Am. J. Int'l L. 824, 824 (1999) ("[U]nilateral intervention, even for what the intervening state deems to be important humanitarian ends, is and should remain unlawful.") *with* Ruth Wedgewood, *NATO's Campaign in Yugoslavia*, 93 Am. J. Int'l L. 828 (1999) (questioning the view that the intervention was unlawful and concluding that legality is "a complex cultural process not confined to the Council chamber"). *Compare* Ian Brownlie & C.J. Apperley, *Kosovo Crisis Inquiry: Memorandum on the International Law Aspects*, 49 Int'l & Comp. L.Q. 880, 904 (2008) ("Humanitarian intervention . . . has no place either un the United Nations Charter of in customary international law.") *with* Christopher Greenwood, *International law and the NATO Intervention in Kosovo*, 49 Int'l & Comp. L.Q. 926, 934 (2000) ("[R]esort to force in this case was a legitimate exercise of the right of humanitarian intervention recognised by international law and was consistent with the relevant Security Council resolutions."). *Compare* Jonathan I. Charney, *Anticipatory Humanitarian Intervention in Kosovo*, 93 Am. J. Int'l L. 841 (1999) (stating that the invasion's "legality remains questionable, at best") *with* Abraham Sofaer, *International Law and Kosovo*, 36 Stan. J. Int'l L. 1, 15 (2000) (arguing that although no factor taken alone establishes the legality of the invasion, "under all the relevant circumstances," the military action was "reasonable in light of Charter's provisions and purposes"). *Compare* Bruno Simma, *NATO the UN and the Use of Force: Legal Aspects*, 10 Eur. J. Int'l L. 1, 22 (1999) (arguing, prior to the invasion, that "only a thin red line separates NATO's actions in Kosovo from international legality") *with* Julie Mertus, *Reconsidering the Legality of Humanitarian Intervention: Lessons from Kosovo*, 41 Wm. & Mary L. Rev. 1743, 1787 (2000) (arguing that a closing reading of the UN Charter implicitly mandated NATO's air campaign for humanitarian purposes, but the campaign was disproportionate and therefore became illegal).

[83] *See* Antonio Cassese, *Ex Iniuria Ius Oritur: Are We Moving Towards International Legitimation of Forcible Humanitarian Countermeasures in the World Community*, 10 Eur. J. Int'l L. 23, 24 (1999)

As the footnotes accompanying the paragraph above show, much ink has already been spilt by eminent scholars appraising the legality of the invasion. This book will briefly describe their legalist arguments, as the author agrees with many of them. International law as codified in the Articles 2(4) and 51 of the UN Charter prohibits unilateral military force.[84] The two exceptions are individual or collective self-defense, or authorization by the Security Council under its Chapter VII powers. These rules are interpreted strictly, because loose constructions of these prescriptions risk sliding back to prior eras where states easily turned to violence against each other to resolve their disputes.[85]

NATO's bombing was not an exercise in individual or collective self-defense because no NATO state was under attack. Indeed, no state at all was under attack because Kosovo was part of the FRY, and the conflict was purely internal in 1999.

There was also no Security Council resolution authorizing the use of force. Resolution 1199 adopted in 1998 stated that if FRY did not comply with the measures imposed by the Council, the Council would consider further measures. It did not delegate its authority to maintain peace to states to enforce its commands.[86] Although the Council had authorized military action in some internal conflicts, such as Somalia, Haiti, and Rwanda,[87] thereby limiting the scope of Article 2(7) of the Charter prohibiting interference with matters "within the domestic jurisdiction of any State," the Council did not do so in the Kosovo conflict.[88]

It is true that the Security Council failed to condemn the bombing. On March 26, 1999, Russia, Belarus, and India sponsored a resolution condemning the NATO campaign as unlawful. That resolution was defeated by 12 votes to 3, with only China and Namibia joining Russia in favor of the resolution.[89] Resolution 1244 did

(stating that the "breach of the United Nations Charter occurring in this instance cannot be termed minor"); Tarcisio Grazzini, *supra* note 81, at 434 ("[T]he operation found no legal basis in the Charter and can hardly be justified on the basis of the controversial right to intervene on humanitarian purposes under general international law."); Peter Hilpold, *Humanitarian Intervention: Is There a Need for a Legal Reappraisal?*, 12 Eur. J. Int'l L. 437, 448 (2001) (rejecting purported legal justifications for NATO's invasion); Enrico Milano, *Security Council Action in the Balkans: Reviewing the Legality of Kosovo's Territorial Status*, 14 Eur. J. Int'l L. 999, 1020 (2003) (stating that NATO bombing was "beyond the limits set by international law"); Christine Chinkin, *International Law and the NATO Intervention in Kosovo*, 49 Int'l & Comp. L.Q. 876, 924 (2008) (unilateral humanitarian intervention remains controversial under international law and the NATO bombing did not come under any Charter exception prohibiting force).

[84] Vaughan Lowe, *International Legal Issues Arising in the Kosovo Crisis*, 49 Int'l & Comp. L.Q. 876, 935 (2008).

[85] W. Michael Reisman, *Kosovo's Antinomies*, 93 Am. J. Int'l L. 861 (1999) ("But we all are stricter when it comes to reading Article 2(4), for no one wants a return to the world of classic international law in which states could resort to violence against each other at will.").

[86] S.C. Res. 1199, U.N. Doc. S/Res/1199 (Sept. 23, 1998). *See* Lowe, *supra* note 84, at 936.

[87] Belarus, India and Russian Federation: Draft Resolution, U.N. Doc. S/1999/328 (Mar. 26, 1999).

[88] Lowe, *supra* note 84, at 936.

[89] Kritsiotis, *supra* note 67, at 347. *See* Ray Murphy, UN Peacekeeping in Lebanon, Somalia, and Kosovo 76 (2007) (arguing that the failed resolution "could be interpreted as an endorsement of the NATO campaign").

not even refer to NATO's military action.[90] However, an illegal act is not transformed into a legal one simply because the Security Council does not condemn it. Further, as observed earlier, the UN Charter charges the ICJ and not the Security Council with responsibility to make legal determinations,[91] and so the silence of the Security Council on a point of law is inconclusive.

Likewise, Serbia brought a claim against NATO states before the ICJ, claiming that the military strikes were unlawful. However, the ICJ declined to hear the case on the merits for lack of jurisdiction over the FRY at the time of the bombing.[92] The ICJ's decision thus neither confirms nor denies the legality of NATO's actions.

Ultimately, the legalist justification advanced by NATO states was a novel argument that their actions were lawful because the purpose of the campaign was humanitarian, to stop the growing violence against Kosovar Albanians. In response to questions in the UK Parliament, George Robertson, the Secretary of Defense stated: "Our legal justification rests upon the principle that force may be used in extreme circumstances to avert a humanitarian catastrophe."[93] UK Permanent Representative to the U.N. Jeremy Greenstock took the same position in asserting before the Security Council that the NATO bombing was legal because it "was justified as an exceptional measure to prevent an overwhelming humanitarian catastrophe."[94]

In the ICJ proceedings in the *Legality of Use of Force* cases, the United States, Germany, and Belgium emphasized, among other justifications for their bombing, the humanitarian dimensions of the campaign.[95]

In 1999, humanitarian intervention was not an exception to the prohibition against the use of force. The Charter contains exceptions to the use of force but makes no exception for humanitarian intervention. If the framers of the Charter had wanted to carve out such an exception, they would have done so, as they did for self-defense and Security Council authorization. They did not do so, and it would strain textual interpretation to read such an exception into the Charter's silence.[96]

On balance, therefore, none of the purportedly legalist arguments advanced in support of NATO's bombing withstand scrutiny. The invasion deviated from shared expectations of appropriate uses of military force, thereby damaging the stability of the international legal system.

90 UN Security Council Resolution 1244, *supra* note 75, ¶ 10 (June 10, 999).

91 *Supra*, pt II.A (questioning Security Council Resolution 660, which purported to make a legal determination that Iraq's occupation of Kuwait was illegal).

92 Legality of Use of Force (Serb. and Montenegro v. U.K.), Judgment, 2004 I.C.J. 1307, ¶ 113 (Dec. 15).

93 328 Parl. Deb., H.C. (6th ser.) (1999) 616–17 (*in* Kritsiotis, *supra* note 67, at 347).

94 Brownlie & Apperley, *supra* note 82, at 879–80 (quoting Greenstock).

95 *See* Kritsiotis, *supra* note 67, at 343–45 (discussing legal arguments made by respondents in the *Legality of Use of Force* case); Brownlie & Apperley, *supra* note 82, at 881 (describing the same arguments).

96 *See* Charney, *supra* note 82, at 836 ("[H]umanitarian intervention is not an exception to the Charter's prohibitions on the use of force."). *Cf.* Henkin, *supra* note 82, at 824 (rejecting humanitarian intervention as a ground for unilateral force because of its potential for abuse).

2. Specific Morality

Although officials deviated from their general moral obligation to promote the common good through legalism, their actions were justified because the specific morality of stopping Serbia's mass killings outweighed the general moral obligation. Officials had a specific moral obligation to protect the interests and values of their constituents. Madeline Albright stated on June 28, 1999, before the Council on Foreign Relations, that it was in the interests of the United States to bomb the FRY:

> Our strategy throughout has been grounded firmly in U.S. interests. By meeting massive ethnic cleansing in the Balkans with a red light, we make it less likely that NATO will be called upon to use force in the future. And by supporting democracy and promoting human rights, we contribute to a future of stability and peace throughout Europe. This is fully consistent both with American interests and with NATO's purpose, which is to prevent war while defending freedom.[97]

But more than anything else, it was moral to stop the escalating mass killings and displacement of Albanians from Kosovo. As the Report by the Independent International Commission on Kosovo concluded, bombing was legitimate because "all diplomatic avenues had been exhausted and because the intervention had the effect of liberating the majority population of Kosovo from a long period of oppression under Serbian rule."[98] Albright stated that the campaign supported NATO's purpose, which was "to prevent war while defending freedom."[99] Kofi Annan issued a statement on March 24, 1999, stating that although the Security Council has "primary responsibility for maintaining international peace and security," "force may be legitimate in the pursuit of peace."[100]

It is difficult to quarrel with the morality of promoting peace and defending freedom. The UK Prime Minister stated to the media that the bombing campaign was "fought not for territory, but for values."[101] The House of Commons Foreign Affairs Committee considered the bombing morally justified.[102] Accounting for these moral considerations, along with the interests of NATO states in a stable Balkans and a robust NATO, explains why international legal prescriptions circumscribing the use of military force were ineffective in the Kosovo conflict.

Admittedly, as the bombing progressed, information from the field raised questions about the morality of the invasion. The Report by the Independent International

[97] Madeleine Albright, Sec'y of State, Address to Council on Foreign Relations, 10 Dept. of State Dispatch 3 (June 28, 1999).

[98] Executive Summary, Kosovo Report, *supra* note 50. Richard Falk, who studied policy-oriented jurisprudence with Myres S. McDougal and appears to continue to apply it in some fashion, but was critical of McDougal's substantive positions Cold War issues, chaired the Commission.

[99] Albright, *supra* note 97.

[100] Hilpold, *supra* note 83, at 462 & n.75 (quoting Kofi Annan).

[101] Murphy, *supra* note 89, at 76 & n.106 (quoting UK Prime Minister).

[102] *Id.* at 76 & n.107 (quoting House of Commons Foreign Relations Committee).

Commission on Kosovo observed that although the bombing campaign was supposed to have been for a limited duration, it lasted 78 days. NATO officials also failed to anticipate that bombing would dramatically increase the displacement and expulsion by Serbia of Albanians from Kosovo. War is messy, and the best laid plans go awry. The bombing campaign was probably justified because it was a decisive turning point in stabilizing the Balkans and protecting the most basic goods for Kosovar Albanians.

Even if that were not the case, the reasonableness of a decision must be judged in light of the circumstances and information available at the time of the decision. The justificatory account of international law does not require optimal decisions about how to interpret, apply, or ignore prescriptions. It only requires that decisionmakers exercise their best judgment in good faith, based on what they know, and considering as completely as they can the general morality of legalism along with the specific morality of promoting the values at stake. If decisions made in good faith turn out to be suboptimal, decisionmakers should adjust their actions and expectations of appropriate conduct in future similar international problems.

3. Feedback Loops

The account of international decisionmaking presented here provides a justification for international law that is preferable to insisting on slavish compliance with laws and legalism.[103] The bombing of Kosovo arguably falls into a small minority of exceptional international problems where officials are justified in departing from legalism because deviations from the general morality of international law were justified by promoting the specific morality of stopping mass killings.[104]

A cautionary note is in order, however. When acting upon a moral calculus that justifies departing from legalism, officials may create feedback loops that adjust the legal prescriptions they ignored in unpredictable ways. If they do not authoritatively specify whether and how their conduct adjusts prescriptions, other decisionmakers may subsequently misinterpret the impact of their conduct on applicable legal prescriptions, thereby permitting conduct in subsequent disputes that ought not to be permitted under international law. As discussed later, U.S. Vice President Richard Cheney and Secretary of Defense Donald Rumsfeld persuaded President George W. Bush that no Security Council resolution was necessary to invade Iraq in 2003

[103] *See* Richard A. Falk, *Kosovo, World Order, and the Future of International Law*, 93 Am. J. Int'l L. 847, 853 (1999) ("[T]o regard textual barriers to humanitarian intervention as decisive in the face of genocidal behavior is politically and morally unacceptable[.]").

[104] *Cf.*, Ronald Dworkin, Law's Empire 406–07 (1986) (arguing that a purified interpretation of law seeks not just formal coherence, but also justice, as a special form on integrity, but that this interpretive process "does not declare which officer has which office in that grand project"). Under the justificatory theory of international law, every decisionmaker is responsible for contributing to the process of interpreting it and working toward international law's purified form, to use Dworkin's terminology.

in part because NATO had bombed the FRY without Security Council authorization.[105]

Officials from NATO states appeared to recognize the risk of an uncontrolled feedback loop in their statements after the campaign began. German Foreign Minister Klaus Kinkel cautioned that NATO's unilateral use of force "must not become a precedent. As far as the Security Council monopoly of force is concerned, we must avoid getting on a slippery slope."[106] Albright similarly cautioned against "sweeping conclusions" that Kosovo would become precedent for other interventions because "[e]very circumstance is unique."[107] However, as the arguments of Rumsfeld and Cheney in 2003 indicate, statements by foreign ministers that NATO's intervention was *sui generis* did not prevent a feedback loop.

Officials should explain how their conduct adjusts international legal prescriptions to accommodate moral considerations in future conflicts, rather than claim that the incident at hand is unique and has no effect on international law. As Vaughan Lowe has explained: "Better to define a narrow principle and have it invoked by others than to act on the basis of no principle and encourage unprincipled action."[108] Michael Reisman agrees: "The practical question is whether Kosovo-like decisions . . . will be essentially uncontrolled actions taken by one or more powerful states in their own special interest . . . or whether they will be subjected to the discipline of international law standards and contribute to the major purposes of the UN Charter."[109]

In this regard, it is regrettable that the ICJ found it lacked jurisdiction in the *Legality of the Use of Force* cases.[110] Had it exerted jurisdiction, it would have had an opportunity to authoritatively explain the constitutive effect of the 1999 bombing on the law of war, and to clarify the important restrictions on the use of force that remained unaffected by NATO's unilateral intervention in the FRY.

It is also is regrettable, albeit understandable, that the Security Council did not acknowledge NATO's invasion in Resolution 1244. Even if it had just stated in its preamble that NATO intervened to avert a humanitarian crisis only after all other

[105] *Infra*, pt. II.C.1.

[106] Lowe, *supra* note 84, at 938 (quoting Kinkel).

[107] Albright, *supra* note 97, at 3.

[108] Lowe, *supra* note 84, at 939.

[109] Reisman, *supra* note 85, at 862.

[110] *See* Legality of Use of Force (Yugoslavia v. Spain), Judgment, 1999 I.C.J. 761, ¶ 40 (June 2); Legality of Use of Force (Yugoslavia v. U.S.), Judgment, 1999 I.C.J. 916, ¶ 34 (June 2); Legality of Use of Force (Serb. and Montenegro v. Belg.), Judgment, 2004 I.C.J. 279, ¶ 129 (Dec. 15); Legality of Use of Force (Serb. and Montenegro v. Can.), Judgment, 2004 I.C.J. 429, ¶ 116 (Dec. 15); Legality of Use of Force (Serb. and Montenegro v. Fr.), Judgment, 2004 I.C.J. 575, ¶ 116 (Dec. 15); Legality of Use of Force (Serb. and Montenegro v. Ger.), Judgment, 2004 I.C.J. 720, ¶ 115 (Dec. 15); Legality of Use of Force (Serb. and Montenegro v. It.), Judgment, 2004 I.C.J. 865, ¶ 116 (Dec. 15); Legality of Use of Force (Serb. and Montenegro v. Neth.), Judgment, 2004 I.C.J. 1011, ¶ 128 (Dec. 15); Legality of Use of Force (Serb. and Montenegro v. Port.), Judgment, 2004 I.C.J. 1160, ¶ 119 (Dec. 15); Legality of Use of Force (Serb. and Montenegro v. U.K.), Judgment, 2004 I.C.J. 1307, ¶ 115 (Dec. 15).

diplomatic efforts had failed, that would have at least telegraphed to decisionmakers in future conflicts that if the 1999 incident created a new exception to the prohibition on force, it was limited to humanitarian interventions against ongoing internecine wars, and only in situations where all diplomatic means had failed. This clear threshold for actions would limit the scope of abuse or excessive resort to force except where strictly necessary. It would have helped to create a shared expectation that unilateral force was not permitted against Iraq in 2003 on humanitarian grounds because Saddam Hussein was not committing genocide or other mass killings against Iraqis at that time. As discussed below, the invasion of Iraq was arguably reasonable, but it was not justified on humanitarian grounds, and the 1999 bombing should not have served as a precedent for the 2003 invasion.

C. The 2003 Invasion of Iraq

After the multilateral military force expelled Iraq from Kuwait, the Security Council imposed the terms of Baghdad's surrender in Resolution 687. It was adopted on April 3, 1991, with 12 votes, with Cuba opposing and Ecuador and Yemen abstaining.[111] It communicated its prescriptions in the legalistic fashion of Council resolutions, invoking Chapter VII and affirming prior resolutions against Iraq.[112] The resolution consolidated shared expectations among international decisionmakers about appropriate intrusions on Iraq's sovereignty. It demarcated the boundary between Iraq and Kuwait,[113] created a demilitarized zone,[114] ordered Iraq to destroy all chemical and biological weapons and nuclear material,[115] controlled Iraq's oil exports,[116] and established Iraq's responsibility for war damages.[117]

Several more resolutions followed in the 1990s, each attempting to box in Saddam Hussein with measures such as "no fly zones"[118] and sanctions. Saddam was partly able to circumvent sanctions. Baghdad was permitted to sell oil in order to finance humanitarian efforts. Instead, Saddam used these oil sales to give out patronage and underwrite his personal expenses. The Sanctions Committee that had been set up by Resolution 661 was aware of this corruption but did not clamp down on it because the United States did not wish to alienate Iraq's smuggling partners, Jordan and Turkey, which were U.S. strategic allies in the Middle East.[119]

[111] S.C. Res. 687, U.N. Doc S/RES/687 (Apr. 3, 1991).

[112] *Id.* at pmbl, ¶ 1.

[113] *Id.* at ¶ 3.

[114] *Id.* at ¶ 5.

[115] *Id.* at ¶ 8–13.

[116] *See* S.C. Res. 687, *supra* note 111, at ¶ 20–24.

[117] *See id.* at ¶ 15–19. *See also* Malone, *supra* note 3, at 74–75.

[118] S.C. Res 688, U.N. Doc S/RES/688 (Apr. 5, 1991). *See also* Zacklin, *supra* note 1, at 15 ("In order to enforce and monitor compliance with their respective interpretations of 688 the United States, United Kingdom and France unilaterally created an air exclusion zone north of the 36th parallel. This was later extended to a southern air exclusion zone below the 32nd parallel.").

[119] *See* Zacklin, *supra* note 1, at 131. *See also* Gray, *supra* note 42, at 172 (stating that "[t]hese experiences with Resolution 687 highlight the lack of clear enforcement mechanisms to respond to

The Islamist terrorist attacks on the United States of September 11, 2001, changed everything.[120] George W. Bush had just been inaugurated the 43rd President of the United States of America earlier that year. The attacks of September 11, 2001, made President Bush realize that the prior strategy of containing Iraq posed high risks for the United States. Saddam Hussein had a history of stockpiling and using weapons of mass destruction. An intelligence report concluded:

> Since the end of inspections in 1998, Saddam has maintained the chemical weapons effort, energized the missile program, made a bigger investment in biological weapons, and has begun to try to move forward in the nuclear area.[121]

President Bush feared that Saddam Hussein might pass his weapons of mass destructions to terrorists, who would then use them against the United States. He stated in his memoir:

> Before 9/11, Saddam was a problem America might have been able to manage. Through the lens of the post-9/11 world, my view changed. . . . With threats flowing into the Oval Office daily—many of them about chemical, biological, or nuclear weapons—that seemed like a frighteningly real possibility. The stakes were too high to trust a dictator's word against the weight of the evidence and the consensus of the world. The lesson of 9/11 was that if we waited for danger to fully materialize, we would have waited too long. I reached a decision: We would confront the threat from Iraq, one way or another.[122]

President Bush also stated in an interview with the English television network ITV in April 2002:

> The worst thing that could happen would be to allow a nation like Iraq, run by Saddam Hussein, to develop weapons of mass destruction, and then team up with terrorist organizations so they can blackmail the world. I'm not going to let that happen.[123]

non-cooperation by Iraq" and discussing, *passim*, the problems with operationalizing the resolution); George W. Bush, Decision Points 226–29 (2010) (discussing difficulties faced in securing Iraq's compliance with Resolution 687 and subsequent resolutions).

[120] Bush, *supra* note 119, at 136 ("The attacks on the World Trade Center in New York and other targets in the United States transformed the international security environment."); Thompson, *supra* note 4, at 135–36 (discussing how 9/11 shaped the United States' policy towards Iraq). *See also supra* ch. 4, pt. VII.B.1.

[121] Bush, *supra* note 119, at 229 (quoting intelligence report).

[122] *Id.*

[123] Bob Woodward, Plan of Attack 120 (2004). *See also* President George W. Bush, Keynote Address at the United States Military Academy at West Point (June 1, 2002) ("The war on terror will not be won on the defensive . . . We must take the battle to the enemy, disrupt his plans, and confront the worst threats before they emerge.") (*quoted in* Woodward, *supra* note 123, at 132).

Other U.S. officials also expressed concern about a daily barrage of worldwide threats against the United States. These threat assessments led them, in good faith, to consider stronger measures in order to prevent another attack after the destruction of the World Trade Center and a wing of the Pentagon by terrorists.[124]

The pursuit of values for Americans and other communities reinforced the administration's strategy of preemptive force. President Bush explained to West Point cadets:

> Our nation's cause has always been greater than our nation's defense. . . . We have a great opportunity to extend just peace by replacing poverty, repression and resentment around the world with hope for a better day.[125]

By September, Bush had combined national security, moral imperative, and geopolitical concerns. He told U.S. congressional leaders in a private meeting: "Saddam Hussein is a terrible guy who is teaming up with Al Qaeda. He tortures his own people and hates Israel."[126] A top secret memo titled "Iraq: Goals, Objectives and Strategy," signed two months later on November 29, 2002, added another goal in invading Iraq: "to minimize disruption in the international oil markets."[127]

National interests and moral considerations might not fully explain why the United States attacked Iraq. Personal considerations are difficult to tease apart from policy decisions because, ultimately, policymakers are human, and human considerations often influence good faith judgments. At a private briefing on September 19, 2002, Richard Burr, a North Carolina Republican, emphasized that Saddam Hussein gassed his citizens. Bush responded: "I am well aware . . . He tried to kill my Dad."[128]

The confluence of some or all of these factors resulted in the Bush administration adopting a doctrine of using preemptive military force against putative enemies.[129] On November 21, 2002, President Bush instructed Secretary of Defense Donald Rumsfeld to update their war plan for Iraq.[130] On March 20, 2003, the United States

[124] Jack L. Goldsmith, The Terror Presidency 71–72 (2007) (describing the daily "threat matrix" reviewed by U.S. officials and how it shaped their analysis of measures necessary to prevent another attack).

[125] Woodward, *supra* note 123, at 132. *See also* A Project for the New American Century ("That American Leadership is good both for America and for the world; that such leadership requires military strength, diplomatic energy and commitment to moral principle.") (*quoted in* Malone, *supra* note 3, at 188).

[126] Malone, *supra* note 3, at 188.

[127] Memorandum from The White House Situation Room to the Vice President et al., Iraq: Goals, Objectives, and Strategy (Nov. 29, 2002) (*quoted in* Woodward, *supra* note 123, at 229).

[128] Woodward, *supra* note123, at 187.

[129] *See* The White House, The National Security Strategy of the United States of America 23 (Mar. 2006), *available at* http://www.strategicstudiesinstitute.army.mil/pdffiles/nss.pdf (articulating the Bush Doctrine). *See also* Tai-Heng Cheng & Eduardas Valaitis, *Shaping an Obama Doctrine of Preemptive Force*, 82 Temp. L. Rev. 737, 753 (2009) (discussing the Bush Doctrine).

[130] *See* Woodward, *supra* note 123, at 1–3.

invaded Iraq, beginning with heavy aerial bombardments and the V Corps and First Marine Expeditionary Force charging to Baghdad from Iraq's southern border.[131]

The decision of the United States to invade Iraq in March 2003 is not so surprising. The United States was militarily far superior to Iraq. The U.S. administration adopted a new policy to seek out and eradicate national security threats after the attacks against the United States on September 11, 2001. Congress gave approval to the U.S. President to use military force in Iraq well before any UN Security Council resolution could be passed authorizing a new invasion, unlike the 1990 invasion where President George H.W. Bush relied on Council Resolution 678 to persuade Congress to allow him to start war.[132]

What is remarkable is that it took so long to do so, after having decided in November 2001, almost 18 months prior, to invade Iraq because of the risk that it would arm terrorists against the United States. What is even more remarkable is that during those 18 months, the United States tried not once, but twice, to obtain legal authorization from the Security Council to invade Iraq. It succeeded in its first attempt and failed in its second, but it never claimed to invade Iraq without regard for international law.

Although U.S. Vice President Dick Cheney opposed seeking UN authorization,[133] in his speech at the UN General Assembly on September 12, 2002, President Bush outlined Iraq's violations of Council resolutions and concluded that the United States "will work with the UN Security Council for the necessary resolutions."[134] He did so because major coalition partners in the invasion, UK Prime Minister Tony Blair, Australian Prime Minister John Howard, and Spanish President Jose Maria Aznar needed a new Security Council resolution authorizing the invasion in order to win over their domestic constituencies to support the U.S. war effort.[135] This affirms the observation from the study of the 1990 invasion that Chapter VII resolutions are in the central case of international law because they shape expectations of appropriate conduct among decisionmakers and their constituencies.

The United States proposed to the Security Council that it adopt a U.S. draft resolution giving Iraq a final chance to disarm; failing to do so would make it legal to invade Iraq.[136] Cheney proposed a tactical move to tighten the vice around Saddam. At his suggestion, the U.S. draft proposed that Iraq be required to provide a full and

[131] BUSH, *supra* note 119, at 254–55.

[132] H.R.J. Res. 114, 107th Cong. § 3 (a) (2002) (authorizing force as the President "determines to be necessary and appropriate") (passed with 296 to 133 votes in the House and 77 votes to 23 in the Senate.).

[133] *See* WOODWARD, *supra* note 123, at 157.

[134] President George W. Bush, Speech to United Nations General Assembly (Sept. 12, 2002) (*cited in* WOODWARD, *supra* note 123, at 184). *See also id.* at 183 (reporting that over the opposition of Secretary of Defense Donald Rumsfeld, President Bush "chose the resolution option").

[135] *See* WOODWARD, *supra* note 123, at 183. BUSH, *supra* note 119, at 232 (recollecting that Tony Blair suggested the United States seek a resolution when he met with President Bush in April 2002).

[136] *See* WOODWARD, *supra* note 123, at 181–82.

accurate declaration of its armaments in 30 days. If it did not do so, this would be treated as failing to disarm.[137]

France, Russia, and China all had commercial ties with Iraq and opposed removing Saddam by force.[138] The French ambassador, Dominique de Villepin, preferred a two-step process in which the Council first would issue a resolution giving Iraq a final chance to comply, and then it would convene to decide if Iraq had complied and what measures to take if it had not complied.[139]

The permanent five members eventually resolved the question about whether there ought to be a two-step or one-step process by elision. Resolution 1441, whose provisions are discussed below in detail, avoided stating whether the Council would be required to reconvene to authorize force. Instead, it recalled that the Council had "previously warned Iraq that it will face serious consequences as a result of its continued violations of its obligations."[140]

The final point of contention came down to whether the disjunctive "or" or the conjunctive "and" would be used in the test of whether Iraq had complied with Resolution 1441. The United States wanted to state that a material breach would be "false statements or omissions in the declarations submitted by Iraq pursuant to this resolution *or* failure by Iraq at any time to comply with, and cooperate fully with the implementation, of this resolution. . . ." (emphasis added). France, on the other hand, wanted to state that a material breach would require both false statements and a failure to fully cooperate with implementation.[141] The United States eventually acceded to the French position after National Security Advisor Condoleezza Rice persuaded President Bush and his key advisors that whatever the language of Resolution 1441, Council members would argue over whether Saddam had complied with it.

The importance that decisionmakers placed on the legalism of Security Council resolutions is underscored by the involvement of governments at the highest levels in a fight over a single conjunction. Bob Woodward's narrative of the final negotiation prior to the formal Security Council meeting adopting Resolution 1441 is illuminating and reproduced here:

> Sometime during the night of November 6 or early the morning of November 7, Powell finally received the final okay from Rice. He called de Villepin, who was on an airplane with Chirac. 'Dominique, we can go with 'and' but only if that's the end of it. There is nothing else to discuss. It is over. And I have to have your approval of that and your president's approval.' 'The president is sitting here with me.' De Villepin said. 'I will ask him. I think this is it.' Powell waited as they conferred. He thought de Villepin sounded

[137] *Compare* S.C. Res. 1441, ¶ 3, U.N. Doc. S/2002/1441 (Nov. 8, 2002) *with* Woodward, *supra* note 123, at 222 (citing the American draft of Resolution 1441).

[138] *See* Thompson, *supra* note 4, at 104 (noting that China was a major supplier of military equipment to Iraq, and France and Russia were eager to restore the "prewar status quo").

[139] S.C. Res 1441, *supra* note 137, at ¶ 2.

[140] *Id.* at ¶ 13.

[141] *See* Woodward, *supra* note 123, at 222–23 (discussing the American draft of Resolution 1441 as opposed to the French draft); Thompson, *supra* note 4, at 143.

> so relieved that either solution would have been acceptable. 'Yes,' de Villepin finally said. 'Yes.' 'Wonderful,' Powell replied. 'That's a deal with you.' He immediately called the Russian foreign minister, Igor Ivanov. 'Igor, I just made a deal with Dominique and it's going to be 'and.' 'That's a major breakthrough.' Ivanov said. 'How wonderful! I must hang up and go see the president immediately.' He apparently rushed off to walk with Vladimir Putin. Ivanov called back a half-hour later. Putin approved. 'It is wonderful, it is a breakthrough.' No, Powell realized, it wasn't. The seeming compromise was just getting everybody off the hook. But hey, he thought to himself, you take it when you can get it.[142]

Presidents of great nations have more than enough affairs of state requiring their decisions. If Council resolutions were unimportant, the presidents of the United States, France, and Russia would not have diverted their attention to wordsmithing.

On November 8, 2002, the Council unanimously adopted Resolution 1441. Even Syria, the sole Arab state on the Council, voted in favor, testifying to Saddam's eroding support in the Arab world, and the diplomatic skills of the United States.[143]

Resolution 1441 makes broad prescriptive claims. The resolution expressed determination to "secure full compliance" with the decisions of the Council,[144] invoked "Chapter VII of the Charter of the United Nations,"[145] and remained "seized of the matter,"[146] which was legal code for retaining authority over the dispute and claiming to displace any other UN organ—such as the General Assembly or ICJ—from addressing the matter. It decided that Iraq remained in "material breach of its obligations under relevant resolutions."[147] It used the mandatory language of legal orders, stating that Iraq "shall provide . . . not later than 30 days from the date of this resolution"[148] a full weapons declaration. Resolution 1441 also referred to "false statements and omissions" constituting "a further material breach of Iraq's obligations."[149] Finally, it alluded to enforcement measures and consequences of noncompliance but stated that Iraq "will face serious consequences as a result of its continued violations of its obligations."[150]

Immediately after Resolution 1441 was adopted, John Negroponte, the U.S. Permanent Representative to the U.N., issued an Explanation of Vote. This statement clarified the drafting intentions of Resolution 1441, which had been prepared by the United States. Negroponte explained:

> As we have said on numerous occasions to Council members, this Resolution contains no "hidden triggers" and no "automaticity" with respect to the use of force. If there is a

[142] Woodward, *supra* note 123, at 225–26.

[143] *See also* Bosco, *supra* note 4, at 228–31 (discussing negotiations leading to the adoption of Resolution 1441).

[144] *See* S.C. Res. 1441, *supra* note 137, pmbl.

[145] *Id.*

[146] *Id.* at ¶ 14.

[147] *Id.* at ¶ 1.

[148] *Id.* at ¶ 3.

[149] *Id.* at ¶ 4.

[150] *Id.* at ¶ 13.

> further Iraqi breach, reported to the Council by UNMOVIC, the IAEA, or a member state, the matter will return to the Council for discussions as required in paragraph 12. The Resolution makes clear that any Iraqi failure to comply is unacceptable and that Iraq must be disarmed. And one way or another, Mr. President, Iraq will be disarmed. *If the Security Council fails to act decisively in the event of a further Iraqi violation, this resolution does not constrain any member state from acting to defend itself against the threat posed by Iraq, or to enforce relevant UN resolutions and protect world peace and security.*[151]

The United States' position was thus that Resolution 1441 did not constrain any state from using military force in self-defense against the threat posed by Iraq, to enforce relevant UN resolutions, and to protect world peace and security.

The United Kingdom, the key coalition partner in the invasion and a cosponsor of Resolution 1441, did not explicitly endorse the U.S. view that no further authorization was needed in the UK's statement after Resolution 1441 was adopted. Greenstock, the UK permanent representative, stated:

> There is no "automaticity" in this Resolution. If there is a further Iraqi breach of its disarmament obligations, the matter will return to the Council for discussion as required in Operational Paragraph 12. We would expect the Security Council then to meet its responsibilities.
>
> [. . .] But if Iraq chooses defiance and concealment, rejecting the final opportunity it has been given by the Council in Operational Paragraph 2, the UK—together, we trust, with other Members of the Security Council—will ensure that the task of disarmament required by the Resolutions is completed.[152]

Greenstock's statement is a model of diplomatic obfuscation. It did not state whether ensuring disarmament would involve obtaining another Security Council resolution or not.[153]

However, France, China, and Russia issued a joint statement explicitly stating the opposite of the U.S. interpretation of Resolution 1441:

> Resolution 1441 (2002) adopted today by the Security Council excludes any automaticity in the use of force. . . . In case of failure by Iraq to comply with its obligations, . . . such

[151] Press Release, United States Explanation of Vote on UN Security Council Resolution 1441, (Nov. 8, 2002), *available at* http://www.staff.city.ac.uk/p.willetts/IRAQ/US081102.HTM (emphasis added).

[152] United Kingdom Explanation of Vote on Security Council Resolution 1441, (Nov. 8, 2002), *available at* http://www.staff.city.ac.uk/p.willetts/IRAQ/UK081102.HTM (emphasis added).

[153] *Cf. Attorney General's Advice on the Iraq War Iraq: Resolution 1441*, 54 Int'l & Comp. L.Q. 767, 775 (2005) ("[T]he language of resolution 1441 leaves the position unclear and the statements made on adoption of the resolution suggest that there were differences of view within the Council as to the legal effect of the resolution.").

> failure will be reported to the Security Council. . . . It will be then for the Council to take a position on the basis of that report.[154]

These attempts to control the interpretation of Resolution 1441 show how international law is a process of communicating and interpreting prescriptions to shape expectations of appropriate conduct, in order to control decisions and outcomes in international disputes.

On December 7, Iraq submitted an 11,807 page declaration.[155] The United States regarded this declaration as a tactic by Iraq to delay war rather than meaningful compliance.[156] However, at a January 20, 2003, Security Council meeting on terrorism, de Villepin stated that France remained opposed to war against Iraq.[157]

The events that followed are remarkable not because the United States invaded Iraq without a second resolution, but because it tried so hard to get one. The language of Resolution 1441 invoking Chapter VII, prior resolutions, and "serious consequences" was sufficiently vague to be interpreted as both authorizing force and not authorizing force. As with most legal arguments, advocates of war had enough linguistic room to interpret the prescription, apply it to their selected facts, and justify their decision. Although he did not use legalese, President Bush used this legalistic approach when he responded to President Chirac's opposition to war on a private telephone conversation, stating: "When the United Nations Security Council says something, it's important that it mean something."[158] Further, as the most powerful nation, the United States could have gone to war, as a practical matter, without a further resolution, as indeed it eventually did. Yet avoiding a second resolution was not the first strategic option. It was Plan B.

Plan A was to obtain a second specific resolution expressly authorizing war. Although Bush and his key officials did not wish to seek a second resolution, on January 31, 2003, Blair explained to Bush, in what Bush later called "the famous second resolution meeting," that it was politically necessary for Blair to obtain a

[154] Press Release, French Embassy, Iraq/UNSCR 1441—Joint Statement by the People's Republic of China, France and the Russian Federation (Aug. 11, 2002), *available at* http://www.ambafrance-uk.org/Iraq-UNSCR-1441-Joint-statement-by.html.

[155] *See* The Secretary-General, *Report of the Secretary-General on the Declaration submitted by Iraq on 7 December 2002, ¶ 6, delivered to the Security Council,* U.N. Doc. S/2003/232 (Feb. 23, 2003) ("Responding to the requirement in paragraph 3 of Security Council resolution 1441 (2002) to provide a "currently accurate, full and complete declaration of all aspects of its programmes to develop chemical, biological, and nuclear weapons, ballistic missiles, and other delivery systems", on 7 December, Iraq submitted a declaration to UNMOVIC and the IAEA and, through its President, to the Security Council. The declaration, including supporting documents, comprised more than 12,000 pages.").

[156] Woodward, *supra* note 123, at 240 (quoting President George W. Bush stating "The declaration is nothing, it's empty, it's a joke, but we will be measured in response."); *id.* at 235 ("Wrap the whole thing up in red tape as it's been done for 12 years previously, pass another resolution, call it good, everybody goes home and nothing happens.").

[157] *See* U.N. SCOR, 58th Sess., 4688th mtg. at 26, U.N. Doc. S/PV/4688 (Jan. 20, 2003).

[158] Woodward, *supra* note 123, at 313 (quoting President Bush).

second resolution.[159] This was because Blair needed to shore up support in his Parliament, in the same manner that George H. W. Bush had used Resolution 678 to persuade Congress to authorize war. Blair also needed to manage its bilateral relationship with France, its immediate neighbor, as well as manage its broader relations with Europe, which was decidedly less enthusiastic about war than the United States.[160]

By February 22, Bush, Blair, Spanish President José Aznarm, and Italian President Silvio Berlusconi agreed that they would seek a second resolution.[161] This tentative consensus was all the more remarkable because the United States' diplomatic efforts in the Security Council for a second resolution had not gone well, and yet it was willing to choose the difficult diplomatic route of seeking another resolution. On February 5, Secretary of State Colin Powell had given a lengthy presentation to the UN Security Council that was intended to present strong evidence that Saddam still had weapons of mass destruction in violation of Resolution 1441. The evidence, however, was nothing new and in any event, largely circumstantial and inconclusive.[162] The French remained free to take the position that war should be avoided, which Chirac communicated by telephone to Bush on February 7.[163]

Even with that lukewarm reception to Powell's speech, the United States continued to pursue a second resolution. Before then, it had only prepared resolutions providing ultimatums for military action. The United States, the United Kingdom, and Spain circulated a draft Chapter VII resolution to the Council which stated simply that "Iraq has failed to take the final opportunity afforded to it in resolution 1441 (2002)."[164] Russia, Germany and France offered a competing resolution stating that "So far, the conditions for using force against Iraq are not fulfilled."[165] There was no compromise in sight.

Early in the morning on March 12, Bush finally decided that the United States would invade Iraq without a second resolution. At Blair's request, he personally called Mexican President Vincente Fox and Chilean President Ricardo Lagos, asking if they would lend their key support as nonpermanent members on the Security Council for a second resolution. They did not give their support, and Bush concluded to Blair: "It's over."[166] There would be no further resolution. At 10:16 p.m.

[159] *See id.* at 297.

[160] *See id.*

[161] *Id.* at 319–20.

[162] *See* U.N. SCOR, 58th Sess., 4701st mtg., U.N. Doc. SC/7658 (Feb. 5, 2003). *See also* Woodward, *supra* note 123, at 307–11.

[163] Woodward, *supra* note 123, at 313. *See also* Bosco, *supra* note 4, at 231–36 (discussing Powell's presentation and quoting reactions of diplomats from other states).

[164] Bosco, *supra* note 44, at 237; S.C. Draft Iraq Res. 2003/215, U.N. Doc. S/2003/215, at 2 (Feb. 24, 2003).

[165] Bosco, *supra* note 4, at 237; Letter dated 24 February 2003 from the Permanent Representatives of France, Germany and the Russian Federation to the United Nations addressed to the President of the Security Council, U.N. Doc. S/2003/214 (Feb. 24, 2003).

[166] *See* Woodward, *supra* note 123, at 343–45.

on March 20, 2003, President Bush appeared on television and announced to America and the world that the military invasion of Iraq had begun.[167]

Although the Security Council did not issue a second resolution authorizing war, events just before the invasion indicate that the Security Council and international law were very much on the minds of officials. Four days before the declaration of war, Bush, Blair, and Aznar were hosted in Portugal by its president, José Manuel Durão Barroso, to discuss the imminent war. In private, they discussed whether there was legal authorization to go to war based on Resolution 1441, and concluded that the language of "serious consequences" authorized the invasion. At 5:30 p.m., the leaders jointly participated in a news conference. Durão framed the meeting as "a last opportunity for a political solution."[168] The solution, however, was founded in not just politics, but also in law. Bush explained the justification for war as the "inescapable" logic of Resolution 1441. Blair reiterated that there was a "responsibility to uphold the will of the United Nations set out in Resolution 1441 last November." International law was sufficiently important that, four days before war, the heads of state were interpreting prescriptions legalistically to justify war![169]

Law may be used for political ends. Nevertheless, decisionmakers look to prescriptions to express and consolidate expectations of appropriate conduct. Without Resolution 1441 to interpret as a prescription for military force, the United States would have had a much harder time justifying its actions to other nations, to domestic constituencies, and foreign audiences whose support was necessary to build a multilateral coalition for invasion.[170]

Even if the Security Council's claim to legal authority was manipulated in the invasion of Iraq, it was never disavowed. Rather, the unique authority of the Security Council continued to be invoked.[171] The invading coalition further relied on the authority of the Security Council in the aftermath of the invasion. The United States and United Kingdom sought and obtained Security Council Resolution 1483 on May 22, 2003. Resolution 1483 "recognize[ed]" the United States and the United Kingdom as occupying powers with "specific authorities, responsibilities and obligations under applicable international law."[172]

[167] *Id.* at 398; *Bush speech in full*, BBC News (Mar. 20, 2003), http://news.bbc.co.uk/2/hi/americas/2866715.stm (full transcript).

[168] *Id.* at 360.

[169] *See* Woodward, *supra* note 123, at 357–58. *But see* Zacklin, *supra* note 1, at 7 (noting Kofi Annan stated the invasion was illegal and violated the UN Charter). *See also* Thompson, *supra* note 4, at 117–22 (surveying similarly legalist criticisms and defenses of Operation Desert Fox).

[170] *See* Bush, *supra* note 119, at 237–38 ("[A]lmost every ally I consulted—even staunch advocates of confronting Saddam like Prime Minister John Howard of Australia—told me that a UN Resolution was essential to win public support in their countries. [Secretary of State] Colin [Powell] agreed.").

[171] *But cf.* Bosco, *supra* note 4, at 242–48 (arguing that the United Nations Security Council quickly became relevant again after the invasion).

[172] S.C. Res. 1483, pmbl., U.N. Doc. S/RES/1483 (May 22, 2003).

1. General Morality

Although there are strong arguments that the invasion of Iraq was legal, the better view is that officials deviated from legalism when they claimed that the war was lawful.

William H. Taft, IV, Legal Advisor of the U.S. State Department, and Todd Buchwald, Assistant Legal Advisor for Political-Military Affairs, mounted a spirited defense of the 2003 invasion in the *American Journal of International Law* in July 2003. They claimed that the invasion was "certainly lawful," and U.S. actions did not "show a disregard for international law."[173] They argued that Resolution 1441 used the "same terminology" of a "final opportunity" that was present in Resolution 678. Because Resolution 678 authorized force, and the language in the two resolutions were similar, Resolution 1441 "operated in the same way to authorize coalition forces to bring Iraq into compliance with its obligations."[174] Their legalist method is familiar to advocates: find an authoritative interpretation of a prior prescription (Resolution 678), identify similar language in the prescription to be interpreted (Resolution 1441), and conclude inductively that therefore the present prescription carries the same meaning as the prior prescription (authorizing force).

Critics, however, pointed out that the operative language was different. Resolution 678 explicitly authorized the use of "all necessary means," whereas Resolution 1441 contained no such explicit authorization. It only recalled the Council's prior warning that Iraq will "face serious consequences" for violating its obligations. Therefore, the argument goes, Resolution 1441 cannot be interpreted as authorizing force.[175] This argument reached the opposite conclusion as Taft and Buchwald but deployed the same mode of reasoning: select the relevant language in two prescriptions for comparison; if the language differs, then the two prescriptions must have different meaning.

Indeed, Taft and Buchwald used a similar legalist method of reasoning to bolster their argument that Resolution 1441 authorized force. They pointed out that in earlier drafts of Resolution 1441, paragraph 12 stated the Council would convene immediately "to decide any measure to ensure full compliance." The adopted resolution replaced the decision function of the meeting with a decision "to consider the situation and the need for full compliance. . . ." Taft and Buchwald reasoned that if the draft resolution called for a second meeting, and that language did not appear in

[173] *See* Todd F. Buchwald & William H. Taft, IV, *Preemption, Iraq and International Law*, 97 AM. J. INT'L L. 557, 563 (2003).

[174] *Id.* at 563.

[175] *See* Thomas M. Franck, *What Happens Now? The United Nations After Iraq*, 97 AM. J. INT'L L. 607, 612 (2003) ("[W]hat Resolution 1441 did was to purchase unanimity for the return of the inspectors by postponing to another day, which the sponsors hoped might never be reached, the argument as to whether Resolutions 678 and 687 had authorized further enforcement at the sole discretion of one or more of the Council's members.").

the final resolution, then the final resolution must be interpreted as not requiring a second decision.[176]

However, as Taft and Buchwald in all likelihood knew, the real reason for the softened language was to achieve through elision consensus between the United States on one hand, and France, Russia, and China on the other hand for the resolution.[177] A confidential "Downing Street Memorandum" of July 2002 noted the opinion of UK Foreign Secretary Jack Straw that the plan for an ultimatum for Iraq to disarm would "help with the legal justification for the use of force."[178] This ultimatum was Resolution 1441, which was intended to legitimize invading Iraq. However, its text was vague in order to obtain support from the permanent members of the Security Council, who had divergent interests in Saddam's regime. The United States subsequently tried and failed to secure a new resolution explicitly authorizing the invasion of Iraq in 2003. It nonetheless invaded Iraq, claiming that Resolution 1441 authorized force.

However, the United States' interpretation of Resolution 1441 probably stretches legalism too far. Resolution 678 had had a constitutive effect in shaping expectations of decisionmakers that if the Security Council wished to authorize force, it would do so explicitly.[179] The United States' invocation of Resolution 1441 as implicitly authorizing the invasion deviated too far from the community expectations about legalist interpretations of Chapter VII resolutions.

Negroponte's arguments, made on the day that Resolution 1441 was passed,[180] that the United States has an inherent right of self-defense, also do not withstand scrutiny. Under Article 51 of the UN Charter, a state may only act in self-defense against an armed attack.[181] Even assuming that Article 51 extended to an armed attack that had not occurred but was imminent, self-defense did not apply because there was no intelligence report indicating that Saddam was planning an imminent attack against the United States or that he had supplied weapons to terrorists who were planning an imminent attack. The intelligence reports simply stated—wrongly—that Saddam had weapons of mass destruction and that "experience shows that Saddam produces weapons of mass destruction to use, not just to deter."[182] Such a risk of a future attack, without any details of when or how or by

[176] *See* Buchwald & Taft, *supra* note 173, at 562.

[177] *See* Woodward, *supra* note 123, at 221–23 (describing French opposition to unilateral military action and Powell's decision to propose vague language in the final draft resolution in order to persuade France not to exercise its veto, citing Powell quote from final negotiations); William H. Taft IV, *The Bush (43rd) Administration—William H. Taft IV*, *in* Michael P. Scharf & Paul R. Williams, Shaping Foreign Policy in Times of Crisis 127, 132 (2010) (acknowledging differing interpretations of Resolution 1441 between the United States and other states) [hereinafter Shaping Foreign Policy].

[178] *See* Malone, *supra* note 3, at 191.

[179] Vaughan Lowe, *The Iraq Crisis: What Now?*, 52 Int'l & Comp. L.Q. 866, 866 (stating that "it is simply unacceptable" to invade Iraq based on "silences in Resolution 1441").

[180] *Supra*, pt II.C.

[181] *See* UN. Charter art. 51.

[182] Bush, *supra* note 119, at 236.

whom, does not meet the legal threshold for the legal exception of self-defense as it existed in 2003.

Negroponte's claim that the United States could unilaterally act to protect international peace and security also had no basis in law. Articles 39 and 51 of the UN Charter explicitly allocates to the Security Council sole authority for protecting peace and security through military force, except in disputes where a state acts in self-defense before the Council is seized of the matter.[183]

On final analysis, the U.S. officials deviated from their general obligation to promote the common good through legalism when they invaded Iraq on questionable legalist grounds.[184] This deviation from legalism damaged the common good. Academics have observed that the invasion risks destabilizing world order as other states may claim similar unilateral military rights.[185] It also may harm international cooperation because states would be hesitant to agree to anything in the future out of a fear of "their words being twisted afterwards."[186]

2. Specific Morality

Waging wars is presumptively immoral because they result in death, injury, and destruction. This presumption is rebuttable if there are strong moral reasons for going to war. Here, a key reason to go to war was to disarm Saddam Hussein of weapons of mass destruction. It turned out that he had no such weapons.

It remains unclear whether the UK officials reasonably believed that Saddam had weapons of mass destruction. At the time of this writing, there is an ongoing inquiry in the United Kingdom to consider the evidence of what officials there knew or did not know. The evidence emerging from that inquiry is not yet conclusive one way or the other.[187]

However, there is some evidence that suggests that President Bush believed in good faith that Iraq had chemical and biological weapons. His statements that he believed Saddam had weapons of mass destruction are supported by the fact that the U.S. military prepared its troops for biological counterattacks from Iraqi forces and

[183] *See* UN Charter arts. 39, 51.

[184] *See* Malone, *supra* note 3, at 195 (describing Resolution 1441 as "a convenient but substantively meaningless improvisation that immediately spawned new wrangles over its interpretation"); Bosco, *supra* note 4, at 241; Zacklin, *supra* note 1, at 144–46.

[185] *See* Franck, *supra* note 175, at 617.

[186] Alexander Orakhelashvili, The Interpretation of Acts and Rules in Public International Law 491 (2008).

[187] *Compare* Testimony of Sir William Ehrman, Iraq Inquiry, Nov. 25, 2009, Tr. 95:21–96:4 (revealing the United Kingdom received an intelligence report on March 17, 2003 stating that Saddam did not have chemical weapons, a few days before the invasion) *with* British Government, Iraq's Weapons of Mass Destruction: The Assessment of the British Government [the "Iraq Dossier"] (revealing intelligence indicating that Iraq had weapons of mass destruction) *and* Letter from Tim Dowse to Margaret Aldred, Iraq Inquiry, Dec. 14, 2009, at 1 (stating that officials who worked on the Iraq dossier "did so in good faith.").

provided U.S. military personnel with hazmat suits.[188] The belief was also reasonable, given Saddam's history of procuring and using weapons of mass destruction and his persistent refusal to permit inspectors to verify that he no longer had any.

The evidence also suggests that President Bush in good faith believed that Iraq would provide chemical and biological weapons to Al-Qaeda terrorists for them to use against the United States. When Madeline Albright was Secretary of State under the Clinton administration, she too was concerned that Saddam might arm terrorist groups with his weapons of mass destruction.[189] She was informed by intelligence officials at that time that Saddam did not have links to Al-Qaeda.[190] However, after September 11, 2001, President Bush received intelligence reports that Abu Musab al-Zarqawi, an Al-Qaeda affiliated terrorist, was operating a biological laboratory in northeastern Iraq.[191] Although this report did not establish that Saddam knew about this, when the CIA, working with a major Arab intelligence service, asked Saddam to extradite Zarqawi, he refused. These facts provide circumstantial evidence of links between Iraq and Al-Qaeda.[192] Even if the evidence was inconclusive on its own, an official responsible for the security of his constituencies must take this evidence and its possible implications seriously.

These facts indicate that there was a risk that Iraq would use its weapons against the United States or supply them to terrorists planning an attack against the United States. The consequences of a chemical or biological attack are catastrophic. Therefore, even if the risk is less than certain, it is not a risk that an official should take.[193] Faced with over a decade of noncompliance by Saddam, and a failure of the Security Council to effectively disarm Saddam through its numerous resolutions, it was understandable for the United States to take matters into its own hands, for its own survival. The general moral obligation to obey international law cannot outweigh the moral obligation to protect the well-being and lives of constituencies. This moral calculus does not make lawful an illegal invasion. However, unlawful actions may, in acute circumstances, nevertheless be reasonable.

There has been no credible allegation, backed by sufficient proof, that President Bush acted in bad faith or without sufficient deliberation. He deliberated for 18 months. During this time, government officials, including Secretary of State Colin Powell, a military general, reviewed intelligence reports. Using their judgment based on the best, but nonetheless imperfect, information available, the administration concluded that the risk that Iraq would pass biological and chemical weapons was real. After 9/11, that risk was not one that a U.S. President could take.[194]

[188] *See* Bush, *supra* note 119, at 235–36.

[189] *See* Albright, *supra* note 69, at 658.

[190] *See id.*

[191] *See* Bush, *supra* note 119, at 236.

[192] *Id.*

[193] *Cf.* Albright, *supra* note 69, at 351–52 (describing risks of a chemical attack by Saddam and concluding: "This was scary stuff.").

[194] *Cf. id.*, at 352 & n.2 (noting that prior to 9/11 Dick Cheney favored continuing the Clinton policy of containing Iraq and explaining that the decision not to invade Iraq in 1990 was to avoid

President Bush could have determined, based on these facts, that there was a real risk Iraq had weapons of mass destruction and would supply them to terrorists, who would use them to attack the United States. These terrorists had already attacked U.S. embassies in Africa, U.S. military warships—such as the USS Cole—and had attacked the United States on its own soil on September 11, 2001. Even though Iraq did not in the end have weapons of mass destruction, it could have been reasonable for U.S. officials to have also concluded that Saddam did have weapons of mass destruction and was prepared to use them or supply them to terrorists. Thus, officials had a moral obligation to disarm Saddam, by force if necessary, to protect their constituencies.[195] This moral calculus justified deviating from strict legalist interpretations of limited authorizations to use force even if those departures from legalism would damage the common good.[196]

Officials, like other Herculean decisionmakers in international law,[197] ought to exercise their best judgment in balancing the competing moral considerations when deciding how to interpret prescriptions and what to do. Correspondingly, unless their actions are patently unjustified, they should be allowed to exercise their discretion in good faith.

3. Feedback Loops

Although the 1999 bombing of NATO was a completely separate incident from the 2003 invasion of Iraq, NATO's decision to bomb Serbia without even trying to obtain a Security Council resolution authorizing force was a constitutive event creating an unregulated feedback loop that influenced the United States to invade Iraq in 2003.

The legal consequences for the unauthorized NATO bombing were never clarified. Resolution 1244 simply established an UN interim administration after Belgrade capitulated, without acknowledging, let alone accepting or condemning, NATO's unilateral war against Serbia.[198] The ICJ concluded that it lacked jurisdiction to hear claims brought by Serbia against NATO states that their bombing had

other states perceiving the United States "as an imperial power, willy-nilly moving into capitals in that part of the world, taking down governments").

[195] *See id.* at 177 (noting that executive decisionmaking involves "mak[ing] our decisions based on the best information available each day, inevitability influenced by the effect of decisions reached the previous day, week, or year. . . . sometimes stepping wrong and having to retrace."); *cf.* Reisman, *supra* note 85, at 860 (1999) ("[D]ecision makers must act on current facts, not wishful if-onlys and wistful might-have-beens.")

[196] *Cf. Attorney General's Advice on the Iraq War Iraq: Resolution* 1441, *supra* note 151, at 776 ("[O]n a number of previous occasions, including in relation to Operation Desert Fox in December 1998 and Kosovo in 1999, UK forces have participated in military action on the basis of advice from my predecessors that the legality of the action under international law was no more than reasonably arguable.").

[197] *See supra* ch. 3, pt. V.D.

[198] *See* S.C. Res. 1244, *supra* note 75.

been illegal.[199] Consequently, it was left to scholars to determine whether the bombing was lawful, and if it was lawful, under what circumstances in the future would unilateral force also be lawful. Not surprisingly, academic consensus was not reached.[200]

Thus, when President Bush was deciding whether he needed explicit authorization from the Security Council to invade Iraq, he considered the Clinton administration's bombing of Serbia without even trying to get authorization. Donald Rumsfeld and Dick Cheney argued that based on that precedent, and the fact that 16 resolutions had already been passed attempting to neutralize the security threat that Iraq posed, further authorization to invade Iraq was not needed. President Bush concluded: "From a legal standpoint, a resolution was unnecessary."[201]

It is also easy to see how officials could conflate the two events. The 1999 campaign was principally to neutralize an ongoing humanitarian crisis in Kosovo involving mass killings and displacements of Kosovars. Saddam Hussein had gassed minorities in Iraq and had continued to abuse his constituents and repress them. If it was justified to invade Serbia on humanitarian grounds, it might seem reasonable to invade Iraq on humanitarian grounds as well.

However, whatever constitutive effect NATO's bombing on Serbia had on international law, officials ought not to have claimed that it changed the law to permit the United States to invade Iraq without Security Council authorization. In the 1999 bombing, there was a temporal nexus between the bombing and the ongoing mass killings. In the 2003 invasion of Iraq, there were no ongoing mass killings. Without a temporal nexus between a humanitarian crisis and the use of force, the right to use force for humanitarian reasons would be open to abuse as a pretext for invasion, as well as errors of judgment that human rights abuses were sufficiently grave to require intervention.

Had the Security Council, the ICJ, or another authoritative body clarified the legality and criteria for unilateral force after the bombing of Serbia, Cheney and Rumsfeld would have had a more difficult time persuading President Bush that the 1999 campaign established a precedent for U.S. military action without Security Council authorization. In 1999, some scholars feared that not taking the prohibition on military force seriously was the thin end of the wedge. Now their fears had materialized, because the international community insufficiently clarified and regulated the feedback loop created in a key international incident, the bombing of Serbia.

By comparison, the Security Council has controlled the feedback loop created by the 2003 invasion. Decisionmakers and constituencies in other countries have imposed high diplomatic and reputational costs on the United States for the 2003

[199] Legality of Use of Force (Serb. and Montenegro v. Ger.), Judgment, 2004 I.C.J. 720, ¶ 115 (Dec. 15).

[200] *See supra* pt. II.B.

[201] Bush, *supra* note 119, at 237.

invasion, thereby limiting its power in future disputes.[202] The international process of communication about Resolution 1441 and the invasion of Iraq also reinforced community expectations that Security Council authorization to use force must be explicit. The effect on U.S. power and the constitutive dimensions of the 2003 invasion of Iraq were demonstrated in 2006, when the United States obtained a Security Council Resolution 1696 calling on Iran to suspend its nuclear enrichment activities.[203] Although it is a Chapter VII resolution, it explicitly requires further authorization for sanctions. Paragraph 8 states that the Security Council:

> *Expresses* its intention, in the event that Iran has not by that date complied with this resolution, then to adopt appropriate measures under Article 41 of Chapter VII of the Charter of the United Nations to persuade Iran to comply with this resolution and the requirements of the IAEA, and *underlines* that further decisions will be required should such additional measures be necessary[.]

According to Orakhelashvili, the United States had sought authorization for sanctions in the resolution if Iran did not comply with the resolution's prescriptions to cease nuclear enrichment. Because the United States had previously read Resolution 1441 to implicitly authorize force, other members of the Security Council insisted that Resolution 1696 explicitly require further authorization to impose sanctions.[204] In diplomacy, like in life, credibility can only be lost once.

Comparing the feedback loops from the 1999 war and the 2003 invasion, a reasonable question to ask is: why did the international community fail to control the feedback loop in 1999 but did try to do so in 2003? There are complex reasons for the different international responses to the two respective wars, which may have to do as much with rational appraisals of each incident as with political interests of decisionmakers and the demands of their constituents. However, a reasonable explanation may be inferred from important differences between the two wars.

The 1999 invasion was widely judged by officials and constituents as legitimate because the horrifying acts of violence in Serbia had to be stopped, and the risks of widening instability in the Balkans was significant. In contrast, the 2003 invasion has been criticized worldwide, especially since no weapons of mass destruction were found in Iraq afterward, and violence in Iraq increased under Coalition occupation.

This difference in legitimacy between the two wars may explain the different reactions in the ongoing process of communication among decisionmakers that establishes legal prescriptions and gives them meaning. In response to the 1999 invasion, decisionmakers simply acquiesced and the Security Council never addressed it, leaving ambiguity as to its legality and scope of future application.

[202] *See* Cockayne & Malone, *supra* note 32, at 405 (one key reason why "[c]osts for the US, for Iraq, and for the UN have been staggering" in the 2003 invasion was because it took place "without clear international legal sanction.").

[203] *See* S.C. Res. 1696, UN Doc. S/RES/1696 (July 31, 2006).

[204] Orakhelashvili, *supra* note 186, at 492.

In response to the 2003 invasion, decisionmakers took explicit steps to clarify that Security Council resolutions do not implicitly authorize force, in order to reject the United State's legalist view of implict authorizations in resolutions.

A lesson to draw from a comparison of the two feedback loops is that regardless of the legitimacy of an international decision to go to war, if it deviates from shared expectations of appropriate conduct, decisionmakers and authoritative institutions should always clarify what, if any, constitutive effect the incident had on extant prescriptions. Failing to do so leaves room for ambiguity. It makes state actions in the future less predictable. This uncertainty undermines international law as a system for promoting the common good. Consequently, in an international incident, authoritative decisionmakers have a moral obligation to clarify the scope and limits of adjustments they make to prescriptions, to minimize the risk that decisionmakers will haphazardly apply these modified prescriptions in future disputes.

With the benefit of hindsight, it would be best not to regard the 2003 invasion as altering the international legal prescriptions on the use of force to permit preemptive attacks. It should, instead, be viewed as a mistake of good faith lapse of judgment, with awful and irreparable consequences for the Iraqis and U.S. soldiers who were injured or killed.

Some good can come from bad mistakes when decisionmakers learn from them. The 2003 invasion has demonstrated that international legal prescriptions on the use of force are archaic. The legal triggers authorizing military force come too late to stop terrorist attacks or attacks using weapons of mass destruction. No state with military capabilities to stop an attack will obey legal prescriptions that do not permit it to successfully defend itself. Therefore, scholars and officials should methodically consider how to authoritatively adjust the laws of war to permit states to effectively defend themselves against enemies using highly destructive technologies in unconventional ways, while preserving minimum order and preventing abuses of those laws. The alternative of insisting on archaic laws of war simply risks another catastrophic error when another state decides it has to cast aside present laws in order to protect itself from terrorists with weapons of mass destruction.

One alternative to consider is adjusting international law to impose on states, which have been proven to possess weapons of mass destruction and that have carried out unlawful armed attacks within a limitations period of say 20 years, the burden of proving to an international organization, such as the International Atomic Energy Agency, that they no longer have such weapons. Where the errant state fails to do so, the law should permit an international coalition of states to invade the errant state to forcibly disarm it without further Security Council authorization. The logic of this new approach is that a state that has nothing to hide will come clean about its disarmament. Making the consequences of failing to discharge the burden of proving disarmament explicitly clear in a legal prescription ahead of time, before the next international dispute, should encourage rational decisionmakers in errant states to disarm and discharge their burden of proof.[205]

[205] This proposal updates and supplements the author's prior recommendations, which were published in Cheng & Valaitis, *supra* note 129.

This adjustment to international law is likely to better manage recourse to force than the present legal prescriptions that absolutely prohibit attacking a state that is reasonably feared to possess weapons of mass destruction and thought to be willing to use them. The alternative regulatory regime proposed provides a way for responsible states to protect themselves. Under this proposal, the 2003 attack would have been legal. It would also have been legitimate on legalist grounds, because the facts met the proposed threshold for preemptive force proposed. Such legalism provides a formal footing for the reasonable assumption in 2003 that Iraq had weapons of mass destruction and would use them after it evaded international inspection efforts and multiple Security Council resolutions for decades.

The difference that this proposal may have made, had it been the law in 2003, is that Saddam Hussein may have realized that invasion was legal and inevitable if he did not prove he had disarmed. If he was a rational actor, he may have provided such proof to remain in power, especially because, as it turns out, he had nothing to hide. While the proposed adjustment provides no guarantee that Saddam Hussein would have acted in this way, it would have increased the likelihood that he would have. That could have avoided the 2003 war and its terrible consequences.

Projecting into the future, the proposed legal prescription could potentially authorize attacking North Korea. The IAEA has determined that North Korea has nuclear weapons.[206] If the Security Council passes a resolution that North Korea's attacks on South Korea in 2010 were unlawful,[207] or if North Korea engaged in unlawful uses of force in the future, that would place upon North Korea the burden of proving that it has disarmed. If it failed to discharge that burden, the proposed prescription would authorize the use of force against North Korea.

This does not mean that it would be wise to attack North Korea. It may be catastrophic to do so, and policymakers must be cautious about the risk of a nuclear war. However, if the proposed criteria for preemptive force are met, and policymakers and military experts determine in their best good faith judgment that forcible disarmament is the necessary and wise course, such forcible measures ought to be legal, even without direct Chapter VII authorization.

The adjustment proposed is preferable to an expansive doctrine of preemptive self-defense, such as the Bush Doctrine, under which a state reserves for itself the absolute self-judging right to attack any other state thought to pose an incipient threat. A balance must be struck between, on the one hand, respecting a state's sovereign territory and right to be free from attack, the need to minimize violence, and a state's legitimate interests in a strong defensive military; and, on the other hand, other state's interests in self-defense.

[206] *See* IAEA Director General, Implementation of the NPT Safeguards Agreement Between the Agency and the Democratic People's Republic of Korea, U.N. Doc. GC(46)/16 (Aug. 16, 2002). *See also* The DPRK's Violation of its NPT Safeguards Agreement with the IAEA, *available at* http://www.iaea.org/newscenter/focus/iaeadprk/dprk.pdf (providing historical context).

[207] *See* Remarks by Ambassador Susan E. Rice, U.S. Permanent Representative to the United Nations, at a Security Council Meeting on the Situation on the Korean Peninsula (Dec. 19, 2010), *available at* http://seoul.usembassy.gov/p_rok_121910.html ("On November 23, North Korea launched a premeditated and unprovoked attack on the island of Yeonpyong.").

The author proposes that a reasonable conclusion is to prohibit unilateral preemptive attacks against other states that either do not have weapons of mass destruction, have not indicated their willingness to use them through prior unlawful attacks, or have proven that they have disarmed. Thus, the proposal would also not permit attacking Iran at the present time, if intelligence reports confirm that it has not acquired nuclear weapons, or if Iran has not carried out any unlawful attack.

There is an additional reason why the regime of managed preemptive force proposed is preferable to an unregulated, self-judging right of states to unilateral force. Allowing states to judge for themselves, without any international criteria, when a threat is sufficiently grave to require early intervention, risks abuse by decisionmakers acting in bad faith, without any international standard to hold them accountable. Michael Reisman and Andrea Armstrong have surveyed international responses to the Bush Doctrine, and found that many other states copied the United States and declared for themselves corresponding rights to use preemptive force.[208] Even if the United States and some other states will exercise an unchecked right to preemptive force responsibly, it cannot be assumed that all states would do so. The possibility that Iran would claim such a right, on the basis that the United States has done so, to attack Israel, or that Israel would justify preemption against Iran with similar reasoning, would be unacceptably destructive to world order and the common good it promotes.

From a U.S. perspective, the proposal here is not without potential problems. Suppose an international decision is made that the limitations period for prior unlawful attacks, which requires a state to disarm and prove that it has done so, is not 20 years but a longer period of 30 years: the United States would be required to disarm because the ICJ determined in 1986 that the United States committed unlawful attacks against Nicaragua.[209] This decision is highly questionable on multiple grounds and was discussed in Chapter Four. But the reason for a 20-year limitations period is not to avoid catching the United States within the disarmament regime. It is because the Cold War ended in 1990, and, writing in 2010, it is reasonable to propose international regulations that consider only the actions of states after the Cold War, which was a period of unique conditions and exigencies. In the alternative, decisionmakers could adopt these adjustments to the law of war prospectively, so that actors can adjust their behavior accordingly.

Supposing decisionmakers accept that the alternative proposed here provides workable standards to guide them in determining the narrow circumstances in which preemptive force is legitimate and legal, there is still the question of how to adjust the existing laws on the use of force to make the proposal legally effective. It is unlikely that the UN Charter can be amended because there are too many state

[208] Andrea Armstrong & W. Michael Reisman, *The Past and Future of the Claim of Preemptive Self-Defense*, 100 Am. J. Int'l L. 525, 548 (2006) ("[M]imesis may accelerate the drift away from the binary formulation of Article 51."); *id.* at 550 (highlighting the dangers of "legal mimesis").

[209] Military and Paramilitary Activities In and Against Nicaragua (Nicar. v. U.S.), 1986 I.C.J. 14, ¶ 292 (June 27).

parties to achieve consensus. The ICJ could adopt this proposal, but that would require an innovation of law arguably beyond its legalist authority.

It will therefore be up to decisionmakers in states to adjust prescriptions on the use of force. They may interpret the 2003 invasion as adjusting expectations that states may use preemptive force under the narrow circumstances proposed, in light of the fact that the United States invaded Iraq after it failed to prove that it had disarmed. Government officials may also declare that they accept these proposals in their military doctrine, which may provide a basis for concluding that the customary law of force has changed. The ICJ, scholars, or other authoritative decisionmakers may subsequently acknowledge and accept this change. This process of adjustment will take time. Decisionmakers ought to collectively work out the particulars of this proposal, such as the applicable standard of proof of disarmament. But these adjustments are preferable to the present obsolete restrictions on force. It is better to have new clear standards known to all decisionmakers and constituents in advance than to repeat the error of the 2003 invasion of Iraq.

III. CONCLUSION

The close examinations of the 1990 Gulf War, the 1999 NATO bombing of the FRY, and the 2003 invasion of Iraq have demonstrated how the justificatory theory of international law applies to officials. Like all other decisionmakers, they ought to balance the general morality of promoting the common good through legalism with specific moral considerations of each particular international problem, and the need to make claims that other decisionmakers will accept so that their claims are at least minimally effective. However, unlike judges or arbitrators, officials represent the constituents of their states and have a special moral obligation to promote the preferred values of their constituents, in addition to their other moral obligations.

When making decisions about the optimal balance of these considerations in an international problem, officials have to make decisions based on the best available information at that time. In retrospect, decisions may turn out to be wrong because intelligence was flawed, as was the case with Iraq; or because other decisionmakers respond in unanticipated ways, as was the case with Serbia. In some circumstances, hindsight may lead observers to judge earlier actions as illegitimate. However, bearing in mind what information was available when an operational decision had to be made under immense pressure, a decision that led to bad outcomes may have been reasonably justified at the time it was made

Whether a decision was legitimate or not, if it departed from interpretations of legal prescriptions accepted as appropriate, officials ought to clarify—in authoritative institutions such as the Security Council or ICJ if possible—the standards for departure and the adjustments to prescriptions. Such authoritative clarifications are necessary to prevent unintended feedback loops that alter the law in unexpected ways in future disputes, even potentially undermining basic struts of the international legal system that are necessary to secure the common good, such as the prohibition on the use of military force except in tightly circumscribed and regulated exceptions.

9 Law Beyond Laws

I. REFRAMING DEBATES

In order to justify international law's claim to regulate decisionmakers, this book offers guidance to decisionmakers about what they should do and how they should make decisions in international problems. In the central case of the international legal system,[1] decisionmakers share expectations of appropriate conduct expressed as laws and other prescriptions, but nevertheless have to interpret those expectations when they apply prescriptions to concrete problems. This interpretative process simultaneously adjusts shared expectations for the future and authoritatively influences outcomes in problems at hand. In order to justify international law, decisionmakers involved in its interpretative process ought to take legalism seriously to maintain minimum world order, while trying to effectively secure the other values at stake in international problems, within the limits of their institutional functions.[2]

This project was undertaken to try to ease the gridlock among some liberals and conservatives about international law. In an extreme version of the disagreement, conservatives have been accused of seeking greater executive discretion unfettered

[1] *See supra* ch. 1, pt. III.A; ch. 3, pt. III (both discussing the concept of a central case).

[2] *Cf.*, Ronald Dworkin, Law's Empire 405 (1986) ("Hercules must fold back, into his calculations about what the law is, the best interpretation of his community's principles of fairness, which define his own powers against those of other institutions and officers.").

by international law,[3] and liberals stand charged with using international law as a tool to constrain powerful actors and promote ideological views.[4] Although these accusations oversimplify political disagreements and obscure points of agreement, they highlight the polarization of views about international law. This book attempts to mediate between the views by asking not whether international law can control decisionmakers, but how should decisionmakers harness the international legal system to good ends.

Scholars also occasionally appear to be gridlocked about international law. Some realists who are politically aligned with some forms of conservatism have sought to minimize the perception of international law as law and have emphasized that it is subordinate to politics.[5] In contrast, some liberals have tried to justify international law as law,[6] emphasizing that "there is a system of norms, a system of reciprocal obligations that most countries obey."[7] The justificatory theory of international law presents an alternative to debates about whether international is law. It focuses instead on how decisionmakers should effectively use the interpretative processes of the international legal system for good ends, and what they ought to do when faced with international problems. If THE LIMITS OF INTERNATIONAL LAW by Jack Goldsmith and Eric Posner was a conservative thrust, and THE POWER AND PURPOSE OF INTERNATIONAL LAW by Mary Ellen O'Connell was a liberal parry, this book proposes a conciliatory alternative to battle.

II. SITUATING AMONG THEORIES

Policy-oriented jurisprudence provides a way to ease the gridlock by situating important insights from other theories of international law within a framework for

[3] *See* Thomas Franck, *Is International Law Really Law*, Remarks at the American Society of International Law Annual Meeting (March 27, 2009), 103 AM. SOC'Y INT'L L. PROC. 161, 162 (2009) (describing "exceptionalists of the sole superpower" who prefer "avoiding being shackled by the ties of [international] law when one has the capacity to get what one wants and getting done what needs to be done").

[4] JOHN BOLTON, HOW BARACK OBAMA IS ENDANGERING OUR NATIONAL SOVEREIGNTY 22 (2011) (claiming that the "Left has seized on customary law as a fertile field for imposing its own ideological standards internationally and binding countries to 'laws' they never explicitly approved").

[5] *See* Franck, *supra* note 3 at 162 ("[E]xceptionalists . . . question whether international law is law.").

[6] *See* Sean D. Murphy, *The Concept of International Law*, 103 AM. SOC'Y INT'L L. PROC. 155, 169 (2009) (observing that international law "has a rather striking array of ways in which rules are made, interpreted, monitored and complied with, suggesting the presence of a system of 'law,' albeit an unusual one"). *See also* D. Stephen Mathias, Anthea Roberts, & Carlos M. Vazquez, *An Introduction: International Law as Law*, 103 AM. SOC'Y INT'L L. PROC. 1 (2009) (seeking to "renew our focus on 'International Law as Law'").

[7] Franck, *supra* note 3 at 163. *See also* Jose Alvarez, *But is it Law?*, Comments at the American Society of International Law Annual Meeting, *in* 103 AM. SOC'Y INT'L L. PROC. 163, 165 (2009) ("Now one can say, as I do, that this enforcement problem [of international law] does not prevent international regimes (whether those involving trade, investment or human rights) from casting their shadow over the behavior of states and deterring unlawful behavior or nudging states into settling, even if for ten cents on the dollar.").

understanding and refining the international legal system to solve actual problems.[8] The core thesis of this book is that in the central case of the international legal system, decisionmakers identify relevant prescriptions, which may take the form of laws, guidelines, principles, articulated practices, or even just shared expectations. They then interpret and apply those prescriptions to the facts. Finally, they have to make a claim about which interpretation to follow, or to ignore or change the prescriptions all together. Other decisionmakers respond to that claim with their own claims interpreting prescriptions. Eventually, decisionmakers may agree on an interpretation, resulting in an outcome in an international problem. This consensus on relevant prescriptions helps to guide future conduct and shape outcomes in other problems, subject to further interpretations by decisionmakers. Although this is a policy-oriented account of the international legal system, international legal process theory has long-accepted that processes such as the ones described above are the foundations of the international legal system,[9] and constructivist international relations theory has recently come to also view international law as a product of social practice and shared expectations.[10]

Thinking about the international legal system in this way turns on its head the usual question about what laws require of people, and reformulates the inquiry as what should people do about law. This inversion is necessary to set up a justificatory theory of international law that guides decisionmakers, so that building and refining the international legal system is a worthwhile enterprise.

In every international problem, a decisionmaker has a general moral obligation to interpret prescriptions according to legalist reasoning and procedures because that helps to produce clear and stable prescriptions, thereby promoting minimum global order,[11] or the "common good" in John Finnis' natural law terminology.[12] That allegation also promotes legitimacy, which, according to Thomas Franck's international

[8] *Cf.* W. Michael Reisman, Siegfried Wiessner & Andrew R. Willard, *Commentary: The New Haven School: A Brief Introduction*, 32 Yale J. Int'l L. 575, 582 (2007) (quoting "the Chinese proverb which Chairman Deng Xiao Ping made famous: It does not matter whether a cat is black or white but whether it catches mice").

[9] *See* Oscar Schachter, *Toward a Theory of International Obligation*, 8 Va. J. Int'l L. 300, 308 (1968) (acknowledging that the processes Schachter described as the basis of legal obligations "are similar to those suggested by Lasswell and McDougal").

[10] *See* Jutta Brunnée & Stephen J. Toope, Legitimacy and Legality in International Law: An Interactional Account 56 (2010) (stating, from the constructivist international relations perspective, that "for law to guide human interaction is must be broadly congruent with the practices and patterns of society. Law must rest on a foundation of shared understandings").

[11] Steven Ratner, *Between Minimum and Optimum World Public Order: An Ethical Path for the Future, in* Looking to the Future: Essays in Honor of W. Michael Reisman 195, 196 (Arsanjani ed., 2011) ("Minimum public order derived from the observation that human beings can best advance their individual and collective goals with minimal coercion and with a set of authoritative procedures for the deployment of force in situations when it is necessary.").

[12] John Finnis, Natural Law and Natural Rights 156 (1996) (referring to the common good as "some set (or set of sets) of conditions which needs to obtain if each of the members is to attain his own objectives," and that "this definition neither assets nor entails that the members of a community must all have the same values or objectives").

legal process theory, comes from adherence, coherence, and determinacy.[13] This form of morality is a "morality of duty," to use Lon Fuller's phrase.[14] This emphasis on legalism should go some way to reassure positivists who see rules as a tool to restrain arbitrary political decisions.[15]

Additionally, however, in each international problem, a decisionmaker has a specific moral obligation to promote a reasonable balance of the values at stake in that problem. The goal is similar to "maximum world order" in policy-oriented jurisprudence,[16] or the "morality of aspiration" in Lon Fuller's natural law theory.[17] The optimal balance of values at stake should take into account the preferred values of the decisionmaker's constituencies as well as the values common to all communities affected by the decision. This approach tries to find a balance between the preferences of sovereigntists who favor national interests,[18] and cosmopolitans who are concerned with the well-being of everyone in every state.[19] The decisionmaker's institutional responsibilities and limits of his authority should guide his determination of a reasonable balance of values and legalism. Judges and arbitrators should emphasize legalism whereas officials, regulators, and legal advisors have a heavier moral duty to promote their constituents' preferred values.

Moreover, a decisionmaker should also choose a decision that is likely to have some minimum threshold of effectiveness. As realists would agree, if other decisionmakers completely reject a claim that they must act or refrain from acting because

[13] Thomas Franck, The Power Of Legitimacy Among Nations 49 (1990) (stating that the "indicators of rule-legitimacy in the community of states are: *determinacy*, *symbolic validation*, *coherence*, and *adherence*") (emphasis in original).

[14] Lon Fuller, The Morality of Law 5 (Revised ed. 1969) (explaining that the morality of duty "lays down basic rules without which an ordered society is impossible, or without which an ordered society directed towards certain specific goals must miss its mark").

[15] *See* Alexander Orakhelashvili, The Interpretation of Acts and Rules in Public International Law 53 (2008) ("Positivism and consensualism are necessary in international law owing to the need for coherency and predictability in the legal system[.]"); *id.* at 583 (criticizing "indeterminacy being used for political interests").

[16] Ratner, *supra* note 11, at 197 ("The concept of optimum world order . . . was said to be the global order that allowed for maximal production and sharing of the eight base values identified early in the work of McDougal and Lasswell: respect, power, wealth, skill, enlightenment, rectitude, affection and well-being.").

[17] Fuller, *supra* note 14, at 5 ("The morality of aspiration is most plainly exemplified in Greek Philosophy. It is the morality of the Good Life, of excellence, of the fullest realization of human powers.").

[18] *See* Jack L. Goldsmith & Eric A. Posner, The Limits of International Law 226 (2005) ("[S]tates speak the language of obligation while following the logic of self-interest . . . and 'liberal democracies are unlikely to support a cosmopolitan foreign policy.'"); Eric Posner & John Yoo, *International Law and the Rise of China*, 7 Chi J. Int'l L. 1, 14 (2006) ('The FTAA [Free Trade of the Americas Agreement] has the *virtue* of both enhancing the economic strength of the US and furthering its hegemonic role in the Americas.") (emphasis added).

[19] Ratner, *supra* note 11, at 201 ("Cosmopolitans scholars are committed to justice based on the equal concern for individuals everywhere, regardless of whether the individual is in one's community or another community.").

of a prescription, that prescription does nothing to promote the common good or values at stake because it is merely academic.[20]

In many international problems, decisionmakers will be able to select an interpretation of a prescription that harmonizes their general and specific moral obligations in an effective manner because legalism tends to yield several possible interpretations of prescriptions. This appreciation for the formal indeterminacies in law is shared with critical legal studies scholars, such as David Kennedy and Martti Koskenniemi.[21]

Where no legalist interpretation of a prescription would harmonize general and specific moral obligations and effectiveness, elites ought to adjust the prescription by proposing an interpretation that deviates from legalism, or, if necessary, disobeying the prescription and proposing an alternative. What they should not do is simply claim an exception for themselves because that encourages other decisionmakers to do the same in an unregulated fashion. This undermines the common good and risks misallocating the values at stake.

III. RESULTS FROM CASE STUDIES

The case studies in this book illustrate how the justificatory theory of international law guides and appraises decisionmaking. Decisionmakers ought to promote the common good by making and interpreting prescriptions to regulate international problems. Aside from formal laws, decisionmakers can consolidate shared expectations of appropriate conduct through informal prescriptions, especially where interests and values are aligned, such as the Basel III Accords and other Financial Stability Board guidelines.[22] Decisionmakers ought to favor informal prescriptions over formal laws where informal prescriptions are just as likely to strengthen shared expectations and are easier to negotiate swiftly, where outcomes are insufficiently determinate and informal prescriptions permit elites to tentatively test the prescriptions, or where vital interests of other decision makers would cause them to block formal prescriptions.

When prescriptions exist, decisionmakers will need to interpret and apply them. In easy cases, where general and specific moral obligations, as well as effectiveness, were aligned, decisionmakers appropriately made decisions with strict fidelity to legalism. It was moral for U.S. officials to condemn the cruel treatment of detainees

[20] *See* Hans Morgenthau, Politics Among Nations 277 (3d ed. 1960) ("To recognize that international law exists is, however, not tantamount to asserting that it is . . . effective in regulating and restraining the struggle for power on the international scene.").

[21] David Kennedy, International Legal Structures 294 (1987) ("[T]he field of rhetorical maneuver [in international law] . . . seems to extend itself virtually to infinity. To a certain extent it results from what seems to be the fluidity and logical indeterminacy of rhetorical frameworks characteristic of each discourse."); Martii Koskenniemi, From Apology to Utopia 610 (2005) ("Now most of *From Apology to Utopia* is devoted to the demonstration of the indeterminacy thesis.").

[22] *See supra* ch. 6, pt II.B.

at Abu Ghraib,[23] to acknowledge violations of the Vienna Convention on Consular Relations and to take measures to stop further violations by state and local law enforcement officials,[24] and to liberate Kuwait from Iraq by force and to end the 1990 Gulf War.[25] It was appropriate for the ICJ to interpret legalistically laws about sovereignty over territory in the *Pedra Branca* case,[26] and it was moral for Singaporean and Malaysian officials to comply with the judgment of the ICJ in that decision. Judge Feliciano acted properly when, serving as an arbitrator, he legalistically determined that the United States had 11 months plus 10 days from the date of Appellate Body decision to comply with the ruling of the WTO appellate body decision, by applying the legal principles contained in relevant treaty texts and prior WTO arbitral decisions.[27]

Complying with appropriate legalist prescriptions strengthens future compliance, because it consolidates expectations of compliance in other similar situations, both by the complying elite and by other elites. The Bush administration acknowledged its obligations under the Vienna Convention on Consular Relations in the *Avena* case.[28] In addition to serving U.S. interests to do so, another possible reason was that the U.S. federal government had committed itself to that position in the prior *LaGrand* case involving violations of the same provisions of the treaty.

Where, however, legalist interpretations of prescriptions would inadequately promote the specific values at stake in an international problem, decisionmakers ought to deviate from legalism so long as they reasonably appraise their specific moral obligations to protect relevant values at stake to be greater than their general moral obligation to promote the common good. Thus, the 1999 bombing of Serbia was probably illegal, but legitimate.[29] If the United States and United Kingdom believed in good faith and with sound judgment that Iraq had weapons of mass destruction based on intelligence information available to them, then the 2003 invasion of Iraq was a reasonably moral decision even if it stretched legalism and damaged the common good that legalism promotes.[30] This book showed that waterboarding did not violate applicable international prescriptions prohibiting torture. Even if waterboarding constitutes unlawful torture, U.S. legal advisors would be justified in authorizing interrogators to waterboard terrorists under strict recorded conditions on a case-by-case basis, if necessary for national security. This is because legal

23 *See supra* ch. 7, pt. II.A.

24 *See supra* ch. 4, pt. II.C.

25 *See supra* ch. 8, pt. II.A.

26 Sovereignty over Pedra Branca/Pulau Batu Puteh, Middle Rocks and South Ledge (Malay./Sing.), Judgment, 2008 I.C.J. 12 (May 23). *See supra* ch. 4, pt. II.A.

27 Final Anti-Dumping Measures on Stainless Steel from Mexico, Arbitration Report, WT/DS344/15 (Oct. 31, 2008). *See supra* ch. 5, pt. II.A.

28 Avena and other Mexican Nationals (Mex. v. U.S.), 2004 I.C.J. 12 (Mar. 31); Request for Interpretation of the Judgment of March 31, 2004 in the case concerning Avena and other Mexican Nationals (Mex. v. U.S.), 2009 I.C.J. 1, 16 (Jan. 19). *See supra* ch. 4, pt. II.C.

29 *See supra* ch. 8, pt. II.B.

30 *See supra* ch. 8, pt. II.C.

advisors have a special duty to promote the preferred values of their constituents, which includes, fundamentally, their lives.[31]

When deviating from legalism, decisionmakers ought not to simply claim exceptions. This risks encouraging other elites to do the same and undermining the common good that comes from legalism. Because NATO claimed that the 1999 bombing of Serbia was *sui generis* without clarifying the criteria for humanitarian intervention, U.S. officials later considered that incident as precedent for the 2003 invasion of Iraq, even though there was no immediate humanitarian crisis in Iraq.[32]

Decisionmakers should instead clarify the reasons for their deviation and propose adjustments to obsolete prescriptions. If the laws authorizing military force are outdated and do not adequately allow states to protect themselves against terrorists or modern weaponry, decisionmakers ought to clarify new regulations authorizing or restricting force, rather than giving states *carte blanche* to attack each other. Decisionmakers can avoid unregulated feedback loops from the 2003 invasion of Iraq by interpreting that incident as proposing an adjustment to the law of force rather than a rejection of it entirely. One adjustment to consider is permitting states to forcibly disarm another state that has previously used force unlawfully and later failed to prove that it no longer had weapons of mass destruction. Such a change to the law of force is better than giving states a wide right to preemptive force, which is more prone to abuse and errors of judgment.[33]

If a decisionmaker fails to correct his inappropriate deviations from legalism, then other decisionmakers should make those corrections, to the extent it is appropriate within their institutional roles. The ICJ in the *Nicaragua* case restricted the basis for self-defense to an armed attack by another state, even though nothing in Article 51 of the U.N. Charter required the armed attack to come from another state.[34] This restriction is archaic because armed attacks often now come from terrorists or state-supported militias. In the *Wall Opinion*, Judge Higgins could not authoritatively correct that deviation because of a shared expectation that the ICJ abides by its prior jurisprudence.[35] However, it was within her judicial authority to point out in the separate opinion the error that the court in the *Nicaragua* case had made,[36] starting an ongoing process to reconsider the *Nicaragua* standard for self-defense.

This justificatory account of international law offers decisionmakers a framework to balance legalism with universal values and the preferred values of constituencies. This is a middle road among viewpoints and may annoy others with more extreme preferences. The proposal that the legal advisors ought to authorize waterboarding of suspected terrorists in individual cases, with strong checks in place, might not

[31] *See supra* ch. 7, pt. II.B.

[32] *See supra* ch. 8, pt. II.C.

[33] *See supra* ch. 8, pt. II.C.

[34] Military and Paramilitary Activities (Nicar. v. U.S.), 1986 I.C.J. 14, ¶ 139 (June 27).

[35] Legal Consequences of the Construction of a Wall in the Occupied Palestinian Territory, Advisory Opinion, 2004 I.C.J. 136, 215, ¶ 33. (July 9) (Separate opinion of Judge Higgins).

[36] *Id. See supra* ch. 4, pt. II.B.

please some neoconservatives and liberals. So, too, the appraisal that absent undue influence from the United States on one arbitrator in the *Loewen* arbitration,[37] the decision of the tribunal was reasonable. These are controversial positions on difficult issues. The author hopes readers will see that the appraisals are reasonable, even if readers disagree with them.

It is hoped that, collectively, the case studies illustrate how the justificatory theory of international law provides guidance to decisionmakers. It provides a framework for discussing what decisionmakers ought to do, and for thoughtfully engaging with each other about the answers to any specific international problem, from the perspectives of decisionmakers who actually have to find solutions that affect lives, instead of merely criticizing problems.

IV. CONCLUSION

The justificatory theory of international law provides a framework for analysis based on theory and backed by case studies to guide but not coerce elites. Constituents expect decisionmakers to exercise their judgment, and this book offers decisionmakers a way of thinking about international problems to decide what to do.

The justificatory theory of international law does not predict outcomes, nor does it give controlling instructions to decisionmakers.[38] These are not its goals. Such a high degree of regulation is practically impossible in an international legal system that lacks centralized authority to enforce laws. It is also normatively unattractive in a world populated by individuals and communities, which, aside from some basic values, have diverse preferences. A shopkeeper in Singapore probably has little patience for officials from foreign liberal democracies lecturing him about political rights, just as a rancher in Tucson probably dislikes Germany interfering with Arizona's death penalty.[39] But they both want to be able to sell their goods to each other and to travel overseas should they wish to do so. The international legal system ought to help individuals and communities cooperate and compete with each other to pursue their respective preferred values.

In seeking to offer guidance to elites by drawing on prior theoretical insights of eminent scholars and testing them against contemporary case studies, the author is acutely aware that there are other important fields of research not yet traveled, such as environmental law and criminal law. These and other adventures are left for another day and the author invites other scholars to join the endeavor.

[37] Loewen Group, Inc. v. U.S., ICSID Case No. ARB(AF)/98/3, 42 I.L.M. 811 (June 26, 2003).

[38] *See, e.g.*, ch. 5, pt. II.C. (discussing different possible appraisals of the ad hoc committee's decision on annulment in CMS v. Argentina). *See also* CMS Gas Transmission Co. v. Argentine Republic, ICSID Case No. ARB/01/8, Award (May 12, 2005); CMS Gas Transmission Co. v. Argentine Republic, ICSID Case No. ARB/01/8, Annulment Proceeding (Sept. 1, 2006).

[39] *See* Fed. Rep. Germany v. United States, 526 U.S. 111 (1999) (denying petition of habeas corpus to stop the execution in Arizona of a murderer who was a German citizen). *See also* LaGrand (Ger. v. U.S.), Judgment, 2001 I.C.J. 466, 511, 516 (June 27).

This book ends where it begins, with the politics of theorizing. The account of the international legal system offered here has political consequences if decisionmakers adopt it. It rejects a blanket disapproval of international law and so it will not resonate with trenchant exceptionalists or other scholars who radically challenge existing international power structures reflected in the international legal system. It also distances itself from an extreme liberal view that international law ought to constrain executive power even where acute national interests are at stake. Hopefully, most readers will agree with this book's rejection of those extreme views.

The justification for international law does not depend on whether it is law. It depends on whether the international legal system is effective and good. International law works best when decisionmakers interpret prescriptions to balance values and the common good, within their institutional responsibilities, and in ways that at least some other decisionmakers accept. On final analysis, international law is what we make of it, for it is nothing more or less than the sum of our decisions.

Bibliography and Sources

BOOKS

MADELEINE ALBRIGHT, MADAM SECRETARY: A MEMOIR (2003).

MOHAMED SAMEH M. AMR, THE ROLE OF THE INTERNATIONAL COURT OF JUSTICE AS THE PRINCIPAL JUDICIAL ORGAN OF THE UNITED NATIONS (2003).

R. P. ANAND, STUDIES IN INTERNATIONAL LAW AND HISTORY: AN ASIAN PERSPECTIVE (2004).

JOHN AUSTIN, THE PROVINCE OF JURISPRUDENCE DETERMINED (David Campbell & Philip Thomas eds., 1998)(1832).

JAMES A. BAKER, THE POLITICS OF DIPLOMACY: REVOLUTION, WAR, AND PEACE, 1989–1992 (1995).

AHARON BARAK, JUDICIAL DISCRETION (1989).

STEPHANE BEAULAC, THE POWER OF LANGUAGE IN THE MAKING OF INTERNATIONAL LAW (2004).

DAVID J. BEDERMAN, INTERNATIONAL LAW FRAMEWORKS (3d ed. 2010).

DAVID J. BEDERMAN, INTERNATIONAL LAW IN ANTIQUITY (2001).

R. DOAK BISHOP, JAMES CRAWFORD, & W. MICHAEL REISMAN, FOREIGN INVESTMENT DISPUTES: CASES, MATERIALS, AND COMMENTARY (2005).

JOHN BOLTON, HOW BARACK OBAMA IS ENDANGERING OUR NATIONAL SOVEREIGNTY (2011).

GARY B. BORN, INTERNATIONAL ARBITRATION: CASES AND MATERIALS (2011).

GARY B. BORN, INTERNATIONAL COMMERCIAL ARBITRATION (2009).

DAVID L. BOSCO, FIVE TO RULE THEM ALL: THE UN SECURITY COUNCIL AND THE MAKING OF THE MODERN WORLD (2009).

JAMES BOUVARD, TERRORISM AND TYRANNY (2003).

IAN BROWNLIE, PRINCIPLES OF PUBLIC INTERNATIONAL LAW (7th ed. 2008).

JUTTA BRUNNÉE & STEPHEN J. TOOPE, LEGITIMACY AND LEGALITY IN INTERNATIONAL LAW: AN INTERACTIONAL ACCOUNT (2010).

GEORGE BUSH & BRENT SCOWCROFT, A WORLD TRANSFORMED (1998).

GEORGE W. BUSH, DECISION POINTS (2010).

MICHAEL BYRES, CUSTOM, POWER AND THE POWER OF RULES (1999).

BENJAMIN N. CARDOZO, THE NATURE OF THE JUDICIAL PROCESS (1921).

ANTHONY CARTY, THE DECAY OF INTERNATIONAL LAW?: A REAPPRAISAL OF THE LIMITS OF LEGAL IMAGINATION IN INTERNATIONAL AFFAIRS (1988).

ABRAM CHAYES & ANTONIA HANDLER CHAYES, THE NEW SOVEREIGNTY: COMPLIANCE WITH INTERNATIONAL REGULATORY AGREEMENTS (1995).

TAI-HENG CHENG, STATE SUCCESSION AND COMMERCIAL OBLIGATIONS (2006).

COMMENTARY ON THE ROME STATUTE OF THE INTERNATIONAL CRIMINAL COURT: OBSERVERS NOTES, ARTICLE BY ARTICLE (2d ed. Triffterer ed., 2008).

JOHN DAVIES, THE QUESTION CONCERNING IMPOSITIONS (1656).

MARTIN S. DAY, THE MANY MEANINGS OF MYTH (1984).

ALAN DERSHOWITZ, SHOUTING FIRE: CIVIL LIBERTIES IN A TURBULENT AGE (2002).

ALAN DERSHOWITZ, WHY TERRORISM WORKS: UNDERSTANDING THE THREAT, RESPONDING TO THE CHALLENGE (2002).

ERIKA DE WET, THE CHAPTER VII POWERS OF THE UNITED NATIONS SECURITY COUNCIL (2004).

EMERRICH DE VATTEL, THE LAW OF NATIONS (Kapossy & Whatmore eds., Liberty Fund 2009).

CHARLES DE VISSCHER, THEORY AND REALITY IN PUBLIC INTERNATIONAL LAW (P.E. Corbett trans., 1968).

JUERGEN DEDRING, THE UNITED NATIONS SECURITY COUNCIL IN THE 1990S (2008).

RONALD DWORKIN, LAW'S EMPIRE (1986).

EXPLORING LAW'S EMPIRE: THE JURISPRUDENCE OF RONALD DWORKIN (Hershovitz ed., 2006).

JEREMY M. FARRALL, UNITED NATIONS SANCTIONS AND THE RULE OF LAW (2007).

AARON FICHTELBERG, LAW AT THE VANISHING POINT: A PHILOSOPHICAL ANALYSIS OF INTERNATIONAL LAW (2008).

JOHN FINNIS, NATURAL LAW AND NATURAL RIGHTS (1996).

ROGER FISHER, IMPROVING COMPLIANCE WITH INTERNATIONAL LAW (1981).

THOMAS M. FRANCK, FAIRNESS IN INTERNATIONAL LAW AND INSTITUTIONS (1995).

THOMAS M. FRANCK, THE POWER OF LEGITIMACY AMONG NATIONS (1990).

LON FULLER, THE MORALITY OF LAW (Revised ed. 1969).

RICHARD K. GARDINER, TREATY INTERPRETATION (2008).

FREDERICK HENRY GAREAU, STATE TERRORISM AND THE UNITED STATES: FROM COUNTERINSURGENCY TO THE WAR ON TERRORISM (2004).

CHINMAYA R. GHAREKHAN, THE HORSESHOE TABLE: AN INSIDE VIEW OF THE UN SECURITY COUNCIL (2006).

YUVAL GINBAR, WHY NOT TORTURE TERRORISTS (2010).

JACK L. GOLDSMITH, THE TERROR PRESIDENCY (2007).

JACK L. GOLDSMITH & ERIC A. POSNER, THE LIMITS OF INTERNATIONAL LAW (2005).

BRANDT GOLDSTEIN, STORMING THE COURT (2005).

GREGORY GRANDIN, EMPIRE'S WORKSHOP (2007).

ROBERT D. GREENBERG, LANGUAGE AND IDENTITY IN THE BALKANS: THE SERBO-CROATIAN DISINTEGRATION (2004).

ALAN GREENSPAN, THE AGE OF TURBULENCE (2008).

ANDREW T. GUZMAN, HOW INTERNATIONAL LAW WORKS: A RATIONAL CHOICE THEORY (2007).

JÜRGEN HABERMAS, BETWEEN FACTS AND NORMS: CONTRIBUTIONS TO A DISCOURSE THEORY OF LAW AND DEMOCRACY (1997).

H. L. A. HART, THE CONCEPT OF LAW (2d. ed. 1994).

LOUIS HENKIN, HOW NATIONS BEHAVE: LAW AND FOREIGN POLICY (1968).

LOUIS HENKIN, HOW NATIONS BEHAVE: LAW AND FOREIGN POLICY (2d ed. 1979).

ROSALYN HIGGINS, PROBLEMS AND PROCESS: INTERNATIONAL LAW AND HOW WE USE IT (1995).

ROSALYN HIGGINS, THEMES AND THEORIES: SELECTED ESSAYS, SPEECHES AND WRITINGS IN INTERNATIONAL LAW (2009).

WILLIAM SEARLE HOLDSWORTH, A HISTORY OF ENGLISH LAW (7th ed., rev. vol. 1956).

ALLAN C. HUTCHINSON, THE PROVINCE OF JURISPRUDENCE DEMOCRATIZED (2009).

INTERNATIONAL LAW AND THE THIRD WORLD (R. Falk et al. eds., 2008).

INTERNATIONAL REGIMES (S. Krasner ed., 1983).

International Rules: Approaches from International Law and International Relations (Beck et al. eds., 1996).

Shunmugam Jayakumar, Diplomacy: A Singapore Experience (2011).

Shunmugam Jayakumar & Tommy Koh, Pedra Branca: The Road to the World Court (2009).

Philip C. Jessup, A Modern Law of Nations (1959).

Philip C. Jessup, Transnational Law (1956).

Douglas M. Johnston, The Historical Foundations of World Order: The Tower and the Arena (2008).

Hans Kelsen, General Theory of Law and State (Wedberg trans., 1945).

Hans Kelsen, Pure Theory of Law (Knight trans., 1989).

Hans Kelsen, Principles of International Law (1952).

Hans Kelsen, Principles of International Law (3rd prtg.1959).

Hans Kelsen, The Communist Theory of Law (1999).

David Kennedy, International Legal Structures (1987).

Robert Keohane, International Institutions and State Power (1989).

Bernhard Knoll, The Legal Status of Territories Subject to Administration by International Organizations (2008).

Martti Koskenniemi, From Apology to Utopia (2005).

Martti Koskenniemi, The Gentle Civilizer of Nations: The Rise and Fall of International Law (1870–1960) (2001).

Nicola Lacey, A Life of H. L. A. Hart: The Nightmare and the Noble Dream (2004).

Harold D. Lasswell & Myres S. McDougal, Jurisprudence for a Free Society (1992).

Hersch Lauterpacht, International Law: Collected Papers (1975).

Hersch Lauterpacht, International Law (1970).

Hersch Lauterpacht, Private Law Sources and Analogies of International Law (1927).

Edward C. Luck, UN Security Council: Practice and Promise (2006).

David M. Malone, The International Struggle Over Iraq: Politics in the UN Security Council, 1980–2005 (2006).

Gerard Malynes, Lex Mercatoria, the Ancient Law-Merchant (Hamilton ed., 2d ed. 2001).

Kenneth Manusama, The United Nations Security Council in the Post-Cold War Era: Applying the Principle of Legality (2006).

John Norton Moore, The Secret War in Central America and the Future of World Order: Sandista Assault on World Order (1987).

Hans Morgenthau, Politics Among Nations (3d ed. 1960).

John F. Murphy, The United States and the Rule of Law in International Affairs (2004).

Ray Murphy, UN Peacekeeping in Lebanon, Somalia, and Kosovo (2007).

Terry Nardin, Law, Morality, and the Relations of States (1983).

Neil MacCormick, Rhetoric and the Rule of Law (2009).

Arthur Nussbaum, A Concise History of the Law of Nations (1954).

Mary Ellen O'Connell, The Power and Purpose of International Law (2008).

Lassa Oppenheim, International Law: A Treatise (1905).

Oppenheim's International Law (Lauterpacht ed., 1970).

Oppenheim's International Law (Jennings & Watts eds., 9th ed. 1996).

Alexander Orakhelashvili, Peremptory Norms in International Law (2006).

ALEXANDER ORAKHELASHVILI, THE INTERPRETATION OF ACTS AND RULES IN PUBLIC INTERNATIONAL LAW (2008).

MARK OSIEL, THE END OF RECIPROCITY: TERROR, TORTURE AND THE LAW OF WAR (2009).

HENRY M. PAULSON, JR., ON THE BRINK (2009).

COLEMAN PHILLIPSON, THE INTERNATIONAL LAW AND CUSTOM OF ANCIENT GREECE AND ROME (1911).

RICHARD A. POSNER, HOW JUDGES THINK (2008).

ERIC A. POSNER & ADRIAN VERMEULE, TERROR IN THE BALANCE (2007).

PRACTICAL REASONING: READINGS IN PHILOSOPHY (Raz ed., 1978).

JAMES BENNETT PRITCHARD, ANCIENT NEAR EASTERN TEXTS: RELATING TO THE OLD TESTAMENT (3d ed. 1969).

SAMUEL PUFENDORF, OF THE LAW OF NATURE AND NATIONS (Kennett trans., 3d ed. 1717).

DIETRICH RAUSCHNING ET AL., KEY RESOLUTIONS OF THE UNITED NATIONS GENERAL ASSEMBLY 1946–1996 (1997).

JOSEPH RAZ, PRACTICAL REASON AND NORMS (1999).

W. MICHAEL REISMAN & AARON M. SCHREIBER, JURISPRUDENCE (1987).

W. MICHAEL REISMAN ET AL., INTERNATIONAL LAW IN CONTEMPORARY PERSPECTIVE (2d ed. 2004).

W. MICHAEL REISMAN, LAW IN BRIEF ENCOUNTERS (1999).

W. MICHAEL REISMAN, SYSTEMS OF CONTROL IN INTERNATIONAL ADJUDICATION AND ARBITRATION: BREAKDOWN AND REPAIR (1992).

W. MICHAEL REISMAN & ANDREW R. WILLARD, INTERNATIONAL INCIDENTS: THE LAW THAT COUNTS IN WORLD POLITICS (1988).

SHABTAI ROSENNE, PRACTICE AND METHODS OF INTERNATIONAL LAW (1984).

PHILIPPE SANDS, TORTURE TEAM (2008).

MICHAEL P. SCHARF & PAUL R. WILLIAMS, SHAPING FOREIGN POLICY IN TIMES OF CRISIS (2010).

WILLIAM SCHULZ, TAINTED LEGACY (2003).

JAMES BROWN SCOTT, LAW, THE STATE, AND THE INTERNATIONAL COMMUNITY, VOL. 1 (2002).

SELECT CASES CONCERNING THE LAW MERCHANT, VOL. 1 (Gross trans., 1908).

ANNE-MARIE SLAUGHTER, A NEW WORLD ORDER (2004).

ANDREW ROSS SORKIN, TOO BIG TO FAIL (2010).

GEORGE SOROS, THE NEW PARADIGM FOR FINANCIAL MARKETS (2008).

HENRY J. STEINER & DETLEV F. VAGTS, TRANSNATIONAL LEGAL PROBLEMS (1968).

KENNETH R. STEVENS, BORDER DIPLOMACY: THE *CAROLINE* AND MCLEOD AFFAIRS IN ANGLOAMERICAN-CANADIAN RELATIONS, 1837–1842 (1989).

MARGARET THATCHER, THE DOWNING STREET YEARS (1993).

THE IRAQ WAR READER: HISTORY, DOCUMENTS, OPINIONS (Sifry & Cerf eds., 1991).

THE METHODS OF INTERNATIONAL LAW (Slaughter & Ratner eds., ASIL 1999).

THE TORTURE PAPERS: THE ROAD TO ABU GHRAIB (Greenberg & Dratel eds., 2005).

THE UNITED NATIONS SECURITY COUNCIL AND WAR: THE EVOLUTION OF THOUGHT AND PRACTICE SINCE 1945 (Lowe et al. eds., 2008).

ALEXANDER THOMPSON, CHANNELS OF POWER: THE UN SECURITY COUNCIL AND U.S. STATECRAFT IN IRAQ (2010).

THUCYDIDES, HISTORY OF THE PELOPONNESIAN WAR (Warner trans. 1954).

MARK TUSHNET, A COURT DIVIDED: THE REHNQUIST COURT AND THE FUTURE OF CONSTITUTIONAL LAW (2006).

TOM TYLER, WHY PEOPLE OBEY THE LAW (1990).

JEREMY WALDRON, TORTURE, TERROR, AND TRADE-OFFS (2010).
C.G. WEERAMANTRY, UNIVERSALISING INTERNATIONAL LAW (2004).
RALPH WILDE, INTERNATIONAL TERRITORIAL ADMINISTRATION: HOW TRUSTEESHIP AND THE CIVILIZING MISSION NEVER WENT AWAY (2008).
BOB WOODWARD, PLAN OF ATTACK (2004).
LEE KUAN YEW, THE SINGAPORE STORY (1998).
JOHN YOO, WAR BY OTHER MEANS (2006).

ARTICLES

Kenneth W. Abbott, *International Relations Theory, International Law, and the Regime Governing Atrocities in Internal Conflicts*, 93 AM. J. INT'L L. 361 (1999).
Kenneth W. Abbott, *Modern International Relations Theory: A Prospectus for International Lawyers*, 14 YALE J. INT'L L. 335 (1989).
Guillermo Aguilar Alvarez & W. Michael Reisman, *How Well are Investment Awards Reasoned?*, *in* THE REASONS REQUIREMENT IN INTERNATIONAL INVESTMENT ARBITRATION: CRITICAL CASE STUDIES (Alvarez & Reisman eds., 2008).
Kern Alexander, *Global Financial Standard Setting, the G10 Committees, and International Economic Law*, 34 BROOK. J. INT'L L. 861 (2008-09).
José E. Alvarez, *But is It Law?*, 103 AM. SOC'Y INT'L L. PROC. 163 (2009).
José E. Alvarez, *The Return of the State*, 20 MINN. J. INT'L L. 223 (2011).
Kofi Annan, *Forward in* RALPH ZACKLIN, THE UNITED NATIONS SECRETARIAT AND THE USE OF FORCE IN A UNIPOLAR WORLD. POWER V. PRINCIPLE (2010).
Kenneth Anderson, *Remarks by an Idealist on the Realism of the Limits of International Law*, 34 GA. J. INT'L & COMP. L. 253 (2006).
Antony Anghie & B. S. Chimni, *Third World Approaches to International Law and Individual Responsibility in Internal Conflict*, *in* B. S. CHIMNI, INTERNATIONAL LAW AND WORLD ORDER: A CRITIQUE OF CONTEMPORARY APPROACHES (1993).
Andrea Armstrong & W. Michael Reisman, *The Past and Future of the Claim of Preemptive Self-Defense*, 100 AM. J. INT'L L. 525 (2006).
James E. Baker, *Use of Force: Jupiter as Everyman: Michael Reisman and the Scholar as Teacher*, 34 YALE J. INT'L L. 533 (2009).
Luiz Olavo Baptista, *Interpretation and Application of WTO Rules: Florentino Feliciano and the First Seven*, *in* LAW IN THE SERVICE OF HUMAN DIGNITY: ESSAYS IN HONOUR OF FLORENTINO FELICIANO (Charnovitz et al. eds., 2005).
David J. Bederman, *Appraising a Century of Scholarship in the American Journal of International Law*, 100 AM. J. INT'L L. 20 (2006).
John B. Bellinger III, *The Bush (43rd) Administration–John B. Bellinger III (2005–2009)*, *in* MICHAEL P. SCHARF & PAUL R. WILLIAMS, SHAPING FOREIGN POLICY IN TIMES OF CRISIS (2010).
John B. Bellinger III & Vijay M. Padmanabhan, *Detention Operations in Contemporary Conflicts: Four Challenges for the Geneva Conventions and Other Existing Law*, 105 AM. J. INT'L L. 201 (2011).
Frank Berman et al., *Foreign Legal Advisers' Roundtable*, *in* MICHAEL P. SCHARF & PAUL R. WILLIAMS, SHAPING FOREIGN POLICY IN TIMES OF CRISIS (2010).
Paul Schiff Berman, *Seeing Beyond the Limits of International Law*, 84 TEX. L. REV. 1265 (2005-06).
Daniel Bodansky, *The Legitimacy of International Governance: a Coming Challenge for International Environmental Law*, 93 AM. J. INT'L L. 596 (1999).
John R. Bolton, *Is There Really "Law" in International Affairs?*, 10 TRANSNAT'L L. & CONTEMP. PROBS. 1 (2000).

Christopher J. Borgen, *The Language of Law and the Practice of Politics: Great Powers and the Rhetoric of Self-Determination in the Cases of Kosovo and South Ossetia*, 10 Chi. J. Int'l L. 1 (2009).

Herbert W. Briggs et al., *Appraisals of the ICJ's Decision: Nicaragua v. United States (Merits)*, 81 Am. J. Int'l L. 77 (1987).

Herbert W. Briggs, *Nicaragua v. United States: Jurisdiction and Admissibility*, 79 Am J. Int'l L. 373 (1985).

Charles Brower, *The Ethics of Arbitration: Perspectives from a Practicing International Arbitrator*, Keynote Address at the Riesenfeld Symposium, 5 Berkeley J. Int'l L. Publicist 1 (2010).

Ian Brownlie & C.J. Apperley, *Kosovo Crisis Inquiry: Memorandum on the International Law Aspects*, 49 Int'l & Comp. L.Q. 880 (2008).

Chris Brummer, *Post-American Securities Regulation*, 98 Cal. L. Rev. 327 (2010).

Todd F. Buchwald & William H. Taft, IV, *Preemption, Iraq and International Law*, 97 Am. J. Int'l L. 557 (2003).

Thomas Burgenthal, *Proliferation of International Courts and Tribunals: Is It Good or Bad?*, 14 Leiden J. Int'l L. 267 (2001).

Julien Cantegreil, *Legal Formalism Meets Policy-Oriented Jurisprudence: A More European Approach to Frame the War on Terror*, 60 Me. L. Rev. 98 (2008).

Julien Cantegreil, *The Final Award in Mondev International v. United States of America*, *in* The Reasons Requirement in International Investment Arbitration (Reisman & Alvarez eds., 2008).

Robert F. Carolan, *An Examination of the Role of Hybrid International Tribunals in Prosecuting War Crimes and Developing Independent Domestic Court Systems: The Kosovo Experiment*, 17 Transnat'l L. & Contemp. Probs. 9 (2008).

Anthony Carty, *Critical International Law: Recent Trends in the Theory of International Law*, 2 Eur. J. Int'l L. 66 (1991).

Antonio Cassese, *Ex Iniuria Ius Oritur: Are We Moving Towards International Legitimation of Forcible Humanitarian Countermeasures in the World Community*, 10 Eur. J. Int'l L. 23 (1999).

Antonio Cassese, *The Role of Legal Advisers in Ensuring that Foreign Policy Conforms to International Legal Standards*, 14 Mich. J. Int'l L. 139 (1992).

Eric C. Chaffee, *Finishing the Race to the Bottom: An Argument for the Harmonization and Centralization of International Securities Law*, 40 Seton Hall L. Rev. 1581 (2010).

Anupum Chander & Randall Costa, *Clearing Credit Default Swaps: A Case Study in Global Legal Convergence*, 10 Chi. J. Int'l L. 639 (2009-10).

Jonathan I. Charney, *Anticipatory Humanitarian Intervention in Kosovo*, 93 Am. J. Int'l L. 841 (1999).

Abram Chayes, *A Common Lawyer Looks at International Law*, 78 Harv. L. Rev. 1396 (1965).

Hilary Charlesworth, *Feminist Methods in International Law*, *in* The Methods of International Law (Slaughter & Ratner eds., ASIL 1999).

Tai-Heng Cheng, *Power, Authority and International Investment Law*, 20 Am. U. Int'l L. Rev. 465 (2005).

Tai-Heng Cheng, *Power, Norms and International Intellectual Property Law*, 28 Mich. J. Int'l L. 109 (2009).

Tai-Heng Cheng, *Precedent and Control in Investment Treaty Arbitration*, 30 Fordham Int'l L.J. 1014 (2007).

Tai-Heng Cheng, *Renegotiating the Odious Debt Doctrine*, 70 Law & Contemp. Probs. 7 (2007).

Tai-Heng Cheng, *Why New States Accept Old Obligations*, 2011 U. Ill. L. Rev. 1 (2011).

Tai-Heng Cheng & Robert Trisotto, *Reasons and Reasoning in Investment Treaty Arbitration*, 32 Suffolk Transnat'l L. Rev. 409 (2009).

Tai-Heng Cheng & Eduardas Valaitis, *Shaping an Obama Doctrine of Preemptive Force*, 82 Temp. L. Rev. 737 (2009).

Christine Chinkin, *International Law and the NATO Intervention in Kosovo*, 49 Int'l & Comp. L.Q. 876 (2008).

Christine Chinkin, *Normative Development in the International Legal System*, *in* Commitment and Compliance: The Role of Non-Binding Norms in the International Legal System (Shelton ed., 2000).

James Cockayne & David M. Malone, *The Security Council and the 1991 and 2003 Wars in Iraq*, *in* The United Nations Security Council and War: The Evolution of Thought and Practice since 1945 (Lowe et al. eds., 2008).

Harlan Grant Cohen, *Finding International Law: Rethinking the Doctrine of Sources*, 93 Iowa L. Rev. 65 (2008).

Jules Coleman, *Incorporationism, Conventionality, and the Practical Difference Thesis*, *in* Hart's Postscript (Coleman ed., 2001).

Arthur Corbin, *The Judicial Process Revisited: Introduction*, 71 Yale L.J. 195 (1971).

James Crawford, *The International Court of Justice*, Judicial Administration and the Rule of Law, *in* Bowett et al., The International Court of Justice: Process, Practice and Procedure (1997).

John R. Crook, *Contemporary Practice of the United States Relating to International Law: U.S. Strategy for Responding to ICJ's Avena Decision*, 99 Am. J. Int'l L. 489 (2005).

Charles Hall Davis, *Preamble to Constitution of the League of Nations*, 5 Va. L. Reg. New Ser. 14 (1919).

Kenneth W. Dam, *The Subprime Crisis and Financial Regulation: International and Comparative Perspectives*, 10 Chi J. Int'l L. 581 (2009-10).

Ronald Dworkin, *Response*, *in* Exploring Law's Empire (2006).

Richard A. Falk, *Kosovo, World Order, and the Future of International Law*, 93 Am. J. Int'l L. 847 (1999).

Richard A. Falk, *Legality & Legitimacy: The Quest for Principled Flexibility and Restraint*, 31 Rev. Int'l Stud. 33 (Supp. 2005).

Richard A. Falk et al., *Myres Smith McDougal (1906–1998)*, *in* 2 Rosalyn Higgins, Themes and Theories: Selected Essays, Speeches, and Writings in International Law (2009).

Richard A. Falk, *The Role of Law in World Society*, *in* Toward World Order and Human Dignity: Essays in Honor of Myres S. McDougal (Weston & Reisman eds., 1976).

Ulrich Fastenrath, *Relative Normativity in International Law*, 4 Eur. J. Int'l L. 305 (1993).

Florentino P. Feliciano, *The Application of Law: Some Recurring Aspects of the Process of Judicial Review and Decision Making*, 37 Am. J. Juris. 17 (1992).

W.J. Fenrick, *Targeting and Proportionality during the NATO Bombing Campaign against Yugoslavia*, 12 Eur. J. Int'l L. 489 (2001).

John Finnis, *H.L.A. Hart: A Twentieth-Century Oxford Political Philosopher: Reflections by a Former Student and Colleague*, 54 Am. J. Juris. 161 (2009).

Gerald Fitzmaurice, *Legal Advisers and Foreign Affairs*, 59 Am. J. Int'l L. 72 (1965).

Susan D. Franck, *An Empirical Analysis of Investment Treaty Awards*, 101 Am. Soc'y Int'l L. Proc. 459 (2007).

Susan D. Franck, *Development of Outcomes of Investment Treaty Arbitration*, 50 Harv. Int'l L. J. 435 (2009).

Thomas M. Franck, *Icy Day at the ICJ*, 79 Am. J. Int'l L. 379 (1985).
Thomas M. Franck, *Is International Law Really Law*, 103 Am. Soc'y Int'l L. Proc. 31 (2009).
Thomas M. Franck, *What Happens Now? The United Nations After Iraq*, 97 Am. J. Int'l L. 607 (2003).
Tom Ginsburg, *Bounded Discretion in International Judicial Lawmaking*, 45 Va. J. Int'l L. 631 (2004–05).
Mario Giovanoli, *The Reform of International Financial Architecture After the Global Crisis*, 42 N.Y.U. J. Int'l L. & Pol. 81 (2009).
Joseph Gold, *Strengthening the Soft International Law of Exchange Agreements*, 77 Am. J. Int'l L. 443 (1983).
Michael D. Goldhaber., *NAFTA Suit is Alive, Kicking*, Nat'l L.J., Mar. 1, 2004.
Christine Gray, *After the Ceasefire: Iraq, the Security Council and the Use of Force*, 65 Brit. Y.B. Int'l L. 135 (1994).
Christine Gray, *The Charter Limitations on the Use of Force: Theory and Practice*, *in* The United Nations Security Council and War, The Evolution of Thought and Practice since 1945 (Lowe ed., 2008).
David Gray, *Rule-Skepticism, "Strategery," and the Limits of International Law*, 46 Va. J. Int'l L. 563 (2005-06).
Tarcisio Grazzini, *NATO Coercive Military Activities in the Yugoslav Crisis (1992–1999)*, 12 Eur. J. Int'l L. 391 (2001).
Christopher Greenwood, *International law and the NATO Intervention in Kosovo*, 49 Int'l & Comp. L.Q. 926 (2000).
D.W. Greig, *Nicaragua and the United States: Confrontation Over the Jurisdiction of the International Court*, 62 Brit. Y.B. Int'l L. 119 (1991).
Randall D. Guynn, *The Global Financial Crisis and Proposed Regulatory Reform*, 2010 BYU L. Rev. 421, 422–34 (2010).
Andrew T. Guzman, *Rethinking International Law as Law*, 103 Am. Soc'y Int'l L. Proc. 155 (2009).
Andrew T. Guzman, *The Promise of International Law*, 92 Va. L. Rev. 522 (2006).
Gunther Handl et al., *A Hard Look at Soft Law*, 82 Am. Soc'y Int'l L. Proc. 371 (1988).
Oona A. Hathaway & Ariel N. Lavinbuk, *Rationalism and Revisionism in International Law*, 119 Harv. L. Rev. 1404 (2006) (book review).
Oona Hathaway & Scott J. Shapiro, *Outcasting: Enforcement in Domestic and International Law*, 121 Yale L.J. (draft of Nov. 3, 2010) (forthcoming 2011).
Laurence R. Helfer & Anne-Marie Slaughter, *Why States Create International Tribunals: A Response to Professors Posner and Yoo*, 93 Cal. L. Rev. 899 (2005).
Louis Henkin, *Comment*, *in* Abram Chayes, The Cuban Missile Crisis (1974).
Louis Henkin, *Kosovo and the Law of Humanitarian Intervention*, 93 Am. J. Int'l L. 824 (1999).
Chaim Herzog, *Sir Hersch Lauterpacht: An Appraisal*, 8 Eur. J. Int'l L. 299 (1997).
Rosalyn Higgins, *Integrations of Authority and Control: Trends in Literature of International Law and International Relations*, *in* Toward World Order and Human Dignity: Essays in Honor of Myres S. McDougal (Weston & Reisman eds., 1976).
Rosalyn Higgins, *Introductory Statement: Diverging Anglo-American Attitudes to International Law*, 2 Ga. J. Int'l & Comp. L. 1 (1972).
Rosalyn Higgins, *The Benign First Mate*, *in* Law in the Service of Human Dignity: Essays in Honour of Florentino Feliciano (Charnovitz et al. eds., 2005).
Peter Hilpold, *Humanitarian Intervention: Is There a Need for a Legal Reappraisal?*, 12 Eur. J. Int'l L. 437 (2001).

Robert Howse & Ruti Teitel, *Beyond Compliance: Rethinking Why International Law Really Matters*, Global Policy (Online), Vol. 1, No. 2; NYU School of Law, Public Law Research Paper No. 10-08 (Feb. 2010).

John Ikenberry, *The Limits of International Law*, FOREIGN AFFAIRS, Mar./Apr., 2005, (book review).

Dick Jackson, *Interrogation and Treatment of Detainees in the Global War on Terror*, *in* THE WAR ON TERROR AND THE LAWS OF WAR: A MILITARY PERSPECTIVE (Lewis ed., 2009).

R.Y. Jennings, *The Caroline and McLeod Cases*, 32 AM. J. INT'L L. 82 (1938).

Robert Jennings, *Hersch Lauterpacht: A Personal Recollection*, 8 EUR. J. INT'L L. 301 (1997).

Robert Jennings, *The Role of the International Court of Justice*, 68 BRIT. Y.B. INT'L L. 1 (1998).

Robert Jennings, *The Judiciary, International and National, and the Development of International Law*, 102 INT'L L. REPORTS ix (E. Lauterpacht et al. eds.,1996).

Mark J. Kadish, *Article 36 of the Vienna Convention on Consular Relations: The International Court of Justice in Mexico v. United States (Avena) Speaks Emphatically to the Supreme Court of the United States about the Fundamental Nature of the Right to Consul*, 36 GEO. J. INT'L L. 1 (2004).

Sanford H. Kadish, *Torture, the State and the Individual*, 23 ISR. L. REV. 345 (1989).

Kaiyan Homi Kaikobad, *Self Defence, Enforcement Action and the Gulf Wars*, 63 BRIT. Y.B. INT'L L. 300 (1992).

David Kennedy, *The Last Treatise: Project and Person (Reflections on Martti Koskenniemi's From Apology to Utopia)*, 7 GERMAN L.J. 982 (2006).

David Kennedy, *The Mystery of Global Governance*, 34 OHIO N.U. L. REV. 827 (2008).

David Kennedy, *Tom Franck and the Manhattan School*, 35 N.Y.U. J. INT'L L. & POL. 397 (2003).

Benedict Kingsbury, *Legal Positivism as Normative Politics: International Society, Balance of Power and Lassa Oppenheim's Positive International Law*, 13 EUR. J. INT'L L. 401 (2002).

Benedict Kingsbury, Nico Krisch, & Richard B. Stewart, *The Emergence of Global Administrative Law*, LAW & CONTEMP. PROBS., Summer/Autumn 2005.

Henry A. Kissinger, *The Pitfalls of Universal Jurisdiction*, FOREIGN AFFAIRS, July/August 2001.

Nico Krisch & Benedict Kingsbury, *Introduction: Global Governance and Global Administrative Law in the International Legal Order*, 17 EUR. J. INT'L L.1 (2006).

Rosalyn Higgins, *Closing Remarks at the Conference To Honor the Work of Professor Michael Reisman*, 34 YALE J. INT'L L. 605 (2009).

Harold Hongju Koh, *Bringing International Law Home*, 35 HOUS. L. REV. 623 (1999).

Harold Hongju Koh, *Is there a "New" New Haven School of International Law?*, 32 YALE J. INT'L L. 559 (2007).

Harold Hongju Koh, *Forward* to MICHAEL P. SCHARF & PAUL R. WILLIAMS, SHAPING FOREIGN POLICY IN TIMES OF CRISIS (2010).

Harold Hongju Koh, *Michael Reisman, Dean of the New Haven School of International Law*, 34 YALE J. INT'L L. 501 (2009).

Harold Hongju Koh, *The 1988 Fraenkel Lecture: Bringing International Law Home*, 35 HOUS. L. REV. 623 (1998).

Harold Hongju Koh, *Transnational Legal Process*, 75 NEBRASKA L. REV. 181 (1996).

Harold Hongju Koh, *Why Do Nations Obey International Law?*, 106 YALE L.J. 2599 (1997).

Martti Koskenniemi, *Letter to the Editors of the Symposium*, *in* THE METHODS OF INTERNATIONAL LAW (Ratner & Slaughter eds., ASIL 1999).

Martti Koskenniemi, *The Politics of International Law*, 1 Eur. J. Int'l L. 4 (1990).

Martti Koskenniemi, *The Politics of International Law—20 Years Later*, 20 Eur. J. Int'l L. 7 (2009).

Dino Kritsiotis, *The Kosovo Crisis and NATO's Application of Armed Force against the Federal Republic of Yugoslavia*, 49 Int'l & Comp. L.Q. 330 (2008).

Hajredin Kuci, *The Legal and Political Grounds for, and the Influence of the Actual Situation on, the Demand of the Albanians of Kosovo for Independence*, 80 Chi.-Kent L. Rev. 331 (2005).

Harold D. Lasswell & Myres S. McDougal, *Legal Education and Public Policy: Professional Training in the Public Interest,* 52 Yale LJ. 203 (1943).

Hersch Lauterpacht, *The Grotian Tradition in International Law*, 23 Brit. Y.B. Int'l L. 1 (1946).

Brian Leiter, *Legal Realism, Hard Positivism, and the Limits of Conceptual Analysis, in* Hart's Postscript (Coleman ed., 2001).

Janet Koven Levit, *A Bottom-Up Approach to International Lawmaking: The Tale of Three Trade Finance Instruments*, 30 Yale J. Int'l L. 125 (2005).

Janet Koven Levit, *Bottom-Up Lawmaking though a Pluralist Lens: The ICC Banking Commission and the Transnational Regulations of Letters of Credit*, 57 Emory L.J. 1147 (2008).

Karl Llewellyn, *How Appellate Courts Decide Cases*, 17 Penn B. Ass'n Q. 54 (Oct. 1945).

Vaughan Lowe, *Preface* to Matthew Craven, The Decolonization of International Law (2007).

Vaughan Lowe, *International Legal Issues Arising in the Kosovo Crisis*, 49 Int'l & Comp. L.Q. 876 (2008).

Vaughn Lowe, *The Iraq Crisis: What Now?*, 52 Int'l & Comp. L.Q. 859 (2003).

R. St. J. MacDonald & Douglas M. Johnston, *International Legal Theory: New Frontiers of the Discipline, in* The Structure and Process of International Law (MacDonald & Johnston eds., 1983).

Jennifer Martinez, *Towards an International Judicial System*, 56 Stan. L. Rev. 429 (2003).

D. Stephen Mathias, Anthea Roberts & Carlos M. Vazquez, *An Introduction: International Law as Law*, 103 Am. Soc'y Int'l L. Proc. 155 (2009).

Myres S. McDougal & Harold D. Lasswell, *Identification and Appraisal of Diverse Systems of Public Order, in* International Law Essays: A Supplement to International Law in Contemporary Perspective (McDougal & Reisman eds., 1981).

Myres S. McDougal, Remarks at the 79th Annual Meeting of the American Society of International Law, 103 Am. Soc'y Int'l L. Proc. 283 (1985).

John O. McGinnis, Review Essay, *Principle versus Politics: The Solicitor General's Office in Constitutional and Bureaucratic Theory*, 44 Stan. L. Rev. 799 (1992).

Darrel Menthe, *Legalization and the Mediation of International Disputes: The Balkan Experience*, 23 Conn. J. Int'l L. 83 (2008).

Theodor Meron, *Judicial Independence and Impartiality in International Criminal Tribunals*, 99 Am. J. Int'l L. 359 (2005).

Julie Mertus, *Reconsidering the Legality of Humanitarian Intervention: Lessons from Kosovo*, 41 Wm. & Mary L. Rev. 1743 (2000).

Enrico Milano, *Security Council Action in the Balkans: Reviewing the Legality of Kosovo's Territorial Status,* 14 Eur. J. Int'l L. 999 (2003).

John Norton Moore, *The Secret War in Central America and the Future of World Order*, 80 Am. J. Int'l L. 43 (1986).

Trevor Morrison, *Stare Decisis in the Office of Legal Counsel*, 110 Colum. L. Rev. 1448 (2010).

Liam Murphy, *The Political Question of the Concept of Law*, in HART'S POSTSCRIPT (Coleman ed., 2001).

Liam Murphy, *Better to See Law This Way*, 83 N.Y.U. L. REV. 1088 (2008).

Sean D. Murphy, *Contemporary Practice of the United States Relating to International Law*, 93 AM. J. INT'L L. 161 (1999).

Sean D. Murphy, *The Concept of International Law*, 103 AM. SOC'Y INT'L L. PROC. 165 (2009).

Mikael Nabati, *International Law at a Crossroads: Self-Defense, Global Terrorism, and Preemption (A Call to Rethink the Self-Defense Normative Framework)*, 13 TRANSNAT'L L. & CONTEMP. PROBS. 771 (2003).

Mary Ellen O'Connell, *The International Law of Drones*, 14:30 ASIL INSIGHTS, (Nov. 12, 2010).

Lassa Oppenheim, *The Science of International Law: Its Task and Method, 2* AM. J. INT'L L. 313 (1908).

Hari M. Osofsky, *A Law and Geography Perspective on the New Haven School*, 32 YALE J. INT'L L. 421 (2007).

Eric J. Pan, *Challenge of International Cooperation and Institutional Design in Financial Supervision: Beyond Transgovernmental Networks*, 11 CHI J. INT'L L. 243 (2010-11).

Colter Paulson, *Compliance with Final Judgments of the International Court of Justice Since 1987*, 98 AM J. INT'L L. 434 (2004).

Jan Paulsson, *International Arbitration and the Generation of Legal Norms: Treaty Arbitration and International Law* (May 21, 2006), *available at* http://www.transnational-dispute-management.com/article.asp?key=883.

Andreas L. Paulus, *International Law After Postmodernism: Towards Renewal or Decline of International Law?*, 14 LEIDEN J. INT'L L. 727 (2001).

Henry H. Perritt, Jr., *Final Status for Kosovo*, 80 CHI.-KENT L. REV. 3 (2005).

Stephen R. Perry, *Hart's Methodological Positivism, in* HART'S POSTSCRIPT (Coleman ed., 2001).

Stephen R. Perry, *The Varieties of Legal Positivism*, 9 CAN. J. L. & JURIS. 361 (1996).

Eric Posner, *Evaluating the Effects of International Law: Next Steps*, 1:3 GLOBAL POLICY 334 (Oct. 2010).

Eric Posner & John Yoo, *International Law and the Rise of China*, 7 CHI J. INT'L L. 1 (2006).

Eric A. Posner & John C. Yoo, *Judicial Independence in International Tribunals*, 93 CAL. L. REV. 1 (2005).

Aseem Prakash & Matthew Potoski, *The International Organization for Standardization as a Global Governor: A Club Theory Perspective, in* WHO GOVERNS THE GLOBE? (Avant ed., 2010).

Balakrishnan Rajagopal, *Martti Koskenniemi's From Apology to Utopia: A Reflection*, 7 GERMAN L. J. 1089 (2006).

Steven Ratner, *Between Minimum and Optimum World Public Order: An Ethical Path for the Future, in* LOOKING TO THE FUTURE: ESSAYS IN HONOR OF W. MICHAEL REISMAN (Arsanjani et al. eds., 2011).

Stephen Ratner and Anne-Marie Slaughter, *Symposium on Method in International Law: Appraising the Methods of International Law: A Prospectus for Readers, in* THE METHODS OF INTERNATIONAL LAW (Slaughter & Ratner eds., ASIL 1999).

Joseph Raz, *Two Views on the Nature of the Theory of Law, in* HART'S POSTSCRIPT (Coleman ed. 2001).

Paul Reichler, *Holding America to Its Own Best Standards, Abe Chayes and Nicaragua in the World Court*, 42 HARV. INT'L L. J. 15, (2001)

W. Michael Reisman, *No Man's Land: International Legal Regulation of Coercive Responses to Protracted and Low Level Conflict*, 11 Hous. J. Int'l L. 317 (1988–89).

W. Michael Reisman, *The Manley O. Hudson Lecture: Why Regime Change Is (Almost Always) A Bad Idea*, 98 Am. J. Int'l L. 516 (2004).

W. Michael Reisman, *Kosovo's Antinomies*, 93 Am. J. Int'l L. 860 (1999).

W. Michael Reisman, *Law from the Policy Perspective*, *in* International Law Essays: A Supplement to International Law in Contemporary Perspective (McDougal & Reisman eds., 1981).

Michael Reisman, *McDougal's Jurisprudence: Utility, Influence, Controversy*, 79 Am. Soc'y Int'l L. Proc. 266 (1985).

W. Michael Reisman, *Old Wine in New Bottles: The Reagan and Brezhnev Doctrines in Contemporary International Law and Practice*, 13 Yale J. Int'l L. 171 (1988).

W. Michael Reisman, *On the Causes of Uncertainty and Volatility in International Law*, in The Shifting Allocation of Authority in International Law: Considering Sovereignty, Supremacy and Subsidiarity (Broudy & Shany eds., 2008).

W. Michael Reisman, *Preface to* Douglas M. Johnston, The Historical Foundations of World Order (2008).

W. Michael Reisman, *Theory About Law: Jurisprudence for a Free Society*, 108 Yale L.J. 935 (1999).

W. Michael Reisman & Andrea Armstrong, *The Past and Future of the Claim of Preemptive Self-Defense*, 100 Am. J. Int'l L. 525 (2006).

W. Michael Reisman, Siegfried Wiessner, & Andrew R. Willard, *Commentary: The New Haven School: A Brief Introduction*, 32 Yale J. Int'l L. 575 (2007).

David B. Rivkin Jr., et al., *Remember the Caroline!*, Nat'l Rev. (July–Dec. 2002).

Davis R. Robinson, *The Reagan Administration–Davis R. Robinson (1981–1985), in* Michael P. Scharf & Paul R. Williams, Shaping Foreign Policy in Times of Crisis (2010).

Davis R. Robinson et al., *Some Perspectives on Adjudicating Before the World Court: The Gulf of Maine Case*, 79 Am. J. Int'l L. 578 (1985).

Shabtai Rosenne, *Sir Hersch Lauterpacht's Concept of the Task of an International Judge*, 55 Am. J. Int'l L. 825 (1961).

Shabtai Rosenne, *The Influence of Judaism on the Development of International Law*, 5 Neth. Int'l L. Rev. 119 (1958).

Steven E. Sachs, *From St. Ives to Cyberspace: The Modern Distortion of the Medieval "Law Merchant,"* 21 Am. U. Int'l L. Rev. 685 (2006).

Oscar Schachter, *Toward a Theory of International Obligation*, 8 Va. J. Int'l L. 311 (1968).

Michael P. Scharf, *Earned Sovereignty: Juridical Underpinnings*, 31 Den. J. Int'l L. & Pol'y 373 (2003).

David Schneiderman, *Judicial Politics and International Investment Arbitration: Seeking an Explanation for Conflicting Outcomes*, 30 NW. J. Int'L L. & Bus. 383 (2010).

Stephen M. Schwebel, *Reflections on the Role of the International Court of Justice*, Jurisprudential Lecture at the University of Washington, 61 Wash. L. Rev. 1061 (1986).

Stephen Schwebel, *Remarks on the Role of the Legal Adviser of the U.S. State Department*, 2 Eur. J. Int'l L. 131 (1991).

Malcolm N. Shaw, *The International Court of Justice: A Practical Perspective*, 46 Int'l & Comp. L.Q. 831 (1997).

Dinah L. Shelton, *Case Concerning Avena and Other Mexican Nationals (Mexico v. United States)*, 98 Am. J. Int'l L. 559 (2004).

Bruno Simma, *NATO the UN and the Use of Force: Legal Aspects*, 10 EUR. J. INT'L L. 1 (1999).

Bruno Simma & Andreas L. Paulus, *The Responsibility of Individuals for Human Rights Abuses in Internal Conflicts: A Positivist View*, 93 AM. J. INT'L L. 302 (1999).

Abraham D. Sofaer, *International Law and Kosovo*, 36 STAN. J. INT'L L. 1 (2000).

Abraham D. Sofaer, *Terrorism and the Law*, FOREIGN AFFAIRS, (1986).

Peter J. Spiro, *A Negative Proof of International Law*, 34 GA. J. INT'L & COMP. L. 445 (2006).

Rochelle L. Stanfield, *Looking Beyond the Guns of August*, 22 NAT'L J. 1959 (1990).

Nicos Stavropoulos, *Hart's Semantics*, *in* HART'S POSTSCRIPT (Coleman ed., 2001).

Arthur A. Stein, *Coordination and Collaboration: Regimes in an Anarchic World*, *in* INTERNATIONAL REGIMES (Kranser ed., 2d prtg. 1984).

Richard H. Steinberg & Jonathan M. Zasloff, *Power and International Law*, 100 AM. J. INT'L L. 64 (2006).

Milena Sterio, *The Kosovar Declaration of Independence: "Botching the Balkans" or Respecting International Law*, 37 GA. J. INT'L & COMP. L. 267 (2009).

Brigitte Stern, *Custom at the Heart of International Law*, 11 DUKE J. COMP. & INT'L L. 89 (2001).

Edward T. Swaine, *Restoring (and Risking) Interest in International Law*, 100 AM. J. INT'L L. 259 (2006).

William H. Taft IV, *The Bush (43rd) Administration–William H. Taft IV (2001-2005)*, *in* MICHAEL P. SCHARF & PAUL R. WILLIAMS, SHAPING FOREIGN POLICY IN TIMES OF CRISIS (2010).

The Role of the Legal Adviser of the Department of State, 85 AM. J. INT'L L. 358 (1991).

Theresa Tobin, *A Terrorist Attack: Response and Reflection*, *in* PERSPECTIVES ON 9/11 (El-Ayouty ed., 2004).

Matthew Turk, *The Perils of Global Legalism. By Eric Posner*, 42 INT'L LAW & POL. 344 (2009) (book review).

Detlev F. Vagts, *International Law in the Third Reich*, 84 AM. J. INT'L L. 661 (1990).

Detlev F. Vagts, *The Financial Meltdown and Its International Implications*, 103 AM. J. INT'L L. 684 (2009).

Reynaldo Anaya Valencia et al., *Avena and the World Court's Death Penalty Jurisdiction in Texas: Addressing the Odd Notion of Texas' Independence from the World*, 23 YALE L. & POL'Y REV. 455 (2005).

Jure Vidmar, *International Legal Responses to Kosovo's Declaration of Independence*, 42 VAND. J. TRANSNAT'L L. 779 (2009).

Jeremy Waldron, *Hart and the Principles of Legality*, *in* THE LEGACY OF H. L. A. HART (Kramer et al. eds., 2008).

Jeremy Waldron, *Normative (or Ethical) Positivism*, *in* HART'S POSTSCRIPT (Coleman ed., 2001).

Colin Warbrick & Dominic McGoldrick, *Kosovo: The Declaration of Independence*, 57 INT'L & COMP. L.Q. 675 (2008).

Ruth Wedgewood, *NATO's Campaign in Yugoslavia*, 93 AM. J. INT'L L. 828 (1999).

Prosper Weil, *Towards Relative Normativity in International Law?*, 77 AM. J. INT'L L. 413 (1983).

Harry Wellington, *Common Law Rules and Constitutional Double Standards: Some Notes on Adjudication*, 83 YALE L.J. 221 (1973).

Edith Brown Weiss, *Introduction*, *in* INTERNATIONAL COMPLIANCE WITH NONBINDING ACCORDS 1 (Weiss ed., 1997).

Burns H. Weston, *The Role of Law in Promoting Peace and Violence: A Matter of Definition, Social Values and Individual Responsibility*, *in* TOWARD WORLD ORDER AND HUMAN DIGNITY: ESSAYS IN HONOR OF MYRES S. MCDOUGAL (Weston & Reisman eds., 1976).

Siegfried Wiessner, *Law as a Means to a Public Order of Human Dignity: The Jurisprudence of Michael Reisman*, 34 YALE J. INT'L L. 525 (2009).

Siegfried Wiessner & Andrew R. Willard, *Policy-Oriented Jurisprudence & Human Rights Abuses in Internal Conflict: Toward a World Public Order of Human Dignity*, 93 AM. J. INT'L L. 316 (1999).

Paul R. Williams, *Earned Sovereignty: the Road to Resolving the Conflict Over Kosovo's Final Status*, 31 DENV. J INT'L L & POL'Y 387 (2003).

Elizabeth Wilmshurst, *The Best Defense? Legitimacy & Preventative Force*, 105 AM. J. INT'L L. 390 (2011) (book review).

Jason Webb Yackee, *The Reasons Requirement in International Investment Arbitration: Critical Case Studies*, 103 AM. J. INT'L L. 629 (2009) (book review).

Lee Kuan Yew, *Forward* to SHUNMUGAM JAYAKUMAR & TOMMY KOH, PEDRA BRANCA: THE ROAD TO THE WORLD COURT (2009).

John Yoo, *International Law and the War in Iraq*, 97 AM. J. INT'L L. 563 (2003).

John Yoo, *Using Force*, 71 U. CHI. L. REV. 729 (2004).

David Zaring, *International Institutional Performance in Crisis*, 10 CHI J. INT'L L. 475 (2009-10).

Rex J. Zedalis, *On the Lawfulness of Forceful Remedies for Violations of Arms Control Agreements: "Star Wars" and Other Glimpses at the Future*, 18 N.Y.U. J. INT'L L. & POL. 73 (1985).

TREATIES

Agreement between the Government of the United States of America and the Government of the Republic of Honduras Concerning the Encouragement and Reciprocal Protection of Investments, July 1, 1995, Senate Treaty Doc. No. 106-27.

Agreement on Encouragement and Reciprocal Protection of Investments, Czech/Slovk.-Neth., Aug. 1, 1975.

Bilateral Investment Treaty Concerning the Reciprocal Encouragement and Protection of Investment, U.S.-Arg., Nov. 14, 1991, 31 I.L.M. 124 (1992).

Convention Against Torture and Other Cruel, Inhuman or Degrading Treatment or Punishment, 1465 U.N.T.S. 85 (Dec. 10, 1984).

Convention on the Prevention and Punishment of the Crime of Genocide, Dec. 9, 1948, 78 U.N.T.S. 1021.

Convention on the Recognition of Enforcement of Foreign Arbitral Awards, June 10, 1958, 330 U.N.T.S. 3.

Convention on the Settlement of Investment Disputes Between States and Nationals of Other States, Mar. 18, 1965, 575 U.N.T.S. 159.

Geneva Convention [I] for the Amelioration of the Condition of the Wounded and Sick in Armed Forces in the Field, Aug. 12, 1949, 6 U.S.T. 3114, 75 U.N.T.S. 31.

Geneva Convention [II] for the Amelioration of the Condition of the Wounded, Sick and Shipwrecked Members of Armed Forces at Sea, Aug. 12, 1949, 6 U.S.T. 3217, 75 U.N.T.S. 85.

Geneva Convention [III] Relative to the Treatment of Prisoners of War, Aug. 12, 1949, 6 U.S.T. 3316, 75 U.N.T.S. 135.

Geneva Convention [IV] Relative to the Protection of Civilian Persons in Time of War, Aug. 12, 1949, 6 U.S.T. 3516, 75 U.N.T.S. 287.

International Covenant on Civil and Political Rights, G.A. Res. 2200A (XXI), U.N. Doc. A/2200 (Dec. 16, 1966).

League of Nations Covenant

Marrakesh Agreement Establishing the World Trade Organization, Apr. 15, 1994, 33 I.L.M. 1144 (1994).

North American Free Trade Agreement, U.S.-Can.-Mex., Dec. 17, 1992, 107 Stat. 2057 (1994).

Rome Statute of the International Criminal Court, Jul. 17, 1998, U.N. Doc A/CONF.183/9.

United States-Section 129(C)(1) Uruguay Round Agreements Act, WT/DS221/R (July 15, 2002).

Statute of the International Court of Justice, 33 U.N.T.S. 993 (1945).

The General Agreement on Tarrifs and Trade, Oct. 30, 1947, 61 Stat. A-11, T.I.A.S. 1700, 55 U.N.T.S. 194.

Treaty on the Establishment of German Unity 1990, 30 I.L.M. 463 (1991).

Treaty of Westphalia, Peace Treaty between the Holy Roman Emperor and the King of France and their Respective Allies (1648), *available at* http://Avalon.law.yale.edu/17th_century/westphal.asp.

United Nations Charter

Vienna Convention on Consular Relations, Apr. 24, 1963, 21 U.S.T. 77, 596 U.N.T.S. 261.

Vienna Convention on Diplomatic Relations, Apr. 18, 1961, 23 U.S.T. 3227, 500 U.N.T.S. 95.

Vienna Convention on the Law of Treaties, May 23, 1969, 1155 U.N.T.S. 331

RESOLUTIONS

Universal Declaration of Human Rights, G.A. Res. 217A, U.N. Doc. A/810 (Dec. 12, 1948).

G.A. Res. 3314 (XXIX), U.N. Doc. A/3314 (Dec. 14, 1974).

G.A. Res. 3452(XXX), U.N. Doc. A/3452 (Dec. 9, 1975).

G.A. Res. ES-10/14, U.N. Doc. A/RES/ES/10/14 (Dec. 12, 2003).

S.C. Res. 384, U.N. Doc. S/RES/384 (Dec. 22, 1975).

S.C. Res. 501, U.N. Doc. S/RES/501 (Feb. 25, 1982).

S.C. Res. 660, U.N. Doc. S/RES/660 (Aug. 2, 1990).

S.C. Res. 661, U.N. Doc. S/RES/661 (Aug. 6, 1990).

S.C. Res. 662, U.N. Doc. S/RES/662 (Aug. 9, 1990).

S.C. Res. 664, U.N. Doc. S/RES/664 (Aug. 18, 1990).

S.C. Res. 665, U.N. Doc. S/RES/665 (Aug. 25, 1990).

S.C. Res. 666, U.N. Doc. S/RES/666 (Sept. 13, 1990).

S.C. Res. 667, U.N. Doc. S/RES/667 (Sept. 16, 1990).

S.C. Res. 669, U.N. Doc. S/RES/669 (Sept. 24, 1990).

S.C. Res. 674, U.N. Doc. S/RES/674 (Oct. 29, 1990).

S.C. Res. 677, U.N. Doc. S/RES/677 (Nov. 28, 1990).

S.C. Res. 678, U.N. Doc. S/RES/678 (Nov. 29, 1990).

S.C. Res. 686, U.N. Doc. S/RES/686 (March 2, 1991).

S.C. Res. 687, U.N. Doc S/RES/687 (Apr. 3, 1991).

S.C. Res. 688, U.N. Doc S/RES/688 (Apr. 5, 1991).

S.C. Res. 1199, U.N. Doc. S/Res/1199 (Sept. 23, 1998)

S.C. Res. 1203, U.N. Doc. S/RES/1203 (Oct. 24, 1998).

S.C. Res. 1244, U.N. Doc. S/RES/1244 (June 10, 1999).
S.C. Res. 1272, U.N. Doc. S/RES/1272 (Oct. 25, 1999).
S.C. Res. 1441, U.N. Doc. S/2002/1441 (Nov. 8, 2002).
S.C. Res. 1483, U.N. Doc. S/RES/1483 (May 22, 2003).
S.C. Res. 1696, UN Doc. S/RES/1696 (July 31, 2006).
S.C. Res. 1863, U.N. Doc. S/RES/1863 (Jan. 16, 2009).
S.C. Res. 1483, U.N. Doc. S/RES/1483 (May 22, 2003).

INTERNATIONAL CASES AND AWARDS

Accordance with International Law of the Unilateral Declaration of Independence in Respect of Kosovo, Advisory Opinion, 2010 I.C.J. 141 (July 22).

Admission of a State to the United Nations (Charter, art. 4), Advisory Opinion, 1948 I.C.J. 57 (May 28).

Al-Adsani v. United Kingdom, Eur. Ct. Hum. Rt., Application No. 35763/97 (Nov. 21, 2001).

Al-Saadoon v. U.K., App. No. 61498/08 (Eur. Ct. H.R., Mar. 2, 2010).

Application of the Convention on the Prevention and the Punishment of the Crime of Genocide (Bosn. & Herz. v. Serb. & Montenegro), 2007 I.C.J. 1 (Feb. 26).

Armed Activities on the Territory of the Congo (Democratic Republic of the Congo v. Uganda), Judgment, 2005 I.C.J. 168 (Dec. 19).

Brazil—Measures Affecting Patent Protection, Request for Establishment of a Panel by the United States, WT/DS199/3 (Jan. 9, 2001).

Cambodia's Application for Interpretation by the ICJ, Preliminary Objections, 1961 I.C.J. 17 (May 26).

Case 323/87 Comm'n v. Italy (taxation of rum), 1989 E.C.R. 2275.

Case Concerning Avena and Other Mexican Nationals (Mex. v. U.S.), 2004 I.C.J. 12 (March 31).

Case Concerning Avena and Other Mexican Nationals (Mex. v. U.S.), Application, 2004 I.C.J. 12 (Jan. 9, 2003).

Certain Norwegian Loans (Fr. v. Nor.), 1957 I.C.J. 9 (July 6).

CMS Gas Transmission Co. v. Argentine Republic, ICSID Case No. ARB/01/8, Annulment Proceeding (Sept. 1, 2006).

CMS Gas Transmission Co. v. Argentine Republic, ICSID Case No. ARB/01/8, Award (May 12, 2005).

Corfu Channel (U.K. v. Alb.), 1949 I.C.J. 244 (Dec. 15).

Delimitation of the Maritime Boundary in the Gulf of Maine Area (Can. v. U.S.), 1984 I.C.J. 246 (Oct. 12).

Final Anti-Dumping Measures on Stainless Steel from Mexico, Arbitration Report, WT/DS344/15 (Oct. 31, 2008).

Final Anti-Dumping Measures on Stainless Steel from Mexico, Appellate Body Report, WT/DS344/AB/R (Apr. 30, 2008).

GAMI Investments, Inc. v. United Mexican States, Final Award (B) (UNCITRAL, Nov. 15, 2004).

Helnan Int'l Hotels A/S/ v. Arab Republic of Egypt, Decision of the Ad Hoc Committee, ICSID Arb/05/19 (June 14, 2010).

Interhandel Case (Switz. v. U.S.), 1959 I.C.J. 6 (Mar. 21).

International Status of South-West Africa, Advisory Opinion, 1950 I.C.J. 128 (July 11).

Island of Palmas Case (Neth./U.S.), Award of the Tribunal, 2 R.I.A.A. 828 (1928).

Japan—Countervailing Duties on Dynamic Random Access Memories From Korea, Award of the Arbitrator, WT/DS336/16 (May 5, 2008).

Klöckner Industrie-Anlagen GmBH v. Rep. Cameroon, 1 ICSID Rev. FILJ 89 (1986).

LaGrand (Ger. v. U.S.), Judgment, 2001 I.C.J. 466 (June 27).

Legal Consequences for States of the Continued Presence of South Africa in Namibia (South-West Africa) Notwithstanding Security Council Resolution (1970), Advisory Opinion, 1971 I.C.J. 16 (June 21).

Legal Consequences of the Construction of a Wall in the Occupied Palestinian Territory, Advisory Opinion, 2004 I.C.J. 136 (July 9).

Legality of the Use by a State of Nuclear Weapons in Armed Conflict, Advisory Opinion, 1996 I.C.J. 66 (July 8).

Legality of Use of Force (Serb. and Mont. v. Belg.), Preliminary Objections, Judgment, 2004 I.C.J. 279, (Dec. 15).

Legality of Use of Force (Serb. and Mont. v. Can.), Preliminary Objections, Judgment, 2004 I.C.J. 429, (Dec. 15).

Legality of Use of Force (Serb. and Mont. v. Fr.), Preliminary Objections, Judgment, 2004 I.C.J. 575, (Dec. 15).

Legality of Use of Force (Serb. and Mont. v. Ger.), Preliminary Objections, Judgment, 2004 I.C.J. 720, (Dec. 15).

Legality of Use of Force (Serb. and Mont. v. It.), Preliminary Objections, Judgment, 2004 I.C.J. 865, (Dec. 15).

Legality of Use of Force (Serb. and Mont. v. Neth.), Preliminary Objections, Judgment, 2004 I.C.J. 1011, (Dec. 15).

Legality of Use of Force (Serb. and Mont. v. Port.), Preliminary Objections, Judgment, 2004 I.C.J. 1160, (Dec. 15).

Legality of Use of Force (Serb. & Mont. v. U.K.), Preliminary Objections, Judgment, 2004 I.C.J. 1307, (Dec. 15).

Legality of Use of Force (Yugo. v. Spain), Request for the Indication of Provisional Measures, Order, 1999 I.C.J. 761, (June 2).

Legality of Use of Force (Yugo. v. U.S.), Request for the Indication of Provisional Measures, Order, 1999 I.C.J. 916, (June 2).

Loewen Group, Inc. v. U.S., ICSID Case No. ARB(AF)/98/3 (June 26, 2003).

Metalclad Corp. v. United States, ICSID Case No. ARB(AF)/97/1, Award (Aug. 30, 2000).

Military and Paramilitary Activities in and against Nicaragua (Nicar. v. U.S.), Declaration of Intervention of the Republic of El Salvador (Aug. 15, 1984).

Military and Paramilitary Activities in and against Nicaragua (Nicar. v. U.S.), Judgment on Jurisdiction of the Court and Admissibility of the Application, 1984 I.C.J. 392 (Nov. 26).

Military and Paramilitary Activities in and against Nicaragua (Nicar. v. U.S.), Judgment on Merits, 1986 I.C.J. 14 (June 27)

Military and Paramilitary Activities in and against Nicaragua (Nicar. v. U.S.), Order on Intervention of the Republic of El Salvador (Oct. 4, 1985).

Military and Paramilitary Activities in and against Nicaragua (Nicar. v. U.S.), Order on Provisional Measures, 1984 I.C.J. 169 (May 10).

Order of July 16, 2008, Request for Interpretation of the Judgment of 31 March 2004 in the case concerning Avena and other Mexican Nationals (Mex. v. U.S), 2008 I.C.J. 311.

Prosecutor v. Furundija, Int'l Crim. Trib. Former Yugoslavia, Case No. IT-95–17/1-T (Dec. 10, 1998).

Prosecutor v. Jean Paul Akayesu, Int'l Crim. Trib. Former Yugoslavia, Case No. ICTR-94-T (Sept. 2, 1998).

Prosecutor v. Tadic, Judgement, Case No. IT-94–1-A (July 15, 1999).
Request for Interpretation of the Judgment of 31 March 2004 in the case concerning Avena and other Mexican Nationals (Mex. v. U.S.), 2009 I.C.J. 1, 16, (Jan. 19).
Reservations to the Convention on the Prevention and Punishment of the Crime of Genocide, Advisory Opinion, 1951 I.C.J. 15 (May 28).
Sovereignty over Pedra Branca/Pulau Batu Puteh, Middle Rocks and South Ledge (Malay./Sing.), Judgment, 2008 I.C.J. 12 (May 23).
The Application of the Convention on the Prevention and Punishment of the Crime of Genocide (Bosn. & Herz. v. Serb. & Mont.), 2007 I.C.J. 1 (Feb. 26).
The Barcelona Traction, Light, and Power Co., Limited (Belg. V. Spain), Second Phase, 1970 I.C.J. 3 (Feb. 5).
United States—Final Anti-dumping Measures on Stainless Steel From Mexico, Award of the Arbitrator, WT/DS344/15 (Oct. 31, 2008).
United States – Laws, Regulations and Methodology for Calculating Dumping Margins ("Zeroing"), Appellate Body Report, WT/DS294/R (9 May 2006).
Vienna Convention on Consular Relations (Para. v. U.S.), Provisional Measures, 1998 I.C.J. 248 (Apr. 9).
Voting Procedure on Questions Relating to Reports and Petitions Concerning the Territory of South-West Africa, Advisory Opinion, 1955 I.C.J. 67 (June 7).
Western and Eastern Fronts Ethiopia's Claims, (Permanent Court of Arbitration 2005).
Western Sahara, Advisory Opinion, 1975 I.C.J. 12 (Oct. 16).

NATIONAL LAWS

Arbitration Act of 1996 (Eng.).
Authorization for Use of Military Force, Pub. L. No. 107-40, S.J. Res. 23, 107th Cong. (2001).
Exec. Order No. 13,491 Fed. Reg. 4893 (Jan. 22, 2009).
Fed. R. App. Proc. 32(B)(i).
Federal Arbitration Act, 9 U.S.C. §§ 1–16, 201-08.
Military Commissions Act of 2006, 42 U.S.C. § 2000dd.
Foreign Sovereign Immunities Act, 28 U.S.C. § 1604.
H.J. Res. 114, 107th Cong. (2002).
Sherman Antitrust Act, 15 U.S.C. §§1-7.
Torture Convention Implementation Act, 18 U.S.C. §§ 2340-2340B.

NATIONAL CASES

Anonymous v. Sheriff of London, Y.B. 13 Edw. 2, fol. 9, Pasch, pl. 5 (Ch. 1473).
Bevill, Bresler, & Schulman v. Spencer Sav. & Loan, 878 F.2d 742 (3d Cir. 1989).
Breard v. Greene et al., 523 U.S. 371 (1998).
Browning v. Johnson, 422 P.2d 314 (Wash. 1967).
Fed. Rep. Germany v. United States, 526 U.S. 111 (1999).
Hamdan v. Rumsfeld, 548 U.S. 557 (2006).
Medellín v. Texas, 552 U.S. 491 (2008).
R. v. Cook, [1998] 2 S.C.R. 507 (Can.).
United States v. Belfast, 611 F.3d 783 (11th Cir. 2010).
United States v. Nippon Paper Industries Co., 109 F.3d 1 (1st Cir. 1997).

OTHER SOURCES

184 Parl. Deb., H.C. (6th ser.) (1991).
216 Parl. Deb., H.C. (6th ser.) (1993).

328 Parl. Deb., H.C. (6th ser.) (1999).

Madeleine Albright, Sec'y of State, Address to Council on Foreign Relations, 10 Dept. of State Dispatch 3 (June 28, 1999).

Alistair Darling's Northern Rock Statement Text, The Telegraph, (Feb. 17, 2008), *available at* http://www.telegraph.co.uk/news/uknews/1578940/Alistair-Darlings-Northern-Rock-statement-text.html.

American Bar Association Report to the House of Delegates, *in* The Torture Papers: The Road to Abu Ghraib (Greenberg & Dratel eds., 2005).

Amnesty International, EUR 70/046/1998, Federal Republic of Yugoslovia: A Human Rights Crisis In Kosovo Province: Document Series A (June 1998).

Kofi Anan, *A More Secure World: Our Shared Responsibility: Report of the High-Level Panel on Threats, Challenges and Change*, UN Doc. A/59/565, (2004).

Attorney General's Advice on the Iraq War Iraq: Resolution 1441, 54 Int'l & Comp. L.Q. 767 (2005).

Basel Committee on Banking Supervision, Basel III: International Framework for Liquidity Risk Measurement, Standards and Monitoring (2010), *available at* http://www.bis.org/publ/bcbs188.pdf.

Belarus, India and Russian Federation: Draft Resolution, U.N. Doc. S/1999/328 (Mar. 26, 1999).

John B. Bellinger III, Legal Adviser, U.S. Sec. of State, Luncheon Address at the 6th Annual International Law Conference hosted by the U.S. Naval War College, International Legal Public Diplomacy, 82 Int'l L. Stud. Ser. US Naval War Col. 205 (2007).

John B. Bellinger, Speech to the Int'l Law Assoc: Reflections on Four Years as Legal Advisor (Oct. 17, 2008).

Senate Testimony of John B. Bellinger, III, Legal Advisor, Dep't of State, Apr. 15, 2008 at 3, 110th Cong. Rec. 2007–2008.

Ben S. Bernanke, Chairman of the Bd. of Governors of the Fed. Reserve Sys., Statement before the United States Senate Committee on Banking, Housing, and Urban Affairs (Sept. 23, 2008).

Tony Blair, UK Prime Minister, Speech Spelling Out the Terror Threat Facing the UK and Defending the Iraq War (March 5, 2004) *available at* http://news.bbc.co.uk/2/hi/uk_news/politics/3536131.stm

Günther Bräunig et al, *Financial Statements and Management Report 2007/2008*, IKB Deutsche Industriebank AG (Jul. 4, 2008), *available at* http://www.ikb.de/content/en/ir/financial_reports/annual_report_2007_2008/AG_englisch_080814_sicher.pdf.

British Government, Iraq's Weapons of Mass Destruction: The Assessment of the British Government [the "Iraq Dossier"] (2002).

Chip Brown, *The Search for Cleopatra*, Nat'L Geographic Magazine, July 2011.

Bush speech in full, BBC News (Mar. 20, 2003). http://news.bbc.co.uk/2/hi/americas/2866715.stm (full transcript).

President George W. Bush, Keynote Address at the United States Military Academy at West Point (June 1, 2002).

President George W. Bush, Speech to United Nations General Assembly (Sept. 12, 2002).

Chronology of the Financial Crisis: USA–Europe–Switzerland, Institut für Bankrech, http://www.ibr.unibe.ch/unibe/rechtswissenschaft/ibr/content/e9490/e9491/files9571/total.ChronologyoftheFinancialCrisis.pdf.

Hillary Clinton Senate Confirmation Hearings as Nominee for Secretary of State (2009), *video available at* http://foreign.senate.gov/hearings/hearing/?id=7b16fc93-0c92-41f5-5e17-a09abc461b1c

Michael Corkery, *Basel III: And the Biggest Winners Are . . .*, Wall. St. J. (Sept. 13, 2010), http://blogs.wsj.com/deals/2010/09/13/basel-iii-and-the-biggest-winners-are/.

Correspondence Between Great Britain and the United States, Respecting the Destruction of the Steamboat *Caroline*, 30 B.S.P. 193 (1858).

Draft Articles on the Responsibility of States for Internationally Wrongful Acts, Report of the ILC on the Work of its Fifty-third Session, art. 25, U.N. GAOR, 56th Sess, Supp No 10, U.N. Doc. A/56/10 (2001).

The Economist, Economist Intelligence Unit, Country Profile: Bosnia and Herzegovina (1998).

Testimony of Sir William Ehrman, Iraq Inquiry, Nov. 25, 2009, Tr. 95:21–96:4.

Eyes on Iraq; In Cheney's Words: The Administration Case for Removing Saddam Hussein, N.Y. Times (Aug. 27, 2002), http://query.nytimes.com/gst/fullpage.html?res=9505E3D9113CF934A1575BC0A9649C8B63.

Fax to Office of Legal Counsel, Latest OMS Guidelines, Jan. 15, 2005.

Financial Stability Board Charter.

Financial Stability Board, Improving Financial Regulation: Report of the Financial Stability Board to G20 Leaders (2009).

Financial Stability Board, Progress since the Washington Summit in the Implementation of the G20 Recommendations for Strengthening Financial Stability (2010).

Financial Stability Board, Promoting Global Adherence to International Cooperation and Information Exchange Standards (2010).

Financial Stability Board, Reducing the Moral Hazard Posed by Systemically Important Financial Institutions: FSB Recommendations and Time Lines (2010), *available at* http://www.financialstabilityboard.org/publications/r_101111a.pdf.

Financial Stability Forum, Principles for Sound Compensation Practices (2009), *available at* http://www.financialstabilityboard.org/publications/r_0904b.pdf.

Financial Stability Forum, Report of the Financial Stability Forum on Addressing Procyclicality on the Financial System (2009), *available at* http://www.financialstabilityboard.org/publications/r_0904a.pdf.

Financial Stability Forum, Thematic Review on Compensation: Peer Review Report (2010) *available at* http://www.financialstabilityboard.org/publications/r_100330a.pdf.

David Fischer, *The DPRK's Violation of its NPT Safeguards Agreement with the IAEA*, *available at* http://www.iaea.org/newscenter/focus/iaeadprk/dprk.pdf (providing historical context).

Andrew Forbes & David Henley, *China's "Ancient Tea-Horse Road" in Historical Perspective*, CPAmedia, http://www.cpamedia.com/trade-routes/tea-horse-road-historical-perspective/.

Morrison Foerster, Basel Framework (March 2010).

Frontline: The Gulf War: Part B (PBS television broadcast Feb. 4 1997) *transcript available at* www.pbs.org/wgbh/pages/frontline/gulf/script_b.html.

Further Written Observations of the United States of America, Request for Interpretation of the Judgment of 31 March 2004 in the Case Concerning Avena and Other Mexican Nationals (Mex. v. U.S.) 2008 I.C.J. (Oct. 6).

Lourdes Garcia-Navarro & Stevie Inskeep, *Libya: Coalition Is Overstepping Its U.N. Mandate*, NPR (Mar. 29, 2011) http://www.npr.org/2011/03/29/134943154/Libya-Latest.

Germany Clinches Bank Rescue Deal, BBC News (Oct. 06, 2008), http://news.bbc.co.uk/2/hi/7653868.stm.

Germany Seeks to Reassure Savers, BBC News (Oct. 5, 2008), http://news.bbc.co.uk/2/hi/7653317.stm.

Lord Goldsmith, *Legal Basis for Use of Force Against Iraq* (Mar. 17, 2003) *available at* http://www.number10.gov.uk/Page3287.

Jeanne J. Grimmett, Congressional Research Service, WTO Decisions and Their Effect in U.S. Law (2007).

José Viñals & Martin J. Gruenberg, Report to the Financial Stability Board: Note by the Staffs of the International Association of Deposit Insurers and the International Monetary Fund on Unwinding Temporary Deposit Insurance Arrangements (2009).

Andrew Guzman, Antonia Chayes, Jose Alvarez, Thomas Franck, & Sean Murphy, Panel Discussion: *In What Sense is International Law Law?*, 103 Am. Soc'y Int'l L. Proc. 155 (2009).

High-Level Panel on Threats, Challenges & Change, *A More Secure World: Our Shared Responsibility: Report of the High-Level Panel on Threats, Challenges and Change*, U.N. Doc A/59/565 (Dec. 2, 2004).

IAEA Director General, Implementation of the NPT Safeguards Agreement Between the Agency and the Democratic People's Republic of Korea, U.N. Doc. GC(46)/16 (Aug. 16, 2002).

I.C.J. Practice Directions, Practice Direction III (Order of Oct. 2001) (as amended Jan. 20, 2009).

International Law Commission, Fragmentation of International Law: Difficulties Arising from the Diversification and Expansion of International Law, U.N. Doc. A/CN.4/L.682 (Apr. 13, 2006).

Joint Press Statement on the 5th Malaysia-Singapore Joint Technical Committee (MSJTC) Meeting on the Implementation of the ICJ Judgment on Pedra Branca, Middle Rocks and South Ledge, November 30, 2010 (Dec. 2, 2010).

Michael T. Kaufman, *Crisis in the Balkans: The History; Two Distinct Peoples With Two Divergent Memories Battle Over One Land*, N.Y. Times, April 4, 1999.

Jakob Kellenberger, *Official Statement of the International Committee for the Red Cross: Sixty Years of the Geneva Conventions: Strengthening Legal Protection for Victims of Armed Conflicts* (Sept. 21, 2010), *available at* https://www.icrc.org/web/eng/siteng0.nsf/html/ihl-development-statement-210910.

Greg Keller & Frank Jordans, *Basel III Rules: Banks Given Until 2019 to Fully Comply with Global Regulations*, Huffington Post (Sept. 13, 2010).

Harold Hongju Koh Biography, U.S. Dep't of State, http://www.state.gov/r/pa/ei/biog/143262.htm.

Harold Hongju Koh, Legal Adviser, U.S. Dep't. of State, Remarks at the American Society of International Law Annual Meeting: *The Obama Administration and International Law* (Mar. 25, 2010), *available at* http://www.state.gov/s/l/releases/remarks/139119.htm.

Hervé Hannoun, Presentation: The Basel III Capital Framework: A Decisive Breakthrough, at 2 (Nov. 22, 2010), *available at* http://www.bis.org/speeches/sp101125a.htm.

Independent International Commission on Kosovo, The Kosovo Report: Conflict, International Response, Lessons Learned (2000).

Interview by Harry Kreisler with Harold Hongju Koh, Legal Adviser, in Berkeley, CA. (Oct. 3, 2003) *available at* http://globetrotter.berkeley.edu/people3/Koh/koh-con1.html.

Investment Company Act Release No. IC-29092 (Dec. 16, 2009).

Kosovo: Historical Chronology, UN Security Council, http://www.securitycouncilreport.org/site/c.glKWLeMTIsG/b.2693009/.

Charles Krauthammer, *The Reagan Doctrine*, Time, Apr. 1, 1985.

First Interview with Professor Sir Elihu Lauterpacht, Squire Law Library, Cambridge University (Jan. 29, 2008).

Letter dated 24 February 2003 from the Permanent Representatives of France, Germany and the Russian Federation to the United Nations addressed to the President of the Security Council, U.N. Doc. S/2003/214 (Feb. 24, 2003).

Letter from Daniel Webster, Secretary of State, United States, to Henry Fox, Minister, United Kingdom (Apr. 24, 1841), *in* 29 B.S.P. 1129 (1957).

Letter from Daniel Webster, Secretary of State, United States, to Lord Ashburton, British Plenipotentiary, United Kingdom (Aug. 6, 1842), *in* 2 A DIGEST OF INTERNATIONAL LAW (John Bassett Moore ed., 1906).

Letter from Tim Dowse to Margaret Aldred, Iraq Inquiry, Dec. 14, 2009.

Larry May, *Jus Cogens and Procedural Rights in International Law*, Presentation at the Foundation of International Law Conference (Apr. 24, 2010).

Member States of the United Nations, THE UNITED NATIONS, http://www.un.org/en/members/index.shtml.

Memorandum for John Rizzo, Acting General Counsel of the Central Intelligence Agency, (Aug. 1, 2002) (Memorandum entitled "Interrogation of al Qaeda Operative") (on file with author).

Memorandum for the Vice President et al., Humane Treatment of al Qaeda and Taliban Detainees (Feb. 7, 2002), *in* THE TORTURE PAPERS: THE ROAD TO ABU GHRAIB (Greenberg & Dratel eds., 2005).

Memorandum from Colin L. Powell to Counsel to the President, Draft Decision Memorandum for the President on the Applicability of the Geneva Convention to the Conflict in Afghanistan, *in* THE TORTURE PAPERS: THE ROAD TO ABU GHRAIB (Greenberg & Dratel eds., 2005).

Memorandum from Daniel Levin, Acting Assistant Attorney General, to James B. Comey, Deputy Attorney General (Dec. 30, 2004) (on file with author).

Memorandum from Donald Rumsfeld, U.S. Secretary of Defense, to Commander USSOUTHCOM (Jan. 15, 2003), *in* THE TORTURE PAPERS: THE ROAD TO ABU GHRAIB (Greenberg & Dratel eds., 2005).

Memorandum from Donald Rumsfeld, U.S. Secretary of Defense, to James T. Hill, Commander, U.S. Southern Command (Apr. 16, 2003), *in* THE TORTURE PAPERS: THE ROAD TO ABU GHRAIB (Greenberg & Dratel eds., 2005).

Memorandum from Jay S. Bybee, Assistant Attorney General, U.S. Department of Justice, to Alberto R. Gonzales, Counsel to the President, U.S. Department of Justice, (Aug. 1, 2002), *in* THE TORTURE PAPERS: THE ROAD TO ABU GHRAIB (Greenberg & Dratel eds., 2005).

Memorandum from Steven G. Bradbury, Principal Deputy Assistant Attorney General, to John A. Rizzo, Senior Deputy General Counsel, Central Intelligence Agency (May 10, 2005).

Memorandum from William J. Haynes II, General Counsel, U.S. Department of Defense, to General Counsel of the Department of the Air Force (Jan. 17, 2003), *in* THE TORTURE PAPERS: THE ROAD TO ABU GHRAIB (Greenberg & Dratel eds., 2005).

Memorandum from The White House Situation Room to the Vice President *et al.*, Iraq: Goals, Objectives, and Strategy (Nov. 29, 2002).

Jackie Northam, *Popularity Of Drones Takes Off For Many Countries*, NPR (July 11, 2011) http://www.npr.org/2011/07/11/137710942/popularity-of-drones-takes-off-for-many-countries.

President Barack Obama, Speech to the United Nations General Assembly (Sept. 24, 2009).

Outrage at "Old Europe" Remarks, BBC NEWS WORLD EDITION (Jan. 23, 2003), http://news.bbc.co.uk/2/hi/europe/2687403.stm.

Pac Rim Cayman LLC v. El Salvador, expert opinion of W. Michael Reisman, ICSID Case No. ARB/09/12 (Mar. 22, 2010).

Henry M. Paulson, Jr., Sec'y of the Treasury, Testimony Before the Senate Banking Committee on Turmoil in US Credit Markets: Recent Actions Regarding Government Sponsored Entities, Investment Banks and other Financial Institutions (Sept. 23, 2008).

Jan Paulsson, John E.C. Brierley Memorial Lecture at McGill University, Montreal: *International Arbitration is Not Arbitration* (May 28, 2008).

Jan Paulsson, *Moral Hazard in International Dispute Resolution,* Inaugural Lecture as Holder of the Michael R. Klein Distinguished Scholar Chair, (Apr. 29, 2010) available at http://www.arbitrationicca.org/media/0/12773749999020/paulsson_moral_hazard.pdf.

Jan Paulsson, Symposium, *Making the Most of International Investment Agreements: Indirect Expropriation: Is the Right to Regulate at Risk?* (Dec. 12, 2005), available at http://www.oecd.org/dataoecd/5/52/36055332.pdf.

Press Release, Bank for International Settlements, Group of Governors and Heads of Supervision reach broad agreement on Basel Committee capital and liquidity reform package (July 26, 2010), *available at* http://www.bis.org/press/p100726.htm.

Press Release, French Embassy, Iraq/UNSCR 1441—Joint Statement by the People's Republic of China, France and the Russian Federation (Aug. 11, 2002), *available at* http://www.ambafrance-uk.org/Iraq-UNSCR-1441-Joint-statement-by.html.

Press Release, G-7 Finance Ministers and Central Bank Governors Plan of Action (Oct. 10, 2008), *available at* http://www.treasury.gov/press-center/press-releases/Pages/hp1195.aspx.

Press Release, Secretary-General Says United Nations Has Duty to Exhaust All Possibilities of Peaceful Settlement Before Resorting to Use of Force, U.N. Doc. SG/SM/8600 (Feb. 12, 2003) (cited in RALPH ZACKLIN, THE UNITED NATIONS SECRETARIAT AND THE USE OF FORCE IN A UNIPOLAR WORLD (2010)).

Press Release, United States Explanation of Vote on UN Security Council Resolution 1441, (Nov. 8, 2002), *available at* http://www.staff.city.ac.uk/p.willetts/IRAQ/US081102.HTM.

Provisional Rules of Procedure of the Security Council, U.N. Doc. S/96/Rev.7 (1983).

Proxy Disclosure Enhancements, Exchange Act Release Nos. 33–9089; 34–61175.

Ronald Reagan, Address at the National Association of Evangelicals (Mar. 8, 1983).

Ronald Reagan, Address Before a Joint Session of the Congress on the State of the Union (Feb. 6, 1985).

W. Michael Reisman, United States of America v. Canada, Opinion with Respect to Selected International Legal Problems in LCIA Case No. 7941 (May 1, 2009), *available at* http://ita.law.uvic.ca/documents/ReismanExpertOpinion.pdf

Condoleezza Rice, U.S. Sec'y of State, Remarks at the 99th Annual Meeting of the American Society of International Law (Apr. 1, 2005), *reported in* 21:3 AM. SOC'Y INT'L L. Newsletter 7 (May/July 2005).

Susan E. Rice, Remarks as the U.S. Permanent Representative to the United Nations, at a Security Council Meeting on the Situation on the Korean Peninsula (Dec. 19, 2010), *available at* http://seoul.usembassy.gov/p_rok_121910.html.

Rules of the International Court of Justice, 1978 I.C.J. Acts & Docs. 4 (as amended Apr. 14, 2005).

S.C. Draft Iraq Res. 2003/215, U.N. Doc. S/2003/215 (Feb. 24, 2003).

S.C. Draft Res. 18250, U.N. Doc. S/18250 (July 31, 1986).

Oscar Schachter, Remarks at the American Society of International Law Annual Meeting (Apr. 26, 1985), *in* 79 AM. SOC'Y INT'L L. PROC. 266 (1985).

Schlesinger Report, Final Report of the Independent Panel to Review Department of Defense Detention Operations (Aug. 2004), *in* The Torture Papers: The Road to Abu Ghraib (Greenberg & Dratel eds., 2005).

Serge Schmemann, *Confrontation in the Gulf: Kohl Says He'll Seek to End Curb on Army's Role*, N.Y. Times, Sept. 10, 1990.

Kevin M. Stack, *The Concept of Law in the Age of Administration* (Oct. 14, 2009)(on file with the author).

S.C. Provisional Records, S/PV.2693, at 92 (Nov. 29, 1990)

The Secretary-General, *Report of the Secretary-General on the Declaration submitted by Iraq on 7 December 2002, delivered to the Security Council,* U.N. Doc. S/2003/232 (Feb. 23, 2003).

Sovereignty over Pedra Branca/Pulau Batu Puteh, Middle Rocks and South Ledge (Malay./Sing.), Special Agreement, 2003 I.C.J. 2 (July 24).

The Fay-Jones Report, Investigation of Intelligence Activities at Abu Ghraib (Aug. 2004), *in* The Torture Papers: The Road to Abu Ghraib (Greenberg & Dratel eds., 2005).

The White House, The National Security Strategy of the United States of America (Mar. 2006).

Timeline: Banking Crisis, CNN (Oct. 22, 2008), http://edition.cnn.com/2008/BUSINESS/09/30/us.bailout.timeline/index.html.

Christopher Towe & Martin J. Gruenberg, Exit from Extraordinary Financial Sector Support Measures: Note for G20 Ministers and Governors Meeting, (2009).

Jean-Claude Trichet, President of the ECB; Lucas Papademos, Vice President of the ECB; Statement at Frankfurt am Main: Introductory Statement with Q&A (Oct. 2, 2008).

Jean-Claude Trichet, President of the ECB, Statement at the European American Press Club Paris: The ECB's Response to the Crisis (Feb. 20, 2009).

Senate Armed Services Committee, 110th Congress, Inquiry into the Treatment of Detainees in U.S. Custody (Nov. 20, 2008), *available at* http://armed-services.senate.gov/Publications/Detainee%20Report%20Final_April%2022%202009.pdf.

UK Office of Legal Advisor to the Ministry of Foreign Affairs, Report to Committee of Legal Advisors on Public International Law, Council of Europe.

U.N. SCOR, 58th Sess., 4688th mtg., U.N. Doc. S/PV/4688 (Jan. 20, 2003).

U.N. SCOR, 58th Sess., 4701st mtg., U.N. Doc. SC/7658 (Feb. 5, 2003).

UN Convention Against Torture, Declarations, *available at* http://treaties.un.org/Pages/ViewDetails.aspx?src=TREATY&mtdsg_no=IV-9&chapter=4&lang=en.

UN Convention Against Torture, Objections to Declarations, *available at* http://treaties.un.org/Pages/ViewDetails.aspx?src=TREATY&mtdsg_no=IV-9&chapter=4&lang=en.

United Kingdom Explanation of Vote on Security Council Resolution (Nov. 8, 2002), *available at* http://www.staff.city.ac.uk/p.willetts/IRAQ/UK081102.HTM.

U.S. Dep't of the Treasury, Financial Regulatory Reform: A New Foundation (2009).

Anton R. Valukas, Report of Anton R. Valukas Volume 1 (Mar. 2010), *available at* http://online.wsj.com/public/resources/documents/LehmanVol1.pdf.

Christopher Weeramantry, Acceptance Speech at The Right Livelihood Awards (Dec. 7, 2007), *available at* http://www.rightlivelihood.org/weeramantry_speech.html (last visited Aug. 1, 2011).

Working Group Report on Detainee Interrogation in the Global War on Terrorism: Assessment of Legal, Historical, Policy, and Operational Considerations (Mar. 6, 2003), *in* The Torture Papers: The Road to Abu Ghraib (Greenberg & Dratel eds., 2005).

Index